Governing Europe

edited by

JACK HAYWARD

AND

ANAND MENON

OXFORD

UNIVERSITY PRESS

OXFORD
UNIVERSITY PRESS

Great Clarendon Street, Oxford ox2 6DP

Oxford University Press is a department of the University of Oxford.
It furthers the University's objective of excellence in research, scholarship,
and education by publishing worldwide in

Oxford New York

Auckland Bangkok Buenos Aires Cape Town Chennai
Dar es Salaam Delhi Hong Kong Istanbul Karachi Kolkata
Kuala Lumpur Madrid Melbourne Mexico City Mumbai Nairobi
São Paulo Shanghai Taipei Tokyo Toronto

Oxford is a registered trade mark of Oxford University Press
in the UK and in certain other countries

Published in the United States
by Oxford University Press Inc., New York

British Library Cataloguing in Publication Data

Data available

Library of Congress Cataloging in Publication Data
Governing Europe / edited by Jack Hayward and Anand Menon.
p. cm.
Includes bibliographical references.
1. European Union. 2. European Union countries—Politics and government.
3. Europe–Politics and government—1989 I. Hayward, Jack Ernest Shalom. II. Menon,
Anand, 1965–

JN30 .G6784 2003   320.94–dc21   2002038197
ISBN 0–19–925014–6 (hbk.)   ISBN 0–19–925015–4(pbk.)

1 3 5 7 9 10 8 6 4 2

Typeset by Newgen Imaging Systems (P) Ltd., Chennai, India
Printed in Great Britain on acid-free paper by Biddles Ltd
www.biddles.co.uk

Contents

vi   *Contents*

Notes on Contributors

Sonia Alonso, Researcher at Universidad Carlos III, Madrid.

Rudy B. Andeweg, Professor of Political Science at Leyden University.

Sabino Cassese, Professor of Administrative Law, Department of Law, University of Rome 'La Sapienza'.

Paul Craig, Professor of English Law, St. John's College, Oxford.

Colin Crouch, Chairman of Department of Social and Political Sciences and Professor of Sociology at the European University Institute, Florence; and External Scientific Member of the Max Planck Institute for Social Research, Cologne.

Maurizio Ferrera, Professor of Public Policy and Administration at Pavia University and Director of the Centre for Comparative Policy Research at Bocconi University in Milan.

Klaun H Goetz, Senior Lecturer in Government, Department of Government, London School of Economics and Political Science.

Peter A. Hall, Krupp Foundation Professor of European Studies and Director of the Minda de Gunzburg Center for European Studies at Harvard University.

Jack Hayward, Emeritus Professor of Politics, University of Oxford and Research Professor, Hull University.

Anton Hemerijck, Deputy Director of the Netherlands Scientific Council for Government Policy in the Hague.

Andrew Hurrell, University Lecturer in International Relations and Fellow of Nuffield College, Oxford.

Hussein Kassim, Senior Lecturer in Politics, School of Politics and Sociology, Birkbeck College, University of London.

Patrick Le Galès, CNRS senior research fellow at CEVIPOF and Associate Professor of Politics and Sociology at Sciences Po, Paris.

Giandomenico Majone, Emeritus Professor of Public Policy, European University Institute, Florence.

José María Maravall, Academic Director and Professor of the Centre for Advanced Study in the Social Sciences, Juan March Institute, Madrid.

Sonia Mazey, Faculty Lecturer in Politics and Tutorial Fellow, Hertford College, Oxford University.

Anand Menon, Professor of European Politics and Director of the European Research Institute at the University of Birmingham.

Yves Mény, President, European University Insitute, Florence.

Wolfgang Müller, Professor of Political Science at the University of Vienna.

Neill Nugent, Professor of Politics and Jean Monnet Professor of European Integration at Manchester Metropolitan University.

Edward Page, Professor of Political Science, London School of Economics and Political Science.

William E. Paterson, Director of the Institute of German Studies at the University of Birmingham.

B. Guy Peters, Maurice Falk Professor of American Government, University of Pittsburgh.

Martin Rhodes, Professor of European Public Policy at the European University Institute in Florence.

Rod Rhodes, Professor of Politics (Research) at the University of Newcasle-upon-Tyne; Professor Politics and Public Policy in the School of Politics and Public Policy, Griffith University (Brisbane, Australia) and Adjungeret Professor, Institut for Statskundskab, Kobenhavns Universitet (Denmark).

Jeremy Richardson, Fellow and Senior Tutor at Nuffield College, Oxford.

Gordon Smith, Emeritus Professor of Government at the London School of Economics and Political Science.

Sidney Tarrow, Maxwell M. Upson Professor of Government and Sociology at Cornell University.

Mark Thatcher, Lecturer in Public Administration and Public Policy, London School of Economics and Political Science.

Loukas Tsoukalis, Jean Monnet Professor of European Organization, University of Athens, and President of the Hellenic Foundation for European and Foreign Policy (ELIAMEP).

List of Abbreviations

ART	Autorité de Régulation des Télécommunications
CFSP	Common Foreign and Security Policy
COGs	Centres of Governments
CET	Common External Tariff
CCP	Common Commercial Policy
CAP	Common Agricultural Policy
CSA	Conseil Supérieur de l'Audiovisuel
CECEI	Comité des établissemente de credit et des enterprises d' investissement
COREPER	Committee of Permanent Representatives
CIE	Committee of Independent Experts
DM	Deutschmark
EC	European Communities
EU	European Union
EMU	Economic and Monetary Union
ECJ	European Court of Justice
EP	European Parliament
ECB	European Central Bank
EMI	European Monetary Institute
ECOFIN	Council of Economics and Finance Ministers
EEA	European Economic Area
EGE	European Group on Ethics
ESDP	European Security and Defence Policy
ECSC	European Coal and Steel Community
EEC	European Economic Community
EMS	European Monetary System
ERM	Exchange Rate Mechanism
EdF	Électicité de France
GMOs	Genetically Modified Organisms
ICFP	Inter-ministerial Conference for Foreign Policy
IGC	Inter Governmental Conference
IMF	International Monetary Fund
JHA	Justice and Home Affairs
MEP	Members of the European Parliament
MFA	Movimento das Forcas Armadas
NPM	New Public Management
NGOs	Non-Governmental Organizations
NSF	National Salvation Front
OMGUS	Organization of Military Government, US
OFT	Office of Fair Trading
PFI	Public Finance Initiative

QMV   Qualified Majority Vote
QUANGOs   Quasi Non-Governmental Organizations
SEM   Single European Market
SEA   Single European Act
SMEs   Small and Medium-sized Enterprises
TNCs   Transnational Corporations
TEU   Treaty on European Union
TECs   Training and Enterprise Councils
UKREP   UK Permanent Representation to the European Union

Foreword

Vincent Wright: Engagement with History, Political Science, and Economics

TONY ATKINSON

Vincent and I both contributed to *A New Handbook of Political Science* (Goodin and Klingemann 1996) chapters subtitled 'Old and New'. (His chapter, with Guy Peters, was on Public Policy and Administration.) It seems to me, as an outsider (an economist, not a historian or a political scientist.), that this subtitle is a good description of Vincent's own intellectual style. He combined all the virtues of the classical historian with intellectual curiosity about new ideas in political science. He was as much at home writing about the first four years of the Mitterrand Presidency as he was studying the biographies of nineteenth century prefects. He was keenly interested in old institutions such as freemasonry, yet was among the first to understand the significance of new developments such as privatization. He encouraged students to pursue the archival work he loved, but was tolerant of those who adopted a quite different approach. (In both cases, of course, their work was subjected to close and sceptical examination.) It is highly appropriate, in a volume in memory of Vincent, that Peter Hall should quote the statement attributed to Santayana that those who neglect history are doomed to repeat it. But Vincent was also receptive to what could be learned from a theoretical framework. When interviewing prospective prize research fellows, he could always be relied on to engage with even the most abstract presentation.

Engagement is, for me, the key. One of the pleasures of talking to Vincent was his openness to cross-disciplinary exchange. He did not like the methods adopted by most economists and was—rightly—suspicious of their influence on policy making. But he was willing to engage. As is reflected in a number of the chapters in this volume, he worked on key issues of economic policy-making, such as regulation, industrial policy, and privatization, the last of which he described as 'a gold mine for political scientists' (1999: 173). Moreover, he was willing to work with economists, notably in his collaboration with John Vickers on *The Politics of Privatization in Western Europe* (1989). Today, the subjects being studied by economists and by political scientists often overlap, but they seem too often to be talking past each other. Economists are unduly reliant on simplistic models that lack institutional grounding (median voter models seem to have too large a role); political scientists seem often to work with implicit models of the economy that lack the insights of modern economic theory or fail to capture general equilibrium reactions. What is needed is more genuine engagement of the kind that Vincent practised.

Turning to the volume's overall theme, *Governing Europe*, I am impressed by how well the different chapters convey the dynamics of political change in Europe: the changing European State and the changing state of Europe. Much has happened even in the period since he died, and one would like to know how he would have interpreted these events. As Sudhir Hazareesingh and Karma Nabulsi observe in their obituary, Vincent had 'a resolute appreciation of the role of individuals' (2000: 377). How far is the success or failure of the euro going to depend on the choice of the President of the European Central Bank? Has progress on the European social agenda been the result of a few key ministers of social affairs? Echoing the contributors to this volume, I wish that Vincent were still here so that I could discuss these questions—and many more—with him.

Preface

Grappling with Untidy Reality: Vincent Wright's Comparative Complexities

JACK HAYWARD

The explicit comparison of European politics is methodologically rooted in the conviction that the analyst should avoid taking for granted the implicit assumptions of one's own political culture. The systematic exploration of their similarities and differences has been the means of imparting the necessary distance between the investigator and the subject investigated. While Benthamite utilitarianism relied upon an abstract and deductive scientism that has been revived in American-led rational choice techniques, mainstream British political science preferred a historically based inductive approach (Hayward 1999: 3–6, 23). In France, the dominance of public law meant that the implicit comparisons of a Tocqueville were neglected for a century in favour of an introvert study of judicial phenomena. By the second half of the twentieth century, a scholar like Vincent Wright could range across the length and breadth of political science, adapting his initial institutionalist inductivism to suit the varied subject matter examined. So the state, courts and constitutionalism, public administration and public policy, governments, parties and organized interests, democracy and popular participation, which are later successively discussed, were his simultaneous concerns. Western and Southern Europe remained the focus of his personal research, because for most of his working life East-Central and Eastern Europe did not lend themselves to comparisons with which he was intellectually comfortable.

Invited to describe the development of his personal contribution to the proliferating publications on comparative European politics in his lifetime, Vincent Wright called his retrospective 'The path to hesitant comparison' (Wright 1999: ch. 15). What he self-deprecatingly described as his 'intellectual schizophrenia', (ibid: 176) to account for the hesitancy, could be less defensively described as a sustained duality. Resolutely shunning synthetic generalizations based upon spurious oversimplifications, he was not content to fall back upon the reassuring singularities of historical description. While the subject matter was complex, explanation necessitated recourse to analytic conceptual categories. Although he retained a historically sensitive allergy to models and a reluctance to let methodological concerns dictate the problems to be investigated, as a social scientist he accepted the challenge that model building and methodological rigour posed. So, while conceding that 'comparison and history are intrinsically ill-suited partners' (Wright 1999: 176), he did not allow the historian's 'ingrained 'scepticism' and eye for detail to paralyse his concurrent work on comparative politics.[1] In fact, the two sides of his research were interdependent. His historical work protected him from the universalizing fallacies which some political scientists have sought to import from economics—which Richard Rose calls 'landless theory'—while his comparative politics protected him from the historian's tendency to assume uniqueness (Rose 1991: 452). Vincent Wright's systematic analyses combined the respect for national and subnational diversity with the circumspect use of generic concepts capable of crossing national borders. He adopted what Richard Rose has dubbed a 'bounded variability' that avoided accumulating 'empirical data that will sink under its own weight' (Rose 1991: 447, 448).

Stylistically, Vincent Wright's splitter's predilection for stressing diversity means that his writings are replete with words such as complexity and cleavage, tension and dissension, variety and fluidity, diffuseness and chaos, incrementalism and fragmentation, precariousness and fragility, contradiction, competition, and confrontation. It is also reflected in the enumeration of impressively long checklists that are a distinctive feature of his attempts to avoid glib generalizations. However, while he is insistent on the need to particularize, Wright showed, first in the case of France and then in his more explicitly comparative work, that a superficial knowledge might rigidly separate what a more profound awareness could reunite. Paradoxically, Wright ultimately minimizes the peculiarity all too frequently attributed and self-attributed to French politics by showing that when one descends to the detailed cases of what actually happens, French practice is not so different from that of other countries as French principles would lead one to believe. As such, it is a salutary corrective to a culturalist emphasis on what is irreducibly special and reunites the study of politics after appearing to dismember it. Thus, the impulse towards systematic comparison existed implicitly in his single country work, becoming capable of incorporation as a case study because it was intrinsically comparable. As we shall see, it was only in his later work that Wright accepted that the systematic comparison of a limited number of West European countries meant starting, as Rose puts it, from 'the logic of a matrix'. 'Whereas case studies may arrive at concepts and generalizations at the end of research, comparative analysis of more than one country requires the specification of concepts at the beginning in order to identify what is to be examined in different national contexts' (Rose 1991: 453, 455).

Wright preferred to initiate and edit most of his comparative work in collaboration. Given the need to mobilize a vast amount of information from a range of countries and his concern that only a specialist could be relied upon to have access to the detailed data and the understanding of how to evaluate it, there was a great temptation to recruit a team rather then undertake the work himself. However, it was also consistent with his inductive type of analysis, with the capacity to generalize coming at the end rather than at a beginning. To pull the various contributions together, not merely the conclusion

---

[1] One may consider that Vincent Wright was too ready to concede the incapacity of political scientists to do creative work in comparative political history. The names of Sammy Finer, Stein Rokkan, and Charles Tilly, amongst others, come to mind.

but the introduction to the edited book or special issue of a journal had to await the findings of the others. Wright preferred to run the risk of a loss of overall coherence. To avoid the whole becoming less than the sum of the parts, Wright's own contribution would seek to compensate for the divergences between authors by incorporating as much as possible of their diversity into his comprehensive comparative analysis. The resulting complexity underlined the fact that the truth is seldom simple once it is subjected to close investigation.

When Vincent Wright commented on a paper by Edward Page, which could not detect a distinctive British comparative politics tradition, he offered two revealing suggestions. First, he thought that British attitudes towards comparatism were characterized by a 'querulous criticism', which sceptically subjected the hypotheses advanced to rigorous logical empirical analysis, that might be traced to the influence of philosophical and historical investigative styles characteristic of the dominant universities of Oxford and London. As Vincent Wright had studied and taught at the London School of Economics before moving to Nuffield College, Oxford, he was speaking *en connaissance de cause*, as well as reflecting the formative influences upon his own approach. The second fault-finding feature was an appeal to the 'Zanzibar principle', according to which it is always possible to point out at least one country to which a comparative generalization did not apply (Page 1990: 441; citing Daalder 1987: 19). Once again, this type of objection would commend itself both to a particularising historian, as well as conforming to Popper's conception of correct scientific method. So, although typically couched in light hearted fashion, Wright was being particularly serious about his own reservations towards comparative politics as it was generally practised in North America.

Vincent Wright described the LSE Government Department (he was always keener on 'government' rather than politics as a focus) as his 'intellectual home' (Wright 1999, 164). Rather than William Robson (who commissioned his *The Government and Politics of France*) it was Michael Oakeshott who was acknowledged by Wright as the predominant intellectual influence upon him, first as a student and later as a colleague. 'A profound scepticism and pessimism pervade all his teachings', which Vincent Wright recalled, 'reinforced my love of history and my natural leanings to scepticism' (Wright 1999: 165). Oakeshott's visceral insularity precluded meaningful comparison, exercising a persisting inhibition. It also ensured that initially comparative government would be absent from his training. Although Robson had been active in the International Political Science Association and was not indifferent to making institutional comparisons, the undergraduate course in comparative government was in fact devoted to major foreign governments. French was taught by William Pickles (he delivered the lectures and Dorothy wrote the textbooks) and it was he who aroused Vincent Wright's lifelong preoccupation with the French and encouraged him to engage in postgraduate studies in France. It was by his personal example that Bill Pickles reinforced Wright's 'instinctive dislike for the pompous and pretentious ... intellectual scepticism' and 'pugnacious and argumentative style' (Machin and Wright 1985: ix). It was to Dorothy and William Pickles that he gratefully dedicated *The Government and Politics of France*.

SUCCESSIVE APPROXIMATION: FROM SINGLE COUNTRY SPECIALIST TO CROSS-NATIONAL COMPARISON

Vincent Wright's move to Sciences Po in Paris reinforced rather than counteracted his initial revulsion from comparative research. Not only was politics conceived there as almost exclusively Franco-French but it was extremely narrow in focus. Although it had partly escaped from the grip of the Faculty of Law, political science retained the strong bias towards electoral geography which had been imparted to it by André Siegfried. So, after some preliminary exploration in other directions, Wright allowed himself to be steered by the historian of the French Right, René Rémond, and electoral analyst François Goguel towards a study of electoral mobilisation in the Basses-Pyrénées during the Second Republic and Second Empire. From that unlikely starting point began Wright's successive steps, taking at first tentative and then more confident strides, from local and national singularity towards cross-national generality.

Micro-politics from below: The View from Pau

While France is very diverse, Wright could hardly have landed in a more peculiar corner of that country. It was located in the extreme south-west, the Basque part having much more in common ethnically with their Spanish counterparts than with the rest of Frenchmen. He was studying them in the mid-nineteenth century, before the centralizing efforts of the French state had been deployed to full effect, so the scope for generalization was even more problematic. The micro-political character of the doctorate (Wright 1965) was accentuated by being based primarily on two years research in the local archives of the capital of Basses-Pyrénées, Pau. Wright testified that '[i]n writing my thesis I explored and even discovered themes which remain central to my intellectual interests. I also acquired a taste for detailed archival work which has never deserted me' (Wright 1999: 167). The commitment to original, detailed investigation ensured that he was inoculated against the practice of repeating the received wisdom of those who usually had not bothered to put their sixth-hand statements to the test of the evidence. He was to apply the spirit of such research methods when he turned to subjects which were not susceptible to this treatment.

Although Wright's research might have become another one of 'those great monuments to the excellence of the French historical tradition' which he read with delectation, he was already beginning to make intra-national French comparisons. He asked: 'how far did the elections in this area reflect the national situation? How were similarities and specificities to be explained?' (Wright 1999: 166–7). To answer these questions, he had to go beyond the electoral aspects of the process of national integration into studying the administrative links between local notables and state officials revealed by the national and local archives. This led him to write two books, which were a follow-up from his thesis, on the Council of State and the Prefects of the Second Empire. They demonstrated that despite the appearance of centralized authoritarianism, there was the 'practice of constant negotiated accommodation' between Paris and the Provinces, between local politicians and national officials, that was shown to be still operative a century later by the *Centre de Sociologie des Organisations* researchers in the 1960s and 1970s (Worms 1965; Wright 1972, 1973; Grémion 1976). As Wright was to put it more forthrightly in his textbook about the Fifth Republic, 'Parisian bureaucrats and their provincial agents, prefects and locally elected officials are condemned to live together in a chaos of surreptitious bargaining, illicit agreements, hidden collusion, unspoken complicity, simulated tension and often genuine conflict' reflecting 'a fragmented power structure in the capital and the splintered power structure in the provinces' (Wright 1978: 225).

Macro-politics from Above: The View from Paris

Before publishing his general book on France in 1978, Wright—who in 1969 had returned to LSE—showed himself ready to generalize about the contemporary French politico-administrative system. With a self-assurance born of close contact with thoughtful state officials, as well as his solid grounding in administrative history, Wright successfully challenged in a highly influential article the view that senior civil servants occupied a hegemonic position in the French Fifth Republic. He forcefully made six points, of which three can be picked out. First, the Gaullist Republic had no consistent theory of administration because its proponents 'could not decide whether the basic aim of their measures was to make the administration more autonomous, more efficient, more subordinate or more democratic' (Wright 1974: 50, cf 51–2). Second, 'the French civil service is particularly prone to internal tensions and dissensions', between and within fragmented ministries (Wright 1974: 52, cf 53–5). Third, the politicization of the senior civil service was not new and had been both exaggerated and oversimplified.

Wright used the insight into the workings of the French state provided by his historical perspective to show that 'the political and administrative traditions accumulate and survive in unhappy and precarious balance'(Wright 1974: 63). Combining *Ancien Régime*, Napoleonic and post-Napoleonic, parliamentary and post-parliamentary sedimentations, 'it is a world composed of entrenched traditions, half-remembered rules and conveniently forgotten stipulations, of complicity and conflict, ideological clashes and masonic collusions, political chicanery and petty administrative corruption, personal rivalries and political alliances, unabashed self-interest and embarrassing idealism, compromising commitments and watchful opportunism, unforgivable cowardice and praiseworthy courage, naked ambition and calculated disinterest. It is a highly *personalized*, complex and confused world, rendered difficult to analyse and defiant of comparison by the unceasing interplay of irritating human imponderables' (Wright 1974: 65). Wright ends by ridiculing the 'adepts of overarching theories of comparative administration, those unrepentant builders of models' whose ranks he was still refusing to join in 1974 (Wright 1974: 65).[2]

---

[2] By 1990, in a chapter on 'The Administrative Machine: Old Problems and New Dilemmas', Wright would structure his argument around 'The Napoleonic Model of Administration' and 'The Distortion of the Napoleonic Model' (Wright 1990: ch. 6).

The Government and Politics of France generalized this analysis by a Jacobin fearful of the fissiparous tendencies that were persistently turning the myth of a 'One and Indivisible Republic' into the reality of a dissensual and divided one. Wright's self-proclaimed 'Jacobinism' was exacerbated precisely by the fear that, despite its arrogant pretensions, the centre might not hold. Having demythologized the claims of the French state to omnipotence and omnicompetence, he proceeded to hand out lessons in modesty which prompted in his informed French audience an unsuspected masochism as this verbally sadistic foreigner held up for their contemplation a mirror in which they recognized familiar features which they were too discreet to make explicit. 'Power is diffused' with the government resembling 'a huge Byzantine court riddled with feuding factions', interacting or mutually avoiding each other at the centre of 'a chaos of decision-makers', 'enmeshed in a concatenation of competing and contradictory forces . . . and if they are not always the helpless spectators of the fate of their country . . . their freedom of action is often singularly limited' by history and the outside world (Wright 1978: 231–2).

While Wright was at this stage more inclined to Franco–French comparison, indeed suggesting—in words that mock the habitual examination question—that there was 'more to compare than to contrast' between the Fourth and Fifth Republics in their susceptibility to 'fitful and supine incrementalism' (Wright 1978: 230, 232; cf. 106), he was prepared to extrapolate his comparison much further. His visceral scepticism led him to assert that in a world of perpetual flux (with much of it remaining in darkness, while most of the rest is impenetrably complex) the political analyst was hard put to locate where and by whom decisions were being taken. 'Analysing the political process in France—as in any complex industrial society—is rather like peering down a dimly-lit kaleidoscope, held in a gently inebriated hand: after a while it is possible to distinguish some of the more significant pieces, but the pattern is ever changing and is sensitive to the slightest shudder. Furthermore, there are pieces that remain in obstinate obscurity' (Wright 1978: 231). One could be forgiven for despairing to the point of being deterred from engaging in so hazardous an investigation but Vincent Wright regarded the difficulties as a challenge to intellectual ingenuity rather than an alibi for defeatism.

At a time when it was customary to stress the omnipotence of the President of the Fifth Republic, Wright characteristically emphasized that 'he is enmeshed in a complex web of personal, historical, constitutional, and political restrictions' (Wright 1978: 227, cf. 228–9). Even before the 1986 advent of 'cohabitation' between an adversarial President and Prime Minister—a situation that Wright later called 'cohabitension' (Wright 1993: 116)—he stressed that presidential power 'rests on precarious constitutional and political foundations . . . which may not last' (Wright 1978: 57; cf. Wright 1993: ch. 4). Even when the Prime Minister and most ministers were selected by the President 'there has emerged around the President a system of institutionalized tension, not only between them[3] but also between his staff and theirs, between Prime

---

[3] The subtitle that Wright gave to a chapter on 'The President and the Prime Minister' is characteristic: 'Subordination, conflict, symbiosis or reciprocal parasitism?' (Wright 1993).

Minister and the other ministers as well as among them and with their junior ministers' (Wright 1978: 80, cf. 81–2). Wright pointed out that while such tension damaged policy coordination and could result in vacillation or paralysis, it avoided the 'stultifying search for consensus' that he detected in pre-Thatcherite Britain (Wright 1978: 83). At the bottom of the hierarchy, Wright noted that in France in the early 1970s, 'an application for a loan or subsidy normally involved no fewer than sixty procedures in nine ministries', demonstrating the problems of coordination that made nonsense of governmental monolithic pretensions (Wright 1978: 214).

Wright catalogued the fragmentation, not only of the political and administrative executive but also the parties and parliament, rejecting the claims of the latter's Fourth Republic omnipotence and its Fifth Republic impotence. In the case of French pressure groups, he was not content with a simple dichotomy but presented four models . . . only to argue that 'all are inadequate and somewhat simplistic in their explanations'; saying of one of them that 'like most models, it raises more questions than it answers, and it is too neat and too selective in its choice of facts to convey the full complexity of the situation' (Wright 1978: 174, 176). Going on to describe 'the untidy reality' in all its complexity with delectation, Wright concludes: 'In short, the relationship between the state and the groups during the Fifth Republic is like the rest of government—infinitely complex and intrinsically untidy' (Wright 1978: 198, cf. 185–7).

Wright was unduly dismissive of his 'textbook' (not all of which are born free and equal), which he only reluctantly updated (Wright 1999: 168), preferring to concentrate upon first-hand research that did not force him to make generalizations and even implicit cross-national comparisons that still made him feel uncomfortable. Believing as he did that reality was always shifting, he did not relish the unending pursuit of a description and analysis that reduced a dynamic process to a misleadingly static picture. He preferred instead to reiterate that 'the biggest decision-maker in any political system is the past' (Wright 1978: 229–30) and was later to look with favour on the approach theorized as 'historical institutionalism' which he had been unconsciously practising for many years. However, further staging posts in his successive approximations to explicit reconciliation with comparison were necessary before a reluctant and minimalist theorist would be willing to accept some sacrifice of his intellectual scruples and enduring reservations.

Bilateral and Circumscribed Comparison

Vincent Wright explained his concurrent 1970s ventures into comparison in part by 'the constant stream of invitations to lecture in French universities on British politics, which forced me into constant, if largely implicit, Franco-British comparison. These invitations extended my contact to that tiny band of French academics who were beginning to be interested in explicit comparison' (Wright 1999: 168). This led him to co-edit a book on *Local Government in Britain and France*, which did not attempt to conceal 'the revealing fact that different approaches to apparently similar subjects betray the differing preoccupations and priorities of France and Britain' (Lagroye and Wright 1979: viii). The introduction succinctly compares the functions, problems, and attempted reforms in the two systems, dwelling on their differing historical experiences and institutional arrangements. It has a circumspect tone, as though the authors are unsure of their footing as they venture into treacherous territory. The final paragraph bears the hallmark of Wright's determination not to be defeatist. 'Pointing out these very real difficulties of comparison should induce caution not despair. The exercise of comparison may prove fruitful if ambitions are limited, for the ultimate value of comparison lies less in the spurious generalizations it might provoke than in the intellectual curiosity that triggered off the comparison, and in the insights it might provide about the basic premises, mechanisms, functioning, and ends of each of the systems compared' (Lagroye and Wright 1979: 9). This is no stirring affirmation of faith in comparison to move mountains in terms of generalization. Rather, it is to better understand differences that we compare.

More ambitiously, in February 1978 appeared the first issue of *West European Politics*, the brainchild of Vincent Wright and Gordon Smith, his LSE colleague in the Government Department. Smith had already committed himself much more firmly to comparative politics in the first edition of his *Politics in Western Europe* (Smith 1972). Mutual empathy led them first to create a Master's degree in West European Politics and then the journal. At the outset, they decided to confine its coverage to only part of Europe and to exclude European integration, although over the years they became more willing to publish outside the original criteria whilst retaining the restrictive title of what had deservedly become a highly successful journal (Smith 1999: 158). 'It reflected Vincent's approach to comparative politics via the best inductive route: an initial comprehensive grounding in the study of a single country, from bottom to top and then from top to bottom' (Hayward 2000: i). Smith's German specialism and Wright's French specialism were extended and expanded pragmatically in latitudinarian fashion. In retrospect, Wright was fully entitled to confess: '*West European Politics* remains an object of some pride: its breadth, eclecticism and accessibility, its openness to young academics (and even to research students), convey, however unwittingly, a plea for pluralism and tolerance within the European comparative politics community' (Wright 1999: 169).

Shortly before launching the journal, Vincent Wright moved to Nuffield College, Oxford, where he supervised and advised many of the doctoral students who were to become some of the liveliest members of that comparative politics community. He now enjoyed the resources to conduct a sustained programme of seminars and collaborative research that drew him ever deeper into explicit comparison. However, further impetus to this process was imparted by his two years at the European University Institute in Florence from 1980 to 1982.

From Incipient into Explicit Comparison: The Shift to Political Economy

Wright's receptiveness to the persistent pressures 'to adjust to the exigencies of a changing political science' responded to the close contact he had at the EUI with four colleagues: a Frenchman, a Dutchman, an Irishman, and an Italian. With Yves Mény, he organized a weekly seminar on centre–periphery relations in Western Europe. More significantly, they launched a cross-national comparison of the political management of the steel crisis in Belgium, Britain, France, Italy, and West Germany that resulted in two edited volumes, an abridged French version and a full English version (Mény and Wright 1985*a*, 1987). In the case of Hans Daalder, who had played an active part in the establishment of the European Consortium of Political Research that sought to Europeanize political science under American inspiration, the influence was facilitated by being combined with a historical sensitivity that Wright appreciated. The arguments with Peter Mair and Stefano Bartolini, who made fewer concessions to his continuing misgivings, compelled him to accept the consequences of a more overt use of comparative method. 'In retrospect, my relatively brief time at the Institute proved crucial in forcing me to address the methodological problems involved in comparison as well as taking into consideration the need for some basic theorizing. It also convinced me that good comparative work probably required collaborative effort' (Wright 1999: 170) which was reflected in the fact that so many of his subsequent publications were edited collections, prepared by congenial attempts at securing convergence in workshops. Vincent was now not inclined to smile indulgently on the Oakeshottian superciliousness towards the methodological concerns of the comparatist. Once his rearguard action was over, there was no holding Vincent Wright back in the 1980s and 1990s, manifestations of which were his active role as General Editor of the Macmillan Comparative Government series from 1986 and Co-editor of its European Community series from 1992.

However, he did not abandon his firm anchor in French politics. 1984 saw the publication of an edited book (to which he contributed a third of the content): *Continuity and Change in France*, in which continuity of the Mitterrand presidency was emphasized institutionally, in its personnel and in its policies. 'The Socialists may claim that they are inaugurating a new régime but, in truth, they are merely strengthening the existing one' (Wright 1984: 67, cf. 64–74). While his heart was not in electoral analysis, he demonstrated that he could undertake it with both the comprehensive clarity and mastery of detail that he showed with more enthusiasm in his studies of administration and public policy. He also attached great importance to the personality of political leaders as a contingent factor that disrupted attaching undue weight to the forces of anonymous determinism. His ability to sum up an important politician in a lapidary pen portrait is flamboyantly evident in the extended introduction to this volume. On the Right, Prime Minister Barre was described as 'a pragmatic liberal with a dogmatic style' (Wright 1984: 18, cf. 35–6), while his 'attenuated liberalism' masked 'the progressive transformation of President Giscard d'Estaing from an enlightened reformer into an apprehensive conservative' (Wright 1984: 18, cf. 14–17). On the Left, Prime Minister Mauroy was 'conciliatory, jovial, extrovert, overtly political, and avuncular' (Wright 1984: 53), while President Mitterrand was 'better as a manoeuvrer than as a manager' (Wright 1984: 42, cf. 43). He concluded his 1984 review of the 1981 change of president: 'François Mitterrand inherited from his predecessor a long list of problems, broken promises and unsolved contradictions. The early evidence suggests that he may bequeath his successor with a similar record' (Wright 1984: 75). Events were to show that Vincent Wright's scepticism was well directed.

A year later, *Economic Policy and Policy Making under the Mitterrand Presidency*, subjected a pivotal u-turn to searching criticism and heralded an increasing concern with political economy that would take a more comparative turn after nationalization gave way to privatization, following the new Socialist love affair with big firms. Owing to an 'overestimation of the potential of the public sector as an instrument of *dirigisme*' further nationalization did not provide the leverage over industry anticipated, partly because government control was often ineffective and the firms were financially weak: frequently 'vast, fragile, and incoherent holding companies' (Machin and Wright 1985: 17, 21, cf. 23). 'This post-1981 complex Hapsburgian industrial mosaic of some 4,300 firms, employing 2,400,000 people in France (or 22 per cent of the industrial workforce) and 24,000 abroad' exacerbated problems of coordinating state action by a proliferation of actors pursuing divergent purposes (Machin and Wright 1985: 20). As a result, 'the processes of decision making accentuated the disjointed, reactive, confused, piecemeal, contradictory, and often irrational nature of the decisions' (Machin and Wright 1985: 17). Although none of this was new, the Left's ambitions made matters worse. 'In 1982, there were no fewer than 300 industrial policy mechanisms, 150 different procedures for aid to industry (including sixteen different categories of help for exports, eleven for boosting employment and eight for energy and saving)' so that piecemeal intervention frustrated the claims to planning (Machin and Wright 1985: 11, cf. 10–16). Wright was to return to these problems in a comparative context when first privatization and then core executive coordination were subjected to searching analysis.

Before doing so, the results of the EUI collaboration with Mény in the early 1980s, involving the mobilization of an international and interdisciplinary group of researchers, were published as *The Politics of Steel: Western Europe and the Steel Industry in the Crisis Years (1974–84)*. Steel was selected as 'the obvious arena in which the interplay of Community, national, regional, and local forces could best be observed' (Mény and Wright 1987: vii). The editors frankly faced the difficulties. 'Was it meaningful to compare the five countries' "political management of the steel crisis" when countries differ so greatly in their political systems, their industrial culture, the structure of their industrial policy networks, and in their financial capacity to cope with the crisis? . . . How, indeed, to tackle an industry which displays such great variety even *within* each of the states studied? Similarly, was it possible to propound generalizations about industrial policy making based on the study of an industry which was in the throes of an enduring and dramatic crisis' (Mény and Wright 1987: viii)? Despite the fact that a common methodology had not been imposed on the contributors, the conclusions had not been contradictory, thanks in no small part to the efforts of the editors, reflected in their 110 page introduction to an 810 page book! It should come as no surprise that a major constraint upon state crisis intervention was found to be 'the multiplicity of decision points within, and the fragmentation and compartmentalization of, the State apparatus which is involved in industrial policy making' (Mény and Wright 1987: 45).

Back in Oxford, the subject of 'The Politics of Privatization in Western Europe' was chosen for a conference that led to the publication of a tenth anniversary special issue of *West European Politics* (Vickers and Wright 1988). Edited by Vincent Wright with his

Nuffield colleague, John Vickers, it was the political scientist rather than the economist who played the leading role. As Wright subsequently explained the choice: 'privatization is a gold mine for political scientists, for it raises profound philosophical and moral questions about property rights, about the concept of the state and of the nature of public goods, and about the balance between state, market, and society. For public policy specialists, it provides valuable material for analysing well-known phenomena, ranging from policy diffusion and policy reversal to policy slippage and policy fiasco, as well as enabling the testing of rational choice theory, theories of regulation, interest group theory, and approaches based on policy networks and policy communities. My own interest in privatization is twofold. First, as with public-sector reform generally, I am interested in the unintended and paradoxical nature of the reform programmes. Second, as a comparatist, I am interested in explaining the differences in the privatization programmes' (Wright 1999: 173). The now customary practice of an analytic tidying up of the diverse reality in an extended introduction, was followed by eight chapters on privatization in Britain, France, West Germany, Belgium, Italy, Austria, the Netherlands, and Sweden. The 1988 anniversary issue concern with the shift towards the policy preferences of profit-seeking entrepreneurs from the budget-maximizing bureaucrats and vote-maximizing politicians that had been the preoccupation of political scientists, signposted a research focus that remained active until Vincent Wright's death.

His fullest exposition of his views on the subject came in *Privatization in Western Europe. Pressures, Problems and Paradoxes*, one of many publications of the *Observatoire du Changement Social en Europe Occidentale*, of which Vincent Wright was a founder member with Henri Mendras and Arnaldo Bagnasco, that held frequent conferences at Poitiers from 1990 to 1997. His introduction preceded two chapters on Britain, followed by others devoted to France, Germany, Italy, Spain, Austria, Sweden, the Netherlands, and Portugal. To the convergent fiscal, technological, financial and EU pressures, he added the diffusion of the British privatization model. There were a mix of ideological, electoral, financial, fiscal, and managerial motives which encountered political, legal, and institutional constraints. Against the marketizing mania that had taken hold in the 1990s, Wright suggested that 'we may be witnessing less the process of state retreat then of state reshaping' (Wright 1994a: 40, cf. 1–43). This became the subject of a special issue of *West European Politics*, co-edited with Wolfgang Müller.

American political scientists belatedly decided from the mid-1980s to bring back the state they had unceremoniously expelled from the behavioural analysis of politics, while from the mid-1970s, European political scientists were empirically downgrading the role of the state, victim simultaneously of domestic overload and European integration. In their generalizing introduction to 'The State in Western Europe: Retreat or Redefinition?' Müller and Wright identified five major interconnected pressures combining to reduce the role of states. They were ideological, political (including public opinion), international, European Union, and technological. More specifically in a characteristic Wright enumeration, 'state retreat may be seen in the adoption of a wide range of policies: budgetary squeeze; privatization (a multi-dimensional phenomenon); deregulation (which ranges from the removal of controls to the reduction in administrative formalities); marketization (the introduction of competitive market forces to some sectors to replace bureaucratic systems of allocation); devolution of state authority to non-elected state officials at the territorial level, in public sector industries or in semi-autonomous administrative agencies, or to private agents charged with the implementation of public policy; territorial decentralization to subnational "governments" ' (Müller and Wright 1994: 8). While willing to concede that West European states were compelled to bargain under constraint, their actions, in conformity with the redefinition hypothesis, were indirect—notably through regulation—rather than reduced (Majone 1994: 77–101). In his personal contribution on 'Reshaping the State: the implications for public administration', Wright insisted that 'each West European country has a unique blend of factors which explains persistent divergences in spite of clear evidence of convergence. In short, national contexts matter' (Wright 1994a: 122). Specificities could not simply be submerged under generalities.

Vincent Wright returned to this theme in his 1997 introduction to the special issue of *Modern and Contemporary France*. Asking whether we were witnessing the end of *dirigisme*, he 'emphasized that, *in comparative terms* [his emphasis], extensive *dirigisme* was a distinctive feature of the French system' (Wright 1997a: 151). However, he pointed out that '*dirigisme* was probably always more powerful as a rhetorical mobilizing device and as a pervasive myth—hence the persistent nostalgia for a politically constructed golden age—than as a strategy or coherent set of matching policies. In truth, the French model masked a messy reality in which public and private intertwined, in which private interests were often more powerful than public actors, in which the latter were fragmented and divided, in which macro- and micro-economic objectives were frequently in conflict, and in which "industrial policy" was inconsistent and sometimes incoherent, reactive, and defensive rather than proactive and strategic . . .' (Wright 1997a: 151). However, 'the state has retained its role as travelling *salesman* (and is especially active in France's important arms trade), as *advocate* (in trade negotiations and in the European Union generally), as *regulator*, and as *cushion* for its companies (through tax relief, subsidies, grants, research contracts, export aid, and public procurement, and various ill-concealed protectionist devices) . . . In short, *dirigisme* has been transformed, but this had entailed neither the end of the state nor of French exceptionalism' (Wright 1997a: 152–3). What Wright described as his 'instinctive and intellectual Jacobinism (which survived the years of mindless centralisation in my own country)' (Wright 1999: 194), achieved a more landless, theoretical, and comparative formulation in the 'new institutionalism', particularly in its historical institutionalist variant, which became the final resting place for this tireless champion of the resurgent state.

THE HISTORICAL INSTITUTIONALIST RECONCILIATION: THE EMPIRICAL ANALYSIS OF INERTIAL REALITY

In his last, posthumously published contribution to *West European Politics* (a special issue on 'The Changing French Political System', a project that he supported from its inception), Vincent Wright expressed his pleasure that 'Political scientists have once again become more interested in institutions, and even at last, in the law. It is now generally accepted that individual and group preferences are embedded in and shaped by institutions, an historically forged amalgam of bodies, rules, procedures, norms, customs, rites, which generates its own conventions, path dependencies and notions of appropriateness' (Wright 2000: 92). While common to all West European countries, this was especially true of France, as he had shown in his work on bureaucratic reform. However, when it came to explaining cross-national differences in privatization programmes, 'Historical institutionalism is without doubt a good explanatory starting point, but my research suggests two caveats. The first is that in an area such as privatization institutionalism needs to be extended beyond the already broad category of political and governmental institutions, conventions, rules, customs, prejudices, instincts, and culture, in order to embrace economic and financial institutions . . . The second caveat relates to the growing impact of the cumulative and intense pressures of an economic, ideological, political, financial, and technological nature—some international or European Union in character, others purely domestic—that are sweeping aside some of the impediments rooted in historically embedded institutionalism' (Wright 1999: 174). The 'indispensable bedmates' of history and political science (Wright 1999: 172) were proving to be turbulently inclined to tumble each other out of bed.

Vincent Wright was persuaded, partly as a result of his increasing encounters with American political science in its non-rational choice manifestations, to countenance the use of theoretical frameworks, but being allergic to abstraction, he did so in a highly circumspect manner. He acknowledged in particular the influence of Peter Hall, James March, Johan Olsen, and Guy Peters in the final approximation to a theorized cross-national comparison. It was the ultimate stage in an ongoing dialectic between the 'intellectual indolence' of confinement to historical singularity and the intellectual exertions of generic conceptual frameworks providing guidelines to bounded variability (Wright 1999: 173, 176). Thus, of one of several unfinished ambitious pieces of research, 'Governing from the Centre: Core Executive Policy Co-ordination', a six country comparative project that adopted the comparative 'logic of the matrix' referred to earlier, Wright could not refrain from declaring: 'As with all comparative work, an apparently straightforward project, based on a relatively simple matrix, quickly ran into a methodological and definitional quagmire . . .' (Wright 1999: 175) from which it has, fortunately been possible to reemerge, even if not unscathed (Hayward and Wright, 2002).

The attraction of historical institutionalism for Wright was its inductive and eclectic approach to institutional activity in shaping policy over time. The emphasis on path dependency as structuring nation state responses to new challenges and of the unintended consequences which arise from crises, have directed attention to the operative forces in social causation being 'mediated by the contextual features of a given situation often inherited from the past' (Hall and Taylor 1996: 941, cf. 954–5). There is a presumption that institutional inertia will only be overcome if sufficiently strong force is exerted or if resistance to change can be bypassed (Hayward 1975: 341–59; Peters 1999: 64–5). There is a further presumption that, except in crisis situations (such as led to the foundation of the Fifth Republic in 1958), the routine practices of 'muddling through' will prevail, with incremental adjustments being made to accommodate change. Wright would not have been unduly disturbed by Peters' judgement that historical institutionalism is more descriptive than predictive (Peters 1999: 76), except that he would have stressed the need to be analytical.

An insatiable intellectual curiosity in exploring differences comparatively provided the motivating impetus to Vincent Wright's many-sided activities as a committed political scientist. To the end, Vincent Wright remained willing to pay the price in complexity of exerting a grip on political reality. In the tireless task of tidying up reality, he was finally prepared to work with matrices and models, at least as points of departure. His typologies clarified without simplifying because tidiness came second to authenticity. The dialectical clash of interpretative thesis and antithesis of strategic interaction in shaping political outcomes was more important than building an ephemeral synthesis.

As is appropriate to Wright's institutionalist approach to European government, the following essays begin with examinations of its constitutional, governmental, and administrative aspects and end with the state in its domestic and international contexts. Although Wright never concealed the fact that he considered parties and popular participation less central to the workings of politics than many of his colleagues, they were not neglected. What particularly excited his interest was the public policy interface and interaction between the public authorities and the economic and social policies (more than the foreign and defence policies) that occupied the forefront of everyday political life. So the breadth of discussions that follow reflect the ambitious scale of the work of the scholar to whom they are dedicated. In the depth of their analysis they reflect his commitment to the most rigorous research standards, as well as his infectious enthusiasm for subjects to which he maintained a sustained dedication.

1

Institutions and the Evolution of European Democracy

PETER A. HALL

Although democracy is often seen as an achievement secured once and for all at one point in time, when the suffrage was extended to the bulk of the population, for instance, in the late nineteenth or early twentieth century in western Europe, in fact, it is the product of an evolving process in which the institutions and ideals of representative government adapt to recurring challenges.[1] Democratic institutions are not static features of the political space but subject to continuous challenge and change.

Institutional flux is as evident today as it was a century ago. In Italy, strenuous efforts were made in the 1990s to cope with the collapse of the political formula established after the Second World War. In nations as diverse as Britain, France, Spain, and Belgium, power has been devolved to regional bodies, some of which have many of the attributes of states. Across much of Europe, authority is being transferred to agencies that are virtually independent of popular control, including central banks, courts, and regulatory commissions. States that once relied on a civil service accountable to the political executive and legislature to ensure that policies are responsive to the populace now make increasing use of market competition and private-sector providers for that purpose. An expanding European Union is conferring substantial power on supranational institutions far-removed from the people, if not fully independent of them. These developments raise questions about the character and future of democracy in Europe that are addressed in many of the essays in this volume.

The purpose of this chapter is to place contemporary debate about European democracy in a wider historical context by considering how analyses of the institutions that underpin democracy in Europe have evolved over time in tandem with political developments. It is said that those who neglect history are doomed to repeat it.[2] That can be also true of social science. We depend on the insights of successive generations of scholars for much of what we know about democracy. By examining how their analyses shifted as European governance itself evolved, we can develop

---

[1] This point is a powerful theme of Beer (1965), where it was first impressed upon me, but it is also exemplified in the work of Vincent Wright, to whom this volume is dedicated and who has charted both the transformation of France from the Fourth into the Fifth Republic and the 'retreat of the state' across Europe in more recent years. (See especially Wright 1989; Vickers and Wright 1989).

[2] This observation is generally attributed to George Santayana (1905: ch. 12).

perspectives with which to understand the problems confronting Europe today. Although I restrict myself to a brief survey, those interested in the subject can follow the references back to deeper debates.

THE FEASIBILITY OF POPULAR GOVERNMENT

In many European nations, substantial strides towards democratic governance had already been taken by the last decades of the nineteenth century. With measures such as the 1890 repeal of the anti-socialist laws in Germany and the passage of a French law on associations in 1901, basic civil rights of free speech and assembly were being secured across much of the continent (Goldstein 1983). However, the legislative politics of the time tended to follow models that left disproportionate political power in the hands of relatively small economic and political elites. In nations that concentrated power in an elected assembly or parliament, as Britain did, the right to vote for members of the legislature was often restricted by property qualifications, not to mention resistance to female suffrage, which left two-thirds of the adult population without a vote. In nations, such as France or Germany, where universal male suffrage gave most households a vote, the power of the assembly was restricted, often by powerful second chambers whose members were chosen on terms that privileged the old elites. Most European nations were still making a transition to democracy that was far from complete (Moore 1966; Rueschemeyer *et al.* 1992; Ertman 1998; Bermeo and Nord 2000).

In this context, the extensions of the suffrage that followed the end of the First World War came as a radical development, one that moved the continent from the elite-based politics of the previous century into an era of mass democracy in which the majority of the populace were to become the arbiters of who formed the government and made policy. Those seeking political power now had to win the votes of ordinary people, and political parties became increasingly important vehicles for their campaigns. On the left of the political spectrum, the continent saw the rise of what Duverger (1954) termed 'mass political parties' characterized by extensive organizations designed to mobilize working-class electors, alongside the looser groupings of 'cadre' parties that relied more heavily on the reputation of their candidates to attract votes. Mass politics and the mobilization of votes became a serious business.

At the same time, governments became larger and more interventionist. The effort to wage 'total war' between 1914 and 1918 had forced many states to take extensive control of the private sector. The early years of the century saw the first imposition of income taxes, new ministries of labour oriented to manpower planning, and the development of social policies aimed at those suffering from unemployment or old age. Although governments scaled down their activities after the war, levels of taxation and public spending remained substantially higher and demands for state intervention acquired a new legitimacy. The era of mass democracy coincided with the rise of the interventionist state, raising the hopes of some and fears of others that pressure from the masses would force governments to intervene ever more forcefully into society and the market economy.

This was the setting for the analysis of democratic institutions just before and during the inter-war years. Well-aware that the world was changing, the most perceptive observers developed analyses of political institutions that reflected contemporary concerns about the feasibility of popular government. Prominent among them were the Italian sociologists Mosca and Pareto. Influenced by an Italian political system that was democratic in form but dominated by the political class of Piedmont, they argued that power is always distributed unevenly and that elites enjoy disproportionate power, even in democratic polities, by virtue of their privileged access to office or resources. In Mosca's view, societies differed primarily according to how their institutions provided for a 'circulation of elites'. Both saw democracy as a political system that offers the public some voice in the selection of the political elite but cannot erase fundamental inequalities of power, especially given the uneven distribution of resources in a capitalist economic system.

Like Machiavelli, Mosca, and Pareto injected into analyses of democracy a realist note that was to be influential in subsequent decades. Schumpeter (1942) took up their perspective to describe democracy as little more than autocratic governance punctuated by periodic electoral campaigns. During the 1950s and 1960s, scholars undertook a series of empirical studies to establish whether democratic polities were dominated by a 'power elite' drawn from those of high economic and social standing (Mills 1956; Dahl 1961; Lindblom 1977). Their emphasis was on the discrepancy between the formal rules of democracy and its realities flowing from the embeddedness of the polity in social or economic systems marked by great disparities in power and resources.

In this work, we can see the precursors to rational-choice analyses that treat politics as little more than a struggle for material resources among self-interested elites. It is a reminder, relevant to current debates about the European Union, that even the most democratic regimes leave more power in the hands of the elites than the masses and that one of the key issues in any institutional design is whether it allows for an adequate circulation of elites, both to bring new ideas into government and to ensure that those entrusted with power remain accountable to a broader electorate. Elite theory also reminds us that political institutions cannot be understood in isolation from the economic and social systems in which they operate.

Max Weber (1962; 1968), perhaps the greatest institutional analyst of the early twentieth century, approached the developments of that era from a different perspective. He was struck by the growing organization of politics, marked by the rise of professional politicians and the progressive rationalization of the state, whose endeavors were now influenced by social science and implemented by large bureaucracies. Although Weber greeted these developments with some ambivalence, seeing them as part of a process of disenchantment whereby an 'iron cage' of reason settles over social life, he was one of the first to draw attention to the potential of bureaucracy as an organizational device for harnessing the collective action of many people to the service of a single set of goals. The contrast he drew was with patrimonial regimes that relied on clansmen, clerics, or aristocrats to carry out the ruler's will. Weber's work suggests that effective bureaucracy is the indispensable concomitant to democracy, as many emerging democracies have found, and that the formal rules of law and regulations can be as effective as the traditional or charismatic forms of authority characteristic of earlier regimes.

In its most optimistic version, the Weberian perspective sees democracy as a system of rule that uses modern forms of organization to identify and serve the popular will, harnessing the power of science to the collective good. In the similar formulation of Beer (1974), the democratic state is seen as a political form that marries 'rationalism' to 'voluntarism'. As such, democratic nation states are the quintessential political vehicles of modernity, forged from enlightenment ideals and agents for the implementation of such ideals. This vision of democracy is considerably more inspiring than that of elite theory, but vulnerable to the critiques of a post-modernist age dubious about the power of reason and attentive to the repressive features of modern organizations (Foucault 1977; Herf 1984).

THE IMPORTANCE OF CULTURE, ORGANIZATION, AND SOCIAL CONDITIONS

In the two decades after 1945, the defining fact for virtually all analyses of European democracy was the collapse of Germany's nascent democracy into fascism, holocaust, and world war. Until then, it had seemed plausible that, once a nation secured democratic government, it would maintain it. But this notion, like other progressive visions of history, collapsed with the Weimar Republic. As a result, issues of stability became central to political analysis. Scholars turned their attention to the problem of identifying conditions that might assure the stability of democratic regimes.

Moreover, the collapse of the Weimar republic called into question traditional types of institutional analysis oriented to the constitutional or legal systems of nations. After all, Weimar had had a democratic constitution, carefully designed to balance the need for decisiveness, epitomized by the observation of Mendès-France that 'to govern is to choose', and the desire to ensure responsiveness to a popular will. One of the legacies of Weimar was a new concern about powerful presidencies and electoral systems built on proportional representation that feeds a literature of continuing importance (Sartori 1976; Shugart and Carey 1992; Lijphart 1999; Skach 1999). But the central reaction of the field was to turn away from constitutional issues to look toward society for the bases of democratic stability.

The problem was to decide which features of society most matter to the survival and functioning of democracy. This issue led many scholars to develop an intense interest in the study of political culture, on the premise that popular support for democratic values is a crucial bulwark for democracy. In some cases, this work moved well beyond institutional analysis. The pioneering studies of Almond and Verba (1963) used cross-national opinion surveys to develop models of the attitudes likely to be most supportive of democracy. Other works integrated the cultural dimensions of politics into analyses of institutions, seeing institutions as crucial to the construction of culture or culture as integral to the operation of institutions. In general, however, these analyses shifted attention away from constitutional arrangements toward the institutions found within a broader political arena, including political parties and interest groups.

The studies undertaken in this period reflect substantial variation in views about which institutions matter, how they matter, and in what culture consists. Eckstein (1961; Eckstein and Gurr 1975) developed a theory of the stability of democracy in which authority relations were central. He associated democratic culture with egalitarian authority relations of the sort developed by membership in secondary associations and argued that they could be used to consolidate democracy (see also Dahrendorf 1967; Hoffmann *et al.* 1963). Beer (1965; 1982*b*) put more emphasis on the effectiveness of political parties and interest groups as vehicles for the representation of interests and saw culture as the set of attitudes and operative ideals indispensable to a particular system of representation.

Some of the most important debates of this era centred on the contributions that political parties or interest groups can make to democracy and on the types of parties or interest organizations likely to be most effective. Michels' (1915) classic study of the German social democrats called into question the extent to which mass parties could support internal democracy, while others applauded their capacities to draw citizens who might otherwise be quiescent into active political participation (Verba *et al.* 1978; cf. Lipset *et al.* 1956). In the most influential contribution to this literature, Kirchheimer (1966) observed that the era of 'mass' and 'cadre' parties was over and that both types of parties were giving way to 'catch-all parties' built on the direct appeals of their leaders to the electorate rather than the involvement of the party rank and file.

Others focused their attention on interest groups (Ehrman 1957; LaPalombara 1964). How these groups contribute to the stability of democracy, however, became an object of contention. Dahl (1956; 1971) and others formulated a pluralist position, which held that democracy will be more stable where citizens are involved in many groups with overlapping memberships whose cross-cutting cleavages limit the development of factions rigidly arrayed against each other. But Lijphart (1977) pointed out that the stability of many nations divided along ethnic or religious lines, such as the Netherlands, Switzerland, Austria, and Belgium, seemed to depend on a different type of political organization that aligns each group into cohesive pillars under leaders who agree to share power in order to avoid social conflict (cf. Barry 1975). He drew attention to the 'consociationalism' of the smaller European democracies in terms that would influence scholars of 'neo-corporatism' (Schmitter and Lehmbruch 1979; Katzenstein 1985).

Social conditions came to the foreground of political analysis in other ways as well during this period. Many believed that the principal threat to political stability stemmed from the potential for conflict among social classes. Memories of mass unemployment during the inter-war years were still fresh; communist parties were sizeable in many nations; the rhetoric of right and left was often strident; and a cold war lent urgency to the claims of each side. Partisan support fell largely along class and religious lines, and the dominant conceptions of political parties developed in these years saw them as reflections of social cleavages (Converse and Dupeux 1962; Butler and Stokes 1969; Lipset and Rokkan 1967; Przeworski and Sprague 1986). Accordingly, many believed that the stability of democracy depended heavily on socioeconomic conditions. Prosperity or shifts in social conditions that dissolve class divisions were expected to reduce the divisiveness of politics as well.

Throughout the 1950s, many waited with bated breath to see whether the class-based conflict that had been so divisive in inter-war Europe would reassert itself. By the early 1960s, however, Europe was experiencing levels of affluence never seen before as well as the growth of a prosperous and porous middle class. Analysts soon associated these developments with the growing moderation of party platforms on both the left and right, symbolized by 'Butskellism' in Britain and the Bad Gödesberg programme of the German SPD (Graubard 1964). Some went so far as to proclaim the 'end of ideology' (Bell 1960). In short, this was an era when politics was seen, for the most part, as an expression of socioeconomic conditions and the success of democracy widely associated with economic prosperity.

TECHNOCRACY, NEO-CORPORATISM, AND THE ROMANTIC REVOLT[3]

With the stability of democracy in western Europe apparently assured, political analysts turned their attention, during the late 1960s and 1970s, towards issues of institutional engineering. There was much to attract their attention. With the rise of 'catch all' parties dominated by their leaders, the influence of legislators began to decline in favour of the political executive. A series of studies documented the growing power of the Prime Minister and the erosion of ministerial responsibility to parliament in Britain (King 1969). Wright (1989) showed how the constitutional changes that moved France from the Fourth to the Fifth Republic and the initiatives of Charles de Gaulle reinvigorated executive governance, drawing a fractious party system into two blocs (Williams 1964).

At the same time, others were reexamining relations between politicians and civil servants. The adage that politicians make policy while civil servants implement it, if ever true, was clearly inadequate to describe the division of labour in an age of complex governance (Gordon 1971). Many observed that the upper civil service was becoming increasingly politicized (Suleiman 1974; Dogan 1975) and new models were sought to describe relations among politicians and officials (Heclo and Wildavsky 1974; Aberbach et al. 1981; Suleiman 1985; Kingdon 1990). What these analyses documented was the end of a quintessentially European system of checks and balances in which a highly trained civil service equipped with its own *esprit de corps* was supposed to serve as an independent guardian of the public interest, against the more partial interests even of politicians. Least developed in Britain, where the public was thought to be protected by lines of accountability that render the civil

---

[3] I borrow the term 'romantic revolt' from Beer (1982b).

service subordinate to ministers responsible to parliament, but most developed in Germany where the concept was prominent enough for Hegel to label civil servants the 'universal class', this ideal had long been part of European conceptions of the state (Dyson 1981). Buttressing it were systems of administrative law dictating how authority should be exercised and agencies, such as the French Council of State, charged with ensuring those rules were followed. Although the probity of the civil service continues to be a valuable feature of European democracy, the days when officials could provide strong checks on their political masters were passing.

As the size, spending, and scope of the state increased, notably through social programmes that turned all European nations into 'welfare states', many analysts began to reconsider the dynamics driving policy making (Rose 1981; 1985). The 'end of ideology' celebrated by some seemed, to others, to herald the rise of 'technocracy'—government by experts overly dedicated to science or a purely professional ethos rather than the well-being of the people whom governments were supposed to serve (Ellul 1964). As the endeavors in which governments were engaged became increasingly specialized, many asked how politicians with limited expertise could oversee policy effectively without becoming prisoners of the specialists they were supposed to direct. The civil service had become more political, but politicians were finding it more difficult to cope with the technical intricacy of their briefs. Concerns such as these were fueled by even more important developments in the nature of modern governance. The volume of technical regulations issued by governments was gradually exceeding the number of laws passed by legislatures, and states were creating increasing numbers of semi-independent agencies endowed with substantial regulatory power and specialized missions that could be difficult for laymen to understand, let alone supervise (Benveniste 1972; Bell 1973; Jacoby 1973).[4]

On the left, developments such as these provoked a lively debate about the nature of the state in capitalist society that inspired a resurgence of institutionalist analysis. There was general agreement that states served the interests of the capitalist class, but the issue was how and why. Miliband (1969) argued that states were responsive to business interests because the latter command more resources in the arenas of electoral and pressure-group politics than do workers. Poulantzas (1972) and others (O'Connor 1973; Althusser 1984; Block 1987), however, argued that the relevant outcomes were conditioned by the very structure of a state that is embedded in capitalist society, contending that the institutional structures of a liberal democracy force its leaders to maintain 'business confidence' in order to secure reelection. These debates inspired a wider revival of interest among political scientists in states and institutions (Lindblom 1977; Bornstein *et al.* 1984; Evans *et al.* 1985).

Others responded to these developments by inquiring more deeply into the networks that link specialists to governments, generating conceptions of 'policy networks', 'issue networks', and 'epistemic communities' to describe the relationships between professional communities and states and to chart the influence that professionals had acquired over policy making (Heclo 1974; Rhodes 1981; Haas 1992).

---

[4] In Britain, these agencies are often termed 'quasi non-governmental organizations' or QUANGOs.

Observing how dependent governments had become on the advice and cooperation of organized interest groups if their complex policies were to be successful, Beer (1965) has described the rise of a new 'collectivist politics', showing how increases in the scope of policy had been accompanied by shifts in conceptions of representative government that accorded a new legitimacy to regular interaction between producer groups and governments.

Schmitter (1974) and others (Winkler 1976; Schmitter and Lehmbruch 1979; 1985; Berger 1981; Streeck and Schmitter 1985) expanded on this theme to note that governments were often now devolving authority to producer groups in return for their cooperation in the administration of policy. This 'neo-corporatism' became especially prominent when governments sought agreement from employers and trade unions to incomes policies designed to stem rising rates of inflation. Although a feature of governance across Europe during the 1970s, neo-corporatist arrangements were seen as most important and durable in nations whose producer groups were cohesively organized (Goldthorpe 1984; Katzenstein 1985). Analyses such as these provided the inspiration for many of the institutionalist analyses of the 1970s and 1980s that linked patterns of policy to the organization of labour, capital, and the state (Zysman 1983; Hall 1986; Cox 1986). Some saw neo-corporatism as an arrangement that delivers superior levels of economic performance (Przeworski and Wallerstein 1982; Alvarez *et al.* 1991; Cameron 1984). However, others were suspicious of such arrangements from a democratic perspective, seeing them as political cartels in which governments, no longer responsive to legislatures, now formed tight alliances with producer groups that suppressed dissent among the rank and file and limited the influence of other groups entitled to a voice in policy making (Panitch 1981; Offe 1984; 1985).

Popular concern about issues such as these erupted in the public arena during the late 1960s. In May 1968, barely four years after a distinguished group of scholars (Graubard 1964) had celebrated the political stability of postwar Europe, an unexpected alliance between students and workers almost toppled the French Fifth Republic. The revolt was initially sparked by a protest against government restrictions on student residences; and, in the weeks that followed, material demands were less prominent than the existential reaction of the young against the hierarchical structures of a state that seemed unresponsive to the concerns of ordinary people. Although demands about wages and working conditions fueled the strikes that hit many European nations in the following years (Crouch and Pizzorno 1978), there was an anti-establishment character to protest in this period that lent political force to intellectual critiques of 'technocracy' (Inglehart 1977).

Concerns such as these acquired institutional vehicles in the 'new social movements' that developed rapidly across Europe during the 1970s, as citizens mobilized against nuclear power or the stationing of nuclear missiles in Europe and in support of measures to protect the environment (Offe 1985; Cooper 1996). Reacting against a centrist establishment and 'grand coalitions' that seemed to shut many out of politics, these movements became important new institutions in the political arena and revivified European democracy. Efforts to explain their appearance and fate in institutional terms led to new bodies of scholarship emphasizing the 'political opportunity structures' facing such movements, the resources central to mobilization, and the 'collective action frames' on which they drew (Kitschelt 1986; Tarrow 1994; Kriesi *et al.* 1996; McAdam *et al.* 1996; Klandermans *et al.* 1988; Tarrow this volume). Others saw these new social movements as evidence of an emerging cleavage between an older generation preoccupied with material concerns and a new one born to enough affluence that it could be drawn to 'post-materialist' issues (Inglehart 1977).

This reaction against traditional social norms coincided with an intensification of distributive conflict that was fuelled by and reflected in high levels of inflation (Goldthorpe and Hirsch 1978; Crouch and Pizzorno 1978). Facing lower rates of economic growth after the oil shocks of 1974, European governments struggled to satisfy the expectations for higher incomes and public spending that 30 years of continuous economic expansion had generated. In most cases, the growth increment no longer left room for private incomes and public spending to grow substantially at the same time. As a result, electorates became increasingly dissatisfied with governmental performance.

The academic response to these developments was a set of works arguing that contemporary governments were 'overloaded' (Crozier *et al.* 1975; King 1975*a*; cf. Offe 1982; Beer 1982*b*). The capacity of governments to supply collective goods no longer seemed to match the demands made upon them. Some attributed this imbalance to an erosion in traditional norms of authority that left the institutions normally responsible for social order unable to regulate popular demands. Others observed that many of the institutions regulating the distribution of resources were functioning badly in a context of high inflation. Industrial relations, for instance, had become increasingly conflictual. But, as the efforts of governments to rectify these problems failed, the state itself was widely perceived to have become inefficient. Politicians who had once been happy to take credit for economic growth began to seek a rationale for shifting responsibility for economic sacrifice away from the state. The result was a sea-change in the politics of Europe, during the 1980s, that can be characterized as a 'move to the market'.

THE MOVE TO THE MARKET

The relevant political developments are striking. Inspired by neo-liberal ideas that were expressed most forcefully in Britain by the Thatcher governments of 1979–90, many European states began to sell off the public enterprises they had nationalized after the war. This 'privatization' was accompanied by widespread 'deregulation' designed to intensify competition in markets, including financial markets where governments had once exercised substantial control over the flows of funds (Vogel 1996).[5] Most governments now encourage firms to seek finance on newly expanded stock exchanges or international capital markets. As a result, governments have less

---

[5] As Vogel (1996) and Majone (1996) point out, of course, what I term 'deregulation' usually entails reregulation.

capacity than they once had to direct industrial development or stimulate economic expansion. In most countries, the rates of increase in levels of public spending and taxation have declined.

The point of most of these measures is to reduce the role of the state in the alloca-tion of resources and expand the role of markets. The premise is that organizations facing more intense competition operate more efficiently, using fewer resources to produce goods or services of equivalent or higher quality. Some governments are now applying these principles to their own services, forcing their agencies to compete with private-sector providers or with other agencies, and sub-contracting many endeav-ours that were once the responsibility of public employees to private firms. Public day-care centres now compete with private providers in Sweden, and health authorities in Britain compete with one another for clients.

From the perspective of democratic theory, these are consequential steps. To ensure that their actions are responsive to the needs of the populace, democratic gov-ernments have traditionally relied upon a chain of authority that links the providers of public services to superiors in a civil service hierarchy who are, in turn, respons-ible to Ministers reporting to a legislature elected by the people. Demands for better services flow from the electorate to the government through the political system. Market institutions, by contrast, render service providers responsive by allowing their clients to turn to other providers if they are dissatisfied with what they receive. One system relies on the 'voice' of the citizen to ensure responsiveness, while the other relies on the capacity of the client to 'exit' (Hirschman 1970). In some respects, then, the 'new public management' is changing the posture of the individual *vis-à-vis* the state from one associated with the role of a 'citizen' to one that more closely resembles that of a 'client'.

In large measure, it was the international dimension of this move to the market during the 1980s that rendered it so forceful and durable. Dissatisfied with poor lev-els of economic performance, the member states of the European Community agreed in 1985 to create a single continental market and to reinforce it in 1999 with an eco-nomic and monetary union that gave most of them a single currency. They disman-tled barriers to trade and allowed the new European Union to make many decisions by (qualified) majority vote, effectively removing the veto each nation once had over decisions affecting it. At the same time, the European Court of Justice has increased its jurisdiction *vis-à-vis* national governments. In combination with the liberaliza-tion of world markets, these steps have increased the impact of market forces on most Europeans and reduced the capacities of national governments to counteract those forces (Hirst and Thompson 1996; Streeck 1995; Scharpf 1999; Cerny 1999).

The recent analysis of democratic institutions in Europe has been deeply influenced by these developments. Privatization, deregulation, and governmental reform are now the subject of large literatures documenting their progress (Vickers and Wright 1989; Vogel 1996; Feigenbaum *et al.* 1998; Thatcher 1999). They have led some to reconsider the criteria used to determine whether an activity should be provided by the public or private sectors, which traditionally assigned to the state those likely to lead to a 'natural' monopoly or to generate significant 'public goods' (Self 1993). Others focus on the 'new public management' to explore the advantages of sub-contracting public services to private firms and the consequences of encouraging competition among government agencies (Kingdon 1990; Barzelay 2001).

A large body of scholarly work is now devoted to the European Union. For some years, this literature was dominated by debates about the factors that condition further political integration, of special interest to institutional analysis because it ranged those who maintain that national governments control the process against others who argue that some elements of the dynamic escape government control because each step towards integration in one sphere generates unanticipated consequences that intensify pressure for integration elsewhere (Moravcsik 1991; 1998; Keohane and Hoffmann 1991; Pierson 1996). The latter often emphasize the orchestrating role of the European Commission and the importance of initiatives from the business community (Sandholtz and Zysman 1989; Streeck and Schmitter 1991; Ross 1995).

In recent years, this debate has waned in favour of more intensive studies of how the European Union operates and its effects on national policy (Héritier *et al.* 1996; Liebfried and Pierson 1995; Wallace and Wallace 1996; Héritier 1999; Scharpf 1999). In an influential series of works, Majone (1994*a*; 1996) explores the implications of a regime that operates primarily through regulation. Tsebelis (1994; 1995) charts the shifts in power that have followed changes to the EU's rules for decision making, stressing the importance of agenda control and veto points to the outcomes. Scholars have begun to compare the quality of governance in the European Union to that of a nation state, considering how multi-tiered governance structures affect the character of policies and responsiveness to the citizenry (Hayward and Page 1995; Marks *et al.* 1996; Hooghe 1996; Scharpf 1999). Some argue that, because the European Union has been more effective at market-building than state-building, it lacks the capacity to provide social protection expected of states and is eroding the ability of its members states to provide such protection as well (Streeck 1995). Others question how democratic the European Union is and explore the state of developments that might render it more so, including the construction of a European public sphere, the emergence of a transnational party system, transparency in decision making, and a stronger parliament (Williams 1991; Perez-Diaz 2000; Goetz and Hix 2000).

CONTEMPORARY EUROPEAN DEMOCRACY

As this survey indicates, the themes that figure most prominently in analyses of European democracy have changed substantially over fifty years in tandem with political developments. The insights this literature has generated remain relevant today but, considered together, they reveal subtle but pervasive shifts in the configuration of European democracy. Moreover, for all its power, democratic theory has not fully caught up with the realities of European governance. There are still substantial discrepancies between the classic concepts used to describe a democratic system and the actual operation of European polities. Consider a few examples.

1. We normally describe the relationship of the individual to the democratic state as one based on 'citizenship'. But the transformation of the state over the past 50 years now limits the adequacy of this description. In some nations, almost half of the populace receives the bulk of its income from the state in the form of pensions, social benefits, or salary. Government services are now so extensive that many individuals approach the state primarily as its clients, whether for day-care, health-care, agricultural support, or social services.

2. The state is traditionally defined as an entity that is 'sovereign' over its territories, but sovereignty has little meaning in a context where the European Union has the authority to enforce regulations on its member states, without the agreement of their national governments. Some suggest that the emerging system of European governance resembles that of the feudal era more than that of the post-Westphalian system of sovereign states (cf. Krasner 1999*a*).

3. The European Union is usually seen as a democratic enterprise, but its governing institutions are more similar to those of the Second German Empire (1871–1914) than to those of most contemporary democratic states. The EU's rules for decision making are so complex that few beyond those who operate them understand them. Its parliament, although elected, has limited powers and operates without an effective party system. Executive power rests with a Commission that is not subject to direct election.

4. We normally think of the legislature as the seat of political power in a nation and the body representative of the citizenry. Most European nations, however, now delegate substantial regulatory power to para-public agencies that make policy without consulting the legislature. Much of the activity we associate with 'representative government' now takes place, not around the legislature but in negotiations between officials and interest groups that by pass it, and sometimes political leaders, altogether.

5. The essence of effective democracy lies in clear lines of accountability running from the government to an electorate that can use competition among political parties to hold it responsible for policy. In many parts of Europe, however, central governments now share so much power with state, regional, or EU authorities that a good deal of policy is determined in inter-level negotiations so intricate that electorates cannot readily determine who is responsible for the results (Scharpf 1991; Marks *et al.* 1996).

6. Although democracy is usually associated with government by representatives of the people or institutions responsible to them, many nations are now vesting greater powers in non-elected bodies, such as courts and central banks, that have been deliberately insulated from political control. As a result, an increasing number of matters that were once decided by governments are now being determined by bodies unaccountable to the electorate (Hall and Franzese 1998; Stone Sweet 2000).

Observations such as these lead some theorists to describe the political systems of Europe as 'post-democratic' (Pasquino 1998).[6] This may be premature. Representative government has always been imperfect, and liberal democracy deliberately places

---

[6] I am grateful to Richard Tuck for drawing my attention to this work.

limits on popular rule. What is less certain is whether the governments of Europe are now limited in the best possible ways. Despite the accomplishments of the literature surveyed here, conventional democratic theory is still somewhat at odds with the operation of European democracies. As European governance changes, we need new accounts of how governments work that can be used to assess the state of European democracy and, by the same token, democratic theories that take full cognizance of the dilemmas of contemporary governance.

Scholars are now studying these problems from a variety of perspectives (Hoffmann 1982; Beck 1986; Held 1987, 1995; Hayward 1995; Gray 1998; Giddens 1998; Krieger 1999; Scharpf 1999). Although this body of work encompasses many diverse approaches, a good deal of it revolves around four sets of issues widely seen as central to a more complete understanding of European democracy. Since they define much of the contemporary research agenda, I will conclude by briefly identifying each.

Many analysts are looking into the impact of international integration on the capacity of modern states to provide the kind of counterweight to market forces that Polanyi (1957) once identified as essential to the success and stability of democracy. In his classic formulation, Polanyi argued that states must temper market competition with social protection, but many question whether governments can still deliver such protection in a context where their instruments have been depleted by more intense international integration (Rodrik 1997; Berger and Dore 1996; Hirst and Thompson 1996; Garrett 1998b). As Scharpf (1999) notes, when governments are less effective, their legitimacy may decline. Some argue that the devolution of power to sub-national and supra-national levels of governance may provide solutions to these problems, but others contend that devolution simply intensifies the dilemmas by rendering policy making less transparent or purposive. Assessments of the political impact of globalization carry great implications for our understanding of European democracy.

Others are studying changes to the meaning of citizenship and the 'nation' inspired by the decline of traditional solidarities based on class or religion, the multiethnic character of European societies, and the expectation that people and foreign cultural forms will continue to flow across open borders. To paraphrase Anderson (1991), many European nations are 'reimagining themselves' and reconsidering the meaning of citizenship (Brubaker 1996; Favell 1998; Krieger 1999). Some analysts expect new forms of European citizenship to emerge that may be a prerequisite for the democratization of the European Union (Soysal 1994; Benhabib 1999; Feldblum 1999). These works remind us that national ideals are an important component of the institutions that structure political life in Europe.

A very different body of literature is applying theories of delegation to the traditional problem of establishing lines of accountability in democratic polities. Pollack (1997) and others use principal-agent analysis to explain the structure of the European Union and patterns of delegation within national polities (Tsebelis 1994; Moravcsik 1998; Przeworski *et al.* 1999). Some employ it to assess the ways in which relations among the executive, legislature, and civil service are being reconfigured in nation states, drawing on extensive work on these problems in the United States

(Huber 1996; Barzelay 2001). These inquiries provide useful tools for assessing the degree to which the many non-elected agencies of contemporary states remain responsive to the electorate.

Finally, a number of analysts are reconsidering the contribution that the organization of civil society makes to the performance of democracies. Putnam (1993; 2002) argues that regular interchange among ordinary citizens generates a body of 'social capital' that can be used to improve policy and the accountability of governments. Rothstein (1998a) explores the way in which levels of trust among the leaders of key social organizations and their followers affect neo-corporatist negotiations. Extending an existing literature about political participation, others assess the conditions that underpin civic engagement or trust in government (Hall 1999; Offe 1999; Norris 1999; Pharr and Putnam 2000). Such analyses link the organization of contemporary society to longstanding issues in the republican tradition of democratic theory.

In sum, we have learned a great deal about the institutions underpinning democracy in Europe over the past fifty years, but there is much still to be investigated. Because the character of democratic governance itself shifts over time, as the institutions and ideals underpinning it respond to changing circumstances, each new generation faces the challenge of devising and implementing an understanding of democracy appropriate for its time.

2

National Courts and Community Law

PAUL P. CRAIG

This chapter examines the way in which national courts have reacted to Community law, in particular to the claim to supremacy over national law contained in the jurisprudence of the ECJ. The discussion begins with a brief account of the Community's supremacy doctrine. This will be followed by an analysis of the reaction of national courts to this claim. The focus will then shift from positive law to the normative evaluation of a number of issues which are central to this topic. The chapter concludes with an overview of the political science literature which has considered the reasons for the reaction of national courts to the claims made by the Community judicial institutions.

SUPREMACY: THE ECJ'S JURISPRUDENCE

It is readily apparent that there will be clashes between Community law and national law. These will often be inadvertent. More intentional recalcitrance on the part of the Member States will be less common, though it is not by any means unknown. In any event some rules must exist for such cases. Not surprisingly the ECJ has held that EC law must be supreme in the event of any such conflict. This principle was first enunciated in *Costa* v. *ENEL*[1] where the ECJ responded to an argument that its preliminary ruling would be of no relevance to the case at hand because the Italian courts would be bound to follow national law. It held,

> By creating a Community of unlimited duration, having...powers stemming from a limitation of sovereignty, or a transfer of powers from the States to the Community, the Member States have limited their sovereign rights, albeit within limited fields, and thus have created a body of law which binds both their nationals and themselves.

The Community's supremacy was given added force by the ECJ's ruling in the *Simmenthal* case,[2] where the Court made it clear that Community law would take precedence even over national legislation which was adopted after the passage of the relevant EC norms. The existence of Community rules rendered automatically inapplicable any contrary provision of national law, *and* precluded the valid adoption of

---

[1] Case 6/64, [1964] E.C.R. 585, 593.
[2] Case 106/77, *Amministrazione delle Finanze dello Stato* v. *Simmenthal SpA* [1978] E.C.R. 629.

any new national law which was in conflict with the Community provisions. It followed, said the ECJ, that 'every national court must, in a case within its jurisdiction, apply Community law in its entirety and protect rights which the latter confers on individuals and must accordingly set aside any provision of national law which may conflict with it, whether prior or subsequent to the Community rule'.[3] The ECJ has, moreover, made it clear that not even a fundamental rule of national constitutional law could be invoked to challenge the supremacy of a directly applicable Community rule.[4] The reasoning of the ECJ concerning supremacy has been subjected to critical scrutiny, notably by de Witte (1984).

SUPREMACY: THE REACTION OF NATIONAL COURTS

All legal systems in the Community have had to deal with the claim by the ECJ to supremacy over national law. In some systems this has been unproblematic. In others there has been greater controversy or difficulty. The very nature of these difficulties has differed between the Member States which belong to the Community. These differences themselves stem from differing constitutional traditions. Space precludes extensive treatment of all the Member States of the Community. The analysis which follows will, however, seek to convey a spectrum of the more important views on this issue. (Schwarze, 2001)

In reading the material which follows it should be recognized that there are four more particular issues which arise for resolution within national legal systems. First, how far have national courts accepted the supremacy of Community law, and have they placed any limits on this acceptance in relation to clashes between Community law and the national constitution? Second, what was the conceptual basis for the national judicial decisions? Did the national court base its acceptance of supremacy on some provision in the national constitution, or did it accept the more *communautaire* reasoning of the ECJ which grounds supremacy on the very nature of the Community legal order? Third, what position does a Member State take on the issue of *Kompetenz–Kompetenz*? It is clear that the European Union is based on attributed competences, and that it only has the powers accorded to it in the constituent treaties. The very scope of those competences is however open to differing interpretations. The key issue is therefore who should have ultimate authority to decide whether some action is *intra* or *ultra vires* the Community? Should this power reside with the ECJ or with national courts? Fourth, it is important to understand that supremacy in continental national legal systems will often be connected with a related but distinct issue. This concerns the court before which the matter can be raised. It is common in such legal systems that only the constitutional court can pronounce on the validity of national legislation. The case law concerning, for example,

---

[3] Case 106/77, *Amministrazione delle Finanze dello Stato* v. *Simmenthal SpA* [1978] E.C.R. 629. para. 21.
[4] Case 11/70, *Internationale Handelsgesellschaft mbH* v. *Einfuhr-und Vorratsstelle fur Getreide und Futtermittel* [1970] ECR 1125.

Italy can only be understood against this background. The objections of the defend-
ants were as much concerned with the court before which the issue could be raised,
as they were with supremacy itself.

Belgium provides a suitable point of departure since it furnishes one of the best
examples of acceptance of the supremacy of Community law based upon reasoning
which is closest to that employed by the ECJ itself. There have been numerous unsuccessful attempts to insert a provision in the Belgian Constitution which would provide for the primacy of treaties over conflicting statutes. Notwithstanding the
absence of any such provision, the Cour de Cassation accorded supremacy to EC law
in the famous *Le Ski* case.[5] The case concerned a conflict between Article 12 of the
EC Treaty, which forbade the introduction of new customs duties, and a later Royal
decree which imposed taxes on milk products imported from EC countries. The
Cour held that in the event of a conflict between a norm of an international treaty
which produces direct effect in the domestic legal order and domestic law, the treaty
must prevail. The primacy of the treaty flowed from the very nature of international
law. This reasoning applied, said the Cour, with particular force in the event of a clash
between Community law and national law, since the EC treaties instituted a new legal
system in whose favour the Member States have restricted the exercise of their sovereign powers in the areas determined by those treaties. The Cour was strongly influenced by the submissions of the Procureur General Ganshof van der Meersch. He
argued that the very nature of international law implied its superiority: the subjects
of international law were the states, and it followed that the international legal order
was superior to national legal orders. The argument was premised on a strong monist
view of the relation between international law and national law: both comprised a
single legal order and hence a norm could not be valid and invalid at the same time.
While the reasoning in *Le Ski* is very *communautaire* there are indications of a more
circumspect approach being taken by other Belgian courts. The Cour d'Arbitrage,
which is the Constitutional Court, has indicated that the constitution is superior to
international treaties, and interpreted *Le Ski* to apply only to the clash between
national laws and the EC Treaty. It has been argued that the logic of the approach
adopted by the Cour d'Arbitrage is that it regards the issue of *Kompetenz–Kompetenz*
as lying within its jurisdiction, not that of the ECJ (Bribosia 1998: 21–2).

In *France*, the Cour de Cassation accepted the supremacy of Community law over
French law as early as 1975.[6] It held that the question was not whether it could review
the constitutionality of a French law. Instead, when a conflict existed between an
'internal law' and a properly ratified 'international act' which had thus entered the
internal legal order, the Constitution itself accorded priority to the latter. The Cour
thus based its decision on Article 55 of the French Constitution,[7] rather than

---

[5] *Fromagerie Franco-Suisse Le Ski* v. *Etat Belge* [1972] CMLR 330.
[6] Decision of 24 May 1975 in *Administration des Douanes* v. *Société 'Cafés Jacques Vabre' et SARL Weigel et Cie.* [1975] 2 CMLR 336.
[7] 'Treaties or agreements duly ratified or approved possess, from the moment of their publication, a superior authority to those of laws under the condition, for each treaty or agreement, of its application by the other party'.

adopting the *communautaire* approach advocated by Procureur Général Adolphe Touffait. The Conseil d'Etat took a different view in *Semoules*,[8] where the problem was cast in jurisdictional terms. The Conseil d'Etat ruled that, since it had no jurisdiction to review the validity of French legislation, it could not find such legislation to be incompatible with Community law, nor could it accord priority to the latter.[9] It was not until 1989 that the Conseil d'Etat shifted its position in the *Nicolo* case.[10] Commissaire du Gouvernement Frydman took the view that Article 55 of itself necessarily enabled the courts, by implication, to review the compatibility of statutes with treaties, and that, therefore, treaties should be given precedence over later statutes. Although it did not expressly adopt the view expressed by the *Commissaire*, the Conseil d'Etat appeared to accept the premises on which that view was based. It ruled that the relevant French statutory rules were not invalid on the ground that they were 'not incompatible with the clear stipulations of the above mentioned Article 227(1) of the Treaty of Rome'. The Conseil d'Etat has also, more recently, recognized the priority of both Community regulations and directives over French statutes, without discussing the theoretical basis for that supremacy.[11] However, as in the case of Belgium, so too in the case of France, the Conseil Constitutionnel has made it clear that there are limits to France's acceptance of supremacy. In its *Maastricht I*[12] decision it confirmed that France could transfer competence to an international organization, provided that it did not thereby violate the essential conditions for the exercise of national sovereignty, and provided that the international agreement did not contain clauses contradictory to the Constitution. If the government does wish to transfer power not allowed by the existing constitutional norms it will therefore have to modify the Constitution. Moreover in its *Maastricht II* decision[13] the Conseil Constitutionnel made reference to Article 89 of the French Constitution which stipulates that the republican form of government may not be open to revision. While the issue of *Kompetenz–Kompetenz* has not been squarely addressed by the French courts, the indications are that the Conseil Constitutionnel regards the final competence as residing within the Member States (Plottner 1998: 52–4).

The approach of the *Italian* courts has been affected by their dualist perspective on the relationship between national and international law. Under this view national and international norms are separate, each regulates its own sphere of competence, and the latter do not become part of national law until they have been transformed or adopted into the national legal system. The national jurisprudence has also been

---

[8] Decision of 1 March 1968 in *Syndicat Général de Fabricants de Semoules de France* [1970] CMLR 395.

[9] Although the French Constitution provided for the primacy of certain international treaties over domestic law, the Conseil d'Etat was of the view that decisions on the constitutionality of legislation were matters for the Conseil Constitutionnel to make before the legislation was promulgated.

[10] [1990] 1 CMLR 173.

[11] See *Boisdet* [1991] 1 CMLR 3, on a reg. which was adopted after the French law, and *Rothmans and Philip Morris and Arizona Tobacco and Philip Morris* [1993] 1 CMLR 253 on a dir. adopted before the French law.   [12] C.C., 9 April 1992.

[13] C.C., 2 September 1992.

shaped by Article 11 of the Constitution which provides that Italy can accept, on the same conditions as other countries, those limitations of sovereignty that are necessary to take part in international organizations aimed at fostering peace and justice among nations. The initial approach of the Italian courts nonetheless denied supremacy to Community law, the Constitutional Court holding that in the event of a clash between two norms, the one later in time should take precedence.[14] It was indeed this national decision which prompted the ECJ to give its famous ruling in the *Costa* case.[15] During the 1970s the Constitutional Court modified its position. It was willing to accord primacy to Community law if it was later in time than the relevant national law. Where the Community norm preceded the national law the former would be applied only after a finding of unconstitutionality by the Constitutional Court. This too did not satisfy the ECJ and led to the *Simmenthal* ruling[16] wherein the ECJ made it clear that every national judge must be able to give full effect to the supremacy of EC law. It was not until 1984, and the decision in *Granital*,[17] that the Constitutional Court modified its approach. It accepted that Community norms which had direct effect should take precedence over national norms, and should be applied by ordinary judges, irrespective of the time when two norms were enacted.[18] However it is clear from the case, and from subsequent jurisprudence,[19] that the Constitutional Court has limited its acceptance of Community law supremacy. It will not bow to the ECJ, or indeed to Community legislation, where this transgresses the fundamental values of the Constitution, such as fundamental rights, democratic principles, and the like (Gaja 1990). It seems that Community norms can derogate from national constitutional provisions provided that they respect the fundamental values of the constitutional system as a whole (Cartabia 1998). Moreover, the Constitutional Court appears to assert that it has the competence to decide on the division of competence between national law and Community law (Petriccione 1986).

In *Germany* there have been different problems. Article 24 of the German Constitution allows for the transfer of legislative power to international organizations, but there have been questions as to whether this Article permitted the transfer to the EC of a power to contravene certain basic principles protected under the Constitution itself. This question arose in *Internationale Handelsgesellschaft mbH.*[20] The German Federal Constitutional Court held that Article 24 nullified any amendment of the EC Treaty which would destroy the identity of the valid constitutional structure of the Federal Republic of Germany by encroaching on the structures which constituted it. The part of the Constitution which dealt with fundamental

---

[14] *Costa/ENEL*, Dec. 14, 7 March 1964.   [15] Above n. 1.   [16] Above n. 2.

[17] *SpA Granital* v. *Amministrazione delle Finanze*, Dec. 170, 8 June 1984.

[18] National law was not held to have been repealed in such cases. The rationalization was rather that national law was deemed not to be relevant in such cases.

[19] *SpA Fragd* v. *Amministrazione delle Finanze*, Dec. 232, 21 April 1989.

[20] *Internationale Handelsgesellschaft mbH.* v. *Einfuhr und- Vorratstelle für Getreide und Futtermittel* [1974] 2 CMLR 540.

rights was an inalienable, essential feature of the German Constitution. The Court held that the Community at that time did not have a codified catalogue of fundamental rights. Given this state of affairs the guarantee of fundamental rights in the Constitution prevailed as long as the competent organs of the Community had not removed the conflict of norms in accordance with the Treaty mechanism. However, by 1986, having considered, *inter alia*, the development by the ECJ of the fundamental rights doctrine (Craig and de Burca 1998: ch. 6), the German Federal Constitutional Court ruled that[21] *so long as* the EC generally ensured effective protection of fundamental rights, which was to be regarded as substantially similar to the protection of fundamental rights required unconditionally by the German Constitution, the Federal Constitutional Court would no longer review Community legislation by the standard of the fundamental rights contained in the Constitution (Frowein 1988).

However, the German court has since then indicated limits to its acceptance of Community law supremacy in its 'Maastricht judgment',[22] in which it ruled on the constitutional relationship between European Community law and German law when the constitutionality of the State's ratification of the Treaty on European Union was challenged (Herdegen 1994; Everling 1994; Weiler 1995a; MacCormick 1995; Kokott 1996; Zulegg 1997; Kumm 1999). It held that ratification was compatible with the Constitution. It did however make it clear that it would not relinquish its power to decide on the compatibility of Community law with the fundamentals of the German Constitution, and that it would continue to exercise a power of review over the scope of Community competence. In the course of its decision the court stated that 'if European institutions or agencies were to treat or develop the Union Treaty in a way that was no longer covered by the Treaty in the form that is the basis for the Act of Accession, the resultant legislative instruments would not be legally binding within the sphere of German sovereignty'.[23] The court also gave a similar warning to the Community judicial institutions, saying that the Union Treaty distinguished between the exercise of a sovereign power conferred for limited purposes and the amendment of the Treaty. Treaty interpretation which had effects equivalent to an extension of the Treaty would not produce any binding effects for Germany.[24] The 'banana' litigation has shown that the German courts are less likely to use this reserved power than suggested by the 'Maastricht judgement'. (Everling 1996; Reich 1996; Kokott 1998; Elbers and Urban 2001; Peters 2000).

The supremacy of Community law was always felt to pose particular problems for the *United Kingdom*. This is because Parliamentary sovereignty is a cornerstone of UK constitutional law. The traditional formulation of this doctrine holds that Parliament has the power to do anything other than to bind itself for the future (Wade 1955). Moreover, the United Kingdom has always adopted a dualist view about the relationship between international treaties and national law. Such treaties,

---

[21] *Re Wünsche Handelsgesellschaft*, Dec. of 22 October 1986 [1987] 3 CMLR 225, 265.
[22] *Brunner v. The European Union Treaty* [1994] 1 CMLR 571.   [23] *Ibid.* para. 49.
[24] *Ibid.* para. 99.

although signed and ratified by the United Kingdom, are not part of the domestic law of the United Kingdom. To be enforceable at the domestic level, they must be domestically incorporated in an Act of Parliament. This then makes it very difficult to guarantee the supremacy of Community law over later national statute, since the Act of Parliament which incorporates EC law and makes it domestically binding would seem vulnerable to any later Act of Parliament which contravenes or contradicts it. The traditional principle of Parliamentary sovereignty would not permit the earlier statute to constrain Parliament, which might wish to contradict its earlier measure in a later statute. The courts would be obliged to give effect to the latest expression of the will of Parliament and to treat the earlier statute as having been repealed or disapplied by implication (Wade 1996*b*).

The European Communities Act 1972 incorporated EC law in domestic law. It provides through section 2(1) that Community rights and obligations will be recognized and enforced. There need not be a fresh act of incorporation to enable UK courts to enforce each EC regulation. Section 2(4) stipulates that 'any enactment passed or to be passed . . . shall be construed and have effect subject to the foregoing provisions of this section'.

The leading decision on the supremacy issue is now *R.* v. *Secretary of State for Transport, ex p. Factortame Ltd.*[25] in which Spanish fishermen claimed that the criteria for registration of vessels under the Merchant Shipping Act 1988 were discriminatory and incompatible with the EC Treaty. Whether the 1988 statute was in fact in breach of EC law was clearly a contentious question, and all agreed that a reference should be made to the ECJ under Article 177 (now 234). The question which remained for decision in the first *Factortame* case concerned the status of the 1988 Act pending the decision on the substance of the case by the ECJ. The House of Lords decided that there was no jurisdiction under English law to grant interim injunctions against the Crown, and the applicant claimed that this was itself a violation of Community law. The ECJ decided this issue in favour of the applicants.[26] It held that, the full effectiveness of Community law would be impaired if a rule of national law could prevent a court seised of a dispute governed by Community law from granting interim relief.[27]

The case then returned to the House of Lords to be reconsidered in the light of the preliminary ruling given by the ECJ, *R.* v. *Secretary of State for Transport, ex p. Factortame Ltd (No. 2)*.[28] Lord Bridge had this to say [29]

Some public comments on the decision of the Court of Justice, affirming the jurisdiction of the courts of the member states to override national legislation if necessary to enable interim relief to be granted in protection of rights under Community law, have suggested that this was a novel and dangerous invasion by a Community institution of the sovereignty of the United Kingdom Parliament. But such comments are based on a misconception. If the supremacy within the European Community of Community law over the national law of member states

---

[25] [1990] 2 A.C. 85.

[26] Case 213/89, *R.* v. *Secretary of State for Transport, ex p. Factortame Ltd.* [1990] 3 C.M.L.R. 867.

[27] [1990] 3 C.M.L.R. 867, para. 21.   [28] [1991] 1 A.C. 603.   [29] [1991] 1 A.C. 603, 658–9.

was not always inherent in the EEC Treaty it was certainly well established in the jurisprudence of the Court of Justice long before the United Kingdom joined the Community. Thus, whatever limitation of its sovereignty Parliament accepted when it enacted the European Communities Act 1972 was entirely voluntary. Under the terms of the 1972 Act it has always been clear that it was the duty of a United Kingdom court, when delivering final judgment, to override any rule of national law found to be in conflict with any directly enforceable rule of Community law. Similarly, when decisions of the Court of Justice have exposed areas of United Kingdom statute law which failed to implement Council directives, Parliament has always loyally accepted the obligation to make appropriate and prompt amendments. Thus there is nothing in any way novel in according supremacy to rules of Community law in areas to which they apply and to insist that, in the protection of rights under Community law, national courts must not be prohibited by rules of national law from granting interim relief in appropriate cases is no more than a logical recognition of that supremacy.

The *EOC* case [30] serves to demonstrate the ease with which the highest national courts have slipped into their new role. The case concerned the compatibility of UK legislation on unfair dismissal and redundancy pay with EC law. Under the relevant UK law [31] entitlement to these protections and benefits operated differentially depending upon whether the person was in full-time or part-time employment. Full-time workers were eligible after two years; part-time workers only after five. The great majority of part-time workers were women and the Equal Opportunities Commission took the view that the legislation discriminated against women, contrary to Article 119 EC (now Article 141) and to certain Community directives. The EOC sought a declaration that the UK legislation was in breach of EC law. The House of Lords found for the applicant. It held that the national legislation was indeed in breach of Article 119 and the directives. The House of Lords went on to make it clear that this power to review primary legislation resided in national *courts*. It was not only the House of Lords itself which was to have this species of authority. The Divisional Court could itself exercise this power. [32]

Space precludes a thorough analysis of the effects of these cases on the traditional concept of sovereignty. This can be found elsewhere (Craig 1991; Wade 1996*b*; Allan 1997). A distinction should be made in this respect as between the substantive impact of the decision and its conceptual foundation.

In terms of its substantive impact, it seems that the concept of implied repeal or disapplication, under which inconsistencies between later and earlier norms were resolved in favour of the former, will no longer apply to clashes concerning Community and national law. If Parliament ever does wish to derogate from its Community obligations then it will have to do so expressly and unequivocally. Whether our national courts would then choose to follow the latest will of Parliament, or whether they would argue that it is not open to our legislature to pick and choose which obligations to subscribe to while still remaining within the Community, remains to be seen. It is also unclear precisely how are courts would deal with the *Kompetenz–Kompetenz* issue which will be discussed more fully below (Craig 1998).

---

[30] R. v. *Secretary of State for Employment, ex p. Equal Opportunities Commission* [1994] 1 All E.R. 910.
[31] Employment Protection (Consolidation) Act 1978.   [32] *Ibid.* p. 920.

There is more dispute as to the conceptual foundation for, or explanation of, what the courts have done (Craig 2000a). For some it is possible to rationalize what the courts have done merely as a species of *statutory construction*. All would agree that if a statute can be reconciled with a Community norm through construing the statutory words without thereby unduly distorting them then this should be done, more especially when the statute was passed to effectuate a directive. However the species of statutory construction being considered here is more far-reaching. On this view accommodation between national law and EC law is attained through a rule of construction to the effect that inconsistencies *will* be resolved in favour of the latter *unless* Parliament has indicated clearly and ambiguously that it intends to derogate from Community law. The degree of linguistic inconsistency between the statute and the Community norm is not the essential point of the inquiry. Provided that there is no unequivocal derogation from Community law then it will apply, rather than any conflicting domestic statute. Counsel for the applicants framed their argument in this manner in the first *Factortame* case.[33] This view was posited by Lord Bridge in the same case where he stated that the effect of section 2(4) of the European Communities Act 1972 was that the Merchant Shipping Act 1988 should take effect as if a section were incorporated in the later statute that its provisions would be without prejudice to directly enforceable Community rights.[34] His Lordship relied on the effect of the 1972 Act as part of his argument in the second *Factortame* case.[35] A similar argument has been made extra-judicially by Sir John Laws (1995: 89), and by Hartley (1999). The construction view is said to leave the essential core of the traditional view of legal sovereignty intact, in the sense that it is always open to a later Parliament to make it unequivocally clear that it wishes to derogate from EC law. In the absence of this, section 2(4) serves to render EC law dominant in the event of a conflict with national law. The attractions of this approach are self-evident. Clashes between EC law and national law can be reconciled while preserving the formal veneer of legal sovereignty. This approach is, however, not unproblematic (Wade 1996b; Craig 2000a).

A second way in which it is possible to conceptualize what the courts have done is to regard it as a *technical legal revolution*. This is the preferred explanation of Sir William Wade who sees the courts' decisions as modifying the ultimate legal principle or rule of recognition on which the legal system is based. On this view the 'rule of recognition is itself a political fact which the judges themselves are able to change when they are confronted with a new situation which so demands' (Wade 1996b: 574).

There is, however, a third way in which to regard the courts' jurisprudence. This is to regard decisions about supremacy as being based on *normative arguments of legal principle the content of which can and will vary across time*. This is my own preferred view (Craig 2000a, b). A similar argument has been advanced by Allan (1997). On this view there is no a priori inexorable reason why Parliament, merely because of its very existence, must be regarded as legally omnipotent. The existence of such power, like all power, must be justified by arguments of principle which are normatively convincing. Possible constraints on Parliamentary omnipotence must similarly be

---

[33] [1990] 2 AC 85, 96.   [34] [1990] 2 AC 85, 140.   [35] [1991] 1 AC 603, 658–9.

reasoned through and defended on normative grounds. This approach fits well with the reasoning of Lord Bridge in the second *Factortame* case. His Lordship does not approach the matter as if the courts were making an unconstrained political choice at the point where the law stops. His reasoning is more accurately represented as being based on *principle*, in the sense of working through the principled consequences of the UK's membership of the EC. The contractarian and functional arguments used by Lord Bridge exemplify this style of judicial discourse. They provide sound normative arguments as to why the United Kingdom should be bound by EC law while it remains within the Community. These arguments would moreover be convincing and have force even if section 2(4) had never been included in the 1972 Act.

FROM POSITIVE LAW TO NORMATIVE EVALUATION: FOUR CENTRAL ISSUES

The discussion thus far has concentrated on positive law, in terms of how national courts have reacted to the claims to supremacy in the jurisprudence of the ECJ. It is important to stand back from this case law and to evaluate in normative terms four of the central issues which are of relevance in this area.

The Conceptual Basis for the Decisions of National Courts

We have seen that one such issue is the conceptual foundation on which any particular national court chooses to accept the supremacy of Community law. A national court may base its decision on the *communautaire* reasoning of the ECJ. This emphasizes the distinctive nature of the Community legal order and the fact that supremacy is necessary in order to ensure that the EC attains the tasks assigned to it. Acceptance of this reasoning is to be found most clearly in the judgment of the Belgian court in *Le Ski*.[36] The alternative formulation is to make acceptance of supremacy turn on the existence of a provision in the national constitution, or in a primary statute, such as Article 55 of the French Constitution, Article 11 of the Italian Constitution, section 2(4) of the UK European Communities Act 1972, or Article 93 of the Spanish Constitution.[37]

It is clear as a matter of principle that there is nothing to *prevent* a national court from adopting the former 'route' should it wish to do so, and that this is so notwithstanding the existence of a provision such as Article 55 of the French Constitution.

It is equally clear that there is nothing to *compel* a national court to adopt the *communautaire* explanation for supremacy. It is moreover not surprising that most national courts have opted for some version of the second conceptual foundation for supremacy. National courts will, other things being equal, seek to reconcile the supremacy of EC law in a way which entails least disturbance of the existing constitutional order. It is therefore natural for courts to fasten upon provisions such as Article 55 of the French Constitution when adjudicating on this delicate matter.

[36] Above n. 5.   [37] The position in Spain is explained lucidly in de Noriega 1999.

The logical consequence of doing so is that if the national constitution were to be changed, and the relevant provision were to be excised from it, then the supremacy of EC law would be undermined. This problem should nonetheless be kept within perspective. Even if this should occur, it would still be open to a national court, depending upon the precise form of the revised constitution, to continue to accept the supremacy of EC law, basing this on some version of the *communautaire* thesis.

Supremacy: 'Clear' Cases

Much of the discussion about supremacy has focussed on clashes between EC law and constitutional norms, and on the issue of *Kompetenz–Kompetenz*. Both are important and will be considered below. Discussion of these issues should not, however, be allowed to cloud the more straightforward case. This is where there is a clash between EC law and national law in circumstances where neither of the above problems is present. If the national law predates the EC norm then most legal systems would apply the *lex posterior* maxim, or rules of construction, in order to accord supremacy to the Community norm.

The more difficult instance is where the Community has enacted a regulation or directive which conflicts with a later national law in an area which is unequivocally within Community competence. This conflict may be inadvertent, the result of absence of fit between the two norms. In such cases national courts may be inclined once again to use principles of construction to 'square the circle' and make the two norms compatible.

This leaves the most difficult instance of all, which is where the conflict is intentional. What national courts would do, as a matter of positive law, in such a case would be for them to decide in the light of their national constitutional traditions. What is of relevance here is the position in normative terms. When viewed from this perspective the argument for the supremacy of Community law is a strong one.

A number of arguments combine towards this conclusion. In *functional* terms many of the central precepts of the EC are based on the uniform application of its laws in all the Member States. This would be seriously undermined if states could pick and choose as to the norms which they were willing to accept. In *contractarian* terms, for those Member States other than the original six, it can be argued that they joined the EC knowing full well the terms of membership, including the *acquis communautaire*, a central component of which is the supremacy doctrine. For such states to turn round later and to seek to depart from Community norms is therefore to act in breach of the terms on which they made their contract when joining the Community. The fact that successive Treaty amendments have not touched this cornerstone of Community case law provides a contractarian rationale as to why even the original six should be bound. To allow states intentionally to depart from Community norms which are unequivocally within the EC's competence would also *undermine the Community's legislative process* which has been agreed to by all the Member States. Where a norm has been properly enacted by qualified majority, a state which has lost out in the EC's legislative arena should not be allowed to resile from that obligation through the intentional enactment of national legislation to the contrary. This is all the more so given that the legislative process itself may afford opportunities for states to secure some form of differential application of Community law in their own country (Tuytschaever 1999; de Burca and Scott 2000). If they have been unable to do so, then they should not be able to upset the stipulated legislative mechanisms by the intentional enactment of national legislation which is contrary to Community law.

The principal normative argument to the contrary is based on *democracy*: if the national legislature intentionally chooses to pass legislation which is in conflict with EC law, then this should be upheld and applied by the national court since the legislature is the expression of that country's democratic will. This argument is however flawed. If a Member State should choose to exit from the Community because of disagreements with its policies, so be it.[38] It is a good deal more difficult to sustain the argument from democracy where the state wishes to remain in the EC, albeit while not adhering to a norm which it has enacted. The very decision to join the EC made by the national Parliament is itself an expression of national democratic will. This decision has benefits, in terms of access to the single market, free movement, etc. It also necessarily has costs, in terms of some loss of autonomy. This is indeed characteristic of any collective action (Buchanan and Tullock 1962). When viewed in this manner the democratically mandated decision to enter and remain in the EC must necessarily lead to some limitations on what the national Parliament is free to do.

It may of course be the case that the state can advance *other* normative arguments to justify its departure from Community law. It might, for example, wish to argue that compliance with Community law would place it in breach of other obligations derived from another international treaty. Claims of this nature would then have to be assessed in their own right in the light of the relevant norms which govern the relationship between Community obligations and those based on other international treaties.

In the absence of any such argument it is difficult, in normative terms, to defend a state which seeks not to comply with a norm which it dislikes in an area which does fall four square within the sphere of Community law.

Supremacy: Clashes with National Constitutional Norms

We have seen that, for the ECJ, the supremacy of EC law operates even against national constitutional norms.[39] Acceptance of this aspect of the supremacy doctrine has been felt to be particularly problematic for some, if not all, Member States. That clashes of this kind are problematic is undeniable. Closer analysis of this type of case

[38] There is in fact no explicit provision for such exit. Space precludes discussion of the relevant legal issues which arise in this context. Suffice it to say for the present that, in political terms, the other Member States would not seek to force such a state to remain within the EC.

[39] Above n. 4.

is however helpful in order to distinguish the differing normative considerations which are at stake.

Let us begin by understanding what constitutions, for all their variety (Finer *et al.* 1995), actually contain (Raz 1998). Most constitutions will in some way or another address two types of issue which can be regarded as the core of the document. There will be what can be termed *structural constitutional provisions*. These are designed to identify the law-making organs of the state, the composition of the executive, and the relationship between legislature and executive. In nation states which are federal, or where there is some measure of devolution, the structural provisions of the constitution will also identify the powers of the different tiers of government. There will often be *rights-based limitations* on what the organs of government thus specified are able to do. Not all constitutions contain rights-based limits on governmental action. Many constitutions do however have such provisions. The generality or specificity of such Bills of Rights varies significantly. Over and beyond these provisions constitutions vary enormously. Some are 'thin', containing little if anything else. Others are 'fat', with the consequence that many measures are thereby constitutionalized.

There may well be a number of legal consequences of having a written constitution. Two are especially worthy of note. The existence of such a constitution will have *implications for the powers of the courts* (Stone Sweet 2000). It should however be recognized that the existence of a constitution does not inexorably mean that there should be only one form of constitutional review. There are a number of options, ranging from what can be termed strong constitutional review, connoting the power of a constitutional court to invalidate legislation which offends constitutionally enshrined rights, to a rule of construction that primary legislation will be deemed not to offend such rights. Legal systems can adopt a variety of positions along this spectrum. The existence of a written constitution will often also mean that *special rules apply for the modification of the constitutional document*. The nature of these rules will vary from legal system to legal system. Special majorities may be required for constitutional amendment. These may be combined with the need for a referendum, or some form of constitutional convention. The common theme is however that by denominating an issue as 'constitutional' we recognize that it is taken off the agenda of normal politics: the norms enshrined in a written constitution are not at the whim or mercy of the party or parties which happen to control the ordinary legislative agenda at that time. This does not mean that the constitutional norms are ossified and incapable of being changed. It does mean that they cannot be changed simply by the passage of ordinary primary legislation.

With this background we can begin to make some progress as to clashes between EC law and national constitutional law. It is useful to distinguish between four such types of case.

In the first, the state is *willing to accept the modification of its constitutional* status quo. This is exemplified by the French judicial and political reaction to the Maastricht Treaty. The Conseil Constitutionnel decided that the citizenship provisions of the Maastricht Treaty which gave a right to vote in municipal elections to non-French EU citizens infringed Articles 3, 24, and 72 of the French Constitution. The Constitution was amended to remove this difficulty. A similar scenario occurred in Spain (de Noriega 1999: 279). This type of case is further exemplified by the reaction of the Italian Constitutional Court which held that Community norms could derogate in some way from national constitutional norms, provided that they respected the fundamental values of the constitutional system (Cartabia 1998: 139). In these types of case the inconsistency between EC law and national law is regarded as curable or acceptable, because the constitutional rules thereby affected are themselves perceived as open to change without thereby compromising the essential constitutional fabric of that state.

The second type of case is that in which the *state is willing to accept restraint in the exercise of national constitutional norms, provided that EC law develops protections regarded by the state as essential in a democratic polity.* This is exemplified by the jurisprudence of the German Federal Constitutional Court in the fundamental rights' cases. The effect of the decision in *Solange II*[40] is not that the German Court gave up its jurisdiction in such cases. It is rather that it decided that it would no longer control Community regulations and the like on the basis that they infringed rights contained in the German Basic law, provided that the EC itself ensured effective protection for such rights. In this type of case the provisions contained in the national constitutional norms are regarded as sacrosanct, but the state is willing to accept that national enforcement thereof can be held in abeyance where sufficient protection exists at the EC level.

The third type of case is where the *state signals its refusal to accept the supremacy of EC law in the event of a conflict with 'essential' national constitutional norms.* There are judicial utterances from, for example, the French and Italian courts, that EC law will not be allowed to undermine the republican form of government, or derogate from the fundamental principles of the constitutional system, respectively. In these cases the courts are providing a 'long stop' to ensure that the core essence of that state's constitutional tradition is not undermined. There are analogous statements to be found in the Spanish case law where the Constitutional Court has made it clear that Community law does not take priority over the Spanish Constitution (de Noriega 1999). Precisely which issues come within this is, of course, inherently contestable. It has moreover been argued by MacCormick (1999: 115–19) that supremacy of Community law should not be confused with all-purpose subordination of Member State law to Community law, and in particular that it should not necessarily be taken to mean the subordination of the entirety of the state's constitution.

The final type of case is that in which *the state signals its refusal to accept supremacy of EC law because it believes that the subject-matter of the dispute is not within the Community's competence.* This raises the general problem of *Kompetenz–Kompetenz* which will be discussed more generally below. It can arise in a constitutional context where the essence of the national argument is that the EC does not have competence over a particular area because the national constitution reserved this for the state itself, and prevented the matter from being delegated or surrendered to any other institution.

[40] Above n. 21.

Kompetenz–Kompetenz

We have seen that a number of the national courts, explicitly or implicitly, have assumed that the ultimate power to decide on the limits of the Community's competence resides with them. The Danish Supreme Court has adopted the same view.[41] The ECJ for its part has, not surprisingly, taken the opposite view, and has indeed denied that national courts have the power to invalidate Community legislation.[42] Some academics have in the light of this conflict expressed the view that there is no way of resolving this dilemma (Stone Sweet 1998: 319). There has however been a lively doctrinal debate on just this issue.

Schilling (1996) has defended the Member State view and argued that the ECJ is wrong to regard itself as the ultimate authority on the scope of Community competence. He considers that international law is the only viable foundation for the Community legal order. From this he concludes that the ultimate *Kompetenz–Kompetenz* must reside with the states. Schilling's argument is that, in the absence of treaty institutions, the accepted method for the interpretation of international treaties is autointerpretation by the contracting states. He acknowledges that a reading of Articles 220 and 226–40 could be taken to mean that the ECJ has a judicial *Kompetenz–Kompetenz*. Schilling nonetheless rejects that view, arguing that because the Community is limited to the purposes set out in Article 2, the Treaties taken as a whole should not be interpreted so as to accord the ECJ a judicial *Kompetenz–Kompetenz*. On his view the states have preserved their right to autointerpret the Treaties, with the consequence that they individually have the final word on the scope of the competences which they have delegated to the Community.

This view has been vigorously challenged by Weiler and Haltern (1996). They accept for the sake of argument that the Community can be regarded as being grounded in international law.[43] They do not accept that autointerpretation is the accepted method of treaty interpretation in international law, and argue that there is much authority for the view that claims of unconstitutionality are decided by the organs whose acts were challenged (Osieke 1977, 1983). Weiler and Haltern then turn their attention to the interpretation of the EC Treaties. The plain meaning of Articles 220 and 226–40 taken as a whole, and in particular the wording of Articles 226, 227, 230, and 234, is to accord the ECJ the ultimate authority to decide on the issue of Community competence. They then reveal the flaw in Schilling's argument that this natural construction should be rejected because the Community only has authority in the areas assigned to it under Article 2. The argument that a Community without legislative *Kompetenz–Kompetenz* cannot possess a court with judicial *Kompetenz–Kompetenz* is the real centre of Schilling's argument. There is, as Weiler and Haltern state, no reason why an international organization with limited powers,

---

[41] Case 1 361/97, *Carlsen* v. *Rasmussen*, 6 April 1998.
[42] Case 314/85, *Firma Foto-Frost* v. *Hauptzollamt Lubeck-Ost* [1987] ECR 4199.
[43] They do however argue, correctly in my view, that there are many features of the Community legal order which warrant its characterization in constitutional terms.

and hence no *legislative Kompetenz–Kompetenz,* should not contain a court with *judicial Kompetenz–Kompetenz,* which would be the ultimate arbiter of disputes concerning the extent of those limited competences.

There is a further, more theoretical, dimension to the debate about *Kompetenz–Kompetenz.* MacCormick's work is of real significance here. He has, in a series of pieces (1993, 1995, 1996, 1999), addressed the relationship between national and Community legal orders. Space precludes any detailed treatment of MacCormick's thesis, but the essence of his argument and its relevance to the present debate is as follows. The theoretical starting point is one of legal pluralism, 'the idea that there can coexist distinct but genuinely normative legal orders' (1999: 102). Law, as institutional normative order, is clearly to be found in the EC as well as in Member States. Both legal orders possess constitutions, in the sense of norms which establish and empower their regime's institutions. Where 'there is a plurality of institutional normative orders, each with a functioning constitution (at least in the sense of a body of higher-order norms establishing and conditioning relevant government powers), it is possible that each acknowledge the legitimacy of every other within its own sphere, while none asserts or acknowledges constitutional superiority over another' (1999: 104). MacCormick terms this constitutional pluralism.[44] While he accepts that there are other ways in which the relationship between legal orders could be conceptualized, he argues that the pluralistic reading is the most convincing (1999: 116–17). The consequences of this reading are important.

On the one hand, it means that the doctrine of supremacy of Community law 'should by no means be confused with any kind of all-purpose subordination of member-state-law to Community law' (1999: 117), since to hold that membership of the Community necessarily entailed subordination of the state's entire constitution to Community law would be wrong (1999: 116).

On the other hand, the systems are properly to be regarded as interacting; each constitutes in its own context and over the relevant range of topics a source of law superior to other sources. Thus the ECJ should be held to have the 'competence to interpret the norms conferring this interpretative competence, and thus an interpretative, as distinct from a norm-creating, competence–competence' (1999: 117). But equally the highest national courts must be able to interpret their national constitutional and other norms and 'hence to interpret the interaction of the validity of EC law with higher level norms of validity in the given state system' (1999: 118).

The view proffered by MacCormick does of course mean, as he himself admits, that not every problem may be susceptible to simple legal resolution. The ECJ would have an interpretative, but not a norm-creating, *Kompetenz–Kompetenz,* while the supreme national courts would retain authority to test the validity of EC law with their own higher level norms. He does however make it clear that national determinations as to whether EC law is consistent with the essentials of a national legal order should be undertaken 'in accordance with international obligations to other member states and in accordance with essential commitments of the national legal order including the

---

[44] See also Kumm (1999).

commitment to good faith observance of international obligations' (1999: 120). This should affect the standard of review which a national court employs when thinking of rejecting a Community norm which it believes to be *ultra vires*. The national court should only adopt such a course of action if it believes that the Community illegality is manifest.

It should moreover be pointed out that others have sensed the need for moderation in this context. Thus Kumm (1999) has also argued for a pluralist reading of the relationship between the Community and national legal orders. In a different vein, while Weiler and Haltern have argued for the existence of a *Kompetenz–Kompetenz* power in the ECJ, they nonetheless maintain that the legitimacy of decisions about Community competences would be enhanced if a new body were to be created to adjudicate on such matters, which would be composed of representatives from national judiciaries as well as from the ECJ (1996).

EXPLAINING NATIONAL COURT ATTITUDES TO ECJ JURISPRUDENCE: THE CONTRIBUTION OF POLITICAL SCIENCE

The Contending Views

There have been a number of interesting and conflicting explanations of national judicial attitudes to the ECJ's jurisprudence on supremacy and direct effect.

A *neo-realist* explanation has been advanced by Garrett (1992; 1995a), and by Garrett and Weingast (1993). They see legal decisions at both the national and the European level as being shaped by national interest calculations. On this view national actors have a variety of tools at their disposal to influence the way in which courts exercise their power. These tools include constitutional amendment, alteration of the court's jurisdiction, and passive resistance to judgments which are disliked. The very possibility that these tools might be used causes courts such as the ECJ to remain within the sphere which is acceptable to Member States, and even promotes the interests of the more powerful states. While all courts will be influenced in general terms by what is 'acceptable' to their constituency, there is no consistent evidence to sustain the neo-realist assertion that national interests are the principal factor in shaping judicial behaviour (Alter 1998: 236).

A *neo-functionalist* rationalization has been put forward by Burley and Mattli (1993). The thesis is that the ECJ created a structure which made it rational and advantageous for a number of different actors to use Community norms and thereby to foster legal integration. Private citizens were given Community rights which they could use in their own name in their own courts to challenge national norms. National courts, particularly lower level courts, were accorded increased power because the ECJ made it clear that its doctrines of direct effect and supremacy could be pleaded before any national court. Many national courts gained powers to challenge primary legislation which they had not possessed before. National courts became Community courts in their own right, a feature expressly emphasised by the ECJ. Lawyers specializing in EC law were willing advocates in this process, as were scholars of Community law. The neo-functionalist thesis has been criticized by Alter (1998: 239–41). She argues that not all legal actors see themselves as empowered through EC law. Some supreme courts have had their monopoly over national law diminished. The fact that 'some actors gain through legal integration cannot explain why those actors which saw themselves as net losers in the process accepted the outcome of legal integration' (Alter 1998: 240). She argues further that many potential plaintiffs choose not to avail themselves of EC law even though it would advance their interests, and that the neo-functionalist argument cannot explain significant time lags or variation in legal integration as between different countries. The neo-functionalists have more recently modified their position to accommodate some of these arguments (Mattli and Slaughter 1998).

Alter's own preferred account is the model of *inter-court competition* (Alter 1998). Her thesis is that different courts have different and often competing interests in legal integration. Lower national courts will often be in competition with higher national courts. The former can use ECJ jurisprudence to circumvent decisions of higher national courts which they dislike. Lower national courts also gain by expanding their own power to include an element of constitutional review which they did not possess hitherto. Higher national courts, by way of contrast, have an interest in 'thwarting the expansion and penetration of EC law into the national legal order' (Alter 1998: 242), because this will diminish their monopoly of influence over national law. For Alter it is therefore the lower national courts which have cajoled higher national courts to accept the supremacy of EC law over national law. On this view it is the lower national courts which make the references to the ECJ to 'challenge existing national jurisprudence or to challenge high court decisions' (Alter 1998: 243). National high courts to which legal questions were appealed had either to accept ECJ doctrine or to reject. They accepted it provided that it did not encroach too far on their own autonomy. Lower courts continued to make references to the ECJ, and higher national courts, Alter argues, 'repositioned themselves to the new reality' (1998: 243). The national high courts adjusted their constitutional doctrine to make it compatible with the supremacy of EC law over national law, but did so on grounds which were most compatible with that doctrine.

Political scientists tend to take a dim view of *legalistic explanations* as being of importance in explaining legal integration. The very way in which the 'legal view' is presented is clearly of importance. Thus, Alter, for example, regards the paradigm legal perspective as one in which EC law has its own inherent legal logic which both justifies the decisions made by the ECJ and compels national courts to apply that jurisprudence. National court decisions which do not do so are seen as unintended mistakes to be 'cured' by better information (1998: 230). This view is then criticized on the ground that the inexorable legal logic driving the process does not exist. She acknowledges a more nuanced version of legalism in which it is accepted that ECJ decisions have a prima facie authoritative force. This is found wanting as an explanation of legal integration on the grounds that there is much that it fails to explain, including time lags in the acceptance of supremacy and the continued variation in national court behaviour in relation to ECJ doctrine (Alter 1998: 231).

A Lawyer's Response

Analysis of these matters by political scientists is valuable. They bring skills and a perspective to bear which lawyers lack. This does not of course preclude lawyers from subjecting such theories to critical scrutiny. My comments will be limited to explanations 2–4, since I have nothing to add to the criticism already made of the neo-realist model.

My own view is that an admixture of the *legalistic and neo-functional theory* provides the best explanation for what has occurred, that properly understood they are not separate theories at all, and that the criticisms thereof are largely misplaced.

Lawyers do not generally believe that there is some inexorable logic driving us towards acceptance of Community law supremacy. Few legal issues are capable of being stated this definitively, and the relationship between Community law and national law is certainly not one of them. What lawyers might well believe with justification is that there is some force in the claims to legal supremacy propounded by the ECJ, even if this should be qualified in the ways considered above. It is significant that we do not find national constitutional courts seeking to argue positively or normat-ively that national law should take precedence over Community law in circumstances where there is no conflict with national constitutional norms, and no issue of *Kompetenz–Kompetenz*. We do not, in other words, see normative claims by such national courts to justify recalcitrance by a Member State in relation to an issue which is unequivocally within the EC's sphere of competence, where issues of fundamental rights, etc. are absent. In this sense the legalistic arguments have weight.

But lawyers would also regard the factors which form the neo-functionalist argument as being of importance. To exclude such considerations is to somehow reify legal systems and legal argumentation in a way which few, if any, lawyers would seek to do. Courts hear cases because people bring those cases to them. This is a trite but important proposition. People bring such cases because they believe that there is some advantage in doing so. They rely on EC law where it is helpful to their claim. It was the Community law doctrine of direct effect which allowed them to bring their actions in national courts. It was indeed this very doctrine which was of principal importance in allowing supremacy claims to be litigated before national courts. Direct effect, combined with the preliminary reference mechanism and the doctrine of precedent enunciated by the ECJ, provided a powerful tool to enable individuals to challenge national norms which were inconsistent with EC law (Weiler 1981, 1991; Craig 1992). This fostered legal integration in the general manner argued for by the neo-functionalists. It was especially important at a time when the Community legislative process was suffering from malaise, and hence when integration in this way was beset with difficulties.

The arguments against the combined legalistic and neo-functionalist view are not convincing. It is of course the case that there were 'losers' from the Community law regime. The 'winners' nonetheless outnumbered the losers by a large measure. Direct effect gave all those in the Community rights which they could employ against the state or other private parties. It created roughly 300 million potential plaintiffs who had the optimal incentive to use rights in their own name in their own national courts. It was difficult for the state itself to deny that individuals should have such rights. This was in part because of the incremental development of the direct effect doctrine by the ECJ. It was in part because it would have been difficult politically for a state to argue that such rights should not be accorded to its citizens. National supreme courts might be losers to some degree, insofar as their monopoly over national law was compromised. Yet their acceptance of the supremacy of Community law, albeit subject to the limits discussed above, is nonetheless explicable. The legalistic argument in the sense presented above was of significance in this respect. So too was the fact that while their adjudicative monopoly over national law was diminished, their overall power was also increased to the extent that they could now rule against national law for inconsistency with EC law. The argument that neo-functionalism fails to explain time lags or variation in the acceptance of supremacy in different states is difficult to understand. Courts are not machines. Legal systems are not identikit computers. The forces which operate in legal systems are diverse and eclectic. There is no reason to expect uniformity in this respect. In one legal system the high courts may, for example, rest content with accommodation of EC law through rules of construction which obviate any tension between national law and Community law, thereby avoiding the necessity of passing judgment on the supremacy issue directly for some time. In other legal systems the style and manner of adjudication may be different, leading to an earlier confrontation of such matters. Moreover, the factual foundation for the claim that actors choose not to avail themselves of EC legal argument, even though it would help their cause, is wanting.

The premises of the *inter-court competition thesis* are open to challenge in a number of respects. It is true that the interests of lower and higher national courts might diverge to some degree. The reality of their interrelationship is more complex. The idea that lower national courts were eager to arrogate power to themselves, and that this was the main driving force behind legal integration, does not ring true. The argument assumes implicitly that only national constitutional courts had concerns about the relationship between EC law and the domestic constitution, and that lower courts would not be concerned with the possibility that EC law would impinge on national constitutional provisions. This is counter-intuitive to say the least. Most important is the fact that the thesis fails to take account of the mechanics of adjudication introduced by the EC Treaties. Cases come before domestic courts. They are brought by parties who desire a resolution of their dispute as expeditiously as possible. The cases may involve a clash between EC law and a primary national statute. The clash may be between a different national norm, an executive act, or an administrative order, and an EC rule. It may be unclear whether a primary statute is really at stake at all. The parties begin their case in the relevant lower national court. They have no desire to fight their way through the entire national judicial hierarchy in order to get an answer. Their natural interest is to have the case referred to the ECJ as quickly as possible, or even better to ask the national court to pass judgment itself in the light of a ruling on the matter already given by the

ECJ. It is true that *Simmenthal*[45] facilitated the exercise of this power by lower national courts. It is true also that lower national courts may have been content to use the power thus accorded to them, more especially, as would often be the case, where there was no clash with a primary statute. This is however far from saying that the main feature driving legal integration was competition between lower and higher national courts. The reality is that *Simmenthal*, combined with direct effect, gave individuals the opportunity to use their EC rights in any national court, and gave those national courts the power to pronounce on the relation between national law and EC law. It is not surprising that individuals should seek to avail themselves of these opportunities in the manner argued for by the neo-functionalists.

CONCLUSION

It is clear that the EC has posed, and continues to pose, real problems for the relationship between the Community legal order and those which subsist within the Member States. The broad claims to supremacy contained in the ECJ's jurisprudence have been accepted only in part by the Member States. National courts have, by and large, not adopted the conceptual rationale for supremacy preferred by the ECJ, but have based their acceptance on provisions within their own domestic legal order which have been interpreted as according priority to EC law in the event of a clash. National courts have, moreover, imposed a variety of substantive limitations on their acceptance of supremacy.

When considering this material it is important to be clear as to the positive law enunciated by the various national courts. We must, however, also press further and take on board the normative dimension of the debate, since without this it is impossible to come to any satisfactory conclusion on the issues raised in this chapter.

We should also keep the tensions revealed by this discussion within perspective. The ECJ and national courts have always engaged in a discourse which has shaped the doctrine which now exists. They will continue to do so. The fact that some Member States send strong signals to the ECJ to the effect that they will not accept Community legislative or judicial determinations which they believe to be *ultra vires* does not mean that they will readily find them to be so. Such national judicial statements are intended to serve as a warning to the Community institutions, which the latter will recognize as such. Neither the Community legislature, nor the ECJ, has an interest in provoking a clash with the essential provisions of Member State constitutions.

---

[45] See above n. 2.

PART I

THE CORE EXECUTIVE

3

On Studying Governments

RUDY B. ANDEWEG

IN DEFENSE AND IN SEARCH OF GOVERNMENT

Government, both good and bad, is the theme of some of the largest and most impressive frescoes in Siena's Palazzo Comunale. They date back to 1337–9. Could Lorenzetti, their creator, still have painted 'government' had he lived today? States, and governments in particular, so it is argued, are 'hollowed out' both from within through privatization, decentralization to autonomous agencies, etc., and from without by globalization and European integration (e.g. Rhodes 1994). As a result, the sovereignty of government is said to be eroding, and we are gradually but inexorably moving to a situation in which we are ruled by shifting coalitions and networks of several governmental and non-governmental actors and institutions. The thesis has been the topic of some debate (e.g. between Saward 1997; Rhodes 1997b); a recent echo of an earlier debate in political science about the distribution of power, between elitists and pluralists. However, even if we accept the existence of a trend from 'government' to 'governance', obituaries of government are premature.

We should not overestimate the changes. Many of the public services that are now being hived off were relatively recent and controversial acquisitions by governments. In most countries it is not clear whether privatization and agencification actually have resulted in a retreat of government, or rather to a change in the instruments used by governments: from ownership and direct control to regulation. Even where governments have abolished particular tasks, it is sometimes argued that this was a conscious decision to reduce overload, to have more control over less. There is most consensus with regard to the erosive effects on governmental sovereignty of globalization and European integration. Here too, we should not overestimate the changes. A Golden Age of fully sovereign and omnipotent governments probably never existed; there has not been a linear development from economic autarky to global interdependence, and both the autarky of the past and the interdependence of the present need to be qualified (see Hurrell and Menon this volume). Moreover, we should distinguish between spontaneous globalization (of trade, communication, pollution, crime, etc.) and European integration. The latter can also be seen as

I thank the editors and Peter Mair for their valuable comments and helpful suggestions.

a partial answer to globalization, as governments pooling their resources to maintain or regain control over these developments (e.g. Milward 2000). Although the nature of the European Union as primarily intergovernmental or increasingly supranational continues to be debated, no one denies that governments remain privileged actors in EU decision making. In short, as Müller and Vincent Wright conclude, governments 'remain central actors—arguably *the* central actors, even if they are increasingly prisoners of an interlocking network of bargained situations: they are not bypassed or eliminated but rather more constrained. They retain a nodal decision-making power but their action is more indirect, more discreet and more bartered' (Müller and Wright 1994: 7–8).

Capturing these changes in the position of government need not be out of the reach of a modern-day Lorenzetti, but there is another challenge. The frescoes of Siena depict both the allegories and the effects of good and bad government, *not* government itself. Similarly, political scientists writing about government rarely offer an explicit definition (not even Finer in the 'conceptual prologue' to his monumental historical overview (1997)). Two problems appear to contribute to the conceptual elusiveness of government. First, the term 'government' is used to describe both a systemic function or activity, and the structure or institution that is supposed to perform such activity. To define a structure by a function is asking for trouble, as it is rare to find a perfect match between the two: structures are usually multi-functional and functions are rarely monopolized by a single structure. Government is no exception (King 1975b: 175–9). It is curious that most synonyms for the 'government' are also functionally defined: the 'executive', or (in the United States) the 'administration'. More recent approaches that define government by the currently fashionable function of 'co-ordination' (e.g. Rhodes and Dunleavy 1995: 12) do not solve the problem. One of the consequences of using a functional definition is that the borderlines of the object of study are poorly marked. This is the second definitional problem. Some authors have argued that more people or institutions are involved in the function of government than the relatively small group of people formally comprising the government: political advisers or *cabinets ministériels*, senior departmental officials, central government agencies, etc. This then leads to the use of terms that have a broader scope than 'government', such as 'the cabinet system' (e.g. Burch and Holliday 1996) or 'the central executive territory' (Madgwick 1991). Others have taken the opposite approach and, in an attempt to peel the onion and find the place where (as President Truman put it) 'the buck stops', have introduced terms with a narrower scope, such as 'the core executive' (Rhodes and Dunleavy 1995) or 'COGs': 'Centres of Government' (Goetz and Margetts 1999).

There is no ready solution to the problem of definition, but a first step would be to separate structure from function. One of the few synonyms of government that is not functionally defined is 'cabinet'. Bagehot famously defined cabinet by its location: as a 'hyphen which joins, a buckle which fastens' the political arena to the administrative apparatus (Bagehot 1993: 68). As a term, 'cabinet' may not travel far outside parliamentary systems of government (however, see Warsaw 1996; Bennett 1996), but Bagehot's definition of cabinet suggests what is probably the best way to conceive of 'the government' in general: the most senior constitutional body, politically responsible (to parliament or president) for the activities of the state bureaucracy. This is the definition I shall use in the following overview of approaches to the study of governments.

This survey explicitly builds upon King (1975*b*) and Campbell (1993) as predecessors. King suggests three broad categories in the key research questions that students of governments have posed: recruitment, internal dynamics, and external relations. For King, questions about recruitment dealt with the individuals making up the government (the causes and effects of various selection procedures, selection criteria, and differential tenure and turnover). Curiously, he did not mention the composition of governments in partisan terms, although there was already no shortage of literature on that topic in 1975. I shall broaden this category of 'government composition' to include such questions. Questions about the internal dynamics led most often to descriptive constitutional or historical studies, and dealt with both the decisionmaking processes and the distribution of power within the government. For King, external relations were about the relationship between government and parliament. There were then, as there are now, many other 'external relations' that have attracted the attention of students of government: the relations with governments of other states (international relations), with sub-national governments (what, in the United States, are called intergovernmental relations), and, in the European Union, supra-national government ('multi-level governance'), with organized interests (neo-corporatism, policy networks/communities), etc. Given the Bagehotian definition of government I have just proposed, it seems logical to focus here on both 'executive–legislative relations' and the relationship between government and bureaucracy.

In another, more recent, review of the field, Campbell (1993) confines himself to that last question (the relations between 'political executives and their officials'), but contrasts various theoretical perspectives: institutionalism, 'public choice thinking', and 'a pinch of personality' (in his review King too had included a paragraph on 'the executive psyche'). These three would indeed seem to be the dominant theoretical perspectives in the study of governments (if not in political science in general) today. Institutionalism, inspired by constitutional studies, has the oldest credentials in political science. Public choice, rational choice, formal theory, and game theory form a cluster of overlapping approaches that are inspired by economics in the sense that they have adopted some of the key assumptions and methods of micro-economic theory. The third perspective is usually labelled behaviouralism. Strictly speaking, behaviouralism is not a theoretical perspective, but in practice, sociology (first) and psychology (more recently) inspire the theories of behaviouralists.

If we now cross-tabulate the trichotomy of research themes adapted from King with the trichotomy of theoretical perspectives adapted from Campbell, we have a map of the study of governments. The content of the cells in Figure 3.1 consists of illustrative examples, without any pretension to be exhaustive. Figure 3.1 also serves as an outline of the remainder of this chapter. Starting with the composition of government, we shall discuss the contribution of the various theoretical approaches to each of the three clusters of research questions, using the illustrative examples mentioned in the cells of the three-by-three table.

THEORETICAL PERSPECTIVE	FOCUS OF RESEARCH QUESTION		
	Composition	*Internal Dynamics*	*External Relations*
Institutionalism	—	Prime-ministerial v. cabinet gov't	Executive–legislative relations
Rational Choice	Coalition formation	—	Control over the bureaucracy
Political Sociology/ Political Psychology	Recruitment/ motivation	Political roles/ groupthink	—

Figure 3.1 *Overview of approaches to the study of governments*

GOVERNMENT COMPOSITION

Party Composition

Of all governments between 1945 and 1987 in twelve West-European countries, only 6 per cent were composed of ministers from a single political party with a majority in parliament (Laver and Schofield 1990: 70). If we take into account that two out of three *minority* governments consist of ministers from only one party (Strøm 1990: 61), the proportion of single-party governments goes up, but still between two-thirds and three-quarters of all governments are based on a coalition of parties. The search for an explanation of the composition of these coalitions has been largely the province of rational choice theory (for more extensive overviews, see Laver and Schofield 1990; Laver 1998). After all these years, the most important proposition is still that only minimal winning coalitions will form (e.g. Riker 1962), that is, that governments will not include political parties that are not necessary for obtaining a majority in parliament. After all, the number of ministerial positions in the government is limited, with the consequence that adding new parties to the coalition will reduce the number of positions for the other governing parties. Assuming that parties act rationally and in their own interest, they will shun unnecessary partners. It is a plausible hypothesis, but it has two major weaknesses: first, election results usually allow a large number of different minimal winning coalitions to form, so that the theory does not result in a unique prediction; second, minimal winning coalitions form in only 40 per cent of the situations in which no single party has won a parliamentary majority; in almost as many cases, minority governments form, and in a quarter of the cases an 'oversized' or 'surplus majority' coalition (containing 'unnecessary' parties) forms (Laver and Schofield 1990: 70).

One of the ways in which scholars have tried to remedy these two problems is by refining the theory. For example, a 'bargaining proposition' has been added to the minimal winning hypothesis: coalitions should be not only minimal winning, but also 'minimum number', that is, they should consist of the smallest number of parties that can still command a majority in parliament, because the transaction costs are lower when the number of negotiating parties is smaller (Leiserson 1966).

Theorists have also refined the theory by differentiating the parties: because of the distribution of seats in parliament, some parties are a necessary partner in more minimal winning coalitions than other parties are, or it may even be impossible to form a majority coalition without a particular party. Such parties with a high 'power index' or 'dominant' parties are more likely to be found in governing coalitions (e.g. Van Deemen 1989). Such refinements greatly reduce the number of 'predicted' coalitions although they still do not always result in a unique prediction nor help to explain the occurrence of oversized coalitions and minority governments.

The second strategy to improve the predictive power of coalition theory has been more radical. The minimal winning hypothesis and its refinements assume that what is at stake is the distribution of ministerial positions; in other words, that parties are 'office seeking' and that the parties' ideologies or programmes are not relevant. Most modern coalition theorists now assume that parties are (also) 'policy seeking'. This new assumption reduces the set of predicted coalitions considerably: when forming a government, parties will try to get as many of their policy preferences translated into government policy as possible. For that reason they will prefer as their coalition partners parties that are as like-minded as possible. Thus we expect coalitions of ideological neighbours, or coalitions that span the shortest possible ideological distance ('closed minimal range') to form (e.g. De Swaan 1973). Moreover, assuming parties to be policy seeking helps us to understand why oversized coalitions and minority governments form. The number of ministerial positions are relatively constant, so that adding parties to the coalition dilutes the spoils. This is not true for government policy. As long as adding coalition partners does not increase the ideological span of the coalition, a party's chances of realizing its policy preferences are not affected and oversized coalitions can be the result. Where the rules and institutions allow parties to influence public policy even without government membership (e.g. through their affiliated interest groups in neo-corporatist institutions, or through their MPs in parliamentary committees), some parties may actually prefer to stay on the opposition benches, and a minority government will form when insufficient parties join (Strøm 1990). The parties can also be ordered according to their ideological preferences (usually on a Left–Right scale). Some parties may be desirable or necessary partners in more ideologically inspired coalitions than other parties, for example, if a party includes the median voter in parliament ('centre', 'pivotal', or 'strong' parties, depending on the definition; see e.g. Van Roozendaal 1992; Laver and Shepsle 1996). Such a party may, for example, be able to choose between a minimal winning centre–right and a minimal winning centre–left coalition. Within both coalitions, however, it would be on one of the flanks. The party can keep the pivotal position it occupies in parliament also in government by adding a (numerically unnecessary) party and forming an oversized coalition, enabling it to play the two flanks within the government off against each other.

However, the switch from office seeking to policy seeking also has its drawbacks. For some theories it suffices to order the parties from Left to Right, but for others we also need to know the exact ideological distances between parties, and these are not easy to measure. Expert judgements are sometimes used, or the number of words devoted to individual items in party programmes is counted, but neither approach is ideal. In addition, many coalition theorists assume that only three parties exist and that only one ideological dimension is relevant to construct their models, but reality is more complex (for a rare study involving more than one dimension, see Laver and Shepsle 1996). More fundamentally, the policy seeking assumption is still just an assumption. It is an empirical question whether parties are office seeking or policy seeking, or both (and then, in what mixture) (Müller and Strøm 1999).

Personnel Composition

So far, rational choice theory says little about the individual ministers who make up the government, implicitly assuming that the party composition is more important than the composition in terms of personnel. There are empirical studies of the government's composition in this regard, but they are considerably less in number, and they are not part of an ongoing debate or driven by a single theoretical concern. Roughly speaking, three different questions can be discerned. The first is still closely linked to the literature on party composition, and is about the party affiliation of ministers in a particular portfolio. If parties are policy seeking, some ministerial portfolios are likely to be of greater importance to them than others are. Indeed, studies have found that, when their party is in government, socialists tend to take portfolios such as Social Affairs, Public Health, or Labour, that liberals are often in charge of Economic Affairs or Finance, that conservatives opt for Interior, Foreign Affairs, or Defence, that Christian-Democrats are likely to be found in Religious Affairs or Education (e.g. Budge and Keman 1990).

The second question is about the social background of ministers. The theoretical concern can be sociological and pertain, for example, to the impact of long-term societal change on the composition of the government, but more often it is normative, seeking to explain the lack of representativeness of governments. The sociological concern usually leads to longitudinal studies of ministers' social backgrounds in one country (e.g. Secker 1991). Depending on the time frame and the country, such studies show that the personnel composition of governments has become more diverse: from older, exclusively male, predominantly aristocratic members of the dominant religious or ethnic group in nineteenth century governments, to slightly younger, occasionally female, middle class ministers with some members of the working class, from various religious denominations in contemporary governments (ministers from ethnic minorities are still exceptional).

The concern with representativeness often leads to comparative studies of incumbents or ministers in a particular period (e.g. Thiébault 1991*a*). Recently, the concern has focused on the under-representation of women in government. Scandinavians and leftist parties appoint more female ministers, but one of the most interesting explanatory factors is the recruitment process itself. Where only incumbent MPs are eligible for ministerial office, fewer women are appointed because women are still under-represented in parliament, and they have not (yet) risen to positions such as committee chairs where they can advertise their *ministrabilité*. For similar reasons, where recruitment favours technocratic expertise rather than political experience, the proportion of women in government is higher (Davis 1997; Siaroff 2000).

Such factors are the central concern of the third cluster of studies, which take a more dynamic approach, and look at the career paths of ministers prior to their appointments. Some authors combine the study of previous careers with social background (e.g. Prewitt and McAllister 1976; Blondel 1985), but increasingly authors concentrate on the type of positions held before ministerial office (e.g. Armingeon 1986; Dogan 1989). Previous experience in sub-national politics is important in most countries, but it plays a particularly strong role in ministerial recruitment in federal countries (e.g. Thiébault 1991*b*), with an interesting exception for the United States (e.g. Wyszomirski 1989). Most ministers are recruited from parliament (in some parliamentary systems of government this is a constitutional requirement), but there is considerable variation across countries (De Winter 1991). The location of government between the political arena and the administrative apparatus can lead to conflicting job requirements: as heads of departments ministers may need technocratic specialization, and as their parties' representatives in the government, ministers may need to be generalists with political experience (Blondel 1991). In some countries, such as the Netherlands, technocratic expertise has traditionally been highly valued in ministerial recruitment, but more and more in combination with political experience (Bakema and Secker 1988). This fits with the more general observation that the composition of government has become more politicized (Cotta 1991). In that sense there is a curious paradox: whereas ministerial recruitment has become more open in terms of social background, it shows signs of a development towards a closed political class when one looks at the career paths towards ministerial office.

Motivation

In a related argument, King has asserted 'the rise of the career politician': government is increasingly in the hands of people who are totally committed to politics as a way of life (King 1981). These career politicians are politically seasoned and hard working, but without much experience in the world outside politics, and lacking detachment. It raises the question what motivates individuals to devote their life to politics and to seek its highest prize: governmental office. One of the most influential answers to that question is given by Lasswell, who argued that 'the political personality' seeks office in search of power to compensate for low self-esteem (Lasswell 1948). This 'compensation hypothesis' has found support in psychobiographic accounts of governmental leaders: the US president Woodrow Wilson sought power because his self-esteem as a child was undermined by a stern and over-demanding father (George and George 1956); the self-esteem of president Richard Nixon suffered when his beloved mother temporarily left the family in search of a better climate for one of his brothers who eventually died of tuberculosis (Mazlish 1973); British prime minister Winston Churchill's self-esteem was dented by an extreme lack of attention from his parents (Rintala 1984).

What we do not know is how generalizable the findings from such case studies are. The kind of governmental leader that attracts the attention of psychobiographers may not be representative of all members of governments. Moreover, the 'compensation hypothesis' stands radically opposed to one of the best documented findings about *mass* political behaviour: that high efficacy leads to political activity. Studies of the motivation not of one, but of a sample of governmental leaders are rare, but the few that are available would seem to indicate that the 'compensation hypothesis' applies to some, but not to all of them. Barber (1992) has famously distinguished four types of 'presidential character', using attitude towards the office (positive or negative) and level of activity in office (active or passive). The 'active-negatives' are close to Lasswell's compensators for low self-esteem, and include Wilson, Hoover, Johnson, and Nixon. Barber's typology has generated considerable controversy (see e.g. Pederson 1989), but it should be noted that he used his typology to predict Nixon's demise before the Watergate scandal unfolded (the first edition was published in 1972). Barber bases his typology primarily on a (given his number of cases, inevitably) impressionistic analysis of biographical data. Others have employed more systematic content analyses of public speeches and interviews in search of the motivation for governmental office. Here too we find evidence that more than one motive may fuel political ambition. For example, Winter distinguishes three motives: 'power' (the impact one may have on the behaviour or motives of others when holding governmental office); 'achievement' (the opportunity the office provides for pursuing excellence, quality of output, innovation); and 'affiliation' (the experience of warmth, friendship, team spirit when in government). All US presidents studied by Winter exhibit all three motives, but the mixture varies considerably (Winter 1987). Interestingly, Winter is less concerned with 'power-hungry' politicians, but warns that those US presidents who are primarily motivated by 'achievement' are likely to become frustrated and may resort to dishonest or even illegal tactics to achieve their goals (Winter 1995).

GOVERNMENTS' INTERNAL DYNAMICS

Hierarchy and Collective Decision Making

The institutional approach to the internal dynamics of governments is characterized by a preoccupation with the role of the head of the government *vis-à-vis* its other members. In semi-presidential systems of government both the president and the prime minister claim to lead the government, and this bicephalous leadership creates its own, occasionally conflictual, dynamics during periods of *cohabitation*, but perhaps even more when both leaders belong to the parliamentary majority (e.g. Wright 1993). However, apart from that rather special case, the literature in this field is dominated by the debate over 'prime ministerial' vs 'cabinet' government, particularly, but by no means exclusively, in Britain. It is argued that the Prime Minister is no longer the *primus inter pares* facilitating collective decision making. The argument has evolved from Crossman's original discussion of the prime minister's role in cabinet (e.g. Crossman 1972) to Foley's analysis of the public role (Foley 1993), but if we disregard important differences between various approaches, the argument is that the prime minister's formal powers (to select, reshuffle, and dismiss the other ministers, to decide the agenda, and to give instructions to ministers) and support structure (an increasing number of advisers, including political appointees, as well as patronage), combined with party leadership (and control over the party's machinery) and media exposure, have 'presidentialized' the office. Others have dismissed the importance of such factors, and argue that even with a sizeable staff, the prime minister's span of control simply cannot encompass all the government's actions, or they point to the fact that even Mrs Thatcher had to step down when she lost the support of her cabinet colleagues. Apart from the fact that there is considerable variation across countries in the degree of monocratic leadership, depending on factors such as single-party or coalition government, the degree of ministerial specialization, and neo-corporatism (see Baylis 1989; Jones 1991), there is increasing dissatisfaction with the contradistinction between prime-ministerial and cabinet government itself (Weller 1991).

One of the grounds for this dissatisfaction is that the debate confuses two dimensions of government. Prime-ministerial government refers to the degree to which government deviates from what still is the constitutional norm in many countries: that all ministers are equal and all have one vote in cabinet. Cabinet government refers to another constitutional norm: that ministers decide collectively (or at least are collectively responsible). Deviations from (collective) cabinet government do not result in prime-ministerial government, but in fragmented government. If we crudely dichotomize both dimensions, in combination they form a typology of governments (Andeweg 1993, 1997a).

DISTRIBUTION OF POWER	ARENA OF DECISION-MAKING	
	Fragmented	*Collective*
Monocratic	e.g. US presidential governments	E.g. Swedish single-party governments
Collegial	e.g. the Swiss Federal Council	e.g. Dutch coalition governments

Figure 3.2 *A two-dimensional typology of governments*

The lower right-hand corner of figure 3.2 represents the case where the constitutional norms of ministerial equality and collective decision making fully apply. The upper left-hand corner is furthest removed from this situation: the head of government takes decisions after consulting ministers individually. Historically, many cabinets originated from this cell, when ministers were merely individual advisers to the monarch. Today, the US government fits this description, although some presidents have sought to breathe life into the cabinet as a collective. It is not an accurate description of most governments in parliamentary systems of government, however. There, prime ministers may be quite powerful, but exercise that power in meetings of the full cabinet (e.g. in Sweden) or at least in cabinet committees (e.g. in the United Kingdom, although Blair is reported to favour bilateral meetings over cabinet and cabinet committees, Holliday 2000: 91–2). The two dimensions have been used not only to measure variation across countries, but also within a political system over time, related to the parties and personalities involved (e.g. Aucoin 1994; Burch and Holliday 1996: 142–6).

The disadvantage of this approach to the government's internal dynamics is that it does not capture these dynamics themselves, but rather the government's structure that constrains them. We now turn to two rival accounts of the internal dynamics themselves, interestingly both generalizing from case studies of US foreign policy involving the same island, and the same president.

Conflicting Roles?

Allison's classic case study of the 1962 Cuban missile crisis (Allison and Zelikow 1999; the first edition, written by Allison alone, was published in 1971) can be read as a step by step penetration into the government's internal dynamics. Allison presents three models, in the first of which government decisions are explained as the calculated acts of a unified rational actor. In the second, 'organizational behaviour' model, the emphasis is on the various organizational divisions and standard operating procedures within the government, but these are still co-ordinated by a unified leadership. In the third, 'governmental politics' model, it is recognized that diverging preferences and priorities can be found even within the governmental leadership. In this last model, the emphasis is clearly on the internal dynamics of the government: the government consists of 'players in positions', and 'propensities and priorities stemming from positions are sufficient to allow analysts to make reliable predictions about a player's stand' (Allison and Zelikow 1999: 298). Or, in words made famous by this study: 'Where you stand depends on where you sit' (Allison and Zelikow 1999: 307).

The impact of 'position' on 'propensities and priorities' is likely to be greatest when the position resembles a 'total institution', monopolizing the holder of that position's time, social contacts, etc. This is what Searing calls a 'position role'. 'While the scripts of these formal roles always leave some room for interpretation, they specify not only the many tasks to be performed but also the chief goals that constitute the roles' motivational cores' (Searing 1994: 15), and being a government minister usually constitutes such a position role. According to our Bagehotian definition of government, the 'position role' of a minister is moulded by being the interface between political arena and administrative apparatus. Searing argues that the overload of ministers is such that they cannot fully meet the expectations of both the political and administrative sides of their position. As a result, within the 'position role' of being a minister, 'preference roles' have developed around these two sides and ministers specialize in being either a 'Politician' or an 'Administrator' (Searing 1994: 321–6). Some such role specialization may occur, but given their two-sided position as ministers, Searing's 'Politicians' can ill afford to ignore the fact that they are also head of a department, and his 'Administrators' can hardly be successful without paying attention to the fact that they are put in that position by their party. There is some evidence that ministers do not so much specialize in either role, but constantly shift gear between the two roles, acting as a politician or as an administrator depending on whether the government is dealing with a politically controversial issue or not (Andeweg 1988). Also, the relative saliency of the two embedded roles may vary across political systems. In coalition governments, for example, ministers are constantly reminded that they are their party's bridgeheads in the government and part of their job is to look over the shoulders of ministers from other coalition parties. The relative lack of political heterogeneity in single-party governments reduces the scope of political conflicts within the government and thus lowers the saliency of the minister-as-politician. In most governments, ministers are heads of departments and many debates within the government are about conflicting departmental interests. In such conflicts, ministers are expected to fight their department's corner in cabinet, emphasizing the minister-as-administrator. However, in the rare case that ministers are not heads of executive agencies, as in Sweden, we should expect a lower saliency of this role (Andeweg 1988).

Groupthink?

Starting from a case study about the decision making which led to the disastrous 1961 Bay of Pigs invasion, Janis developed a theory of the government's internal dynamics based on its homogeneity rather than its heterogeneity (Janis 1982). He argues that a combination of high stress (e.g. in a crisis situation) and a cohesive group of decision-makers (e.g. sharing the same social background and ideology) results in a process of concurrence seeking, in which the maintenance of group solidarity becomes more important than a critical evaluation of information, alternative courses of action, and risks. This 'groupthink' is characterized by an overestimation of the group's strength and morality, by closed-mindedness, and pressures towards uniformity. As a result, decision making is defective and the probability of a successful outcome decreases. Despite evident weaknesses in the theory (e.g. group cohesion being both an antecedent condition and a characteristic of groupthink), it has been highly influential. The theory has been amended to include among the antecedent conditions not only situations of high stress, but also situations of over-optimism, such as during the 'honeymoon' period following the inauguration of a new government. An even more fundamental amendment, illustrated in a case study of the 1985–6 Iran-Contra affair, points to the possibility that it is not necessarily an increasing identification with the decision making group which fuels groupthink, but also collective anticipatory compliance with the assumed wishes of the leader ('T Hart 1994).

So far, most studies of groupthink have focused on the United States, leading Janis to wonder whether groupthink is essentially an American phenomenon (Janis 1982: 186–7). Tentatively, he offers the British government's decision making about the 1938–9 appeasement policy as a European example, but there are reasons to expect a lower incidence of groupthink in most European governments. First, in governmental decision making, conflicting roles (ministers representing different parties as well as different departments) prevent most European governments from developing into cosy and homogeneous groups. Second, European governments are more institutionalized than the US government, in which the cabinet is easily ignored and many crucial decisions are taken in small informal and ad hoc groups. Thus, depending on such structural characteristics, the internal dynamics of some governments are more likely to be characterized by conflicting roles, and those of others by concurrence seeking. Of course, the immediate situation may also trigger one of the two modes of decision making. It is tempting to hypothesize that conflicting roles dominate routine decision making, while stressful situations such as crises prompt groupthink, but it is curious to note that it was Allison who derived his model from a case study of a crisis, whereas Janis' case study hardly qualifies as such.

GOVERNMENTS' EXTERNAL RELATIONS

Executive–legislative Relations

For most institutionalists, the two principal models of the relationship between the government (the 'executive') and parliament (the 'legislature') are parliamentary and presidential government. The pros and cons of both models have been fiercely debated, especially when democratizing countries had to make fundamental choices of institutional design during the early 1990s. However, the debate is marred by—at least—three problems.

First, there is conceptual confusion (e.g. Elgie 1998). Most (but not all) authors agree that it is a characteristic of parliamentary government that the government is dependent on the confidence of a parliamentary majority, while it is a characteristic of presidential government that neither the president nor his government can be dismissed by parliament (impeachment notwithstanding). However, most authors add other elements to the definition, and differ on what these additional characteristics should be: direct or popular election of the president in a presidential system; multi-member governments in parliamentary systems and single-member governments in presidential systems; the separation of head of state and head of government in parliamentary systems. These definitional differences also lead to different classifications of existing political systems, but lack of consensus is not the only problem here. The additional characteristics are irrelevant to what these two systems are supposed to model: executive–legislative relations. Moreover, when more than one variable is used in the definition of the models, even if these extra variables are simple dichotomies, the number of permutations grows exponentially and we end up with numerous intermediate types. The most famous of these intermediate types, semi-presidential government (introduced as a concept by Duverger 1980; Elgie 1999), nicely illustrates the point. In semi-presidential systems (of which the French Fifth Republic is the most notorious example), an elected president appoints and may dismiss the ministers, but the ministers are also dependent on parliamentary confidence. Much paper has been wasted on the question whether semi-presidentialism is a true intermediate model, or whether it is alternating between two phases; presidential government when the president is, in effect, the leader of the parliamentary majority, and parliamentary government when the president's party belongs to a parliamentary minority (*cohabitation*).

The answer to the question of whether there are two phases, or which phase the system finds itself in at a particular moment, is interesting because it tells us whether the president or the prime minister is the effective head of the government, but this is a question about the government's *internal* dynamics (hence I mentioned it above under that heading), not about its *external* relations with parliament. With regard to the latter aspect—and that is what semi-presidentialism is supposed to be a model of—there is no difference between *cohabitation* and congruence between the presidential and parliamentary majority: in both cases there is a government that can only survive as long as it has the confidence of a parliamentary majority. Even the French Fifth Republic is a parliamentary system of government.

Second, it is extremely difficult to disentangle the consequences of having a parliamentary or presidential government from a host of other institutional factors and political contingencies. Let me confine the discussion of the advantages and disadvantages of both systems to the consequences of whether the government can be censured by parliament or not (see e.g. the contributions by Linz and others in Lijphart 1992; Shugart and Carey 1992). Advocates of presidential government argue that dependency on parliamentary confidence engenders governmental instability, which may eventually lead to the collapse of the democratic regime (as in Weimar Germany). Advocates of parliamentary government reply that, while such governments are indeed less stable, the degree of instability depends on many other factors (such as the party system, whether the government is single-party or coalition, whether the coalition is minimal winning or not, etc.) and may be effectively reduced by constitutional rules such as the German constructive no confidence vote, in which parliament can only bring down the government if there is an alternative government that has the support of a parliamentary majority. They then go on to argue that the risk of democratic collapse is actually greatest in presidential governments because of its lack of flexibility. The system may work as long as the president and (preferably both houses of) parliament are in the hands of the same party, but if they are not, there is no conflict resolution mechanism and deadlock ensues. The resulting immobilism erodes the legitimacy of the regime which, eventually, may collapse. Such collapses indeed have occurred more often in presidential systems than in parliamentary systems, but depending on the exact operationalization and time frame used, the differences are not very pronounced. Moreover, presidentialists argue, other factors are at work (e.g. many parliamentary governments are found in the western industrialized countries while many presidential governments rule in developing countries). The risk of immobilism when different parties have won the presidency and the parliamentary majority should not be overstated: in the United States, such 'divided government' has been argued to have little impact on the 'production' of legislation and major parliamentary inquiries (Mayhew 1991; Elgie 2001). The effects of divided government can be mitigated by having weakly disciplined parties, or by constraining the legislative powers of the president, and its occurrence can be significantly reduced if the electoral cycles of the president and the parliament coincide. So, the answer to the question whether parliamentary or presidential government is better with regard to the relations between government and parliament must be 'it depends'.

Third, the debate suffers from an overdose of Montesquieu. It treats 'the' government and 'the' parliament as two bodies that only interact as such. In an influential attempt to deconstruct this 'two-body image', King has suggested a typology of different 'modes of executive–legislative relations' on the basis of the experience in Britain, France, and Germany (King 1976). The various modes deal with the relations between ministers and the opposition, ministers and their own party's backbenchers, ministers and parliamentary committees, etc. More recently, King's typology has been adapted to distinguish the three most dominant patterns of interactions between ministers and MPs (Andeweg and Nijzink 1995):

1. A non-party mode, in which, akin to the Montesquieu formula, the interactions are between government as such and parliament as such: ministers act as members of the government when they interact with MPs who act as the people's representatives, regardless of which party a minister or an MP belong to, and regardless of the portfolio of the minister and the policy specialization of the MP.
2. An inter-party mode, in which executive–legislative relations constitute an arena for the incessant struggle between the parties over the next elections: party-membership is more predictive of the interactions in this arena than membership of either government or parliament, or than portfolio. Two 'submodes' can be distinguished within the inter-party mode: an opposition mode for the relations between the governmental majority and the opposition, and a coalition-mode (where applicable) for the relations between the parties making up the governmental majority.
3. A cross-party mode, in which executive–legislative relations constitute a market place for the 'trading' of social interests: the policy area for which a minister or an MP is assigned responsibility is more predictive of the interactions in this market place than membership of either government or parliament, or party affiliation.

Although the typology is designed with parliamentary systems of government in mind, it travels to presidential systems without difficulty. In the United States, for example, the inter-party mode may be less in evidence (but by no means absent) than the two other modes, just as the cross-party mode may be less pronounced in the United Kingdom. Despite such differences in emphasis, all three modes can probably be discerned in all political systems, with the non-party mode occasionally emerging during parliamentary inquiries of government scandals or fiascos, the inter-party mode most visible in plenary debates and Prime Minister's question time, and the cross-party mode practised most in meetings of specialized parliamentary committees with 'their' ministers. Depending on the political agenda, governments and parliaments shift gear from one mode to another.

Executive–Bureaucratic Relations

The study of the relations of government with the state apparatus differs in two important respects from the analysis of its relations with parliament. First, rational choice approaches are much more important in this field, although there is also a size-able institutionalist literature (e.g. Page 1992; Farazmand 1999). Second, the study of the relations between ministers and civil servants is coloured by a strong normative concern: that the government should control the bureaucracy. Thus, formal theory models the relationship in a principal-agent framework, with the government as the principal and departments as the agents to which the government delegates the implementation of its policies (e.g. Hammond 1996; Huber 2000). This normative slant does have the effect of narrowing the perception of executive–bureaucratic relations: more attention is paid to the top–down process of implementation than to the bottom-up process of policy advice and formulation, and the relations are modelled in terms of hierarchies rather than of policy networks. The argument in agency theory is that any principal always runs the risk that the agent will maximize his own utility rather than that of the principal ('shirking'). In the case of the relationship between government and bureaucracy this agency loss is caused by the advantage the bureaucracy has in terms of specialized knowledge and expertise ('information asymmetry'), exacerbated by the sheer size of the span of control a minister faces and by the greater continuity in office of civil servants compared to ministers.

The government relies on two strategies to reduce agency loss: *ex ante* controls and *ex post* controls. A well known *ex ante* control is to appoint only (senior) civil servants who share the government's political preferences: a spoils system or the politicization of the bureaucracy. There are three problems with this strategy: first, the emphasis on political loyalty assumes that bureaucrats' personal political preferences are the main source of shirking. There is no empirical evidence to support this assumption. Second, although the government may want to appoint officials who are (in the terminology of the former Soviet Union) 'red ànd expert', there is likely to be a trade-off between political loyalty and expertise. It is this trade-off that has been one of the arguments for the reduction of the spoils system in the United States. Third, it is assumed that the preferences will be stable after appointment, and that the political appointees will not 'go native' in their department. A second form of *ex ante* control is to give the bureaucracy little discretionary power by specifying their mandate. Here, the drawback is the risk of a Kafkaesque inflexibility in the application of the rules in specific situations, of 'red tape'. The *ex post* controls consist of reporting requirements and monitoring, either of a routine or random nature ('policy patrol') or when there are signals from citizens, interest groups, the media, or the courts that something has gone wrong ('fire alarms').

There are signs that governments increasingly relax their *ex ante* controls and give more autonomy to bureaucratic agencies, while at the same time reinforcing their *ex post* controls through inspectorates, ombudsmen, auditors, internal regulators, etc., amounting to what has been called an 'audit explosion' (e.g. Hood *et al.* 1999). Governments vary in the use they make of these various controls, but so far, there is little systematic and comparative research into this variation and its effect on agency loss (an example is Peters 1991). However, all these controls, whether *ex ante* or *ex post*, involve enforcement costs for the government (screening candidates for appointments, drafting detailed legislation, paying for all those inspectors and auditors, and reading their reports) and compliance costs for the bureaucracy (writing annual reports, giving information to inspectors, etc.). So, the most important lesson of principal-agent theory is that there is a point at which the benefits of control no longer outweigh its costs. In other words, no rational government will seek total control over its bureaucracy.

Principal-agent theory also shows that the costs of political control of the bureaucracy vary considerable with the institutional and political context. Generally speaking, the costs are lowest when a third party has a vested interest in monitoring the agent and informing the principal. Often, such a third party is a competitor of the agent. Thus, the parliamentary opposition has an interest in keeping track of the governmental majority's actions and in revealing any agency loss to the principal, in this case the voters. In the relationship between government and bureaucracy, however, the departments usually monopolize the position of agent of the government, despite occasional calls for the introduction of competition within the state apparatus. If competition does exist, it is usually the result of overlapping jurisdictions of departments or of divisions and bureaux within departments. At the other end of the equation, the costs of controlling the bureaucracy are highest when there is more than one principal (e.g. Waterman and Meier 1998). If these principals have divergent preferences, this creates a window of opportunity for the bureaucracy, within which it can follow its own preferences, playing one principal off against the other. A frequently cited example is the US political system in which the bureaucracy is formally subordinated to the president and his ministers, but at the same time dependent on Congress for legislation and funding. The result is a 'war of control of administration' (Kaufman 1981: 181) between president and parliament and lots of room for manoeuvre for astute bureau chiefs.

Although a coalition government formally constitutes a single principal, it may resemble a situation of multiple principals: when a minister needs cabinet approval, dissenting departmental civil servants may mobilize the coalition partner against their own minister if that is to their advantage. The widespread practice in coalition government of divided portfolios (with ministers from different parties sharing responsibility for a portfolio, or with junior ministers from one party being appointed to a department led by a minister from another party) also provides such opportunities and drives up the costs of control. A special case of multiple principals is governmental instability or high turnover, where the government is not even long enough in office to be able to use *ex post* controls, and bureaucrats can stall the implementation of governmental policies in the knowledge that a new government will be in office soon (but see Huber and Lupia 2001). Here the experience of the French Fourth Republic is frequently mentioned.

Throughout this analysis in terms of principals and agents, the assumption is that, without controls, the bureaucracy will follow preferences that are different from those of the government. As noted above, the underlying assumption of a spoils system is that civil servants have *political* preferences that are different from those of their ministers. There can be little doubt that this occurs, but it is highly unlikely that all civil servants share the same political persuasion, even if self-selection and recruitment may result in some political views being over-represented. If the bureaucracy as such has divergent preferences at all, these must be related to the very membership of the bureaucracy. The most influential hypothesis in this respect has been formulated by Niskanen (1971: esp. 36–42). Some civil servants may prefer high salaries, while others prefer job security, or power, or status, or perquisites. The maximization of all of these preferences, however, requires the maximization of the bureau's budget. So far, however, the empirical testing of the budget-maximizing hypothesis has found some, but by no means overwhelming, support (see contributions to Blais and Dion 1991). In response to criticism, Niskanen later specified his hypothesis: bureaucrats do not maximize their bureau's overall budget, but only the discretionary part, or surplus budget (Niskanen 1991). This qualification brings Niskanen closer to Dunleavy, who argues, among other things, that above a certain threshold, further maximization of the budget is unlikely to be attractive to senior civil servants. Once that optimal budget size is achieved, bureaucrats prefer interesting and important work, and they follow 'bureau-shaping' strategies: to do staff rather than line work, to be geographically close to the centre of power, to work in small collegial units, etc. (Dunleavy 1991: 174–248). This, according to Dunleavy, explains the bureaucratic support for the Thatcher government's public sector reforms. However, whether bureaucrats are budget-maximizers or bureau-shapers, these preferences refer to internal, administrative policy making, not to the government's substantive policy making (Egeberg 1995). Important as 'office politics' may be, it is the civil servants' influence over 'real politics' that forms the core of fears of agency loss and rule by bureaucrats.

SO WHAT?

The Theoretical Approaches Compared

At the end of this *tour d'horizon*, inevitably, the question arises what the relative merits of each of the three theoretical perspectives (institutionalism, rational choice, political sociology/psychology) are for the study of the three research themes (the composition, the internal dynamics, and the external relations of governments). A first answer is that, to some extent, it is a matter of different horses for different courses. Figure 3.1—the map of the study of governments presented at the beginning of this chapter, contains three interesting blanks, suggesting that 'institutionalism' has little to contribute to the study of the government's composition, that 'rational choice' is silent about the government's internal dynamics, and that 'political sociology/ psychology' have little to say about the government's external relations. Of course, like any map, Figure 3.1 is an oversimplification: the borderlines between the cells are less clear-cut in reality. For example, most modern rational choice theorists and behaviouralists are (neo-) institutionalists, in that they recognize institutions as constraints on the maximization of utility, or even as agents of role socialization (Peters 1999). Moreover, the interesting blanks on the map may not be completely virgin territories, although I do maintain that they represent a relative lack of emphasis in a particular theoretical perspective. In the institutionalist perspective, for example,

institutions are the units of analysis, and not much attention is paid to the composition and recruitment to those institutions, but the institutionalist distinction
between presidential government and parliamentary government, while focusing on
executive–legislative relations, is nevertheless based on different rules for the composition of governments. Similarly, for most rational choice approaches, 'the game is
over' after the formation of a coalition until the 'equilibrium' is disturbed by new
elections or other exogenous shocks, leaving little room for internal dynamics, but
rational choice is not completely silent on this aspect of government because of the
applicability of, for example, game-theoretical models to decision making within
governments. Behaviouralists tend to take the individual member of the government
as the unit of analysis and are therefore less inclined to take the external relations of
the government as such into account, but a government's internal dynamics and its
external relations are difficult to disentangle when ministers represent their department or their parliamentary party in cabinet debates.

Apart from these different emphases that are inherent to the three theoretical perspectives, however, it is curious to note the lack of overlap in Figure 3.1: each theoretical perspective appears to monopolize particular research questions. The study of
coalition formation constitutes an obvious example of such exclusiveness, in this case
of the rational choice approach. There is no reason why behaviouralists, and the political psychologists among them in particular, could not develop and test hypotheses
about coalition formation, allowing us to contrast their explanations or predictions
with those generated by rational choice theory. There is actually a whole literature on
coalition formation available in psychology (e.g. Komorita 1984; Wilke 1985) that has
been largely ignored by political scientists. Only by applying several theoretical perspectives to the same research question can we improve our understanding of both
that research question, and of the strengths and weaknesses of the various theoretical
perspectives (a strategy persuasively advocated by Dunleavy 1995).

Meanwhile, our survey of the study of governments does illustrate some of the
advantages and disadvantages associated with the three theoretical perspectives in general. One of the clearest examples that emerges concerns the question of political preferences. Rational choice theories have relatively little to say about the nature of political
preferences, other than that they should be stable and transitive. Preferences are merely
the starting points of the strategic behaviour that the theory seeks to elucidate. In the
case of coalition theory, for example, it was assumed originally that political parties are
office seeking. When the predictions that were based on that assumption proved inadequate, the assumption about the preferences was altered from office seeking to policy
seeking. Of course, some parties may be more interested in office and others may prefer to have an impact on government policy. Some rational-choice theorists include
such possibilities and make no assumption about the content of the preferences (the
so-called 'thin' rational choice), but if the outcome of the coalition formation depends
as much on the preferences that the parties seek to maximize as it depends on their
strategic behaviour in doing so, the question why parties pursue those particular preferences cannot be ignored. The same problem was illustrated in the discussion of the
relations between the government and the bureaucracy: whether agency loss will affect

the ideological direction of governmental policy, or will result in budget-maximizing, or rather in budget-shaping, depends on the dominant preferences within the civil service, and as such is out of the reach of principal-agent theory.

Not only the preferences themselves, but also their stability constitutes a problem, especially in neo-institutionalist rational choice theories. Earlier in this chapter we saw how, in Allison's 'governmental politics' model, preferences are not only determined by personality and personal interests, but also by the position of the actor: 'Where you stand depends on where you sit'. For rational choice theorists, this violates the assumption of invariant preferences: when an individual becomes a member of a particular governmental branch or bureau, this is assumed not to affect the pre-existing preferences. These preferences are *exogenous* to the institution, and institutional rules and positions are only 'constraints' on a rational actor's options for realising her preferences. For behaviouralist neo-institutionalism (the most important variety of which is known as 'historical neo-institutionalism'), the institutional context not only provides rules but also roles, and thus forms not only a constraint, but also a source of preferences. Preferences are *endogenous* to the institution when they change as the result of recruitment into an institutional position; the actor may strive to behave as is expected of someone in that position. This 'logic of appropriateness' (March and Olsen 1989) is not at variance with, and may help to explain, Allison's governmental politics model. To illustrate this controversy between rational choice and historical neo-institutionalism: as part of their 'portfolio allocation approach' to government, Laver and Shepsle apply principal-agent theory to the relationship between a party and its ministers. They argue that political parties are ill-equipped to monitor and control the decisions of their ministers, but they can influence a department's policies through a form of *ex ante* control: by appointing a minister to that portfolio whose manifest personal preferences coincide with the party's preferences (Laver and Shepsle 1996: 13–15). This implicitly assumes that the minister's personal preferences before and after appointment will be identical. Although there are ministers for whom this assumption turns out to be valid, there are many others whose preferences do change with changes in the positions they occupy. Hence the adage that *'Un Jacobin ministre n'est pas un ministre Jacobin'*.

Government as Independent Variable

So far, government has been the dependent variable in this overview: we have discussed the contributions made by three theoretical perspectives to research questions about the government's composition, its internal dynamics, and its external relations. The ultimate 'so what?' question, however, moves one step further down the causal chain, treats the varieties of composition, internal dynamics, and external relations as independent variables, and wonders what their impact is on, for example, the stability, legitimacy, and policy of the government. Here, the evidence is still patchy, to say the least.

The partisan composition of the government is clearly linked to its duration: even taking into account differences in the operationalisation of government duration, and debates over the relative impact of coalition 'attributes' and random 'events', single-party governments are more stable than coalition governments; minimal-winning coalitions are in office longer than surplus-majority or minority governments; and ideologically compact coalitions have a higher survival rate than ideologically more heterogeneous coalitions (e.g. Warwick 1994). Whether the government's policy output is also related to its partisan composition, or whether economic factors in particular constrain governments to such an extent that 'politics does not matter', is the subject of fierce debate. The provisional outcome would seem to be that economic circumstances have a high explanatory power, but that the composition of the government still makes a considerable difference. That difference, however, is much more pronounced in majoritarian democracies than in consensus democracies (e.g. Schmidt 1996). Even that conclusion probably underestimates the overall impact of the government's party composition. Empirical studies in this field usually focus on policy outputs that can be measured in financial terms (overall budget size, percentage of GDP spent on education, transfer payments, etc.). It seems plausible that, by their nature, such policy outputs are more subject to economic constraints than policies that cannot be measured in dollars or euros: decisions to allow abortion, to abolish the death penalty, to introduce conscription, the selection of countries that will receive development aid, etc.

The impact of the government's composition in terms of personality was already mentioned: presidents who are 'active-negative' or who score high on the 'achievement' motive are more prone to scandal and failure than other presidents. Obviously, it is more difficult to establish a relationship between personality and policy in governments that are more collective and collegial in nature, but studies have suggested such effects on the foreign policy decisions of European prime ministers (e.g. Kaarbo and Hermann 1998). In contrast, there is no evidence linking the social background of ministers to the government's legitimacy or policy. What little evidence is available looks at the effects of legislative rather than ministerial recruitment and has only found some impact for gender.

Hardly any research has been done linking the government's internal dynamics to its stability or policies. Hierarchy and collective decision making within governments can be seen as alternative strategies for policy co-ordination, and the variation in these respects provides an interesting laboratory to test the relative effectiveness of vertical and horizontal coordination, but it is difficult to separate the effects of the internal dynamics from contextual factors. Baylis, for example, presents data to show that, compared to 'monocratic' government, 'collegial' government correlates with higher GDP, lower unemployment and inflation rates, fewer days lost because of strikes, etc., but he hastens to add that 'It is plausible that certain intervening variables, for example, the presence of a "culture of accommodation" or a neo-corporatist structure of interest group representation, help to explain *both* collegial decision making *and* relatively strong performance (...)' (Baylis 1989: 160). In fact, Lijphart has incorporated such factors in his distinction between majoritarian and consensus government and found that, depending on the indicators, consensus governments perform as well as, or better than, majoritarian governments (Lijphart 1999: 258–74).

In combination, Janis' story of the Bay of Pigs disaster and Allison's story of what many regard as the successful management of the Cuban missile crisis, have led to a strong belief among scholars and policy-makers that internal dynamics do matter. Recommendations to ensure multiple advocacy within government, such as appointing someone to play 'devil's advocate', are taken to heart. However, the empirical evidence is not all that strong. Students of groupthink usually identify a policy fiasco and retrospectively analyse the decision making that preceded the fiasco; they do not attempt to find groupthink in policy success, nor do they first categorise decision making as groupthink or not and then wait to see whether it leads to success or failure (for a review of some exceptions, see Riggs, Fuller, and Aldag 1997). It seems plausible that both vigorous debate and concurrence seeking can have beneficial effects, but at different stages of the policy process: multiple advocacy first, to improve the quality of decision making, and consensus later, to mobilise all group-members to join forces in the implementation of a decision.

With regard to the government's external relations, the inconclusive debate over the legitimacy and stability of presidential versus parliamentary systems of government has already been mentioned. Another claim about the difference between the two systems is that presidential government improves the quality of democracy, because the head of government is directly elected. Even advocates of parliamentary government acknowledge presidentialism's superiority in this respect. However, it appears to be a highly theoretical advantage: whatever indicators of legitimacy, trust in government, or satisfaction with the way democracy works is used, presidential government does not seem to lead to higher scores (Pharr and Putnam 2000). With regard to policy making capabilities, Weaver and Rockman conclude that although institutional variation does matter, the distinction between presidential and parliamentary studies is relatively unimportant (Weaver and Rockman 1993: 460). This is in line with my criticism of the 'two-body image' as too crude, but unfortunately so far there is no evidence linking the relative emphasis on different modes of executive–legislative relations to outcomes.

The same applies to the principal-agent approach of executive–bureaucratic relations: 'Such an assessment entails measuring the objectives of cabinet ministers, measuring the expected outcomes from actions taken by civil servants (because the best plans can go astray), and measuring the actual outcomes of actions taken by civil servants (because ultimately the proof is in the pudding). There are myriad factors that, to say the least, make this very difficult' (Huber 2000: 397). This, however, is a problem besetting all studies of the effects of particular aspects of government: how to isolate these effects from those of other aspects of government and from contextual factors.

Apart from that general caveat, the results are mixed: the social composition of governments and the presidential/parliamentary distinction do not seem to have a great impact, but the partisan composition of governments and the psychological make-up of heads of government do play a role. There is some evidence about the impact of the government's internal dynamics, but it could be stronger, and there is little or no research into the effects of the modes of executive–legislative relations and into the predictions of principal-agent theory with regard to relations with the bureaucracy.

CONCLUSION

It is twenty-five years since King wrote his survey of the state of the discipline with regard to the study of governments, and they have been productive years: the list of references could easily be augmented with recently published studies, but even without further additions, less than 10 per cent of the references in this chapter predate King's review, and the average publication cited dates from the last decade. At the end of his survey, King predicted that future research in this field would be based on detailed investigation, and that it would be comparative (King 1975b: 243). However, it still is customary for reviews of the literature on governments to lament its descriptive (historical or formal-legal), a-theoretical, and non-comparative nature (e.g. Bowles 1999: 1–7; Weller and Bakvis 1997: 7–11), and there still are many single-country studies in this field (e.g. Elgie 1993; Pfiffner 1996; Smith 1999), and many supposedly comparative books deal with their subject on a country-by-country basis (e.g. Laver and Shepsle 1994; Elgie 1995; Blondel and Cotta 1996; Blondel and Müller-Rommel 1997, 2001; Müller and Strøm 2000a). On the other hand, and in line with King's predictions, such books increasingly address a set of common, theoretically inspired questions. Books that deal with the governments of several countries are increasingly structured thematically (e.g. Baylis 1989; Shugart and Carey 1992; Laver and Shepsle 1996), even when they are multi-authored (e.g. Weller *et al.* 1997; Blondel and Cotta 2000), and they are increasingly based on empirical research (e.g. Blondel and Thiebault 1991; Blondel and Müller-Rommel 1993).

In short, the study of governments is coming of age. If I may end with my own prediction (or rather wishful thought), it is that these trends continue, with fewer aspects of government being colonised by just one theoretical perspective (notwithstanding the fact that some theoretical perspectives are simply more suited to some research questions than others), and with more attention to the impact of varieties of government on performance.

4

What is New about Governance and Why does it Matter?

R. A. W. RHODES

INTRODUCTION

Commenting on research into British central government, Peter Riddell, political editor of *The Times*, said:

The language in which political scientists operate is divorced from that of practitioners and commentators. Every time I see the word 'governance' I have to think again what it means and how it is not the same as government. Terms such as 'core executive', 'differentiated polity' and 'hollowed out executive' have become almost a private patois of political science, excluding outsiders, rather like the jargon of management reform in the civil service. The current generation of political scientists should look back a century to the elegance and clarity—though not the views—of Dicey and Bryce, and even perhaps the wit of a Bagehot.

This chapter defends the 'private patois of political science', revisiting the notions of: governance, the core executive, hollowing out, and the differentiated polity. There are already formal academic statements aplenty.[1] I want to provide an informal guide to one way of understanding British government; to what we are trying to understand and how we understand it. I do so because I am convinced the old vocabulary for describing Westminster and Whitehall is at best a partial description of how British government works. We need a new language to capture the changes which have and are taking place. And here lies both a puzzle and a danger. The puzzle is that the new vocabulary is not acceptable until approved by everyday use but it cannot be so approved until we start using it. The danger in this defence is that I simplify the ideas to make them clear to the point where I do not accept my own analysis.

In defending this patois, my objective is not to repair the wounded pride of political science. It matters how we understand British government. Such understandings are not the privilege of the chattering classes. If our existing map of our institutions

---

[1] On governance see Rhodes (1997a, 2000a,b). On policy networks see Rhodes (1988) and Marsh and Rhodes (1992). On the core executive see Rhodes and Dunleavy (1995). On power-dependence see Rhodes (1999 [1981]). On hollowing out see Rhodes (1994) and Weller *et al.* (1997). On Britain as a differentiated polity see Rhodes (1988, 2001). Readers who want the full academic paraphernalia supporting my interpretation of British government will find the references in these books.

and how they work is faulty, we mislead citizens and undermine representative democracy. Such maps are about how we are governed and politicians with faulty maps will make promises they cannot keep, not because they are venal, but because, unwittingly, they travel in the wrong direction. I am trying to make corrections to the existing map of British government so citizens and politicians alike know what journeys they can and cannot take.

TELLING STORIES

The shorthand name for the conventional story of how British government works—and the story is shared by academics and practitioners alike—is the Westminster model. This model focuses on such features as cabinet government and the role of the prime minister, majority party rule, parliamentary supremacy, and a neutral permanent civil service. It would be foolish to deny that these are important characteristics of British government but the Westminster model paints an incomplete picture. For example, the growth of the welfare state made many professions powerful. They could change and at times openly resist the policies of the elected government. If a powerful executive could pass new policies, it could not always make sure those policies would be put into practice as intended. So, if the Westminster model is characterized by a strong executive and a tradition of 'leaders know best', an interesting puzzle is why do so many of their policies fail. The much-vaunted, seemingly all-powerful Mrs Thatcher 'handbagged' the professions of the welfare state. Yet, as I write, the newspapers are filled with stories about arrogant consultants in the NHS and the problems of holding them to account. What is missing from the Westminster model is an account of 'the sour laws of unintended consequences' (Hennessy 1992: 453).

To compound the problems of the Westminster model, much has changed in the half a century from Attlee to Blair. The Empire is no more. The European Union exercises an influence few anticipated when Britain joined in 1972. Respect for authority and falling trust in government go with the decline of class and the growing importance of race, gender, religion, and nationality as cleavages in British society. Globalization is the cliché of the present day, with nation states seemingly powerless to resist (see Hurrell and Menon, this volume). The Westminster model acts as a symbol of continuity in this sea of change, a tribute to the eternal verities of British government and its capacity to adapt. It is a myth, but in so saying I do not seek to trivialize the Westminster model. Myths express truths and help us to impose some order on a complex, anarchic world. So, like John Wayne in an American Western, the Westminster model encapsulates shared values about British government, including our heroic qualities. But the brute fact of life is that Britain can act alone only rarely. In an interdependent world, diplomacy, agreement, and compromise are unavoidable and many of the economic and political decisions which impact on Britain are taken in forums where we are one voice among many.

Of course, academic colleagues are not blind to the changes. Many identify the weaknesses of the Westminster model and seek to assess whether it remains useful.

But they do so within this map of British government. The language they use is the language of the Westminster model and they often call for a return to the eternal verities of cabinet government and parliamentary sovereignty. Again as I write, there are debates about Blair's presidentialism, about the death of cabinet government, and about whether No. 10 has become a prime minister's department in all but name. These debates assume the issues and problems confronting the British executive concern institutional positions and their current incumbents. Again I do not dispute these trends are important. I do dispute that they can be adequately explored using the language of the Westminster model.

The past two decades have seen a second language widely used to talk about British government, commonly referred to as either managerialism or the New Public Management (NPM). Managerialism encompasses disparate reforms (see e.g. Wright 1994*b*). They include: privatization or selling the assets of the former nationalized industries; regulating both public utilities and the internal workings of the bureaucracy; the political control of the civil service by ministers; and decentralization which initially referred to decentralization within government departments but latterly has also covered devolution to Scotland, Wales, and Northern Ireland. But marketization and corporate management are of greatest relevance for explaining the rise of governance. Marketization refers to the use of market mechanisms in the delivery of public services to strengthen competition and increase choice (e.g. contracting-out). Corporate management refers to introducing private sector management methods in the public sector (e.g. setting objectives and measuring performance, value for money, and 'Investors in People'). More recently the emphasis has shifted to responsiveness and closeness to the customer (e.g. the Citizens Charter and its successor, Service First).

British government has undertaken reforms in both these areas and many commentators employ such phrases as the managerial state, the state under stress, and the audit explosion to capture the changes in the Westminster model. A pervasive storyline of British government is the clash between the Westminster model and the emerging managerial state. Thus, the search for greater economy, efficiency, and effectiveness led to agencification and separating policy from management. Ministers delegated responsibility to agency chief executives but remained accountable to parliament for policy. For many commentators this trend weakened ministerial responsibility to parliament. But the concerns of NPM are often too narrow, focusing on, for example, the internal management of central departments rather than managing the links between departments, the rest of the public sector, the voluntary and private sectors. The reforms have been evaluated but rarely and when they are evaluated the emphasis falls on narrow financial and efficiency indicators, not their effectiveness. Reforms are often reformed before we can assess what impact they have had. The supporters of managerialism claim much but prove little. The outcomes of managerialism may include greater efficiency and less accountability, but analysis cannot be confined to these normal concerns of the Westminster model.

How one sees the Westminster model and managerialism depends in part on one's view of political science. If the aim of political science is to test hypotheses, then the Westminster model can be a fruitful source of questions about, for example, the effects of different electoral systems, the incidence of backbench revolt in the House of Commons, and changing patterns of recruitment in the higher civil service. Similarly, managerialism poses hypotheses about, for example, the accountability of agencies and the factors improving efficiency in service delivery. However, political science can be seen, not as a 'social science' with the ambition to state general laws and predict, but as a 'human science' which uses narratives to construct explanations rooted in individual beliefs and actions.[2] The aim is to tell a story in ways which pose new questions and open new avenues of exploration.

Narratives may have a chronological order and contain such elements as setting, character, actions, and happenings, but their defining characteristic is that they explain actions by reference to beliefs and preferences. These narrative structures are akin to those found in works of fiction. However, the stories told by the human sciences are not fiction. They must meet conventional standards of evidence; that is, encompass known and agreed facts and use consistent, logical argumentation. But these standards are conventional, not objective. The analogy is with a lawyer addressing a jury. A jury hears different accounts of the same crime. The skills of the political scientist are then forensic, teasing out inconsistencies in existing explanations, and creative, telling a different story to explain the same facts. The jury is the rest of the political science community and other interested audiences such as politicians and civil servants. Does the new story change existing stories? Does it account for more of the 'facts'? Is the new story persuasive? So the political scientist must also be skilled in the arts of rhetoric and persuasion.

The key point for this chapter is that, in constructing a narrative, political scientists can choose which language they will employ for telling their story. Just as the social sciences can employ the language of hypothesis testing, so the human sciences can employ literary forms such as irony, tragedy, or romance.[3] The choice of language influences how we tell our story. In this chapter I seek to provide a language which

---

[2] The notion of narratives is not used in the analysis of British government, although there are at least two related notions. Tivey (1988: 3) uses 'the image' ... 'to denote the consequences of an interpretation'... of 'a set of assumptions about 'the system'... and how it works'. This image contains 'operative concepts' or 'operative ideals': 'the views of the authors are taken to be of some influence; what they have said has to some extent become operative ... they have gained currency among those who study politics, and diluted and distorted they have reached the practitioners' (Tivey 1988: 1; see also Beer 1982a: xiii, 404). Gamble (1990: 405) employs the notion of an 'organizing perspective' which precedes epistemology and theory and provides 'a map of how things relate, a set of research questions'. It provides the language with which we draw the map and pose the questions. An image, organizing perspective, or narrative is not falsifiable; it is more or less accurate. It never provides a definitive account; it is an approximation, a map where maps 'can guide ... even when they are and are known to be grossly inaccurate' since they can be corrected on the way (MacIntyre 1983: 32).

[3] This chapter does not explore the argument that the choice of language or tropes (White 1973: ch. 1, 1978: ch. 2) prefigures both the story (and its plot) and, therefore, the explanation (see also Barthes 1981). Lacking a shared technical language, politics, and history, rely on familiar figures of speech (or ordinary language) to create meaning. So the way in which we tell our stories is 'dictated by the dominant figurative mode of the language he has used to *describe* the elements of his account *prior* to his composition of the narrative'. In effect, 'historians *constitute* their subjects as possible objects of narrative representation by the very language they use to *describe* them' (White 1978: 94–5).

helps us to understand the sour laws of unintended consequences. There is no one language suitable for all analyses of British government. And I stress, although my language may be tinged with the tragic, it is not built on neologisms. I use no invented words. Every word is in the Oxford English Dictionary (OED) and, where it has several meanings, I make it clear which one I am using.

The Westminster model and managerialism provide narratives of British government which influence, indirectly, how practitioners and citizens view the system. This chapter offers a different narrative which opens new avenues of exploration by seeking to show that the sour laws of unintended consequences are inevitable using the existing maps of British government. To do so, I employ the language of *governance, core executive*, and *hollowing out* to provide a map of *the differentiated polity*.

GOVERNANCE

Finer (1970: 3–4) defined government as: 'the activity or process of governing' or 'governance' (as in the OED); 'a condition of ordered rule'; 'those people charged with the duty of governing' or 'governors'; and 'the manner, method or system by which a particular society is governed'. Present-day use does not treat governance as a synonym for government. Rather, governance signifies a change in the meaning of government, referring to a *new* process of governing; or a *changed* condition of ordered rule; or the *new* method by which society is governed. How has the Westminster model changed? But what is new in British government?

To answer this question I must start with the notion of policy networks. The term refers to those sets of organizations clustered around a major government function or department. These groups commonly include the professions, trade unions, and big business. Central departments need their cooperation to deliver services. They need their cooperation because British government rarely delivers services itself. It uses other bodies. Also there are too many groups to consult, so government must aggregate interests. It needs the 'legitimated' spokespeople for that policy area. The groups need the money and legislative authority which only government can provide.

Policy networks are a long-standing feature of British government. They have developed a consensus about what they are doing which serves the aims of all involved. They have evolved routine ways of deciding. They are a form of private government of public services, scathingly referred to by the New Right as producer groups using government for their own sectional interests.

The government of Margaret Thatcher sought to reduce their power by using markets to deliver public services, bypassing existing networks, and curtailing the 'privileges' of professions, commonly by subjecting them to rigorous financial and management controls. But these corporate management and marketization reforms had unintended consequences. They fragmented the systems for delivering public services and so created pressures for organizations to cooperate with one another to deliver services. In other words, and paradoxically, marketization multiplied the networks it was supposed to replace. Commonly, welfare state services are now delivered by packages of organizations. So what is new is the spread of networks in British government. Fragmentation not only created new networks but it also increased the membership of existing networks, incorporating both the private and voluntary sectors. Also, the government swapped direct for indirect controls and central departments are no longer either necessarily or invariably the fulcrum of a network. The government can set the limits to network actions. It still funds the services. But it has also increased its dependence on multifarious networks and devolution to Scotland, Wales, and Northern Ireland simply adds a further layer of complexity which will fuel territorial networks.

In short, governance refers to the changing role of the state after the varied public sector reforms of the 1980s and 1990s. In the UK context, where there is no state tradition comparable to the continental tradition of *Rechtsstaat*, the literature on governance explores how the informal authority of networks supplements and supplants the formal authority of government. It explores the limits to the state and seeks to develop a more diverse view of state authority and its exercise.

If networks are the defining characteristic of governance, how do they differ from such more widely understood notions as markets and hierarchies (or bureaucracies)? Table 4.1 shows the distinctive features of networks compared with markets and hierarchies as mechanisms for allocating and coordinating resources and public services.

Again, my aim is not to bore the reader with endless definitions but to provide an at a glance characterization to show that networks are a distinctive coordinating mechanism and, therefore, separate from markets and hierarchies. Of these characteristics, trust is central because it is the basis of network coordination in the same way that commands and price competition are the key mechanisms for bureaucracies and markets, respectively. It is 'the most important attribute of network operations' (Frances *et al.* 1991: 15). Shared values and norms are the glue which holds the complex set of relationships together; trust is essential for cooperative behaviour and, therefore, the existence of the network. As a working axiom, networks are high on trust and contracts are low on trust. With the spread of networks there has been a recurrent tension between contracts on the one hand with their stress on competition to get the best price and networks on the other with their stress on cooperative behaviour.

Table 4.1 *Characteristics of markets, hierarchies, and networks*

	Markets	Hierarchies	Networks
Basis of relationships	Contract and property rights	Employment relationship	Resource exchange
Degree of dependence	Independent	Dependent	Interdependent
Medium of exchange	Prices	Authority	Trust
Means of conflict resolution and coordination	Haggling and the courts	Rules and commands	Diplomacy
Culture	Competition	Subordination	Reciprocity

So, governance refers to governing with and through networks or, to employ shorthand, it refers to *steering networks.* I use governance in three ways. First, it describes public sector change; it refers to the fragmentation caused by the reforms of the 1980s and 1990s. Second, I use it to interpret British government. To talk of the governance of Britain is to say the Westminster model is no longer acceptable and we have to tell a different story of the shift from government (the strong executive) to governance (through networks). Third, I use governance to prescribe the next round of reforms; for example the terms holistic governance or joined-up governance refer to measures designed to improve coordination between government departments and other agencies. But whether I use the term to describe, interpret, or prescribe, it still refers to the changing form of the British state in general and the ways in which the informal authority of networks supplements and supplants the formal authority of the state in particular.

CORE EXECUTIVE

There is a conventional debate about the British executive which focuses on the relative power of prime minister and cabinet. Many have pointed to its limited nature but it continues to this day as commentators rail against Blair's presidentialism. This analysis assumes the best way to look at the executive is to consider key positions and their incumbents. Instead of such a positional approach, the executive can be defined in functional terms. So instead of asking which position is important, we can ask which functions define the innermost part or heart of British government. The core functions of the British executive are to pull together and integrate central government policies and to act as final arbiters of conflicts between different elements of the government machine. These functions can be carried out by institutions other than prime minister and cabinet; for example, the Treasury and the Cabinet Office. By defining the core executive in functional terms, the key question becomes, 'who does what?'

There is a second strand to the argument favouring a focus on the core executive rather than prime minister and cabinet. The positional approach also assumes that power lies with specific positions and the people who occupy those positions. But power is contingent and relational; that is, it depends on the relative power of other actors and, as Harold Macmillan succinctly put it, 'events, dear boy, events'. So, ministers depend on the prime minister for support in getting funds from the Treasury. In turn, the prime minister depends on ministers to deliver the party's electoral promises. Both ministers and prime minister depend on the health of the American economy for a stable pound and a growing economy to ensure the needed financial resources are available. This power–dependence approach focuses on the distribution of such resources as money and authority in the core executive and explores the shifting patterns of dependence between the several actors.

So, the term 'core executive' directs our attention to two key questions: 'Who does what?' and 'Who has what resources?'. If the answer for several policy areas and several conflicts is that the prime minister co-ordinates policy, resolves conflicts, and controls the main resources, we will indeed have prime ministerial government. However, as Wright and Hayward (2000: 33) concluded, core executive coordination is in practice modest. It has four characteristics.

1. It is largely negative, based on persistent compartmentalization, mutual avoidance, and friction reduction between powerful bureaux or ministries...
2. Even when cooperative, anchored at the lower levels of the state machine and organized by specific established networks, coordination is sustained by a culture of dialogue in vertical relations and of integration at the horizontal level.
3. It is rarely strategic, so almost all attempts to create proactive strategic capacity for long-term planning... have failed...
4. It is intermittent and selective in any one sector, improvised late in the policy process, politicized, issue-oriented, and reactive.

The endless search for the holy grail of coordination continues in British government and it lies at the heart of New Labour's reforms. As Kavanagh and Seldon (2000) point out, under New Labour we have seen prime ministerial centralization in the guises of: institutional innovation and more resources for No. 10 and the Cabinet Office; and strong political and policy direction as No. 10 seeks a firm grip on the government machine. The pendulum swings yet again as the centre promotes coordination and strategic oversight to combat Whitehall's departmentalism and the unintended consequences of managerialism. Such 'power grabs' are 'a reaction to felt weakness, a frustration with the inability to pull effective levers'. For as Norton (2000: 116–7) argues, 'Ministers are like medieval barons in that they preside over their own, sometimes vast, policy territory'. Crucially, 'the ministers fight—or form alliances— with other barons in order to get what they want' and they resent interference in their territory by other barons and will fight to defend it. So, the core executive is segmented into overlapping games in which all players have some resources with which to play the game and no one actor is pre-eminent in all games.

In sum, power–dependence characterizes the links both between barons and between the barons and prime minister. Looking at the heart of the machine as if it is a core executive characterized by power dependence and game playing reveals the limits to the Westminster model view that Britain has a strong executive. Coordination is intermittent, selective, and sectoral. Reforms to strengthen the core executive reflect the strength of the barons and the core's past weakness, not its current strength (for we do not know if these reforms will work, only that previous reforms did not). Wright and Hayward (2000: 34) argue core executives lack political will, time, information, cohesion, and effective instruments. Also, the weight of 'urgent' political issues needing attention and multiple constitutional and administrative constraints further limit the capacity of the core executive to coordinate effectively.

The argument about the strength of the British executive is overstated. It is clear there were always many constraints. But with the trend from government to governance the constraints become ever more insistent. The storyline of the past twenty years is one of fragmentation confounding centralization as a segmented executive seeks to improve horizontal coordination among departments and agencies and vertical coordination between departments and their networks of organizations. The unintended consequence of this search for central control is a hollowing out of the core executive. It is a present-day illustration of Enoch Powell's comment that in politics 'the test of success or failure is so unsure that one is tempted to wonder whether there is such a thing as true political success at all: failure, or frustration, or reversal, seems so much to be the essence of any political career' (cited in Hennessy 1996).

HOLLOWING OUT

I attended a Moravian (Protestant) church school. We celebrated Christmas with a Christingle service. This involved slicing the top of an orange, scooping out the flesh to make an empty space inside which was filled with a small candle. There were no electric lights in the chapel as we sang carols, just hundreds of flickering candles. Hollowing out of the state is an equally straightforward event. It means simply that the growth of governance has scooped the flesh (or the ability to act effectively) out of the core executive (or orange) and replaced it with the candle of diplomacy.

In what ways has the capacity of the British core executive been eroded? The state has been hollowed out from above (e.g. by international interdependence), from below (by marketization and networks), and sideways (by agencies). Internally, the British core executive was already characterized by baronies, policy networks, and intermittent and selective coordination. It has been further hollowed out internally by the unintended consequences of marketization which fragmented service delivery, multiplied networks, and diversified the membership of those networks. It will not be long before devolution to Scotland, Wales, and Northern Ireland impose further constraints. Indeed, there may be a demonstration effect which gives added momentum to the demand for regional devolution in England.

Externally, the state is also being hollowed out by membership of the European Union and other international commitments. Menon and Wright (1998) conclude: there is 'no doubt' the United Kingdom has 'forged an efficient policy making and coordinating machine' because the government speaks and acts with one voice. It has also been successful in its 'basic strategy of opening up and liberalizing the EU's economy'. However, its 'unjustified reputation' for being at the margins of Europe is justified for EU constitution building and 'an effective and coherent policy-making machine becomes ineffective when it is bypassed' for the history-making decisions.

Few would consider the problems of steering an ever more complex, devolved government machine, and being bypassed for constitutional, history making decisions as evidence of the core executive's ability to act effectively. It is important to distinguish between intervention and control. Indisputably the British centre intervenes often but its interventions do not always have the intended effects and so cannot be considered control. New Labour recognizes the problem. Improved central coordination lies at the heart of its policy agenda. Blair (1998) stated the aims succinctly: 'joined-up problems need joined-up solutions' and this theme runs through the *Modernizing Government* White Paper with its frequent references to 'joined-up' government and 'holistic governance' (Cm 4310 1999; see also Cabinet Office 2000). Both phrases are synonyms for steering networks and the White Paper is a response to the government's belief that 'too little effort has gone into making sure that policies are devised and delivered in a consistent and effective way across institutional boundaries'. It describes the challenge as 'to get different parts of government to work together' by, for example: 'designing policy around shared goals'; 'involving others in policy making'; and 'integrating the European Union and international dimension in our policy making'.

Joining-up takes various forms. For example, there are area-based programmes or 'action zones' (twenty-six in health, twenty-five in education) linking central and local government, health authorities, the private sector, and voluntary organizations; and group focused programmes such as the 'Better Government for Older People' pilot (Cm 4310 1999: 18, 26–7, and 29). New Labour stresses developing networks to promote cooperation and these networks are supposed to be based on trust. Blair describes such trust as 'the recognition of a mutual purpose for which we work together and in which we all benefit' (Blair 1996: 292). Quality public services are best achieved through cooperative relations based on trust and the Labour government's reform proposals base the delivery of public services on such networks.

However, the practice of British government remains familiar. Ministers, the barons at the heart of British government, continue to defend their fiefdoms; it was ever thus. Equally, action zones show the limits to vertical coordination. There is an epidemic of zones, to the point where the solution (to fragmentation) becomes part of the problem (by adding to the bodies to be coordinated). For example, John Denham (1999), a junior minister in the Department of Health, concedes that 'zones can sometimes make government look more, rather than less complicated to the citizen' and there is the danger of 'initiative overload' because the zones do not join-up.

Zones show the government adopting an instrumental approach to network management which assumes the centre can devise and impose ways to foster integration in and between networks and realise central government's objectives. The reforms have a centralizing thrust. They seek to coordinate departments and local authorities by imposing a new style of management on other agencies. So, they 'do not want to run local services from the centre' but '[T]he Government is not afraid to take action where standards slip'; an obvious instance of a command operating code (Cm 4310 1999: 35, 37, 45, 53, 55). Zones are owned by the centre and local agendas are recognized in as far as they help the centre. Such a code, no matter how well disguised, runs the ever-present risk of recalcitrance from key actors and a loss of flexibility in dealing with localized problems. Gentle pressure relentlessly applied is still a command operating code in a velvet glove. When you sit at the top of a pyramid and you cannot see the bottom, control deficits are an ever-present unintended consequence.

'Diplomacy' or management by negotiation is the hands-off alternative to hands-on management. Such skills lie at the heart of steering networks. Network structures are characterized by a decentralized negotiating style which trades off control for agreement. This style of hands-off management involves setting the framework in which networks work but keeping an arm's length relationship. For example, a central department can: provide the policy framework and policy guidance; prod the network into action by systematic review and scrutiny of its work; use patronage to put 'one of its own' in key positions; mobilize resources and skills across sectors; regulate the network and its members; and provide advice and assistance (Cm 2811 1995). Such steering is imperfect but just as there are limits to central command, there are limits to independent action by networks. Above all, such management by negotiation means agreeing with the objectives of others, not just persuading them that you were right all along or resorting to sanctions when they disagree.

THE DIFFERENTIATED POLITY

The Westminster model treats Britain as a unitary state but this term is a black hole in the political science literature. It is a taken-for-granted notion, all too often treated as a residual category, used to compare unitary with federal states to highlight the characteristics of the latter. However there are several types of unitary state and Britain differs in that, for Scotland, Wales, and Northern Ireland, pre-Union rights, institutional structures, and a degree of regional autonomy persisted throughout the post-war period. In other words, administrative structures are not standardized; there is a maze of institutions and a variegated pattern of decentralized functions. I refer to Britain as a differentiated polity to make it clear that political integration and administrative standardization have been and are incomplete. British government has grown by becoming specialized in both the functions it delivers and the territories it governs. So the term also draws together the changes of the 1980s and 1990s which saw significant changes in the functional and territorial specialization of British government. The arguments that networks have multiplied as an unintended consequence of marketization; that the degree of international interdependence is greater and that, as a result, the core executive's capacity to steer is reduced or hollowed-out, serve to reinforce the interpretation that centralization and control are incomplete and Britain is best viewed as a differentiated polity—an unruly disUnited Kingdom.

It is important to place this differentiated polity in an historical perspective. Referring to the 1960s, Lowe and Rollings (2000) conclude: 'political and administrative fragmentation may have sapped the ability of the core executive to coordinate a strong central policy, but the fundamental impediment to modernization remained the power of vested interests within the broader governance'. Moreover, this trend is specific to the post-war period. There was no straightforward increase in state intervention after 1900 and a hollowing out after 1945. The prominence of governance (as networks) rose and fell during the twentieth century. Governance was pre-eminent at the turn of the century, obsolete in the 1960s, and reinvented in the 1980s.

Devolution will provide further impetus to these swings in the pendulum from centralization to governance and back. It may be one of the most significant reforms of the post-war period because it reinforces functional decentralization with divided political authority. Devolution to the English regions will not take place in the life of the second Blair parliament. But the new Regional Development Agencies have not stilled the clamour of regional voices for devolution. So, political decentralization remains on the political agenda and the civil service may soon confront a patchwork quilt of regional assemblies and directly elected mayors in England (as well as Scotland, Wales, and Northern Ireland) with new machinery of government to manage intergovernmental relations both for domestic matters and the European Union. Diplomatic skill in intergovernmental bargaining will become a prominent part of a civil servant's repertoire. Britain will get a taste of the federal-provincial diplomacy so characteristic of other Westminster systems such as Australia and Canada. In the words of the Head of the Home Civil Service, Sir Richard Wilson (1998) the civil service 'are going to have to learn skills that we haven't learned before'.

In short, the networking skills increasingly required to manage service delivery will also be at a premium in managing the intergovernmental relations of devolved Britain. The task is to manage packages; packages of services, of organizations generally, and of governments in particular. This is not the picture of British government painted by the Westminster model. Its account of Britain as a unitary state emphasizes political integration, centralized authority, a command operating code implemented through bureaucracy, and the power of the centre to revoke decentralized powers. The differentiated polity narrative emphasizes political devolution, fragmentation and interdependence, and functional decentralization. The contradictions between authority and interdependence, bureaucracy and networks, and political and functional politics underpin the sour laws of unintended consequences.

CONCLUSIONS

When trying to repair a gap in the map of British government there is always the danger of appearing one-sided. I seek to counter a view of British government which stresses Britain as a unitary state with a strong executive. I do not dispute the British executive can act decisively. Obviously, the centre coordinates and implements policies as intended at least some of the time. But the Westminster model attaches too little importance to the sour laws of unintended consequences. Governments fail because they are locked into power-dependent relations and because they must work with and through complex networks of actors and organizations. To adopt a command operating code builds failure into the design of the policy. Such centralization will be confounded by fragmentation and interdependence which will, in turn, prompt further bouts of centralization. It is time to break free of the shackles of the Westminster model.

Devolution is the first step and it is proving a hard pill to swallow. Devolved governments do their own thing. They elect first ministers the UK government does not want to deal with. They adopt policies the UK government does not approve of and embroil the centre in disputes not of its making. Similarly, if at a more mundane level, policy networks implement and vary policies in ways the centre dislikes. DfES battles long and hard with the Treasury for extra money for the education service only to see local authorities spend that money on services other than education. Trusting devolved governments, local authorities, indeed any decentralized agency, to deliver the services people want and to be accountable to those whom it serves is a big step for a British centre habituated to intervening at will. Hands-off is a lesson no government has been willing to heed since 1945 but hands-on controls are no way to manage a differentiated polity. Unless governments grasp this nettle and devise a central operating code which fits an institutional structure characterized by functional and political decentralization, the sour laws of unintended consequences will prevail and public cynicism will spread.

Vincent Wright (1997*b*: 13) remarks that the interactions of state, market, and society throw up many contradictions and dilemmas, but a distinguishing feature of governing is its 'overarching and integrative function'. It provides 'ballast', 'a semblance of coherence', 'occasional steering ability' but 'above all' it provides 'a degree of legitimacy to governance'. Recent reforms and faulty maps threaten that legitimacy. The analysis of governance seeks to identify the intended and unintended consequences of the reforms of the 1980s and 1990s and to correct faulty maps. Whether it succeeds is a judgement that will be made by others, but analysing governance is important precisely because it focuses on the interaction of state bureaucracy, markets, and networks, and their consequences for government legitimacy.

5

Executives in Comparative Context

KLAUS H. GOETZ

FOUR IMAGES OF THE EXECUTIVE

The comparative study of European executives stands at the interface of two subdisciplines of political science: comparative government and comparative public administration. The first—comparative government—focuses on the primarily political and governmental aspects of the executive. It deals, for example, with the role of prime ministers and government ministers; cabinets and cabinet committees; coalition governments, including how they are formed and terminated, how portfolios are allocated, and political decisions made; or the relationships between governments and governing parties. One could characterize this perspective as executive studies 'from above', in that the executive territory is typically surveyed from the vantage point of political and governmental leadership.

By contrast, accounts from the perspective of comparative public administration are interested, first and foremost, in the bureaucratic parts of the executive that extend beneath its thin political veneer. Such studies concentrate on the executive 'machinery', in particular, the ministerial administration and other types of central agencies; the status, organization, and role of non-elected executive personnel, notably the civil service; and, increasingly, the importance of administrative law in governing executive action. With an emphasis on the bureaucratic foundations of executive power, comparative public administration studies the executive 'from below'.

This, admittedly, rather simplified divergence in perspective and empirical focus reflects the duality of executives as political and administrative entities. As political institutions, executives are oriented towards acquiring, securing, and exercising political power. This function often predominates at the centre of government, where the requirements of political management drive the organization (Peters *et al.* 2000*a*). At the same time, however, executives are administrative institutions, which typically form the apex of a hierarchically structured administrative organization. Thus, in Germany, for example, the Federal ministries are classed as supreme Federal authorities (*oberste Bundesbehörden*) and the minister is the head of the authority. The 'old time religion' of traditional public administration (Peters 1996; Peters and Wright 1996) has, of course, been subject to sustained attack over the least two decades, most notably in the Anglo-Saxon world. Yet, efforts to replace 'bureaucracy' with 'New Public Management' have been aimed more at the formal organization of public administration than its underlying rationality, guided by the ideas of impartiality, objectivity, regularity, and legality (Wright 1994*b*). The latter principles and, in particular, the identification of a permanent civil service with the public good, remain central to the self-image of the ministerial public service, and career services continue to be the norm in Western ministries.

The tension between politics and administration is central to understanding the institutionalization of executives. This tension is not only about the tasks executives are expected to perform, but also, perhaps more importantly, about the most appropriate organization of the executive, including its personnel. Much of the contemporary discussion surrounding the reform of executives in both Western and Eastern Europe is, at its core, concerned with the relative weight that is to be accorded to politics vs. administration and the institutional designs best-suited to accommodate the tension between them. For example, where and how should a line be drawn between the powers and responsibilities of elected executive politicians, on the one hand, and officials, on the other? To what extent and in what form should the former be involved in decisions concerning the appointment and career prospects of the latter? How these boundaries have fluctuated over time and across countries and how the political and administrative spheres have interacted (or, at times, coalesced) is at the centre of some of the most insightful comparative writing on European executives (Wright 1996*a*).

A second basic tension in the executive concerns the relation between the formal office (including elected offices) and office holders. It has been argued that political institutions, in general, and the political parts of the executive, in particular, are distinguished by the exceptionally close connection between office and office holder (Göhler 1994). Certainly, mainstream executive studies, especially of chief executives (i.e. heads of government) and ministers, regularly note the importance of the personal qualities, dispositions, and motives of incumbents and the extent to which individuals shape the office they occupy. In fact, much of the literature concerned with political leadership in Western democracies revolves around this theme (Elgie 1995). There are, of course, great differences in the degree to which individuals can remould or reinterpret the formal position that they occupy. But at the top levels of the executive, consisting of heads of government and core ministers, it would appear that the 'man maketh the office' as much as the 'office maketh the man'. This is particularly the case where, as in much of Central and Eastern Europe after 1989 or in Germany after 1945, new or fundamentally revised constitutions needed to be brought to life and discredited institutional legacies had to be overcome. Under such conditions, enterprising elected executives may be able to define their office in a way that sets the path for decades to come. The impact of Chancellor Adenauer on the long-term development of the German chancellorship is a case in point (Padgett 1994).

Whether executive politicians 'make a difference' to the offices that they hold has long been subject to a lively debate, which, more recently, has spilled over to the administrative realm. Thus, from a rational choice perspective, attempts have been made to model the behaviour of officials with reference to individual utility calculations; in this connection, the debate between those who understand officials as either 'budget maximizers' or 'bureau shapers' has been particularly fruitful (Dunleavy 1991; Marsh *et al.* 2000). With a less theoretical bent, biographical approaches that seek to examine the impact of specific officials, usually drawn from amongst the top of the bureaucratic hierarchy, are also gaining in prominence (Theakston 1999, 2000). But the assumption that officials, just like executive politicians, have considerable scope for moulding the posts they occupy is not undisputed and the evidence indecisive. Thus, Egeberg and Sætren (1999: 96) suggest that 'It seems as if government bureaucracies (...) are able to endogenize officials' preference formation to a considerable degree (...) when the content of the proposals and decisions they make in their capacity as officials is to be explained, knowledge of their private interests seems to add little to our understanding'.

The degree to which office and office holder are separated or merged, that is, the extent to which it is possible to analyze, and to generalize about, the former without reference to specific office holders, constitutes the second key dimension of executive institutionalization. For example, is the position of the head of government defined primarily by convention and open to political reinterpretation, as in the United Kingdom, or does it appear more hemmed in by legal norms, notably in the form of a written constitution and political constraints, such as the dynamics of coalition government, as appears the case in Germany or the Netherlands? Are the powers and duties of officials, especially senior officials operating at the apex of the ministerial bureaucracy, subject to extensive legal regulations that are strictly enforced or are they operating in a 'grey zone', where practice is moulded by individuals rather than formal norms? Again, European countries differ significantly in the emphasis they place on clear role differentiations within the executive; the intensity with which they seek to regulate political and administrative offices and the behaviour of office holders; and the changeability of organizational arrangements over time.

With reference to these two dimensions of institutionalization, we may then distinguish four images of the executive. These images also stand for the four principal ways of approaching the comparative study of executives, and most contemporary analyses can be placed somewhere in the space described by the four images (Figure 5.1).

1. *Image I*: 'Big beasts in the jungle'. The primary concern here is for the actions of individual political actors. The executive is equated with government, an arena in which individuals driven by the desire for political power clash and vie for influence. Both the development of public policy and the development of the executive itself are

Dimension of institutionalization	Incumbent/office holder	Office
Political	Image I: 'Big Beasts in the Jungle'	Image II: 'The Art of Government'
Administrative	Image III: 'Sir Humphrey Rules'	Image IV: 'The Art of Administration'

Figure 5.1 *Four images of the executive*

seen to be inextricably bound up with the actions of individual political actors. Not surprisingly, such an approach to executive studies is perhaps most pronounced in countries that have a tradition of 'strong' chief executives, as found in presidential or prime ministerial democracies.

2. *Image II*: 'The art of government'. Here, too, the political–governmental rather than the administrative features of the executives are of principal concern, but more systematic attention is paid to the institutional as opposed to the individual aspects of governing. Thus, one finds an interest with the structures and processes of governing; patterns of co-operation and coordination in executive systems that emphasize collegiality and collectivity; and, more broadly, the political conditioning of executive action, notably as a consequence of the interaction between coalition, party, and parliamentary government. To comprehend policy development in the executive and the latter's developmental trajectory, the complexity of its political institutional foundations must be taken into account.

3. *Image III*: 'Sir Humphrey rules'. From this perspective, it is individual officials (or small cliques of officials sharing a common outlook) who provide the key to unravelling the actions of the executive. Since 'officials matter', it is important to examine their values, beliefs, and attitudes. Accordingly, a good deal of comparative work has been done into the degree of cultural homogeneity of administrative elites and cross-country differences in the composition and orientations of senior civil servants (Armstrong 1973; Suleiman 1974; Dogan 1975; Aberbach *et al.* 1981).

4. *Image IV*: 'The art of administration'. Finally, there is a body of writing that emphasizes the administrative institutional foundations of the executive. This approach is of special import in European countries that are thought to have a 'strong state tradition', such as France or Germany (Dyson 1980), highly developed systems of public law (which includes administrative law), and protected career civil services. For example, Renate Mayntz and Fritz W. Scharpf (1975), in their authoritative study of policy making in the German Federal administration, highlighted the extent to which policy outcomes could be explained as a result of hierarchical and functional specialization and organizational fragmentation inside Germany's Federal bureaucracy.

The following addresses in more depth some of the issues and arguments raised so far. The four images just set out will help us to structure this discussion, although they provide at best a rough map to the territory of executive studies. The key aim is to open up the executive 'black box' by examining the internal life of European executives rather than engage with the debate on the appropriate location of the executive within the political system (see Andeweg this volume). To this end, the following section will analyze in more detail how the two constitutive tensions in the institutionalization of executives play out in different countries. This issue is discussed with reference to executive coordination and the organization of centres of government. Whilst this discussion shows that a good deal is by now known about cross-country variations in the institutional configurations of executive power, systematic comparative evaluations of the effects of different institutional arrangements are rare. This observation applies, in particular, when it comes to differences in bureaucratic structure. Predictably, the dearth of solid comparative evaluation has not stopped efforts at executive reform. In Western Europe, evidence suggests that the majority of countries are moving towards more personalized forms of exercising executive power, at both political and administrative levels. By contrast, in post-Communist Central and Eastern Europe, the thrust of domestic reform initiatives and assistance provided by international organizations has pointed in precisely the opposite direction, that is, depersonalization. But empirical research into executive development in the region raises doubts over whether depersonalization is really occurring[1]. Indications of a growing de-institutionalization of Western executives and barriers to effective institutionalization in the East must not be taken as evidence that European executives are 'in decline'. Rather, they are a reminder that comparative executive studies must not focus exclusively on explaining differences in the institutional *configurations* of executives, but should become more sensitive to different *degrees* of institutionalization and change over time.

INSIDE THE EXECUTIVE

Executive Coordination

Coordination is one of the 'classic' themes in executive studies that has received renewed attention in recent years, not least owing to the comparative research undertaking initiated by the late Vincent Wright in the context of the British Economic and Social Research Council's Whitehall Programme (see, in particular, Wright and Hayward 2000). This work has close links to the concept of the 'core executive', developed by Rhodes and Dunleavy to capture 'all those organizations and structures which primarily serve to pull together and integrate central government policies, or act as final arbiters within the executive of conflicts between different elements of the government machine' (Dunleavy and Rhodes 1990: 4). Since then, the concept of the core executive—encompassing both an activity and an institutional arrangement—has inspired a range of comparative (Weller *et al.* 1997; Peters *et al.* 2000*a*) and single-country studies (Rhodes and Dunleavy 1995; Smith 1999; Hayward and Wright, 2002).

This revival of academic interest in the manner in which executives seek to coordinate their activities is not difficult to explain. In common with much of the research agenda of comparative government and public administration, it closely mirrors and follows empirical trends in the political systems of the major Western democracies. Functional specialization and institutional differentiation are, of

---

[1] The observations on executive development in Central and Eastern Europe are principally informed by a research project on 'Executive Capacity in Central and Eastern Europe', which is funded by the Volkswagen Foundation and led by the author. The other participants in this project include Martin Brusis, Hellmut Wollmann (both Humboldt University Berlin), Vesselin Dimitrov, and Radoslaw Zubek (both LSE). More detailed findings of this project can be found in a special issue of the *Journal of European Public Policy*, Vol. 8, No. 6, 2001, which is devoted to governance in Central and Eastern Europe.

course, the signs of modern organizations, and the complexity of contemporary executive bureaucracies reflects the continued influence of these organizing principles. The challenge of re-integrating the activities of highly specialized organizations is, thus, inherent in the institutional set-up of modern executives. However, as Peters *et al.* point out (2000*b*: 8ff.), pressures for effective coordination appear to have increased significantly over the last two decades or so, not least because of increased sectorization of policy making; growing budgetary pressures that force prioritization; and a changing public policy agenda, in which cross-cutting issues that do not fit neatly into existing departmental structures have gained in salience. The importance of such issues, and the barriers that may prevent successful coordination across institutional boundaries within the executive, are highlighted in a report by the Performance and Innovation Unit of the British Cabinet Office. It notes that 'budgets and organizational structures are arranged around vertical, functional lines (education, health, defence, etc.) rather than horizontal, cross-cutting problems, and issues (social exclusion, sustainable development, etc.)' (Cabinet Office 2000: 6). European integration has added a further key dimension to national executive coordination requirements: 'These arise from the general characteristics of the European Union, from specific duties and obligations incumbent on the member states, and from the politicization of European matters in domestic political life' (Kassim *et al.* 2000: 6; see also Goetz 2000*a*).

Reflecting the twin political and administrative nature of the executive, one may broadly distinguish two perspectives in the discussion of executive coordination. The first, taking its clues from comparative government, revolves around the notions of party government, coalition government, and parliamentary government. Such accounts stress the interwoveneness of executives, governing parties, and parliamentary parties in the modern governing process and point to their consequences for executive coordination (Blondel and Cotta 1996, 2000). The prevalence of 'consensus democracies' (Lijphart 1999), with their orientation towards power-sharing and consensus-building, increases the need for coordination within executives (often constituted by coalitions) and between executives and other political institutions on whose active support or at least acquiescence they rely. In consensus democracies, there is also typically little scope for the non-negotiated unilateral imposition of political decisions, that is, coordination by fiat. But even in political systems that seem more closely to resemble Lijphart's second ideal-type, that is, the Westminster model, of which the British political system was long the leading exponent, executive autonomy appears to be in decline with far-reaching implications for traditionally inward-looking executive coordination cultures.

Viewed from this perspective, executive coordination is principally understood as a consequence of the overriding need for political compromise in increasingly differentiated and complex policy making frameworks. It is a means of resolving conflicts over political preferences and priorities, both within the executive and between the executive and the political forces and institutions with which it must cooperate. Cross-national variations in coordination mechanisms are, accordingly, chiefly to be explained with reference to political variables, such as the party-political makeup of government, the nature of executive–legislative relations, the dynamics of party competition, and/or the degree of centralization in the political system. A recent detailed comparative study of coalition governments in Western Europe (Müller and Strom 2000*b*: 572ff.) shows the diversity of the devices that are being employed for political coordination. They include, *inter alia*, written coalition agreements; coalition committees that manage the relations amongst the governing parties; inner cabinets; coalition working groups composed of members of the government and the governing parliamentary parties to prepare major legislative initiatives; or party summits, 'that is, meetings of the leaders of the coalition parties, whether or not these hold portfolios in the cabinet' (*ibid.*: 583).

It is sometimes implied that political coordination mechanisms of this type have largely undermined cabinet (the council of ministers) as the central institution of executive conflict resolution; cabinet has been reduced to rubberstamping decisions taken elsewhere. However, it is easy to overstate the extent to which the growing use of political coordination devices of the type mentioned by Müller and Strom has altered the reality of modern executive government. On the one hand, there is nothing especially new about such mechanisms, as the experience of long-standing consensus democracies such as the Belgium (de Winter *et al.* 2000) and The Netherlands (Timmermans and Andeweg 2000) illustrates. On the other, as Blondel argues in his comparative survey of Western European cabinets, even in countries where non-cabinet based coordination devices are used extensively, the council of ministers 'remains an arena in which final appeals can be and are made, as well as (at least in some countries) a place where ideas are discussed' (Blondel 1997: 14–15).

Whereas comparative government explanations stress political coordination requirements and highlight the importance of political arrangements for conflict resolution, discussions from the perspective of comparative public administration take the organizational features of the executive system as their point of departure. Here, the need for coordination is, in the first instance, understood as a reflection of the division of labour within modern bureaucracies. Thus, coordination is the attempt to cope with the tensions between specialization, decentralization, departmentalism and hierarchy on the one hand, and the real-life interdependence of policy issues, on the other, as expressed in the above quotation from the British Performance and Innovation Unit. Careful institutional design can help to minimize the need for interinstitutional coordination, but it cannot eliminate it altogether. Accordingly, comparative public administration is interested in the principles underlying the interministerial division of labour and the internal organization of ministerial departments and other central agencies; analyzes how these affect coordination requirements; and studies administrative coordination devices, such as task-specific working groups staffed by officials or formal procedural guidelines governing the preparation and interministerial coordination of legislative initiatives within the executive.

The politics–administration distinction has its use in helping to impose some order onto the bewildering array of coordination arrangements; yet, the reality of coordination practice does not easily fit any neat categorization. Thus, the seemingly clear dividing line between political and administrative coordination is, in fact, regularly blurred and, in some countries, obliterated altogether. Not only is it often difficult to distinguish political conflicts in the executive from those generated by technical arguments; a classification of coordination devices that relies on the distinction between executive politicians and officials also quickly runs into difficulties, since, in many Western European countries, no easy line can be drawn between the two (Page and Wright 1999*a*; Bekke and van der Meer 2000). As Guy Peters (1997*a*: 239) notes, one of the key issues at stake here 'is the extent to which the two groups are conceptualized as being fundamentally different sets of actors, as opposed to a part of the same governmental elite in common service to the state'. Partly, this is about the recruitment of both groups, partly about the degree of differentiation in their functions. Thus, Germany and France are given as examples for a 'merger of the two branches of an executive elite' (*ibid.*: 236), whilst the United Kingdom (Wright 1996*a*) or Denmark (Jensen and Knudsen 1999) are often held out as examples of strict separation. Yet, whilst in the case of France, movement from the elite civil service *grands corps* into the sphere of electoral politics is, indeed, a well-recognized route to ministerial office (Wright 1974), in Germany, the typical career paths of politicians and senior officials divide very early on (Goetz 1999, 2000*b*).

If one can speak of a degree of merger in the latter case, it is not because of common recruitment or shared social characteristics, but rather because German administrative practice and law explicitly recognize that a distinction between the political and administrative dimensions of officials' work is very difficult to draw. Thus, the top two ranks in the Federal ministerial civil service hierarchy, administrative state secretaries and heads of divisions, are in law classed as political civil servants (*politische Beamte*), who, according the provisions of the Law on Political Civil Servants, may legitimately be expected to be in basic agreement with the political objectives of the government of the day and can be sent into temporary retirement by the political executive at any time. Under such conditions, it is not surprising that in a sample of Federal ministerial officials covering the top four ranks in 1987, some 86 per cent agreed with the statement that 'it is at least as important for senior civil servants to possess political skills as it is to have technical expertise' (Derlien 1994). In short, the functional division between politicians and bureaucrats is often indeterminate, in particular at the level of political civil servants, and political and administrative roles in coordination overlap (Goetz 1997).

Two major points should have emerged from this discussion of executive coordination. First, the four images of the executive identified in the previous section find their expressions in diverse coordination practices. Image I lays the stress on highly personalized networks of political coordination, as they are, for example, described by Molina (2000) for the case of EU policy coordination in Spain. Image II accords with the continued importance of both classical devices of institutionalized political coordination, and the proliferation of supplementary institutional arrangements, notably in the sphere of coalition governance. Image III is associated with personalized systems of administrative coordination, as they are, for example, provided by the integrative capacity of *grands corps* in France or the partisan ties that link senior officials in consociationalist systems such as Austria (Liegl and Müller 1999). Finally,

Image IV points to the significance of depersonalized administrative coordination mechanisms, as they are exemplified by the multitude of interministerial committees staffed by officials that typically prepare political decision taking in cabinet.

The second point to note is that personal institutional, political, and administrative coordination mechanisms do not exist in neat boxes; rather, they are complementary and interact closely. In practice, 'pure' types are rare and hybrids the norm (Wright and Hayward 2000).

Centres of Government

Centres of government (COGs) are generally understood to comprise the institutions that provide direct support and advice to the head of government and to the council of ministers. The COGs combine a range of distinct tasks, which, considered together, single them out amongst other institutions of the central executive. Thus, they typically carry out political, policy-related, and administrative functions; deal with both routine and non-routine matters; are involved, in one form or another, in all stages of the policy process, including policy initiation, formulation, decision making, implementation, monitoring, and evaluation; possess a cross-sectoral remit, which covers a broad, if not the entire, spectrum of domestic and foreign policy; have a special responsibility for ensuring policy coherence and consistency; are expected to combine reactive capacities with an ability to launch and promote new initiatives; and play a central role in 'selling' the government's achievements to the media. However, there is a good deal of cross-country variation in the relative weight accorded to these tasks and in the organizational arrangements in place to perform them. Organizing for the complexity of these responsibilities involves difficult decisions on institutional structures, procedures, and also the status of the personnel working at the COG.

Drawing on recent surveys of COGs in both Western and post-Communist Central and Eastern Europe (Goetz and Margetts 1999; Peters *et al.* 2000*a*), one may identify three distinct conceptions of the place of the COG in the executive and the political system more broadly. The first, which derives from the experience of prime ministerial systems, conceives of the COG as the vanguard of the head of government. The COG is regarded as the apex of the ministerial hierarchy, acting as a kind of superministry. Its foremost task is to secure the effective control of the head of government over the members of the council of ministers. The COG acts as the eyes, ears, and, where necessary, the iron fist of the chief executive. In so doing, it represents the chief executive's authority, and prime ministerial power provides the COG's chief resource in dealing with other parts of the executive machinery. This conception conforms to a policy process that is top-down rather than bottom-up and in which policy coherence ultimately relies on the authoritative imposition of the Prime Minister's will on reluctant ministers. The Prime Minister's Office in Spain appears to correspond quite closely to this model (Heywood and Molina 2000).

The second conception—the COG as the government's clerk—provides almost a mirror image of the vanguard model, and is informed by traditions of cabinet government, based on collegiality and collective responsibility. Here, the COG supports the government as a collegiate body and seeks to secure the smooth preparation and implementation of collective decision making by the cabinet. The COG acts on the authority of the government; but in dealing with ministries and other executive institutions, it relies not so much on hierarchy, but on two-way flows of information and communication. It must refrain from pushing a particular line, but assist in organizing a government-wide deliberation process that leads to a consensual collective decision. This view of the COG is associated with a bottom-up policy process, in which individual ministries drive policy development. Interministerial coordination is horizontal rather than vertical and based on negotiation and bargaining. Examples of countries in which the COG has traditionally tended to approximate this model include the Netherlands, in which the Prime Minister has long acted as the chief moderator of the government rather than a powerful leader (Andeweg 1997*b*) or Denmark, where the compromise nature of politics 'makes it possible for a prime minister to survive for a long period provided he quickly realizes that leadership of the government does *not* mean posing as a strong leader' (Knudsen 2000: 154; emphasis in the original).

A third conception of COGs—the executive's management core—is most explicitly linked to consensus democracies. Prime ministerial government and cabinet government may be useful concepts for understanding political decision making inside the political executive. Yet, their exclusive focus on the internal dynamics of government is in danger of ignoring the consequences that flow from the interwovenness between government, governing parties, and majority parliamentary parties. Under the conditions of party government and parliamentary government, the COG's remit cannot be limited to organizing decision making within government; rather, it needs to synchronize the work of the executive with the political forces on whose continued consensus the survival of the government depends, notably the majority governing and parliamentary parties. Executive autonomy is low, the policy process is open to non-executive actors, and interministerial, executive–party, and executive–legislative coordination are strongly interconnected. Accordingly, the COG is engaged in the management of governance networks that extend well beyond the executive. In so doing, the COG employs a varied repertoire of resources, including authority, information, and political and technical expertise. The German Chancellor's Office may serve as an illustration.

No Western European country has adopted any of the institutional models in pure form. But there appears to have been a fairly uniform trend towards the strengthening of the powers and resources of the centre over the last two decades or so. This trend cannot only be observed in countries such as the United Kingdom (for details see Lee *et al.* 1998), where traditionally powerful centres have further gained in centrality; it has also affected executives in which the COG's role tended to be closer to that of a government's clerk than to the Prime Minister's vanguard or a management core. Most observers link this development directly to what is widely regarded as the growing centralization of power within Western executives in the office and person of the head of government. Thus, it has been suggested that in Spain, for example, we have witnessed the emergence of a 'quasi-presidential' executive, in which 'the prime minister is constitutionally empowered to monopolize the most important decisions of national policy' (Heywood and Molina 2000). Similarly, it has frequently been proposed that the UK's political system is becoming increasingly presidentialized. But even where constitutional provisions, tradition, and political conditions have been less favourable to a concentration of executive power, signs of prime ministerialization appear unmistakable. For example, the progressive concentration of executive power in the German chancellorship that could be observed during the 1990s under Chancellor Helmut Kohl (Clemens and Paterson 1998) does not appear to have been reversed under Chancellor Schröder (Korte 2000). If anything, the latter's domination over his cabinet, including members of the smaller coalition partner, is more resolute. It may also be interesting to note that in those Central and Eastern European executives where clear indications of advancing institutionalization can be found, this development is closely associated with prime ministerialization and an effective COG. Hungary, under the leadership of Prime Minister Viktor Orbán serves as a case in point (Goetz and Wollmann 2001).

If one seeks to arrive at generalizations about developmental trends in terms of the two-dimensional space of executive studies introduced earlier, at least two points deserve underscoring. First, it appears justified to speak about a growing personalization of power in European executives, which is one of the reasons why academic analysts have become increasingly interested in the study of 'leadership'. But it is clear that such personal leadership can only be exercised with appropriate institutional backup; hence the attention to the quality of resources available to COGs. Institutional support does not, however, equal a high degree of formalization— perhaps more than anywhere else in the executive, official organizational charts are unreliable guides to the operation of COGs. Knudsen's (2000) question about the Danish COG—'how informal can you be?'—often commands a brief answer: very. Even where, as in Germany, the basic formal organization at the Chancellery has remained fairly stable over the years, chains of command and influence at the COG can vary greatly over time.

Second, at the COG, politics and administration meet directly and sometimes uncomfortably; the tension between the two can be minimized, but not altogether eradicated, and institutional arrangements designed to combine the political and administrative aspects of COG work are, accordingly, always open to challenge. For example, the French executive has long been able to draw on a rich repertoire of institutional devices to strengthen the politics–administration nexus (Wright 1974), including, as noted earlier, a high degree of integration between political and administrative elites, and *cabinets ministériels*, which are made up of 'a small (and sometimes not very small) group of close, politically sensitive and policy-oriented advisers which are recruited by the Minister and which expires on his or her departure'; their role is 'to act as the eyes and ears of the Minister, to define and push through his programme, and to look after his parliamentary and constituency work' (Wright 1996a: 306). Yet, despite such institutional support, the integration of politics and administration can prove very difficult, as Menon's (2000) study of the Secretariat General of the French Interministerial Committee for EU Matters demonstrates. Although the

Secretariat is part of the Prime Minister's Office, Menon has found clear evidence of '*décalage* between the organs of technical coordination and political initiatives' (*ibid.*: 95), with the result that 'political initiatives can on occasion be nonsensical' (*ibid.*). Tensions between the Prime Minister and the President and their respective offices reinforce this dynamic (Wright 1993).

EVALUATING EXECUTIVES

The preceding discussion should have given some indication of the complexity and variation in the institutionalization of European executives. The revival of institutionalist approaches in comparative political science (Peters 1999), combined with the major comparative research efforts of the last decade, has meant that we do, by now, know a great deal about cross-country commonalities and differences in the internal life of executives (even though the established democracies of Western Europe are much better covered than the post-Communist states of Central and Eastern Europe). Much can also be learned from single-country studies, especially if the questions are framed with comparative concerns in mind. It may, of course, be argued that, for all the effort to gather information on executive practices across countries, *systematic* comparisons—as opposed to illustrations of commonalities and differences—are rare; usually cover only a small number of cases (and thus run into the well known 'small *n*' problem); and, if they attempt any quantification at all, rarely go beyond fairly crude measures, such as numbers of ministers or rates of ministerial turnover. One can, therefore, have some sympathy with Weller and Bakvis's (1997: 9) *cri de coeur*: 'when (are) comparative volumes on executives (...) going to contain some genuinely comparative conclusions, rather than setting out yet again a future research agenda'?

Certainly, scholars of the executive have tended to be reticent about the effects of variations in executive arrangements. Thus, Wright and Hayward's (2000) summary of the key findings of their comparative study of executive coordination provides many insights into types and styles of coordination, but offers little in the way of concrete guidance for 'institutional engineering', since ' "optimal" coordination will depend on a host of variables', such as the nature of coordination ambitions and constitutional, institutional, political and administrative opportunity structures' (*ibid.*: 45). Similarly, Wright's comparative analysis of the national coordination of EU policy making (Wright 1996*b*: 165; quoted in Kassim 2000*a*) is extremely cautious about linking institutions and effects, noting that 'the effectiveness of a country's domestic EU coordination capacity must be judged according to the issue, the policy types, the policy requirements, and the policy objectives. Merely to examine the machinery of coordination is to confuse the means and the outcomes'. The conclusions of a more recent comparative effort on the same subject, in which Wright participated, are equally modest as regards the effectiveness of different national coordination systems: 'The question of effectiveness—what it means in a EU context and whether there is a recipe for success in the form of a particular national strategy—though undoubtedly an important concern, is extremely problematic' (Kassim 2000*a*: 254).

These examples underscore the conclusions of Egeberg's (1999) critical assessment of the state of research on central government bureaucracies, namely that too little is known about the policy effects of differing executive structures and procedures (Andeweg this volume). It is not surprising to find, therefore, that contemporary policy oriented work in comparative political economy, which seeks to establish systematic links between cross-national variations in political institutions and policy outputs, treats the executive largely as a 'black box'. Put differently, variations in the internal organization of executives are rarely employed to explain variations in policy outcomes (see, e.g. Beck *et al.* 2000). It is worth noting that the World Bank has recently become increasingly interested in developing 'diagnostic sets' and 'toolkits' that would allow its own staff and the national governments with whom they work to assess executive capacity on the basis of criteria that are open to some form of qualification and quantification (Manning *et al.* 1999; Evans and Manning 2001). But the contributions of comparative government and comparative public administration to such an enterprise must remain strictly limited, as long as the institutionalist agenda of executive studies is principally concerned with capturing different executive configurations rather than their effects.

THE QUEST FOR EXECUTIVE REFORM

The lack of comparative evidence-based studies of the linkage between executive configurations and the quality of government or policy (however defined) might be regarded as a rather academic problem. It has not stopped governments from reforming and reshaping the executive machinery; indeed, executive reform seems a perennial and ubiquitous obsession (Wright 1994*b*; Heywood and Wright 1997).

How could one characterize the consequences of these reforms with reference to our two-dimensional executive space? Developments in Western Europe, on the one hand, and Central and Eastern Europe, on the other, appear to follow opposite directions. In Western Europe, the overall trend is clear: it points towards both growing individualization and growing politicization. Increasing individualization is most apparent at the level of the senior civil service, affecting both conditions of employment and conceptions of accountability. Thus, in many European countries, there has been a move away from uniform regulations covering terms and conditions to individual—often fixed-term, though renewable—contracts that may also specify specific performance targets. Moreover, elements of performance-related pay have been introduced in many countries (see Bekke and van der Meer 2000). This individualization and contractualization of the relationship between senior officials and the state has been inspired by the idea that classical bureaucrats need to be turned into public managers, who ought to be individually held accountable—and that means both rewarded and, if things go wrong, penalized—for the performance of the organizations they manage (rather than administer).

Such a shift towards individualized forms of accountability not only affects the relations between ministers and officials, but also leads to a redefinition of accountability relationships in the political system more broadly. This is perhaps most evident in the case of the United Kingdom. Whereas the traditional British constitutional doctrine of ministerial accountability assumed that only ministers (not their civil servants) were accountable to Parliament for the actions of their departments, the creation of a range of executive agencies by successive British governments has to some extent undermined this convention. Heads of executive agencies have increasingly been held directly accountable before parliamentary committees, although there is a degree of ambiguity surrounding the nature of this novel type of accountability relationship (Giddings 1995; Polidano 1999).

There is a further aspect to individualization, beyond employment conditions and formal accountability relationships, and this refers to what Page and Wright (1999*b*: 277) have termed 'a *deinstitutionalization or personalization of political trust*' (emphasis in the original). The relationship between senior officials and executive politicians is, they argue, subtly changing as trust in the institution of the civil service is progressively replaced in many countries by an emphasis on personal trust. The latter 'does not have to be defined strictly in party-political terms (...) The central point is that increasing political influence in senior appointments suggests the possibility that membership of a 'neutral' civil service is decreasing as a guide to trust among political elites' (*ibid.*: 278).

The case for growing individualization and personalization should not be overstated. It does not hold everywhere and, like every trend, is capable of being reversed. In the Netherlands, for example, the creation of a unified Senior Public Service (ABD) in 1995 would appear to point to further institutionalization rather than individualization of the administrative part of the executive and, as van der Meer and Raadschelders (1999: 227) suggest, 'it may well limit politicization of top appointments'. Moreover, as Richards (2000) points out in respect of top civil service appointments in the United Kingdom, the strong involvement of Prime Minister Thatcher in the appointment of top officials and her insistence on the kind of personal-political trust mentioned by Page and Wright was much less in evidence under her successor, John Major. But while these examples caution against overstretching the individualization thesis, they do not invalidate it.

Individualization in the administrative sphere and the relationships of politicians and officials is an important contributor to the second trend noted above, that is, politicization. In the present context, this refers to the successful quest by executive politicians for reasserting political authority over ministerial administrations. From the 1960s to the 1980s, arguments about the rise of technocratic–bureaucratic rule were much *en vogue* amongst Western European political scientists; by contrast, the last decade or so has witnessed determined efforts on the part of executive politicians to strengthen their hold over the ministerial administration. The driving forces behind this trend are complex and not easy to disentangle, but they fall broadly into the same categories as those that have led to a renewed emphasis on the need for executive coordination. As parliaments and governing parties in many Western European countries have sought to strengthen their proactive role in public policy making (Norton 1998; Blondel and Nousiainen 2000), the scope for unilateral executive action—that is, executive autonomy—has tended to decline and the need for executive–legislative coordination and cooperation grown. Pressures on heads of government and ministers to act as policy mediators rather than decision makers have mounted and they have responded to this development by seeking to reinforce mechanisms for political steering in the executive. Such efforts have varied in form. They have included both organizational changes aimed at strengthening political direction (e.g. through the upgrading of COGs and, at the level of individual ministries, the creation or reinforcement of political support offices resembling *cabinets ministériels*); and personnel policy measures of the type noted earlier that have endeavoured to increase the responsiveness and accountability of individual civil servants to the holders of elected offices.

If we turn to post-Communist Central and Eastern Europe, the gist of official reform initiatives appears to point in the opposite direction of the Western European agenda, at least in those countries that belong to the first wave of EU Eastern enlargement. If, in the West, we find personalization and politicization, then the Eastern programmes centre on fortifying the institutional foundations of the executive and on its depoliticization. Spurred in part by external pressures—notably the EU's accession criteria and the World Bank's 'good governance' agenda—the creation of non-partisan career civil services has been the core plank of public sector reform in much of Central and Eastern Europe and relevant legislation has been introduced in most of the region (Nunberg 1999; Verheijen 1999). The institution of a civil service did not exist under Communism and its creation has been regarded as a key prerequisite for the strengthening of executive capacity. Institutionalization of the ministerial civil service is closely tied to a depoliticization agenda. State administration under Communism was subordinated to the will of the Communist party; partisan loyalty and reliability were expected both of individual administrators and the state administration as a whole. Given this inheritance of partisan state administration, official reform documents have focused on the need to 'push politics out' of administration and to establish clear boundaries between the political and administrative components of the executive.

Despite early political backing for the institutionalization of ministerial career civil services, more than ten years after the first freely elected post-Communist governments came to power, very little real progress appears to have been made. A recent comparative survey on the development of post-Communist administrative capacity concluded: 'Civil service laws have seldom been the expected catalysts for the stabilization, de-politicization and professionalization of the central administration. Rather than being a starting point for the development of civil service policies, the adoption of laws has become an objective in itself. Apart from Hungary, none of the candidate countries has come close to the development of a civil service policy, in addition to the necessary legal framework' (Verheijen 2000: 29).

The failure to implement legislation designed to establish a non-partisan professional civil service is generally put down to a lack of political resolve. After all, tightening the criteria for recruitment, promotions, and dismissals, amongst other things, restricts politicians' ability to shape their offices and to reward party-political and personal loyalty. However, bearing in mind the trend towards individualization in the ministerial personnel systems in Western Europe, an alternative explanation suggests itself. Briefly, attempts to 'push politics out' by defining clear boundaries between politics and administration are inspired by a mistaken reading of both the past and the problems of the present. Under Communism, partisanship in the government bureaucracy was indeed enforced (though to varying degrees in different countries and policy sectors); but the ministerial bureaucracy was also non-political, in that it was not geared towards the preparation and assessment of policy alternatives. To the extent that the latter were discussed, it was the party bureaucracy rather than the state bureaucracy that fulfilled this task. In other words, government was an executive in the literal sense.

This legacy persists. In particular, officials used to work in an environment in which political direction was imposed from outside find it difficult to make an active contribution to preparing political decisions and to the management of conflict resolution inside the government and between the government and other political actors, notably parliament, political parties, and civil society. Executive politicians are, therefore, often tempted to seek policy advice and management skills from outside the executive bureaucracy and to bypass the latter in favour of more informal networks or small entourages placed outside the line administration. Civil service development strategies that are principally geared towards strengthening the boundaries between politics and administration are likely to exacerbate this problem, for they raise the danger that executive politicians see the civil service as an obstacle, rather than a resource, to effective governmental decision making. This is particularly the case where executive politicians operate under conditions of coalition government and fragile parliamentary and societal support. Under such circumstances, professionalization of the civil service must also imply to 'bring politics back in', in the sense of paying sustained attention to the need for fostering 'political craft' amongst senior officials (Goetz 1997).

THE STUDY OF EXECUTIVES: A MATTER OF DEGREES?

The above analysis of the state of, and trends in, executive development suggests that the institutional foundations and fortifications of the executive may be less solid than is generally assumed. For Western Europe, it has been argued that core executives increasingly resemble 'hollow crowns' (Rhodes 1997*b*; Saward 1997), as political power is dispersed in complex governance networks. In the East, executive capacity is thought to be low, and there is talk about institutional shells and façades; parallel governance structures that undermine official executive arrangements; endemic corruption; and low public trust in both politicians and officials (for a review see Goetz and Wollmann 2001).

Neither the stability nor the effectiveness of executive arrangements can, therefore, be taken for granted. This may be an obvious point to make, but it has far-reaching implications for comparative executive studies. While comparing differing institutional configurations is part of the staple diet of executive research, institutionalist approaches do not usually pay systematic attention to differing degrees of institutionalization. Thus, students of the executive are principally interested in variations in institutional design. As was noted above, there is also some concern with the effects of these institutional variables on political and policy outcomes; but we know very little about how strongly institutionalized these variables themselves are.

To gain a better understanding of the interaction between institutional configurations and degrees of institutionalization and of their combined effect on outcomes, the conceptualization of degrees of institutionalization and, in particular, their operationalization need to move centre stage in executive research (Peters and Goetz 1999). The two-dimensional space introduced at the outset can provide some modest guidance for such an endeavour. Turning first to the tension between office and office holder, sociologically inspired institutional theory, with its emphasis on enactment, internalization, and habitualization of institutional norms and values, directs attention to the potential incongruence between formal institutions and the people who bring them alive. Claus Offe, for example, has stressed this aspect in his account of institutional design in post-Communist transitions. Where institutional norms, embedded in specific organizational arrangements, deviate permanently and substantially from those held by the people acting within an institution, institutionalization is precarious. Such dissonance appears particularly likely in the case of 'consequentialist' institution-building that follows a logic of 'imitating, importing, and transplanting': 'As a result, the new institutions are in place, but they fail to perform in anticipated ways, and thus become subject to ever more hectic cycles of renewed institutional engineering and concomitant efforts to "reeducate" people so as to make them fit for their roles in the new institutions' (Offe 1996: 212).

One attempt to capture this possible conflict between formal institutions and individuals, and, thus, degrees of institutionalization, has been elaborated by Nedelmann (1995) who sets out a continuum of high and low institutionalization along five dimensions. In her scheme, high institutionalization is associated with the habitualized reproduction of institutional norms (enacting); internalization of norms and values; a stress on the intrinsic value of institutions; the facilitation of choice as institutions 'relieve' individuals from the burden of choice; and depersonalization. By contrast, low institutionalization is found where strategic action predominates; norms and values must be justified and defended; the institution is justified on the basis of instrumental utility; actors face the full burden of choice; and the reproduction of institutional patterns depends on specific individuals.

This understanding of institutionalization is attractive, since it allows the analysis to go beyond the mere existence of formal institutions. However, whilst of considerable heuristic value, such an approach can only provide part of the answer. It needs to be integrated into a broader framework that pays equal attention to the 'hardware' that constitutes an important part of executive capacity, notably legal, financial, organizational, and personnel resources. In so doing, it is worth keeping in mind the second tension highlighted above, that is, between politics and administration. With reference to classical sociological modernization theory, Lepsius, for example, has argued that 'If under typical circumstances one finds a "syncretism" of guiding ideas, then one cannot assume that behaviour will become regular, predictable and typical. The degree of institutionalization will then be low' (Lepsius 1997: 59; my translation, KHG). Viewed from such a perspective, the only way of creating a highly institutionalized executive would either be comprehensive politicization or comprehensive bureaucratization in the form of a ruling mandarinate. Neither option is attractive or likely in a liberal democracy. Consequently, the institutionalization of executives is necessarily precarious and a measure of instability inbuilt—good news for students of the executive, whose subject is unlikely to go stale.

6

The Political System of the European Union

NEILL NUGENT AND WILLIAM PATERSON

INTRODUCTION

The single most striking feature of government and politics in Western Europe in the modern era has been the creation of a European-level political system. Embodied in what was formerly known as the European Communities (EC) and which since the entry into force of the Maastricht Treaty in 1993 has been known as the European Union (EU), this political system has been forged through two parallel and mutually reinforcing processes. First, there has been an extensive transfer of policy powers and responsibilities from national political systems to the European level, with virtually all spheres of public policy now on the EU agenda to at least some degree. Second, there has been the development of European-level institutions and decision-making processes.

This chapter examines the EU's political system. In so doing it does not attempt to provide a comprehensive or detailed guide to all aspects of the nature of the system. Rather it seeks to highlight its key features. One of these features underpins much of the explanation and analysis of the chapter: the European Union is at the centre of what is becoming a European system of governance, in which different levels of government are increasingly interpenetrated and in which boundaries between the European Union and its member states are becoming eroded.

We begin with an analysis of the nature of EU policy activity. This is followed by an examination of EU decision making, focused particularly around the question of who governs. Next, there is an analysis of the nature of the European Union as a political system, with particular consideration given to the extent to which it displays the characteristics of a state on the one hand and features of new governance on the other. There is then an examination of an issue that concerns all political systems and which has become increasingly debated in EU circles—the nature of the EU's legitimacy. The chapter ends with some concluding remarks.

THE NATURE OF EU POLICY ACTIVITY

Incremental Growth

Since the EC was established in the 1950s there has been an enormous increase in the range and depth of European-level policy responsibilities. This growth has not occurred at a steady rate—there having been rapid and slow periods of policy expansion—but it has been constantly ongoing. It has been so for three, in practice inter-related and overlapping, main reasons.

First, an increasingly expansive view has been taken of what needs to be done if the Single European Market (SEM) (initially known as the Common Market)—which may be thought of as being at the heart of 'the European project'—is to be fully established and operating with maximum efficiency. Early hopes that the creation of a customs union (which was established in 1968 with the removal of internal tariffs and quotas and the creation of a Common External Tariff (CET) and Common Commercial Policy (CCP)) would lead to an open, competitive, and efficient market were not realized. That this was so was recognized with the 'relaunch' of the Community in the mid-1980s, which was largely focused on integrating the still fractured national markets into a European market that could compete globally. As part of this integrating of fractured national markets, an enormous volume of rules and regulations have been put in place (some of them through EU legislation, many of them through European standards agencies), to force, to underpin, and to facilitate free and fair competition within the EU market place. The rules and regulations are concerned both with direct market issues, such as product specifications and company mergers, and also with less direct issues such as social welfare provisions and environmental standards (both of which have important implications for business overheads). In recent years the policy area that has received the greatest attention in terms of the claimed benefits it can have in helping to promote a fully and properly integrated internal market is Economic and Monetary Union (EMU).

Second, some policies have been developed because the EU's decision makers are, for the most part, drawn from the centre of the political spectrum and subscribe to a political philosophy in which decent public standards and reasonable levels of public protection for citizens are supported. Insofar as it is necessary or desirable for such policies to be pursued at the EU level—and one reason it is so is that without EU protection market forces may result in a lowering of standards and provisions—then so have policies tended to be developed. Examples of policy areas where development has been at least partly driven by a desire to directly assist and protect standards and citizen welfare are regional policy, social policy, environmental policy, equal opportunities policy, and consumer protection policy.

Third, just as an increasingly expansive view has been taken of what is required to complete the internal market, so a broader view has come to be taken over the years of what other policies ought to be dealt with at EU level in the interests of effectiveness and efficiency. Foreign policy has been a beneficiary of such thinking, with the EU's interests in this area gradually expanding from very hesitant and cautious beginnings in the early 1970s to the situation today wherein, though there is still very far from being a comprehensive or integrated European foreign policy, there are few major foreign policy issues on which the European Union does not at least pronounce within its Common Foreign and Security Policy (CFSP) framework. Moreover, foreign policy has come to be joined on the EU agenda by the related, but even more sensitive, policy area of defence, with the 1997 Amsterdam Treaty identifying 'soft' defence policy goals, with the creation of a 60,000 rapid reaction force being agreed at the December 1999 Helsinki summit, and with the building of a broader European strategic defence identity and capability very much on the EU policy agenda. Another 'non-market' policy area that has developed as a result of expansive thinking about what the European Union should and could be doing is justice and home affairs (JHA) policy, which has seen, since the mid-1980s, the development of a raft of policies and initiatives to tackle such transnational policy problems as drug trafficking, money laundering, and illegal movement of persons.

Key Features

The factors that have made for policy expansion have combined to create an EU policy portfolio characterized by the following key features:

There is some involvement in all areas of public policy. There is no major area of public policy that does not feature to at least some extent on the EU's agenda. In the early years of the EC the focus was primarily on market-related policies, but over the years there has been a progressive embracing of both broader economic policies and of policies—such as in the CFSP and JHA spheres—that have no direct economic content at all.

The extent of EU policy involvement varies considerably. Although the European Union has some involvement in all spheres of public policy, the extent of that involvement varies between policy areas. A spectrum may be envisaged, at one end of which the European Union is the main policy maker, at the other end of which member states are so, and in between which policy-making powers are shared between the European Union and the member states. External trade, agriculture, and competition are examples of policy areas at the EU end of the spectrum; education, health, and law and order are examples at the member state end; and regional policy, environment policy, and research policy are examples of policy areas stretched between the two ends.

EU-level policy involvement varies not only in terms of policy making but also policy implementation. There are some EU policies, most particularly in the competition sphere, where the European Union—mainly through the Commission—implements itself directly. So, for example, the Commission decides on the permissibility of certain types of mergers between companies and on the legality of state aid, of restrictive practices, and of abuse of dominant trading positions. More generally, however, the EU's implementation role takes the form of monitoring and overseeing frontline policy implementation that is undertaken on its behalf by national agencies.

These agencies include customs and excise authorities (which, amongst other duties, collect EU tariffs and levies and apply EU laws on indirect taxation), ministries of agriculture and agricultural intervention agencies (which deal directly with farmers and agricultural traders in the context of the Common Agricultural Policy (CAP)), and health and safety agencies (which apply EU environmental, consumer protection, and working conditions legislation). In just what form and with what intensity the monitoring and the overseeing actually occurs varies widely, with the Commission doing little more than receiving periodic reports from national agencies in spheres such as consumer protection, but engaging in constant two-way communications and sitting on committees with national and subnational officials where decentralized funding programmes are involved.

There are variations in the extent to which policies have a supranational or an intergovernmental base. EU policies are often thought of as being *either* supranational *or* intergovernmental in character, but this is not the case.

The more policies display the following characteristics the more they are supranational in character:

(1) the Commission, the European Court of Justice (ECJ), and the European Parliament (EP)—all of which are independent from national governments—exercise significant powers;
(2) decisions can be taken in the Council of Ministers by qualified majority vote (QMV);
(3) they are located in pillar one—the EC pillar—of the Treaty on European Union (TEU) which, amongst other things, means that EU laws can be made.

By contrast, the more policies display the following characteristics the more they are intergovernmental in character:

(1) decision-making powers are located in the two institutions which bring together the representatives of the national governments, the European Council, and the Council of Ministers;
(2) the Council of Ministers must take decisions by unanimity (by tradition, the European Council almost invariably proceeds in this way);
(3) they are located either in the second pillar (CFSP) or third pillar (Provisions on Police and Judicial Cooperation in Criminal Matters) of the TEU, or are not located in any pillar at all.

A policy area such as external trade may be thought of as being supranational in that all three of the supranational 'qualifying criteria' apply to it, just as defence may similarly be thought of as being intergovernmental. However, there are many policy areas, such as aspects of JHA, which meet the first and third of 'the supranational criteria', but where QMV is not always available in the Council. Similarly, there are policy areas, such as CFSP, which meet the first and third of 'the intergovernmental criteria', but where QMV is possible for certain types of decisions.

Since the mid-1980s supranationalism has made major advances. It has done so most notably through treaty reforms that have provided greater powers for the EP, more use of QMV in the Council, and extensions to the explicit policy remit of the first pillar. However, even after the treaty reform agreed at the December 2000 Nice summit, intergovernmentalism is still a very important feature of the EU's policy base with, for instance, the non-governmental institutions being at best mere supportive participants in some areas of policy activity and with unanimity in the Council still applying to almost fifty treaty articles. Amongst the policy spheres that remain primarily intergovernmental in character—and where therefore, national sovereignty may be said to still exist—are the traditionally sensitive areas of foreign policy, defence policy, law and order policy, and taxation policy.

Policies are primarily regulatory in character. At first sight, a rather odd feature of the European Union is that although it has a very wide ranging policy portfolio, EU spending is very small in relation to national spending: amounting to only around three per cent of total public expenditure in the European Union and just over one per cent of total EU Gross Domestic Product. The explanation for this seeming imbalance between the importance of EU policies and EU expenditure is that the policy areas which have heavy expenditure implications—such as health, education, social welfare, and defence—remain largely in national hands. The European Union does have some responsibilities for policy areas with significant expenditure implications—most notably the CAP (which accounts for almost half of EU expenditure) and parts of regional, social, research, and overseas aid policies—but always on a shared, and most commonly on a junior partner, basis.

EU policies are not, therefore, generally of a redistributive character. That is to say they do not involve directly moving significant resources from one geographical area to another or from one part of the population to the other. Rather, most EU policies are primarily of a regulatory character (Majone 1996). This means that they lay down a regulatory framework for public activity—be it concerned with the operation of the market, the protection of the environment, or the rights of EU citizens to work and live in member states other than their own. In so doing they involve the European Union, as Hix (1998: 42) has put it, 'in the allocation of social and political values throughout Europe'. Some EU regulatory policies and measures do, of course, have very significant distributive and expenditure implications. EU laws on, for example, air and water quality, can require considerable investment to meet specified standards. But in such cases the investment does not have to be made by the European Union itself but rather by public and private sector companies and agencies in the member states.

An important reason why EU regulatory policies have so increased in scope in recent years is that they are necessary for the successful operation of the SEM: without a level regulatory playing field—on the likes of product contents, competition rules, and workers' entitlements and protection—there cannot be fair and open competition. A second reason is that with member states being unwilling to countenance significant increases in the size of the EU budget, the expansion of regulatory policies has been the most obvious way forward for those who wish to see a broadening in scope of the EU policy agenda. And a third reason is that the implications of regulatory policies are not so easy to calculate as the consequences of redistributive policies and, consequently, are not so politically charged.

DECISION MAKING IN THE EUROPEAN UNION

A Multi-Actor, Multi-Process System

EU decision making involves a multitiplicity of actors and processes. There are three main types of actor. First there are the five main EU institutions: the European Council, which consists of the fifteen Heads of Government or State of the member states, the fifteen Foreign Ministers, and the President and one other member of the Commission; the Council of Ministers, which at its most senior level brings together ministers of the member states in different policy formations; the Commission, which is headed by a twenty member College of Commissioners; the EP, which is made up of 630 directly elected Members of the European Parliament (MEPs); and the ECJ, which comprises one judge per member state. Second, there are the governments of the member states, each with their own interests and preferences, each with their own organizational arrangements for dealing with EU business, and each usually harbouring internal differences between parts of the governmental machinery over aspects of the European Union, and would-be EU, policy. Third, there are a host of other actors who also actively participate in EU policy processes. This third category of actors, which can be sub-categorized in many different ways, includes non-member state governments, subnational levels of government, business corporations, national interest groups, and Eurogroups—that is, interest groups that seek to organize and represent interests at the European level.

As for EU decision-making processes, the number that can be said to exist depends on the degree of precision that is used in making distinctions between them. If attention is focused just on legislative processes, there are four main procedures—consultation, cooperation, co-decision (the most used procedure since the Amsterdam Treaty entered into force in May 1998), and assent—with differences within them (mainly concerning the powers of the EP and whether QMV is available) that results in a total of almost thirty detectably different procedures. Beyond legislative procedures, there are many additional procedures, which again are themselves subject to many variations. These include procedures used by the European Council for conducting its business, by the Council of Ministers in the framework of the second and third pillars, and by the Commission when it issues administrative rules and regulations.

It is not possible here to examine in detail the nature of the EU's many actors and processes. Amongst the sources available for readers who wish for such examinations are Dinan (1999), McCormick (1999), Nugent (2003), Peterson and Bomberg (1999), and Wallace and Wallace (2000). Attention below will be focused rather on identifying some of the most important overall features of EU decision making.

The Institutional Balance

The balance of decision-making power between the EU's institutions has become increasingly complex over the years. In the early days of the EC most decision making pivoted on a Commission–Council axis with, in broad terms, the former making policy and legislative proposals and the latter making decisions on the basis of the proposals. However, not only have the relations between these two institutions gradually become more entangled, but they have also been joined by the European Council and the EP as key decision-making institutions. This may be briefly illustrated by outlining institutional roles in three different decision-making contexts.

What may be thought of as *strategic directional decisions*—on such issues as treaty reform, enlargement, and major economic initiatives—are taken by the European Council. Since, however, the European Council only meets twice a year for 'normal' sessions and rarely more than twice a year for special sessions, and since too it does not have its own administrative machinery, it is unavoidably heavily dependent on preparatory work being undertaken on its behalf by other institutions. In particular, it is much reliant on the Commission to undertake studies for it and to present policy papers to it, and it is reliant on the Council of Ministers—especially the Foreign Ministers in the General Affairs Council and the Economic and Finance Ministers in the Ecofin Council—to clear as much negotiating ground as possible in pre-summit meetings. The June 2000 Feira European Council meeting illustrated this process, with many negotiations focused around papers submitted by the Commission—on such topics as the internal market and 'e-Europe'—and with many of the summit's decisions—including those on permitting Greece to join the single currency in January 2000 and the creation of a European research area—being little more than ratifications of agreements already reached in the Council of Ministers (European Council, 2000).

The ECJ has no jurisdiction over European Council pronouncements or decisions.

Legislative decisions, all of which are made under the first—EC—pillar of the TEU, are taken by the Council or by the EP and the Council on the basis of proposals submitted by the Commission. The EP's role used to be restricted to consultation, but treaty reforms since the mid-1980s have so extended its legislative powers that it is now, under the co-decision procedure, a co-legislator with the Council in respect of most EU legislation. The European Union may thus be said to have a bi-cameral legislature. Like all such legislative systems, but even more so given the Commission's initiating powers, EU decision-making processes are heavily dependent on inter-institutional negotiations and cooperation. Informal processes within an inter-institutional triangle, in which much business is conducted away from set-piece occasions such as ministerial meetings and EP plenary sessions, is thus a central feature of EU legislative decision making.

All legislative decisions are subject to the jurisdiction of the ECJ. It is a jurisdiction that has often been used in a way that has had the effect of shaping, usually in an expansive manner, the nature of EU law.

Decisions taken under the second and third pillars of the European Union are primarily a matter for the Council of Ministers. The Commission is 'associated' with these pillars but does not have the exclusive right of proposal that it has under the first pillar, whilst the EP has certain consultation rights but not the power of veto that it has over much proposed legislation.

Although the powers of the Commission and the EP are not as great under the second and third pillars as they are in respect of legislation under the first pillar, the two institutions are, in practice, nonetheless often able to 'punch above their [treaty power] weight' under these pillars. So, to take the second pillar, one way in which the Commission is able to exercise influence is via the linkages which exist, or which it is able to make, between the CFSP on the one hand and trade and aid (where its treaty powers are much greater) on the other. The EP is able to exercise influence under the second pillar via debates and exchanges with the Council in plenary and committee sessions and also via its position as co-authority with the Council for the EU budget—which, since the Amsterdam Treaty, has been the source from which most EU foreign policy actions are financed.

The Court has no jurisdiction under the CFSP pillar but does have some limited competence under the Police and Judicial Cooperation pillar.

The European Union–Member State Balance

Since the early days of the EC, scholars have debated where power lies between the European level and the member states level. There have been, in broad terms, two main schools of thought.

On the one hand, those subscribing to an intergovernmental view—of whom Andrew Moravcsik (1993, 1998) has been the most forceful proponent in recent years—have argued that decision-making power on major issues rests with the governments of the member states. The states may have ceded some policy implementation powers to European-level bodies and may sometimes be guided on particular policy matters by such bodies, but the national governments are the decision makers on issues that are of particular importance to them and retain their sovereignty in these issue areas. This is so by virtue of a mixture of: (a) many important policy areas—including defence, taxation, and law and order—still essentially being national-level policies; (b) many important policy areas that are very much on the EU agenda—including CFSP, JHA, indirect taxation, treaty reform, and enlargement—being subject to a unanimity requirement for decisions to be taken in the European Council and/or the Council of Ministers; (c) the existence of a series of controls exercised by the national governments over the supposedly supranational institutions, especially the Commission.

On the other hand, those subscribing to a supranational view—such as Sandholtz and Stone Sweet (1998)—have emphasized how the increased use of QMV has made it increasingly difficult for individual governments to control events in the Council of Ministers, and also how non-governmental actors exercise extremely important decision-making roles. On this latter point, much of the thrust of the supranationalist approach is to emphasize how intergovernmentalism takes too restrictive a view of how decisions are made. The European Council and the Council of Ministers are, it is readily acknowledged by supranationalists, key actors in the later stages of decision making, but in the earlier stages—when agendas are set and framed—other actors, especially the Commission, are seen as often exercising an influential role. An important way in which the Commission's agenda-setting role is seen as being exercised is via its ability frequently to set the parameters of policy debate through the issuing of papers/recommendations/communications/proposals that indicate not only what may be desirable but also what may and may not be—politically and technically—possible. Beyond agenda-setting, some commentators—such as Schmidt (1997, 2000)—have suggested that the Commission's influence on decision making is also important at the decision-making stage, with it being able to take advantage of informational and political resources at its disposal not only to help mediate decisions within and between other institutions but to be able to insert its own policy preferences into final decisions.

A useful tool in evaluating the merits of intergovernmental and supranational interpretations of EU decision making is principal-agent analysis (see Pollack 1997*a*, *b*). An intergovernmental interpretation is given credence insofar as the national governments, operating primarily through the European Council and the Council of Ministers, can be shown to be the principal EU decision makers and other institutions can be shown to be of limited importance and/or to be but agents of the national governments. By contrast, a supranational interpretation has force insofar as non-governmental actors can be shown to be principals, or if they are acknowledged as agents but can be shown to be not overly confined by restrictions that principals seek to place on them.

As the above outline of the intergovernmental and supranational positions implies, there is some force in both interpretations. Which one is closest to capturing 'the true nature' of EU decision making depends very much on the decision-making context. Clearly on a few major decisions, such as treaty reform, the governments are very much the principal and other policy actors exercise at best a subsidiary role. On other major decisions, however—such as the size of the EU budget and the enlargement process—guidance provided by the Commission is crucial in influencing, if not determining, the final decisions of governments. And as for decisions that are not major decisions—meso and even more so micro decisions—it is clear that non-governmental actors can be very influential, especially in respect of decisions falling within the EC pillar. For example, the Commission takes many important decisions—covering such matters as company mergers, state aid, abuse of dominant trading positions—in the sphere of competition policy; the EP occasionally vetoes Council-approved legislative proposals, and enjoys considerable success in amending proposals; and ECJ rulings have obliged the national governments to do many things they would not otherwise have done—such as be more progressive in respect of equal opportunities.

Who Decides?

It is clear from what has been said so far in the chapter that decision-making power in the European Union is dispersed and fragmented. It has been shown to be so both as regards the balance of power between EU institutions and between the European Union and the member states. A fuller and more detailed analysis of EU decision making would reveal even further dispersal and fragmentation, with the main policy actors being shown often to be far from monolithic and cohesive entities, and with a host of other, subsidiary but not unimportant, actors—including interests and interest groups—being shown to be significant in some contexts.

An indication of the extent of the dispersal and fragmentation of power in the European Union is seen in the varying positions of policy actors according to the type of decision being taken, the policy area concerned, and the decision-making procedure applying. (These three dimensions of variation are, of course, in practice closely related). As regards the type of decision being taken, variations are seen, for example, in the way in which the European Council is a central actor when major directional decisions are being made but is not much involved in middle range or micro-decisions, and in the way in which the EP has a key role in legislative decision making but only a consultative role in most other types of decision making. As regards the policy area concerned, illustrations of variation include the much stronger position of the Commission under the first pillar than under the second and third pillars, and the correspondingly stronger positions of national governments—on an individual as well as a collective basis—under the second and third pillars. And as regards the decision-making procedure applying, amongst examples of variation are the greater powers of national governments on an individual basis when unanimity rather than majority voting applies in the Council of Ministers, and the greater strength of the EP when the co-decision procedure applies in respect of legislative decision making.

Dispersal and fragmentation of power is also occasioned by the importance of coalition politics in the European Union. All of the four main decision-making institutions—the European Council, the Council of Ministers, the Commission, and the EP—contain a wide range of opinion amongst their ranks. This means that it is usually necessary to accommodate a broad range of views before individual institutions can take decisions, especially when decision-making rules are tight (as when unanimity applies in the Council and when the support of an absolute majority of all members is required in the EP) or when the operating practice is to seek consensus if possible (as it almost invariably is in the European Council and usually is in the Commission and in the Council of Ministers even when QMV can be used). When institutions have established a position, it is then often necessary for them to reach accommodations with the—usually different—positions of other institutions to enable a final decision to be taken.

The importance of coalition building results in informal politics being a striking feature of EU decision making. Much is decided, or at least many decisions are in effect prepared, away from formal decision-making settings in less structured and more relaxed settings. Examples of these settings are bilateral meetings between national leaders, telephone conversations between representatives of the Council Presidency and Commission officials, and the countless ad hoc gatherings—in corridors, bars, and on the margins of formal occasions—that are such a part of 'the Brussels circuit'.

THE EUROPEAN UNION AS A POLITICAL SYSTEM

'European integration has produced a new and complex political system' (Hix 1999: 5). There are many ways in which the European Union is a political system. It has, for example, as has been noted above, well-developed and complex institutional and decision-making frameworks. There is a wide and expanding set of executive, legislative, and judicial powers—with, in comparative terms, the judicial powers being especially strong, conferring as they do supremacy and direct effect on EU law within the scope of the EU treaties (Dehousse 1998). The policies which emerge as a result of the interaction between the various levels of the EU system cover most areas of public policy and are dominant in the rules which govern the exchange of goods, services, and capital in the member states' markets.

But what sort of political system is the European Union? Early attempts to theorize about European integration presented it as a subset, albeit a highly important and developed subset, of regional integration. This approach proved, however, to be extremely difficult to sustain given the increasing scope and depth of European integration. As an example of regional integration the European Union turned out to be without serious emulation. It has represented an *n* of 1 (see Caporaso *et al.* 1997 for a debate on the *n* of 1 question).

The *n* of 1 problematic has created difficulties for comparative, theoretical, and conceptual work on the European Union, but it has not disabled it. There may be no direct comparator for the system as a whole, but the constituent elements of the Euro polity can be compared with the analogous elements of other political systems. For, as Helen Wallace has observed, the European Union is a political system with 'more features of normality than of abnormality—politics like any other, and policy-making like any other, *except* when strikingly distinctive patterns are observed' (Wallace 2000*a*: 66).

A full review of the comparative, theoretical, and conceptual work undertaken on the European Union is, of course, not possible here. However, it is possible to give an indication of how such work can be useful in furthering understanding of the nature of the European Union as a political system by looking at two conceptual approaches that are increasingly used to frame the debate on the nature of the European Union.

On the State-Like Nature of the European Union

'[The European Union] is not a state and there are few areas of policy in which it is the exclusive location for generating collective action or solving policy dilemmas' (Wallace 2000*a*: 66). Notwithstanding the authority of Helen Wallace's statement, the succession of grand reforming treaties since the mid-1980s—the 1986 Single European Act (SEA), the 1992 Treaty on European Union (TEU), the 1997 Treaty of Amsterdam, and the 2001 Treaty of Nice—have stimulated a debate as to the degree to which the European Union has developed, and is likely to further develop, state-like characteristics. The debate itself is often confused since it runs alongside and interacts with a much wider debate about the (eagerly) anticipated demise of the Westphalian state and the degree to which it has already been hollowed out by globalization, regional integration, and the inability of all states, with the arguable exception of the United States, to meet the claim that they can provide for their own external security.

There are a number of obvious senses in which the EU possesses or aspires to possess state-like characteristics. At a symbolic level it has a flag, an anthem, and virtually a common passport. Through its treaty-established institutions and processes it takes authoritative decisions that control economic and social activities within its territory. Many of these decisions are taken on the basis of QMV in the Council, which means the preferences of the governments and citizens of one or a group of states can be overruled—a situation that is normally associated with states since it pre-supposes the existence of a political community.

Since the early 1990s these 'established' state-like characteristics have been joined by other such features. One of these features is EU citizenship, which was created by the Maastricht Treaty and strengthened by the Amsterdam Treaty. Citizenship is a concept that has been linked inextricably to the development of the modern state since the eighteenth century, with assumptions about citizenship invariably being framed in the logic of statism. The institution of an EU citizenship was therefore a considerable departure from established norms and arguably represented a very significant step in state-building. Other recently developed features that may also be thought of in this way include: EMU and the euro (states conventionally have a single currency); the series of moves to create a European defence capability (control of defence is usually thought of as being at the very heart of national sovereignty); and the Schengen Protocol, which has a dual character in which the abolition of internal controls is associated with increasingly hard border regimes in the east and south to deal with illegal migration and organized crime (states are normally at least partly defined by the hard character of their borders). The increasing public discussion on the need for an EU constitution is also relevant here, with the matter clearly having moved up the EU's list of priorities.

These various developments have excited a fevered and overheated debate in a number of member states, particularly the United Kingdom and Denmark, about whether or not a European super state is emerging. It is important at this point to provide some perspective. The citizenship provisions in the Maastricht and Amsterdam Treaties are extremely modest and complement rather than threaten state-based citizenship provisions. Similarly, the defence conclusions of the Nice Treaty fall a very long way short of a European army, with it as yet being unforeseeable that the European Union could enjoy the monopoly of physical coercion which has long been seen to be a defining feature of states. As for EMU it is often forgotten that the Irish Republic had a long standing currency union with the United Kingdom and that Benelux was also a currency union.

The debate about a possible constitution is similarly misleading. Constitutions are not exclusively associated with states. Most organizations have a set of rules, commonly called the organization's constitution, which possess a more binding character than ordinary organizational rules. Whether having a document entitled a constitution would strengthen the state-like character of the European Union would thus depend very largely on its contents, though the procedural rules for treaty revision are also important. Were, for example, the European Union to abandon unanimity in favour of QMV for treaty revision, an important rubicon would have been crossed (Hine 2001). At present, the leading advocates of an EU constitution are the German Federal and Länder governments, which are primarily concerned to establish a clearer division of competences and a check on the inherently expansive character of the EU system. In German conceptions of statehood, a key role is assigned to a *Staatsvolk* or demos: that is, the emphasis is on a citizenry which owes exclusive loyalty to a particular state. Without such a citizenry there is no state. It was this thinking that impelled the German Constitutional Court in its Maastricht judgement to describe the European Union as a *Staatenverbund* (confederation of states) rather than a *Bundestaat* (federal state) (See Weiler 1995*b*).

The debate about the supposed state-like character of the European Union is, moreover, rendered more complex by the changing character of the modern state itself, with many of its core features having become blurred. For example, no European state can convincingly claim to provide complete external security on its own borders. Either manifestly in NATO or unspokenly as free riders, all European states rely ultimately on the protection offered by the United States. Similarly, it is clear that the economic and welfare aspirations of states have required ending the state's exclusive claim on a very wide range of economic and social powers. This has resulted in both the extensive pooling of sovereignty and an increased porousness of states, the latter being particularly associated with the growing leverage of international capital and corporations.

The EU and New Governance

An extensive body of academic literature takes a 'new governance' approach to the study of political systems. Although encompassing a number of different perspectives, this approach is based on several shared assumptions. A core assumption is that the state no longer possesses a monopoly in relation to governance functions, but shares it with other actors. Another assumption is that governance is no longer hierarchical in the conventional state-centric mode. And a third assumption is that governance is increasingly centred on regulation rather than redistribution. The general accent in new governance is on 'government beyond the state'.

Aspects of the new governance approach have been utilized and developed by a number of EU scholars (see e.g. Kohler Koch 1996; Heritier 1996). One prominent example of the application of new governance thinking to the European Union is seen with the concept of multilevel governance, the point of departure for which is 'the existence of overlapping competencies among multiple levels of governments and the interaction of political actors across those levels. Member state executives, while powerful, are only one set among a variety of actors in the European polity. States are not an exclusive link between domestic politics and intergovernmental bargaining in the European Union' (Marks *et al.* 1996: 41). This multilevel governance depiction of the European Union has a number of attractions. In particular, it avoids the assumption that the European Union is only a Brussels-level game and it avoids also a too reductionist state centrism. In doing so, however, it is in danger of presenting the system as too flat and not sufficiently recognizing that some actors are better placed and are more powerful and influential than others. It can be argued that whilst intergovernmental approaches to conceptualizing the European Union over-privilege the role of key states, multilevel governance runs the risk of seriously underestimating their influence.

Similar criticisms can be made of network approaches to explaining EU governance. Such approaches emphasize the role and influence of a wide range of actors—formal and informal, institutional and non institutional, national and transnational—in EU processes (see e.g. Peterson 1995; Rhodes *et al.* 1996; Peterson and Bomberg 1999). Whilst valuable in helping to identify the variety of EU policy-making activity, network-based approaches can underplay the role of formal actors—especially the member states—and can underestimate the political dimension of EU processes. Indeed, the criticism of network theory that it underplays the political can be levelled at the new governance literature more widely, for the fact is that the European Union is a political system where the allocation of values and resources are decided.

Paradoxically, one of the most influential approaches to new thinking in EU governance has been to follow a 'back to the future' route. A number of analysts, most notably Ole Waever (1995), have gone behind the Westphalian state model and employed the neo-medieval metaphor to describe a political system characterized by overlapping authorities, divided sovereignty, diversified institutional arrangements, multiple identities, and soft border zones that undergo regular adjustment (Zielonka 2000: 104). This line of thinking is represented in Table 6.1 (Zielonka 2000). The neo-Westphalian State, the features of which are outlined in the first column of Table 6.1,

Table 6.1   *Two contrasting models of the future EU system*

Neo-Westphalian state	Neo-Medieval empire
Hard and fixed external border lines	Soft border zones in flux
Relatively high socioeconomic homogeneity	Socioeconomic discrepancies persist without consistent patterns
A pan-European cultural identity prevails	Multiple cultural identities coexist
Overlap between legal, administrative, economic, and military regimes	Disassociation between authoritative allocations, functional competencies, and territorial constituencies.
A clear hierarchical structure with one centre of authority	Interpenetration of various types of political units and loyalties
Distinction between EU members and non-members is sharp and it is most crucial	Distinction between the European centre and periphery is most crucial, but blurred
Redistribution centrally regulated within a closed EU system	Redistribution based on different types of solidarity between various transnational networks
One single type of citizenship	Diversified types of citizenship with different sets of rights and duties
A single European army and police force	Multiplicity of various overlapping military and police institutions
Absolute sovereignty regained	Divided sovereignty along different functional and territorial lines.

Source: Zielonka (2000: 104). Reproduced by kind permission of the Foreign Policy Centre, the original book may be purchased from http://fpc.org.UK

does not fit the present European Union and for the reasons we have already argued seems extremely improbable in the future. As with any attempt to capture a system by a declension of features, there are some elements which do correspond—for example; the distinction between members and non-members—but this is not true of almost all the other features. The second column, which Zielonka chooses to label neo-medieval, seems initially to be more promising. This is hardly surprising since it is a metaphor designed to capture a loosely coupled system lacking the centralized authority of the neo-Westphalian executive. While this neo-medieval model has a seductive appeal, it is, however, analytically weak and open to a number of objections. One key objection relates to borders: Zielonka's identification of soft border zones in flux as a defining feature seems at variance with developments in the European Union where the pressures of international migration and fear of crime are pushing the European Union in the direction of ever harder borders towards the east and the south (Grabbe 1999). More critically, the neo-medieval model fails to account for the role of the member states or the impact of globalization and does not capture the regulatory dimension which has been at the heart of the developing EU governance system since the introduction of the SEM.

New governance approaches are thus useful, but have limitations. In an influential article on new governance, Simon Hix (1998) has argued for an approach which would unify the insights of the new governance school and his own approach which focuses on the European Union as a political system. So far no such unified account has appeared, but there are indications that the study of 'Europeanization'—that is, how domestic level institutions adapt to the emergence and development at the European level of distinct structures of governance—will provide a fertile ground for such an account. Here we are looking at an intensely political process of the redefinition of how the state performs its functions and who performs them. 'The misfit between European and domestic processes provides societal and/or political actors with new opportunities and constraints in the pursuance of their interests' (Börzel and Risse 2000: 2). In seeking to explain change here, we necessarily have to explore the supranational, state, and substate levels and the centrality of inter and intra level relationships since institutions in the EU's dynamic environment can no longer rely on formal allocations of competences. Europeanization is a theme which gripped Vincent Wright in his later years and which played to his strengths of a broad theoretical grasp on the one hand and a fine ground knowledge of the French and British systems on the other. In Wright's approach, context was crucial 'in explaining why it is that the various member states have reacted differently to and been affected in contrasting ways, by European integration' (Menon 2001a: 250) Sadly, his untimely death prevented him from working out fully the implications of this approach.

THE LEGITIMACY PROBLEM

There are many reasons to expect legitimacy to be an acute problem for the EU. It is a new and unfamiliar political system; it has substantial powers to go into the nooks and crannies of member societies; its rules override those made by national institutions; it takes decisions that effect ordinary lives; it demands sacrifice, sometimes with uncertain long-term reward; it takes from some in order to give to others; it affects deeply held values, including basic feelings of identity; and it is a large political system that often seems physically distant to its citizens. (Lord 2000: 2)

The European Union is not a state but is a political system of fairly ambitious scope. All political systems have to be perceived as legitimate if they are to be stable. The quotation by Lord indicates the reasons why legitimacy has increasingly become an issue in the EU system.

Joseph Weiler makes a useful preliminary distinction between formal and social legitimacy. Formal legitimacy in Weiler's terms is legality understood in the sense 'that democratic institutions and processes created the law on which the European Union is based' (Weiler 2000: 80). Social legitimacy is not concerned with procedures but implies a broad social acceptance of the system.

Weiler argues that the European Union has always been legitimate in the formal sense, since it was established and has been extended on the basis of treaties ratified by member states. There has, however, always been an incipient problem of democratic control and, therefore, of social legitimacy in the operation of the institutions. This is seen, for example, with the Council of Ministers, whose members are ultimately responsible to their national parliaments, but only in a very weak manner in regard to most EU matters, including the making of EU legislation. The fact is that an effect of European integration has been to strengthen national executives and weaken legislatures. This relative strengthening and weakening has increased over the years, not least because of the extended provisions for, and use of, QMV in the Council since the mid-1980s. QMV has made the legitimacy problem increasingly manifest, for it has raised the question of the circumstances and areas in which mass populations are prepared to accept majority rule. Acceptance of majority rule presupposes a *Staatsvolk* or demos, but Europe is clearly at some considerable distance from having such a foundation. This absence is at the heart of why social legitimacy is an important issue.

Unsurprisingly, this has not been seen as a major problem by national governments, which have relished their EU autonomy and have been prepared to trade democratic control for increased effectiveness. It has similarly not generally disturbed national oppositions, which have hoped to become governments, or other elites, which have normally been predisposed in favour of effectiveness and more favourable to European integration than mass opinion. Nonetheless, in recent years, a great deal of thinking has gone into how the legitimacy problem ought to be addressed. Although the European Union may be formally legitimate by virtue of its treaties being ratified at national levels, most ratifications are channelled via national parliaments so democratic criteria may be thought to be met only in an indirect and weak sense. In some member states this has been felt to be insufficient, hence the usage in Denmark and Ireland of referenda for ratifying major treaty changes. Referenda on major 'constitutional' issues are possible in other states in the future, with Sweden and the United Kingdom likely to follow Denmark's example of holding a referendum on EMU should their governments decide that there is a positive economic case for entry. The use of referenda is even being discussed seriously in Germany, where the democracy-destroying potential of referenda in the Weimar Republic has ensured a taboo status for referenda at federal level.

Obviously, occasional referenda on major issues do not, however, meet the problem of democratic control on ongoing, 'everyday' integration. There are two possible routes here. One is to strengthen the EP, a process that has been ongoing since the SEA. Unfortunately, this appears to have little or no effect on the social legitimacy of the European Union, given the public's rooted lack of enthusiasm for the Parliament as demonstrated by low turnouts in EP elections. The other route is to strengthen national parliaments along Danish lines or to establish a Senate of national parliamentary representations. The main problem with these solutions, especially the second, is that they have potentially damaging implications for decision-making efficiency and could compromise the output of the European Union.

A quite different and alternative approach to the legitimacy problem is suggested by what is known in 'Euro-speak' as flexibility or enhanced cooperation. This is the notion, which was given treaty-status at Amsterdam, that certain policies may be developed at European level without all EU member states participating. Clearly this would avoid the difficulty of national populations being overridden and taken in directions to which they are deeply opposed.

Another possible approach is to build a European demos by strengthening the identity function. The criteria for Union membership laid down at the 1993 Copenhagen summit constitute a proto-civic identity grouped around respect for democratic principles and individual rights, whilst the invocation of sanctions against the inclusion of the party led by Jorg Haider in the Austrian government in 1999 also assumed a European community of values. Proposals for a European constitution are also often couched in terms of encouraging a constitutional patriotism. None of these attempts, however, seem likely to be very effective at the mass level: they are simply too dry and abstract. Identities are normally created either by an external 'other' or by performance. Post-war West Germany, for example, relied on both, with the Soviet threat and sustained economic growth. The European Union is not seriously threatened and attempts to build an EU identity in terms of anti-Americanism are highly divisive and self-defeating. Performance criteria continue to be the most attractive route. EMU has possibilities in this context, for if it is successful it is likely to be much more effective than any other single factor in creating social legitimacy. If, however, it fails, the negative effect on mass opinion could be extremely damaging.

CONCLUDING REMARKS

The overall picture that emerges of the EU's political system is of a system characterized by complexity, fragmentation, and continuing evolution. This is an inevitable consequence of the shifting balance between the national and European levels, and of the competition between the EU's many political actors to establish strong positions for themselves within the EU's still developing political system.

Given this situation, it is perhaps surprising that a system which might have been expected to produce stasis has in practice produced much purposive, decision-making, and policy expansion. Since the mid-1980s the European Union has been associated with a number of history-making decisions, such as the creation of the European Union itself on the basis of a three pillar structure, the establishment of multi-annual budgetary programming, and the launching of EMU. At a more everyday level, the SEM has acted as a catalyst for a very marked process of policy expansion.

It remains to be seen whether the European Union is capable of carrying through the major project that now faces it, namely its own expansion to nearly thirty members. The prospect of including so many new states, all at different stages of economic and political development, will clearly strain many of the EU's founding contracts, not least in the complications it will create for the processes of arriving at inter-state agreements. Issues of institutional architecture will probably have to be grasped more firmly than they have been hitherto if gridlock is to be avoided. Nevertheless, past history suggests that the difficulties will be overcome.

PART II

PUBLIC ADMINISTRATION

7

Dismantling and Rebuilding the Weberian State

B. GUY PETERS

The title of this chapter reflects an important question about the contemporary development of public administration and its role within the contemporary state.[1] It is clear that the public sectors in most contemporary countries have been recast through accepting some version of the 'New Public Management' (see Pollitt 1993). The traditional public sector has been, to a great extent, dismantled through this process of administrative reform, although the character of the emergent system for governing is not always clear. The question that is posed by these reforms is whether that earlier version of government can, or should, in any way be recaptured. The implicit and explicit argument is that a good deal of value has been lost through these changes in the style of governing but that it may well be impossible to rebuild anything approximating the older version of the state and the public bureaucracy.

PRELIMINARY ISSUES

Before we embark on the place of Max Weber in a redefined public sector, there are several preliminary issues that should be addressed. These issues will not so much be resolved as acknowledged. The same intellectual issues that we will cope with in this manuscript have been dealt with by others a number of times and they are still far from resolved (see, e.g. Mommsen 1974; Page 1985; Derlien 1999). In our acknowledgement of these continuing intellectual issues, we can identify some of the complexity of coping with change within the contemporary public sector. In addition, we

---

This chapter is an attempt to write the manuscript that Vincent Wright and I could never quite get on paper. We spent a number of hours in his room discussing 'good old Weber' and the place of Weber in understanding both the (once) traditional public bureaucracy and its role in managing the State. The more we read and talked, the more complex this subject became and hence the paper never appeared, other than to be listed as 'forthcoming' in several other papers. It will inevitably be weaker by my not being able to continue those discussions, and to have Vincent cast his skeptical, albeit enthusiastic, eye over this product. It will be forced to simplify, for the sake of clarity and completion, some of the issues that vexed us as we worked together.

[1] Although certainly not using this title, Vincent did identify the question of recapturing the nature of the Weberian state and in some lectures (especially those given once at El Colegio de Mexico) wrestled with the subject.

have to identify the role that the intellectual roots of government in contemporary industrial democracies in Weberian theory may have in understanding the reformed system that is currently emerging. Again, there is always the question of what of importance has been lost through the reforms implementing the New Public Management, despite their other contributions to the performance of the public sector, and what any values that have been lost may mean for the continuing reform of the public sector (see Peters 2001*a*). In particular, have subsequent changes in the public sector been able to recapture some of those lost values?

WEBER AND WEBERIAN ARE NOT NECESSARILY THE SAME THING

The first point about the use and abuse of Weberian concepts in discussing the State is that there is a difference, and often a vast difference, between what Weber himself wrote and what the advocates and defenders, as well as the critics, of a Weberian State have taken those ideas to mean. This discrepancy between the formal statement of the concept of bureaucracy and the political reactions manifested in response to those ideas is particularly evident when Weber's ideas are used with reference to institutions outside the cultural and political context for which they were intended. Indeed, as we will point out below, to some degree there is a direct correspondence between Weber's own writings and the social and intellectual conditions within Germany at his time.

The primary question then is what did Weber actually say about the State and the role of bureaucracy within it? Weber himself was at once quite clear and ambiguous about these two points. On the one hand, a reader can rather easily extract a set of characteristics of a bureaucracy, covering both structural and behavioural characteristics. The academic literature addressing this issue is voluminous. One of the more important attempts to identify what Weber actually wrote, and to determine the extent to which several European governments are indeed Weberian, is Ed Page's book (1985) examining the nature of power and authority within the public sector in Britain, France, and Germany. Likewise, Hans-Ulrich Derlien (1999) identifies a number of formal and behavioural aspects of the Weberian ideal type model of bureaucracy, whether that is in the public or private sector.

Page identifies several elements that are central to the concept of bureaucracy and which exist to some degree in virtually all administrative systems. These points include familiar terms such as hierarchy, tenure in office, and the development of neutral competence. In particular, however, Page focuses on the power of 'bureaucrats' relative to their nominal political masters and the relative influence that both sides of this equation have on public policy. Page focuses on the question of '*Beamtenherrschaft*', or dominance of the political system by the bureaucracy and the extent to which that dominance is inherent in complex contemporary political systems. This is a central political as well as analytical question for understanding some of the conflicts arising from contemporary administrative reforms, especially because the explicit goal of some reformers was to devalue the public service (Peters 1986; Savoie 1994).

Page attempts to identify rather clearly what Weber said, but others have added more of their own interpretations to the concept of bureaucracy. These numerous differences in interpretation and analysis are not just the consequences of alternative linguistics and academic interpretations of the text, but they also represent a political project. On the one hand, if one accepts what has come to be the received version of the Weberian model of rationality and the place of formal bureaucracies in ensuring that rationality in the political system, then there is a very different role assigned to the democratic political process and the role of civil servants within that process. In particular, civil servants are expected to be very much the ancillaries of their political masters rather than more central components of the policy-making process.

Also, the 'Weberian state' is to some extent a short-hand term for a particular version of governance, some of which is now considered outdated by many modernizers in government, but some of which may need to be revived. This form of governance reflects the sense in which both scholars and practitioners have conceptualized the public bureaucracy in rather formalistic terms, and believed that government actually performed much as Weber had assumed that his 'Ideal Type' bureaucrats would behave. For example, the hierarchical authority at the centre of Weberian conceptions of management has long been known to have been circumvented as much as it is followed by participants in formal organizations. Thus, for many people a conception of government that was intended largely as an intellectual model (see below) was transformed into a mental image of how real governments performed.

OTHER 'BUREAUCRATIC' FORMS OF GOVERNMENT

Although Weber is the focus of most debates about the meaning of bureaucracy and its position in government, there is an interesting set of analogous writing about Woodrow Wilson and his role in defining public administration in the United States (Stillman 1991). Wilson is perhaps most famous for his definition, and advocacy, of the politics/administration dichotomy (1887), a concept that has continued to haunt Anglo/American public administration (Redford 1969). What is perhaps most interesting about the politics/administration dichotomy is that it is often interpreted as an argument on behalf of political control of public policy, and the subservience of civil servants. While in terms of control over public policy that characterization is correct, it is equally correct that Wilson argued for the supremacy of administration. Administration was assumed to be a superior concern, given that it was amenable to scientific analysis, while politics only functioned at the level of an art.[2] Therefore, despite the democratic imperative of politicians remaining in charge of policies, there is an equal efficiency imperative that supports the role of public administration in managing those policies once adopted. Further, although operating within the American context that even at his time was skeptical about government and

---

[2] An interesting comment for one who was also a successful politician.

bureaucracy, Wilson took in essence a statist position, praising the capacities of non-democratic governments of the time such as Prussia.

The British style of administration, as well as those of countries derivative from this tradition (see Peters 2001c), is not Weberian *per se*, but yet the formal, hierarchical style found prior to administrative reform shares many characteristics with the Weberian model. The traditional model of the state and public administration, was captured well by Walsh and Stewart (1992) in a discussion of the basis of reform in British government. They enumerated four fundamental characteristics of that traditional model. These were:

1. *Self-sufficiency.* The idea was that when government undertook a task it would provide the service in question itself. This is to some extent the French concept of *services publics*, meaning that there are certain services that should be publicly provided. This idea is in marked contrast to contemporary mechanisms of providing services such as contracting out, vouchers, and public–private partnerships.
2. *Hierarchy.* This is a familiar concept to describe management within the public sector, and is certainly seen as Weberian. The idea is simply that within government there will be strong hierarchical control exercised within organizations. In addition, there is a hierarchical style of dealing with clients, so that services are provided with little or no involvement of the public for whom they are intended. Again, this conception of control within the public sector is changing rapidly, with more 'empowerment' of both workers and clients (Peters and Pierre 2000).
3. *Equality.* The Weberian civil servant is meant to respond to the public in an impersonal and objective manner. Likewise government as a whole is meant to treat citizens—defined by ethnicity, gender, class, and region—in an equal manner. Reforms are also loosening this constraint, and the idea of differential levels of service to different segments of the public is becoming more acceptable.
4. *Routinized Establishment Procedures.* This is a very British means of saying that there should be a civil service, with recruitment, promotion, and retention on the basis of merit criteria. Deregulation of the public service, and others aspects of government, is weakening this criterion of the traditional state as well.

In addition to these points, one dominant feature of bureaucracy in the Anglo-American tradition is the separation of politics and administration. The associated value is that of the political neutrality of the civil service, and its insulation from direct political influence. The civil service is assumed to be able to serve any political master and to be able to remain in office regardless of changes in the political complexion of the government. The neutrality of the civil service has come under increasing pressure in many Anglo-American systems (Savoie 1994), but that norm remains central to much of the discourse about public administration in this group of countries.

This paper will focus on what the Weberian State came to mean, whether because of what Weber actually wrote or what that term has been interpreted to mean by scholars and to some extent by practitioners. It is also concerned with what has happened to the Weberian State in light of numerous political and administrative critiques that have been launched against bureaucracy. The wide scale efforts at reform are to some extent directed at the Weberian system, whether by name or not, and what is happening in government represents some response to the ills of that format for governing.

MAX WEBER AND BUREAUCRACY

The scholarly work of Max Weber is perhaps forever associated with the concept of bureaucracy. The debate over the meaning of this term has gone on for decades in the German-speaking world, and after his work came to be known outside that cultural area the debate spread and perhaps even intensified, perhaps because the administrative tradition in Anglo-American countries is markedly different. This debate concerning the actual meaning and intention of Weber's writing continues to this day. There are at least four interpretations of the meaning and importance of Weber's work on bureaucracy:

1. *Description.* One interpretation of bureaucracy is that it is a description of the administrative structure of Prussia in the late nineteenth century. It is perhaps an exaggerated description of that administrative structure, taking its tendencies to the extreme and neglecting the extent to which those structures did not fulfill the expectations of the author (see Page 1985), but it might yet be seen as descriptive.
2. *Theory.* Another view of bureaucracy is that it is a theory, grounded in the development of capitalism and state legitimacy. That is, bureaucracy could be seen as the highest form of development of the capitalist state, legitimated by the rational–legal acceptance of the superiority of this form of governing.
3. *Process.* Another way of thinking about bureaucracy is as representing a process of change, rooted in a particular conception of history and development. The important concept in this interpretation is that bureaucratization is a process of social change (see Eisenstadt 1965). It may be that no organization will ever attain the (presumed) goal of full bureaucratization, but the process is teleological, moving always towards the development of a more bureaucratic state.
4. *Ideal Type.* Finally, the conventional interpretation of bureaucracy is as an ideal type model, and therefore a concept more than a theory. This also is a methodological tool, a concept that can be employed as a standard against which to compare real world administrative systems.

There is good evidence to support each of these four notions of what is implied by the term bureaucracy, and each of the four has utility for understanding public administration and the capitalist state. In addition, they function both historically and in the contemporary period. Also, although these uses of the term are presented as mutually exclusive, there are actually some points of tangency among the approaches, so that an interest in process may actually be derived from a broader theoretical interest in the notion of bureaucracy, and the focus on formal organizations in public administration.

Academic Interpretations. As well as these four views of bureaucracy, there are a variety of more substantial academic interpretations on Weber's work and the role of bureaucracy in that work. There are two major interpretations found here, each now associated with a major scholar of Weber. On the one hand Reinhard Bendix argues for the virtual inevitability of bureaucracy and that once created it will be virtually impossible to dismember. In other words, for Bendix bureaucratic administration is permanent, inevitable, and indispensable in industrialized capitalist societies. Further, bureaucracy is rooted in capitalism and can be seen as a means of state legitimation. This is true in part because it can make the state more effective and that effectiveness can legitimate government (Lipset 1959). Also, the legality and equality associated with the *Rechtstaat* helps to justify the capitalist order.

Bureaucracy helps to justify the capitalist order, but it is also necessary for the development of that economic order. Economic modernization and rationalization requires overarching concepts of order, ensured by bureaucratic administration. From the simple matter of ensuring performance of contracts to more demanding tasks of creating effective markets and ensuring law and order in society more generally, bureaucracy is a central feature of a successful capitalist state. Further, the equality and universalism of bureaucracy could be seen as a foundation for more egalitarian political programmes. Of course, the evidence is that formal bureaucracy has also been central to the functioning of socialist states, and in some ways reached its most extreme form in those systems.

Mommsen has advanced a substantially different interpretation of the nature and role of bureaucracy in the contemporary state. He emphasizes Weber's ambivalence towards rationalism and capitalism, and hence towards bureaucratization. Despite its possible virtues, Weber saw that bureaucracy could constitute a threat to individualism and freedom, through its uniformity and rationalization. In contrast to the view of uniformity as egalitarian, Mommsen has seen this trait of bureaucracy as more restrictive, and as stifling for individuals seeking to advance alternative views of the political world. Being treated with absolute equality may simply mean that individual traits, and individual needs, are ignored.

Another problem arising in the role of bureaucracy in the public sector is that its rationalizing elements may lead bureaucrats to attempt to expand their influence (individually and collectively) in policy making. The expansion of this style of administration and policy making can be seen as a means of controlling externalities among organizations to smooth the working of the machinery of government. In this view even private sector organizations that deal with public bureaucracies may find that they need to adopt a more bureaucratic form in order to be able to cope with the demands of bureaucracy.[3] Further, bureaucracy and capitalism are not so complementary in this view as they were for Bendix; bureaucracy may stifle the entrepreneurship and freedom required for successful capitalism, especially when bureaucratization is associated with the development of a univeralistic welfare state.

---

[3] This is an example of the isomorphism of organizations in a field noted by Dimaggio and Powell (1991*a*).

Therefore, for Mommsen, bureaucracy was not an inevitable outgrowth of (or condition for) modernization. It was rather more of an intellectual construct than any reflection of the real world of administration in the public sector. The concept is no less useful analytically in this view, but it is different from reality. Therefore bureaucratization is contingent on very particular patterns of development, particularly those found in Prussia. Indeed, this could be a self-denying hypothesis about development, much as Orwell's *1984* had been. The knowledge of the potential negative nature of bureaucracy may be enough to prevent governments from becoming excessively bureaucratized, and may make citizens in democratic regimes more vigilant about bureaucratization.

These alternative conceptions of bureaucracy make the analytic task more difficult. Rather than a single concept, we appear to be coping with many, or at least many possible interpretations of that one concept. Further, the concept is itself multifaceted so that an organization may be 'bureaucratic' along one dimension but not so on others. For example, while much of the public sector remains bureaucratic in the sense of maintaining rather formalistic rules and regulations about policies, it may debureaucratize its public personnel management or recruit personnel from the public sector rather freely.

THE CRITIQUES

The critiques of the Weberian model of bureaucracy are numerous and varied. They are normative, empirical, as well as both normative and empirical. For the normative criticisms, what is perhaps most interesting is that there are a number of almost directly contradictory critiques of the approach. On the one hand bureaucracy is frequently seen as an excessively rigid and conservative social institution, and is argued to be a barrier to change. On the other hand the concern with fairness and equity within bureaucracy can be seen as a means of administering government in a more democratic manner than would be possible with other conventional forms of implementing public programmes. In addition, the emphasis on merit recruitment is a mechanism for democratization in societies that have been dominated by a class or ethnic group.

NORMATIVE

There are normative critiques of bureaucracy intertwined with many of the other critiques mentioned here, and indeed perhaps the most important questions concerning the bureaucratic state are normative. These questions are based on concern about the demands for the willing suspension of individual ethical choices. At the extreme, the behaviour of many members of the German bureaucracy during the Nazi period could be regarded as the epitome of acting in a Weberian manner (Friedrich 1962). The rules were certainly followed and there were meticulous files retained.

The problem is that the actions being recorded were offensive to any sense of moral behaviour in government.

The normative problem for bureaucracy, therefore, is to find ways of balancing norms of obedience to, and support for, appropriate actions by superiors with individual evaluation of the content of those actions. The need to balance those values has led, for example, to the institutionalization of 'whistle-blowing' opportunities in the public sector, and to the creation of offices such as Inspectors General in the US federal bureaucracy designed to give individual bureaucrats a safe way of questioning the actions of superiors. The difficulty, of course, is that even these offices place the major burden of identifying abuses of power on the least powerful and most vulnerable members of the bureaucracy.

ORGANIZATION THEORISTS

Organization theorists have raised a number of critiques of the Weberian perspective on public bureaucracy. There is a rather large literature on each of those numerous critiques, so we can only present these ideas here in a rather brief form. The first and perhaps most common question raised by organizational theorists of the Weberian approach is the reality and utility of the politics/administration dichotomy implied in the approach to the public sector. This conception of the nature of public organizations has been common in the Anglo-American countries, where the notion of this separation is most deeply ingrained. The problem is that, empirically, it is difficult to identify this separation: politicians play a role in administration and, perhaps more importantly, administrators play major roles in policy advice and policy implementation. Normatively, it can be argued that administration will perform better if it—especially in the upper echelons—is infused with some political commitment and is not empowered to resist the ideas of its political 'masters'.

A second separation coming from Weberian doctrine about bureaucracy (as commonly interpreted) is the separation of the public and private sectors. Again, it is increasingly difficult to identify the dividing line between these two sectors in practice, as governments come to utilize the private sector for implementation and private sector organizations become dependent upon the public sector for funds, political influence, and perhaps their very existence. Again normatively it is not clear that a total separation of the two sectors would be functional for either sector, given that each one's existence tends to depend upon the other.[4] Still, there is the need to protect the public's interest in the face of policies and administration that heavily involve private sector interests and actors.

Organizational theorists have also wondered if hierarchy is as pervasive a feature of organizational life as Weberian thinking would make it appear. This question has

---

[4] The point that has been made by many institutional analysts within economics is that the market is itself a political construction, so that without a properly functioning public sector there is unlikely to be a properly functioning private sector.

been asked for some time but is becoming more significant, given the increasing need for participation within organizations and increasing cultural rejection of hierarchy in most industrialized societies (Hofstede 1984; Inglehart 1997). Further, hierarchy as a characteristic of organizations often does not covary with the other attributes of organizations that Weber argued were features of bureaucracy (Constas 1958; Udy 1959). For example, hierarchy may be inversely related to the use of formal rules for control behaviour within organizations. Having both formal means of regulating behaviour may be redundant, although the Ideal Type model argued that they were both essential elements.

Finally, although we will argue below for the importance of restoring some public interest and public service values into the public sector, these are by no means the only values that are relevant in managing in the public sector. Even in the most process-oriented and bureaucratic organization (in the pejorative sense of the term) there was always some concern with efficiency, or at least with the effectiveness of programmes. Further, Weber was not as apolitical as he is sometimes depicted[5] and was aware that bargaining over values was almost inherent in the public sector. Further, there is often a need to trade off some of the public interest for other important values being pursued through the public sector, or to trade different conceptions of the public interest. Certainly Weberian scholars who followed the master, for example, Robert Merton, have also noted that the displacement of public interest goals by more personal goals occurs within many public sector organizations.

CRITIQUE FROM THE RATIONAL CHOICE PERSPECTIVE

Rational choice theories of politics have gained substantial importance in contemporary political science. Given that theoretical trend, it is important to note that the image of the public servant advanced by Weber, certainly in the tabloid version and perhaps in the more genuine version as well, is rather different from what would be expected from the rational choice perspective. The bureaucrat in the extreme model of bureaucracy could be seen as an agent functioning without appreciable agency loss (see Brehm and Gates 1999). This self-denying behaviour is very different from the self-interested behaviour assumed without question in rational choice views.

Even if individual bureaucrats may not be self-serving, as they have been in works such Niskanen's (1971) now classic conception of bureaucrats, there may be manifest organizational interests involved in the bureaucracy. Thus, good bureaucrats (perhaps even in Weberian conception) may attempt to promote the policy perspectives of their organization and to increase the standing of the organization for all the right reasons. In that process, however, he or she may behave as a political animal—the bureaucratic politician—rather than as a detached, legalistic bureaucrat.

---

[5] See, for example, his notable work on 'Politics as a Profession'.

CRITIQUE FOR INADEQUATE OPENNESS
AND PARTICIPATION

There is also a political, democratic critique of bureaucracy. Here the closed nature of bureaucracy and its use of hierarchy and rules appears to deny citizens the opportunity to influence the outcome of decisions, even those decisions affecting them directly. On the one hand, this critique does imply that bureaucracies are using criteria of equality and fairness in making decisions that might actually be undermined by permitting higher levels of participation. The fairness criterion implied by this critique should be valued, but in the extreme this does appear to limit the ability of citizens to be active members of the political community at the output stage, with their influence apparently being confined to voting. As governments become more concerned about using participative, and even deliberative, instruments this hierarchical mode of decision making becomes increasingly less viable.

The participation critique has been common in Anglo-American and Scandinavian countries, but also has become more common in German administration with its more strictly Weberian roots. This change reflects in part the growth of more citizen-based organizations in Germany and the greater openness of German government to public participation. Thus, even in the land of its birth the formality of bureaucracy and its insulation from public pressures now confront political realities that push in populist directions. This pressure may be even more important with the Greens becoming a more significant political force.

REPRESENTATIVENESS

Finally, there are critiques of bureaucracy from another democratic perspective, that of representativeness (Selden 1996). The argument against bureaucracy being advanced on the ground of representativeness is that the use of testing and other means of enforcing merit tend to favour members of the dominant communities in society. This is especially true given that any tests used for recruitment to the bureaucracy (especially when those merit tests are requirements for senior positions) often have strong cultural elements. Therefore, although the system appears, and is intended to be, eminently fair, in fact it may be seriously biased. Further, the use of merit systems provides less opportunity to use the public sector as a 'model employer' and a leader in creating greater social opportunity.

The difficulty with traditional merit-based recruitment is that it has a tendency to perpetuate any class system or any other social hierarchy that exists within the society. Government in some ways reflects its society but it can, and perhaps should, also be a powerful means of altering its society. When bureaucracy and public management are divorced from political realities then, it is argued by critics of conventional bureaucratic recruitment and retention policies, that capacity to produce change is squandered. The bureaucracy then simply comes to reflect the dominant political and economic groups. Of course, as we will point out, some of the alternatives to Weberian conceptions of bureaucracy may be even less amenable to making value

choices in the bureaucracy than is the traditional recruitment by merit and management by hierarchy.

DISMANTLING THE WEBERIAN STATE

The administrative reforms of the 1980s and 1990s, and continuing into the new century, have produced substantial changes in the Weberian state or however that structure should be typified. Most of those reforms have been directed at fundamental
features of that administrative state, although the particular targets of change have varied dramatically. Some have been directed at the emphasis on public service, as opposed
to efficiency and effectiveness. Other have attempted to make bureaucracy more democratic and more representative. Still other reforms have attempted to lessen the
verticality of the public sector and to coordinate the multiple organizations that
build their own internal cultures to control the behaviour of participants.

The state that is emerging from all this change is quite different than the one inherited by the reformers. The emerging state form answers many of the critiques that have
been raised against Weberian bureaucracy and other forms of traditional public
administration. For example, the use of market-based ideas to manage within the public sector tends to reduce the power of assumptions about hierarchy and authority.
Rather, it depends upon the individualistic motivations to guide actions by civil servants, so that rather than depending upon formal rules and regulations, performance
will depend upon the desire of individual civil servants to advance their own careers.
That individualistic motivation may, however, leave the public interest in doubt, despite
the optimistic assumptions of much of the market-based and rational choice literature
on bureaucracy. In particular, that literature assumes that efficiency is the dominant
issue in the minds of the public, while in reality the values of the public are more
diverse and often focused on quality of services rather than their costs.

Closely associated with the loss in formal accountability is the loss in a concept of the
public interest. In fairness this concept is perhaps more derivative from the workings of
the traditional bureaucracies described by Walsh and Stewart than it is explicitly stated
as a part of the Weberian ideal.[6] In some ways the strict legalism of Weber's conceptions
might be taken to mean that the law was the more appropriate focus for the public interest, with the bureaucracy being concerned more with the implementation of that law in
a fair and impartial manner. Still, the statecraft that was practised prior to the reforms
associated with New Public Management did have a more manifest concern with the
public interest than does the managerialist practice that has become the norm in most
industrialized democracies, and many less developed countries as well.

Finally, although we could extend this argument to a much greater length, the
dominant strand of reform during the past several decades tended to subordinate
quality and ideas of public service to ideas of efficiency and economy. This may be

---

[6] This concept is more evident in Woodrow Wilson's writings on bureaucracy and government than it
is in Weber's.

simply another way of stating the point of a loss of concern with the public interest, but in this case it is manifested as much in what governments do as in how they do them. One of the interesting questions that surfaces when these administrative and policy questions are raised is the extent to which the Weberian State is linked to the Welfare State. On the one hand these two might be thought to be entirely different conceptions, reflecting very different notions of administration and political economy. On the other hand, however, the latter to some extent depends upon the former, especially if that Welfare State is to be equitable in the manner in which it distributes its benefits, and is to maintain a sense of procedural and well as substantive fairness in its actions.

This final issue also points to some of the differences between what Weber himself wrote and how he has been interpreted. The assumption is often made that Weber's idea of rationality would be related to a concern for efficiency in government. Derlien (1999) points out that rationality in organizational life meant something quite different to economic efficiency to Weber, He was more concerned with predictability, precision, and the intensity and extensiveness of services (again, concern related in part to the contemporary Welfare State) than with simple economic efficiency. Indeed, the Weberian state might be extremely inefficient in that it requires getting each case settled correctly, in for example the delivery of social programmes, rather than just settling the most cases in the least amount of time.

PUTTING IT BACK TOGETHER

After the traditional state has been dismantled, the issue must become what can be salvaged, or what could be recreated, from the remnants of the old administrative system and the innovations of the new. We have argued here and elsewhere that a great deal of value has been lost in the dismantling of what we have come to think of as the Weberian state. Those losses of values have occurred despite (or in some cases because of) the benefits created through the numerous administrative reforms. The question is whether it is possible to have some of the improved efficiency associated with reforms while reinstitutionalizing ideas such as equality, security, and commitment to public service.

As noted above, one lost value that may need to be recaptured in any subsequent reform of the State is the centrality of accountability by the public sector. While the contemporary state is hardly divorced entirely from the need to account for its actions, at least within democratic regimes, still the form of governing that has emerged is hardly as directly accountable as that which it replaced. This degradation of traditional accountability is to some extent by design, given the desire to create greater managerial autonomy, along with greater freedom for lower echelon bureaucrats (see Peters and Pierre 2000). As with other versions of market-based changes in the public sector, there is assumed to be a hidden hand that tends to optimize outcomes, perhaps even in accountability terms.[7] Importantly, however, governments are making more concerted efforts to enhance their accountability.

[7] For a thorough critique of this optimistic assumption about the efficacy of the market see Peter Self (1993).

The form of accountability that is being implemented in many contemporary states is rather different from the legal formalism implied by Weber or the parliamentary accountability typical of Westminster regimes. One emerging form of accountability externalizes this crucial function of government, and depends upon political processes outside the state, rather than on those within the public sector, to provide accountability. For example, the current interest in 'regulating government' (Hood *et al.* 1999) relies in part on inspectorates and other formalized means of enforcing accountability. It also relies in part on political processes and the activation of the consumers of government services to place pressure on the providers of those services for better services and fairer implementation of the programmes. For example, publicity used to 'name and shame' failing schools and hospitals often depends upon the clients of those facilities to mobilize and to place pressure on the providers.[8] This at once provides a means for redress of any problems, while divorcing the State from direct responsibility.

The other means of providing for accountability in the contemporary state is through invoking the values of performance and quality management. The primary assumption of these approaches is that what really matters in accountability is what is being produced by government for citizens. This conception of accountability then differs rather markedly from the Weberian norms that focus more on process, fairness, and legality than on the substance of benefits being produced. Despite that deviation from the historical concept of accountability, the emphasis on performance is a powerful means of ensuring the accountability of government organizations as well as individual public servants. It forces actors in government to account for what they have produced for the public and to explain, if targets are not reached, why they have failed. Further, this process of setting standards, measuring achievement, and requiring explanation can be linked directly to the budgetary process, thereby giving the process more teeth.[9]

The notion of performance as central to reforming the public sector may also help to restore the concept of the public interest to a more central place in governing contemporary societies. While providing a clear and accepted definition of 'the public interest' has been one of the philosopher's stones in political science (see Friedrich 1962), one useful operational approach may be the quality and quantity of the services being provided to citizens by the public sector. Thus, if public administration can focus on what government is doing for citizens, then it has some means of assessing the extent to which the public interest is being provided for. This is a very utilitarian conception of the public interest,[10] in contrast to the more legalistic and procedural

---

[8] This mechanism has a pronounced class bias, given that middle-class, educated parents and patients are more likely to be effective in expressing their grievances than are the less educated and the less affluent. Thus, an apparently democratic attempt to empower clients of public programmes may have quite undemocratic consequences, see Peters 2001c.

[9] Perhaps the clearest example of that linkage is in the Government Performance and Results Act of 1993, and the role that performance plans and annual results are intended to play in future budget allocations (Radin 1998; Peters 2001b).

[10] This notion of the public interest has many of the same assumptions as cost-benefit analysis—the standard economist's conception of the public interest. For a critique of that utilitarianism embedded in the model see Peter Self (1977).

one inherent in Weber's writings, but it does have the virtue of restoring some conception of the public to the driving seat in the assessment of government. This is in contrast to managerialist, at least vulgar managerialist, programmes that emphasized simple economic logic and cost-savings as the means of providing best for citizens.

Much of what I have been discussing has been centred on the industrialized democracies, and properly so given that this is the class of countries that has most closely approximated the Weberian ideal type. In addition this is the set of counties in which managerialist paradigm for reform has been most widely accepted. That having been said, some attention should be given to the countries of the Third World and the impact of reform on administration there. These countries appear to have been pushed very quickly into accepting the managerialist agenda without first having gone through the Weberian/Wilsonian stage of development of administration (Hentic and Bernier 1999). This (often imposed) attempt to skip stages in the process of development[11] means that public administration in these regimes has been asked to abandon many legal and procedural controls in order to promote efficiency without having institutionalized a set of values that can restrain abuse and corruption. The dysfunctions of such changes are likely to be manifested in increased corruption, with the danger that what is almost inherently corruption may be sanctioned because it appears to be related to a more marketized version of governing.

CONCLUSION

As we have discussed recapturing values as a function of continuing changes in the public sector, it is apparent that the Weberian characterization of the traditional public bureaucracy will not be recreated, nor should it. That Weberian State was a particular form of governing suitable for a particular time and place but not necessarily timeless. On the other hand some of the virtues associated with that style of governing are more timeless and deviations from those values should be suspected. There were certainly numerous dysfunctions in this form of governing, as have been pointed out above, and even advocates of some aspects of this system have recognized those dysfunctions.

The bad news is that those values of concern for legality, probity, and predictability of outcomes were threatened rather severely by the reforms implemented during the 1980s and 1990s. We have detailed earlier some of those assaults, albeit generally well-intentioned assaults. Some were much less well-intentioned and were direct attacks on the concept of a neutral, competent civil service. No matter how well-intentioned the changes may be, however, there must still be concerns about restoring the central values that have motivated administration in the public sector. The logic of restoring those values is not simply to resist change in the public sector, but

---

[11] The imposition comes primarily from international donor agencies, and individual countries operating as donors, attempting to promote managerial efficiency.

rather because those values were functional for maintaining administration in both a democratic and effective manner.

The good news, however, is that there has been some reassertion of the importance of the values that had been threatened. The changes noted above are restoring a greater sense of accountability to administration. Likewise, the separation of political and administrative actions that is so central to Anglo-American thinking about administration has been identified as a major casualty of the former changes and there are attempts to identify the proper scope for each type of activity. That being said, many of the concerns that Vincent Wright identified remain viable and as time passes become even more pressing. As the number of civil servants and politicians who have participated in the Weberian state diminishes, then the questions about whether the managerialist construction is really the best way in which to run government are likely to wane. This is not to argue that the Weberian State is necessarily the only, or even best, solution for the problems of governing. It is, however, to argue that these questions should be considered and considered carefully when attempting to make government work.

8

The Age of Administrative Reforms

SABINO CASSESE

INTRODUCTION

'Administrative reform' indicates a series of interventions that are promoted by political or administrative bodies and introduced to adapt public administrations to economic and social change. There is no equivalent to such interventions in the private sector, where the word reform is not used. Here, such words as change or transformation are used and adapting to the market and the surrounding environment is an ongoing process. It has been calculated that private enterprises modify their structures and procedures every 5–8 years.

The need for reform in the public sector and the stress laid on interventions in this area depend on various factors. First of all, public administrations are usually bigger than private organizations and tend to be more stable. As far as size is concerned, it should be remembered that public administrations in European countries with fifty to sixty million inhabitants employ from four to six million people. As far as stability is concerned, public administrations are more or less meticulously regulated by laws, that is, by the acts of the legislature. For this reason, they are bereft of complete power to regulate themselves. Because of their size and the stability of their functioning and organization, public administrations change less quickly than the political, economic, and social framework in which they have to operate. In order to reduce the differential, special public policies known as administrative reforms are usually adopted. Through such policies any difficulties arising as a result of size and stability may be overcome.

Second, frictions periodically emerge between the two components of public administrations, political oversight and the administration proper. These frictions call for adjustments. This situation is especially evident when changes occur in the political majority in government. If the new majority wants to avoid having to govern with the instruments used by the previous majority, it needs quickly to change the administrative instruments at its disposal. This is another reason why administrative reforms are launched.

A TWENTIETH CENTURY PHENOMENON

Administrative reform is not just a problem peculiar to the public sector. It is also a twentieth century phenomenon. In the past, public administrations were relatively limited in size. In the nineteenth century they employed from around fifty thousand to three hundred thousand people in countries with twenty to thirty million inhabitants. This meant that there was no need for a special policy to change them. Furthermore, a clear line distinguishing politics from administration had not yet been drawn, as bureaucracy was made up either of people selected by the political body (e.g. through political patronage in the United Kingdom until the mid-nineteenth century) or of people who were members of parliament at the same time (until mid-nineteenth century in France). It can therefore be said that political control over the organization and functioning of the public sector meant that implementing government policies posed no problems.

The need for administrative reform emerged in the course of the twentieth century. This came about partly at the political level. In France, for example, it started to mature during the Popular Front led by Léon Blum (1936–7), which attributed its failure to the inability to communicate its reforming intentions to administrative institutions. Administrative reform was an instrument for adapting administrative structures and procedures to the new policies of a left-wing government. In France the idea of administrative reform drew its inspiration not simply from the political need for reform but also from the studies of American-inspired rationalist industrial organization known as 'Taylorism' (Rials 1977).

But the need for administrative reform also developed within public administrations. One example of this was the 1968 Fulton Report, which proposed that British public administrations had to abandon the model based on amateur, all-round civil servants in favour of greater professionalism amongst specialists and administrators. This led to the setting up of a Civil Service College for training civil servants and the introduction of greater mobility for employees between departments (The Civil Service 1968).

In the first three quarters of the twentieth century, administrative reform nevertheless remained an episodic phenomenon in Europe. Governments focused their efforts on more tangible service reforms (health, pensions, education, homes, and employment). As a result, although there had been plans for administrative reform, these did not lead to specific public administrative reform policies.

Things have changed in the last quarter of the century. First, administrative reforms acquired a place of their own, becoming an autonomous public policy assigned to members of government entrusted solely with this task. Second, administrative reforms have become a permanent public function linked to the implementation of a project conceived as a series of continuous, not episodic, interventions. Third, administrative reforms have been put at the top of the political agenda, with a powerful, ongoing commitment needed to ensure that state machinery for implementing government policies was fully effective. Fourth, administrative reform policies spread to become a common element of government action in many countries.

The main reasons for developing administrative reforms were the result of the rediscovery, affirmation, and diffusion of market forces, the enterprise and private law, and of the role of consumers. The user is no longer an *administré*, but a customer who has to be satisfied.

Thanks to the free market philosophy, administrative reforms have changed from being policies involving the public sector internally to interventions aimed at improving the efficiency and effectiveness of services for citizens and, as such, policies external to the machinery of state.

The administrative reforms launched in the last quarter of the century in many European countries have numerous characteristics in common. First, they are presented in emphatic terms to highlight their newness: '*Neue Steuerungsmodell*' in Germany since 1978; 'New Public Management' in the United Kingdom since 1979; '*Renouveau du service public*' in France since 1989; '*Modernizacion*' in Spain since 1992; and 'Re-inventing government', the apt formula employed by Osborne and Gaebler in the United States in 1992 and widely used in many European countries. Second, administrative reforms in the last quarter of the twentieth century have been just as widespread in countries with right-wing governments (as was the case in the United Kingdom in the years 1979–97) as they have in countries with left-wing governments (e.g. in France in the periods 1981–6, 1988–93, and 1997–2002) and in countries with permanent coalition governments (e.g. Germany and Italy). Third, administrative reforms have been extensively applied in countries with widely varying public administrations and also in terms of the context in which they operate. For example, the United Kingdom and France are countries with high-performance public administrations, while in Italy they are Byzantine. Fourth, the reforms experimented in European countries have nearly always been devised by the government but hardly ever contested by the opposition. This is considered to be a 'bipartisan' public policy. For example, administrative reforms were started in France by Chirac in 1986, continued by Rocard in 1988, and developed by Balladur and Juppé from 1993 to 1997. Administrative reforms have therefore been a vehicle for modernizing public administrations, regardless of the majority in government, whether performance is satisfactory or not. There is a consensus of opinion between majority and opposition on the issue.

REFORM MOTIVATIONS AND OBJECTIVES

The first motivation is the financial crisis of the state: increased activities, especially in the four sectors of education, health, social security, and promoting employment; difficulties for the Exchequer in financing these activities; resorting to increased public indebtedness; and the fear of state bankruptcy (Rose and Peters 1978). This has highlighted the need to curb the state's role in terms of management and disbursement whilst developing its role as contractor and regulator. The second important factor that has given rise to administrative reform policies is the result of dissatisfaction with the public sector's performance. It is considered to be cumbersome, intrusive, and politicized. It offers a wide range of services, but ineffectively and slowly. It imposes too many direct and indirect burdens (taxes and the time consumed by administrative formalities). The third factor: internationalization, makes it essential for national systems to come into line with those of other countries and for coordination between the various systems. Each national administration has to adapt to the developments of other administrations, under penalty of creating disadvantages for its own users.

Under the pressure of these motivations, four parallel lines of reform have been developed since 1975. First, public administrations are moving towards a European model, imposed by the European Community (and later by the European Union). It has two sides: national administrations have had to adjust to the new supranational body, while there is a quest for appropriate ways of influencing EC decisions. For about twenty years, the European Community only influenced the constitutional frameworks of States. Only since the late 1970s (and, in particular, in the 1990s) did it radically influence national administrative systems, through directives on the contracts of public administrations, public services, banks, and insurance, for example. Second, in direct contrast with the one we have just mentioned, a tendency developed to devolve former state powers to sub-state bodies. This devolution has come about in favour of regions, as well as smaller provinces and municipalities. While the first and second tendency give rise to a relocation of duties within the network of public powers, the third, on the other hand, involves the privatization of public functions to private hands. This is to a large degree a privatization of enterprises, which has been made necessary due to the difficulty encountered by states in balancing their accounts and the free market philosophy, which favours giving public authorities powers of regulation but not management.

The latest tendency is more complex and consists of a unitary but not coherent set of policies, New Public Management, and has now spread to all European countries. It embraces several elements:

(1) 'agencification', the tendency to assign to special bodies (agencies or independent authorities) duties that were previously performed by special units belonging to the state organization, which acquires the stellar organization typical of industrial groups;
(2) 'process re-engineering', the revision of procedures inside public administrations so as to simplify them and thus reduce the burden of the administration on citizens;
(3) 'value for money', introducing commercial accounting in public administrations with a view to analysing costs and keeping them under control, and increasing the productivity of public services;
(4) 'result-oriented budgeting', drawing up accounts of public administrations less geared to procedures and more to maximizing the product;
(5) 'public–private partnership', the collaboration of private organizations in managing public services in various ways or contracting out such services and assigning them in full, or alternatively enlisting the financial collaboration of private organizations;

(6) 'marketization', opening public services to competition. This can be achieved in a number of ways, but primarily by entrusting the management of public services to several operators competing with each other;

(7) 'customer orientation', identifying quality indicators and productivity standards, ensuring compliance with them and assessing the satisfaction of users of public services.

'New Public Management' has been facilitated as a result of developing these techniques, many of which have been tested in private enterprises and then, duly adapted, applied to public administrations.

ADMINISTRATIVE REFORM IN WEST EUROPE

The United Kingdom was the first country to embark upon a substantial and radical programme of reforms. Although it was late joining the European Community, it quickly adapted its public administration. This has produced two results. It is one of the countries that enforces EC directives most rapidly and effectively and that most deeply influences the shaping of EC policies. An example of both these points is the EC directives on liberalizing public services (telecommunications, rail transport, gas, electricity). After a period of centralization (1979–97), during which the financial dependence of local authorities on the centre was increased and management principles and rules were extended from the centre to the periphery, in 1998 the United Kingdom granted asymmetrical devolution to Scotland and Wales. It also pioneered and implemented, from 1979 onwards, a wide-ranging privatization programme, under which most of the public industrial sector was transferred to private ownership. Furthermore, the United Kingdom has developed New Public Management further than any other country. In 1980 it launched market testing procedures (competitive tendering and best value). In 1982 it launched the Financial Management Initiative and used private managers in public administrations. Since 1988 it has experimented with a programme of agencification, gradually setting up about one hundred 'Next Step Agencies', each one being assigned its own target, budget, and performance objectives. Since 1991, the Citizens' Charter has established standards in the provision of public services and corresponding citizens' rights.

The process of adapting French administration to the European system has involved both legislation and jurisdiction. Over half of the legislation of recent years has been to enforce EC directives. In 1989, the Council of State, in the *arrêt Nicolo*, established the supremacy of EC law. Furthermore, two important laws, in 1982 and 1992, have implemented decentralization. The first (Defferre law) transferred state functions to local authorities, elevated the regions into local authorities, eliminated state controls on local authorities, and reinforced the local executive. The second (Pasqua law) established that central administrations only have guidance functions, while responsibility for execution is vested in state field offices. It consolidated the powers of the regional prefect, and established the principles of deconcentration from Paris and subsidiarity. In addition to these laws, there is also the 1991 law on the delocalization of central offices, under which the activity of the *Ecole Nationale d'Administration* has been partly transferred to Strasbourg.

From 1986 to 1988 and from 1993 onwards, French governments implemented a wide-ranging privatization programme, but this has not as yet involved the main public services (postal services, gas, electricity, rail transport). As in the United Kingdom, numerous private management techniques have been introduced in public administrations (Massenet 1975). The basic steps introducing the new techniques have been as follows. In 1986 the Chirac government and in 1993 the Balladur government launched programmes aimed at improving the quality of public services. In 1989, the Rocard government issued a circular with a view to launching a modernization programme to be implemented by ministries and services. The aim of the plan was to improve the quality of services and place offices at the service of users. In 1992, the charter of public services was issued. Following the 1993 Prada report and the 1994 Picq report, in 1995 the Juppé government issued a circular geared to redefining state functions and improving the transparency, quality, and rapidity of public services and access to such services by citizens. However, these projected reforms have had only limited implementation.

Germany was one of the first European countries to adapt its institutions to the European Community. On the one hand, it promptly enforced EC directives (especially those on public services), thereby allowing EC law to penetrate national administrative law, while, on the other, it set up offices so that it could enhance its presence in Brussels and better coordinate national action at the EC level. At the local level, Germany already had a highly decentralized framework. In the years from 1979 to 1985, the central government focused its attention on boosting local powers and encouraging the amalgamation of smaller authorities, and in so doing changed the administrative map of local government. This has led to important consequences for other organizations, too, which have had to adjust accordingly. After the wave of privatizations in 1959–65, the German public sector was smaller than that of other European countries. In the period from 1982 to 1989, however, further privatizations were implemented. Those carried out in the car and energy sectors were particularly important, as were the local and *Länder* privatizations and those of public enterprises in Eastern Germany after unification, which proved to be a very considerable operation.

From 1978 to 1979, attempts were made to accelerate, simplify, and modernize, with the aim of remedying bureaucratic malfunctions and administrative inflexibility at the level of the *Länder* and local authorities. These were followed, in 1983, by programmes aimed at simplifying legislation and administration, with the assistance of a special committee for identifying pointless rules. These programmes led to the deregulation of the labour market in 1982 and later of postal services, telecommunications, insurance companies, transport, and power. At the local level, various functions such as the cleaning of public buildings and parks maintenance are now contracted out. Although these steps are not derived from an elaborate theoretical model, despite the use of terms like *Neue Steuerungsmodell*, and in spite of the fact that they are less visible, as they operate mainly at local and *Länder* level, all these interventions have provided a substantial contribution towards administrative reforms.

After being admitted in 1985, Spain has speedily adapted its structures to the EU system. The regional decentralization contemplated by the 1978 Constitution, which envisaged self-governing communities, has moved on with the approval of their statutes in 1981–3, the passing of the 1981 and 1985 laws on local powers, and the 'local pact' in 1997 which has increased the responsibilities of local authorities. The privatization process, which was launched during the eleven years from 1985 to 1996, was further extended subsequently. Reforms of the state machinery commenced in 1990 with the 'Reflections on the modernization of State Administration' followed by the drafting, in 1992, of the 'State Administration Modernization Plan', which contains 204 projects. These developments were the result of the institution in 1986 of a special Ministry for Public Administration. This was followed in 1992 by the law on public administrations and administrative procedure, the law on the organization and functioning of the general administration of the state in 1997, and a new law on public administration and administrative procedure in 1999. These projects and laws alternate structural and substantive reforms which are all directed towards making administrative organization and functioning flexible and guaranteeing greater protection to private citizens.

In Italy, the Europeanization process has been a discontinuous one. Ministerial staffs have never managed to coordinate public intervention in the European context, in spite of the appointment of a minister without portfolio for EC affairs. The enforcement of EC directives is also a slow-moving process but there have been sudden accelerations, such as those concerning access by foreigners to public offices (1994), tenders for selecting public contractors (1995 and 1999–2000), and the liberalization of telecommunications (1997). Decentralization, which was started in 1970–2, when regional authorities were set up and state functions were transferred, continued in 1977 with the second decentralization and in 1998 with the third decentralization (yet to be implemented). The privatization process, which was made easier by the type of organization existing in the Italian public industrial sector (organized mainly in the form of private companies with state participation), got off to a late start (1993) compared to other countries, but went on to produce significant results which were even better than those achieved in many other European countries, especially after 1996–7.

Administrative reform, which was launched in 1979–80 (with the Giannini Report), remained inoperative until 1990 when a law on administrative procedure was approved and some of the most important administrative independent authorities were set up. The year 1992 marked the introduction of contractual bargaining in respect of employment by public administrations. This was followed in 1993 by a 'Report on the conditions of public administrations' and 'Policies for modernizing public administrations', which were implemented by re-organizing a number of ministries, introducing a system of controls and simplifying one hundred procedures (1994). In 1997–9 further attempts at reform were introduced in order to reduce the number of ministries (which are nevertheless increasing in size) and efforts to simplify procedures continue.

COMPARATIVE CONTRASTS IN ADMINISTRATIVE REFORM

The common tendencies we have identified are, however, being implemented in different ways, according to different starting-points and frameworks, 'policy-mixes', methods of preparation and implementation, start-dates and time-spans, and the diversity of dimensions. Let us start with differences in starting-points and frameworks. Although the Europeanization process is based on similar requirements in all countries, the driving force at the root of reforms is quite different. First, reforms have been promoted in countries like the United Kingdom, France, and Germany where efficient public administrations already existed, as well as in countries like Spain and Italy where the efficiency of public administrations was not up to standard. Second, decentralization has occurred in different contexts. Some countries, like France, Spain, Italy, and the United Kingdom, start with a centralized state structure, while in other countries, like Germany, the process is applied in an already decentralized structure. Third, the significance of privatizations vary as there are some countries that had an extended public sector, like the United Kingdom and Italy, and others with a limited public sector, like Germany. Finally, reforms directed towards modernizing management have different characteristics in countries where a distinction between public and private law exists and in countries where this is less marked or non-existent. In the former, problems arise when it comes to introducing managerial techniques in public administrations, which by tradition are governed by public law.

A second element of differentiation stems from two factors, which both involve the policy-mix: the variable importance attributed to the components of administrative reform programmes and the ways in which administrative reforms are linked to other reforms. So, as far as the first aspect is concerned, four different configurations of reform policies can be identified. In the United Kingdom, reforms focus mainly and essentially on privatizations and New Public Management; Europeanization is a secondary issue and decentralization has come late and is partial. In France, on the other hand, reforms are conducted with less urgency, with decentralization and the modernization of the public service taking priority. Germany and Spain are pursuing ambitious objectives on the basis of numerous, albeit modest, initiatives. But in both cases, important events have provided the backdrop, with the transition to the new constitutional regime in Spain and unification in Germany, developments for which administrative reform policies are very relevant. Finally, in Italy stress has been laid on ministerial reform, simplification, and achievements produced indirectly as a result of privatizations.

Administrative reforms are hardly ever promoted on their own but there are significant differences in the way they have been combined with other reforms. In the United Kingdom, for example, the process of administrative reform is closely linked to liberalization policies. In Italy, on the other hand, for most of the period considered, it is correlated with the need to re-organize public finances, and this also applies partly in Spain.

A third difference is the way in which reforms are prepared and implemented. First of all, in some cases the impulse is mainly external (the case in Italy, where the main driving force is the government), whereas in others it comes from within (the case in Germany and France, where bureaucracies play an important role). Furthermore, the venue and methods of elaboration vary from country to country. In France, due to its traditional administrative culture, reforms are elaborated primarily within the administrative corps. At the other end of the scale we find the United Kingdom, where private consultants play an important role, and Italy, where an important role is played by legal culture outside the administration. Another important difference concerns the institutions entrusted with elaboration of reforms within the administration, which were once either the Treasury Ministry or ministries set up ad hoc. But over the past few years, there has been an increasing tendency to assign the arduous task of administrative reform either to prime ministers or to public service ministers.

Implementation depends on the role of the three main motive forces: the bureaucracy, the trades unions, and the users. The role of bureaucracy is not neutral and is decisive. Sometimes it adopts a receptive or adaptive approach towards reform projects. This applies in the United Kingdom, where, thanks to a deference towards political power and the modernizing senior civil service, reform objectives and projects have been internalized. In Italy, by contrast, an inadequate bureaucracy either hinders the reforms or tries to steer them in its own favour. In the case of the trades unions, whereas in the United Kingdom administrative reforms were adopted against the opposition of the trades unions, in Italy reforms are often promoted by the trades unions with a view to gaining joint decision-making powers in public administrations. Users play a lesser role. Although everywhere reforms proclaim the purpose of putting customers first, users are for the most part absent from the reform process.

A fourth difference derives from the starting date and duration of the reforms. There is a clear difference between the United Kingdom, where reforms began in 1987 with the Thatcher Government (even though decentralization only came about in 1998 with the Blair Government) and France and Germany, where the first important reforms started about ten years later and other countries, where reforms began in the 1990s. Furthermore, in the United Kingdom, there has been a continuous and constant commitment during the last twenty years of the century. In Italy, on the other hand, major projects have been proposed and widely publicized. They have given rise to great expectations but due to the modest results achieved they have quickly generated disillusion from public opinion and the section of the civil service most affected by the reforms.

Finally, there is a contrast between British radicalism and the 'macro' approach aimed at redesigning the state and the Spanish micro-reforms which have led to a gradual, step-by-step change. On the one hand, we have the centralized method selected in the United Kingdom and Italy, while, on the other, we have the decentralized method chosen by Rocard in France in 1989, which is based on the capacity of departments to innovate from within. Laws are used, especially in Italy and Spain, while in other countries, especially in the United Kingdom and France, administrative circulars are utilized.

CONCLUSIONS

Public administration and administrative law start by acknowledging basic and original differences between administrative systems and then go on to indicate the convergence brought about by factors such as the European Community or policy emulation. Experience suggests reversing this model. This would mean recognizing that, under the pressure of the same problems, similar solutions are chosen. But once adopted these solutions fit into different frameworks. They are selected and elaborated by different political actors and are implemented at different times, which means that differences arise at a later date and are juxtaposed with the uniformity of policies. This is not, therefore, a case of separate and different systems converging, but, on the contrary, a case of similar policies, which on implementation acquire a different connotation and produce different results.

Administrative reform programmes have been defined as 'festivals of visions' and 'marketing devices'. There have often been complaints of 'reform euphoria', which give rise to grand announcements but end up in disaster when it comes to implementation (Jann 1997). 'Most administrative reforms disappoint. They start off with much fanfare and promise so much (too much, of course) that they are bound to disappoint when the realities set in' (Caiden 1999). As Brunsson and Olsen (1993) have argued, organizations are creatures of their institutional framework. Reforms are brought about by external expectations and are difficult to implement because they are remote from the complex realities.

The reforms undertaken in European countries in the last quarter of the twentieth century provide examples of successes and failures, genuine achievements, and ineffectual rhetoric. They have adapted public administrations to the new European system. They have transferred more power to the periphery. They have transferred a conspicuous part of the public industrial sector to private hands. They have reduced the dimensions of the public sector, which has slowed its growth in all European countries. They have re-organized central structures, which are today less like a pyramid and more like a stellar organization. They have introduced private sector principles and methods into public administrations, accustoming them to evaluation according to performance indicators and inducing them to pay more attention to the voice of users.

Not all the changes announced have been realized and even those achieved have not been realized exactly as announced. However, even the unimplemented reforms have had results, as they have at least played an educational role, teaching the value of change. Nevertheless, the results of the change should not be overestimated. These have often been the consequence of simplifications based on the belief that the public sector and the private sector can be managed the same way. As Vincent Wright put it: 'While it is highly laudable to make government more business-like, it is highly problematic to make it more like business. The public sector has always had to juggle with many conflicting sets of values, including democracy (hence accountability), equity (involving uniformity), and efficiency (minimizing costs). Too much current radical reform of the public sector is obsessed with efficiency, narrowly defined, and is based on a simplistic view of bureaucracy, a naïve view of the market, an idealized view of the private sector, an insensitivity to the hidden cause of reform, an over-optimism about outcomes, and perhaps more fundamentally, a misleading view of the state' (Wright 1998a: 137). It is an illusion to believe that it is possible to reduce the dimensions of the state, which, even though it has abandoned the management of many enterprises, has acquired new and broader powers of regulation (Cassese and Wright 1996).

9

The European Administration: Between Europeanization and Domestication

HUSSEIN KASSIM

'There is a broad consensus that public administrations are as much a "product"' as a "characteristic feature" of what we call the "state". In all phases of the state's formation, the change in its characteristics are closely linked with respective developments of public administration.'

(Wessels 1990: 229)

The above statement has an important resonance in the case of the European Union. The European administration, comprising European and national elements, has made a substantial contribution to the development of the Union, but also reflects, and has reinforced, its peculiarities. As a political system (Hix 1998, 1999)—it is not yet, and may never become, a state—the Union is characterized by the complex inter-meshing and interpenetration of the European and the national (Laffan *et al.* 2000: 74; Kassim and Wright 1991). On the one hand, European level institutions and structures have been penetrated by national officials, who are present at all levels of decision making and in all areas, and dependent, in the absence of dedicated front-line services in the member states, on national administrations for the implementation of EU policy. On the other, national administrations are both active *subjects* of the EU policy process, as participants, and *objects*, as national actors affected by the outcomes of that process.

This chapter examines the structure of the EU's administrative system. It puts forward three general arguments: that the development of the EU's administration has been conditioned by the nature of the European Union as a political system, but that the EU administration has similarly had an impact on the European Union as a political system; that the entrenchment of national administrations in the EU bureaucratic system has had important consequences for its functioning and operation; and that national administrations have been affected, but not transformed, by the development of the European Union. After outlining the features that characterize the Union's political system, the chapter examines how national administrations have penetrated EU decision-making structures and institutions, and looks at the impact of this process at the European level. It then considers how national administrations have been affected by the development of the European Union. Finally, the chapter provides an assessment of the EU's administrative capacity.

THE EUROPEAN UNION AS A POLITICAL SYSTEM

In all advanced industrialized states, the administration both influences, and is influenced by, the broader features of the political system. The European administration is no exception. What is unique, however, is the nature of the political system in which it is implanted. Five characteristics of the European Union as a political system are especially relevant. The first, and perhaps the most fundamental, is the lack of an agreed demarcation of competencies and powers between the European Union and the member states. The EU government is collective—'the national and the European are no longer *separate*' (Bulmer and Wessels 1987: 10, cited in Laffan *et al.* 2000: 74)—but there has been no authoritative division of responsibilities between the two levels.

The second is its fluidity. The European Union has been described as 'fluid, ambiguous, and hybrid' (Olsen 1997: 165; see also Wright 1996*b*). Since 'there is no shared vision or project, or common understanding of the legitimate basis of a future Europe' (Olsen, *ibid*), the Union 'is always in the process of *becoming*—its constitution, institutions, and policy remit have not yet reached, and may never reach, a stable equilibrium' (Laffan *et al.* 2000: 73). Its membership, its rules, the relationships between, and authority of, its institutions are constantly evolving (Wright 1996*b*; Olsen 1997), and its competencies and functions ever-changing. Moreover, the European Union is 'not based on a single treaty, a unitary structure, or a single dominating centre of authority and power. Rather, the Union is built on several treaties and a complex three-pillar structure ... [where] the pillars are organized on different principles and supranational/intergovernmental mixes' (Olsen, *ibid.*). The official description of the European Union as a unified system—three pillars within a single institutional framework—is misleading in view of the differential allocation of decision-making power to the institutions, the differences in structure, and the procedures that apply in each pillar.

Institutional fragmentation is a third feature. Power at the European level is shared between a multiplicity of institutions, and there is no single authoritative legislator (Scharpf 1994, 1999). Legislative power is shared by two institutions—the Council and the European Parliament—that form 'a classic two-chamber legislature' (Hix 1999: 56), and executive authority is spread between the member states (individually and collectively) and the Commission.[1] Each institution is internally differentiated,

---

[1] According to Hix, where executive power has two elements: '*political*, the leadership of society through the proposal of policy and legislation; and *administrative*, the implementation of law, the distribution of public revenues, and the passing of secondary and tertiary rules and regulations' (1999: 21). The member states' executive responsibilities involve setting the long-term policy goals of the EU (Council), setting the medium-term policy agenda (European Council), implementing EU legislation through their own bureaucracies, and managing the day to day administration of EU policies with the Commission through comitology (Hix 1999: 25); the Commission' responsibilities include developing medium-term strategies for the development of the European Union, drafting legislation and arbitrating in the legislature process, making rules and regulations, managing the EU budget, and scrutinizing the implementation of the Treaty of secondary legislation (Hix 1999: 32).

and has its own methods, procedures, and culture, exercises varying degrees of power, and commands different resources. Lines of division within the Commission, for example, run between the political level—the College of Commissioners and their *cabinets*—and the administrative level—the services, which in 1999 numbered twenty-four Directorates-General, each with its own responsibilities and identity (Abélès *et al.* 1993). The Council of the European Union is also an extremely complex body. Its tripartite structure—working groups, COREPER, and ministerial meetings— is differentiated along sectoral lines, the various bodies operate according to differing norms (Lewis 1999) and, with the decline of the General Affairs Council as a co-ordinator (Gomez and Peterson 2001), there is a strong tendency towards fragmentation. Both the Commission (Metcalfe 2000) and the Council (European Council 1999; Gomez and Peterson 2001), moreover, suffer from weak horizontal coordination. Finally, the work of the European Parliament is carried out in seventeen committees. Its policy position, not to mention its organization and procedures, must be agreed by several party groups that threaten continuously to fragment along national lines.

A fourth characteristic is the complexity of the EU policy process. Although the European Commission has a formal monopoly over the initiation of legislation, items on the EU's policy agenda come from a variety of sources, there are a number of influential policy advocates and the policy menu is long, constantly changing, and more varied than at the national level (Peters 1994). Decision making involves a multiplicity of actors, including, besides the fifteen member governments, the EU institutions and other European bodies and agencies, representatives of regional and local authorities, and a host of lobbyists of varying size and importance (Mazey and Richardson 1993*a*; Pedlar and Van Schendelen 1994; Greenwood 1997; Greenwood and Aspinwall 1998). Each is at once an actor with its own interests, an institution with its own rules, code of conduct and operating style, and an arena in which individuals, groups, and associations compete for influence. Decisions are rarely the result of action on the part of a single actor or institution. Interested parties must search for allies and create coalitions, despite the precariousness of the exercise: 'alliance-building is unpredictable and time-consuming . . . [and] the cleavages which shape the coalitions are often cross-cutting' (Wright 1996*b*: 152). Moreover, legislative procedures are long and complex and, combined with the different decision rules that apply to the Council in different policy sectors and sub-sectors, present those involved with a bewildering array of formal processes.[2] Each distributes the power between institutions in a different way, creating variations in the inter-institutional balance according to which procedure is used (Garrett 1995*b*; Scully 1997), encouraging different strategies and imposing different 'bargaining requirements' (Pollack 1994), and privileging certain outcomes over others (Tsebelis 1990). The most intricate of these procedures—co-decision—retains its complexity even after the simplifications introduced at the Amsterdam IGC and has been extended to a wider range of policies (Falkner and Nentwich 2000).

---

[2] The Commission in its review of the operation of the Treaty of the European Union uncovered twenty-four combinations (CEC 1995).

Sectoralization is the fifth feature of the European Union (Mazey and Richardson 1993a; Menon and Hayward 1996). Although a feature of domestic policy making, 'the extent and nature of these problems in Brussels is of a different order' (Wright 1996b: 130). A broad distinction can be drawn between polity issues—constitutional matters such as treaty negotiations, institutional reform, and enlargement, which involve heads of state and government, and foreign ministers—and routine policy (Derlien 2000; Maurer and Wessels 2001). The latter includes at least three policy types—regulatory, redistributive, and distributive policy (Lowi 1964)—each with a specific logic and conflict potential. Beyond these general categories, there are differences concerning the extent of EU competence and authority in any particular area. As Laffan *et al.* observe, 'the Union has extensive regulatory powers in relation to the movement of the factors of production but weak instruments of macroeconomic management. In the social policy domain, there is a consensus about collective action in the area of health and safety, but deep division about redistributive policies' (2000: 88). Sectors and sub-sectors are further differentiated in terms of how responsibility is shared between EU institutions, which decision rules and legislative procedures apply, and the number and type of actors that are involved.

These features of the EU's political system have to a large extent shaped the European administration. However, the permanent involvement and pervasive presence of national administrations in EU decision making has also profoundly influenced its development and help to explain its unique character. The European administration is a curious hybrid, the outcome of continuous interaction between the supranational and the national.

NATIONAL ADMINISTRATIONS IN EU DECISION MAKING[3]

National administrations are omnipresent at the European level. They are important participants at all levels of decision making, and involved at all stages of the policy cycle. Their most obvious institutional presence at the European level is in the form of the permanent representations (Kassim *et al.* 2001). These Brussels-based missions, headed by the permanent representative and his or her deputy—the former of ambassadorial rank—and composed of seconded national officials, perform a number of important front-line functions. At a minimum, they act as a post box for official correspondence with other policy actors, provide a formal point of contact with EU institutions and other governments, are a base for national negotiators, and relay the information they collect in Brussels to interested parties at home. Some permanent representations are entrusted with additional 'upstream' and 'downstream' responsibilities. These include: providing the main negotiators at working group level (Spence 1995), sensitizing EU institutions to national policy stances (Wright 1996b), interacting directly with representations of other member states (Spence 1995), attempting to influence the EU policy agenda (Wright 1996b),

---

[3] This Section draws from, and updates, some of the arguments made in Kassim and Wright (1991).

conducting negotiations in Council working groups, maintaining contact with private interests, maintaining links with the press (Spence 1995), advising the capital, and participating in domestic coordination (Wallace 1973: 57).

National officials are key participants in the Council of European Ministers—the main legislative institution of the Community and the primary venue for the defence of member state interests, particularly in Council working groups, the broad base of the Council's pyramidal structure, where Commission proposals are first debated (Hayes-Renshaw and Wallace 1997; Westlake 1995). Governments are represented by delegations that are composed of officials from the permanent representation or civil servants from the national capitals. The number of working groups—about three hundred (Secretariat General of the Council 1997)—and the frequency with which they meet have increased substantially since the mid-1980s (see Table 9.1). When a working group has completed its deliberations on a file, the dossier passes up the line to the Committee of Permanent Representatives (COREPER). Member states are represented in this key body by the permanent representative or deputy permanent representative. COREPER plays a crucial role in the Council machinery, providing the filter through which all business must pass before discussion by ministers (Barber 1995; de Zwann 1996). Its task is to resolve, where possible, outstanding political issues in order to minimize ministerial workloads. COREPER also connects the European Union directly to the administrations of the member states. Its members occupy a unique position, providing a gateway between the European Union and their respective national administrations, and acting as senior policy makers at both European and national levels.

National influence also extends to the Commission. Although nominally independent—its autonomy ensured by the oath taken by Commissioners and by the creation of a permanent administration whose officials are recruited by merit—the Commission has never been free of member state interference. First, there has long been an implicit and unwritten rule that sanctions national quotas in senior posts. This 'geographical balance' has been jealously protected by the member states, typically by 'their' Commissioner and his or her *cabinet*, who have actively sought to ensure the right number of national flags are placed in senior positions. Although this practice was formally brought to an end by the Prodi Commission as part of the reform process initiated since 1999, it remains to be seen whether governments will be prepared to give up guarantees of a national presence in top positions. Second, national administrations have traditionally laid claim to key positions in areas that are salient domestically, creating *chasses gardées à la française*. In the College, for example, France has often held the development portfolio and, more recently in the transition to monetary union, economic and monetary affairs. Spaniards have been responsible for relations with Latin America, and British Commissioners for competition and external relations. At the level of the services, the DG for competition has often been headed by German, the DG for agriculture by a Frenchman, and the internal market DG by a British official. Here, again, the Prodi Commission has taken action to bring this tradition to an end. Third, national governments may block the appointment of their own members of the Commission, whom they consider have

Table 9.1   *Number of meetings of the council of the European Union*

	Council	COREPER	Working groups
1958	21	39	302
1959	21	71	325
1960	44	97	505
1961	46	108	655
1962	80	128	783
1963	63.5	146.5	744.5
1964	102.5	229.5	1002.5
1965	35	105.5	760.5
1966	70.5	112.5	952.5
1967	75.5	134	1233
1968	61	132	1253
1969	69	129	1412.5
1970	81	154	1403
1971	75.5	127.5	1439
1972	73	159	2135
1973	79.5	148	1820
1974	66	114.5	1999.5
1975	67.5	118	2079.5
1976	65.5	108.5	2130
1977	71	122	2108.5
1978	76.5	104.5	2090
1979	59	107.5	2000
1980	83	106.5	2078.5
1981	83	110	1976
1982	86	107	1885
1983	121.5	105.5	1912.5
1984	133	86	1868.5
1985	118	117	1892
1986	107	118.5	1842.5
1987	123	120.5	1828
1988	177.5	104	2000.5
1989	119.5	100	1932
1990	138	107	2021.5
1991	115.5	145.5	2239
1992	126	133.5	2147
1993	119	115.5	1105.5
1994	98	127	2662
1995	98	112	2364.5
1996	106	100	2596

Source: General Secretariat of the Council of the European Union (1999) *Review of the Council's Work in 1996*, Luxembourg: Office of Publications of the European Communities.

'gone native'. Lord Cockfield, the UK Commissioner for the Internal Market, whose reappointment was blocked by the then Prime Minister, reputedly for his excessive zeal for this European project, is perhaps the best-known example. Fourth, some national administrations—for example, France and the United Kingdom—endeavour to ensure that they are represented in strategic positions in the services by monitoring vacancies for detached national experts and proposing suitably qualified candidates. More generally, governments actively support the practice of *parachutage*—parachuting nationals, who have been seconded from the home civil service to a *cabinet* position, posts that are formally the preserve of Commission officials (Stevens and Stevens 2001).

As well as establishing a presence within the Commission, some member states attempt to mobilize networks of nationals within the institution. Whilst taking action to influence the Commission is regarded as taboo by some national administrations, who regard the institution's independence as sancrosanct, others have no qualms about using 'their' Commissioner and his or her *cabinet* as a source of information about the progress of particular dossiers or personnel issues, or to exercise leverage within the College. The use of *cabinets* as a channel for national interests has attracted considerable comment. In 1979, for example, the Spierenburg Report criticized the member states for encroaching on the prerogatives of the Commission officials by attempting to advance their interests in this way. More recently, the *cabinets* have been described as 'mini-Councils within the Commission' (senior official, quoted by Peterson and Bomberg 1999: 39), demonstrating that member states continue to regard them as national advocates. It remains uncertain whether efforts by the Prodi Commission to make the *cabinets* more multinational will prevent them from serving as conduits for national capitals. At the level of the services, a number of member states try to maintain close relations with their nationals. The British and the French permanent representations, for example, both offer career advice and support, and organize social events. They remain ready to explain the government position on any particular issue or dossier.

National administrations also act as lobbyists of the Commission (Spence 1993). Working through their permanent representations, member states attempt systematically to cultivate relations with administrators in the services. Through these contacts, national officials hope to discover when policy initiatives are to be launched. When activity is detected, the Brussels-based officials alert ministries in the capital, so that a national position can be defined and communicated rapidly to the relevant unit in the Commission. The United Kingdom, in particular, aims to intervene early in the decision-making process in the knowledge that about eighty per cent of an original proposal is likely to remain in the text that is finally adopted by the Council (Hull 1993).

The efforts of national administrations to influence policy are not restricted to the Commission. The European Parliament has been increasingly targeted since the introduction of the co-decision procedure. Some member states, including France, the United Kingdom, Ireland, and the Netherlands, have designated liaison officers in their permanent representations, who are expected to maintain contact with MEPs, ensure that government concerns are communicated, and monitor the progress of dossiers, though, of course, other officials are free to establish their own links. In the UK case, contacts made by UKREP are supplemented by briefings from Whitehall that are sent to MEPs on all legislative proposals before the EP, the detail of which depends upon the importance of the issue to the United Kingdom, as well as by specific briefs sent to members on particular committees. Others, such as Germany's Permanent Representation, require all desk officers to liase with MEPs. Whichever approach is taken, officials at the permanent representation are likely to make contact with their own nationals in the first instance, particularly MEPs from the governing party or coalition, or officials holding positions in the Parliament administration. Nationals in influential positions—committee chairs or *rapporteurs*—are especially likely to be targeted. Some member states—the United Kingdom and the Netherlands among them—spread their net beyond these 'natural assets', and appeal to like-minded MEPs from other states. A third group that includes Greece and Sweden regards contact with the EP as a low priority.

The proliferation of committees at the European level has extended the penetration of EU decision making by national administrations. EU government is government by committee, and as Wright (1996*b*: 151–2) has noted, '[t]hese committees are largely responsible for the mass of micro-level sectoral decisions . . . and . . . are interwoven with a set of overlapping bargaining networks'. The multiplication of committees by both Commission and Council has ensured the involvement of national administrations at all stages of the policy cycle (Buitendijk and Van Schendelen 1995; Van Schendelen 1996, 1999; Dogan 1997). For example, national officials are important actors in the consultative committees whose opinions are solicited by the Commission in the pre-proposal phase. These committees—some of which are standing, some ad hoc; some composed entirely of civil servants, others that are hybrid in nature—enable national governments to monitor and influence policy formulation at this crucial phase. National officials also participate in the comitology committees that control, with varying degrees of authority, the exercise by the Commission of its executive powers in areas of EU activity (Pedlar and Schaefer 1996; Dogan 1997). These committees are of three basic types: advisory committees, which must be consulted by the Commission, but whose opinion is not binding; management committees, which can postpone or remit a matter to the Council for decision if there is a qualified majority against the Commission; and regulatory committees, where the Commission requires a qualified majority in order to adopt a measure.

National administrations are extensively involved in the implementation of EU policy, where they play a crucial role. The Commission was given overall responsibility for implementation by the treaty, but, with no field services of its own, it is 'agencies in the member states [that] undertake most of the front-line implementation of EU policies' (Nugent 2001: 276). National administrations are charged with the task of putting Community policies into practice on the ground. Thus, 'customs authorities collect duties on goods entering the European Union from third countries; national agricultural officials deal with farmers and traders on matters such as milk quotas, the quality of foodstuffs, and payments for produce and set-aside; and [officials at national, regional or local level] . . . consider applications for financial assistance from the Structural Funds (Nugent 2001: 276).

In extending its scope of action and intensifying its activities, the Union has become increasingly dependent on collaboration with national actors, administrations, and agencies. This collaboration takes place in a number of forums and across different levels, and in and between different areas of the decision making process. This has enabled national administrations to develop webs of influence across the Community systems. These nationally organized unofficial networks take a variety of forms. They may operate within the Commission and within the Council, between the Commission and the Council, within and between sectors and sub-sectors, and across different stages of the policy cycle. Member states attempt to locate nationals at strategic points along policy pathways, and mobilize networks to short-circuit or reduce the complexity of the EU process.

The above survey of Community institutions and structures demonstrates that the European Union system is 'shot through with national officials and influences' (Kassim and Wright 1991: 835). How can the spread of national influence, which is far more extensive than the founders intended, be explained? At least three reasons can be identified. The first is the assertiveness shown by the member states in the mid-1960s, which was a formative period for the European Communities. Although the status of the Luxembourg Compromise on national government vetoes and its precise impact remains contested, there is general agreement that it had the consequence of extending national influence and enabling the more reluctant member states to slow down the pace of integration. The transition from unanimity to qualified majority voting in the Council that had been anticipated in the Treaties was effectively postponed. As Garrett and Tsebelis (1996) have demonstrated, the effect was to promote lowest common denominator agreements by strengthening the position of the government that was most sceptical about the development of Community competencies and weakening the agenda-setting power of the Commission. Although the unanimity requirement has largely disappeared—the Single European Act began a process by which qualified majority voting was extended to a greater number of policy areas and, as importantly, the taboo on adopting a decision, despite opposition on the part of a minority of member states—the Council has retained its collegial ethos. Numerous writers on the Council have described the shared norms and collective identity that have developed in Council forums as a result of repeated interaction and serial exchange (Wallace 1990), and are internalized by national officials negotiating at the European level (Sasse *et al.* 1977; Edwards 1996). Thus Fiona Hayes-Renshaw and Helen Wallace, observe that: 'decision-makers in the Council...become locked into the collective process...this does not mean that the participants have transferred loyalties to the EU system, but it does mean that they acknowledge themselves in certain crucial ways as being part of a collective system of decision-making' (cited in Lewis 1999: 10). COREPER, in particular, has developed a strong collective identity and ethos (Lewis 1998, 1999).[4]

Also in the 1960s, the institutional balance of the Communities began to tilt in favour of the member states. The Council became a more powerful body than was

---

[4] See Wallace (1973), de Zwann (1995), Barber (1995), Edwards (1996), and especially Lewis (1998, 1999).

envisaged in the Treaties, with an increasingly large and elaborate structure. The number of ministerial formations grew, as more business in a wider range of policy areas came to be transacted (see Table 9.2), placing greater demand on Council support structures. COREPER was divided into two bodies—COREPER I (deputy ambassadors), which manages the technical Councils,[5] and COREPER II, the senior body, whose remit includes institutional matters and the preparation of the General Affairs, ECOFIN, Development, Justice and Home Affairs, and Budget Council meetings—and a Special Committee on Agriculture was established, while working groups multiplied and spent more time in session. The Commission found itself confronting a formidably large and complex apparatus that commanded considerable resources. In addition, the rise of summitry from the late 1960s and the institutionalization of the European Council in the 1970s, strengthened the power of the member states. The political leadership role originally entrusted to the Commission was increasingly usurped by the heads of state and government.

A second reason for the increased presence of national administrations, particularly since the 1991 Maastricht IGC, is that the extension of Community competencies into sensitive and delicate areas has been gained only at the expense of greater intergovernmentalism. Learning from the experience of the 1992 project, the member states have become increasingly concerned about the way in which supranational bodies, particularly the Commission, have exploited opportunities to enlarge their powers and extended the range of Community activities. As a consequence, they have exercised greater caution when deciding treaty amendments, limiting the role of the Commission, the Court, and the Parliament, and designing procedures that entrench their own power (Kassim and Menon, 2003). This has been evident in the area of Economic and Monetary Union, where the Commission played a crucial part in initiating the project, but where the member states created structures that entrenched their primacy. The second and third pillars, covering, respectively, the Common Foreign and Security Policy, and Justice and Home Affairs, offer a further example. These new areas of common action were added by the Treaty of Union to the existing Community, which became the first pillar in the newly created European Union, but at the price of domination by the member states. Decision-making power is reserved to the European Council and the Council of Ministers, acting unanimously. The Commission has been largely peripheralized, and the European Court of Justice excluded, at least until the Amsterdam Treaty became effective in 1998. Reflecting a concern to prevent creeping communitarianization, the member states attempted to insulate the new pillars from Community structures, by bringing existing intergovernmental bodies at the official level within the broader framework of the Union. This further complicated the organization of the Council and, despite the rationalization introduced at Amsterdam, the structures remain cumbersome (Monar 2000).

---

[5] These now include: Internal Market, Energy, Research, Industry, Telelcommunications, Fisheries, Transport, Environment, Consumers, Labour and Social Affairs, Health, Education, Culture, Tourism, and Agriculture (veterinary and plant-health questions).

Table 9.2 Development of council formations

	1974	1975	1976	1977	1978	1979	1980	1981	1982	1983	1984	1985	1986	1987	1988	1989	1990	1991	1992	1993	1994	1995
Agriculture	14	15	13	12	13	12	14	11	15	14	16	14	11	16	12	12	16	13	13	12	11	10
External relations/General affairs (since 1988)[a]	13	16	14	15	15	12	13	12	13	12	20	14	11	12	12	14	13	13	15	20	14	14
Economic and financial	7	8	7	12	10	6	2	3	3	3	2	3	3	2	2	2	10	13	11	11	11	9
Development cooperation	5	3	—	3	2	1	1	3	2	2	2	2	2	3	2	2	4	3	2	2	2	2
Education	1	1	1	—	—	—	1	1	1	1	1	1	—	1	2	3	2	1	2	2	2	2
Energy	1	—	—	4	3	6	2	3	3	3	2	3	3	2	2	2	3	3	2	3	2	2
Environment	1	—	1	2	2	3	2	2	2	4	3	3	3	4	3	5	5	5	4	6	5[b]	—
Justice/JHA	—	—	—	—	—	—	—	—	—	—	—	—	—	—	—	1	—	1	3	4[c]	4	4
Taxation	—	1	2	1	—	1	1	2	—	—	—	—	—	—	—	—	—	2	—	—	—	—
Research	—	—	1	2	2	2	—	1	3	—	4	2	4	3	4	5	4	2	3	4	4	3
Transport	—	—	3	3	2	2	2	2	2	4	4	3	4	4	4	4	4	6	4	5	5[d]	4
Budget	—	—	3	3	4	4	3	2	4	4	4	5	5	6	4	2	2	2	2	2	2	2
Fisheries	—	—	5	5	7	4	7	8	7	9	5	3	5	3	5	4	3	4	5	5	5	4
Public health/Health	—	—	1	1	1	—	—	—	—	—	—	—	1	—	2	2	2	2	2	2	2	4
Post and telecom's[e]	—	1	1	1	1	—	—	—	—	—	—	—	—	1	1	3	2	2	3	3	3[f]	2
Social affairs[g]	—	—	—	—	2	2	2	2	4	6[i]	2	6[j]	2	2	2	5	3	3	3	4	4	4
Industry and iron and steel	—	—	—	—	—	—	4[h]	—	—	—	—	—	—	—	—	—	—	—	—	—	—	—
Industry	—	—	—	—	—	—	—	—	2	1	—	—	6	5	2	4	4	2	2	5	5[k]	3
Internal market	—	—	—	—	—	—	—	—	—	6	2	5[l]	8	6	8	10[m]	7	5	7	6	3	3
Consumer affairs	—	—	—	—	—	—	—	—	—	1	—	1	2	3	1[n]	2	2	1	2	2	2	2
Cultural affairs	—	—	—	—	—	—	—	—	—	—	2	2	1	—	1	1	2	2	—	2	2	3

Table 9.2 Continued

	1974	1975	1976	1977	1978	1979	1980	1981	1982	1983	1984	1985	1986	1987	1988	1989	1990	1991	1992	1993	1994	1995
Civil protection	—	—	—	—	—	—	—	—	—	—	—	—	—	—	1	—	1	—	—	—	—	1
Tourism	—	—	1	—	—	1	—	1	—	1	—	—	—	2	1	—	1	—	1	—	—	—
Other	3	2	1	—	1	1	3	1	3	1	—	—	2	2	2	—	1	—	—	1	4	1
	44	57	53	61	63	56	60	63	63	83	84	73	79	80	77	89	90	83	87	94	92	76

Notes:
[a] Includes General affairs and Political cooperation, and Foreign affairs (1984).
[b] Includes 1 joint with Transport.
[c] Justice and Home affairs, and 3 Immigration.
[d] Includes 1 joint with Environment.
[e] Telecommunications from 1988.
[f] Includes 1 joint Industry and Telecommunications.
[g] Includes Labour and Social affairs.
[h] Iron and Steel only.
[i] Iron and Steel only.
[j] Include Telecommunications.
[k] Includes 1 joint with Telecommunications.
[l] Internal market and consumer protection.
[m] Includes 1 joint with consumer protection.
[n] Joint with Internal market.

Source: General Secretariat of the Council of the European Union (various issues), *Review of the Council's Work in 19..* (Luxembourg: Office for Publications of the European Communities).

The role of the member states has also been enhanced by the Commission's structural weaknesses—a third reason. The treaties entrusted the Commission with a number of important functions, including policy initiation, policy implementation, the executive of policy, and policy enforcement. In all areas, however, the Commission depends on other institutions or actors to carry out its responsibilities. Moreover, although there has been a dramatic increase in the number, complexity, and difficulty of its tasks, there has been no commensurate rise in its personnel resources. It remains comparable in size to a small national ministry in France (Kassim and Wright 1991: 837) or municipal authorities in Madrid or Amsterdam (Hay 1989; Laffan *et al.* 2001: 80), employing a staff of approximately 16,000 officials, of which about a fifth are linguists.[6] The mismatch between functions and administrative resources has produced serious task overload (CEC 2000*a*; Metcalfe 2000). Commission dependence on the member states is evident in every phase of the policy cycle. Since only a handful of officials in the Commission have responsibility for complex areas of Community policy across the entire Union, the Commission relies to a large extent on national officials to provide technical expertise and support. As well as the consultative committees mentioned above, Commission officials may make use of their personal contacts in the national administrations in developing policy initiatives. With respect to implementation and enforcement, Commission dependence on the member states is structural, as noted above, in the absence of field services in the national territories.

The Commission is not, of course, the only Community institution that is reliant on the national administrations. The ability of the Council to transact business effectively crucially depends on the quality of national institutions, structures, and processes (Lequesne 1993: 215; Wright 1996*b*). This dependence has long been recognized.[7] More recently, with enlargement pending, the European Council has underlined the importance of effective national coordination to the efficient operation of the Council.[8] At the Helsinki summit on 10–11 December 1999, the Heads of State and Government declared that:

The Council must have an overview of all Union policies. For it to do so, there has to be at the heart of the system a single chain of coordination capable of ensuring that Union action is

[6] As Metcalfe observes, 'By governmental standards the Commission is a small organization. Even in small countries a single ministry may be much larger than the whole Commission with its wide-ranging functions, to say nothing of individual DGs with their staff of only a hundred. From this account it is hard to conjure up the terrifying image of a predatory and ever-expanding 'Brussels bureaucracy' that looms so large in anti-EC political rhetoric' (1992: 121).

[7] See de Zwann (1995: 34–5). The author cites instances, as early as 1974, and the European Council in 1980, where Heads of State and Government called for improvements in national coordination to make decision making at the European level more effective.

[8] Coordination between the various formations of the Council has been a long-standing matter of concern that has grown even more pressing in the 1990s. The ability of the General Affairs Council to coordinate the work of the technical Councils—a role traditionally entrusted to it—has been severely tested by the expansion of EU competencies, the multiplication of Council formations, and, in particular, the increasing prominence of ECOFIN. COREPER has been considering the broader question of Council reform, based largely on the 'Trumpf-Piris' report of March 1999. This provided the grounds for the guidelines and recommendations approved by the European Council in Helsinki in December 1999 (Dinan 2000: 36).

consistent with the will of its political leaders. This chain of command starts in the Member States themselves with effective interdepartmental co-ordination and arbitration, and extends through COREPER, the General Affairs Council to the European Council. The Council's ability to meet the challenges ahead largely depends on strengthening the effectiveness of this channel—the backbone of the system. Action to preserve the Council's ability to act decisively therefore needs to be taken at all levels (European Council 1999: 6).

As the above discussion has shown, the penetration of the Union by national administrations has been extremely far-reaching. It supports the contention made by Laffan *et al.* (2000: 74) that national has become embedded in European administration and challenges the widespread assumption that integration is a process of top-down Europeanization. The ubiquitous presence of national administrations has important consequences for the functioning of the European Union as a political system, and is an important factor in accounting for its unique characteristics, thus substantiating the second part of the quotation cited at the beginning of the chapter. Not only has the uncertain constitutional balance between the national and the European levels been further complicated by the penetration of the EU's bureaucratic system by national officials and the assumption by national bodies of European functions, but also decision making has become more complex. The expansion of competencies and the related extension of decision-making structures have, of course, also played their part in this process. However, the involvement of officials from first six, then nine, eleven, twelve, and now fifteen member states, bringing within one bureaucratic system the differing characteristics—including the weaknesses and deficiencies—of multiple administrative structures, procedures, cultures, and traditions, has produced not only logistical challenges—accommodation issues and translation problems to name but two—but also has significantly complicated its operation, notably Council of Ministers' decision taking. Even if the decision-making structures of the Union were rationalized and hierarchialized, if legislative procedures were less complex, and institutional fragmentation diminished by effective internal coordination, coping with such diversity would be problematic. In the absence of changes in that direction, the involvement of officials from such diverse backgrounds, each endeavouring to further the interests of their own member state, makes even routine processes extremely complex and time-consuming.

Divergent national priorities and differing sensitivities, changing national purposes, influenced by short-term electoral goals in fifteen states, shifting national agendas, and divergent responses to external pressures in addition often produce conflicting visions between the member states about the future development of the Union. Without a central authority or a single vision, competing national preferences contribute to the fluidity of the Union by championing action across a wide front of activities without the capacity to establish priorities or impose discipline.

Penetration by national administrations also exacerbates sectoralized policy making at the European level. The 'vertical brotherhoods' (Derlien 2000) that link technical experts in line ministries at the national (and sub-national) level to their counterparts at the European level are not only often extremely close and well-entrenched, but also resistant to efforts at the national level to enforce horizontal (inter-departmental) coordination. Surveys of coordination arrangements show that in most EU member states line departments take the lead in defining the position adopted by government (Kassim *et al.* 2000; Kassim *et al.* 2001). Only in France and the United Kingdom do the mechanisms exist to ensure that all concerned departments are consulted on legislative proposals from the Union and can a central authority impose solutions where ministries hold conflicting positions, at least in routine policy (Kassim 2001; Menon 2001*b*).

A further consequence is that the processes of policy development at the European level have become increasingly inaccessible. Policy making in the Community lacks transparency and visibility. The basic questions—'who does what, and when?'—are often extremely difficult to answer. The impenetrability of EU decision making, combined with the absence at the European level of mechanisms comparable to those that exist in the member states to ensure accountability, has contributed to anxieties about the democratic credentials of the Union.

National penetration at the European level has affected the structure and operation of the Union in several significant ways. However, the process has not been one-way: national administrations have also been affected. One obvious effect has been the growing number of ministries involved in EU policy making. In the late 1990s, it was remarked that only ministries of defence and education were unaffected by EU business, but by the turn of the century even these two departments have been brought within Brussels's embrace. More broadly, Wessels (1997) has argued that constant interaction between national officials at the European level has brought about a 'fusion' of national administrations. His view is that civil servants no longer consider EU policy making as foreign affairs in which they act as 'guard dogs' (Maurer and Wessels 2001) of national interests, but regard Brussels as an arena in which routine decisions are taken and the officials of other member states as partners. A process of 'post-national socialization' (Maurer and Wessels 2001) has transformed the nature of interaction between national officials from negotiation and interpretation of legal texts to effective transnational collegiality. While fusion theory may overstate the case, the testimony of former officials certainly seems to suggest that the cognitive map of civil servants who work on European matters has changed.

THE IMPACT OF EUROPEAN INTEGRATION ON NATIONAL ADMINISTRATIONS

The nature and extent of the impact that involvement in the European Union has had on national administrations is strongly contested. A widely held assumption, for example, is that national administrations have been 'Europeanized'. However, the meaning of the term is often left unspecified, and the mechanisms through which the process operates rarely defined. Indeed, after an exhaustive examination of the literature, one commentator concluded that purported Europeanization frequently amounted to no more than 'a cause in search of an effect' (Goetz 2000*a*). The approach taken in this chapter is somewhat different. The argument presented below is that there are at least three ways in which the European Union has affected national administration. First, as discussed above, national administrations have, in addition to their national mission, assumed a new role as agencies for the implementation of EU rules. To cite but one example, national ministries responsible for fisheries implement the common fisheries policy by monitoring the official landing of fish and locating unofficial landings. These new responsibilities inevitably require adjustment on the part of the ministry in its structure and operation. As part of the European administration, implementing and enforcing EU legislation may involve it in new actions, the use in unfamiliar instruments, and the recruitment and training of additional personnel. A second type of impact relates to policy. As a consequence of decisions (legislative or judicial) taken by EU institutions, national administrations may be compelled to modify or abandon existing policies, to change or discard traditional policy instruments, or to reorganize structures or procedures. This may result in diminished or enhanced administrative capacities, or in changed relations with public or private actors. Such changes are relatively common, and have been discussed in the policy literature on the environment, telecommunications, and air transport (Kassim and Menon 1996; Heritier *et al.* 1996).

A further effect concerns adaptation on the part of national administrations as a consequence of the practical involvement of government in European-level decision making. National administrations have been encouraged to develop mechanisms to support the participation and coordinate the action of national officials in EU structures. The discussion below examines the way in which national administrations have effected this adjustment. It argues that, although the need to coordinate originates in Brussels, the way in which member states have responded to the demands made of them has been shaped by the structural features of national political systems. 'In this context, it may make more sense to speak of domestication than of Europeanization' (Hine and Kassim 1998; Kassim 2000*b*: 21). For this reason, there is no evidence of the convergence around a single administrative paradigm anticipated by some theoretical perspectives (see DiMaggio and Powell 1991*b*).

National Administrations in EU Policy Making

Involvement in EU decision making subjects national administrations to a set of extremely demanding requirements. Participation in the Council, for example, creates substantial pressure on manpower resources. The number of Council meetings at which national officials are expected to be present has expanded dramatically since the mid-1980s, particularly at working group level (see Figure 9.1). There are, in addition, the committees and meetings, both formal and informal, called by the Commission, where national interests need to be represented. Particular skills, different from those that are usually deployed in domestic processes, are also required. Technical expertise is, of course, important, but mastery of negotiating techniques and other languages are invaluable assets (Bulmer and Burch 1998; Debbasch 1988). Exercising responsibilities on behalf of the Union exerts a further pressure. Holding the Council Presidency, for example, is extremely onerous. EU business must be

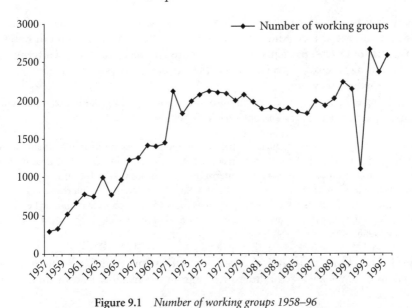

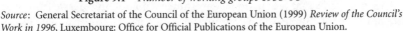

Figure 9.1 *Number of working groups 1958–96*

Source: General Secretariat of the Council of the European Union (1999) *Review of the Council's Work in 1996*, Luxembourg: Office for Official Publications of the European Union.

planned well in advance, hundreds of meetings have to be run, and dossiers advanced in multiple arenas.[9] The official Council guidebook warns ominously that '[m]ajor deployment of the entire national administrative apparatus is required to get the Presidency up and running' (General Secretariat 1996: 6).

Pressures of a different order, which have become more powerful since the mid-1980s, create incentives to 'get things right' in Brussels. In many policy sectors, the Union has emerged as the crucial policy maker or decision-making venue, and the decisions it takes can have far-reaching consequences. The adoption of legislation that is inconsistent with existing domestic policies can be extremely costly, both economically—firms may have to meet the costs of adjusting if new standards are imposed by Europe that are different from national regulations, so harming national competitiveness (Heritier *et al.* 1996; Kohler-Koch and Eising 1999)—and politically governments may be perceived as failing adequately to represent the national interest in Brussels. The same is true in the area of competition policy. State aid or merger cases often assume a high profile, and governments may be damaged if a decision goes against the 'national champion' or other companies with a significant domestic profile. In addition, the European Union has become an increasingly salient political issue. Governments are under pressure to demonstrate to sceptical publics that they have been suitably vigilant in their defence of the 'national interest'. This applies especially

[9] For discussion of the tasks and challenges confronting the Council Presidency, see de Bassompierre (1988), O'Nuallain and Hocheit (1985), Westlake (1995: 37–54), and Hayes-Renshaw and Wallace (1997: 134–57).

to policy sectors that are important domestically—agriculture in France, or fisheries in Spain and the United Kingdom. Furthermore, the European Union disposes of substantial resources, particularly in agriculture and regional policy. Governments have a strong interest, especially given the pressures on public finances, to find money wherever they can.

Ensuring effective national coordination in Union decision making is, however, an extremely difficult task. As Vincent Wright observed:

> the EU is distinctive amongst international organisations in locking its members into a continuous policy-making process of both an active and reactive nature. The co-ordination chain extends from within each ministry and interministerial co-ordination (of both a vertical and horizontal nature) at domestic level, to co-ordinating the domestic-EU interface, and then to co-ordinating within Brussels... [Although] the various levels of coordination may be usefully distinguished for analytical purposes,... in practice, they intertwine in constant fashion... (Wright 1996b: 149).

The features of the European Union as a political system noted above—fluidity, fragmentation, complexity, sectoralization—confront the member states with a serious challenge.

The constraints that face national governments do not only derive from the structure of the Union. Some originate from domestic sources. Governments do not have a free hand in their choice of coordination strategy. Coordination can be strategic, directed towards the common pursuit of an overarching objective, or selective: issue-oriented, reactive, or concerned only with certain stages of the policy cycle. It can be directive, designed to achieve a particular policy goal, or it may be procedural, concerned to ensure that issues are dealt with by the appropriate machinery—or even more modestly that relevant information is circulated to the interested parties. Each has organizational implications, and can only be pursued if the necessary resources are available. Coordination, moreover, must be traded-off against other values, such as stability or inclusiveness. The nature of the political system—for example, the authority of the president or prime minister, whether the state is federal or unitary, and how party competition is structured—the administrative opportunity structure—the degree of centralization or fragmentation, or whether the administrative culture supports information-sharing and cooperation—and the dominant policy style—inclusive and consultative, or exclusionary and statist—are particularly important.

Consequently, although the incentives or the *need* to coordinate national action originates in Brussels, national responses are shaped by attributes of the domestic polity. This explains why the member states have developed rather different structures, processes, and procedures for managing coordination (Kassim *et al.* 2000; Kassim *et al.* 2001). At the European level, this is somewhat less evident, since all member states have permanent representations that appear to perform apparently similar functions. However, the impression of homogeneity is somewhat superficial. There is a set of core responsibilities carried out by all permanent representations (see above discussion). Beyond these similarities, however, there are very significant differences (Kassim and Peters 2001). First, the importance attributed to networking in Brussels, the ambition and the effort expended, differs markedly between representations. The UK Permanent Representation (UKREP), for example, pursues a maximalist strategy, attempting to cultivate relations throughout the Commission and in the European Parliament (Kassim 2001). For Greece and Portugal, though, developing contacts is of secondary importance (Spanou 2001; Magone 2001). Second, whereas the United Kingdom has globalizing ambitions, wishing to push its agenda across all sectors and at all stages of the policy cycle, especially the pre-draft stage, other member states have more selective aims. Ireland, for example, concentrates on 'getting the negotiations right' (Laffan 2001), while Portugal directs its energies at areas that have a special domestic salience. The closeness of the relationship between the permanent representation and the domestic apparatus is a third point of difference. Whereas UKREP is closely involved in coordination in London, Greece's Permanent Representation receives little institutional support from Athens.

At the domestic level also, similarities emerge between national arrangements. For example: heads of government have developed specialist expertise and institutional support to enable them to carry out the increasingly routinized role they perform in EU decision making; foreign affairs ministries continue to occupy a central role in national processes, though their position is being challenged from a number of directions; inter-departmental coordination in EU matters is generally managed by mechanisms that have been specifically devised for the purpose; individual ministries have made adjustments to their internal organization and procedures; and most member states have a junior minister for European affairs or the equivalent, but the office is not typically central to coordination. However, these similarities are relatively superficial. Foreign ministries, for example, may always be involved, but they play very different roles in national systems. In some—Denmark, Portugal, and Spain—the foreign ministry is the dominant actor. In others, it shares power with the economics or finance ministry (Germany and Greece), or with the prime minister's office (Austria, Italy, and the United Kingdom), or is not the central actor at all (France).

More striking are the differences that mark domestic arrangements. First, member states have very different coordination ambitions. Some have far-reaching, strategic, and directive conceptions, and aim to construct an agreed position on every issue and to ensure coherent presentation by all national representatives at every stage of the EU policy process. Others have more modest ambitions that may be substantive—limited to particular policy types or issues—or procedural—filtering out policies that conflict with higher aims or ensuring that more important information is exchanged. France, the United Kingdom, and Denmark are examples of countries that follow the first approach. Even within this small group, however, significant differences are apparent. France's strategy is centred on the SGCI, a small elite unit of 150 officials, attached to the Prime Minister's Office (Lequesne 1993). The United Kingdom, meanwhile, has three central co-ordinators—the European Secretariat of the Cabinet Office, the Foreign and Commonwealth Office, and the UK Permanent Representation (Bender 1991, 1996). In Denmark, although the foreign ministry is a central actor, it manages coordination through a pyramidal committee system (Pederson 2000).

Divergences between member states that have taken the second approach are considerably greater. One difference relates to ambitions. Spain, for example, has 'an explicit desire to speak with one voice' (Hayward and Wright 1998), while Germany appears to take the view that 'hundreds of arrows may be more effective than one shot with Big Berta' (Derlien 2000). A second concerns the identity and status of actors involved in coordination. In Germany, the Länder have become increasingly important participants and have their own 'foreign relations system' (Derlien 2000), but do not boast the co-equal position that the sub-governments in Belgium enjoy with the federal government in EU decision making (Kerremans 2000). Spain has a special committee that brings together representatives from all seventeen autonomous communities, while the Basque Country and Catalonia have an additional channel of access to central government. Coordination in Greece and Portugal, by contrast, is limited to ministries in the central administration. A third difference relates to the choice of coordinating mechanisms. Specialist administrative units have been created in Spain (the SSEU), Italy (the Department for the Coordination of European Community Policies), and Portugal (the DGAC). Committees for managing inter-departmental relations in respect of EU policy exist at the official level in Germany (the Committee of State Secretaries),[10] in Belgium (the P. 11 Committee), in Italy (CIPE, the inter-ministerial committee for economic planning), in Portugal (the CIAC), and in Greece (the Economic Committee). At the political level, Spain has an Inter-ministerial Committee, Greece an Inter-ministerial Committee, Belgium the Inter-ministerial Conference for Foreign Policy (ICFP), and Germany a Cabinet Committee for European Affairs. Weekly meetings take place in Austria, Belgium, and Germany to coordinate policy in advance of COREPER.

This brief examination of systems of national coordination illustrates that the European Union has had an impact on national administrations and that the latter have adjusted to involvement in European decision making. However, even in this key area, it is significant that, although the stimulus came from the European level, the precise form of national arrangements at home and, to a lesser extent, on the front-line in Brussels, has been shaped fundamentally by domestic structures and influences. To paraphrase Metcalfe (1994), national administrations were created to perform domestic functions in a domestic arena, not as participants in a supranational project. It is not surprising that the changes that they have undertaken in order to assume new responsibilities beyond the national realm have been shaped by their pre-existing characteristics and traditions.

ASSESSING THE EUROPEAN ADMINISTRATION

A unique political system has thus emerged with a similarly idiosyncratic administration, characterized by an uneven and complex interpenetration of the European

[10] The Committee is 'chaired by a Junior Minister in the Foreign Office and comprises representatives of that ministry as well as those from the Economics, the Finance and the Agricultural Ministries, from the German Permanent Representation in Brussels, the State Secretary in the Chancellor's Office responsible for European Affairs, and those State Secretaries whose departmental issues are under discussion' (Wright 1996*b*: 158).

and the national. The European administration is not without its weaknesses. In the first phase of the policy cycle, problems arise in policy initiation because of weak coordination within the Commission. The need for horizontal coordination arises, because Directorates-General, like ministries in national administrations, have different views about the appropriate course of action in any given area. Well-known clashes have taken place, for example, between DG Competition and DG Industry (Menon and Hayward 1996), and between DG Competition and DG Regional Policy (Wishlade 1993). Unless differing opinions are reconciled, incompatible objectives or contradictory measures may prevent the emergence of coherent policy initiatives. At the same time, however, the Commission is strongly pillarized, a 'multiorganization' (Cram 1994), where each DG has its own functional responsibilities, operating procedures, and culture (Abélès *et al.* 1993), and interacts with a particular constituency. Inter-service consultation is beset by difficulties—procedures are not always followed or enforced—while the role of the Secretariat General extends no further than ensuring that relevant parties are informed. Moreover, since the College is a collegial body and the President *primus inter pares*, there is no figure in the Commission with the authority to impose a solution where differences arise.

With respect to the output phases of policy making, the structural dependence of the Commission on national administrations creates considerable problems in policy implementation, leading to claims that the Union suffers from an 'implementation deficit' (Metcalfe 1992; Peters 1997*b*). Implementation concerns the incorporation and application of EU law and policy. With respect to the former, the Commission is responsible for ensuring that EU legislation is incorporated into national law, but has no direct powers, so relies on receiving notification from national governments. Where a member state has not complied with its obligations, the Commission may open its own investigation and, if necessary, initiate proceedings before the European Court of Justice. In the recent past, it has adopted a policy of 'naming and shaming' in an attempt to improve compliance. Thus, it publishes a six-monthly internal market scoreboard, showing the percentage of single market legislation that each member state has incorporated into national law. In recent years, the scoreboard has recorded significant progress towards the goal of full implementation of internal market directives.[11]

Implementation and enforcement present particular problems. Not only is it intrinsically more difficult to determine whether a law is being properly applied than discovering whether it has been incorporated into national law, but national administrations may be less enthusiastic about measures that run counter to long-standing policy preferences. Even where they are willing, implementation may be difficult because the legal concepts or methods used are unfamiliar, or because further demands are being made on resources that are already stretched (Nugent 2001: 277–8). The ability of governments to ensure effective implementation has been diminished in some states due to decentralization and agencification. In this area too, the Commission is constrained by a lack of resources and its distance from the front-line.

---

[11] http://europa.eu.int/council/off/concl/index.htm.

A further problem relating to implementation concerns the consistency with which EU laws are applied across the Union. The same law may be implemented and enforced quite differently between member states due to differences relating to national constitutions, legal tradition, administrative culture, and political will. This clearly has serious implications for the claim that an aim of the single market, for example, is to create a level playing field across the Union, and, more broadly, for the nature of integration, which may reveal a pronounced pattern of national differentiation.

The Commission recognized and has attempted to address these weaknesses, particularly since the creation of the internal market. As well as 'naming and shaming', as described above, it has directed efforts towards the creation of networks, linking the Commission officials and national officials that work in the same policy area, to exchange information, ideas, and best practice (Sutherland 1992). The network strategy has been used to improve consistency in a range of areas from anti-fraud to justice and home affairs. In a similar vein, the Commission promotes exchange programmes between member states, and between member states and the Commission.

Policy management has also been an area of weakness. The areas where policy is managed by national governments, such as the Common Agricultural Policy and the Structural Funds, present similar problems to those discussed above. The Commission has tried to create active networks between national administrators, and to raise consciousness of the need to protect Community financial resources. In other fields, ranging from external actions such as PHARE and TACIS, the ACP programmes, and humanitarian aid programme to smaller programmes in research, culture, tourism, education, and transport infrastructure, the Commission has direct responsibility. In some cases, such as the Fourth Framework Programme for Research and Development and the European Development Fund, the relevant DGs have managed the programme directly (Laffan 1997: 178). In others, the Commission has contracted out responsibility. However, serious problems have arisen in both, as highlighted in the two reports presented to the Parliament by the Committee of Independent Experts (CIE 1993*a,b*). The principal deficiencies, addressed by the reform programme adopted by the Prodi Commission (Commission 2000), is that responsibilities have been poorly defined within the Commission and between the Commission and external agencies, that there has been no standard method for contracting out, and that evaluation has been weak or non-existent.

On the input side, coordination within the Commission is likely to remain a problem, until the powers of the Presidency and the Secretariat General are enhanced. On the output side, a number of the difficulties are being addressed, but the range of options is limited by what is politically acceptable. The creation of powerful centralized European agencies, for example, is clearly not a possibility in the post-Maastricht climate of suspicion towards Europe. Strengthening the Commission by expanding its staff resources may, however, offer the best solution for dealing with problems in implementation.[12]

---

[12] For an alternative view, see Metcalfe (2000).

CONCLUSION

'Europe' is portrayed by Eurosceptics as a distant, but powerful, superstate-in-the-making, which is bent on stripping the member states of their remaining sovereignty and whose tentacles reach into every nook and cranny of national life (see, e.g. Siedentop 2001). The Commission is cast as the bureaucratic arm of the European Union. Usually singled out for particular opprobrium, it is criticized on account of its allegedly imperialistic ambitions, its determination to centralize power in Brussels, and its lack of democratic credentials.

Inspection of the European administration, however, reveals a somewhat different and more complex picture. The conflictual image of the European Union against the member states—Brussels locked in a zero-sum game with national governments—does not withstand scrutiny. Examination of its administrative organization shows to the contrary that the European administration is an amalgam of the European and the national, marked by interpenetration and interdependence. National administrations have permeated EU decision-making structures, are present in all areas of EU activity, and to a large degree condition the functioning of EU institutions. At the same time, national civil services have assumed new functions and have been compelled to make adjustments in their operations, structures, and recruiting practices in order to participate at the European level.

Moreover, though it plays an important part in EU decision making (see Nugent and Paterson, this volume), the Commission is in reality far from being the over-mighty, predatory bureaucracy that Eurosceptic critics allege. In practice, the Commission is a small organization that is difficult to coordinate and which is structurally dependant on national administrations, with no administrative presence in the territories of the member states. In addition, although formally independent of the member states, in reality the Commission is in constant contact with the national administrations, and its staffing and appointment practices have responded to, and reflected, national claims.

As with other bureaucracies, the characteristics of the European administration are tightly bound up with the state that it serves. In the case of the European Union, that political system interleaves European and national elements. It is also loose, weakly articulated, and bears the marks of serial improvisation.

10

Europeanization and the Persistence of Administrative Systems

EDWARD C. PAGE

THE ONWARD MARCH OF EUROPEANIZATION?

Europeanization represents something of a paradox. At one level it is impossible to argue that the state has not been 'Europeanized' to some degree. Public policy in a large and expanding range of fields—above all agriculture, trade, and the environment but also social affairs, policing, and education—is shaped by what is decided within the European Union. There can be no doubt that many policy areas in the modern European state have been 'Europeanized' in this sense.

In another sense, there is precious little evidence of 'Europeanization'. A special issue of *West European Politics*, the journal co-founded by Vincent Wright, sought to examine the impact of 'Europeanization'. The conclusions reached gave scant support for the idea that nation states are becoming 'Europeanized'. Hix and Goetz (2000: 20) write that 'most commentators caution against the expectation of growing convergence amongst European political systems' and they endorse this conclusion since 'diverse national and sectoral traditions act as decisive "intervening variables"'. Mair's (2000: 48) contribution concludes that 'Europe fails to have an impact on national party systems'. These verdicts echo much other writing on the subject. For example, Cole and Drake (2000) found at best only a weak and limited impact of 'Europeanization' on the French state and Randall (1997: 362), looking at child care policy, finds only slight convergence and argues that the 'perception of these convergent tendencies should not obscure the substantial remaining differences. There remains much greater polarization in the public provision for under-threes and services for school-age children using private services, the coherence, indeed the whole ethos or philosophy of the child-care system, quality of services and the training, and remuneration of child care staff'.

The difference between these two views can, of course, be explained by the different meanings of 'Europeanization' on which they are based. The first argument is based on the definition of Europeanization as *impact of whatever sort* on the way in which policies are developed in member states. For example, ask any civil servant in, say, an agriculture or environment ministry and they will tell you that what goes on at

European level is crucial for their everyday work. Many domestic civil servants participate in EU policy-making arenas in Brussels and elsewhere. They have to implement EU directives, put other EU regulations into effect, maintain inspection regimes that are initiated by EU laws, and ensure that domestic policy does not infringe or contravene EU law. Moreover, timescales for policy making in member states are shaped by those of the EU (Enkegren 1996)—in Sweden, for example, the relatively slow pace of many of the deliberative processes have had to be changed to suit the demands of EU timetables (see Elder and Page 2000).

The second argument is far more exacting since it is based on a definition of Europeanization as having a *homogenizing* impact on specific institutions and practices across a wide range of state activities. Membership of the European Union is not only producing policies which have to implement, or conform with, EU law, and policy processes in which participation within European decision-making arenas is becoming increasingly important, but also producing greater similarities in political institutions among all member states. If we are to sustain the argument that Europeanization has this homogenizing effect, we must establish that a similar stimulus has similar transformative effects in all countries exposed to the stimulus or that the countries which are 'Europeanizing' are moving towards a common state, possibly from different starting points.

To a very large degree the argument about 'Europeanization', whether and to what extent it is taking place, depends upon the definition used—whether it is Europeanization as impact or Europeanization as homogeneity. The more exacting definition is bound to find less evidence of Europeanization. Yet this observation does not entirely explain the tendency of studies of Europeanization as homogeneity to support a null hypothesis. In fact, there appears to be every reason to expect Europeanization as impact to increase the degree of Europeanization as homogeneity. As member states respond to common EU directives and regulations, we may expect their policies come to resemble those of other member states. The central purpose of this chapter is to examine how it is possible to have Europeanization as impact without Europeanization as homogeneity. In order to do so, the second part of this chapter outlines some of the arguments that lead one to expect greater homogeneity. The tendency to find largely null hypotheses concerning homogenization of state structures and state administration shows that the expectation of growing similarities, derives from a defective understanding of the mechanisms by which the process of homogenization is expected to take place (discussed in Section Expectations Unfulfilled). It also shows that domestic politico-administrative systems to adapt their systems so that Europeanization as impact can remain high while producing little by way of Europeanization as homogenization.

This investigation addresses a central theme in much of Vincent Wright's later comparative work, as well as his work on French politics—the persistence of national difference in the light of wider global as well as European influences on the institutions of individual states. His seminal work on approaches to 'new public management' across Europe (Wright 1994) separated out the genuinely cross-national trends from the nation-specific adaptations, modifications, and forms of resistance to these trends. He had a gift for integrating apparently diverse national experiences into a single, broad theoretical discussion. Yet in such discussions contrasts tended to out-weigh similarities. This tendency to view divergent national state traditions as per-sisting despite trends towards 'Europeanization' and other such forces tending to erode national distinctiveness was at its clearest in a section of his autobiographical discussion of his intellectual development from a love affair with France and along the 'path to hesitant comparison'. In it he describes two recent books (on economic policy) he had been working on. His words go beyond bibliographical description and constitute a more fundamental statement of themes that run through much of his later comparative work:

There is a major process of state restructuring (not demise) at work, that the process is nationally differentiated, that countervailing pressures are evident... that pressures on the nation state are sometimes exploited as opportunities, that within the state apparatus there are winners and los-ers resulting from the reshaping process, that decentralization and Europeanization should not be construed as zero-sum games... and that the nation state, with all its problems, remains, for most citizens, the principal repository of legitimate authority. In arguing this case... I lay myself open to the not entirely unjustifiable accusation of being an old-fashioned Jacobin, perverted by a nos-talgia for the 1950s and 1960s, by a penchant for social democratic distributionalism and an admiration for French prefectoral administration. (Wright 1997: 174)

While Europeanization was not a theme that Vincent Wright treated in the abstract, the issues it raised, and issues related to it, concerning the power and specificity of the nation state were central to his work.

THE EXPECTATION OF HOMOGENIZATION

The notion that states are becoming Europeanized, in both senses, is not new. European states have had profound effects on each others' political systems since their modern origins. The strength of these effects is acknowledged in the historical as well as the modern social science literature on state building. It is natural that authors concerned with understanding the development of the character of political institutions, from Weber (1972), Michels (1915), and Hintze (1962) to Rokkan (1970), Poggi (1978), and Tilly (1990) should construct their explanations in terms of a geo-graphical focus on Europe.

From the early, medieval development of bureaucratic institutions in royal house-holds, feudalism, and the emergence of systems of secular law to the development of estates-based representation, the construction of bureaucratic absolutism, the *Rechtsstaat*, the growth of mass parties and the welfare state, major developments in the politico-administrative structures of the whole continent (including our own islands) can only be explained in a Europe-wide context (see Page 1995). Even in the case of less obviously seminal developments, many political institutions seem to develop at a common pace in many European countries—for example, local govern-ment reform in the late nineteenth century and again after the 1960s (Brans 1992), the elaboration of social insurance schemes after the Second World War (Flora and

Heidenheimer 1981), as well as the post-war nationalizations and privatizations of the 1980s and 1990s (Rose 1985).

Otto Hintze (1962: 216), the German administrative historian, in his account of the development of local government, argues that there are 'two great epochs' in administrative history: the period before 1800 and the period after. Developments after 1800 tended to be shaped by 'theories' including those of the Physiocrats, Turgot and Stein. Before 1800, administrative reforms were shaped less by the power of ideas and more by the conditions facing ruling elites as they sought to establish dominion in often highly fragmented societies. Thus the way institutions such as feudalism, the ministerial structures, as well as the different forms of representation and local government, developed throughout Europe showed striking similarities. Even if it is very hard to prove that such developments involved significant amounts of borrowing, the simultaneous pursuit of similar policies is nevertheless a striking feature of European political development centuries before the creation of the European Coal and Steel Community in 1952 and before the major developments in European integration after the 1980s. It is not fanciful to talk of the development of the 'modern European state'. It is a construct that even those whose work disdains the comparative method of modern political science, such as Michael Oakeshott (1975), find useful in defining and explaining the character of modern politics.

In the nineteenth century Guizot (1846: 252) argued that the similarities between the development of states in Europe was so strong that

Considered in their entirety the Continent and England have traversed the same grand phases of civilization; events have, in either, followed the same course, and the same causes have led to the same effects.

Yet a more accurate description of the character of European development comes from Vincent Wright's own words of 'state restructuring (not demise)' in a 'nationally differentiated' process. We will return to this question of differentiation in the conclusion. However, suffice it to say that part of the problem of the Europeanization thesis is that it fails to take into account the fact that European political development has always been in many senses a common one, and that institutional diversity, and differences in the norms and practices of politics, have persisted throughout.

European states have always displayed strong similarities in their trajectories of political development, yet they have maintained their differences. It is therefore important to outline why the European Union should be expected to produce a widespread process of convergence or homogenizing greater than that produced through centuries of political development based on similar trajectories. In this sense it is not enough to explain Europeanization as the progressive intertwining of the economies of Europe in the EU following centuries of relative isolation of European political systems from each other. Located in the same patch of the globe, European states have always had much in common, so why should membership of the European Union have an especially strong impact on member states' politico-administrative development?

If we look at some of the 'policy transfer' literature we can see why we might expect the development of the European Union to bring with it Europeanization as homogenization to a degree not experienced before the 1950s, transforming traditional institutions and modes of state action. The mechanisms by which such influences can have an impact on individual nation states have increased with the development of the European Union as a major political institution.

The literature on policy transfer has a variety of ways of describing how countries import policies ranging from the abstract sociological (Di Maggio and Powell 1983) to the commonsense (cf. Rose 1993; Westney 1987). However, we can point to four specific mechanisms which would lead us to believe that Europeanization will have increased since the inception of the European Union, and above all after its emergence from a period of 'Eurosclerosis' in the late 1980s.

1. A *'coercive'* mechanism resulting from the fact that the European Union can issue orders. The European Union is the source of initiatives which have the force of law and this produces homogeneity (cf. Dolowitz and Marsh 1995). The term 'coercion' is itself problematic, and is applied to cover circumstances ranging from physical threats to the offer of a conditional grant of money. Moreover it is doubtful whether mechanisms such as EU directives really fall into the category of coercion in a true sense of the term when they are accepted, indeed in many cases welcomed, by member states as valid exercises of EU authority. However, the term is used here because it has some currency in the policy transfer literature and refers to forms of policy transfer where recipient choice is limited.
2. An *imitation* model resulting from the fact that the European Union is the source of initiatives which do not have the force of law and this produces homogeneity. Such initiatives might be EU-level initiatives, individual national practices, or syntheses of different national practices which are imitated by other member states. The imitation may come from the inherent qualities of a particular model or as the result of 'the development of a mainstream consensus, of common paradigms' and the 'development of joint preferences and even identities under the conditions of close political cooperation' which is 'an important element of Europeanization'(Falkner *et al.* 1999: 512). For Bomberg and Peterson (2000) 'EU policy transfer seems to work primarily from the bottom up. It is driven by exchanges between national authorities who share a common concern to solve policy problems, as well as causal understandings and technical expertise. In essence EU policy transfer is a pro-active—and only rarely coercive—approach to the Europeanization of public policy'.
3. An *adjustment* model (member states react in similar ways to conditions created by European Union). This argument was set out by, among others, Hix and Goetz (2000: 20) who sought to assess what they termed the 'adaptive pressures resulting from the lack of fit between EU level institutional and policy arrangements'.
4. A *polydiffusion* model (variety of actors and institutions involved in transfer of ideas and practices in different ways). As Burnham and Maor (1995) have it 'Convergence may come too in a more subtle way for the day-to-day practices of national officials ... especially those meeting their counterparts from other member states ...'

The European Union might be expected to have increased its 'Europeanizing' effect through each of these; not only are there more directives in force than twenty years ago, these directives cover a wider range of areas (Pollack 1994); the expansion in the number of opportunities for national officials and representatives of interest groups to meet colleagues from other countries and compare and learn from the experiences of different countries increases the chances of policies and practices being imitated or spread through polydiffusion, and the increasing range of policies covered by EU policy making means that countries might be expected to have to adapt their institutions and practices to a greater degree than twenty years ago.

EXPECTATIONS UNFULFILLED?

How can we establish that these mechanisms have not produced convergence within European administrative systems? We have already shown that determined efforts to find evidence of Europeanization as homogenization have tended to draw a blank (cf. Hix and Goetz 2000). Another way is to compare a general study of European politico-administrative systems produced before the European Union could begin its homogenizing with a study produced after it. While we lack a common metric to assess how more or less similar countries are becoming, one is unlikely to be able to argue with any conviction that the world presented by Brian Chapman's *Profession of Government* (1952) is more diverse than that presented in the collection I edited with Vincent Wright shortly before his death, *Bureaucratic Élites in Western European States* (Page and Wright 1999). G Montagu-Harris, the author of *Local Government in Many Lands* (1926), could at least identify French, Germanic, and English models of local government in his comparisons. If we take the 'Napoleonic' group of states including France, Belgium, Spain, and Italy, their local government structures have begun, if anything, to diverge to a far greater extent from each other in the period after the 1970s than for nearly two-hundred years (Keating 2000).

Of course Europeanization is not the sole source of possible homogeneity of administrative systems. Since the 1980s, administrative reforms in a wide variety of countries have been grouped under the common label 'new public management'. This wave of reforms is global and, if anything, owes less to Europe and the European Union and more to the United States for its intellectual impetus and bodies such as the World Bank and OECD for its organizational advocacy (see also Pollitt and Bouckaert 2000). While acknowledging some of the similarities between such reforms in many countries, Vincent Wright's (1994) own work called into question the degree to which new public management was recasting traditional politico-administrative structures within a common mould.

Perhaps the most careful and elaborate investigation of the progress of new public management as a basis for administrative restructuring is provided by Pollitt and Bouckaert (2000). They begin by setting out the rather different starting points for administrative reform and outlining the politico-administrative traditions of the ten countries they examine in detail (of which six are EU members—Finland, France,

Germany, the Netherlands, Sweden, and the United Kingdom; the others are Australia, Canada, New Zealand, and the United States). They then discuss the different components of new public management reform, including reform in financial systems (e.g. performance budgeting); personnel management (e.g. promotion on the basis of results); organizational structures (e.g. decentralization and removing layers of management); and performance measurement. They look at the different 'trajectories' of reform taken by different countries and then ask whether 'all ten states were following one, basically similar, route (first mapped out by the Anglo-American countries) or whether, at the other extreme, there was no noticeable pattern to the multiplicity of reforms' (Pollitt and Bouckaert 2000: 93).

Their answer to this question is that there is great diversity with some broad underlying trends. Reform ambitions vary across nations. Pollitt and Bouckaert distinguish between reforms where the ambition is to *maintain* 'as much as possible of the status quo by taking steps to make current structures and practices work better' (they include Germany and the European Commission as main examples), those aiming to *modernize* through making extensive changes to existing institutions (primarily Canada, Finland, France, the Netherlands, and Sweden), those seeking to *marketize* the public sector by introducing private sector conditions into the public sector (above all Australia, New Zealand, and the United Kingdom), and those seeking the goal of a *minimal state* (primarily the United States). They conclude that there 'is a pattern. However, its precision must not be exaggerated'.

Yet for our purposes the similarities do not amount to any evidence of any significant homogenizing process. Even within the group with the largest number of European member states, the modernizers, there are 'different emphases as between managerial modernization (concentrating on management systems, tools, and techniques) and participatory modernization (giving greater salience to devolution of authority to subnational governments and to developing user-responsive, high quality services)' (Pollitt and Bouckaert 2000: 93). Neither as a response to a wave of new public managerial reform, nor to the onward march of the European Union, is there much evidence as yet to sustain the argument that Europeanization as homogenization is a major force underlying the diverse changes in the politico-administrative structures of its member states.

If we accept that membership of the European Union has not produced convergence, then there are two possible implications. One is that we should reserve judgement about the applicability of Europeanization as homogeneity for a few more decades until the processes on which it is based might be expected to have had time to make a more noticeable impact on European political systems. The great transformations of European political systems referred to the above—feudalism, absolutism, and the *Rechtsstaat*—took centuries to develop, so just, say, twenty years of intensive administrative interaction in the European Union cannot be expected to have made a huge dent on long-standing traditions. Lack of time for homogenization to take hold is a plausible answer to the question of why so little evidence of it can be found.

Yet just as plausible is the argument that the mechanisms that are supposed to lead to Europeanization as homogenization are far weaker than is often supposed. It is therefore important to outline this argument. One does not have to look particularly hard in the empirical literature on policy transfer and the impact of the European Union on member states to find out why the different mechanisms discussed above—coercion, imitation, adjustment, and polydiffusion—are unlikely to produce Europeanization as convergence. Let us consider each in turn.

Coercion

To some extent similarities in the standards of service provision mandated by European law might not be regarded as such a guarantee of a wider convergence of political systems as suggested by the term 'Europeanization' if one considers that public policy outcomes in different western European nations appear to have developed in step for much of the twentieth century. There are, for example, systems of education, social security provision, and health care which have developed at a similar pace in terms of the resources devoted to them in different European countries (Rose 1985), but not ended as identical. However, the fact that European nations are now adopting policies, not as a response to directly domestic political pressures but because of a legal obligation to implement judicially enforceable legislation, makes the Europeanization hypothesis appear far more potent.

Are directives and the regulations and decisions that accompany or support them really likely to bring about convergence? This is a more difficult issue to address because it raises fundamental issues about precisely what similarity means. No policies in any one country are likely to be identical in every respect to those in other countries. The whole notion of directives, in fact, builds diversity into the European legislative process because it requires that member states devise their own legislation to give effect to it. Yet directives set limits beyond which member states cannot go (without facing the prospect of being taken to court) when framing their implementing measures, and this creates a degree of homogeneity.

Haas (1998: 33) suggests that our cross-national knowledge about compliance is limited. He writes that

Questions of compliance—to what extent ... states comply, which states are likely to comply ... what patterns of compliance exist within and across areas of regulation ... — have not been extensively investigated and remain poorly understood.

But he still concludes '[c]ompliance is a matter of state choice'. While it is a common argument among public officials that directives are becoming ever more detailed, existing research comparing cross-national implementation of EU directives tends to emphasize their highly uneven implementation. Héritier's work on road haulage showed that the pattern of policy change was different in each of the four European countries she looked at following (among other things) EU directives in the area, and she concluded that in this case 'European policy was only an invitation to change domestic policies in regulating road haulage' (Héritier 1997: 553). Certainly some directives may specify in some detail the levels and standards to be implemented, but even in an area such as environmental pollution, which has been subjected to a substantial volume of detailed directives and regulations, it is still possible to talk of two major member states displaying 'two different regulatory philosophies' in the approach to regulation—the British focus on 'quality' and the Germans on emissions (Lübbe-Wolff 2001).

One of the main reasons for this failure to produce common procedures and outcomes lies in the nature of the policy process, above all in the question of implementation. As Pressman and Wildavsky's (1973) classic statement put it, implementation is about 'forging links in a causal chain'. Once a policy is passed, in terms of a bundle of legislation and money, key decisions about the shape of what actually emerges as a policy outcome depends upon often crucial decisions taken at subsequent stages. Without a single hierarchical–bureaucratic chain of command throughout Europe, with Brussels at the apex, it would require directives of extraordinary detail to create the conditions of 'perfect administration' (Hood 1976) which could remove the discretion of nation states.

Differential implementation is commonly argued to be a limitation on the ability of directives to change national domestic policy. For example, Cole and Drake (2000) in their examination of the 'Europeanization of the French Polity' conclude that

The EU imposed policy orientations on French governments in ways which go against the grain of French policy traditions... On the other hand national traditions were reinforced at the implementation stages and French governments demonstrated their capacity to innovate and recodify in accordance with national traditions.

Imelda Maher (1996: 590), in her Anglo-German comparison of competition policy points out

The implementation practice of UK law is one of implementing EC law within existing institutional arrangements...like the complete veil the state remains...a real barrier for the Community which can pass laws which penetrate beyond the veil but cannot deal directly with those elements of the state which are responsible for the enforcement of those laws.

Implementation structures and procedures have always been acknowledged as a barrier to uniformity, and there is little sign that they are changing or that EU institutions have found effective ways to bypass or counter them, even if they wanted to. For it is quite possible for EU law to be implemented in a variety of different ways throughout member states without identical national laws or institutions to implement them.

Adjustment

Membership of the European Union undoubtedly changes the way in which policy is made within member states. Bureaucrats, interest groups, and politicians have to participate in European forums of decision making. Thus organizations in member states have to adjust to take account of this to some degree. Member states have to send officials to participate in European forums. At a minimum, this implies some form of adjustment in domestic administrative arrangements which establish (whether formally or informally) which particular individuals participate in European decision making, the conditions under which they participate, from whom they receive instructions, to whom they report, and what latitude they have in European policy-making forums. More extensive arrangements for managing the increasingly close relationship between European Union and domestic policy making might even result from this process of adjustment—bodies to coordinate EU negotiating positions across departmental or ministerial boundaries, or bodies to oversee domestic implementation of EU legislation, for example.

There is relatively little comparative work on how domestic politico-administrative structures and practices adjust to the exigencies of participating in a European system of decision making. Dimitrakopoulos' (1997) study compares the European coordinating mechanisms of three member states: Greece, France, and the United Kingdom. It shows two important features of the process of adjustment in this context. First, the exigencies of EU involvement are not sufficiently powerful to bring about similarities between systems at what may be termed a broad 'functional' level. The existence of an apparent 'need' for mechanisms coordinating negotiation between the member state and the European Union (Metcalfe 1988) does not produce such mechanisms. While such bodies exist in France and Britain, primarily through the SGCI and the Cabinet Office European Secretariat, coordination of EU policy 'is exercised in a piecemeal manner through irregular *ad hoc* meetings or through personal contacts … the diffusion of information to other ministries "relies on the patriotism of the official who attended the meeting" as a Greek official put it' (Dimitrakopoulos 1997: 181).

Second, Dimitrakopoulos' study shows for our purposes that institutions like the French SGCI and the UK European Secretariat may fulfil the same functions, but they are very different institutions which reflect their wider domestic politicio-administrative environments. It is characteristic of each that they fit national patterns of coordinating institutions; both rely on the authority derived from their position of serving the Prime Minister, but the SGCI achieves its coordinating role as a distinctive type of secretariat to interministerial committees which include ministers and civil servants, which can mobilize distinctively French forms of intra- and cross-ministerial networks via ministerial *cabinets* and civil service *corps*. It operates in an environment in which its power varies, among other things, according to relationships between not only the Prime Minister and the Minister for Europe, but also between the two parts of the dual executive.

Imitation

The EU administrative structure itself, to a significant degree, has evolved blending structures adapted from member state institutions—the grading system, the names of posts, the principle of advancement through seniority, and the decision making structures of the *cabinet*, for example (Page 1997). This does not prevent the European Union from re-exporting the resultant blend of structures to its member states. A more convincing reason to explain why the administrative structures and practices of the European Union have not so far proved to be a model to be imitated throughout the member states of the Union is that there appears to be manifestly so little to admire about the way the European Union is administered that it would be surprising if anyone would want to copy it. The unattractiveness of the European Union as an administrative model was established even before the 1999 crisis, when the Commission was forced to resign en bloc in the wake of the scandal generated by a report of the Committee of Experts documenting mismanagement and nepotism, if not corruption, at the highest levels of the organization. Its structure was fragmented and seemed to conform to no clear logic (e.g. there were famously three Directorates General, the nearest equivalent to the ministries of member states, concerned specifically with foreign affairs) except that of maximizing the number of senior jobs that could be given to member states, each of which was keen to have as many of their own nationals in top Commission jobs as possible. Agreement on the defects of the EU's politico-administrative structure, above all its fragmentation, had been widespread since at least the time of the Spierenburg Report (Spierenburg 1979), but little action had been taken to address them until the Kinnock reforms after 2000.

Yet it is not only the lack of attraction of the EU as a model (which may or may not diminish if the current reforms do end up producing radical change) that helps explain why the EU has not had a major impact on member state structures and practices through a process of imitation. Rather, we can also question the power of the *mechanism of imitation itself* to generate Europeanization as homogeneity. Perhaps the most striking example of this comes in a sphere where there was both a clear model to be followed and a strong incentive for member states to follow when recasting domestic practices: competition law reform. Eyre and Lodge (2000: 67) identify a European model of competition law which 'relies on a legal prohibition approach, analysing the impact on competition, exercised by a bureaucratic "agent"'. Moreover, the European model was established in the Treaty of Rome. Despite interest in adopting this approach in the United Kingdom after the late 1980s, and a Conservative draft bill in 1996, it was not incorporated into the framework of UK competition law until the passage of the 1998 Competition Act. In Germany the reform of competition law also came in 1998. The process of imitation, nevertheless, did not produce homogeneity. As Eyre and Lodge (2000: 77) conclude

Despite the centrality of EU competition policy both at the European and the national level and the increased decentralized application of competition law by national agencies ... both UK and German competition law, owing to their political institutional patterns, did not fully adopt the EU model.... [This] analysis suggests that national institutions shape the adaptation of these lessons and domestic actors select and apply 'lessons' strategically. Furthermore, it suggests the potential for continued diversity in policy applications owing to institutional inheritance, despite a convergence towards and decentralized application of the EU competition principles.

Even where there is evidence of a clear EU model to imitate and of significant attempts to imitate European patterns, the degree to which imitation is capable of producing homogeneity remains limited. Therefore, when we look at an area like the politico-administrative system of the European Union, where the incentives for member states to imitate EU practices are so much weaker, it is hardly surprising that member states show few signs of convergence through imitation.

Polydiffusion

One significant reason for expecting Europeanization is the increase in popularity in issues connected with policy transfer. According to several takes on Europeanization, the process of interaction between member states of the European Union occurs above all in the context of meetings in the diverse forums in which political, bureaucratic, and interest-group actors from member states meet up (Bomberg and Peterson 2000). One theory that informs much of this thinking about the possibilities for Europeanization through policy transfer is the framework of diMaggio and Powell (1983). They outline three mechanisms which produce 'isomorphism', which they understand as a tendency for organizations to imitate, or adopt similar characteristics to, other organisations; in addition to force and persuasion there is 'mimetic isomorphism' (where organizations are under pressure, perhaps from clients and consumers, to adopt in one sense or another the 'better' practices of other organizations) and 'normative' isomorphism, where ideas and practices spread through professional networks and education.

Mossberger (2000: 96) uses the term 'polydiffusion' to refer to the process of diffusion that takes place through a variety of horizontal as well as vertical channels, and this term applies quite well to the arguments used to describe the wealth of potential contacts among networks of national and European policy makers involved in EU decision making. While polydiffusion as a description of the spread of *ideas* is a highly plausible theory, as a description of how *policies and practices* spread it is less convincing. As Mossberger shows (discussed below), it is much easier for ideas to travel than policies. The central problem with the notion that polydiffusion brings homogeneity is that it invites one to believe that once organizations, or key members of them, become convinced of the merits of alternative practices, they will then successfully apply them. If such an assumption that change is the automatic result of external pressures or contacts may be sustainable in organizational sociology, it is certainly not so in political science. This argument downplays the *political* nature of policy transfer, where drawing lessons from foreign experience and applying them requires commitment, energy, skill, and insight.

Certainly it would be misleading to argue that theories of policy transfer ignore such issues. Marsh and Dolowitz (1996), for example, point to problems of implementation as a reason for the failed transfer of some welfare to work policies under the Conservatives in Britain in the 1980s and 1990s. The issue here is one of emphasis; theoretical approaches to transfer have tended to emphasize the processes and conditions under which ideas may travel. Detailed empirical studies of transfer, such as found in the work of Westney (1987), Jacoby (2000), and Mossberger (2000) emphasize the effort that goes into trying to forge policies that work and to generate political support to put them into effect.

Borrowing and adapting policies from another jurisdiction is a process that involves *choice and deliberation*, unlike the assumption in polydiffusion that it can occur through something resembling osmosis. Westney's (1987) study of how Japanese elites imported European models of the police, the press, the army, and the post office from the late nineteenth century shows it was a result of conscious choice. While choices of which models to import were not pure examples of 'rational shopping'—an exhaustive search of a wide range of alternatives—Japanese elites had some conscious reasons (as well as less 'rational' reasons) for selecting the particular models they chose to emulate. For example, the French model was adopted as a basis for reforming the police system in part because, unlike the other major international model, the English police, it emphasized a social control function. Even where the choice of policies to emulate is even further removed from the 'rational shopping' model than in the Meiji Japanese case, to borrow a policy requires a familiarity with it in its native setting. As Rose (1993) demonstrates, successful lesson-drawing cannot be a casual activity. It requires an understanding of the policy and what makes it work in the exporter jurisdiction, as well as a process of adaptation in response to an understanding of how conditions in the importer jurisdiction force a modification of the programme.

Furthermore, the successful importation of policy models from other countries also requires the *generation and maintenance of political support* for the imported model. Jacoby's study of policy transfer in post-war Germany found that the importation of allied models of trade union organization had effect because the efforts of the allies to shape the union movement in Germany, based on the United States and British concepts, 'helped us to shift the balance of power within existing groups of labour and capital, to the benefit of those Germans whose institutional visions were most compatible with the Allies' own' (Jacoby 2000: 90). In education, the Allies had little or no impact on the shape in which the education system was rebuilt after the war since 'American efforts not only were not geared toward mobilizing indigenous reform forces but also in fact actually discredited some of the Germans who did work with OMGUS [Organization of Military Government, US Zone]'. For Jacoby effective transfer depends upon two pillars. The first pillar is support from groups outside the state. The participation of powerful groups outside the state apparatus is not only a matter of political support but also a means of developing and adapting the imported ideas to the society doing the importing. A 'weak civil society increases the chance that institutions will be transferred unmodified, it also increases the risk that institutions will become ineffective, since there are no powerful groups that can work through them. Transfer usually occurs in established policy domains ... and so the process must usually engage established actors'. The second pillar is flexibility since 'key institutions affect a wide range of interests while confronting complex political problems', meaning that 'some modification is virtually always necessary either before, during or after the transfer'.

Both Westney and Jacoby show the complex political process involved in transferring lessons drawn from the experience of one polity to another. The type of policy transfer implied by the notion of Europeanization—the fundamental alteration of traditional policies and practices in the light of models provided by other countries— is not a casual process in which policies can be picked up from attending conferences or pursued by policy entrepreneurs without substantial mobilization of political support, or without substantial and conscious modification of the imported model to the circumstances of the system in which it is to be applied.

More casual forms of policy transfer can be found, but they are unlikely to have the transformative effect implied by the term 'Europeanization'. In fact Mossberger's (2000) study shows that what may appear to be policy transfer, the widespread adoption of the 'enterprise zone' as a means of addressing urban and regional development problems, could be instead a transfer of *labels*.

Policies become labels when policy characteristics that create ambiguity and promote adaptation combine with forces that encourage diffusion. Labels develop because a loosely bundled or ambiguous concept may be applied to a variety of purposes (Mossberger 2000: 122).

The title of the programme or innovation is almost all these diverse schemes had in common. To draw lessons from another jurisdiction and shape domestic policy on it, especially on the scale implied by the term 'Europeanization', requires far more than a casual borrowing of a name; it requires systematic examination of the model to be emulated and political conditions favourable to such lesson drawing. Such conditions only rarely obtain.

Ideas and slogans can travel, but once they disembark that is only the beginning of the story. They do not find their own way into practice in their new host country, neither can they generally shape policy without themselves being substantially amended in the process. They need the active support of domestic elites and the creative input of policy makers in a what can be, as Jacoby above all shows us, a protracted process. The direct implications of this for Europeanization theory are that while the European Union might expose more policy professionals to the experiences of other countries, merely being exposed to ideas is not likely to lead to imitation, or at least imitation in anything other than a superficial sense. Since lesson drawing is not an automatic result of being exposed to the practices of other countries, participation in international forums of deliberation and decision making such as provided by the European Union is likely to have a more muted impact than authors such as Peterson and Bomberg (2000) have suggested.

CONCLUSION: THE VARIABLES OF ADJUSTMENT

All of these bring us back to Wright's original proposition: that the processes of transformation brought about, possibly at a faster rate than experienced before, by the European Union, represent a restructuring and adjustment rather than a homogenizing Europeanization. In addition, the more we are concerned with establishing commonality and policy transfer, the less headway we make in understanding the character of the transformation and thus the actual impact of Europe. Vincent Wright's work was not content with simply suggesting that 'national differences' persist in the face of these apparent pressures for homogenization, still less is his work based on an assumption that such national conditions are so specific that each country is unique. Rather, throughout his later work there are clear sets of variables which affect the character of adjustment to the kinds of pressures experienced by the state, not only through membership of the European Union but also through wider processes of change such as the 'new public management revolution'.

A variety of features of nation states prevent homogenization. Such features should not be seen as 'blockages' to the adoption of European models of policy or governance. To conceive of such features as barriers suggest that they are stubborn, unchanging features which may, in time, be swept away by a homogenizing process of Europeanization. These features which prevent Europeanization as homogenization are as effective as barriers. A more accurate metaphor would describe them as filters through which pressures for change—whether from Europe or from wider international pressures, or even from broader processes of social, political, economic, or technological change—are perceived and processed by the political system. They produce diverse responses to these pressures, diverse ways of adapting to them. What are these features? To answer this question fully requires no less than the categorization of the variables that make our politico-administrative systems different from each other. However we can outline three major categories here.

As Wright (1994*b*) shows in his discussion of the development of 'new public management', *immediate political interests and constellations* shape the manner in which common types of impetus for change are converted into actual reforms. Party political ideologies and strength, and the relationships with interest groups, are one form of immediate political pressure, and patterns of intra-governmental power, reflecting the balance between different ministers at the political level or different ministries or sections of ministries, are another. *Path dependence*, the notion that a country's starting point when it comes to consideration of types of reform limits the range of alternatives it can consider to those allowed by current institutional patterns, is a name for a concept that has been recognized since at least Aristotle's classification of Greek city states. It has been used to explain developments as diverse as different national approaches to local government reorganization (Wollmann 2000) and the regulation of telecommunications policies (Thatcher 2000). *Basic administrative philosophies*, different conceptions of the role of the public sector in society, the relationship between politicians and bureaucrats, and even wider conceptions of the nature of authority (Hofstede 1979) have shaped patterns of administrative reform for centuries. Such administrative or 'state traditions' (Dyson 1980) remain a significant and powerful explanation for the divergence in approach to common stimuli for change (Pollitt and Bouckaert 2001; Wright 1994; Knill and Lenschow 1998). Ranged against such traditional characteristics producing differentiation, the mechanisms that are supposed to produce Europeanization as homogeneization appear far less formidable than is commonly supposed.

PART III

PARTIES AND ORGANIZED
INTERESTS

11

The Decline of Party?

GORDON SMITH

> Every party must be one-sided and short-lived in comparison with the state. The
> most fitting fate for a party is to dissolve once it has achieved its ends.
>
> (August von Rochau, *Grundsätze der Realpolitik*, 1853)

Political parties would be unlikely to follow the course favoured by von Rochau—
their 'ends' are never fully achieved and are anyway quite flexible. From a present-day
perspective, too, a concern with the central importance of 'the state' as such has been
displaced by the precedence given to the state based on the values of liberal democracy. Those values are supported by the institutions of representative democracy in
which political parties have come to be regarded as a vital component—a standpoint
totally opposed to the conclusion drawn by von Rochau.

Yet, there is no necessary link between the fortunes of liberal democracy and
the role played by political parties; they belong to two quite distinct categories
(though see the implications of supposed party decline identified by Mény and Tarrow,
this volume). The principles of liberal democracy do not automatically point to party
competition and to party government. Nor can the ends that parties pursue simply
be equated with liberal democratic values. In some circumstances the terms of
party competition and the practice of party government may be directly harmful to,
even destructive of, the liberal democratic order.

It is admittedly difficult to visualize the form of a workable and widely acceptable
alternative to the regime of political parties, one that would still be compatible with the
precepts of liberal democracy. Yet, to restrict the assessment to contemporary ideas of
what institutions and arrangements are feasible implicitly assumes that they have
reached an evolutionary dead-end. But the modern forms of party government and
party competition did not just 'happen'; they were themselves products of a long evolutionary process. It seems just as reasonable to believe that the process is continuing even
though there are no firm indications as to the direction it might take. Nevertheless, if it
proves to be the case that there is no workable alternative to political parties as the main-
stay of liberal democracy, then the consequences of party decline would be grave.[1]

---

[1] For Vincent Wright the question of a 'decline of party' was largely irrelevant, and he was sceptical
about their pretensions. Parties only enjoyed the comforting illusion of power. It is a matter of regret that
he failed to elaborate on his views in his writings.

It is in this context that the theme of 'party decline'—together with its near neighbour, the 'crisis of party' (Ignazi 1996)—can best be examined. Particularly over the past forty years or so there have been several studies indicating that political parties generally face mounting problems both in the realm of government and as representative institutions. Howard Reiter (1989), for instance, listed a number of publications of this kind. Thus, the theme of 'neo-corporatism' enjoyed a passing vogue in the 1980s in relation to the former, as did the supposed looming threat of 'ungovernability' to the latter in the same period. Other sources of unease, however, have proved to be long-lasting, especially in relation to the weakening of the linkages of electorates to the political parties.

Given the variety of the perceived sources of party decline, it is useful at the outset to see the whole debate in a wide framework, as Hans Daalder (1992) proposed in his 1991 Stein Rokkan Lecture, 'A Crisis of Party?', with the aim, as he put it, of contributing to a much-needed 'theoretical and conceptual house-cleaning'. He made a primary distinction between normative and empirical judgements concerning political parties. In the present context, the normative group is less relevant for the current discussion, except for those views that lead to an outright rejection of the role of parties in society as essentially inimical to democracy. For Daalder's second group, the problems are different in that the parties are judged as becoming increasingly redundant or ineffective in one or more aspects of their activities, and so are 'in decline'. Thus, one line of criticism is that parties are historically specific phenomena and thus increasingly unsuited to perform in new circumstances. Another is that parties are becoming dominated by market forces, and a further problem they face is that in various spheres they are losing the substance of their power to other actors. It is, indeed, a broad canvas that Daalder presents.

In the following discussion the question of decline is approached rather differently by examining four aspects that have featured prominently in debate: parties as representative agencies; party organization; parties in relation to the state and society; and parties in their 'external' environment. Since this account is concerned with European developments, the effects of European integration on the role of political parties are particularly relevant. First, however, the whole question of decline has to be appreciated in its historical context.

THE MASS MEMBERSHIP PARTY—A DUBIOUS LEGACY

A picture of parties in decline is often one of a gradual decline, and at some stage becoming irreversible. One version is of a final crisis and sudden rupture. Another is undramatic: the parties might well appear to carry on much as before, but in reality would become powerless—a scenario inviting the question as to why anyone would then bother to retain them, except perhaps as a 'dignified façade'. Any version of a final decline is bound to be conjectural, but the important point here is that it draws attention to the implicit assumption that there is something akin to a 'party life cycle', with successive stages following a trajectory and indicating when parties were presumably in some sense at their zenith before taking a downwards course. In this way, we can appreciate the description of parties as 'historically specific phenomena', appropriate to a single era.

At this point discussion takes a step or two backwards, to the period prior to the onset of any apparent party decline, to the era of the mass membership party (Duverger 1954; Neumann 1956). Why should the mass party have this exalted status? Its particular significance undoubtedly lies in the successful mobilization of the newly enfranchised electorates in Europe during the earlier part of the twentieth century and integrating them into the political system; it did so by building up party membership and then retaining a large and loyal electoral support. This loyalty was secured by a party programme that gave prominent place to the interests of its chosen clientele, and strict attention was given to inner-party democracy, and accountability at all levels. Party members were anchored into party life to secure their active involvement and long-term commitment by means of a range of party-related activities, along with a party press to inform and reinforce the bonds with party members.

Such, anyway, is roughly the picture conjured up by the 'model' mass party, and it is this model that has been so influential, regardless of how far it ever accorded with reality. In fact, its features were imperfectly realized in practice and unevenly from one country to another and from one party to another. Thus, the German Social Democrats and the Austrian Socialist Party were probably the most highly organized. The German party had around a million members before the First World War, and the Austrian party built up a formidable network of ancillary organizations with its 'cradle-to-grave' party activities.

These two parties were somewhat exceptional, and the priority given to securing a mass membership was a feature chiefly associated with parties of the left. It was far less prominent for bourgeois and denominational parties—probably because they had less need to do so, since their social links were more secure. Susan Scarrow (2000: 99) in writing of the 'myths' of mass party decline, concludes that one such myth is that: 'The heyday of the democratic mass party was during the first-half of the twentieth century', whereas her finding was that general (as opposed to sporadic) 'membership-based organizing only became a reality during the third quarter of the twentieth century'. If so, it appears that the mass party was fulfilling its prime membership qualification well into the period when it was already being seen as belonging to a past era. We may doubt, too, how far the features ascribed to the mass party ever closely accorded with reality. How democratically accountable were they in practice? It is worth recalling that as early as 1911 Robert Michels formulated his 'Iron Law of Oligarchy' in *Political Parties*, principally based on the real structure of power within the SPD.

These reservations make it difficult to accept the ideal model of the mass party as a reliable basis for judging party development. Yet, it has become a marker, to the extent that the language of 'decline' is employed even though no explicit mention is made of the historical point of reference.

PARTIES AS REPRESENTATIVE AGENCIES

Yet, however one judges the status of the mass party, the fact remains that there are many different signs of a growing distance between parties in relation to their electorates and to wider society. There are two underlying questions. First, what construction should be placed on these trends? Second, what are the implications for political parties, and how may they be expected to respond to the challenge?

There is ample enough evidence that for several years electoral links with parties have been weakening and that it is a process that looks like continuing. Relevant evidence of the lessening of partisan attachments in several respects and across a range of advanced countries has been convincingly detailed in the volume edited by Russell Dalton and Martin Wattenberg (2000). Moreover, although more sporadic in occurrence, there have been waves of outright 'rejection' of the regime of political parties, as seen in the growth of 'anti-party' sentiments (Poguntke and Scarrow 1996).

Various factors have contributed to these developments. Social changes, such as the lower intensity of social-class and denominational barriers, have been the underlying factors. The previously strong social cleavages, buttressed by political organization, enabled parties to encapsulate voters' loyalties, as Lipset and Rokkan (1967) expressed it in the idea of 'frozen' party systems. Rising educational levels enable people to develop their own judgement on political issues and develop their own political skills. This increasing competence is enhanced by the proliferation of mass media, which although biased in one way or another, also provide non-partisan sources of information. More generally, the gradual loosening of previously strong social bonds has resulted in an increasing individualization and privatization of social life. Electoral distance from parties is best shown by surveys that capture expressions of disaffection from parties and party politics, as indicated by the extensive cross-country survey data provided by Dalton and Wattenberg (2000: 19–76). The cumulative effects of all these developments have led in most countries to lower levels of identification with individual parties, although at different rates and with a number of anomalies.

Convincing as the picture of the decline in the linkages with political parties undoubtedly is, a critical question arises, namely, to what extent has this process of electoral detachment carried over to affect actual electoral behaviour? There are various ways in which behaviour may be affected: a secular decline in turnout at elections; increasing electoral volatility from one election to another; the rise of new and possibly radical parties at the expense of established ones. Yet, in all these respects, the evidence appears to be far less conclusive than one might have expected.

Thus, taking the experience of Western Europe over the past forty years or so, there has been a decline in voting turnout, but not a dramatic fall. As Peter Mair has pointed out:

Indeed, despite a modest decline in average turnout levels from just less that 84 per cent to just less than 80 per cent across most of Western Europe between the early 1960s and the early 1990s, the actual numbers of those voting in national elections increased by almost one third... These figures therefore offer little evidence of disenchantment or malaise. (1995: 46)

Nor does it seem that there is any particular level of electoral participation that can be regarded as 'safe', below which there is a danger area. Much depends on such factors as a country's constitutional and other institutional arrangements, the nature of the party system, the political situation at any one time, and not least a country's political culture. Thus in a developed 'civic culture' it is not surprising to find that most people normally regard 'other things' to be more important than politics (Almond and Verba 1963), and that can include voting, without necessarily endangering democracy.

At another extreme, a very high turnout at an election may, in fact, be a sign of dangerous instability and evidence of an unhealthy mobilization of usually apathetic voters, what, in the early 1930s, with the spectacular rise in support for Hitler's National Socialists, leading Social Democrat Kurt Schumacher referred to as 'the mobilization of human stupidity'. By the same token it can be argued that there is no really 'safe' level of electoral support. Thanks largely to its federal structure, Switzerland is perfectly stable with a turnout at the national level of around 50 per cent. In other countries, including federal states, that level of participation would be a cause for concern. Of course, none of this affects the central contention that it is the cumulative effects of a continued decline which indicate a serious weakness, but it does serve to warn against putting too much weight on falling support over short periods and of failing to take into account country-specific factors that may be operative.

Although the number of parties gaining representation has also risen in most countries, usually by around two or three, this rise has not generally affected the 'core' of the larger established parties in the system and has not undermined the stability and functioning of government (Smith 1990). The new entrants, often dubbed 'extreme' or anti-system, may in part account for the maintenance of levels of electoral turnout. Yet their appearance can also be regarded as a way of integrating those voters into conventional participation who otherwise might become quite estranged from it. Moreover, there have been cases where such apparently 'misfit' parties— right-wing populist and new politics Greens—were later incorporated into the governing system. In Austria, the entry into a governing coalition of the right-wing Freedom Party is one example. Another is the case of the German Greens, a party regarded with suspicion when it first appeared, but in 1998 forming a stable coalition with the Social Democrats. More generally, there is the question of post-materialism and the new social movements which at one time were seen as a threat to the 'old politics' parties. This threat has receded partly because the existing parties have been able to take up many new issues without jeopardizing their own sources of support.

Also subject to debate is the interpretation to be placed on the rise in the volatility of party support. Most countries have experienced such a rise over the past fifty years, supporting the connection between lower levels of party identification and its transmission through to electoral behaviour. However, its significance in terms of being part of a very long-term trend can be queried. Thus Stefano Bartolini and Peter Mair (1990) have shown that levels of volatility were actually higher in the inter-war period than in the post-war era.

Furthermore, they make the important distinction between electoral volatility that takes place on an intra-bloc basis, between related parties, and inter-bloc movements, between parties that have nothing in common. Their argument is that shifts of support within a bloc are far less significant than shifts across bloc boundaries.

Since most volatility occurs between related parties, not too much would be read into signs of increased volatility. In more familiar terms, the 'blocs' can be rendered as referring to 'left' and 'right', and the conclusion would then be that party identification in a narrow and specific sense has declined, and that would be one result of the narrowing gap between parties of left and right. Specific attachments are weakening, but voters may well retain a political identification within the wider political spectrum.

How can the apparent disjunction between electoral dealignment and electoral behaviour best be explained? One interpretation is that there is a lagged effect, that the changes which have already taken place in attitudes towards parties will be later followed by a similar negative trend in voting and related behaviour. Why there should be a time-lag at all is another matter, but the 'habit' of voting, for instance, could be one explanation. An alternative interpretation would be that electorates will continue to keep their 'attitudes' towards parties and their voting 'behaviour' in separate compartments. Thus, on the one hand they may well treat party pretensions with scepticism and perceive little difference between party platforms and the labels of 'left' and 'right'. Yet, on the other, they can still be motivated by particular issues coming on to the political agenda, by the personal qualities of rival political leaders, and by the recent performance of parties in government or opposition, or even by expressing a 'negative partisanship'. In other words, an explanation for the disjunction would be that two quite different sets of motivation are involved, one generally based, the other quite specific. Within a wide range it is possible that the two can co-exist.

Not all observers would anyway agree that a hard choice has to be made between the prospect, on the one hand, of continuing electoral dealignment and with it an inevitable decline of party, and on the other hand, the 'rescue' of parties by some outside means. Thus, Svante Ersson and Jan-Erik Lane foresee a dynamic relationship developing between electorates and parties. Faced by electoral instability, much depends on the resilience of the party system and whether parties can maintain their internal stability. They see the relationship as one of 'strategic interaction':

This means that it is neither possible to talk about a frozen electorate and a stable party system, nor to say that it is an unstable party system riding on a highly volatile electorate. Rather it seems to be more appropriate to characterise at least some of the West European electorates and party systems as moving in a cyclical pattern from states of stability to states of instability and back. (Ersson and Lane 1998; 35)

PARTY ORGANIZATION

Despite the vulnerability of parties at the electoral level—or perhaps precisely because of this pressure—they appear to be able to adapt, in terms of their organizational ability, to the changing environment of competitive politics. Yet, a price has to be paid for this adaptation that affects the party as a whole. Can the idea of party decline be applied to the longer-term consequences of developments in party organization?

Our ideas of party organization are still largely modelled on the mass membership party, both in its structure and the ways in which party policies are formed and eventually translated into legislative action. This correspondence is still largely accurate for the form of party organization and the basis of the relationship between the party's component elements, but the reality is quite different. Partly building on Otto Kirchheimer's (1966) earlier work in specifying the character of the catch-all party, Angelo Panebianco (1988: 264) set out several features of the emerging 'electoral–professional party', all of them contrasting with those of the mass party.

The mass party sought to advance the interests of its particular clientele as articulated by the party membership, and the process of decision making was structured to transmit their demands from the bottom upwards. This upwards process was, in fact, hindered by the partial 'insulation' enjoyed by the party in the legislature as well as in government. The electoral–professional party is quite differently placed, since it does not face this double hurdle. Panebianco pointed to the 'pre-eminence of the public representatives' in the party and to its 'personalized leadership' which gears the party to a top-down process of policy making. The primary focus is on the electorate at large, not the aspirations of its own members. The personalization of the party's leader gives the incumbent almost overriding authority, especially when in government. The party leadership will still subscribe to the beliefs central to the party's identity, but in practice needs to take up those issues that have a strong appeal to the wider electorate. Particularly when in government, the leadership has additional resources at its disposal: the ability to shape and redefine party policies, to make a range of party and governmental appointments, to gain financial support from various sources, and to distribute patronage in various ways. All these factors result in a close concentration of power and authority within a small group of politicians and their professional advisers. This portrayal of the electoral–professional party may in some respects be overdrawn, and Panebianco specifically described it as ideal-typical. But the contrasts with the mass membership party are nevertheless striking, and the puzzle is why the mass party model should still be a point of reference, and even more why parties should bother to keep the shell without the substance.

Yet, after all, the 'substance' may still be there. A recent study based on a wide range of countries concluded that the evidence of the data did not support a universal trend towards electoralist party organization and that: 'The remains of the classic mass party model are especially evident in the significant number of cases in which congress delegates decide on the question of leadership' (Scarrow *et al.* 2000: 149). Further, the authors found that ordinary party members continue to have a significant role in selecting legislative candidates and in legitimizing election programmes. On this rendering, it can be reasoned that a healthy balance has been effected between the demands of contemporary party competition on the one side, and on the other, the need to preserve elements of a party's core identity. That could best be secured by expressions of commitment on the part of grass-roots party members and the sense of 'belonging' that they have, rather than just being voiced from within the higher echelons of the party.

On another interpretation, however, moves towards an empowerment of the party base can be regarded as more apparent than real. That may be especially true in the case of the growing practice of giving the power of selecting the party leader to the party membership at large by the use, for instance, of postal ballots for election. This method and other forms of consultation on constitutional matters and policy issues work in the same direction and are also subject to doubt as to whether inner-party democracy works quite as it seems. The argument here is that the direct link between the leadership and ordinary party members is just as much an effective device for sidelining party activists and factional groups that are often the source of troublesome dissent. In contrast, the great majority of individual party members are not at all organized and are much more inclined to follow guidance from the top. Taken to an extreme, this rendering implies that party members have come to resemble a 'stage army', useful for the leadership to display on occasion, but not a proper actor.

In relation to the size of their electorates, party membership in most countries is declining. A recent study (Mair and van Biezen 2001) of party membership in the 1980s and 1990s found unequivocal evidence of a marked decline, especially in the 1990s and particularly evident in the old-established democracies, both in terms of absolute numbers and as a percentage of the electorate. This trend, coupled with a sceptical assessment of the reality of inner-party democracy, lends support to the idea of a general party decline. Yet this conclusion is too narrowly based. The viability of parties has to be judged also on their role more widely in society, on whether, for instance, the character of a party's organization in any way has effects on societal values, such as those of liberal democracy.

PARTIES, SOCIETY, AND THE STATE

If the 'decoupling' of political parties from their social roots continues, how should it be construed? Is it to be understood as a 'decline' of party or rather as an expression of changing relationships between party, society, and the state? One key to appreciating this relationship is the nexus provided by the legislature in parliamentary systems, the meeting point of the two distinct party orientations: one representative of society, the other relating to government and the state. The 'match' or fit between the two is unlikely ever to be perfect. For instance, neither increasing partisan dealignment nor a falling turnout need have adverse consequences for individual parties so long as their legislative representation and governing potential in relative terms is not greatly affected.

This consideration illustrates that there is a form of insulation between parties acting in a representative capacity and their legislative/governmental roles. Moreover, there is a sense in which the latter takes precedence over the former, as Michael Thies concludes:

Party in government is logically primary—indeed, the political party is a purposefully designed organisation of, by and for legislators... Parties existed before elections, but in the age of elections they need to compete for votes in order to retain or enhance their influence in government. (Thies 2000: 256)

An extension of arguments of this kind is that parties are becoming increasingly independent actors, less representative and less 'responsible', but nevertheless with their governing potential unaffected—perhaps even enhanced. Further consequences of this development would not necessarily be detrimental to the parties, as Mair writes:

The disenchantment with parties and even the resentment against parties should therefore not simply be read as a symptom of party decline *per se* ... Rather, the problem appears to lie in a set of contradictory developments, in which parties are at once less able but more visible, less relevant but more privileged. (Mair 1995: 55)

Yet, if it is not a decline of party with the increase in these 'contradictory developments', would the scenario then be in place for a more widespread crisis of the political system itself?

However, this is not how Mair, together with Richard Katz (1995) building on their earlier work (1994), have assessed likely development, as sketched in their formulation of the 'cartel party' as a new party type. Their reasoning is based, first, on the view that parties are no longer as firmly attached to civil society as in the past, and, second, that the role of the state, along with its potential for giving support to parties, has not hitherto been fully appreciated. With the growing distance from civil society, the parties are now turning to the state in order to maintain their position—even as a strategy for survival—by availing themselves of the varied resources at their disposal thanks to their close connection with it. What is more, in so doing the parties effectively act in collusion with one another and as a cartel, since they have a 'mutual interest in their collective organizational survival', whether in government or not. No doubt, however, the parties would rationalize their behaviour in rather different terms.

As for the future outlook, the position taken by Katz and Mair is that the 'interpenetration' of state and party represents a stable outcome and not evidence of party decline. Nor do they regard it as an evolutionary dead-end. The 'limited' and 'contained' competition allowed for by a cartel does imply that a number of issues will be suppressed and bracketed out from the competitive arena, but eventually the operation of the cartel will come under attack with challenges mounted by outsiders—anti-cartel parties. The resulting conflict could result in a crisis affecting a whole party system, but the outcome might equally be some form of accommodation, a radical change of policy forced by the new competitive pressure, or even the break-up of the existing cartel, but it need not lead to an 'ultimate crisis' spelling the end of parties.

As could be expected, the concept of the cartel party—equally to be understood as a kind of 'state party'—as an accurate account of current trends has attracted criticism (Koole 1996). There can be doubts, too, about its status as a full-blown party type but used in the present context, its value lies in showing that parties can compensate for their looser links with civil society by taking advantage of the security offered by the state. However, perhaps the overriding contribution of the cartel (or state) party concept is that it helps redress an imbalance—the one-sided concentration on parties and society relationships—by bringing the state to the forefront.

A focus on the state, in particular the state bureaucracy and its relationship with party government, draws attention to their association in the 'core executive'. The growing importance of the core executive as the foremost steering instrument of a government's policy agenda has increased the need for strong policy coordination. This development has been caused by the growing intensity—and diversity—of electoral demands and is enhanced by the character of modern party competition which encourages party 'outbidding' for votes within a narrowing ideological range. These demands have increased the role of the state along with its rising financial requirements. Inevitably, too, when the amorphous complexity of government organization is exposed at critical junctures, the core executive has to engage in 'crisis management' (Peters *et al.* 2000*a*). Seen in this light, the ever-closer involvement of a party's political leadership with the state machinery supports a conclusion that not only are parties moving towards the state and away from civil society, but also that a party's leadership is becoming more remote from the party itself.

ALTERNATIVES TO PARTY DEMOCRACY?

From the preceding account of the various pressures on party democracy, it would be difficult to conclude that the decline of political parties was becoming inevitable. They have certainly changed the nature of their relationship with electorates, and in consequence their organizational structures and methods of appealing to voters, but many of the changes as much as anything demonstrate their ability to adapt to new conditions. It is the case that parties no longer perform many of their traditional roles, as Rudy Andeweg (1996: 156) puts it: 'Parties may have lost most of their functions with regard to the distribution of services, socialization, communication, aggregation, mobilization, but obituaries are still premature.'

Although a number of functions have been 'lost' to other agencies (and in some respects just as well), among those less easily divested is the key role of parties in 'bringing together' two sets of quite distinctive requirements of a democratic system—those of representation and those of authoritative allocations to be made by government.

Three lines along which alternatives to parties could develop—in principle completely replacing them—have been traced by Kaare Strøm (2000): neo-corporatism, pluralist democracy, and referendum democracy. All three presuppose an initial coexistence with party democracy although eventually supplanting it.

In some ways, neo-corporatism appears to be a credible alternative, since it combines a representative function, albeit primarily of economic interests, with scope for determining policy outcomes. Heisler's portrayal of a 'European Polity Model' goes furthest in showing how popular representation (and hence not restricted to the economic sector) might function in a system of authority segmented on functional lines, and at first acting alongside parties and parliaments (Heisler 1974). Eventually, however, parties would cede their primacy to the new form of representation and presumably also in government.

Attractive as the model is, neo-corporatist modes show little sign of developing further, according to Strøm, and apply only to a limited number of countries. They are likely to be ones that have particular historical features favouring practices of cooptation and interest accommodation. One reason that neo-corporatism has lost its appeal could be that the power of trade unions has weakened and made them far less eligible as partners in neo-corporatist arrangements.

Pluralist democracy would take a quite different course and according to Katz (1986: 50) would come about when, '... emphasis shifted from majority rule to the protection of minorities. This is achieved in part through the incoherence of parties'. Party 'incoherence', brought about by the voice of minorities, would lead to a fragmentation of existing party systems, with all vocal minorities gaining representation. It is far from clear whether this form of pluralism would lead to a stable outcome with existing parties smoothly adapting to a new pattern of representation. There could be difficulty in sustaining majority government. Alternatively, if it were sustained it could be at the price of permanent exclusion of some minorities, and 'minorities' by their nature tend to be self-perpetuating.

A pluralist system of democracy based on forms of territorial decentralization looks altogether more workable. In that case, party incoherence would result from the pressure of territorial minorities on national parties. The course of development would depend on the ability of these parties to maintain control in territorial areas, not least over their own parties in these areas. Ultimately, by a process of 'contagion', national parties would themselves have to change their own basis of representation, with fundamental consequences for the character of party government, that is assuming that a 'central' government still persisted. Even then, however, territorial pluralism would be party-like, although again, as with the minorities option, territorial pluralism would lead to a number of self-contained blocs with little room for change and possibly resulting in the permanent exclusion of some from government, scarcely a recipe for a sound liberal democracy.

It seems implausible to suppose that a pure 'referendum democracy' would be able to meet the conditions for running a complex modern state. Yet, at the same time, of the three alternatives, the extensive use of methods of 'direct' democracy appears to be the most likely path to be followed. In a developed form, it could rob parties of their ability to control the political agenda and shape electoral preferences. Such methods would include the use of popular initiatives to promote new measures, to challenge existing legislation and executive actions, and possibly at an extreme, too, giving the power of 'recall' aimed at removing members of the legislature as well as government ministers.

An obvious limitation to referendum democracy is that its scope is restricted to raising and deciding on specific issues. It would certainly curtail the power of parties, the legislature, and government. Yet referendum democracy could not replace them, but rather act as a powerful counterbalance, as in the Swiss case (Papadopoulos 2001). The danger would be that an uncomfortable coexistence could result in a sharp deterioration of party democracy that outweighed the benefits.

None of these three alternatives to political parties gives much help in analysing developments that are taking place at present, since they are more in the nature of theoretical models that invite interesting speculation rather than being rooted in an assessment of emerging realities. A dimension thus far not considered is the 'external' one, that is, external to the nation state. This aspect is of particular importance in the European context, largely because of the way in which the course of European integration is proceeding.

THE 'PARTY DEFICIT' IN THE EUROPEAN UNION

It can reasonably be objected that introducing this 'external' dimension stretches the idea of party decline too far and that irrespective of the course of European developments, national parties operating in their domestic context will be only marginally affected (Mair 2000). On one level, this argument is valid, but the distinction between 'external' and 'domestic' is steadily becoming less clear-cut for member states. The progressive character of European integration entails an ever-narrowing sphere of autonomy for parties in their domestic arenas. Unless they can find alternative compensation, the term 'decline' has to be appropriate. The question is whether they can gain sufficient compensation within the European context.

From its inception, what is now the European Union has been built up on the basis of inter-governmental negotiation and decision making. This mode can be seen as part of a wider trend, resulting in '... an apparently paradoxical phenomenon: at national level the general erosion of the policy-making capacity of the state has been accompanied by a strengthening of its core executive' (Peters *et al.* 2000*a*: 7). When applied to the situation of national parties and their influence within the European Union, this 'paradoxical' development affects them adversely in two ways. In the first place, the stronger position of the core executive has been primarily to the detriment of parties in their influence and control over government, as already discussed. But the erosion of the independent policy-making capacity of the state itself has led to a further loss of party input.

Although it applies in some degree to all of the state's external relationships, the inter-governmental impetus is particularly marked in the European Union. Besides the formal structures of negotiation and decision making in the European Council and the various councils of ministers, there are frequent, informal bi-lateral meetings, as well as numerous contacts between senior departmental officials. It is only within the core executives of member states that a complete oversight of European matters, and the coordination of the various departments involved, can be attained. Active party control, except over the broadest lines of policy, is not feasible. Nor can the parties be taken into account when compromises have to be negotiated with other member states, or if faced with the imperative of coalition-building with other member states. Once a comprehensive package-deal has been carefully negotiated, it is hardly to be expected that a parliament would try to unpick it at the risk of the entire agreement collapsing.

In its effects, the whole area of European-related matters leaves party and parliamentary input and control deficient, although it is probably the most prominent feature of a more general seepage of parliamentary power to the executive. Some redress of the balance may be had with the establishment of European Affairs Committees, general in the parliaments of member states, with powers of scrutiny over a government's European policies (Raunio and Hix 2000). Yet, by itself, this 'weapon' may be more of a palliative than a genuine cure.

If, along with the deficiency in their control over the executive, the sphere of domestic autonomy is decreasing—and that of the European level increasing—then the European Parliament should provide the means for parties to reassert themselves. That has not proved to be the case. A decisive step, some would say a misguided one, was taken with the introduction in 1979 of direct elections to the European Parliament; previously members had been seconded from the legislatures of member states. The reform was intended to secure popular legitimacy of European institutions by reducing the so-called 'democratic deficit'. The results have been modest: interest in 'European' matters remains low, the persistently low turnout gives European elections a second-order status, electoral choice is still shaped by purely domestic considerations, and scant public interest is taken of the proceedings of the European Parliament. Vernon Bogdanor (1996: 114) goes further: 'It is a paradox that direct elections, intended to help create the political will for European integration, might actually have served to increase popular alienation from European institutions, since the European party system is unable to act as a vehicle for genuine choice at the electoral level'. In part, this outcome can be ascribed to the limited competences of the European Parliament, but it also stems from the fact that the major party groups form an overwhelming 'consensual bloc' cooperating for closer integration.

There is a 'party deficit' at the European level, and the consequence is even more pronounced in the absence of a recognizable 'party system', that is, one based on party interaction. Such 'interaction' could, for instance, be based on the bi-polarity of 'left' and 'right' as the basis of party contestation as typifies national party systems. There are, of course, a number of scenarios that can be constructed of the form in which a European party system might develop (Andeweg 1995). But the underlying problem is whether any realistic scenario would allow party contestation to have full effect, as is the case in the formation of party government in parliamentary systems. It is the absence of such a 'government' that is an indelible feature of the European Union, and national governments could have no rational interest in ceding their authority in this way. As a consequence, a party system at the European level looks set to continue in its present stunted form, and unable to compensate for the deficiency of parties in their national arenas. If not a 'decline', it is not a promising future either.

12

Comparing Economic Interest Organizations

COLIN CROUCH

Organizations representing economic interests within individual nation states peaked in both social importance and academic interest during the 1970s and 1980s. It is often argued that since then they have declined in significance. There are four reasons for this: increasing economic globalization, the dominance of neo-liberal economic ideology, the rise of the individual enterprise, and the challenge of various non-functional interests. The following will assess the significance of each of these, paying attention to both general or convergent trends and those which suggest differences of national experience among European countries.

First we must establish the range of organizations to be included in the discussion. I shall define economic interest organizations as associations representing the joint interests of sectors of producers or consumers of goods or services, whether they are concerned with technical, commercial, or professional issues, or the respective roles of employers or employees. Therefore trade associations, consumers' associations, employers' organizations, and trade unions are all included.

The study of interest associations is often limited to that of voluntary bodies, excluding bodies set up by the state. But there is an important intermediate group—the chambers of trade and commerce in Germany, Austria, and some other countries—which should be included. These are statutory organizations with compulsory membership, but with governing boards elected by member firms and conducting their business autonomously. Although they are set up by the state, they are not controlled by it. Their statutory status does not prevent them from acting as interest representatives, though it may lead them to behave differently from purely voluntary bodies. French chambers, which were previously agencies of central government, have increasingly taken this form too.

During the late 1990s chambers of commerce in the United Kingdom, which had always been voluntary bodies, quite different from the French or German models, responded to government pressure and amalgamated with training and enterprise councils (TECs) (Crouch and Farrell 2001; Bennett and McCoshan 1993). These latter were creatures of government, with managing boards initially appointed by government but subsequently self-reproducing; they were not representatives and had no membership. By amalgamating with them, British chambers gradually gravitated towards the statutory model of interest representation embodied in their German counterparts. TECs were in part public bodies, but they were also private companies; and as they amalgamated with chambers they became membership organizations.[1] They were thus an interesting example of a thoroughly hybrid form of organization, a phenomenon which is likely to be increasingly common in future, as governments and some other actors experiment with new organizational forms. Thus, although the starting point of this account is the study of associations and neither statutory bodies nor firms, we eventually find it necessary to re-examine that distinction.

Firms as such are initially excluded because they do not have a membership which elects representatives or otherwise becomes involved in the determination of policy, but rather sell services to whoever wants them. At least in legal terms, the firm is an organizational form quite distinct from a membership association. In practice the distinction is less clear, for a number of reasons. First, many, perhaps most, membership associations and other voluntary bodies have a trading arm which operates on a market basis, selling certain services. An association may limit such sales to its own members, or it may offer them to all comers, perhaps offering reduced prices to members. Second, many of the services which a firm or individual might acquire through association membership could instead be bought in the market. Technical advice can be bought from consultants; representation in a dispute can be carried out by hired lawyers; even pressing a policy argument on government can be pursued by professional lobbying firms.

Sometimes an individual member's relationship to the decision-making centre of a large association may be so remote that his or her use of its services may be virtually indistinguishable from the purchase of the services concerned in the market. In turn the leadership may feel so remote from the mass of members that its means of maintaining contact with them are identical to those used between firms and customers: advertising campaigns, backed by market research to assess the member-customers' views of the organization and their aspirations for services. This may be true even if the forms of membership participation through electing officers, being elected to governing councils or participating in local meetings, are retained.

We can gain an idea of how a membership organization might turn from an association offering services to members into a firm selling them to customers by examining the history of British building societies (Llewellyn 1997). These organizations make long-term loans for house purchase and provide investment opportunities for lenders in order to fund these loans. They are so-called 'mutual' societies, in that when either borrowing from or lending to a building society one becomes a member of it. They have no external shareholders but are owned by these members, who elect their governing boards. However, within a mass membership of many hundreds of thousands, even millions, it is not clear that these lenders and borrowers find the experience of being a member any different from that of being a customer at a bank—though on

---

[1] In 2000 the UK government abolished the TECs after less than a decade of existence and amalgamated their functions into regional learning and skills councils, a similar kind of hybrid organization but covering more extensive geographical territories and a broader range of responsibilities for education institutions.

average lenders are likely to receive higher interest rates and borrowers pay lower rates than in the case of banks, as no shareholder interest has to be satisfied. In recent years many British building societies have taken advantage of this situation, abolished their 'mutual' status, and become straightforward banks. Former members have become simple customers, and a new class of shareholders has become the owner of the societies and receives the profits. Members had first to be persuaded to vote to give up their rights, and this was usually achieved by paying them some money.

One major difference between an association and a firm is that the former might in certain circumstances be asked, usually by government, to regulate or even discipline its members. It is very unlikely that a firm would be able or willing to do this with its customers,[2] for example, a trade association might be expected to share in the regulation of the quality of the goods or services provided by its members; or a trade union might be expected to secure wage restraint. In the case of associations of firms, the organization's leaders have to be careful that their discipline does not lead their members to prefer simply to buy the services they receive from their association from firms of consultants who will not impose such constraints.

This leads us on to consider different ways in which interest organizations relate to their members and to those with whom they deal in order to represent those members. As Streeck and Schmitter (1985) have shown, this gives a number of different logics of action to such organizations, a trade-off among which has to be achieved. This can then be resolved into a number of alternative relationships. Crouch (1993) identifies four of these, and this model will be used below. The original analysis was concerned solely with industrial relations. This is a rather special case as there are usually three groups to consider: employer interests, employee interests, and government, whereas in many other situations there is only an interest organization and government. This is especially the case where an economic interest is being represented other than in the industrial relations context, that is, where there is as producer or trade interest rather than an employer one. (However, in many of these latter cases there may well be an organized consumer or environmental interest.) It may also be, as frequently in the industrial relations case, that government is not necessarily a central actor. Two 'side' organizations might resolve conflicts between them through private and not legal agreements. The model can therefore be adapted to a number of situations outside industrial relations.

The four types of interest relationships identified are: contestation, pluralism, bargained corporatism, and authoritarian corporatism. Contestation identifies circumstances in which one or another interest organization, or the state, refuses to accept the right of an opposed interest to have any organized expression at all. This is very frequently the approach of employers to the possibility that their workers might form trade unions, and can be found in other contexts too. For example, a large corporation might prevent its suppliers from organizing to represent their interests against it. Interest group activity by the suppressed interest is either very weak and sporadic, or takes the form of expressions of open conflict.

---

[2] Discipline by a large customer firm of its suppliers is however very common; and of course the discipline of employees by an employing firm is routine.

Under pluralism interests have considerable scope for organization, and the organizations that result combine bargaining with other interests with lobbying of government in order to advance the group being represented. They accept no wider responsibility, though they will be expected to accept the right of rival interests similarly to organize. If a large number of interests operate actively in this way, there are likely to be problems of system overload, leading to inflation or even ungovernability (Dahl 1982; Crouch 1993). At some point government is likely to intervene to weaken the capacity of at least some of the interests involved, possibly turning to contestative strategies.

Corporatism refers to situations where, in addition to representing the interests of their members, organizations also discipline them in the interests of some wider general order or in order to fulfill commitments made to bargaining partners. The range of organizations involved is typically smaller than under pluralism, because the kind of control implied is not possible if members have considerable choice to join different organizations; they will tend to choose those which exercise least discipline over them. Historically, corporatist organizations have taken two very diverse forms. They may be established artificially and compulsorily by governments, usually those which have ruthlessly pursued a strategy of contestation and exclusion towards autonomous organizations but wish to leave some structures in place to placate the interest concerned. This was the strategy pursued by fascist and communist governments. It may also be pursued privately by employers who, having refused to accept membership of a trade union by their workers, then establish a representation system which they control themselves. These are all systems of authoritarian corporatism. Obviously, interest representation is in fact very weak.

In a strongly contrasting form of corporatism, autonomous and powerful interest organizations may accept obligations of the corporatist kind, perhaps to avoid the conflict likely to follow if they were relentlessly to pursue pluralist strategies. Alternatively, they may represent such a large proportion of the society concerned that their own members would clearly be among the victims of any major disruption which they caused. Such organizations are known as 'encompassing' (Olson 1982). These forms of corporatism are usually referred to as 'neo-corporatism' to distinguish them from the authoritarian variety.

CURRENT SOURCES OF CHANGE IN INTEREST REPRESENTATION

We can now consider the main forces of change currently affecting the operation of interest representation in western European and other advanced societies.

Economic Globalization

A number of writers have described how the globalization of the economy breaks the link between firms and their national bases (Castells 1997; Beck 1998; Giddens 1999), and in particular reduces considerably the power of organized labour (Boyer 1998; Crouch 1998; Hyman 1998). There are several aspects to this argument.

First, it is argued that globalization reduces the economic significance of nation states and their governments (Ohmae 1991; Castells 1997: ch 5; see also the discussions in Hurrell and Menon, and Thatcher, this volume). These have in the past been fundamental to systems of organized interests, governments normally being major focuses of lobbying and interest-representation activity. If nation states lose their capacity to regulate economies, then national interest associations lose their focus and are likely to decline alongside them. Meanwhile no international political level is replacing that of the nation state. The one global economic authority that does exist, the World Trade Organization, has a mandate to increase the freedom of trade and therefore to reduce national economic regulation without replacing it with an international regulation other than to further free trade. Large corporations are therefore the only actors in global space; they have no political interlocutor (Beck 1998). They do combine with each other for some purposes, but in doing so they do not form associations. The number of global firms involved in any particular area is not large, and they have plenty of internal corporate resources. When they link up they form specific, usually time-limited strategic alliances with each other, which involves a completely different form of organization (Ohmae 1985).

It is further contended that, as large firms move increasingly to this global level, they have no use for membership of their former national associations. They therefore withdraw from these, which find that they are losing their most important members and become associations of small and medium-sized enterprises (SMEs) only. This is particularly problematic for neo-corporatist forms of interest representation, as large firms lose interest in helping to maintain social compromises within a particular nation state. Further still, global firms are said to use their capacity to 'regime shop' in order to locate themselves in countries where labour is prevented from organizing (Boyer 1998; Hyman 1998). This creates a constant downward pressure on labour's strength everywhere.

There is much strength in these arguments, but they may be exaggerated. National governments should not be expected simply to accept their loss of role in the wake of globalization and deregulation. The nation state remains the world's most important *political* level. In democracies national electorates remain fundamental to governments' survival; even in non-democracies regimes are concerned to ensure the economic strength of their national system. If certain areas of former national policy competence are ruled out by global developments, then governments can be expected to seek new ways of assisting national economic performance. Of course, one option is to seek to lead the field in deregulation and liberalization; here the government role will be limited to trying to abolish its own competences as rapidly as possible. But other governments will perceive that not all can play that particular game, and that they themselves have different comparative advantages. They therefore seek alternative approaches.

Not only will new activities often provide a new focus for interest organizations, but the structure of the organizations themselves may change in response. Countries with particularly well coordinated and cooperative corporatist systems may try further to enhance their effectiveness. This has been particularly evident in industrial relations (Schmitter and Grote 1997; Pochet 1999; Boyer 2000; Crouch 2000). In some cases organizations have negotiated new competitive labour-market strategies. In others, looser social pacts have established certain baselines for national cooperation. In these cases the challenge of globalization paradoxically *strengthens* the interest representation system.

Sometimes global corporations present within a country (whether initially 'native' to it or not) will participate in these new national strategies, as their production facilities within the country concerned will gain from any collective achievements of the bargaining. Often, however, they do stand aside from it as predicted by the globalization theorists. For example, the new US-based high-tech firms which have been investing massively in Ireland do not share the new neo-corporatist wage-restraint agreements which bind the rest of the work force, and which have been growing in importance (Murphy and Roche 1997; Hardiman 2000). For a time, government, unions, and SMEs seemed to have decided that having the investment was worth the growing inequalities and social divisions being produced; increasingly however there are tensions. Elsewhere, continuing attempts by governments, unions, and perhaps purely domestic capital to sustain a national model have been undermined by a refusal of global corporations to participate in new national pacts. This is currently the case in Sweden, which for a long time had the curious combination of both a particularly high proportion of multinational corporations and a political preference for imposing a particularly high number of constraints on the freedom of capital (Pestoff 1991, 1995).

The fact that SMEs have little option but to participate in national systems of interest organization is important. Small firms have been the source of considerable economic dynamism in recent years, in both manufacturing and many branches of services, even if they increasingly have to operate as clients of large enterprises. Globalization might if anything strengthen their dependence on the interest representation system of their home-base country, as it requires the collaboration of both firms and governments to enable small enterprises to continue to hold their own within international markets. One explanation of the very different recent developments of neo-corporatist interest structures in Denmark and Sweden is that the former is dominated by SMEs but the latter by multinational concerns. While during the 1960s and 1970s Swedish neo-corporatism was considerably more effective than Danish, today the reverse is the case (Due *et al.* 1994).

This diversity of contexts and past experiences is helping to create a new diversity in interest-organization patterns rather than convergence on a model imposed by globalization.

Further, the argument that there is an institutional vacuum above the nation state can be challenged. A global economy requires a considerable degree of standardization if products from diverse countries are to be used all over the world (Gabel 1987; Cargill 1996). Sometimes these standards are required for health and safety purposes, sometimes in order to enable a facility to be used at all. Sometimes they are worked out, either cooperatively or aggressively, in informal ways among global enterprises themselves, requiring very little in the way of external rules. At other times, however, they require either the formal agreement of governments to implement them within their jurisdictions, or the active participation of governments in determining which standards shall prevail and be globally imposed by some or other international authority. This can become a struggle over which country's preferred practices shall become the global standard; or rather the practices preferred by which country's *firms*.

This competition is becoming a kind of new mercantilism, or at least a version of national champions strategy compatible with an era of deregulation, as governments and leading firms engage in technical diplomacy on behalf of their chosen standard. In many cases there will only be one or a very small number of firms involved along-side an individual government in such struggles (as is the case, e.g. with Microsoft and the US government in the field of computer software). However, at other times a whole group of national-level producers will be seeking to have their preferred pattern imposed as a standard (as with the US Internet provider companies). Their lobbying of government to act on their behalf may require formation of an interest organization of a more or less orthodox pluralist kind.

One of the responses made by governments to erosion of their role is the formation of world-region authorities, by far the most advanced of which to date is the European Union. The extent to which the European Commission has become the focus of organized activity is discussed in the following chapter by Mazey and Richardson. Here we need to consider the relationship between activity at this level and the national scene. This is usually assumed to be a zero-sum one: if one level acquires power over a policy issue, then there is a loss to the other. However, it is possible for the relationship between European Union and national activity to be positive-sum. This works in the following way. If the European Union intervenes in an economic sector, organizations representing firms in that sector often have an interest in lobbying the Commission indirectly via their national governments as well as directly in Brussels. Relations with interest organizations of both Commission and national governments are simultaneously reinforced. Meanwhile, European-level associations draw heavily on the strength of their national affiliates in order to achieve presence in Brussels.

Business associations may even have an interest in strengthening their relations with national trade unions in order to persuade them to join them in lobbying the Commission and the European Parliament, thereby widening the political range open to the lobbying (Dubbins 2002). It is notable that, even though developments in collective bargaining at the European level have been extremely weak and are strongly resisted by most employers and their organizations, the amount of joint activity by employers' associations and unions at the EU level has grown steadily since the launch of the 1992 single market programme. It is not so much that this programme has created a new industrial relations agenda; indeed, much of this programme concerns deregulation. However, as Majone (1993, 1994*b*) argues, deregulation usually takes the form of re-regulation; and even if there is net deregulation, its terms have to be negotiated. The single market programme has therefore created a considerably extended

European agenda of technical and trade issues which deeply concern firms, and which can benefit from union support—provided firms and their associations have good relations with the unions involved. Therefore, there is a curious mixture of contestation (in the refusal of firms to bargain with unions in the normal way), pluralist lobbying, and a limited neo-corporatism as the Commission tries to bind all these representative organizations into a kind of European social compromise.

Neo-liberal Ideology

Since the collapse of the Keynesian consensus under the pressure of the commodity price shocks in the late 1970s, an essentially neo-liberal economic policy consensus has come to dominate, throughout western Europe and far beyond. Its main postulate is that economic activity should be governed by market forces alone. It is therefore hostile not just to government intervention, but also to the operation of organized interests. These are doubly suspect: one, because they are likely to interfere with market forces in their own right; second, because they often put pressure on governments to intervene.

This hostility takes practical form in a variety of ways. It operates directly as ideology: politicians and business leaders who believe that intervention in market processes must always be negative will simply avoid any contact with interest organizations. Perhaps more important than this is the diminution of the political agenda which in principle follows from adoption of neo-liberal assumptions. This covers much of the same ground as the globalization theme, deregulation having been both a product of neo-liberal ideas and a cause of globalization. If governments are prevented from having policy on a certain set of issues, then there is little point in interests organizing around them.

Neo-liberal politics has in particular little time for neo-corporatism, especially in the labour market. If unions have to be accepted, they are forced to operate as closely as possible to the level of the individual workplace, where it will be more difficult for them to avoid the impact of market forces (Crouch 1994). The idea of achieving wage efficiency through some degree of centralized coordination is deeply unattractive.

The situation confronting other interests is more complex. Neo-liberal governments are sympathetic to the lobbying of business interests, especially if this is presented as furthering the extension of markets. But it is more consistent with neo-liberal ideology for firms not to join associations, which are collective bodies, but instead to buy services through the market, including the use of lobbying consultants, who specialize in developing links with politicians, their advisors, and civil servants. Because the relationship between the contracting firm and the lobbying firm takes the form of a market exchange, neo-liberals see far fewer objections to this than they do to associational activity. Paradoxically, in some respects lobbying by consultants is however likely to produce more market distortion than associational activity; the reasons for this will be considered in detail in the following section.

Within Europe the decomposition of membership associations in favour of lobby consultants has gone furthest in the United Kingdom. In Germany and Sweden, while there has been only a partial shift towards neo-liberal policies by governments, there has however been a fuller conversion among business elites. In Germany this has taken the form of a decline in membership of associations. Some firms have argued that, in such areas as vocational training, membership of associations of the German neo-corporatist type imposes obligations on them which mean that they might lose out in competition against firms from countries, like the United Kingdom and United States, which lack such constraints (Bührer 2000; Kohler-Koch 2000). Spokespersons of the German chambers or *Handelskammern* have stressed how they are becoming more like their British counterparts, offering a string of services for sale to member/customers, rather than trying to achieve collective representation and cohesion (Bennett *et al.* 1993).

The strategy of Swedish firms has been quite different, though with the same over-all aim (Pestoff 1991, 1995; Kjellberg 1998). They have remained firm in their membership of their associations, but have sought to turn these into pluralist lobbying organizations, rejecting neo-corporatist involvements. The associations become the weapon in the struggle against neo-corporatism, not (as in Germany) an instrument being discarded as a result of that struggle. However, not all sectors of Swedish employers support the full campaign to destroy the institutional system. And Swedish trade unions and, at least when the social democrats are in office, the government, persist in using neo-corporatist structures and practices for mediating between government and economy. There is therefore a kind of institutional stalemate within the country.

A different situation exists in France. Agriculture has long been subject to a strong neo-corporatist organization. Outside that previously very important sector, however, associations of both business and labour have usually been weak. Relations between government and economy have taken the forms of: (a) legal regulations issued by government and imposed on business without much interaction; and (b) inter-personal links between government personnel and the leaders of major firms, especially the 'national champions' (Cohen 1995). Unions played only a marginal, contestative part (Reynaud 1975).[3]

However, this has been changing for over thirty years, the changes being complicated because they stem from very diverse sources. First, concern among elites at the alienation of organized labour made manifest in the disturbances of 1968 has led to a series of initiatives to encourage business and labour to operate through hitherto virtually non-existent neo-corporatist structures. Second, the advance of neo-liberalism and deregulation has challenged the typical French practices of detailed regulation and the promotion of national champions. In this context, the neo-liberal challenge is paradoxically strengthening neo-corporatist initiatives, which emerge as less unacceptable alternatives than the former *étatisme*.

In Italy too, singularities of the politico-economic context have made neo-corporatism and neo-liberalism into strange bed fellows. The reasons are somewhat similar, and

---

[3] A major exception has been the tripartite management of pension and social insurance funds. For a long time a purely technical matter, these have leaped into political prominence in recent years in France and elsewhere as governments have tried to tackle problems in the funding of pensions (Ebbinghaus and Hassel 1999).

since Italian interest organizations are generally stronger than those in France, the change in Italy has been more significant. As a past history of extreme labour conflict gave way during the 1970s to a contining search for tripartite dialogue and coopera-tion, an important element of consensus was that the state-centred model of the long period of Christian Democratic political dominance had become outmoded. Trade unions and the political left therefore cooperated with some neo-liberal reforms, because they advanced the dismantling of that system (Regini and Regalia).

Some countries present even stronger examples of neo-corporatist institutions being used to achieve reforms of the kind often sought by neo-liberal measures. This is most notably the case in the Netherlands, where a series of changes in labour-market regulation, designed to increase the flexibility of labour, were negotiated through neo-corporatist institutions which had seemed at the time to be in serious decline (Visser and Hemerijck 1997); and in Denmark, where social partners instituted a similar agenda (Kjær and Pedersen 2001). In both cases however the result was a set of innovations that departed considerably from the orthodox neo-liberal policy set.

The relationship between neo-corporatism and neo-liberalism can therefore be far more complex than inspection of the general ideological, or British, German, and Swedish debates suggest. The relationship of neo-liberal policies to lobbying forms of organization is even more ambiguous, as discussion of the British case shows. By advancing the position of those interests which succeed through the market, but sup-pressing those which thrive through its abatement or regulation, neo-liberal policies have non-neutral effects on the political balance of interests within a society. Should they wish to use organization to advance their causes, interests favoured by the mar-ket will find that they face less opposition from the now weakened anti-market forces. Pro-business lobbies will find it easier to exert influence over policy and are therefore likely to grow in power and prominence. Very strictly speaking, this should not be possible, since in a pure market-driven economy there are no policies to be lobbied for once a set of pure markets has been set in place. However, in reality an advanced modern economy is unlikely to be a pure market one. In many sectors there will be highly imperfect competition, and in any case governments can never achieve total deregulation.

The Rise of the Individual Enterprise

Both globalization and neo-liberalism imply something of a shift from business asso-ciations to the individual enterprise as the focus of business politics. Other, separate developments have further strengthened this tendency (Strange 1994; Crouch 1996).

First, in the uncertain product markets and rapidly changing technologies of the contemporary economy, individual firms seek as much freedom as possible from external constraint in order to maintain maximum flexibility for action and cost reduction. While the primary constraints which concern them are pressures from the state and organized labour, they also become resentful of burdens imposed by their own business associations, as we have seen is taking place in Germany. Second, the growth of consultancy firms, replacing services of the kind which enterprises used to acquire from their associations, is both a product of an initial rejection of associational constraints and a facilitator of further subsequent rejections.

Associations seek measures which will assist a whole sector, while individual firms seek their own privileges, such as the award of government contracts. Here firms have no shared interests, only competing ones. They therefore prefer to lobby alone. Large firms either develop their own lobbying departments or draw on the services of consultants who specialize in developing political contacts. Coen (1996) has shown how individual enterprises are becoming increasingly important in lobbying in Brussels, and much the same has been found in some specific national studies. Even where government is consulting, or being lobbied by, firms on matters of general sectoral interest, once firms have started to develop in-house political consultation capacity, it becomes in their interests to keep this activity at firm rather than association level. The firm may subsequently benefit from government favours if its staff members have become known to government personnel through the lobbying process.

These developments, which impart a zero-sum element to relations between firms and their associations, are probably the most potent at eroding the role of the latter. Almost by definition, only a minority of enterprises can gain access to government in this way, except in those sectors dominated by a very small number of oligopolies. It is however then possible that associations become used by firms excluded from the magic circle of political insiders, perhaps backed by government itself not wanting to become too beholden to a small group of individual firms.

A further, quite different factor also favours the rise of representation by firms alone. Current structures of economic interest organizations usually reflect twentieth century industrialism rather than the emerging new sectors, whether these are in services or in manufacturing. This is partly because of an important characteristic of sector-level association-forming: economic 'sectors' rarely have a 'natural' identity. They are social constructs, shaped partly by how government statisticians analyse the economy, and partly by how firms tend to group themselves in interest organizations. For example, firms making steel seem easily identifiable as a group. However, how far up and down the production chain are they likely to extend their organizations? In Germany, following an originally French practice, steel producers have long been associated with both coal and iron ore mining, within a so-called *Montanenbereich*. This means literally 'mountain sector', referring to the fact that originally the iron ore from which steel was made and the coal which powered the first industrial steel furnaces were mined out of the side of mountains, and that the steel works were located nearby. The same link was embodied in the formation of the European Coal and Steel Community, one of the forerunners of the European Union. In many other countries, however, this link has not been made, and the coal and steel industries have always been organized quite separately from each other. On the other hand, in some cases the organization of steel producers moves down rather than up the production chain, extending to include metal products, such as non-powered machinery.

Definitions of the boundaries of sectors will be particularly problematic at times of rapid technical innovation, which often consists precisely in bringing together technologies and processes which were once seen as different. The computing equipment and telecommunications industries are interesting contemporary examples. Only a few years ago computing was regarded as part of the office machinery production industry, and telecommunications as part of postal services. Then they each became recognized as sectors in their own right and ceased to be viewed in their earlier contexts. Now the growth of the Internet and of mobile telephone technology is gradually bringing them together, as what were previously seen as two quite separate sets of both production technologies and final products are becoming fused. It is possible that before long we shall see computing and telecommunications as a single sector.

Related to this is the location of individual firms across sectors. There have long been very large firms which have had holdings across different parts of the economy. The Dutch and British East India Companies were doing this before the end of the seventeenth century, and firms like Société Générale in Belgium behaved similarly in the industrial period. For much of the nineteenth and twentieth centuries, however, most firms at least predominated in one area, or a small number of related areas, of products and production systems. The growing capacity of managerial systems, aided partly by developments in computer and telecommunications technologies, partly by advancing organizational principles, has made possible far more conglomerates, active across not only quite diverse sectors of manufacturing but also across services too. Globalization has assisted this process, and the economic uncertainty of the post-Keynesian economy has also pressed firms to diversify in order to protect themselves against sudden sharp declines in individual industries.

The boundaries between sectors become difficult to discern, and so does the location of firms within sectors, creating a double obscurity of sectoral structure. The idea of economic sectors or branches, which has usually defined the pattern of both trade associations and organizations of employers and employees, is therefore becoming elusive. This makes it even more likely that large firms will prefer to represent themselves, or employ consultancy firms to represent them, rather than remain part of an associational system which relates to outmoded industry boundaries and has little to do with the firm's internal structure.

The Challenge of Non-producer Interests

Economic interests are usually the ones which find it easiest to mobilize power and influence within a political system. Provided government wants the functions concerned to be performed, such interests are able to claim that, unless government policy follows the lines they recommend, efficiency in performing the function is likely to be damaged (Lindblom 1977). They can usually also claim a monopoly on knowledge of how to carry out their functions. If, say, the motor industry tells government that it is not feasible to seek to reduce lead emissions below a certain level, government is likely to believe them unless it has very reliable sources of autonomous expertise available to it.

It is not only economic groups who are able to make claims of this kind, but also the military is certainly in a similar position. So are professions in sectors considered particularly important, such as medicine and the law. However, in contemporary society where governments seem overwhelmingly dependent on economic success, it is normally groups who can claim to speak authoritatively for a particular economic function who can be most effective. Further, the costs of representing a business interest to government are a legitimate business expense, able to be charged to the business activities of the corporation, and probably tax-deductible. This will be true both of membership subscriptions and other costs of associational participation, and of expenditure on company lobbyists.

Groups wishing to challenge a particular economic interest—or economic interests in general, as do some environmentalists—usually have a built-in disadvantage. So do groups who cannot realistically claim any economic advantage if their goals are pursued. Broadly two possibilities are open to these; they are not strictly alternatives, as both could be pursued. First, they can threaten active disruption of some kind if their interests are not met. This overlaps with the implicit threats made by functional groups, but has less legitimacy, because it involves taking action to prevent the supply of a good which would otherwise be available without difficulty. Trade unions fall somewhere between interests of this kind and functional ones. If they threaten that their members will not be willing to carry out their function unless they are, say, paid higher wages, then they are making the same kind of threat as an association of firms. However, firms are able to present their threat, not as a deliberately disruptive action, but as an unavoidable and natural consequence of not taking their advice.

Organizations which can make no threats at all must largely appeal to shared goals, that is make moral appeals to a wider public. This is mainly what environmental groups do, though they sometimes also make use of direct action to prevent, at least symbolically, the carrying out of actions to which they are opposed. Of course, the fact that a cause is raised as a moral appeal does not mean that everyone agrees with it, as the example of rival lobbies over abortion shows. These both make moral claims, but opposing ones.

Many observers would claim that these disadvantages of non-producer groups are particularly strong in neo-corporatist interest systems. Not only are there particularly tight interlocks between government and producer interests, but there is a more or less closed list of accepted and acceptable organizations. This is because within neo-corporatist systems, accepted organizations share certain governance functions with government itself. Non-producer causes, in particular those of green or ecological movements, are likely to be marginalized and even politically excluded. In contrast, it is argued, since within pluralist systems access to government influence does not carry implications of sharing in public authority, it is therefore left open. Where the rewards of being an insider are not so great, there is less distinction between insiders and outsiders.

It is difficult to test this hypothesis, as much depends on what issues are selected. Perhaps the most important case in recent years has been the challenge of green movements. These are a classic case of cause groups claiming to represent a wider public interest confronting functional interests, as many of the issues they want to raise challenge major manufacturing industries—particularly chemicals—whose trade interests as well as trade unions have been strongly represented in both neo-corporatist structures and pluralist lobbying.

If this thesis is correct, we should expect to find green interests making least progress within countries like Germany, the Netherlands, and Scandinavia, and most in France, the United Kingdom, or, outside Europe, the United States. If anything, however, the evidence suggests exactly the opposite, it having been precisely neo-corporatist countries which have taken the lead in green issues within not only Europe but the whole industrial world, while the United States has resisted environmental concerns more resolutely than many European countries. This is true of a number of different issues: atmospheric pollution, the use of non-renewable energy sources, and various forms of chemical and genetic modification of food.

The hypothesis which suggests that producer interests will be particularly powerful under neo-corporatism under estimates the greater power of business lobbies within ostensibly 'open' pluralist systems. Precisely because such systems do not convey official status and are in principle open to anyone capable of getting themselves organized, there is often less constitutional interest in and concern over exactly what goes on within them. Where organized interests do gain obvious political privilege, as is the case in neo-corporatism, both the interests themselves as well as political circles may need to take more explicit care that important public-interest voices are not excluded.[4] This certainly seems to be the view taken by the Swedish industrialists association, SAF. One reason which that organization gives for wanting to move Sweden from a neo-corporatist to a pluralist lobbying form of interest representation is precisely that under neo-corporatism the unions always have to be given parity of participation rights, while under a lobbying system, nothing is guaranteed; SAF believes, probably correctly, that employer interests would then carry more weight than labour ones.

There is some debate over whether, whatever the character of the interest system, producer interests have been under greater or lesser challenge from critics in recent years. One approach to this question draws attention to the importance of manufacturing industry and agriculture in establishing the large interest blocs characteristic of most of the twentieth century. Employers and employees alike of these industries would give priority to their success and therefore support their influence over government. For the past thirty years or so, however, manufacturing (and of course agriculture) has been declining within the advanced economies, especially as a source of employment. Services of various kinds have grown in importance instead. The political power of the interests representing manufacturing should therefore have declined, implying also a change in social values. This is often analysed in terms of a hypothesized movement from materialist to post-materialist concerns, or at least to the liberation of much of the population away from a commitment to manufacturing,

---

[4] There may of course be other explanations for these differences. For example, the proportional representation systems of most continental European countries may have allowed environmentalist parties to gain more influence than in the United Kingdom or United States, so the issue may in fact concern different forms of parliamentary representation rather than of interest representation. Nevertheless, it is certainly difficult to sustain the hypothesis that in neo-corporatist systems non-functional interests are particularly unable to influence government.

enabling them to take up issues of environmental or ethical concern (Eder 1993; Inglehart 1977, 1997; Melucci 1989). These arguments are often also associated with observations of the rising educational level of populations, which, it is argued, enables them to raise their horizons and consider such questions as the future of the planet.

The viability of this thesis depends very much on how the character of the new services sectors is viewed, as they are quite heterogeneous. Much services activity comprises the distributive sector—largely engaged in transporting and selling goods, most of them the products of manufacturing firms; and business services—largely engaged in providing services to firms, prominently including manufacturing ones (Castells 1996, 2000: ch. 4; Crouch 1999: ch. 4). It is doubtful whether there is such a sharp change in economic and social interests away from those of manufacturing in the rise of these sectors. On the other hand, much of the shift towards services, especially in the 1970s and 1980s, took the form of the rise of the so-called social and community services—in particular education, health and other social services, and government administration (Castells *ibid.*; Crouch *ibid.*). It has certainly been demonstrated that persons working in these sectors are particularly strongly represented among the activists of new social movements and environmentalist organizations (Eder 1993; Melucci 1989). This does provide support for at least some forms of the post-materialist thesis.

But one must still be cautious about drawing overall conclusions. There is a tendency to associate services with clean, knowledge-rich, and high-tech activities, and manufacturing with pollution, less educated workforces, and low technology. This is a considerable distortion. Some services employment, particularly some of the most rapidly growing activities, such as domestic service and work in catering outlets, is mainly low-skilled. There is also a good deal of high-technology manufacturing production: the computer industry, telecommunications equipment, and bio-engineering, once it moves beyond the research and development stage.

CONCLUSIONS

Are interest organizations declining or rising in importance? The evidence reviewed above leads us to the conclusion that there certainly are major trends in that direction: globalization, neo-liberalism, and the associated growing autonomy of the individual enterprise all produce that same conclusion, and suggest increasing difficulties in particular for neo-corporatist forms of interest articulation. It is less likely that environmentalist and consumer organizations have contributed to a weakening of the power of economic producer interests, if only because globalization and neo-liberalism have actually served to strengthen those interests, at any rate on the employer side, even if they have weakened the neo-corporatist associational form in which they were often embedded. Possibly the most important single change is the growing role of firms of lobbyists working for individual companies, replacing associations of companies, in corporate representation.

On the other hand, this apparent master tendency is checked at various points and in various ways. As with virtually all social trends, those adversely affected must be expected to react; they will not necessarily do so with great success, but they may be able to do enough to disturb or divert the main lines of change. Therefore globalization produces counter-responses, at national, European, and some other levels. Some of these stimulate organizational activity: the insecurity threatened by neo-liberalism can on occasions perversely strengthen attempts at neo-corporatism. And even if producer interests may usually win in confrontations with their ecological and other critics, their activities are brought under public scrutiny far more than in the recent past.

13

Interest Groups and the Brussels Bureaucracy

SONIA MAZEY AND JEREMY RICHARDSON

Tell me and I'll forget,
show me and I'll remember,
involve me and I'll understand.
(Chinese proverb quoted in the European Commission's
Paper on *Governance and the European Union*)

INTRODUCTION: THE LOGIC OF EUROPEAN LOBBYING

Much has been written about the *sui generis* nature of the European Union. Nevertheless, the relations between the Commission, on the one hand, and an increasingly Europeanized interest group system on the other, appear to have developed along quite predictable lines. The Commission, for its part, exhibits familiar bureaucratic features, such as sectorization, problems of coordination, and a penchant for developing close relations with organized interests. For their part, interest groups have been keen to exploit the Commission (and, of course, other EU institutions, not discussed here, such as the European Parliament and the European Court of Justice) as a new opportunity structure from which to gain influence over public policy making. In practice, most interests are now organized at the European level, yet it seems that there is still scope for new interests to develop a lobbying presence in Brussels. Thus, in March 2000, the American corporation Mattel (the makers of Barbie toys) advertised the post of public affairs analyst 'in order to maintain close contact with various trade, government, and European Union organizations in Brussels' (*European Voice*, 30 March 2000). With Barbie established in Brussels, the EU-level interest group system must surely be approaching saturation point! As the Commission remains at the hub of EU policy making (at least in terms of day-to-day policy making), this chapter focuses upon the links between EC Commission officials, responsible for the formulation (and implementation) of Community initiatives, and the growing number of interest groups affected by them. The founding Treaties of the EC state that the European Commission is the initiator of Community policies and, formally speaking, has the sole right to propose Community legislation. The Commission is also the executive arm of Community governance, ultimately responsible for ensuring the effective implementation of the policies decided upon by the Council of Ministers. Even though the Commission argues that the majority of legislative initiatives emanate from either the Council of Ministers or from national governments, the Commission nevertheless plays the pivotal role in translating initiatives into clear proposals. Administrative officials within the Commission are thus centrally involved in the formulation, management, and application of Community policies.

This fact is now widely appreciated by the very large number of lobbyists in Brussels who—whilst also devoting attention to other EU policy-making institutions and national administrations—generally direct their energies towards the Commission as their first port of call. 'Commission watching' is an essential part of monitoring that crucial stage of the EU policy process—agenda-setting. Moreover, interest groups recognize that often, for them, 'the devil is in the detail'. Again, this leads them to seek a close liaison with Commission officials. This is, of course, not to understate the important role in policy initiation played by other EU institutions, especially the Council of Ministers (Hayes-Renshaw and Wallace 1995; Rittberger 2000; Sherrington 2000; Christiansen 2001), the European Parliament (Corbett *et al.* 2000), and, indirectly, the European Court of Justice (Dehousse 1998; Wincott 2001). National governments, regional authorities, and international agencies also play a key role in the initiation and resolution of European policy proposals. This complex array of actors (which increasingly includes regional governments) makes the EU policy process especially difficult to characterize. The European Union is an extreme case of the US example cited by Kingdon, where a Washington official argued that it was very difficult to identify the actual origin of any policy—the policy process was not like a river, the origin of which could be located (Kingdon 1984: 77).

Thus, in focusing on the Commission in this chapter, we are conscious that we are excluding the important role played by other institutions in policy initiation and policy decision. Effective lobbying (especially since the introduction and extension of the co-decision procedure and QMV) requires a multi-track strategy, that utilizes the multiple access points and venues that the complex EU policy process provides (Mazey and Richardson 1995, 1999). Our focus here, however, is on the role that the Commission plays as a broker, or *bourse*, for the now high levels of interest group mobilization within the European Union. In performing this role, the Commission has also played a crucial role in fostering the institutionalization of interest intermediation in the European Union.

Wherever policy is initiated, it is Commission officials who are charged with the task of drafting legislative proposals that are acceptable to affected interests and governments within (and beyond) the Union. The result is an often symbiotic (though rarely genuinely corporatist) relationship between the Commission and groups. Groups are, of course, drawn to Brussels by a desire to defend and promote the interests of their members in the context of EU policy making. The Commission is, however, equally dependent upon groups. Not only do they provide Commission officials with technical information and advice, the support of cross-national advocacy coalitions (Sabatier 1988) of groups is essential to the successful introduction of Commission proposals. These functional incentives to consult groups are buttressed by the Commission's political need to be able to demonstrate openness and thus enhance its own legitimacy. It is unsurprising, therefore, that the Commission is the focus of so much lobbying by interest groups, independent experts, national administrations, quasi-non-governmental organisations (QUANGOs), and NGOs. Of course, the phenomenon of European lobbying is not at all new (Kirchner and Swaiger 1981; Butt-Philip 1985). Some fairly stable 'policy networks' involving ECSC officials and corporatist interests were apparent as early as the mid-1950s (Mazey 1992). However, the significant expansion of the Community's legislative competence following the adoption of the 1986 Single European Act (SEA), the 1992 Treaty on European Union (TEU), and the 1997 Amsterdam Treaty has prompted a sharp increase in the volume and intensity of interest group activity at the European level. This development is, of course, consistent with neo-functionalist theories of European integration.

In practice, there is considerable variation between sectors in the precise nature of the relationships between Commission officials and groups. The Commission is involved in a wide variety of types of policy networks, some of them so loose and unstructured that the term 'network' may have little utility other than to suggest that there are lots of actors involved. Whilst some interests—for example, in agriculture and IT—have managed to become part of an identifiable 'policy community' (Smith 1990; Peterson 1991), many—for example, in social policy and environment—are involved in loose 'issue networks' of the type identified in the United States by Heclo. (For a discussion of the utility and limitations of network analysis see Richardson 2000). The phenomenon of Euro-lobbying has attracted widespread academic interest; there is now an extensive literature on the EU policy-making role of diverse interest groups (See e.g. Andersen and Eliassen 1991; J Greenwood *et al.* 1992; M.P.C.M. Van Schendelen (ed.) 1993; Mazey and Richardson (eds) 1993*a*; Pedlar and Van Schendelen 1994; Gorges 1996; Coen 1997; Greenwood 1997, 2002*a,b*; Claeys *et al.* 1998; Greenwood and Aspinwall 1998; Bartle 1999; Bennett 1999; Mazey and Richardson 1999, 2001). There is as yet no single, definitive characterization of the nature of the relationship between the Commission bureaucracy and interest groups. However, our own research—conducted over a period of several years—suggests that interest groups have become increasingly institutionalized within the Commission across all policy sectors.

The expansion of EU legislative competence since 1986 has prompted a dramatic increase in the volume and diversity of Euro-lobbyists. The exact number of Euro-lobbyists is unknown. However, back in 1992, the Commission estimated that there were some 3,000 interest groups in Brussels, including more than 500 European associations, and that in total some 10,000 people were employed as lobbyists of one sort or another in Brussels (European Commission 1992*b*). By February 2000, the Commission's own directory of non-profit-making European associations had expanded to include some

800 groups. (http://europa.eu.int/comm/secretariat_general/sgc/lobbies/). Meanwhile, the number of professional lobbyists has also increased since 1992. One firm of political consultants, GPC, now employs forty people in Brussels—ten times more than just eight years ago (*European Voice*, 3–9 February 2000). Direct EU lobbying by firms has also increased significantly: between 1985 and 1997 more than 350 large firms established their own EU affairs office in Brussels (Coen 1999: 9). In addition, international organizations, national federations, trade unions, regional authorities, and voluntary organizations, increasingly have in recent years recognized the need to have a presence in Brussels. Thus, there is now a dense, mature *European* and *transnational* interest group system centred upon the European Union. Indeed, there is probably an *oversupply* of lobbying at the Euro-level (Mazey and Richardson 1996). Certainly, there has been widespread recognition within the Commission for some time now that the Euro-interest group system has become so extensive and well-organized that some more effective system for 'managing' it has to be introduced. Moreover, the 'problem' of the lobby is not merely a technical one; concerns regarding the propriety of Commission–group relations have arisen within the wider context of the debates over the (non-)transparency of EU decision-making procedures and the Union's 'democratic deficit'. These concerns prompted a Commission to review the links between it and special interest groups, which acknowledged the need for these relations to be 'more clearly defined' and to be placed 'on a slightly more formalized footing' (European Commission 1993: 2).

However, the same document also stressed the Commission's continuing commitment to extensive consultation with organized interests. This commitment is not difficult to explain. Popular mythology notwithstanding, the European Commission is still a very small administration. In carrying out their role, officials have somehow to accommodate diverse and often conflicting demands of national governments and sectoral interests within and beyond the European Community. Consequently, there exists a powerful 'logic of negotiation' (Jordan and Richardson 1979). Of course, similar pressures exist at the national level, but they are significantly greater in the multinational context of European policy making. The incremental extension of Community competence and EU enlargement has both increased the need for group consultation and—because of the proliferation of Euro-lobbyists—given rise to a new problem, namely how to balance openness and pluralism against the need for efficiency and stability. As highlighted below, Commission officials have sought to resolve this dilemma by means of diverse forms of institutionalization of group consultation. If the Commission can construct and manage stable transnational coalitions of interest groups and independent experts (in the long run also concerned with policy implementation as well as policy formulation), it will have built one of the classic defence systems predicted by Downs for all bureaucracies—namely a client base willing to defend it in hard times (Downs 1967).

The following discussion is divided into three parts. The first section highlights the organizational and cultural characteristics of the Commission bureaucracy and the implications of these characteristics for groups seeking to develop effective lobbying strategies. All bureaucracies are to some extent shaped by the nature of the environment in which they must operate. The European Commission is no exception. Its historical development as a segmented and pluralistic administration—though contrary to Jean Monnet's ambitions—is perfectly consistent with its role as multiple interest broker and policy initiator. However, this institutional pluralism creates an uncertain and competitive environment for lobbyists. The second section examines in detail recent attempts by the Commission to structure and institutionalize interest group consultation. This analysis highlights the increasing importance of both 'thin' and 'thick' consultative structures. The concluding section briefly considers the utility and limitations of group pluralism within the Commission and asks whether the neo-functionalist predictions have, in the event, turned out to be surprisingly accurate.

THE EUROPEAN COMMISSION OPPORTUNITY STRUCTURE: A LOBBYISTS' PARADISE?

As indicated above, there is a 'logic of negotiation' which encourages groups and Commission officials to seek each other out; the relationship is often a symbiotic one. Thus, groups rarely find it difficult to gain access to officials. However, the disparate nature of the Commission's cultural and administrative style is often unappreciated by groups, many of whom develop a generalized view of 'the Commission' based upon their experiences with one division or section of a DG. Yet, the Commission is a particularly extreme example of a fragmented and compartmentalized bureaucracy. Horizontal coordination within the bureaucracy is often problematic and there is often competition between (and within) DGs over particular policies. Moreover, different parts of the Commission exhibit different cultural and administrative styles. Thus, whilst Commission structures offer many opportunities for group access, effective lobbying of the Commission requires considerable skill and understanding of the disparate nature of the organization.

In many respects, the EU administration resembles a typical bureaucracy. In their classic study of the implementation process in the United States, Pressman and Wildavsky commented that 'an agency that appears to be a single organization with a single will turns out to be several sub-organizations with different wills' (Pressman and Wildavsky 1973: 92). The European Commission is exactly such an organization. The multinational composition of the Commission, the absence of any uniform administrative procedures, democratic mandate, or governing ideology in the political sense of the word (Donnelly 1993) gives rise to an extremely pluralistic and in some respects 'leaderless' executive. At the political level, the Commission President has minimal formal authority and little influence over the composition of either the College of Commissioners or individual Commissioners' *cabinets* (Spence 2000). Moreover, the pluralistic structure and functioning of the Commission bureaucracy is further reinforced by the fragmentation of political authority within the Community as a whole. The Commission shares power with fifteen democratically elected governments and, increasingly, the European Parliament (Rittberger 2000). Within this environment, the Commission performs a pivotal, political brokerage role, without which few EC policies would ever be agreed upon in the Council of Ministers. The brokerage role has been diminished in importance by the (alleged) decline in the Commission's power over policy initiating and agenda setting. In a sense, the 'weakening' of the Commission drives it further down the consultation and mobilization road. In order to perform the brokerage effectively, however, the European Commission needs, therefore, to be able both to draw upon the technical expertise and secure the support and compliance of those interests directly affected by EC legislation, who often have close links with 'their' national administration. This need explains, in part at least, the bureaucratization of the Commission—a development much feared by Jean Monnet, who believed it would undermine the 'supranational' nature of the Commission.

The founding fathers of the European Coal and Steel Community (ECSC), the original European Community, established in 1951, were motivated by a shared commitment to the principle of supranationalism. The creation of the High Authority (executive of the ECSC and predecessor to the Commission) was an attempt to 'operationalize' this principle. Jean Monnet, in particular, hoped to avoid the divisive effects of nationalism by means of collegiate decision making and the separation of administrative and executive functions within the High Authority. Somewhat unrealistically, Monnet drew a distinction between the 'political/decision-making' function of the latter (i.e. the equivalent of the present College of Commissioners) and the 'preparatory/technical' role of the administrative services. Previous experience of national and international administrations had also convinced Monnet of the need to prevent the development of sectoral hierarchies, which he believed would similarly threaten the supranational and collegiate nature of the High Authority. Thus, his ambition was to build up gradually a small, non-hierarchical administration composed of highly qualified (technically and linguistically) officials to support and assist the 'supranational' European executive.

Monnet's aspirations proved somewhat unrealistic. As Gerbet (1992) has observed, the supranationalist principle of the High Authority was, in fact, rapidly eroded by national cleavages and sectoral conflicts within the executive. Such divisions were most visibly reflected in the development of *cabinets* within the High Authority, which tended to be used by member governments and sectoral interests as a vehicle for promoting national interests within the ECSC (Ritchie 1992). Predictably, the internal divisions that developed within the High Authority reached down to the administrative level. Here, national and sectoral cleavages were reflected in the introduction of national quotas governing the allocation of administrative posts, and increasing functional specialization within the bureaucracy (Mazey 1992).

This development was inevitable. As theorists such as Max Weber (1962) and Anthony Downs (1967) have convincingly argued, bureaucracies have an inexorable tendency to grow, both in size and complexity. In terms of its genesis and subsequent development, the administration of the High Authority offers a good example of Down's model of bureaucratic dynamics. By 1954, the rudimentary administrative structures established by Monnet had become ineffective. Increasingly, there were problems of administrative coordination, delays, and overlapping responsibility as all divisions sought in isolation from each other to extend as far as possible their sphere of competence. Administrative reorganization, undertaken in 1954 in the name of efficiency, created a more hierarchical, functionally segmented bureaucracy. This was entirely predictable. Downs (1967) argued that most bureaux have a notion of 'policy space' and are determined to defend and extend the existing borders of their territory. The benefits of expansion far outweigh the disadvantages to the bureaucrat, added to which the pressures for growth are likely to be particularly strong in new bureaux (McKenzie and Tullock 1975). This development was accompanied by the blurring of the distinction made by Monnet between the political and administrative functions of the High Authority. As the scope and complexity of the tasks performed by the ECSC expanded, administrative officials became increasingly involved in the daily management, that is, the execution of Community policies (Mazey 1992). Inevitably, this brought the Commission into direct contact with interest groups.

Since 1957, this process of bureaucratization has continued within the European Commission. The creation of the European Economic Community (EEC) and Euratom in 1957, piecemeal enlargement of the Community in 1973, 1981, 1986, and 1995, and incremental expansion of the Community's sphere of competence have prompted continual enlargement and readjustment of the Commission's staffing and structure and the creation of specialized agencies such as those associated with pharmaceuticals and the environment. More importantly for the purposes of this chapter, each Agency, Division, Directorate-General has become—to varying degrees and in different ways—associated with an expanding base of 'client-groups'. As EU policy has expanded, so has the constellation of groups who are attendant upon each DG and Division in the Commission. Moreover, this dynamic is ongoing: increasing Commission involvement in the second and third pillars of the European Union, the planned eastern and central enlargement of the European Union, internal restructuring of the Commission, and further extension of QMV will undoubtedly prompt further Commission bureaucratization, increased lobbying, and new client groups centred upon the Commission. As we suggested earlier, this fits the Downsian prediction of the behaviour of new bureaucracies—they encourage the development of 'constituencies' loyal to the agency and in some senses dependent upon it. In this sense, there is a good fit between theories of bureaucracy and neo-functionalist theories of integration. Mutual interdependence between the Commission and groups would be predicted by both sets of theories.

The process of European integration has created winners as well as losers amongst interest groups. Unsurprisingly, those who have gained from this process tend to defend further expansion of the Commission's powers. External threats, increasing competitive pressures, and high transaction costs have persuaded many firms of the benefits of further integration. Thus, in November 1999, the 27-member Association of European Airlines called for the European Commission to be given greater authority to negotiate a common EC–US regulatory framework for all carriers (*European Voice*, 25 November–2 December 1999). Early in 2000, the European employers' Association, UNICE, also called on the European Commission to push for more powers to vet mergers and acquisitions, because firms 'preferred the "one-stop shop" offered by the Commission's merger task force' to the multiplication of national merger control authorities (*European Voice*, 27 January–2 February 2000). Meanwhile, within the United Kingdom, many firms have become increasingly impatient with and openly critical of the British government's reluctance (for party political reasons) to sign up to EMU. However, firms are not the only beneficiaries of European integration: environmentalists and women have also tended to favour further European integration as a means of imposing policy change upon recalcitrant national governments (Mazey 1998) and because they see European level solutions as generally more efficient for dealing with both national and transnational problems.

In those sectors where the Commission has no specific Treaty mandate to initiate EC policies, officials have over the years gradually acquired for themselves a de facto policy role. In most such cases, this status owes much to the Commission's cultivation of interest groups and so-called 'epistemic communities' of experts (Haas 1992). Thus, a considerable corpus of environmental law was developed without a strong Treaty base and finally legitimized in the SEA in 1986, long after the event. Only now are member states realizing the huge implementation costs of such environmental policies as the Drinking and Bathing Water Directives, for example. An effective advocacy coalition of Commission officials, the international scientific community, and a vociferous and skillful environmental movement, acting as some kind of 'megaphone for science', made the running. National governments (including Britain, which now leads the opposition to these laws) went along with it, largely in ignorance of implementation problems ahead. Similarly, in the field of EC social policy, much of the work of the Employment and Social Affairs DG has been directed towards mobilizing a constituency of support for policies that the Commission would like to pursue, but which have frequently been blocked by some national governments (Cram 1993: 11–13; Mazey 1995, 1998). To this end, the DG has since the mid-1980s promoted and funded research and networks in the fields of poverty, preventive health care provision, violence against women, and human rights. Although the Commission had no clear legislative competence in these areas, it assiduously cultivated an important constituency and advocacy coalition among voluntary associations, who then campaigned during the 1996 IGC for the Commission to be given greater authority in these policy sectors (Mazey and Richardson 1997). This strategy undoubtedly contributed to the formal strengthening in the Amsterdam Treaty of the Community's competence with regard to the defence of 'human rights and fundamental freedoms' (Article 6). As Peters has observed, 'the politics of the European community is best understood as bureaucratic politics' (Peters 1992: 15). As with all bureaucracies, there are often jurisdictional disputes between different parts of a supposedly unified bureaucracy and problems of horizontal coordination across related policy sectors. A classic example is the lack of coordination historically between the Environment DG and the Regional Policy DG (see Mazey and Richardson 1993a). As a Court of Auditors' report in 1992 confirmed, several DGs have responsibility for specific aspects of EC environmental policy. The report went on to conclude, 'this spread of responsibility requires substantial coordination which is far from being

achieved' (Court of Auditors 1992: 6). In fact, several policies funded by EC structural funds actually contributed to the deterioration of the environment and were
directly at odds with EC environmental policy. The 'co-ordination problem' is now
well recognized by all observers of the Commission and by the Commission itself. In
two areas, environmental policy and gender equality, the Commission has sought to
resolve this problem by the introduction of 'mainstreaming' strategies, designed to
ensure that *all* Commission proposals are based upon an environmental/gender audit.

The problem of coordination within the Commission is not merely a consequence of
institutional fragmentation or competing interests (though these are not unimportant);
it is also due, in part, to the existence of competing cognitive and normative frames
(Surel 2000) within the Commission. As Goldstein and Keohane have argued, ideas and
beliefs are important in determining the way in which policy makers conceptualize
policy problems and policy solutions:

By ordering the world, ideas may shape agendas, which can profoundly shape outcomes. Insofar
as ideas put blinders on people, reducing the number of conceivable options, they serve as invisible switchmen, not only by turning action onto certain tracks rather than others... but also by
obscuring the other tracks from the agent's view. (Goldstein and Keohane 1993: 12)

A policy frame thus provides policy makers with 'a perspective from which an
amorphous, ill-defined problematic situation can be made sense of and acted upon'
(Rein and Schön 1991: 263). Within the Commission generally, there is, for example,
a powerful 'competitive market' frame, which underpins EU regulatory, harmonization, and liberalization policies. However, within this 'meta frame' there exist variations between DGs with respect to policy frames. The Employment and Social Affairs
DG, for instance, has a more interventionist policy frame than the Internal Market
DG and may thus be more willing to restrict the working of the market in order to
realize other policy objectives. Pollack (2000), for instance, argues that differences
between DGs with regard to the implementation of gender mainstreaming of EU
policies are in part due to variation in the 'resonance' of the gender issue with the
dominant frame of the DG in question. As Pollack argues, in order to be effective lobbyists, groups must couch their demands in terms and language that is consistent
with the normative and cognitive frame of the DG with which they are dealing.
Typically, however, more than one DG will have an interest in any policy area. The
overlapping responsibilities of different parts of the Commission further complicate
the lobbyist's task. The 'lead' DG can be identified easily, but this still leaves the problem of how to communicate effectively with other relevant DGs and leaves groups to
cope with the general lack of coordination within the Commission. Moreover,
groups must be able to couch their demands in terms which 'speak to' different—
often competing—policy frames (Dudley and Richardson 1999; Morth 2000). Thus,
the most effective lobbyists are those who, by stimulating a process of frame-
reflection and negotiation between different bureaucratic interests, are able to assist
the Commission in its brokerage role.

There is a tendency for national issues to appear—often quite unexpectedly—on
the Community's own agenda. One reason for this is the concern among sectoral

interests and/or national governments that there should be a 'level playing field' within the SEM. Much Euro-lobbying by groups and national officials is thus designed to ensure that similar technical standards, employment costs, environmental regulations, etc. exist throughout the Community. In September 1990, for instance, the Commission revised proposals for EC legislation on recycling in response to more stringent legislative plans announced earlier that year by the (West) German government. (Mazey and Richardson 1992*a*: 99). Such changes occur because within the framework of the SEM, national interests and governments are anxious to gain a competitive advantage over their EC counterparts. One way of achieving this is to persuade Commission officials to adopt their existing national standards as the basis of EC standards. In May 1993, for instance, the Director-General of the UK Health and Safety Executive, complained that the health and safety EC Framework Directive had been 'entirely written to serve the French system' (*The Guardian*, 12 May 1993). More recently, member-states have campaigned to ensure that European regulations introduced by the newly established European Food Safety Agency are similar to their own. Groups and governments also lobby the European Union in an attempt to make sure the playing field slopes in their favour, for example, the campaign by UK employers' associations and the UK government against those provisions of the EU Charter of Fundamental Rights which strengthened workers' rights. A legal opinion by one Queen's Counsel argued that such a charter would be 'a further lurch away from the "Anglo-Saxon economic model"' (*Financial Times*, 3 August 2000). Thus, groups seeking to monitor policy developments at the EC level need to take account of the fact that the EC policy agenda is to a considerable degree driven by national policy agendas within the fifteen member-states. This competitive agenda-setting in part explains the emergence of an extremely varied EC regulatory system—what Héritier terms a 'regulatory patchwork' created by different states managing to foist their own regulatory regimes for specific policy areas upon the European Union. As no one state *consistently* secures what she calls an 'unqualified home run', a regulatory patchwork is the end result (Héritier 1996).

There is a very strong commitment within the Commission to consult widely with groups. The organizational ideology favouring consultation has been aptly summarized by the Commission's former Secretary General, David Williamson. Introducing the Round Table meeting between the Commission and interest groups, held in Brussels in August 1993, he commented that

from the beginning of the European Community, the Commission has been open to contacts with interest groups and welcomes such contact. A broad spectrum of advice from special interest groups is important in order to arrive at proposals which are practicable. These groups also have a role in relaying information and in helping the understanding of Community action.

This consultative style is illustrated by the process adopted for the development of the so-called 'telecoms package'. Thus, the 2001 White Paper on EU Governance cited this as a typical example of its approach to consultation and listed the seven stages

Figure 13.1   *How the Commission consults: the example of the 'Telecoms Package'*

The Telecoms Package of six measures currently in Council and the European Parliament was developed on the basis of widespread consultation.

1998–9 A number of studies assessing a range of market and regulatory issues launched. Workshops presenting and debating the studies.

May/June 1999 Working Paper on regulatory principles for telecoms reform for consultation.

November 1999 Communication launching the 1999 Telecoms Review setting out general orientations and inviting reaction.

January 2000 Two day Public Hearing with 550 participants.

April 2000 Communication on the results of the 1999 Review. More than 2000 responses from national regulators, trade associations, consumer groups, industry, and individuals.

May 2000 Draft legislation published in the form of five working documents for rapid consultation.

July 2000 Adoption of package of six proposals by the Commission, currently under discussion in Council and European Parliament.

---

through which the package had passed before the Council and EP stages of the legal-ization process—see Figure 13.1.

Moreover, this 'consultation culture' has been reinforced in recent years by the increasing political salience of the EU's democratic deficit, which has prompted the introduction of new procedures and guidelines designed to increase the transparency and effectiveness of Commission–group relations. Yet, notwithstanding this general disposition towards consultation, the multinational composition of the European administration inhibits the emergence of a single, coherent bureaucratic or operational style. In particular, there are as yet no agreed standard operating procedures with regard to interest group consultation. Different national, cultural, and administrative styles remain important in determining the rhythm of the Commission's work. The British sense of humour, the German and Danish tendency to lunch early, the Italian habit of working late, French formality, eleven official languages, and the continental (but not British) tradition of appointing economists and lawyers as senior civil servants combine to create an extremely diverse Euroculture within the Commission (Christoph 1992; de la Guérivière 1992). As McDonald observes 'national identifica-tions and stereotypes *do* occur in the Commission' (McDonald 1997: 61; see also Bellier 1995). These differences contribute to the institutional and cultural fragmentation out-lined above (Cini 1997; McDonald 1997). The mercurial character of the European Commission creates an unstable policy-making environment for groups who, in order to be effective Euro-lobbyists, must first, be able to monitor and respond quickly to changes in a number of policy agendas and second, be able in chameleon-like fashion, to adjust their lobbying strategy to suit different audiences.

It is, however, important to stress that whilst relationships between the European Commission and groups are still in a state of flux, there *is* (as indicated in the following section), evidence of standard operating procedures emerging within the Commission for managing the business of group consultation. As highlighted in the following section, the 'early' rather chaotic and ad hoc consultation system has given way to a more institutionalized and structured pattern of interest intermediation. In large part, this development has been driven by the Commission. However, the interest groups have also become better-organized and more European/international in outlook and structure. EU lobbying strategies generally are becoming more sophisticated as groups begin to appreciate the complex nature of both the EU policy-making process and the nature of the European Commission. In this context two recent developments have significantly enhanced the lobbying capacity of many groups, notably NGOs: the increasing tendency to form effective transnational and/or 'rainbow coalitions'; and the exploitation by groups of the Internet, both as a source of information and transnational mobilization (Keck and Sikkink 1998). For example, there is now a vocal, transnational 'human rights' advocacy coalition based in Brussels, comprising women's groups, environmentalists, refugee and migrant workers' organizations, civil rights groups, pensioners, and disabled associations. This development is, of course, very uneven. Generally speaking, multinational companies and large firms have adapted well to the EU policy-making environment. Some voluntary associations and advocacy groups, used to cooperating on an international scale (e.g. Greenpeace, World Wildlife Fund, Amnesty International) have also developed effective cross-national lobbying strategies as Long's study so clearly demonstrates (Long 1995. See also Mazey and Richardson 1992b, 1993a). However, many smaller firms and national groups still find dealing with the European Commission a rather daunting prospect and may still rely too heavily on contacts with their own national governments. Interestingly, there may be some cross-national variations in the degree of reliance on national administrations as a channel for influencing European policy, with French groups perhaps rather too closely tied to their national government for them to be able to exploit the opportunities of European multi-level games (Josselin 1996).

THE INSTITUTIONALIZATION OF INTEREST INTERMEDIATION WITHIN THE COMMISSION

In recent years, the growth of Euro-lobbying has placed considerable strains upon officials. The key issue, therefore, is how do Commission officials 'manage' the process of consultation? In fact, there is no single or straightforward answer to this question. The nature of the relationship between officials and interest groups at the EC level varies considerably between policy sectors. These differences are the result of the different structural characteristics of individual sectors, diverse bureaucratic interests and administrative styles within the Commission, and differences between groups themselves in terms of their resources, ideology, and objectives. Notwithstanding this diversity, it is nevertheless possible to identify some important general trends now emerging at the EU level with regard to relations between Commission officials and interest groups. More specifically, there are definite signs that consultation is becoming more institutionalized within the Commission in two senses. First, there is clear evidence of the evolution of some formal, but more often informal, behavioural rules, codes, and norms regarding consultation. Second, there has been a gradual emergence of structures, sites, or venues where intermediation can take place at various stages of the policy process. As highlighted below, with respect to both the regulation of lobbying and the preferred form of consultative structures, the Commission's attitude has been determined by it desire to reconcile openness with effective policy making.

In terms of the EU policy process, effective group consultation is functionally beneficial. However, the considerable influence wielded by organized interests within the European Commission and the close—often informal—links which exist between some groups and Commission officials, have served to increase public unease about the Community's 'democratic deficit'. The European Parliament began in 1991 to debate the need for a register of lobbyists. Partly in response to these pressures, the Secretariat General of the European Commission in 1992 reviewed Commission procedures regarding group consultation (European Commission 1992*a*, 1993). Possible legal regulation of lobbying has, therefore, been an important agenda item for both institutions. (For a comprehensive review of these discussions see Greenwood 1997: 80–100; Preston 1998: 222–32.) Throughout this debate, however, the Commission has been greatly concerned to maintain its culture of open consultations with as wide a constituency as necessary. As indicated above, the Commission needs first to ensure that its proposals are technically robust and political feasible. Second, it must strengthen its legitimacy as a transparent and accessible institution. To pursue an *exclusive* rather than an inclusive policy towards interest groups would be conducive to neither objective. The Commission's approach to the formal regulation of lobbying has therefore been extremely cautious and has been designed to discourage extreme forms of abuse. The formal 'licensing' of groups has thus been strongly resisted. Instead, a directory of non-profit-making organizations consulted by the Commission was compiled; the profit-making sector was merely encouraged to draw up its own directory. With regard to regulation, self-regulation has been the Commission's preferred strategy. The Commission has supported the introduction of minimum standards of behaviour and the use of voluntary codes. More specifically, the Commission has included guidance on how to deal with interest groups in the Staff Regulations, which are issued to all officials. Currently, a code of conduct for Commission officials is being discussed with staff representatives. The March 1999 draft of this document includes a brief—and anodyne—section on dealing with interest groups. In addition, the Commission has published a communication entitled *Minimum Requirements for a Code of Conduct between the Commission and Special Interest Groups* (http://europa.eu.int/comm/sg/sgc/lobbies/en/communication/). In fact, the requirements are minimal. The document states that groups should behave honestly and professionally. The only significant 'rules' are that special interest groups 'should neither employ, nor seek to employ, officials who are working for the Commission. Nor should groups offer any form of inducement to Commission officials in order to obtain information or privileged treatment'. Relatedly, the White Paper on Governance in 2001 pledged the Commission itself to produce minimum standards for consultation and to publish them as a code of conduct (European Commission 2001: 7). However, perhaps more important than formal rules regarding group consultation are the informal, unwritten rules of the game, which are essential to effective lobbying and which are widely appreciated by lobbyists and Commission officials. (For a fuller discussion of these norms see Mazey and Richardson 2001; Hull 1993.) Such norms include the need for groups to lobby early in the EU policy-making process, the need to present rational arguments based upon reliable data, the importance of maintaining close professional links with a wide range of Commission officials, the need to formulate European rather than parochial policy solutions, the need to be cooperative and trustworthy, and the need for modesty and discretion. Our own research indicates that these norms have become firmly embedded within the Commission and groups alike and constitute the foundations of an emerging European policy style.

Alongside the evolution of institutional norms and regulatory mechanisms, group participation in EU policy making has become more clearly organized within the Commission. In seeking to structure group consultation, the Commission's strategy has been shaped by the need to demonstrate openness and transparency on the one hand and to establish a permanent, close relationship with (a smaller number of) key interest groups on the other hand. Concerns about openness and transparency of EU decision making had been highlighted in the 1992 Sutherland report, which argued that:

Wide and effective consultation on Commission proposals is essential. The Commission needs to introduce a better procedure for making people aware, at the earliest stage, of its intention to propose legislation. (Sutherland 1992: 30)

In response to this report, the Commission has introduced a number of measures designed to increase openness and transparency. These include earlier publication of the Commission's legislative programme, a commitment to ensure that target groups are aware of any new policy initiatives, and greater use of Green (consultative) Papers. (Prior to 1990, the Commission appears to have published only four Green Papers; in the following eight years approximately fifty were published). Attempts have also been made to make more effective use of the Internet, as a means of relaying information and Commission documents to groups. The Commission has also created a website devoted to its relations with interest groups, reflecting its 'wish to create a single site for the working tools that enable officials to promote the participation of socioeconomic circles and the representatives of civil society in the legislative process' (see Commission Europa Website at *http://europa.eu.int/comm/sg/sgc/lobbies/enindex_htm*). For many years the Commission has partly funded public interest European lobbies, such as the European Women's Lobby and the European Environmental Bureau. However, in an attempt to allay public fears about the EU's democratic deficit, the Commission has, since the early 1990s, increased its efforts to achieve a more balanced institutionalization of interest group intermediation, mainly through the construction of a series of inclusive social networks such as the Social Policy Forum. In 1997, the Commission adopted a Communication, *Promoting the Role of Voluntary Organizations and Foundations in Europe*, which stressed the need for NGOs to be consulted more widely and more systematically. The increasing institutionalization of NGO–Commission relations is also reflected in the considerable financial support that NGOs receive from the Commission. Some 2.65M ECU was set aside for funding environmental NGOs during the period 1998–2001 (OJL 354 of 30 December 1997). Similarly, a single unit (F/2) of DG V provided 5M ECUs for NGOs in 1997. More recently, a Commission discussion paper, *The Commission and Non-Governmental Organizations: Building a Stronger Partnership*, (http://europa.eu.int/ comm/secretariat_general/sgc/ong/en/index.htm), presented by Commission President Romano Prodi and Vice-President Neil Kinnock, reiterated the need for greater and more coherent NGO involvement in the EU policy process, arguing that 'NGOs can make a contribution to fostering a more participatory democracy...within the European Union' (p. 4). More generally, the Commission's White Paper, *European Governance*, published in July 2001, proposed 'opening-up' the policy-making process to get more people and organizations involved in shaping and delivering EU policy (European Commission 2001: 3). The White Paper went on to argue that 'what is needed is a reinforced culture of consultation and dialogue' (European Commission 2001: 17).

The Commission's need to demonstrate openness and transparency is paralleled by its need to mobilize a consensus in favour of technically sound and politically feasible policies. As we argue elsewhere (Mazey and Richardson 2001), these potentially conflicting objectives are typically achieved through different institutional consultative structures used at different stages of the policy-making process. (The 2001 White Paper on Governance stated that the Commission runs nearly 700 ad hoc consultation bodies a wide range of policies (European Commission 2001: 17)). Broadly speaking, the Commission employs two different ways of involving groups in the policy process: large, open gatherings on the one hand and more restrictive committees and forums on the other. Although it is impossible to generalize about the relative importance of these two types of interest aggregation within the Commission, our own research suggests that there is a typical pattern emerging. In the early stages of the policy process, consultative structures tend to be open and inclusive, bringing together all potential stakeholders in an open forum, seminar, or conference. Examples of such structures include: the European Standardization Conference hosted by DGIII (Industry) in 1999; the public hearing for industry and other interested parties on a Green Paper on the Application of Community Competition Rules to Vertical Restraints, held by DGIV (Competition) in May 1999; and the Conference organized by DGXI (Environment) in 1997 on the Environment and Employment, which involved more than 300 participants from a wide range of sectors. Generally speaking, the purpose of this form of consultation is to inform potential stakeholders, try out new ideas, and obtain early feedback on proposals.

However, the subsequent formulation and implementation of detailed proposals usually takes place within the myriad of formal and informal of advisory committees and working parties in the Commission, which are composed of group representatives and technical experts. Formal committees include the Group 1 and Group 2 advisory committees. Group 1, so-called 'expert committees', comprise national officials and experts who are nominated by government departments. In practice, however, these nominees tend to perceive their role as being that of technical experts rather than national government agents. Generally, the Commission *must* consult the relevant expert committee(s) during the policy formulation process (though it is under no obligation to respond to the advice offered by the experts). The Group 2 'consultative committees' represent sectoral interests and are composed of representatives of Euro-associations and national groups. Although the Commission has a procedural ambition to deal primarily with the Euro-associations, the latter are not always able to provide the level of expertise (and cross-national knowledge) required. The *raison d'être* of all these committees is to advise the Commission on the technical details of its proposals. The importance of these committees in the policy process is considerable: it is estimated that there are some 1,000 advisory committees involving some 50,000 representatives from national administrations and the private sector (Greenwood 1997: 41; see also Van Schendelen 1998). In addition, the Commission frequently sets up informal, high level groups or working parties to consider a specific problem. Examples of such structures include: the high level group convened by Commissioner Bangemman to formulate recommendations to the European council on 'Europe and the Global Information Society', involving members of the IT industry (Greenwood 1997: 40); the High level Group on the Economic and Social Implications of Industrial Change, created by DGV in January 1998; and the Auto-Oil Programme set up by DXI in 1992, which brings together the vehicle manufacturing and oil refining industries, member states, NGOs, and other experts within seven working groups of experts.

Thus, it is possible to distinguish between rather open and 'thin' institutions such as very large conferences and seminars and the more restricted 'thick' institutions where only the key players are present. Coen, observing this trend with respect to business interests, refers to the emergence at the EU level of 'the creeping institutionalization of forum style politics' (Coen 1999: 16). The more open structures facilitate legitimation and identification of key actors and likely 'sticking points'. The more restrictive structures facilitate the detailed technical negotiation and bargaining, resulting in practical proposals. Although some consultative structures are temporary in nature, there is an increasing tendency for them to become permanent structures, which meet irrespective of the legislative timetable. This is particularly true of the thicker structures, which become institutionalized sites for permanent consultation, frame reflection, and consensus-building. The fact that it is possible to distinguish between thick and thin institutional structures should not disguise the fact that from the Commission's perspective, consultation is a seamless and long-term process. As one interviewee told us 'we have our style—a *process* of consultation—not just single consultations, but we consult often . . . in order to judge people's views and gauge how far people's views have changed during the process' (Interview, DGXIII 8 July 1999). Thus, institutionalized consultation is as much about mutual learning as instrumental lobbying for short-term, material gain.

The construction of institutions to facilitate learning and consensus-building between competing policy frames and belief systems is *especially* important in the

European Union, because the policy-making system is characterized by multiple cultures, languages, policy traditions, and national agendas. The potential for conflict is great and there is, therefore, a functional need to search for sufficient areas of agreement for workable policies to emerge. For what Sabatier terms 'policy orientated learning across belief systems' (Sabatier 1988: 156) to take place there need to be a forum which is both prestigious enough to force professions from different coalitions to participate, and dominated by professional norms. In this context, the advantage that the Commission has over other institutional venues is that it is widely perceived as an honest broker. It is, therefore, well-placed to create and manage structures of intermediation and frame reflection (Rein and Schon 1991).

An additional pressure for the continuing (and increasingly intense) institutionalization of interest intermediation within the Commission is the evolving nature of the EU's policy style, which has implications for the type of policy instruments used by the Commission (Cram and Richardson 2001). The early 'Community method' of supranational policy making, which was characterized by limited involvement of relatively few, socioeconomic actors, has since the 1980s increasingly given way to an EU regulatory policy style (Majone 1991*a*,*b*; 1996). In the environmental and IT sectors, for instance, the European Commission has sought to establish a European framework of regulation and standards. This policy style has drawn into the policy-making process a much wider range of interests and epistemic communities who supply the type of expertise and knowledge needed to define specific parameters and standards. This shift in policy style has also resulted in the Commission broadening the consultation process to consumer groups and other societal interests, who can claim stakeholder status in the regulatory process. Thus, interest group battles are now routinely fought out in Brussels over such issues as the regulations governing the safety of toys, food production, and water quality, car pricing structures, pensions, and so forth. More recently, however, there are signs that a third, distinctive European policy style may be emerging, which is likely to intensify still further the institutionalization of interest groups within the Commission. This policy style, referred to as the 'OECD technique' by Wallace (Wallace 2000*b*: 32), is characterized by policy coordination, benchmarking, and voluntary codes of practice. As Wallace observes, this approach relies heavily on 'expertise and the accumulation of technical arguments in favour of developing a shared approach. It also relies on efforts to use expertise to promote modernization and innovation' (Wallace 2000*b*: 33). This approach has recently been adopted, for instance, in the field of European employment policy, where the Commission's objective is not to establish a common legislative framework, but rather to compare national practices with the aim of encouraging the spread of best practices. This policy style accords a key role to the Commission as the institution responsible for developing networks of experts, and to experts or epistemic communities as a source of ideas and practices (Radaelli 1999). If, as seems likely, this approach is extended to other policy sectors, it will undoubtedly result in further institutionalization of expertise within the Commission—as well as within the other EU institutions. Moreover, the nature of expertise required by the Commission within this policy style has yet again further broadened the 'reach' of the consultative process beyond narrow sectoral interests and 'scientific' experts to intellectual sources of normative advice. For example, the European Group on Ethics in Science and New Technologies (EGE), which was established by the European commission in 1998, has as its remit 'to advise the Commission on all ethical questions relating to science and new technologies'. Currently, the twelve EGE members include—in addition to biologists, doctors, and a geneticist—a judge from the French Constitutional Council, an Italian lawyer, two professors of philosophy, and a theologian (http://www.europa.euint/comm/secretariat_general/sgc/ethics/composition_en.htm).

GROUPS, EUROPEAN DEMOCRACY, AND INTEGRATION

The developments outlined above represent an unplanned and pragmatic response to the growing importance of European policy making. The steady expansion of the EU's policy-making competence since 1986, combined with piecemeal EU enlargement and institutional reform, have prompted a dramatic increase in the number and range and EU lobbyists. This increase has given rise to the 'problem' of the lobby. As indicated above, this problem is both technical and political in nature. The incentive for both Commission officials and interest groups to continue to develop institutionalized consultative mechanisms is very considerable. As we suggested earlier, there is a functional logic to participation and bureaucratic institutionalization of interests. Yet, this (often restrictive) logic is to some extent counteracted by the apparently contradictory logic—and political imperative—of openness and transparency. Given the multinational nature of the European Union, it is in the Commission's interest to maximize group access to officials. This dependence upon a wide range of interests underpins the Commission's antipathy towards formal regulation of Commission–group relations. Moreover, the EU bureaucracy is under considerable political pressure to broaden its links with NGOs and civil society. Thus, as we have argued elsewhere, the Commission is likely to remain promiscuous in its relationship with groups (Mazey and Richardson 1995, 2001). The Commission has sought to reconcile these two logics by fostering the development of 'thin' and 'thick' consultative structures, both of which have become increasingly institutionalized. As a result, more and more groups are participating in more and more institutions of intermediation centred upon the Commission. However, we do not suggest that these institutions are necessarily stable; European interest intermediation is, like the EU governance system generally, still in a state of flux. Nor are they neutral; all institutions have an inherent bias and create winners and losers. Openness and pluralism do not guarantee influence.

Generally speaking, notwithstanding the Commission's efforts to integrate the so-called civil society interests into the policy process, the most powerful European lobbyists are producer interests, notably multinational firms, whose interests (and policy frames) are deeply embedded within the Commission (Coen 1997, 1999). In part, this difference reflects resource inequalities between groups. In 1992, the Brussels office of COPA, the European association representing EU agricultural producers, employed forty-eight full-time staff and had an annual budget of 120 million Belgian francs. Meanwhile, the Brussels office of BEUC, the European consumers' association, employed just twelve full-time staff and had an annual budget of forty million Belgian francs (Ayberk and Schenker 1998). However, the sources of inequality between groups may be more fundamental. Cohen, for instance, has argued in a constructivist, feminist critique of the EU social programmes, that the deeply entrenched power structure, underlying value system, and working methods of the Commission continue to undermine its rhetorical commitment to building meaningful social partnerships with NGOs and civil society. Nevertheless, Cohen does concede that 'although the European Union is governed by a hidden ethos that is predominantly male, white, and economically competitive, there is a political dynamic taking place that is rather more than social corporatism' (Cohen 2000: 34).

Whether or not this is the case, it is clear that interest groups generally now play a central role in the EU policy-making process. In view of this development, it is appropriate to end this discussion by considering once again the suggestion made some thirty years ago by neo-functionalist theorists that groups would play a key role in the process of European integration (Haas 1958; Lindberg 1963). As we have argued, there is considerable evidence that organized interests (notably the multinational companies) are increasingly active in pressing for standardization, harmonization, and the establishment of a 'level playing field' within the Community. They recognize that in terms of world competition there is little alternative to cross-national collaboration if European industries are to be able to compete with those of the Pacific rim in the next century. Their desire to reduce uncertainty is also leading them to press for greater political as well as economic union within Europe. Indeed, the lead up to the 1996 IGC saw a clear preference on behalf of a whole range of groups—not just business—for a stronger and more effective Europe (Mazey and Richardson 1996b). It would be wrong, of course, to see this type of pressure as *necessarily* leading to more European integration. However, in his discussion of the concept of 'community sentiment' Haas suggested that two of the six necessary conditions for this sentiment to flourish are that:

Interest groups and political parties at the national level endorse supranational action and in preference to action by their national government...[and] Interest groups and political parties organize beyond the national level in order to function more effectively as decision-makers *vis-à-vis* the separate national governments or the central authority and if they define their interests in terms longer than those of the separate nation-state from which they originate. (Haas 1958: 9–10)

Haas goes on to define political integration as 'a process whereby political actors in several distinct national settings are persuaded to shift their loyalties, expectations, and political activities towards a new centre, whose institutions possess or demand jurisdiction over the pre-existing states' (Haas 1958: 16). We believe that this process has already gone a long way and that institutionalization of interests in the Commission bureaucracy has become one of the defining features of the European Union's 'policy style'.

Writing in 1963, Lindberg suggested that European associations were relatively ineffective and that interest groups generally were playing only a limited role in the integration process. However, he went on to argue that:

one can expect that over time the necessity for lobbying will force groups to emphasise collective needs rather than national differences. Such a development can be expected as the central institutions of the EEC become more active, as the types of actions taken involve the harmonization of legislation and the formulations of common policies (rather than the negative process of...barriers to trade), and as...groups become aware that their interests can no longer be adequately served at the national level alone. (Lindberg 1963: 101)

Most of the available evidence suggests that groups in most, if not all, policy sectors now recognize that supranational decisions are required for many policy problems and that it is often in their interests to participate in the formulation of such policies. Groups are therefore beginning to play a significant role in the process of European integration, as predicted by the neo-functionalists. Moreover, this role seems set to expand. For example, the Commission's draft White Paper on *Governance in the European Union* (2000) indicated that one of the reforms it wished to introduce into the processes of preparing and implementing Community rules and policies was '...to improve the interaction between public and private actors...' (http://www.europa.eu.int/comm/governance/index_en.htm, p. 5). Particular emphasis is now being placed on the need to further broaden access. As the Commission paper cited above states, there is a '"right to be involved", which concerns civil society'. The Commission's emphasis on the role of groups in creating a European civic society was also evident in its 1999 *Discussion Paper on the Commission and Non-Governmental Organization*. Thus, one of the four main reasons for its expanding relationship with NGOs is their capacity 'to work as a catalyst for exchange of information and opinions between the Commission and the citizens' (Commission, Brussels, 28 September 1999: 8). Having previously played a key role in the process of creating a European policy space, groups now seem set to play an equally important role in the creation of a European level civil society.

PART IV

DEMOCRACY AND POPULAR
PARTICIPATION

14

Contentious Politics in Western Europe and the United States

SIDNEY TARROW

Modern European history began in contention: with the demand for constitutional rights that led to the French Revolution of 1789 (McAdam *et al.* 2001: ch. 2). Even supposedly 'peaceful' Britain achieved something like its modern form during a not-so-peaceful period of contention. As for the United States, it was created by the first anti-colonial revolution in history. Yet all was not overthrow of inherited authority; in all three episodes there was a mix of extreme and routine politics, transgressive and contained contention, rejection of institutions and the desire to correct them. Contention is the stuff of politics and takes a variety of forms within politics.

For most of its recent history, however, political science has relegated the study of popular protest movements to sociology—or worse, to abnormal psychology. Why is this so? One reason is that attention of most scholars of contention has focussed on social movement organizations—*sustained and crystallized forms of contentious politics on the part of claimants or those who represent them in conflict with authorities, opponents, or rival groups* (Tilly 1995; Tarrow 1998a: ch. 1) and has ignored less crystallized, more episodic, and more interstitial forms of contention. Another reason is that even when their goals were reformist, many of these movements attacked the state or at least adopted a language of militancy towards it. Rhetoric coloured analysis: by both friendly supporters and hostile critics, nineteenth century movements like the labour movement were characterized as being 'against' the system, even as they attempted to enter it. A final reason is the disparity between the methods developed to study contentious and routine politics. The public opinion poll or the study of aggregate election statistics sit poorly with the analysis of protest events or the content analysis of revolutionary discourse.

The inter-war period intensified this tendency to polarization, as a wave of anti-democratic movements from Bolshevism to Fascism rose to attack constitutional governments. Cold War and the establishment social science it fostered added a new aura of outsiderness to the image of popular protest. It was the movements of the 1960s that brought a new generation of activists, many from the incubator of the student

The author wishes to thank his former collaborators Doug Imig and David S. Meyer, for common work cited here, as well as Anand Menon, Davydd Greenwood, and Hanspeter Kriesi for comments on a draft of this chapter.

movement, into political life. Veterans of these movements moved into academia, where they produced a paradigm shift linking contention directly to the polity (Piven and Cloward 1977; Tilly 1978).

The decades that followed reinforced this paradigm shift, with the elaboration on both sides of the Atlantic of models linking popular protest to conventional politics. In the United States, writers like Doug McAdam (1982, 1999), Charles Tilly (1978, 1995), and this author (1989, 1994) elaborated different versions of a 'political process model' that crystallized these changes. In Western Europe, authors like Donatella della Porta (1995), Herbert Kitschelt (1986), and Hanspeter Kriesi and his associates (1995) elaborated their own versions of this approach. More resilient than the much-touted 'new social movement' approach, it has become the dominant approach to contentious politics on both sides of the Atlantic.

As a result of these changes, it is becoming more common to speak of a broad field of 'contentious politics', which I define as *episodic, collective interaction among makers of claims and their objects when (1) at least one government is a claimant, an object of claims, or a party to the claims and (2) these claims would, if realized, affect the interests of at least one of the claimants* (McAdam *et al.* 2001).

Such a definition excludes most routine and bureaucratic political life, but includes revolutions, rebellions, social movements, industrial conflict, civil war, ethno-religious conflict, and related forms. The omnibus term 'contentious politics' does not imply a general covering law for all forms of contention, but it does allow us to examine comparatively a variety of forms of contention and to begin to understand better the relations and transitions between them. It will also, *inter alia*, encourage comparison between American and European social movements and between the most common contentious forms in these two culture areas and those more typical of other parts of the world (McAdam *et al.* 2001).

But in this essay I will limit my comparisons to Western Europe and the United States. Two main distinctions will guide my effort:

- *First*, between *transgressive* and *contained* forms of contention, the first marked by new or hitherto unacceptable forms of action and/or by the representation of new actors or collective identities.
- *Second*, the *degree of opposition to institutions*, ranging from complete acceptance of these institutions to their complete rejection. Figure 14.1 portrays a typology of forms of contention that results from the intersection of these two dimensions.
- By *expressive contention* I refer to episodes of transgressive collective action on the part of social or political actors whose goal is self-representation within an existing polity. These are recognizable from the 'new social movement' paradigm of the 1980s, but can be seen in many previous periods of history (Calhoun 1995).
- By *reformist contention* I refer to contained interaction with elites in the name of claims that are compatible with the existing polity. The majority of contemporary social movements in Western Europe and North America fall into this category.
- By *integral contention* I refer to assaults on the existing polity from new or unrecognized actors using transgressive forms of collective action.

Mode of interaction	Degree of opposition	
	Partial	Total
Transgressive	Expressive contention	Integral contention
Contained	Reform contention	Communal contention

Figure 14.1 *Degree of opposition and mode of interaction of popular protest movements*

- By *communal contention* I refer to groups which turn away from institutions and seek to create alternative communities.

Needless to say, each of the resulting forms of movement is no more than an ideal type. (Later we will explore a hybrid type that seems to be diffusing in contemporary European and American politics.) This means both that several tendencies may exist within the same movement family and that the interaction of a movement with institutions over time can produce transitions from one cell of the typology to another. Consider, for example, the 'identity movements' that have become so common on both sides of the Atlantic: they range from the expressive assertion of difference ('Black is beautiful') to the call for the reform of institutions and public policies to offer benefits to specified groups (e.g. the call for a multiracial census category in the United States), to integralist Islam in North Africa and the Middle East, to communal movements like the renaissance of the hasidim in the Jewish community.

In the *first part* of the chapter, I will use these distinctions to examine these four main types of political contention outlined above. But contentious politics is nothing if not mobile; how it changes in relation to these two dimensions is the topic of *part two*. In *part three*, I will turn to how states interact with movements and consider the hypothesis that Western Europe and the United States are, in some ways, becoming *movement societies*. The chapter will close on a speculative note: how are European social movements—which arose in relation to the national state—being affected by the forces of 'globalization' and European integration in today's world.

FOUR TYPES OF CONTENTIOUS POLITICS

Expressive Contention

In the history of modern Europe, there have been a variety of bases for political protest movements, numerous movement ideologies, many forms of collective action ranging from the most peaceful assemblies all the way to armed struggle, and a range of many types and levels of organization, from near-spontaneity to organized military movements. While some movements arise within institutions, others emerge outside of them. Some movements have goals that are compatible with the institutions that they target, while others aim at the destruction of institutions and still others look to the construction of communities outside the influence of institutions.

We use the term 'expressive' to denote movements whose relation to institutions is both emergent and transgressive. Whatever else is true of them, most episodes of contentious politics arise with strong expressive elements (Alberoni 1968; Melucci 1985) through new forms of dress, speech, habits of life, and forms of interaction. It is only through new or dramatic self-presentation that a movement constructs an identity that will be recognized by both subjects and interlocutors (Melucci 1985). As the term suggests, such movements are unstable in form and are often ephemeral. Since their claims are often limited to a single issue or campaign, they often disappear after the issues around which they organized are surpassed. But more typical is their transformation into one of the more stable forms of interaction with authorities or elites.

Early European labour movements were expressive in this sense, frequently adopting the ritualized forms of earlier movements in the name of often quite modest demands. The adoption of the *charivari* in France, the labour sects in England, the Irish-based 'Molly Maguires' in the American coalfields showed the essentially transitional nature of these early movements. Although expressive elements remained in their evocation of their past and in their desire to hold their members' loyalty, once they discovered their characteristic repertoire of collective action—the strike, the public meeting, and the demonstration—many developed into reformist movements while others were transformed into either integral or communal movements.

European peasant movements had strong expressive elements. Frequently led by opportunities in the larger political system—for example, the Sicilian land seizures that were triggered by Garibaldi's invasion in the 1860s—such movements seldom sought goals more ambitious than the restoration of abusively enclosed common lands or the curtailment of exploitative contracts. Their processions frequently had at their head statues of the Virgin alongside the red or black flag. Rarely were they endowed with a fully-fledged ideology which went beyond their immediate claims, as, for example, was the case for the Andalusian anarchists or the Zapatistas in the Mexican Revolution.

The 'new' social movements of the 1970s and 1980s in Western Europe have frequently been characterized as 'expressive' because of their informal organizations, their lack of fully-formed ideologies, and their focus on what Habermas referred to as 'life-space' concerns (Offe 1985). With the benefit of hindsight, we can see that these characteristics were the results of the *youth* of these movements and did not constitute a historically new type of contention (Offe 1990). By the 1990s most of them had evolved into more stable and less confrontational forms while some—like the various Green parties—had entered parliaments and put on the garb of routine politics. As they aged, expressive new movements transformed themselves into more long-lasting reform movements (Calhoun 1995).

Reformist Contention

Although the term 'reform' was first used in many countries to denote the Protestant Reformation, its contemporary meaning made sense only after the consolidation of the modern state. It is no accident that the first successful modern reform movement was the movement to end the importation of slaves into Britain and the former British empire (Drescher 1987). Beginning among evangelical Protestant groups, this movement was fed by changes in the world economy and by the slave rebellions in the New World. By the 1848 revolution it had spread to the European continent; by 1860, it brought about a Civil War in America. Anti-slavery eventually triumphed in Britain and the Americas, in the wake of official policy advanced by both diplomacy and the British navy.

Although in retrospect reform movements seek only the renovation of existing politics, they often give rise to deep-seated social and political conflicts. This can be seen in the quintessential reform movement of the nineteenth century—the social-democratic labour movement. Beginning as quasi-religious brotherhoods among skilled workers, labour movements sought reforms in the wages and hours of labour, the extension of the suffrage, and, above all, the right to factory representation. Business groups and conservative governments reacted to these demands with hostility, resisting the right to strike and organize, and delaying the expansion of the suffrage to the working class until late in the nineteenth century. Where concessions were made—as in Great Britain under Disraeli—they had the desired effect of 'domesticating' the labour movement and integrating its representatives into routine politics; where they were not or where they were made meaningless by electoral laws—as in Imperial Germany—they drove labour into integral forms of contention.

Anti-slavery had been fed by religious organizations external to its subjects, but the labour movement had both internal and external sources: those created by the discipline of factory work, which produced the trade union as its characteristic form; and those produced by middle-class reformism—as in the case of the British Fabians or French reform socialists. In some cases, like Imperial Germany, unions grew up under the aegis of the Social Democratic party; in others, like France and Italy, left-wing parties and labour syndicates (the term itself is significant) maintained an uneasy and competitive relationship; while in Britain the unions were a constituent in the formation of the Labour Party and remained an influential factor in its policies for decades.

Reform movements flourished with the coming of mass democracy in the twentieth century, especially after the end of the Second World War, when a wide variety of such movements sought reform in the rights of women, minorities, the disabled, and the unborn, and reforms in the regulation of the environment and the workplace. As classical labour movements languished in the wake of the Cold War, new citizens' movements developed around reformist goals ranging from 'Mothers Against Drunk Driving' in the United States to the automobile drivers' movement in Switzerland, hunters in Italy and France, and anti-nuclear and environmental movements all over Europe. Especially successful has been the environmental movement which arose with strong expressive elements but turned rapidly towards reform, with a program that was absorbed by progressive and even moderate political parties (Dalton 1994; Diani 1995).

Why did reform movements flourish in Western Europe and North America over the past twenty years? The answers are biological, cultural, organizational, and institutional:

- *Biologically*, the student and New Left movements of the 1960s left behind a reservoir of activism outside of the declining mass political party system that could be drawn upon by new movements in the 1970s and 1980s—especially by the peace, environmental, and women's movements (McAdam 1988).

- *Culturally*, what some have called 'post-material' attitudes spread among the educated middle class, especially in the service sector, increasingly so as the decline of the Cold War eroded the cleavage between left and right (Inglehart 1977, 1997).
- *Organizationally*, new forms of mobilization and diffusion—and especially the mass media—place expanded resources in the hands of ordinary citizens, giving them a power to influence public policy that only formal bureaucratic organizations could muster in the past (McCarthy and Zald 1987).
- *Institutionally*, the political parties that had created powerful political subcultures in the past lost these as the result of prosperity, secularization, population movement, and the creation of media-driven popular cultures. To a great extent, reformist activism has filled a lacuna opened up by the decline of mass political parties.

In the last three decades, both directly and through their influence on the party system, reform movements have had great success in forcing their programmes onto the agenda of conventional politics. But they have also given rise to counter-movements of people who fear that the foundations of their lives will be undermined by reforms' successes—the so-called 'ugly movements' against immigrants, ethnic and religious minorities, and 'secular humanism' (Koopmans 1995; Kriesi *et al.* 1995). Reacting against the civic and cultural reforms of the 1960s and 1970s like divorce, abortion, the recognition of gay and lesbian rights, and the secularization of religion, these right-wing movements move towards an older model: the 'integral' movements that developed in the inter-war period.

Integral Contention

As in much else, modern integral movements emerged from the Reformation. Michael Walzer has argued that the first modern social movement activists were the Calvinist 'Saints' who spread the gospel by open and clandestine means, made of activism a profession, and built a transnational network of organizers, presses, and churches—much as anarchist and socialist activists would do two centuries later (1971). Integralism was bound up in their doctrine, hardened by repression, and reinforced by their networks and by the states that adopted their faith. When it is combined with peasant land hunger and inter-state rivalry, it produced decades of internecine strife, iconoclasm, and warfare and a powerful countermovement— much like Communism in the twentieth century.

Integralism in its secular form appeared in the late nineteenth century. As the industrial revolution spread from England and France to east-central and southern Europe, competition with Europe's early industrializers required high concentrations of capital and labour, which in turn required large-scale investment, gave rise to investment banks and to state involvement in autocratic regimes like Wilhelmene Germany and Czarist Russia, as well as by semi-autocratic ones like Italy and Habsburg Austria–Hungary. When labour movements arose, they found themselves facing not only large concentrations of capital but also repressive states which regarded strikes and protest demonstrations as dangerous, if not downright treasonous. In Imperial Germany, for example, the Social Democratic Party was declared illegal for eleven years; in Russia, strike leaders were regularly sent to Siberia, where their alienation hardened and they formed the resolve to overthrow the state. In both Russia and Italy, terrorist movements developed which directly targeted the state and the royal families of both monarchies.

Forced to operate in these repressive environments, not only anarchists but also social-democratic and labour movements adopted militant ideologies and forms of organization and rejected the reformism that had come to dominate labour movements in the West. This produced not only anarchism and terrorism, but led to the development of variants of social democracy that closed in upon themselves as 'states within a state' (Roth 1963) or operated clandestinely in quasi-military cells with integral ideologies. The version of social-democracy that moved furthest away from reformism and towards integralism was Leninism.

At its origins, Leninism was one of a number of contentious factions—the Bolshevik one—on the extreme left of the archipelago of radical groups in the vast Russian empire. But its endowment with Lenin's theory of the vanguard party, its utopian commitment to a total transformation of Russia's political and economic life, and its opposition to the First World War allowed it to seize power in the name of a proletarian ideology in a country with a peasant majority that had barely escaped from feudalism. From the struggle to impose Bolshevik rule on such an inhospitable terrain followed many of the distortions of the Soviet route to socialism.

Cheered by the Russians' success and weary of the frustrations and compromises of reformism by the end of the First World War, many European socialists came to see Leninism as a model that could bring the revolution to the West. But other social democrats and reformists had by then become committed to democracy and rejected Lenin's integralist vision. The Bolshevik revolution thus divided the European Left into a reformist and an integralist wing, feeding a process of polarization that weakened the labour movement in general and reformism in particular. Combined with the economic costs of the war and the catastrophe of the depression, this weakening of reformism undermined the weak democracies of Italy and Germany, leaving the way open to a counter-integral movement, fascism.

Mussolini's fasces and Hitler's brownshirts were not the first form of integralism on the Right. In the nineteenth century, as industrialization moved eastward, nationalism—an ideology that was originally associated with the French revolution and reform—turned racial and integral (Kohn 1967). Integral nationalism asserted with equal inaccuracy the absolute uniqueness of each ethnic group, its historical association with a particular slice of territory, and the equally absolute non-right of any other group to share that territory. For the most militant of these movements, this added up to a total rejection of territorial compromise, mobilization around the symbols of folk, race, and language, and a hatred of its neighbours. From the assertion of territorial uniqueness and folk superiority it was a short step to imperialism and—according to Hannah Arendt—a slightly longer one to totalitarianism (Arendt 1958).

Integralism's most recent incarnations are the various forms of religious funda-mentalism that have swept the Islamic, Christian, and Jewish worlds. In Europe, fed by widespread immigration from non-European countries, xenophobic movements have arisen in a number of countries. The French *Front national,* the German *Republicaner,* and the Austrian Freedom Party have garnered millions of anti-immigrant votes and created waves of revulsion throughout Western Europe and the fear of a resurgence of fascism. Even in Britain and the United States, where fascist movements have patently failed to take hold, skinheads and Christian/fascist militia groups reveal a xenophobic substratum that recalls Nazi brownshirts and the American Ku Klux Klan.

Communal Contention

The integral movements surveyed above reject institutions by attacking them; other movements reject institutions by turning away from them and seeking to construct alternative communities. The tendency to create alternative institutions goes back to the monastic movements of the middle ages and to the utopian socialism of the nine-teenth century. We find it again in the communal movements that grew out of the movements of the 1960s, some of which survive to this day, and to an extent in the 'home schooling' movement in the United States. Alternative communities seem to require *physical* separation, which is why so many of them were established in iso-lated or rural areas. Others, like the American Mormons, were forced to isolated areas by the rejection of their practices by the wider community, where it reinforced their solidarity and helped to cement their difference.

The urge to construct alternative communities can easily begin *within* institu-tions—as it did in the monastic communities of the Catholic Church. The early monastic movements organized their rules around the spiritual values represented in teachings of the Church that were ignored in its practice. Catholic doctrine provided them with a frame for rule-making that they would have lacked had they fully separ-ated themselves from its teachings and authority. Even in the 1960s, it was around the teachings of Pope John XXIII that a new wave of religious reformers attempted to create a 'church of the people' in Western Europe (Tarrow 1989) and liberation the-ology in Latin America.

Communalism is not limited to the Catholic Church or to religion in general. The late eighteenth and early nineteenth centuries produced a wave of religious theorizing and alternative community building in Europe and the United States. These commun-ities were often directly religious in inspiration—like the Shakers and Mormons in the United States. But others were inspired by secular reactions to the ills of early indus-trialism—as in the Owenite communities created in Britain and North America. Although most of the early Utopian thinkers were Europeans—like Cabet, Fourier, and Owen himself—because of its openness to new settlements and the absence of an established church, America provided wider spaces for spiritual experimentation.

The construction of alternative communities appears to follow waves of either religious or political enthusiasm, as did the revival movements in the United States in the 1820s and the more recent communal experiments that drew on the activists of the 1960s (Kanter 1972; Kitts 1999). They often emerge from sectors of mass movements that grow disillusioned with reformist or integralist methods and place their hopes for self-transformation in communion with others like themselves in isolation from the temptations of capitalist society. These alternative communities frequently fail, and when they survive, they often do so at the cost of slippage into accepting the forms of behaviour of the dominant society around them.

This paradox is not due to some inherent weakness in the moral fibre of communal activists but results from the fact that their insistence on building total communities requires them to undertake economic activities in which they must compete with actors whose only motive is profit (Kitts 1999). To survive, they make a series of small compromises that eventually leave little but their memories to distinguish them from their competitors. We see this self-transformation into successful businesses in the Israeli kibbutzim, heavily dependent on Arab and foreign volunteer labour and increasingly involved in international trade. The same seems to be the case of the so-called 'alternative scene' which emerged in Western Europe out of the movements of the 1960s: where it has survived, this has largely been due to an acceptance of the rules of the game of competitive capitalism.

DYNAMICS OF PROTEST MOVEMENTS

Expressive movements, reformism, integralism, and communalism: these four variants of contentious politics frequently intersect, combine, and transmute from one form into another. How do such changes come about? Figure 14.1 provided a broad map of the many kinds of popular protest movements that developed in European and American history, but it tells us little about their dynamics. Some observers have seen an inevitable tendency of movements to begin their lives attacking states and institutions only to become institutionalized themselves. But the history of popular protest movements shows other patterns as well as institutionalization: for example, the *radicalization* of once-moderate movements, the creation of *hybrid forms* of organization and strategy, the *privatization* of movement activists and the cultural changes they bring to the life course (Kriesi 1996). Let us begin with the tendency to institutionalization and then turn to these other patterns of change.

The Institutionalization of Movements

Drawing on his own experience with central European socialism at the turn of the twentieth century, the great social theorist, Robert Michels (1915), developed what has come to be called the 'Iron Law of Oligarchy'. This was a model of movement change that described the evolution from anti-system movements to institutions as an inevitable tendency that was built into the nature of popular protest movements. Like much of continental social movement theory, Michels' theory dealt with broad historical tendencies and left little room for politics or for national variations. The model posited

- a trend in movements' ideologies towards de-radicalization;
- a shift from spontaneous forms of organization to centralized bureaucracy;
- a succession from charismatic leaders calling for radical change to organizational specialists more intent on defending their positions, and;
- a movement from violent or disruptive forms of action to electoral, interest group, and parliamentary politics.

Scholars who have followed Michels saw popular protest describing a rough parabola from movement to interest group, from initial surge to one of rational decision making, from principled opposition to institutions to participation in pragmatic politics (Alberoni 1968; Lowi 1971; Piven and Cloward 1977). Michels himself saw history as a 'cruel game: of recurring cycles from democratization and bureaucratization' (Barker, 2001); our epoch suggests that movement dynamics lead in many directions.

The Michelsian model was an apt summary of what happened to many central European social democratic parties in the early twentieth century. But the movements Michels knew best had a peculiarity; they arose in autocratic or semi-autocratic states in rapidly industrializing societies. Representing recently urbanized and poorly educated workers in societies with strong feudal heritages, they had specificities that badly matched the situation of British or American movements or those of the present (Calhoun 1995). Movements like the British CND or the American Civil Rights movement were decentralized and informal, their activists were more likely to take the form of 'transitory teams' than full-time officials, and most of their supporters were recruited on an occasional campaign basis, rather than into the quasi-military ranks of party cells or sections (McCarthy and Zald 1987).

Moreover, many contemporary social movements are *born* with one foot in the world of institutionalized politics. Think of CND, which drew heavily on activists from the British Labour Party; or of the anti-racist group *SOS-Racisme*, which enjoyed the sponsorship of the French Socialist Party; or of the American group called Mothers Against Drunk Driving, whose activities were engaged within institutions from its origins. There must be other patterns of change than those captured by Michels' 'Iron Law of Oligarchy'. Drawing on Hanspeter Kriesi's work (1996), we can identify three others: *radicalization, hybridization, and privatization.*

Becoming More Radical

Radicalization is as recurring a tendency in political protest movements as institutionalization (McAdam *et al.*: chs 2 and 6). Take the episode with which this chapter began—the French Revolution of 1789. After the initial period that Crane Brinton called 'the reign of the moderates' (1938: ch. 5), the more radical members of the revolutionary coalition turned on the moderates, using the tools of state repression and popular mobilization to liquidate them in a 'reign of terror and virtue'. First constitutional moderates were defeated by a coalition of Republicans; then the republican coalition split into competing groups and then into Girondins and Jacobins; and finally, the triumphant Jacobins defeated and eliminated their Girondin colleagues. Through a process of radicalization and polarization, the revolution 'devoured its children' (McAdam *et al.* 2001: ch. 10).

Consider the protest movements that swept across European universities in the 1960s. The year 1968 was a heady period of near-spontaneous protest that brought seasoned political activists into contact with unpoliticized students in marches, demonstrations, and occupations of university faculties. While many of the new recruits faded away quickly, others moved into more professional movement activities, while still others, like the Italian Red Brigades and the German Red Army Faction, took up arms. While radicalization fizzled in Britain and France, the Italian and German cases both show clear evidence of radicalization: first between more moderate and more radical student groups; then between those who adopted armed struggle and those who moved towards a more institutional path; and finally between extreme left and extreme right as they fought to extinguish the republic from opposite extremes (Tarrow 1989; della Porta 1995).

With less dramatic results, a wing of the American civil rights movement also radicalized in the late 1960s. Beginning under moderate , middle-class church-based leadership in the South, as this movement moved into the northern ghettoes it took on a radical colouration, calling for black separatism and developing pretensions to military organization. There was a parallel trend among white radicals when the progressive movement, Students for a Democratic Society, gave birth to the Weathermen, a clandestine organization that dedicated itself to the violent overthrow of the American government. As in Europe, these groups were a minority of a minority, but they show that Michels' 'iron law' is not an inexorable tendency in contentious politics.

Hybrid Movement Forms

Hybridization is the development of forms of organization and strategy which combine disruptive protest and routine forms of activity. This tendency is not new: think of the abolitionist movement of the late eighteenth and early nineteenth centuries. But it was reinforced after the 1960s protest wave because it coincided with the expanding ability of ordinary citizens to organize, to access the media, and to employ discretionary sources of income and fund-raising (McCarthy and Zald 1987). This tendency of expanded 'resource mobilization' reinforced in recent years by the wide diffusion of electronic forms of communication and mobilization; through e-mail, the Internet, and interactive chat groups, organizers with access to electronic communication can form a 'virtual' movement network to organize demonstrations, exchange information, and even obstruct government activities by invading their websites (Hill and Hughes 1998).

Activism that once required the painstaking construction of mass political parties or personal contacts with legislators is now frequently channelled through new and elaborate hybrid movement forms, of which we can enumerate three main subtypes:

1. Among the most widely diffused of these forms is what American political scientists have called 'public interest groups'. These groups are similar in many ways to

traditional associations representing group interests, but they make collective claims around issues of general concern, like the environment, human rights, and women's rights. Relying heavily on direct mail solicitation, electronic mobilization, and lobbying, they also turn from time to time to the classical repertoire of social movements: the petition, the protest demonstration, the march, less frequently the sit in and civil disobedience. This phenomenon has developed more slowly in Western Europe than in America, probably because of the residual strength of mass party organizations; but by the 1990s, as party organizations weakened, even in countries like Italy, public interest groups now cross old ideological lines between secular radicals and Catholics in the name of broad public policy claims. As Donatella della Porta writes; 'groups of citizens who want to attract the attention of public administrators have turned directly to the public sphere through actions of protest that can capture the attention of the media' (2000: 21).

2. A second form of hybrid organization are the community action groups that have flourished in European and American cities since the end of the 1960s. Often drawing on religious activists, they specialize in service provision, distributing information and publicity to constituents, and representing their claims to public officials. More frequently than public interest groups, community organizations use a language and engage in activities redolent of classical movement politics, but they frequently do so more to attract media attention than to force officials to bend to their will. While many types of claims animate such groups, problems like traffic, pollution, drug sales, and physical security are their particular concerns.

3. Finally, coalitional campaigns have become a growing feature of contentious politics on both sides of the Atlantic since the 1960s. These are mass demonstrations animated by movement and movement-related groups, mounted to publicize a particular demand or set of demands. Bringing together sometimes scores of distinct organizations (Gerhards and Rucht 1992), these demonstrations are orchestrated set pieces, often organized in consultation with the police, who advise organizers on parade routes, offer logistical support, and sometimes collaborate in weeding out violent elements. Coalitional campaigns dramatically demonstrate public concern for an issue without the need for large, bureaucratic mass organizations. Like public interest groups and community action groups, they too have eroded the importance of political parties as agencies of mobilization.

Privatization and Culture Shift

In his acclaimed essay, *Shifting Involvements*, economist Albert Hirschman posited that human beings shift periodically from a logic of public involvement to one of privatization and back again (1982). As an economist, Hirschman saw these recurring reversals as akin to consumer behaviour: buy enough home electronic equipment and you will soon desert the market to enjoy the fruits of your acquisitions. Others have seen privatization resulting from the costs and risks of public involvement: spend enough time demonstrating in the streets and you will weary of the costs and frustrations of street politics (Tarrow 1998*a*: ch. 9). In addition, the risks of repression can lead even seasoned activists to desert public politics for private pursuits, or at least for more routine forms of involvement.

The great wave of protest politics in the 1960s in Western Europe revealed just such a parabola of involvement and privatization. After the excitement of the first student occupations in the spring of 1968, many French, Italian, and German student groups left on vacation, drifted into political parties, took up journalism, and entered teaching. A much smaller number, as we have seen, entered clandestine 'integral' groups to follow the path of terrorism. But rather than institutionalization or radicalization, many of the movements of that decade were replaced by privatization.

But although privatization takes people out of active movement politics, it would not be accurate to say that it leaves nothing but memories in the wake of activism. We have already noted that the movements of the 1960s left a reservoir of activists who built a second generation of 'new' social movements. They also contributed to the formation of new political parties like the Greens and to a generation of activists who entered mainstream parties of the left, which in turn adapted their programmes and organizations to attract and hold these new members (Lange *et al.* 1989). Moreover, even those who left the movements of the 1960s developed aspects of their private lives that resonated with movement politics: a preference for natural foods, shopping in cooperative or alternative enterprises, the direct purchase of craft goods from the Third world, contributing to worthy causes descended from their movement careers. Many former activists keep open their network ties to others like themselves, keeping alive a potential for future activism (McAdam 1988).

The influence of great waves of protest like the 1960s one is indirect as well as direct. By daring to challenge convention, waves of protest initiate periods of cultural change affecting even basic cultural expectations, such as assumptions about the roles of men and women, the acceptance of homosexuality, and decisions in the life course. For example, as Doug McAdam found in the United States, a greater incidence of non-traditional family lives and unconventional careers spread from movement activists to the general population of the United States in the decades after the 1960s (McAdam 1999). Culture shift is the quieter but perhaps most durable substatum of the dynamics of contentious politics (Rochon 1998).

PROTEST MOVEMENTS AND THE STATE

Institutionalization, radicalization, hybridization, and privatization: what explains these various mechanisms and processes of change in contentious politics? There are of course many particular changes in every country and epoch of history that contribute to trends in one or another direction. But underlying them all are the relations between movements and political regimes and the strategies of the latter towards contentious politics. The most important state strategy is the particular mix

of repression and facilitation with which states respond to protest; a second important factor is the stability of the political elite and the party system; a third is the extent
to which movements may have become 'normalized'—their once disruptive actions
a predictable and therefore ineffective part of the polity.

Repression/Facilitation

In his 1978 text, *From Mobilization to Revolution*, Charles Tilly points to two characteristic state responses to contentious politics: repression and facilitation:

Repression is *the effort to suppress either contentious acts or groups and organizations responsible for them*. In one form or another, repression is a predictable response to contention which
has relatively predictable effects—generally stiffening resistance on the part of threatened
communities, encouraging evasion of surveillance and shifts of tactics by well organized
actors, and discouraging mobilization or action by other parties. Repression may be selective—
in which case it isolates more militant groups and closes off to them prescribed or tolerated
means of contention. Or it can be generalized, in which case it throws moderates into the arms
of the extremists. (Tilly 1978: ch. 4)

Facilitation, in contrast, is *the provision, purposive or non-purposive, of channels, legal
provisions, and practices which support or tolerate the activities of protest movements*.
Like repression, facilitation can be selective (e.g. tax exemptions that are offered to
'non-political' groups but not to 'political' ones—the definition of what is 'political'
being highly selective) or general (e.g. the right to demonstrate or to strike in a particular society at a particular time). Although in general autocratic states repress dissent while democratic states tolerate it, it is by no means certain that all democratic
states facilitate all kinds of protest. For example, for historical reasons, Germany today
does not permit the display of the swastika or the claim that the Holocaust did not
happen. In Britain, the Defence of the Realm Act sets severe limits on certain types of
expression. And the repression suffered by members of the American Communist
Party in the 1950s tells us that even the most liberal of democracies can be vigorously
repressive when they face those they consider outside the liberal consensus.

Our earlier discussion of nineteenth century British versus Imperial German reactions to the rise of the labour movement show how different mixes of repression and
facilitation lead to divergent trajectories of contentious politics. The early factory
laws, the broadening of the suffrage in 1832 and 1867, and the legalization of trade
unions and of the strike helped lead British workers down a reformist path that eventually produced the domestication of the Labour Party and of the TUC. In contrast,
Bismarck's banning of German Social Democracy for a crucial period of its development led to habits of encapsulation that lasted even after the party was legalized. The
adoption of the 'vanguard' party model was clearly attributed by Lenin to the necessity of struggling against an oppressive autocracy.

Although within a narrower band of variation, the movements of the 1960s were
differentially channelled towards either radicalization or institutionalization according to the mix of facilitation and repression aimed at them by different national governments and their police forces. Driven into clandestinity by repression, the most

militant sectors of the Italian student movement turned increasingly to the only kinds of contention that were available to them—violent attacks on their opponents or on the state (della Porta 1995). In contrast, most American radicals of the 1960s had available a variety of institutional venues that gave them the flexibility to adapt their tactics and innovate in their repertoires (McAdam 1983).

In general, facilitative states encourage institutionalization while repression encourages radicalization and encapsulation. But these trends are not unilinear or irreversible; though western democracies today all employ accommodative police tactics towards protesters (della Porta and Reiter 1998), new waves of protest using unaccustomed or transgressive means may begin the cycle of repression and facilitation all over again. State strategies towards movements depend not only on inherited expectations of toleration, but also on who is in power at the time new waves of contention emerge and what other processes are underway in their societies (McAdam *et al.* 2001).

Elite Unity or Division

A second important aspect of state/movement relations is what Kriesi and his collaborators call the structures of conflict and alignment (1995). Compact elites that rally round the state when protest movements emerge offer fewer openings than elites that are divided, differentiated, or in a process of realignment. This is a typical variation within American and West European politics but it could even be found in 1989 in the authoritarian states of east-central Europe, when divisions among the Communist party elites encouraged dissidents to challenge the foundations of these regimes.

A comparison of the French and Italian elites' responses to the movements of 1968 illustrates how elite stability or realignment affects movement prospects. The failure of the French movement in the face of its tremendous early success in shutting down the economy in May 1968 was not due to its inherent weakness, but to the compact nature of the elite and its rallying behind the Gaullist majority in the June elections that followed. Political economic management reversed the workers' gains in the May conflict, while skillful parliamentary manoeuvering transformed the university reform into a tool of social control (Salvati 1981; Tarrow 1998*b*). Conversely, the Italian protest movement, which started in the same year as the French one, extended well into the 1970s, not because the movement was stronger but because the Italian elite was in a state of disarray. The divisions within the Italian elite weakened the state's response, produced violent but inconsistent repression, and afforded the movement allies in high places whose support encouraged them to continue their struggle.

Towards a Movement Society?

While some scholars of social movements see political regimes as invariably hostile towards popular protest, others see a secular shift towards greater facilitation—or at least towards tolerance of protest—in recent years (della Porta and Reiter 1998; Meyer and Tarrow 1998). Still others see a secular increase in the capacity of ordinary citizens to mobilize on behalf of their interests and values (McCarthy and Zald 1987). If these two trends are correct, it raises the question of whether something fundamental has changed in the politics of contemporary industrial democracies. More people have certainly had experience with contentious politics than their fathers and mothers did; for example, Russell Dalton (1996) points out that increasing numbers of women, retirees, and white collar workers now engage in forms of behaviour that used to be limited to workers and students.

Is there a trend to a greater frequency, to broader diffusion, and perhaps to greater institutionalization of collective action in this new century? Is Western Europe becoming a *movement society*? The idea of a movement society advances three main hypotheses:

- *first*, that social protest has moved from being a sporadic, if recurring feature of democratic politics to a perpetual element in modern life;
- *second*, that protest behaviour is employed with greater frequency, by more diverse constituencies, and is used to represent a wider range of claims than ever before;
- *third*, that professionalization and institutionalization may be changing the major vehicle of contentious claims—the social movement—into an instrument within the reach of conventional politics.

Evidence for these trends has been accumulating (see Meyer and Tarrow 1998; della Porta and Reiter 1998). But there are two problems that have still to be adequately addressed: first, does the trend to normalization apply only to the 'middle age' of the 'new' social movements that arose during of the last movement cycle, or does it also apply to the 'new' movements that have arisen more recently? Second, what is the ultimate effect of these changes? On the one hand, if people protest, they do so because they think such activity will achieve their goals. Recent research on the outcomes of protest suggests that protest indeed 'pays'; but mainly in respect to small changes leading to the acceptance of protesting groups, rather than to broad changes and to the transformation of the polity (Gamson 1990; Giugni *et al.* 1998). On the other hand, to the extent that popular forms of protest have become more acceptable, more legitimate, and more expected, the social movement may be losing its power to inspire challengers and bowl over antagonists and powerholders.

Some analysts already argue that the analytical distinctiveness of social movements is no longer justified (Zald 2000). Others feel that, while distinct from parties and interest groups, their major function is to place new issues on the public agenda, issues that are then worked out in isolation from these movements in the central political process (Tarrow 1998b). Still others argue that too much attention has been paid to 'consensus movements' and that broader attention to other forms of contention show continued reserves of combativeness in newly formed or recently politicized sectors of the public (Piven and Cloward 1992).

We do not yet have clear answers to these issues. What is certain is that as political parties lose their mobilizing function and ordinary citizens gain resources and skills to organize protest movements, the terrain of western political processes is expanding. And if that is the case (to restate the question raised at the outset of this chapter), are popular protest movements distinct from politics or are they becoming simply another form of politics? A final issue takes us beyond the range of domestic politics into spaces where few protest movements have traditionally organized.

TRANSNATIONAL MOVEMENTS AND EUROPEANIZATION

For most of their history, social movements have been part of national political struggles. Indeed, most of our knowledge of contentious politics is centred around the consolidation and the functioning of the national state. Scholars have only recently begun to consider the implications for social and political movements of what some are calling the 'globalization' of world politics and others less ambitiously refer to as 'transnational politics' (Tarrow 2001). Some focus on new forms of activism targeting international targets, like the World Trade Organization; others examine transnational diffusion, like the petrol blockades that swept across Western Europe in mid-2000; while others focus on transnational networks which use their international influence to support popular movements within oppressive national states (Keck and Sikkink 1998).

This is not the place to detail the various versions and properties of the globalization thesis (see Rodrik 1997). In its strong form, it makes four kinds of claims:

- The dominant economic trends of the late twentieth century have been towards international economic interdependence.
- Economic growth of the 1970s and 1980s has brought citizens of the North and West and those of the East and South closer together, making the latter more aware of their inequality.
- Global communications structures are emerging that weave closer ties between core and periphery of the world system. Decentralized and private communications technologies such as computer networking have accelerated the growth of these ties.
- These changes are resulting in the growth of transnational social movements.

If these hypotheses turn out to be true, their implications for contentious politics will be profound. Here are some speculative hypotheses:

- *First*, the national political opportunity structures that constrain and channel national social movements may give way to looser network structures.
- *Second*, the capacity of citizens to mount new forms of collective action beyond borders would increase.
- *Third*, extra-national political involvements will increasingly target international institutions. The Seattle protests of 1999 are a dramatic case in point.

These are major claims, but before embracing them, students should exercise caution. First, the integration of the world economy is not entirely new—and neither are transnational movements. It is enough to think of the Third International or of the spread of nationalism around the globe in the nineteenth century. Moreover, it takes a lot to organize protests transnationally, alongside strangers or through the Internet, and against unfamiliar targets against whom protesters have little direct leverage. Finally, though some students of globalization have dismissed the national state as nearly defunct, states have plenty of power—among other things, over borders. They can also serve as brokers between subnational actors and international institutions. All three of these factors come into play in the case of Europeanization.

Europeanization and Domestication

It is logical to assume that if transnational protest movements are to develop, they will most likely to do so where authoritative institutions regulate the lives of citizens across borders. This is why Western Europe may prove a good proving ground for the globalization thesis. For of all the regions of the world, this is the one in which the most authoritative international institutions can be found, and where social movements, interest groups, and non-governmental organizations cluster around the nerve centre of Brussels (Imig and Tarrow 2001).

But if Western Europe is a proving ground for transnational movements, thus far the theorem has been only partially supported. Although scholars like Sonia Mazey and Jeremy Richardson (1993a) have found increasing numbers of both private and public interest *lobbies* organizing transnationally in Brussels, studies of social movements tell a different story. Apart from a few unusual cases, when Europeans have protested against the policies or institutions of the European Union, they mainly do so *domestically*, choosing national or local interlocutors over whom they have political leverage as their targets (Imig and Tarrow 2001). If the most highly developed set of international institutions in the world continues to produce mainly domestically based protest activities, then the formation of a global civil society is still a good way off.

On the other hand, since the second half of the 1990s there are signs that the primacy of the national state as the locus of contention may be joined by the primacy of transnational and supranational targets. The movement against genetically modified foods, the joint action of French and Belgian workers against the closure of the Renault Vilvoorde plant, the increasing coordination of European farmers' protests, and the petrol boycotts of 2000: these episodes suggest that social actors no longer limit their claims to their national governments. Only more systematic and over-time comparisons will tell us whether the 'domesticated' pattern of European protests is giving way to the formation of transnational social movements.

CONCLUSIONS

These are speculations, more relevant for the future than for the present. What they suggest is that Western European polities—like the United States—continue to possess vigorous civil societies in which social movements operate both inside and around national institutions to defend private citizens' claims and values. We have argued that these movements are best seen not as *exceptions* to normal politics but as part of a field of *contentious* politics. Some forms of movement use more transgressive means while others lean towards contained forms of action; some reject the foundations of western politics altogether while others seek only their reform. Tendencies to institutionalization are countered by shifts towards radicalization; while the privatization of activism often translates into subtle cultural change rather than acceptance of the status quo. Governments repress movements, but also offer them different combinations of opportunity and threat.

If the 'movement society' thesis is correct, we will find more facilitation and less repression, more reform-oriented movements and fewer integral ones in the future than in the past. But this very openness may prove chimerical, for it may neutralize the one factor that gives popular movements their sting: their capacity to disrupt (Piven and Cloward 1977). Popular protest is alive and well in Western Europe and North America, but its character is changing in ways that should be watched by political scientists interested—as Vincent Wright was—in the politics of democracy.

15

From Popular Dissatisfaction to Populism: Democracy, Constitutionalism, and Corruption

The lack of confidence of citizens in their democratic institutions is not new. Among existing democratic systems there has always been dissatisfaction, in some periods or in some places. The twenty-year period between the two World Wars is a particularly dramatic illustration of this situation: most of the new democracies failed to consolidate and most of them had to give way to authoritarian or fascist regimes. Older democracies were also challenged by leftist social movements or extreme right and undemocratic parties. Even during the rosy period between the end of the Second World War and the 1973 oil price shock, dissatisfaction manifested itself in various forms: protest movements of all kinds, especially amongst the young (May 1968), and even the use of violence and terrorism (in Italy and Germany in particular). However, both in the 1920s and 1930s and in the post-war period, these manifestations of discontent with the working of the democratic system were taking place in a different background: many of these movements or anti-system parties were looking for an alternative to Western democracy. The belief that socialism was embodied in the Soviet Union or that 'strong' and nationalistic regimes would realize better the aspirations of the people was helping to build up a credible option for large groups of the population. Western democracies were seen either as unable properly to address the claims of the people or accused of being colonialist, imperialist, or a mere expression of capitalism in its most brutal form.

The competition between alternative models had many implications: in particular, traditional cleavages such as the left/right divide were shaken by an even more dramatic opposition between those parties favourable to the Western-type democratic regimes and those opposed to it (anti-system parties). However, during these periods, the existence of alternative and idealized forms of government does not explain fully the various crises of democracy. Apart from the external dimension ('there is somewhere a better form of government'), many challenges stemmed from the internal dysfunctioning and deficiencies of the democratic system itself. They were deliberately used by the opponents to the Western model as examples and illustrations of capitalist democracy's failure. But in most cases, the Western democracies were able to face the problems and deal with the situation by resorting to institutional reform, extension of political participation and rights, and redistributive policies. These strategies have worked quite well over the forty years of the cold war period and ensured not only the stability of the democratic regimes but also the growing awareness of its superiority up to the fall and collapse of the alternative model. In the long run, democratic regimes were able to overcome the challenges both from outside and inside.

Today, the context for democratic regimes differs in three ways. The first one has already been mentioned: the unchallenged supremacy of the two victorious paradigms of market and democracy. The second is related to the weaker capacity of new or old democracies to deal with the new challenges they have to face: the old instruments, such as the extension of suffrage or expansionist redistributive policies, have exhausted their potential. Third, the relative position of market and democracy (this unhappy couple according to Robert Dahl) has changed in favour of the market and to the detriment of democracy defined as the capacity of the people to control its own fate.

All these trends may constitute good reasons for a redefinition of governments' duties and of the relationship between democratic politics and the economic and social spheres. However, this different approach by the ruling elites is a source of tensions in many political systems. Not only because it often implies a painful redistribution of costs and benefits but also because the expectations of the people might not evolve along the same path as the governments' policies. The adjustment to the new order of things, to the new vision of the world, may put ruled and rulers at odds with the risk of challenging democratic rules and principles.

A first problem to be considered is the nature of the democratic malaise and its manifestations. Has it to do with the democratic principle itself or is it only a temporary dissatisfaction with elites, parties, and political organizations? Two complementary explanations will be then offered to interpret the birth and expansion of this phenomenon: the structural one will emphasize the tension between the constitutionalist and the popular dimension of contemporary democracies; the conjunctural one relates to political corruption, which became so pervasive in the 1990s and contributed to the delegitimation of representatives and of the principle of representation in many European countries.

THE MANIFESTATIONS OF THE *DEMOCRATIC MALAISE*

The so-called *democratic malaise* is rather paradoxical. Never have elections been more frequent, universal (in composition of the electorate), less subject to fraud or questionable practices, or more under the control of impartial judges. Never before has the rule of law been so elaborate or applied with such checks, to the point of sometimes arousing criticism of the excessive bureaucratic development it is said to entail. One cannot help being struck by the development and refinement of legal and procedural techniques of legitimation going hand in hand with major and even growing dissatisfaction with the political system.

To be sure, this malaise is neither constant nor identical from one political system to another. Its forms and manifestations change, as do the policy areas, classes, and groups associated with the dissatisfaction. Legitimacy is something never established once and for all; it must continually be upheld and be achieved either through formal mechanisms (elections), or through the diffuse and therefore more uncertain perceptions of public opinion (expressed through the media, leaders of social groups, support and protest movements, opinion polls, etc.) (Blondiaux 1998). We should therefore not be surprised at these fluctuations and shifts. There are clearly degrees in deficiency of the legitimation process: a fall in the opinion polls is the daily fare of politicians, and does not call the legitimacy of those in government into question. But the persistence of negative opinions may make governability problematic and compel a resignation even if nothing formally requires it.

As long as the legitimacy deficit concerns public action alone, the situation is not serious. It is the very object of democracy to organize divergence of opinions (adversarial politics) and to provide for periodic tests of the legitimacy of pursuing chosen policies, through the ballot box. By contrast, the position becomes more problematic when the legitimacy deficit relates to the institutions or political elites. Taken to the extreme, this deficit is resolved either by reforming the institutions (for instance, the transition from the Fourth to the Fifth French Republic), or by renewing the elites (after the Second World War), or still more radically, by revolution.

After several decades in which most Western democracies had to tackle only those legitimacy problems linked with political choices, they now have to face new challenges. First came the 1968 movements, where modes of political and social participation were radically challenged, even through resort to terrorism, as already mentioned. The Trilateral Commission's pessimism in 1975 has to be seen in this context (Crozier *et al.* 1975). Sometimes it took a dramatic form in the assassinations of Aldo Moro in Italy and the head of the employers' confederation in Germany. For the extreme left radical groups, the regime's fundamental illegitimacy could justify the call for revolution and recourse to political assassination. Some examples of this total denial of legitimacy can still be found in democratic states divided by deep ethnic cleavages or by the existence of territorial minorities (Basque country, Northern Ireland, Corsica).

The new legitimacy crisis that has affected many democracies in the 1990s is different in nature. Despite, or because of, the genuine absence of an alternative to the Western democratic model, the challenge to legitimacy is not inspired by aspirations to a different model of society. Instead, it comes more from dissatisfaction with the institutions, but particularly with political parties or politicians (Majone 1999). Populism has become the catch word to encapsulate this phenomenon (Canovan 1981; Hayward 1996; Taggart 1996; Mény and Surel 2000).

The most fundamental change probably lies in citizen attitudes towards their representatives. Confidence in the parties, in politicians, or in the institutions is at its lowest, something expressed at times in political indifference, sometimes by a fall in the vote for the mainstream parties. Opinion surveys confirm ad nauseam that European voters are converging in their negative or even frankly hostile opinions of what is now commonly pejoratively termed the political class, the *nomenklatura*, the apparatchiks, or the like. As long ago as 1983, Lipset and Schneider were able in their work, *The Confidence Gap*, to discern a widespread anti-élite, anti-power ideology, and a few years later, in 1988, Russell Dalton stressed that 'the feelings of mistrust progressively extended to the assessment of the political regime and the other social institutions. Lack of trust in politics and the institutions became generalized', even if its effect has been highly differentiated (Lipset and Schneider 1983; Flanagan 1987: 1303; Dalton 1988).

Evidence of the phenomenon abounds but its interpretations diverge. Everywhere, political observers have stressed the breadth of this disaffection. In France, this has often been seen as a crisis of representation; in Italy, the perception was more that of failure of a political system, the First Republic, whose end was perhaps rather hastily celebrated. In Germany, from the mid-1990s, a new term made its appearance: *Parteienverdrossenheit* or *Politikverdrossenheit*, denoting the disaffection, shortly after the euphoria of reunification, from parties and from politics. This unfavourable development for the traditional parties, which feeds the increased volatility of electoral choices, thus reflects a reduction in partisan allegiances, for as Piero Ignazi notes, 'the new thing is that citizens now feel freer to move from one party to another; changing one's party allegiance is less and less felt as a traumatic experience. One may go and come without any feeling of betrayal or guilt, previously associated with the fact of abandoning old political allegiances' (Ignazi 1996: 550).

However, the breadth of electoral disaffection does not give the full measure of the discredit most parties faced in the 1990s. Survey findings are still more explicit, and all converge in the same direction: mistrust of parties and politicians is general, and the change is sometimes rapid. Between 1985 and 1991, for instance, the number of Italians disagreeing with the statement that parties are necessary for democracy went from 18 to 35 per cent; among Northern League voters, 5 per cent trusted the parties. At the start of the 1990s, two-thirds of Germans felt the major parties were incapable of solving the country's problems. At the same time, Austrians' opinions were still harsher (three quarters of them felt the parties were interested in nothing but vote-catching). In France the SOFRES surveys, done for ten years now, on the trust of the French in parties and politicians, have gone from mediocre to frankly poor, bringing out a deep, persistent gap between representatives and the represented. The scene is scarcely more inspiring in the United States or the Scandinavian countries apart from Finland.

Susan Pharr and Robert Putnam (2000) seek to go beyond cyclical, ad hoc explanations of this phenomenon of rejection. They first note the generalized, extensive nature of the phenomenon in nineteen democratic countries over the last three decades. Citizens' trust is decreasing practically everywhere, both in politicians (the case in twelve of the thirteen countries where systematic figures are available), the political parties (party identification is declining in seventeen of the nineteen countries considered), and the political institutions themselves (for instance, trust in Parliament has fallen in eleven countries out of fourteen). How is the generality of this phenomenon to be explained? The authors' hypothesis is that the nature and extent of information might have changed, as might the criteria for assessing politics and governmental action, but also stress that it is the performance of the representative institutions that has deteriorated. They end by concluding that this decline in democratic performance might have its source either in governments' inability to satisfy their electors (because of globalization, for instance), or in their lack of fidelity to both their specific commitments (electoral promises) and their fundamental ones (ethical failings for instance).

Further case studies confirm these general trends. Pascal Perrineau has shown how in France the National Front vote emerged among people on the urban periphery living in tough economic conditions and in a dilapidated, unstructured social environment devoid of political reference points. A major part of its support comes from voters whom social isolation, the feeling of being neither listened to nor even heard, and insecurity of living conditions had driven away from political participation (Perrineau 1988, 1997). Hans-Georg Betz describes these attitudes by the term resentment, explained by the fact that these individuals have 'the feeling of having been abandoned by the rest of society and being without material resources to escape the ghettos of old or new poverty' (Betz 1994: 177). In her study on FN voters, Nonna Mayer (1999) also confirms that the National Front tends—especially since the 1995 presidential elections—to attract a proletarian electorate with a clear awareness of being part of the unprivileged. The contrast between the working-class vote in 1988 (presidential elections) and 1995 (legislative elections) illustrates well the voting fluctuations associated with expectations and disappointments: whereas workers had voted massively for Mitterrand in 1988 (61 per cent in the first round, 70 per cent in the second), nearly a third of these voters (30 per cent) moved their votes to Le Pen candidates in 1995 (as against 18 per cent three years earlier).

This diffuse but widespread feeling has often been associated with economic and social crisis. Economic stagnation and the massive increase in unemployment in certain countries or regions of the European Union have indubitably contributed to the emergence of the feeling of mistrust or even hostility. In many countries poor economic performance and the continuous growth of unemployment have been related to the globalization of financial markets, production of goods, and openness of economic borders as well as to the new modes of international governance. The failed meeting of the WTO in Seattle and the protest of variegated groups and NGOs against public international institutions from WTO to IMF, the World Bank, or OECD, as well as multinational corporations or forums (Davos meeting), testify that part of the malaise was attributed to the deep transformations affecting Western economies and democracies.

It could be argued that even during the years of post-war growth, most of the governments in Western Europe had to face dramatic changes which were no less challenging than those of today. Emigration was a matter of routine in Southern Europe; France had to shift from a country of peasants to a more industrial and service-oriented economy; Great Britain, then the so-called 'sick man of Europe', had fully to restructure her industries; Germany had to rebuild the entire country and to absorb the continuous flow of Eastern immigrants. However, these difficulties were counterbalanced by comparing with the past (when the situation was worse) and by a booming labour market first in Northern Europe, later in the Mediterranean countries. Last but not least the growing expansion of the Welfare State contributed to a redistribution favourable to labour and helped to mitigate the transition from the old to the new forms of economic production. The capacity of governments was at its best: economic expansion was providing the resources to redistribute, while the ideological mood was more favourable—at least in Europe—to public intervention than to market forces. The market failures of the 1930s and their political consequences were too fresh to be forgotten, while the association between public intervention (be it in the form of subsidies, public property, or planning) and booming economies was providing the legitimacy for these modes of regulation. It was difficult to attribute the merits of the 'miracle' to the market, to the state, or to the intimate cooperation between the two. What was important was the perception: state intervention was seen as crucial, necessary, legitimate by a large majority of actors, elites, or the population at large. Even among the parties of the right, free marketeers were a rarity and their programmes were paying tribute to the need to temper the market by social considerations.

This European preference for mixed economies and social concerns has been swept away by the neo-liberal policies and the globalization processes. Politicians and parties have been unable to resist market pressures when they have not themselves been instrumental in unleashing economic forces. This more or less deliberate option has, however, clear implications: parties and political elites cannot pretend anymore that they are the motive forces of economic development and growth. Furthermore, the financial capacities of the Welfare State are drastically limited by its continuous expansion, by demographic change, and the impact of unemployment on both resources and spending. In other words, it is not so much globalization itself which causes the problem as the incapacity of public institutions or political elites to cope with the negative side-effects of this great transformation. The ruler is naked.

The anxiety aroused by globalization or the frustrations at new forms of governance are, as we have seen, indisputable ingredients in the malaise, but the economic context gives only a partial view of the phenomenon. How is the emergence of protest movements to be interpreted through recourse to the economic variable alone? The rise of the FPÖ in Austria came in a prosperous country with no economic crisis and where unemployment is among the lowest in Europe; the Belgian National Front remains insignificant in a Wallonia scarred by economic restructuring, whereas the Vlaams Blok is prospering in one of the Europe's richest and most dynamic regions; the Lega Nord sprang up in Lombardy where income per head tops European statistics; Switzerland, Norway, Denmark, Sweden, all champions of economic success, welfare distribution, and collective opulence have also had to face powerful populist protest movements. In other terms, the economic explanation can at best be only one factor in a more complex interpretation.

Faced with the incapacity of ruling elites fully to deliver economic or social policies, many people feel frustrated and betrayed, especially when actual behaviour is at odds with past electoral promises. The political mood is one of actual or perceived failure of the political elites in the tasks entrusted to them and the trust reposed in them. There is, then, among the protest parties, but also in other movements laying claim to a new way of doing politics (like the Greens), a suspicion or even hostility towards representation mechanisms, reflected among the populists by a reaffirmation of leadership (and the supposed direct link between leader and led), and among the others by a commitment to collective leadership and the rapid rotation of posts. One can understand why the first American populist movements might seem modern and progressive. In both cases, there is distrust of the mechanisms of representation, and the representatives, and an attempt to promote direct expression by the people. Everybody acts in the name of democracy but its meaning and substance deeply differ from its actual functioning.

THE STRUCTURAL CONTRADICTION OF DEMOCRATIC REGIMES

When confronted with the establishment of democracy, the Founding Fathers of the American Constitution were faced with a crucial dilemma: how to empower people while not subjecting them to the tyranny of the majority? This delicate problem found its solution in a sophisticated mix of popular input and of checks-and-balances preventing too much power going to any institution and making sure that representatives would be accountable to the people. The French Revolution was less successful. While paying lip service to the separation of powers, it organized, in fact, the ideological and institutional supremacy of the people's representatives. The French solution failed on two counts: on the one hand, the institutions designed by the various republics were unable to avoid the excesses of the majority principle, and to balance it by a proper allocation of powers to distinct institutions; on the other hand, the theoretically all powerful people were expropriated by the political class, given the lack of any proper form of accountability. It is only very lately—and in part by accident—that instruments of checks-and-balances have strengthened the constitutionalist component in the French institutions.

In spite of the diversity of their histories, cultures, and preferences, most, if not all, present democracies reflect this duality. On the one hand, democracies are, above all, the expression of popular will and choice. There is no democracy without free association of citizens, free elections, free expression of political views. Democracy is the power of the demos. Unfortunately, too many citizens are still convinced that democracy is only the power of the demos, and it is rather natural that they think so. Politicians and parties continue to speak about democracy as if it was only about the people's choice through various electoral devices and control mechanisms. This might well be the ideal form of democracy conceived by citizens, as it appears so often in American political debate, for instance. The reality of democracy is far from this dream (or nightmare?).

The problem does not stem so much from the gap between ideal and reality as from the imbalance between popular will and constitutional or procedural limitations, resulting from constitutional or legal devices and the incapacity (or unwillingness) of the elites to take on board demands and claims from the grass roots. The citizens feel that their votes matter less and less, that parties in power do not deliver what they promise while in opposition, that policies do not fit their needs and aspirations. It is not so much democracy which is at stake as the main mechanism of western democracies, representation. The legitimacy of the system is weakened when citizens perceive their representatives as incapable of acting according to the messages they have sent through their votes, protests, or other forms of mobilization. This feeling can be attenuated or exacerbated according to circumstances: capacity of the opposition to propose credible alternatives; international environment; rate of economic growth. However, these variations in time and space cannot hide a paradigm shift in Europe over the years: one pillar of democracy, the popular one has become weaker and weaker while the other one has been strengthened, contributing to the progressive isolation of governing elites from people's pressures. This change has taken various forms.

The power that the courts have acquired through constitutional review is a mighty one since they are in charge of protecting, but also defining and redefining, citizens' rights, without being accountable to the electorate. But this is only a small part of the landscape. Another important element of Europe's development during the second half of the twentieth century has been the progressive and sometimes very detailed and tight control of governmental authorities over the economy through regulation, nationalization, and redistribution. Since the mid-1970s, this magic triangle has been challenged and partly dismantled: deregulation has been the order of the day, privatization has taken place everywhere, and the redistributive policies are under pressure.

Economic regulations, privatization, and the restructuring of redistributive policies are more often than not the responsibility of a new set of institutions accountable vis-à-vis the courts, the market, or a specific regulated sector, but not to the public at large. These institutions are not new by themselves, as the example of central banks indicates. The novelty stems first of all from their multiplication in one form or another (regulating agencies, QUANGOs, quasi-jurisdictional bodies) and also from their status. Most of the time, political authorities are forbidden to interfere, to appoint, or to dismiss members of these bodies, even to try to influence them. The irony is that this transformation has been made by governments themselves, in order to alleviate the pressures arising from all sides and to give them breathing space in an overloaded environment. But by reversing the past trends in a context extremely favourable both to the constitutionalization of politics and to market autonomy, they have considerably reduced their capacity (or willingness) to influence policies which were formally or in substance under their responsibility. Once again these past capacities might have been illusory. A government of the left might have discovered that nationalizing enterprises was indeed a very limited tool to steer the economy. But politicians could offer it as an alternative to the voters and proceed according to their programmes. As admitted bluntly by Jospin—to the dismay of French public opinion used to a different rhetoric—the government is not able to administer the economy. In addition to the trends already mentioned, it is also clear that the globalization of the market economy—and in Europe, the EU integration process—has jeopardized the congruence between the democratic polity and the national market. 'In view of the authority of the market, the *substance* of political democracy turns out to be rather thin, even if the form is strong' (Altwater 1999: 51).

Majone (1999) has defended this shift in regulatory modes from political intervention to agency-type regulation and justified 'why democracies need non-majoritarian institutions'. Policy-credibility and long-term commitments are necessary to the good functioning of the market but poorly provided by political authorities whose horizon is the next electoral race. Therefore, there is a need for regulation by professional and independent bodies. Majone, however, is well aware that the emergence of this fourth branch of government challenges the traditional principle of accountability to the people. To address this question, Majone suggests using the distinction made by the nineteenth century Swedish economist Knut Wicksell to deal with efficiency and redistribution questions through separate processes of collective decision. He writes: 'Efficient policies attempt to increase aggregate welfare, that is, to improve the conditions of all or almost all, individuals and groups in society, while the objective of redistributive policies is to improve the conditions of one group at the expense of another'. While redistribution has to be decided by majority rule (it entails differences in costs and benefits), efficiency policies where everybody can gain should be decided in principle by unanimity. Given the difficulty of using this option with large groups, the second best solution (which reconciles credibility, expertise, and so forth) is to delegate such tasks to expert, non-majoritarian institutions.

Majone does not hide the main difficulty of this solution: the lack of accountability and legitimacy. The legitimacy will be based on the output these agencies achieve (for instance the monetary policy of the central bank) and the accountability guaranteed by a combination of control instruments. There is no lack of examples showing that this difficult problem can be dealt with properly, as shown by the central banks of the United States, Germany, and Italy. However, if people are unhappy with the system, because the chosen solutions privilege market interests rather than citizens' preferences, they have no other option than to manifest their discontent vis-à-vis parties and government authorities which are themselves unable to curb or change the questioned policy.

In Europe, the constitutionalist revolution has gained ground both at the national level and at the European level: the national systems have considerably reduced the input dimension of democracy, while being unable to control its output dimension; they are dependent upon regional or global market forces. The European Union, on the other hand, is the most sophisticated machine of constitutionalist democracy ever invented. There is probably no other example in history of such a complex, balanced, and limited system of government. The 'popular' dimension is reduced to its simplest and elementary dimension: the election every five years of the European Parliament by universal suffrage. Instead of compensating each other through a differentiated emphasis, as it is the case in the United States, the similarity of patterns and trends, nationally and Europe-wide, contribute to exacerbate the problems and to feed the discontent with the actual working of democracy.

PUBLIC EXPOSURE: CORRUPTION AND
ITS DE-LEGITIMIZING EFFECT

Corruption of elites, when it occurs—or rather, when it is unveiled—provides dissatisfied people with a simplistic but extremely powerful tool of interpretation. The basic ideological presupposition is confirmed, illustrated, and justified. The corruption of elites, especially political ones, is for populist movements the most flagrant illustration, the clearest demonstration, of the representatives' betrayal of the represented. The elected have secured the voters' trust and been given a free hand in the name of the general interest they interpret and should guarantee only to find that they have sold out to the interests of the powerful, or still worse, think only of their own financial interests, disregarding the duties of their post. 'They are all rotten!' This is the usual, universal anathema of rising populisms: the mobilizing, vengeful argument, the call for a 'new broom', for a cleansing of the Augean stables. Populism is not just denunciation of corruption, the plague of all political systems and particularly damaging to democracies since corruption denies their values. Populism involves the denunciation of corruption as a generalized, universal, systematic practice of *all* politicians: none escape. It throws out representative democracy along with its corrupt representatives.

Elite corruption offers an ideal platform for populist claims, since it seems to demonstrate the veracity of the betrayal of a mandate by those holding it. However, the existence—even on a large scale—of corruption is not by itself enough to break the link between representative and represented and the trust in people, policies, or institutions. The more or less rampant, more or less widespread corruption that flourished in most Western democracies after the Second World War did not always have negative effects on the legitimacy of politicians and democratic institutions, remaining a 'grey' corruption, tacitly accepted as long as it stayed within acceptable bounds (Heidenheimer *et al.* 1989). Over the years, in Italy, Berlinguer and the PCI were able to raise 'the moral issue' without endangering the Italian political system, or even causing it temporary difficulties. The Flick scandal in Germany had the effect only of amending the party and political campaign financing system. France refused until the mid-1980s to see it as a serious problem, in the name of a cynical conception of political action (Mény 1992). Spain, at grips with the process of democratization, did not look too closely at the origin of the funds its nascent parties needed. The German CDU and SPD continued to be the main purveyors of indirect, hidden resources. Examples and illustrations of these complacent attitudes towards corruption, not just among economic elites and the media but public opinion too, could be multiplied. How is the turnaround that came almost everywhere from the late 1980s to be explained? Several factors might be mentioned, even if one is not always able to evaluate the specific role of each of them (Lascoumes 1997, 1999).

The extent and nature of corruption changed over the last fifteen or twenty years of the twentieth century (Mény 1996: 359–70). From being cases of individual misbehaviour, corruption became organized or even systematic. Political parties, in order to finance themselves, battened on the business world, instituting a sort of unofficial levy (just as compulsory as a tax), collected on transactions between the public sector and the business world. From being a secret deal, corruption became steadily less hidden, to the point that its practice seemed now to form part of an unwritten political convention. It was able to come out in the light of day the more it became systematic and quasi-legitimate. Corruption to benefit an individual remained in principle subject to condemnation; when it was to benefit a party it was seen as a necessity, a lesser evil, and therefore not, ultimately, reprehensible. When the first Italian scandals became public, some politicians, still unaware of the wave that would sweep them away, went so far as to suggest legalizing the '*tangente*', the systematic bribes collected by the parties!

From being a simple exchange, corruption became complex, bringing ever more actors, mechanisms, and levels (local, national, international) into play. This gives rise to a new paradox: corruption is increasingly open because tolerance towards it makes it a quasi-normal practice, yet it is also hard to flush out because of the dovetailing of actors and processes, the apparent respect for formal procedures, and the multiplicity of forms of corruption itself. The universalization of corruption is then strengthened by collusion phenomena within the political class that prevent the normal interplay of institutions, procedures, and political, administrative, or financial checks. The opposition makes no denunciations, since it is itself a partner in the game. At best, each tolerates the other's turpitude and refrains from interfering with practices that have to do with the 'free functioning of the political parties'. At worst, all join happily in the corrupt processes and redistribute the spoils according to agreed scales of distribution. When the scandals became public, revealing the complicity of politicians and parties transcending oppositions and ostensible antagonisms, this collusion gives force and coherence to the simplistic yet convincing argument used by the populist parties: 'they are all rotten'!

The radical shift in attitude towards the question of corruption and its populist exploitation in order to de-legitimize politicians and parties cannot be understood without referring to the context of the 1990s. In Europe, this was first a context of economic crisis where stagnation was accompanied by high unemployment and the apparent inability of governments to rectify the situation. The revelation of political turpitude in this deleterious economic and social climate convinced public opinion that politicians and parties were exploiters, taking liberties with rules and principles while calling on the citizens for rigour. It is significant in this connection that in Italy collusion among political parties and the generalized corruption of the system were tolerated as long as governments in power practised a lax budgetary policy enabling generous distribution to all of the benefits and making people forget the state's disastrous administration by the political class. The Maastricht Treaty, with its budgetary and financial requirements, was what revealed the contradictions, and international business circles, by imposing successive lira devaluations and drastic reform policies, put an end to the pernicious euphoria of the 1980s and the corruption that accompanied it (Recchi 1996: 340–60).

In a context of economic stagnation, the process of delegitimation then becomes cumulative: economic failure renders corruption and collusion intolerable; it gives the press greater freedom of investigation, since the political actors have ever fewer means of direct or indirect pressure to limit or prohibit journalistic enquiry; media revelations heighten the scandal, still further reducing politicians' room for manoeuvre while expanding that of magistrates; enquiries by magistrates and journalistic revelations criss-cross, mutually nourishing and strengthening each other (Pujas and Rhodes 1999: 41–63). Betrayal of the duties of one's post, forgetfulness of principles, violation of rules by those charged with adopting them, these become the leitmotiv of opinion and the writ of impeachment against the rulers. By becoming the justified mouthpiece of business, the media supply all the elements of a potential inquisition.

Faced with hard times, public opinion perceived the lax attitude of some politicians vis-à-vis financial resources as an unacceptable blow to the principles of the democratic order. Sacrifices might be better accepted when they are proposed or imposed by politicians who put their behaviour in conformity with their political declarations or programmes. The unveiling of misbehaviour or malpractice came as a shock and a matter of scandal. It happened in Britain when it was revealed that MPs were making money by acting not only as representatives of the people, but also as efficient lobbyists within Parliament itself, confusing their mandate with personal financial gain. It also happened in France, but the reaction was stronger and lasted longer as the political parties and leaders continued their malpractices while adopting virtuous attitudes and introducing legislation which, supposedly, should have cleared up the matter. The fact that political leaders (who were the main beneficiaries of the corrupt practice related to their political campaigns) succeeded in avoiding blame and punishment has further accentuated the problem. Leaks to the press have shown year after year that all leaders had some direct or indirect involvement in these dirty tricks. Everybody more or less knew the story, but it was another matter when evidence popped up, as happened in October 2000 with the famous 'cassette Méry'. Before dying, one of the main providers of 'soft money' to Chirac's RPR recorded a video tape describing in detail how he had contributed financially to the party whilst it was under the control, direction, and for the benefit of Jacques Chirac. The President's popularity suffered a big drop prior to his 2002 presidential campaign. However, protected as he was by the constitutional and legal rules, he did not fear judicial prosecution. Moreover, public opinion was not strong enough to oblige him to resign as would happen in most democratic systems. Given the lack of judicial or parliamentary control, the main instrument for checking politicians' behaviour remains the media. They become the functional substitutes—with a mix of benefits and drawbacks—of failing traditional instruments of democratic control.

In a study published in 1993, Carlo Ruzza and Oliver Schmidtke (1993: 2–23) show how the *Lega Lombarda* managed to mobilize a sector of opinion in its favour by surfing on the wave of recurrent criticism in the Italian media of the political system. Analysing the main headlines in the newspaper *La Repubblica* (the peninsula's foremost daily and the bitterest critic of *partitocrazia*), the authors show how the journalistic criticisms and the League's slogans concur. Both the League's 'programme' and the newspaper's headlines highlight four main themes: political corruption, the inefficiency of the political system, the waste of public resources, and the inadequacy of public services (transport, hospitals, etc.). To be sure, there are differences in tone, wording, and emphasis, but the League was able to embrace the whole of this discontent and express a widespread perception in public opinion. The League offered solutions, regarded by many as irresponsible, vulgar, and xenophobic no doubt, but nonetheless constituting the only political bid to satisfy an unmet demand for radical change in the party system and government.

It would certainly be ridiculous to claim that the press was the sounding board for the League, if only because of its generally reserved, not to say hostile, attitude to the party and its leader, Umberto Bossi. But there is a parallelism between the virulent critique of a despised regime and the League's capturing of this real, justified political discontent. Nor should one forget that Bossi, like most populist leaders, was able to make full use of the media society's almost pathological interest in scandal. Dubious word-play, semantic or gesticulatory provocation, crudity of vocabulary, or murderous formulae—anything would do to provoke respectable opinion, challenge the rules of coexistence, the social and political conventions, and thus attract media attention by scandalizing it.[1] Conversely, a number of analyses or even semantic inventions by the press can be instrumentalized by populist movements, with intentions of doubtful purity. In Italy, for instance, such buzzwords as *'partitocrazia', 'tangentopoli'* (Bribesville), *'Operazione Mani Pulite'* (Operation Clean Hands), and the Second Republic (to indicate the political, albeit not constitutional, death of the First Republic, which is blithely continuing on its way), were born in the media and have become everyday references, ordinary political slogans, and a reference point for all those—especially the populists—who have made them into instruments of political combat.

In this context, it is easy for populist movements or parties to update criticisms and vocabulary, available and familiar because it has already been used at one time or another in predemocratic or democratic history. The corruption argument is probably the one that most undermines power, even when not democratic. Many non-democratic regimes or governments have in fact endowed themselves with traditional or divine legitimation, or more recently justified themselves through the will to defend and embody the interest of the nation, of the state, or in short, of all. Betraying this aspiration, abusing position in order improperly to enrich oneself, have been illegitimate actions since long before the establishment of democracy. Cicero's accusations against Cataline in Sicily, the Paris people's satirical and rebellious verses against Mazarin, Luther's rebellion, or Savonarola's preaching, show that corruption can be harmful not just to democratic regimes. But history also teaches that it is still more hurtful for them. As Gianfranco Pasquino has noted, 'democracy is struck to the heart' (Mény 1996: 319).

It is questionable whether the denunciation of corruption can be ideal ground for those proposing to regenerate the political system. It is used by democrats in opposition seeking to drive out corrupt authorities through the ballot box, as has often been the case in Latin America or certain Asian countries. But it is also used by the military, finding in past corruption an easy, weighty argument to justify their entry

---

[1] Cf. the importance of the 'scandalized register' that Michel Offerlé (1998) mentions in another context, that of collective action: Offerlé M., *Sociologie des groupes d'intérêt*, Paris, Montchrestien, 1998.

on to the political stage. It is also used by apprentice dictators, who may find in the corruption of democracy the reasons to justify the establishment of an authoritarian regime. The French Third Republic, with the examples of General Boulanger or the upheavals of 6 February 1934 following the Stavisky scandal, survived this risk. It is, finally, true of populist movements and parties proposing to restore democracy by driving out the profiteers and denouncing the elites in power.

POPULIST DICHOTOMY

The corruption of the system, the collusion of politicians and parties, bring out the hollowness of the principles underlying political organization and thereby enable a radical shift in view, something populist parties have always exploited. In a democratic system, the vertical relationship between voters and the elected or elite is a relation founded on trust and organized through an ad hoc structure, the party, which constitutes the common receptacle for the values and aspirations of the representatives as well as the represented. By contrast, in the horizontal dimension, the system presents itself as a fragmented whole made up of units (the parties) that fight among themselves to win power, supported by a fraction of the people.

Populism reverses the equation: the symbiosis is established among the people. It restores and brings back to unity what classical politics had divided. The populists by contrast separate what democratic representation had united, namely the representative/represented twosome held together by common interests, ideologies, and world-views within a political party. It polarizes the elites against the people, the big against the small, them against us. The language signifies this reversal of perspective: there is no longer talk of statesmen but only politicians; no political parties, but political class; not elites, but 'the establishment'; not representative democracy, but power that should be given back to the people.

The weakening of legitimacy in democratic systems is not due to populist movements and parties (Ignazi 1992: 3–34). They are not its cause but an effect. Nonetheless, once got going, this delegitimation movement amplifies under the impetus of the political protest movements. These make the illegitimacy of the government, the elites, the institutions, the system, into the very basis and principle of their claims. Poujade's 'sortez les sortants' is echoed by American populism's 'throw the rascals out', or Bossi's independence demands to separate the good Lombards from 'thieving Rome' or the corrupt Mezzogiorno with its clientelism and its Mafia. Populist parties, being opposition parties with very few chances to get access to power, usually adopt a radical style, a revolutionary rhetoric which excludes concessions and marginal reforms and reminds of fundamentalist appeals and messages. Those which by chance become part of governmental coalitions face hard days in reconciling the constraints of day-to-day politics with their former simplistic discourse (as shown by the FPÖ case in Austria or the Lega in Italy). Moderation is not part of populism's language habits, nor is a spirit of compromise. Intransigence of positions and crudeness combine in a rejection of the system as a whole, whose illegitimacy is not discussed: it is presupposed.

16

Democratizations in the European Periphery

SONIA ALONSO AND JOSÉ MARÍA MARAVALL

In the last quarter of the twentieth century, European politics was dominated by economic integration and democratization. The first was intensified after the political summit in the Hague in December 1969: it first expanded to Great Britain, Ireland, and Denmark in 1973; then to Greece, Spain, and Portugal in 1986; later, to Sweden, Austria, and Finland in 1995; and, eventually, thirteen additional countries were negotiating their admission to the European Union at the end of the century.[1] In the process, the number of countries went up from six to twenty-eight. As for democratization, it unexpectedly started in the three Southern European dictatorships in 1974–5; then, again unpredicted, in Central and Eastern Europe in 1989–90. In half of the latter cases, the new regimes were established in states born after the disintegration of Yugoslavia, the Soviet Union, and Czechoslovakia. The result was a revolution in the European political landscape: the number of democracies more than doubled, from fifteen in 1970[2] to thirty-three in 1994.[3]

Connections existed between the two processes. The 1962 Birkelbach report of the European Parliament declared that only those states that guaranteed truly democratic practices and respect for human rights and fundamental liberties would be admitted into the Community. This political requirement was addressed to the South European dictatorships, and it had an important influence on political events in these countries. The European Community represented, thus, a form of political conditionality. Rewards and sanctions were attached to domestic political developments; the economic rewards of membership depended on democratic reforms. It has repeatedly been argued that to become part of the developed and democratic core of European countries acted as a powerful incentive in the political changes of the poorer and authoritarian periphery. What remains to be explained is why this

---

[1] The thirteen countries were Poland, Romania, the Czech Republic, Hungary, Bulgaria, Slovakia, Lithuania, Latvia, Slovenia, Estonia, Cyprus, Malta, and Turkey.

[2] The fifteen democracies were Austria, Belgium, Denmark, the Federal Republic of Germany, Finland, France, Iceland, Ireland, Italy, Luxembourg, the Netherlands, Norway, Sweden, Switzerland, and the United Kingdom.

[3] The eighteen new democracies were Albania, Bulgaria, Croatia, the Czech Republic, Estonia, Greece, Hungary, Latvia, Lithuania, Macedonia, Moldova, Poland, Portugal, Romania, Slovakia, Slovenia, Spain, and Ukraine.

incentive was effective in 1974–5 and in 1989–90, not earlier or later. But of the different forms of external intervention to promote and protect democracy (Schmitter and Brouwer 2000: 199), 'conditioning' was the more important one in the regime changes of Southern, Central, and Eastern Europe.

'Conditioning' required monitoring. The European Union 1993 summit in Copenhagen opened the door to membership to the new regimes in the East if political and economic conditions, later ratified by the Amsterdam Treaty in 1997, were fulfilled. The political conditions referred to democracy, the respect of minorities, and the rule of law; the economic ones, to a market economy, an independent financial sector, and macroeconomic stability. The Commission submitted regular reports on the fulfillment by each candidate country of such conditions. It noted, for instance, the democratic shortcomings of Slovakia and Romania; or the economic difficulties of Romania, Bulgaria, Lithuania, Latvia, and Estonia.

This monitoring, however, described states of affairs. It did not explain their causes; it just produced exhortations. We intend to examine the two periods of regime change in Southern and Central Eastern Europe. We shall review, with empirical evidence, arguments about economic development, regimes, and political institutions. Our purpose is to understand better the political and economic transformations that went on in what was the southern and eastern periphery of Europe.

A FIRST EXAMINATION OF THE LANDSCAPE

The changes of regime that began in Greece and Portugal in 1974 ended when Ukraine celebrated its first multi-party free elections as an independent state in 1994.[4] Thirteen of the new regimes were classified, according to the Gastil Democracy Scale, as liberal democracies,[5] as opposed to illiberal ones. There were, however, important differences in the points of departure and in the political process, both between and within the southern and eastern regions. We shall discuss the extent to which the past determined the future: whether the preceding regime and the type of transition shaped democracy, or whether democracy was able to overcome birth differences. We shall also examine why democracy was established and sustained in Europe despite the disparity of conditions, and why qualitative differences existed amongst these new democratic regimes.

If we focus first on the point of departure, the process of democratization followed very different paths between and within regions. There were cases of transactions and pacts in Southern Europe (Spain) and in Eastern Europe (Hungary and Poland), as opposed to cases of abrupt and imposed political change (Portugal and Romania). There were different combinations of reforms *from above* and pressures *from*

---

[4] We shall not include in our analysis Bosnia-Herzegovina, given its history of war since independence and the international tutelage of its democratic regime. We shall also exclude the case of the FR Yugoslavia, since the state of war in which it was involved throughout most of the period makes the comparison with the other cases impossible.

[5] The cases of illiberal democracies were Albania, Croatia, Macedonia, Moldova, and Ukraine with only one new dictatorship, Belarus.

below: the latter were much more significant in bringing down the regimes of Czechoslovakia, Poland, Albania, and Romania; the former were important in Hungary, Spain, and the Soviet Union. Some countries, such as Czechoslovakia, showed greater social unrest just before the collapse of the dictatorial regime, while others faced greater social mobilization after the fall of the regime, such as Portugal and Bulgaria. Still other countries did not experience much mobilization from their societies, as was the case of Greece and Hungary, or suffered it both before and after the collapse of the regimes, as in the otherwise very different cases of Spain and Albania. In some countries, the opposition won the first elections, as in Czechoslovakia, Poland, and Hungary; in others, as in Spain, Bulgaria, and Romania, the reformist elites from the previous regime won them. All these different combinations of factors, however, led to the same outcome: the establishment of a polyarchy.

If we examine now the characteristics of our group of countries ten years after the collapse of dictatorship, half of them were new states that became independent in the course of democratization. Czechoslovakia disappeared in January 1993, after its constituent parts peacefully agreed to dissolve the federation. The Soviet Union collapsed in December 1991, after two years of nationalist conflict and separatist demands by the republics and a failed coup by communist hardliners. The disintegration of the Yugoslav federation began in June 1991, when both Croatia and Slovenia unilaterally declared their independence. Macedonia and Bosnia-Herzegovina followed shortly after. The collapse of these three communist federations followed very different paths (from extreme violence in Yugoslavia to a peaceful process in Czechoslovakia), despite sharing nationalist separatism and conflict.

The collapse of the three federations might suggest that federal states can hardly survive democratization. The other culturally heterogeneous countries were unitary states: democracy could be established with no disintegration of the state despite the fact that these cases of Albania, Bulgaria, Hungary, Romania, and Spain had important cultural minorities within their borders, either in terms of numbers and geographical concentration, or of separatist and autonomist demands. The preservation of the state was achieved, however, in quite different ways. In Spain, a federal state was constructed in the course of democratization, whereas in Albania, Bulgaria, Hungary, and Romania the states remained unitary, and different strategies of accommodation of cultural minorities were followed. If we go back to the three federal states that collapsed, Czechoslovakia, the Soviet Union, and Yugoslavia, the new states that emerged from their ruins were by no means internally homogeneous. In these culturally diverse polities of Eastern Europe, politicians adopted in some cases federal-like institutional formulas. Thus, in Moldova and Ukraine, after intense separatist conflict, the governments accepted constitutional recognition of a special autonomy status, for Transdnitria and Gagauzia, in Moldova, and Crimea, in Ukraine. The politics of conflict and accommodation may have been more important than the sociocultural diversity of the country for the outcomes of nationalist demands.

New states did not hamper the creation of liberal democratic regimes. Seven of the thirteen recent liberal democracies that existed in 1999 were established in newly independent states. Yet all illiberal democracies were also located in newly independent states, with the exception of Albania: if not an impediment, these states appear to have encountered greater difficulties or to have needed a longer period of time to become liberal democracies. Hence, Fishman's (1990) thesis that democratization is more difficult when political change affects the state, and not just the regime, seems to find some support in the European cases. However, once in place, none of our thirteen liberal democracies, whether in new states or not, reverted to an illiberal status.

Parliamentary[6] rather than semi-presidential[7] systems appear at first sight to be more congenial to liberal democracy: 80 per cent of the former, against 55 per cent of the latter, were liberal democracies in 1999. Poland, however, provides a counter-example: a semi-presidential system, and conflict between the president and parliament in the years after the establishment of democracy, did not prevent the existence of a liberal democratic regime. Besides, neither the semi-presidential nor the parliamentary system seemed to be related to governmental instability. Two of the countries with the highest governmental instability in the years after the establishment of democracy had semi-presidential systems, Portugal and Poland. But governments in Albania, Estonia, and Latvia were equally unstable during the same period, and yet their systems were parliamentarian. With only the exception of Albania, all of these cases of unstable governments, with either semi-presidential or parliamentary systems, were liberal democracies.

The economic conditions of democratization were different in Southern and Eastern Europe. In Greece, Portugal, and Spain, inflation was considerably lower than in the Baltic Republics or Bulgaria, and economic growth in the first ten years of democratic rule was higher. Compare, for example, the average growth rate of Greece in its first ten years of democracy, 2.6 per cent, with that of Hungary, -0.05 per cent. The economic reforms that were needed in Greece, Portugal, and Spain did not imply, as in their Eastern European counterparts, the total transformation of the economic system. And yet the majority of countries in Eastern Europe persisted as liberal democracies, surviving deep economic crises and profound systemic transformations.

Thus, in this preliminary survey, liberal democracies could be established and sustained in countries with nationalist and separatist conflict, in culturally very heterogeneous societies, under semi-presidential systems where the executive and legislative confronted each other, with governments that were highly unstable, with economies undergoing deep crises, following transitions *from above* and *from below*, in newly independent states, as well as in ones with unitary or federal institutions. Time was crucial in the different trajectories of the new democracies: no initial

[6] Following Shugart's and Carey's measure of presidential power (1992), we have included as parliamentary systems those cases in which a directly elected president has very limited legislative and non-legislative power, if at all: Macedonia, Bulgaria, and Slovenia. There is controversy in the literature concerning the classification of Macedonia and Bulgaria. Contrary to Shugart (1996), Metcalf (2000) thinks that both are semipresidential regimes. Slovenia, however, is unanimously regarded as a de facto parliamentary regime, despite having a popularly elected president.

[7] We have included here all the cases with a president directly elected by citizens and holding moderate to strong legislative or non-legislative presidential power: Belarus, Croatia, Lithuania, Moldova, Poland, Portugal, Romania, and Ukraine.

conditions determined the future. Some countries took longer to become liberal democracies than others. While Greece, Spain, the Czech Republic, Hungary, Lithuania, and Slovenia were liberal democracies soon after the celebration of the first free elections, Latvia, Estonia, Bulgaria, Portugal, Poland,[8] and Slovakia followed a longer, more convoluted path. Time and strategic decision making appear to have influenced a more liberal democratic outcome than initial structural conditions.

A REVIEW OF THE ARGUMENTS

We shall examine three arguments: first, that the emergence of democracy is unrelated to structural variables; second, that the emergence of a democratic regime and its persistence over time require different explanations; and third, that democracy can create, through politics, the conditions of its success or failure, not shaped by legacies of the past, or by the circumstances of birth.

The emergence of polyarchies south and east was not expected by political scientists. Moreover, they were at pains to provide *ex post* explanations. Shortly before the fall of the Portuguese dictatorship, Linz (1973: 176) argued that 'the prediction that nothing dramatic will happen with the death of Franco has been reinforced by recent events in Portugal', considering that the succession of Salazar by Caetano revealed the stability of authoritarian regimes. Influenced by the Southern European and Latin American experiences, political scientists decided that 'objective conditions' were irrelevant for democratization, and turned from structural explanations to political strategies and contingent outcomes. The collapse of the communist regimes of Eastern Europe was equally unpredicted and unforeseen. Before 1989, some authors pointed to factors that could undermine the communist systems: the subversive capacity of nationalism (Collins 1986); economic crisis (Lewin 1988); the incapacity of the regimes to adapt to changes (Brzezinski 1969); the persistence of past memories and loyalties (Brown and Gray 1977; Brown 1984). But, by and large, the analyses did not differ significantly from Huntington's prophecy (1984: 217): 'the probability of a democratic development in Eastern Europe is almost null'.

The collapse of communism, contrary to the Southern European experience, was followed by subsequent explanations in terms of structural preconditions. Unfortunately, the time lag of causality was hardly specified. This did not seem to bother Huntington (1991) when he tried to explain his heterogeneous 'third wave' of democracies by structural preconditions and functional maladjustments: these transitions were 'propelled forward by the extraordinary global economic growth of the 1950s and 1960s'; differences in time lags were simply accounted for by the fact that 'in the less constrained Iberian environment, political development caught up with economic development in the mid-1970s; in Eastern Europe that did not happen until Soviet controls were removed fifteen years later' (1991: 311, 63).

---

[8] In the first elections in Portugal the *Movimento das Forças Armadas* controlled the political process; the 1989 elections in Poland were only to a fraction of the seats in the Sejm under the limitations established by the Magdalenka agreements.

Similar political outcomes were attributed to opposite causes. The prediction that communist regimes were unlikely to change was grounded both on the arguments of 'totalitarianism' (Huntington and Domínguez 1975; Kirkpatrick 1982), and of 'pluralism' (Lane 1976; Hough 1977; Cohen 1985). When the regimes eventually collapsed, the *post hoc* accounts were again contradictory. Some were rooted in old modernization theory: after a long period of growth, the communist economies had become more complex and difficult to manage under authoritarian institutions, society was more plural, and cultural conditions were more favourable to democracy. Other arguments (Maravall 1997) have interpreted the collapse as due to the breakdown of 'goulash communism'. But Przeworski *et al.* (2000) have also demonstrated that neither economic development nor crisis precede changes of regime.

Once the new democracies in Southern and Central Eastern Europe were established, political scientists worried about their 'consolidation'. Schedler (1998: 103) talks of a 'Babylonian chorus of voices singing songs of democratic consolidation'. But this is an obscure and confusing concept (O'Donnell 1996). Some argue that consolidation means both 'survival' and 'quality': the factors that help democracies work also make them last (Diamond 1999). Others (Stepan and Skach 1993: 5) claim that democracy is consolidated when it receives a score of 2.5 or below in the Gastil democracy scale; however, these democracies may or may not last. This is why Schmitter (1994: 59) talks about *persistent unconsolidated democracies*. For Przeworski *et al.* (2000: 7) consolidation is simply an empty term: it maintains that at any level of development the mere passage of time makes the demise of democracy less likely, which is unsupported by evidence. We affirm that what makes these regimes last and what makes them work require different explanations.

We shall discuss what made Southern and Central Eastern European polyarchies work, that is, become more democratic and achieve normatively desirable goals. We have no relevant variability in our cases to examine why they last or not.[9] Thus, the degree of democracy is, at a first stage, our dependent variable. We shall examine in particular whether the degree of democracy can be explained by a political past that shaped the present; by economic conditions; by the presence or absence of ethnic pluralism and nationalist conflict; and by the choice of institutions and its consequences. At a second stage, together with institutional conditions, it becomes the independent variable to interpret other normative goals.

(1) Let us start with the legacies of the past. First, Linz and Stepan (1996: 55–65) have stated that the previous type of regime determines the type of transition and the subsequent development of democracy. Second, Karl and Schmitter (1991) have argued that the mode of transition, and particularly the level of mass mobilization and the use of force, have consequences for institutional choices. Third, Linz and Stepan (1992, 1996) have argued that the sequence of elections influences the nascent regime if the country has a 'stateness problem', as was the case in Spain, the USSR, and

---

[9] These are the two main reasons why we have chosen the Freedom House scale of democracy as our main indicator (Freedom House 1999). First, all our cases are democratic (except Belarus): it is thus necessary to go beyond elections in order to find variation. Second, this scale explicitly includes non-institutional dimensions of democracy and allows us to measure the rights and freedoms de facto enjoyed by individuals in their countries.

Yugoslavia. They think that when the first democratic elections are regional, rather than union-wide, the incentives for the creation of all-union parties and an all-union political agenda are greatly reduced, while politicians can more easily manipulate nationalist and separatist claims. However, while this was the sequence in the USSR, the majority of people still voted to maintain the Union in the 1991 referendum, and the declarations of sovereignty of many of the republics took place before the regional elections (as was also the case in Yugoslavia, with Slovenia, Macedonia, and Croatia). Furthermore, the sequence of elections was the reverse in Czechoslovakia, and yet the state disintegrated. As for Spain, all-union parties were unaffected by the sequence of elections, and many had survived the long period of dictatorship. The fourth and final argument that we shall discuss regarding the past is that previous democratic experiences influence the political stability and the degree of democratization of new regimes. However, as Przeworski (1996: 4) has noted, countries with this past also had the experience of a successful subversion of democracy.[10]

These arguments about the influence of past legacies will be untenable if different types of regimes have led to similar modes of transition and vice versa; if different types of regimes and transitions have given way to polyarchies with similar degrees of democratization in Southern and Central Eastern Europe; or if similar institutional choices have taken place in countries with different conditions of departure.

(2) We now turn to the economic arguments. Przeworski *et al.* (2000) have shown that democracies are extremely vulnerable when their levels of economic development are low. They use as a threshold of poverty a per capita GNP of $3,000. Four of our countries were below that threshold in 1999: Albania, Latvia, Moldova, and Ukraine. Yet none of these countries experienced a democratic collapse, although only Latvia was a liberal democracy at the end of the period. It may be that poor countries, besides being vulnerable to breakdowns, are also more prone than rich ones to undemocratic practices within a polyarchy.

Przeworski *et al.* (2000) have also claimed that what destabilizes regimes of any kind, whether democracies or dictatorships, are economic crises. Maravall (1997) has argued, however, examining several Southern and Central Eastern European regimes, that at similar levels of development democracies were more resilient than dictatorships to economic crises. Such crises were much more acute in the first years of the new democracies, both in Southern and Central Eastern Europe, than in the dictatorships that preceded them; yet democracy survived in these countries while dictatorship did not. Furthermore, the degree of democratization remained high, despite deep economic crises. According to the arguments of Przeworski *et al.* (2000), this was due to the comparatively high levels of development in which democracies experienced the crisis, and to the fact that international conditions predict regime survival better than does the level of development.

(3) We next examine the argument that the presence of cultural and ethnic minorities, and of nationalist mobilization, hinders democratization. As Roeder has

[10] Thus, 'an overthrow of democracy at any time during the past history of a country shortens the life expectancy of any democratic regime in that country' (Przeworski *et al.* 1996: 42).

put it, 'the evidence from post-communist states tells us that democracy is unlikely to survive in ethnically plural societies' (1999: 855). His empirical evidence, however, is unconvincing: his indicator of democracy is the average of each country during the ten years that followed the collapse of communism, and thus the temporal dimension of democratization is ignored. Roeder further argues that ethnicity provides a fundamental identity and engenders conflict that democracy cannot solve, while 'many of the institutions recommended by political scientists for deeply divided societies actually aggravate the problems of political stability and thus undermine democracy' (1999: 867). But incapacity to solve such conflict is different from the possibility of moderating it: this may depend on how the political game is played.

(4) We finally analyse arguments on the effect of three institutional features on the degree of democratization. Such institutions are parliamentarism or presidentialism, the party system, and the nature of the state.

Strong empirical evidence backs the thesis that parliamentary systems work better than presidential ones (Linz 1990*a,b*; Mainwaring 1993; Stepan and Skach 1993; Przeworski *et al.* 1996). The thesis is a well-known one: under presidentialism the stakes are higher; legislative paralysis and minority governments are more likely; there are no deadlock-breaking devices; fixed mandates can turn political crises into crises of the regime, rather than of the government. However, this dichotomy has been criticized on the grounds that it ignores the important number of hybrid or semi-presidential regimes. Only when presidents have high levels of legislative power, or when presidentialism is combined with multipartism and undisciplined parties, are democratic breakdown or failure to become a liberal democracy more likely (Shugart and Carey 1992; Mainwaring 1993; Mainwaring and Shugart 1997; Frye 1997; Metcalf 2000). In our Southern and Central Eastern European countries, we do not have cases of pure presidentialism, only semi-presidential regimes in which the power of the presidency varies. Thus, we will be able to test whether Stepan and Skach's (1993: 5) conclusion that 'there is much stronger correlation between democratic consolidation and pure parliamentarism than between democratic consolidation and pure presidentialism' is also valid for semi-presidentialism. We must consider, at the same time, an alternative thesis: that it is the combination of presidentialism (or semi-presidentialism) and multipartism with undisciplined parties that hampers the capacity of democracies to work[11] (Mainwaring 1993; Przeworski *et al.* 1996).

It has been argued that presidential systems are difficult to change. Przeworski *et al.* (1996: 7) have sustained that 'countries that adopt presidential institutions when they transit to democracy are stuck within them'. Diamond (1999: 99) similarly states that it is difficult to move from presidential to parliamentary systems. However, the Southern and Central Eastern European experiences cast doubts on such institutional 'stickiness': many countries went through substantial institutional

---

[11] According to Przeworski *et al.* (1996) a combination of presidentialism and multipartism 'can expect to live only fifteen years. Presidential democracies in which a single party does have a legislative majority can expect to live twenty-six years' (1996: 43).

alterations in the course of the ten-year period, which modified the distribution of power between the executive and the legislature. Both Portugal and Poland adopted constitutional reforms in order to reduce the powers of the president. Belarus moved towards a stronger presidentialism.[12] In Ukraine the powers of the president were substantially enhanced through a constitutional reform approved by referendum. Slovakia changed from parliamentarism to semi-presidentialism through a constitutional amendment in 1998.

As for the effect of the party system on democratization, we shall consider more particularly two arguments. According to the first, a combination of high electoral and organizational volatility 'harms the quality of democracy and the prospects for democratic consolidation' (Mainwaring 1998: 79). What this argument lacks is an assessment of how the passage of time may affect this volatility (Converse 1969). The second argument is that the degree of democratization depends on whether parties alternate in government (Rose 1995). Of course, this thesis was never used for the cases of Japan, Italy, or Germany. Contrary to these countries, in the Southern and Central Eastern European cases parties alternated in office in the first years of the new regimes; that, nevertheless, did not make them more democratic, and the countries that went further and faster in democratization were not always the ones with an earlier alternation of parties in government.

The last institutional feature is the structure of the state, particularly in countries where national minorities challenge its power. It has been argued that federal states are more vulnerable to disintegration during regime transitions than unitary multinational states (Skalnik Leff 1999); and that federalism aggravates the problems of nationalist conflict and diminishes the likelihood of successful democratization (Roeder 1999). But in Moldova, Ukraine, and Spain, strong nationalist conflict could be accommodated by asymmetrical federalism or quasi-federalism, while the polities became more democratic. Yugoslavia is the exception, not the rule.

The 'newness' of the state also seems to affect democratization. Przeworski *et al.* (1996) have found that the combination of a presidential system and a new state is less stable than a presidential system in an old state. In contrast, parliamentary systems are equally likely to survive in old or new states. But this is an argument about survival, not about whether polyarchies become more democratic, or work better. Our hunch is that the 'newness' of the state affects the degree of democratization only in the first years. With the passage of time, this influence should disappear, and no difference should exist between old and relatively new states.

THE INFLUENCE OF PRECEDING CONDITIONS

With the economic crisis of 1973, the three Southern European countries experienced a sharp economic decline, after a long period of economic growth. At the end

---

[12] Under Shugart and Carey's classification (1992), Belarus moved from a premier-presidential regime to a presidential-parliamentary one.

of the dictatorships, the GNP growth rate per annum dropped to 1 per cent in Portugal, 0.5 per cent in Spain, and −3.6 per cent in Greece. Political factors aggravated the economic crises, in particular the obsession with avoiding economic initiatives that could threaten the regimes' stability. When oil prices went up in 1973, the governments subsidized the increased costs in order that consumers were not affected. Wages in the last decade of the Southern European dictatorships rose significantly faster than the European Community average (Maravall 1997: 52). Increasingly, therefore, the authoritarian regimes came to be seen as an obstacle to further economic development. The answer to the economic crisis in the Central Eastern European dictatorships was remarkably similar. Rather than adjust to the new circumstances, many of the governments sought to maintain rapid growth, resorting to foreign loans, then relatively easy to obtain: as a result, their foreign debts spiralled. Ten years after the beginning of the crisis, foreign debt had risen to $1,113 per capita in Poland and $1,656 per capita in Hungary. If we look at foreign trade, the share of international markets of the communist countries of Europe shrank. Under the crisis, public deficits escalated, as the states protected inefficient enterprises. As for wages, whilst from 1971 to 1980 they rose in nominal terms by an average annual rate of 6.5 per cent in Hungary and 9.5 per cent in Poland, per capita output grew a mere 2.3 and 2.6 per cent respectively (Kornai 1992: 533). As in Southern Europe, economic problems were increasingly interpreted in political terms, as aggravated by obstacles stemming from dictatorship.

Besides similarities, differences existed both between and within each region. If we look at levels of development in Eastern Europe in 1988, the last year of communism, then the GNP per capita was $4,910 in Bulgaria, $5,060 in Poland, $4,650 in Romania, and $6,530 in Hungary, with Albania the poorest of the Eastern European countries. While in Hungary and Poland reforms to improve the economic efficiency of the system were repeatedly attempted, in Czechoslovakia reforms were seen after 1968 as the cause of political crises, rather than as the response, although growth rates fell steadily from 1970 onwards. The same can be said about Romania, Bulgaria, and Albania, where reforms were exceptional and limited.

The nature of the preceding regimes does not seem to explain much of what happened with the transitions, nor after the first elections. If communist regimes were different from Southern European authoritarianism, there were similarities in the political changes of some Eastern and Southern European cases. At the same time, there were radical differences between Eastern European countries. If we look at the relationship between types of regimes and modes of transition, strategies of political survival and responses to economic inefficiency varied considerably among countries of the East and South. At some point, politicians within the regimes saw their survival at risk and reacted to this threat. Some opted for repression; others, for negotiation; still others decided to capitulate. The only factor common to all the countries in Southern and Eastern Europe was this 'threat to survival', which varied in each country. This scenario consisted fundamentally of domestic developments, as in Spain, Portugal, Greece, the Soviet Union, or Hungary; it resulted from external influences in Albania, Bulgaria, Czechoslovakia, Romania, and Yugoslavia.

Change in Eastern Europe was initiated by those countries where liberalization had already started before Gorbachov removed the veto so far exerted by the Soviet Union. Hungary and Poland were closely followed by the other countries in the region. In the latter, where reforms had been repressed, the events in Poland and Hungary indicated that the 'Sinatra doctrine' was indeed a commitment of the Soviet Union not to interfere in the domestic politics of the Warsaw Pact countries. There would not be Soviet protection from the opposition or from the masses. On 9 October in the RDA, on 17 November in Czechoslovakia, on 18 November in Bulgaria, and on 15 December in Romania, the masses began to occupy the streets. The only options were to repress, without the backing of the Soviet Union, to negotiate, or to capitulate.

Variations in the type of regime change in Southern and Eastern Europe did not respond to economic or political differences. If we look at the Southern European cases, economic development had been considerable in the three countries; the regimes have been defined as authoritarian, although their duration and institutionalization had varied. Yet the three transitions were very different. In Portugal the rising of the *Movimento das Forças Armadas* (MFA) brought the dictatorship down in April 1974, making a radical break with the past; in Spain, following a long period of 'pressures from below', a split between hardliners and reformers within the regime eventually led, after the death of Franco, to strategies of consensus to establish the rules of the game and the institutions of the new regime; in Greece, the transition was very short, following the military fiasco over Cyprus, and followed a pattern of transaction between sectors situated within and outside the regime. The existence of nationalist demands and terrorist activity was a fundamental difference between the Spanish case and those of Portugal and Greece; such problems were however present in some of the Eastern European transitions, particularly in the Soviet Union and Yugoslavia.

Poland, Hungary, and the Soviet Union experienced a gradual transformation, in contrast to the abruptness of change in the other cases. In all three countries, a communist leadership with eroded legitimacy accepted profound reforms of the regime and the establishment of power-sharing mechanisms in order to launch economic reforms. In Poland, the strategy of cooptation was initiated by Jaruzelski in 1986 and, eventually, the PUWP began negotiations with the opposition in the Spring of 1989. The objectives were a limited democratization of the Sejm and the establishment of a neo-corporatist strategy in economic policy. But when Solidarnosc won the totality of the seats in the Sejm that were open to competition, the restrictions of the Magdalenka agreement collapsed; in the autumn of the following year, new elections were celebrated, this time without limitations. In Hungary, the political transition also took place through negotiations and pacts. In the Spring of 1988, there was a widespread consensus that some kind of compromise with the opposition was necessary in order to tackle the economic crisis. Six days after the 1989 Polish elections, negotiations with the opposition started, and free elections were held in March 1990. In the Soviet Union a gradual process of transformation began timidly in 1985 after Gorbachov was elected General Secretary of the CPSU; it became more radical with the launching of perestroika in 1987. Restricted elections took place in March 1989: these were the only (all-union) ones to be held before the Soviet Union broke up less than three years later. Nationalist demands and social mobilizations increased between these elections and the celebration of democratic elections to the republics (Alonso 2000). The failed coup by hardline communists in August 1991 precipitated the breakup of the Soviet Union.

Regime change in the other Eastern European countries was much more abrupt. It was triggered by the sudden explosion of mass protests. In Bulgaria, these started on 3 November 1989. On the tenth, Zhivkov, the General Secretary of the Bulgarian communist party, was replaced, in a palace coup, by a soft-liner, the former Foreign Minister Petur Mladenov, who declared that Bulgaria would turn 'into a modern democratic and law-governed state'. In Albania, demonstrations were organized in July 1990, and the government was changed; in November of that year, an electoral law was passed, and multi-party elections were called. Both in Albania and Bulgaria, by calling elections quickly, the reformed communist parties were able to win against a weak and disorganized opposition. But social unrest increased considerably in both countries, forcing coalition governments with the opposition.

Romania was the most abrupt case of political collapse. The Ceaucescu regime was extremely repressive and living conditions had declined dramatically since 1982. Despite this, there were hardly any episodes of social unrest until mid-December 1989 when, amidst the general political collapse in the other Eastern European countries, thousands of people took to the streets in protest against an arbitrary detention in Timisoara. A brutal repression led to further and wider protests in the streets of Bucarest. The National Salvation Front (NSF), organized in the heat of mobilizations by ex-communist leaders, military officers, and a handful of dissidents, brought down the regime and formed a provisional government. When the NSF won the first free elections in May 1990, the opposition claimed that the elections had not been free: the confrontation between anti-government and pro-government groups was very bitter. Only from 1997 has democratization stabilized in a liberal democracy.

In Czechoslovakia, when 500,000 people occupied the streets of Prague, the government could no longer repress. The Prime Minister, Ladislav Adamec, resigned at the beginning of December 1989 and the new government had a majority of non-communist ministers. At the end of the month the federal assembly elected Vaclav Havel President of the Republic. The first democratic elections, in June 1990, were won by the opposition: Civic Forum and Public against Violence. Soon after the elections, Public against Violence, under the leadership of Vladimir Meciar, took up Slovak nationalist demands for an independent state. Two years later, the Czech Republic and Slovakia split. This peaceful separation did not have an impact on democratization in the first case; in the second, it briefly reversed the regime into a lower degree of democracy.

Similar types of regime led to different modes of transition and dissimilar ones, to comparable experiences of change. If we look at Huntington's (1991: 113) distinction of four types of transition, we find for instance the different regimes of Spain, Bulgaria, Hungary, and the USSR sharing a process of 'transformation'; and Greece, Portugal, and the German Democratic Republic, one of 'replacement'. If we take, on the other hand, the typology of regimes developed by Linz and Stepan (1996: 38–54) and relate it with the typology of transitions by Karl and Schmitter (1991), there is no systematic relationship between the type of regime and the mode of transition. Regimes changed through 'pacts' in Spain and Greece, following authoritarianism, but also in Hungary, an example of post-totalitarianism. Transitions by 'imposition' took place in Bulgaria and the USSR, but also in Portugal; and transitions by 'reform' took place in regimes that were as different as the Polish and Albanian.

There is no association either between the types of regime and the modes of transition, on the one hand, and the degree of democracy, on the other. Countries with the higher degrees of democracy in 1999, such as Spain, Portugal, Greece, Hungary, Poland, the Czech Republic, Slovakia, Estonia, Lithuania, and Latvia (all with democracy scores between 1 and 2), correspond to past regimes that were authoritarian, totalitarian, or post-totalitarian. Transitions in these countries followed the paths of 'pacts', 'reforms', or 'imposition'. This last path, shared by the republics of the former USSR, Bulgaria, and Portugal, ended up with substantially different democracy scores.[13] If we compare the mean democracy score in year seven for the different modes of transition, only 'pacts' were significantly different from the rest, with a mean score of 1.6, in contrast with the other types: 2.5 for 'reform', 2.6 for 'imposition', 2.5 for 'revolution'. Thus, the former regimes and the mode of transition were independent from each other; they did not influence the outcomes of democratization either. After a few years, the new regimes could rid themselves of birth conditions.

The past hardly influenced the choice of institutions. There is no association between the type of regime and the system of government[14] that was established. Semi-presidential and parliamentary systems were introduced following all types of regimes. Of the three authoritarian regimes, one was followed by a semi-presidential system in 1999, the other two by parliamentary ones. After the eleven post-totalitarian regimes, in six countries semi-presidential systems existed in 1999; in five, parliamentary ones. Of the two countries with sultanistic regimes (Romania and Albania), one had in 1999 semi-presidentialism and the other one parliamentarism. Only the three totalitarian regimes had similar outcomes in 1999: a parliamentary system. As for the types of transition, only 'pacts' shared the same outcome in 1999: parliamentarism in the three cases. Of the seven experiences of 'reform', five had led in 1999 to parliamentary systems and two to semi-presidentialism. Of the eight transitions by 'imposition', three had concluded in 1999 with parliamentary systems and five with semi-presidentialism. The only transition by 'revolution' (Romania) was in 1999 a semi-presidential system. Furthermore, in one case, Slovakia, the system was changed during democratization. Neither the former regimes nor the types of transitions determined the choice of institutions.

THE EXPERIENCE OF DEMOCRACY

Once the first elections took place, important variations existed in the experiences of democratization of the new polyarchies. We shall use the average of the scores for the

---

[13] Portugal (1.0), Estonia (1.5), Lithuania (1.5), Latvia (1.5), Bulgaria (2.5), Moldova (3.0), Ukraine (3.5), and Belarus (6.0).

[14] The Pearson Chi-Square is 4.29 and is not statistically significant.

political rights and civil liberties scales calculated by Freedom House (1999),[15] that go from one to seven (one represents the highest degree of freedom and seven the lowest). Such scores are provided in Appendices 16.1–16.3. Our last observation is 1999, in which the number of liberal democracies (with an average score below 2.5) was thirteen out of nineteen (68.4 per cent). In the first year after elections, the proportion was lower: 45 per cent of the cases (five[16] out of eleven[17]). If we consider 1993, the first year in which the number of polyarchies was the same as in 1999 (the new states had achieved independence), the proportion was similar to that of the first year after the elections (42 per cent: eight out of the nineteen cases were liberal democracies).

In several countries, democratization had ups and downs. Thus, democratization receded in Slovakia after it became an independent state, between 1993 and 1998. In Albania, the new regime became more democratic in 1993, but quickly turned more restrictive. Estonia and Latvia took some time, after their separation from the Soviet Union, to score as liberal democracies. Some countries, like Romania and Moldova, became slowly but consistently more democratic. By 1996, political change had stabilized: only Albania, Belarus, Ukraine, Macedonia, Moldova, and Croatia remained as illiberal democracies. Thus, the paths of democratization and the pace of change varied. And what explains the degree of democratization achieved in 1993 does not necessarily explain it in 1999.

We shall start examining the effect of the varying degrees of democracy on three groups of dependent variables: economic performance, institutions, and nationalist conflict. Therefore, the first question is whether growth, inflation, and unemployment, as indicators of economic performance, were influenced by variations in democratization. (We use economic data from the World Bank.) The second question is whether institutional choices and governmental stability were affected by the degree of democracy achieved. Finally, we shall see whether nationalist demands depended on the different degrees of democratization, and whether such connections changed with the passing of time.

The regression analyses of the effects of the degree of democracy on growth and inflation[18] (Table 16.1) show that as the rankings in the Gastil scale went up (less democracy), the rates of growth decreased, while those of inflation increased.[19] The correlations between democracy in one year and the rate of growth in the following year show that more democracy was associated with more growth, although the

[15] For those countries which achieved independence after 1991 but which had already held free democratic elections as republics within previous federal states, our observations start in the year of independence, even if it does not coincide with the first democratic elections as an independent state. This affects the following countries: Belarus, Estonia, Latvia, Lithuania, Moldova, Ukraine, Croatia, Slovenia, Macedonia, Czech Republic, and Slovakia.

[16] Czechoslovakia, Hungary, Poland, Greece, and Spain.

[17] Albania, Bulgaria, Czechoslovakia, Greece, Hungary, Poland, Portugal, Romania, Soviet Union, Spain, and Yugoslavia.

[18] We have not included a table for unemployment because, according to the regression and correlation analyses, there is no association whatsoever between the degree of democracy and the rate of unemployment.

[19] Since we have a very small N, we are using the regression analysis basically as a way of measuring effects, rather than to discriminate between variables according to their statistical significance.

Table 16.1 *Regression models for the effects of the degree of democracy on future inflation and growth (years 3–8)*

Independent variable	Growth	Inflation	Unemployment
Constant	6.129	−98.96	15.62
Democracy (years 1–3)	−1.601*	63.44*	−1.77
Signif. F	0.096	0.067	0.388
R^2	0.155	0.184	0.044
N	19	19	19

*Statistically significant at 10 per cent.

strength of the relationship diminished with time. The correlations, beginning by democracy in year one, were as follows: −0.156, −0.534, −0.486, −0.240, 0.171, −0.042.[20] The graphic representation of growth over time reveals that the performance of the more democratic regimes was more consistent and less subject to sudden changes (Figures 16.1 and 16.2).

Those regimes with lower degrees of democratization were more reluctant to reform their economies, and the recovery of growth took longer. This is shown in Table 16.2. Czechoslovakia, Bulgaria, Hungary, and Poland were the first countries to adopt reform packages, between 1990 and 1991. Their regimes were also more democratic than the rest in the first two years: the Gastil scores were 2.2 in Poland, Czechoslovakia, and Hungary, and 2.3 in Bulgaria. Belarus, Romania, Ukraine, and Moldova took much longer to initiate economic reforms, which were also more limited. Gastil scores ranged from 5.5 in Romania to 4.4 in Albania, Belarus, and Ukraine.

The correlations between the degree of democracy in one year and the inflation rate in the following year were always positive through the period: 0.169, 0.420, 0.603, 0.272, 0.207, 0.260. Higher rankings in the Gastil scale (i.e. less democracy) meant more inflation. The inflation rates inherited from the previous regimes were also very different. If we look at the most democratic cases, Bulgaria and Czechoslovakia had low rates before the first democratic elections (6.4 per cent and less than 10 per cent, respectively), the rate was higher in Hungary (16.9 per cent), and dramatic in Poland (58.7 per cent in 1988 and 244.5 per cent in 1989). Early economic reforms led to sharp and short increases in rates of inflation. In Poland, inflation went up to 555.3 per cent in 1990, and began to decline in the following years: 76.7 per cent in 1991 (year 2), 45.3 per cent in 1992 (year 3), and 36.8 per cent in 1993 (year 4). Bulgaria moved from 23.8 per cent in 1990 to 338.5 per cent in 1991 (year 2), the year in which economic reforms were launched. Then the rate began to recede: 91.3 per cent in 1992 (year 3), 72.9 per cent in 1993 (year 4). The experience

[20] Remember that the lower the score, the more democratic the regime. Thus, with one exception, the coefficients are negative.

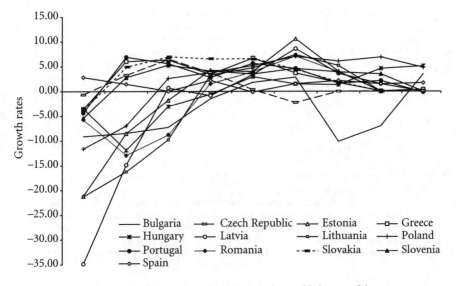

Figure 16.1 *Economic growth in the year since the establishment of democracy*

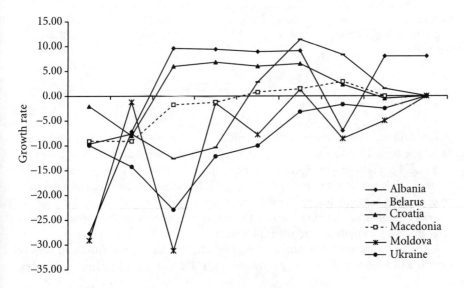

Figure 16.2 *Economic growth in the year since the establishment of democracy*

Table 16.2   *Regression model for the effect of the degree of democracy on economic reforms in 1994[a]*

Independent variable	Economic reforms (1994)
Constant	22.53
Degree of democracy (year 1)	−1.74[***]
Signif. F	0.016
R^2	0.347
N	16

[***]Statistically significant at 1 per cent.
[a]European Bank for Reconstruction and Development, *Transition Report* 1994. The scale is based on six different indicators (large-scale privatization, small-scale privatization, enterprise restructuring, price liberalization, trade and foreign exchange system, banking reform) measured from 1 to 4. The higher the score, the higher the progress in economic reforms. We have used the sum of the scores for the six indicators.

Table 16.3   *Regression models for the effect of economic reforms in 1994 on future economic performance (average after 1994)*

Independent variable	Growth	Inflation	Unemployment
Constant	−5.43	318.57	−0.439
Economic reform (1994)	0.473	−15.78[***]	0.668
Signif. F	0.109	0.007	0.376
R^2	0.173	0.419	0.056
N	16	16	16

[***]Statistically significant at 1 per cent.

of Czechoslovakia was similar: inflation suddenly increased in 1991, from 10 per cent to 58 per cent, and then to 80 per cent in 1992. It also went down in the following years: 20.8 per cent in 1993 (year 1), 10 per cent in 1994 (year 2), 9.1 per cent in 1995 (year 3). This was also the pattern in Hungary. In countries that delayed economic reforms, governments feared the political consequences of such sharp increases in the rates of inflation. Table 16.3 shows the consequences of economic reforms on the rates of growth, inflation, and unemployment.

In order to measure nationalist mobilizations, we have used Gurr's indices of protest and rebellion, based on the Minorities at Risk dataset.[21] The index of protest

---

[21] The Minorities at Risk dataset includes different kinds of minority groups (communal contenders, indigenous peoples, ethnonationalist groups, religious sects, and national minorities). We are only interested in the actions of those minorities with a history of organized political autonomy, with political movements defending autonomy at some time since 1945, or representing a minority in the state in which they reside. The dataset can be downloaded from: http://www.bsos.umd.edu/cidcm/mar.

Table 16.4 *Regression models for the effect of the degree of democracy on nationalist conflict*

Independent variable	Protest		Rebellion	
	(year 3)	(year 6)	(year 3)	(year 6)
Constant	0.719	0.328	−1.643	−1.183
Degree of democracy (year 2)	0.370	—	0.768[**]	—
Degree of democracy (years 2–5)	—	0.573	—	0.624[**]
Signif. *F*	0.290	0.139	0.050	0.019
R^2	0.065	0.124	0.199	0.284
N	19	19	19	19

[**]Statistically significant at 5 per cent.

is an ordinal scale that goes from 0 to 5;[22] the index of rebellion is also an ordinal scale that moves from 0 to 7.[23] The values for each country are annual.

The regression analysis of the effects of the degrees of democracy on nationalist conflict (Table 16.4) shows that democracy increased the levels of nationalist protest and rebellion. It also shows that the less democratic regimes had the higher levels of nationalist conflict, both of protest and rebellion. At the same time, whereas the regression coefficient for protest increased with time, the rebellion coefficient diminished. If we look at the evolution of the rebellion scores, in the first three years of the new regimes three countries had an index higher than 0: Spain, Croatia, and Moldova.[24] Only Spain was at the time a liberal democracy. By the fourth and fifth year after the first free elections, rebellion had spread to Albania and Macedonia, although it had begun to recede in Moldova and Croatia. Ukraine also had to deal with nationalist conflict, but it never reached the dimension of rebellion: it developed at the level of the regional and central elites,[25] while nationalist protests consisted mostly of small demonstrations.

Whereas rebellion was quite exceptional, nationalist protest was present in all those countries with ethnic minorities within their borders: Albania, Bulgaria, Croatia, the Czech Republic, Estonia, Hungary, Latvia, Lithuania, Macedonia, Moldova, Romania, Slovakia, Spain, and Ukraine. It was thus independent from the

[22] The index has been coded as follows: 0—None reported; 1—Verbal Opposition (public letters, petitions, posters, publications, etc.); 2—Symbolic Resistance (scattered acts of resistance or political activity, requests by a regional group for independence); 3—Small demonstrations (rallies, strikes, or riots, with total participation of less than 10,000); 4—Medium demonstrations (total participation of less than 100,000); 5—Large demonstrations (total participation of more than 100,000).

[23] The index of rebellion has been coded as follows: 0—None reported; 1—Political banditry, sporadic terrorism; 2—Campaigns of terrorism; 3—Local rebellions (armed attempts to seize power in a locality, declarations of independence by a minority-controlled government); 4—Small-scale guerrilla activity; 5—Intermediate-scale guerrilla activity; 6—Large-scale guerrilla activity; 7—Protracted civil war.

[24] Spain was suffering a terrorist campaign by the Basque separatist group ETA; Croatia was in the middle of a civil war; and Moldova had intermediate-scale guerrilla activity within its borders.

[25] There were two main conflicts: one between the central government and the Crimean separatists; another within the Crimean region, between the Crimean authorities and the Tartars.

degree of democratization. Rebellion, on the other hand, began to recede with the passage of time. It reached its peak between years four and six of the new regime; however, by the end of the period, in 1999, it had almost disappeared. Polyarchies were able to accommodate the most extreme cases of nationalist conflict; an exception was Spain, where it remained constant over time.

The regression analysis for the effects of the degree of democratization on governmental stability, or on its composition (Table 16.5), shows that none of statistical significance existed. The regression coefficients, although statistically non-significant, suggest that a more democratic regime would be more likely to choose parliamentary institutions, or a presidential system with a weak presidency.

A summary of the evidence so far contradicts the idea that if the economic crisis is very profound, or if ethnic conflict is very deep, new polyarchies will have little chance of becoming more democratic, and will persist only as restricted or illiberal democracies. The evidence suggests that economic growth and the accommodation of nationalist conflict can improve when governments are more democratic.

We now move to examine reverse causality: that is, the effect on democratization of the same three groups of variables (the economy, the institutions of the new regime, and the presence or absence of nationalist demands) that now turn from dependent to independent. The first argument that we want to test is whether bad economic performance limited democratization[26] in the new European polyarchies. The indicators that we use are growth rates, inflation, and unemployment. As for the institutional arguments, we want to discuss (i) whether parliamentary systems were more likely to result in greater democratization of the regimes than presidential or semi-presidential ones; (ii) whether coalition governments and governmental instability brought about lower degrees of democracy; (iii) whether the shorter the experience of an independent state, the lower the degree of democracy. Finally, we also want to see whether nationalist conflict hindered democratization.

Table 16.5 *Regression models for the effect of the degree of democracy on institutions*

Independent variable	System of government	Parties in government	Duration of governments
Constant	2.988	1.855[*]	23.662[**]
Degree of democracy (year 1)	−0.839	0.155	0.198
Signif F.	—	0.567	0.945
Pseudo R^2	0.152	—	—
R^2	—	0.020	0.000
N	19	19	19

[*]Statistically significant at 10 per cent.
[**]Statistically significant at 5 per cent.

[26] Przeworski and Limongi (1997) have shown that the survival of democracies depends on the level of development and on economic performance. We want to test whether this is also valid for the degree of democracy achieved.

Table 16.6 *Regression models for the effect of the economy on the degree of democracy*

Independent variable	Degree of democracy in year 2	Degree of democracy in year 6
Constant	2.538***	1.539***
Growth (year 1)	−0.035	—
Growth (years 1–5)	—	0.0312
Inflation (year 1)	0.00016	—
Inflation (years 1–5)	—	0.0027***
Unemployment (year 1)	−0.038	—
Unemployment (years 1–5)	—	0.038
Signif. F	0.345	0.012
R^2	0.251	0.505
N	15	19

***Statistically significant at 1 per cent.

The regression analysis for economic performance (Table 16.6) indicates that its effects on democratization were very small, both at the beginning and with the passage of time. This is confirmed if we look at those countries with democracy scores lower than 2.5 in 1999 (Appendix 16.1): their inflation and growth rates varied substantially in the years following the establishment of democracy. The range of values of the mean growth rates for the whole period goes from 3.67 in Slovakia to −7.84 in Lithuania. Only half of the liberal democracies in 1999 had positive average growth rates since the new regimes were established. The rest were often in deep crises, with average rates of −7.84 for Lithuania, −4.53 for Bulgaria, −4.64 for Estonia. If we look at inflation, variations among the liberal democracies in 1999 were also vast, with the highest average rates for Lithuania (225 per cent), Bulgaria (212 per cent), Estonia (184.2 per cent), Latvia (164.5 per cent), and Romania (118.3 per cent). However, democratization in these countries was not limited by bad economic performance. As for the five countries classified as illiberal democracies in 1999,[27] they also varied in their average rates of inflation and growth. In none of them, however, did democratization advance in the period. But only Belarus reversed to dictatorship, although average growth rates were −14.14 per cent in Moldova and −13.85 per cent in Ukraine over the period.

In sum, the data have shown that: (a) the new European polyarchies were highly resilient to the economic crisis inherited from the previous regimes and that persisted well into the period of democratic rule; (b) this crisis did not prevent further democratization in thirteen of the nineteen countries in the first decade of the new regimes; (c) the crisis cannot explain the different degrees of democracy achieved by these countries in 1999.

---

[27] Albania, Belarus, Croatia, Macedonia, Moldova, and Ukraine.

Table 16.7   *Regression models for the effect of nationalism on the*
degree of democracy

Independent variable	Degree of democracy in year 2	Degree of democracy in year 7
Constant	2.222	2.205
Protest (year 1)	0.249	—
Protest (years 1–6)	—	−0.132
Rebellion (year 1)	0.187	—
Rebellion (years 1–6)	—	0.447
% minority pop. (year 1)	0.0014	—
% minority pop. (year 6)	—	0.015
Signif. *F*	0.045	0.317
R^2	0.406	0.204
N	19	19

The regression analysis for nationalist protest and rebellion and for cultural heterogeneity (Table 16.7) indicates that nationalist conflict had no significant effects on democratization in year two, although the level of rebellion seemed slightly to affect the degree of democracy achieved in year seven. The regression coefficients for the proportion of the total population of the state that corresponded to a minority were insignificant both in year one and year seven of the new regimes. The level of cultural heterogeneity of the country did not affect democratization.[28] Indeed, the only case in which democratization receded was Belarus, a country without nationalist conflict. Among the five illiberal democracies, Croatia, Moldova, and Ukraine experienced intense nationalist conflict. In the case of Ukraine, however, what hindered further democratic development was the conflict between the executive and legislative branches of power. As for Croatia, the democracy score remained the same during and after the civil war. In Moldova, unilateral and violent declarations of independence by Transdnistria and Gagauzia and guerrilla activity restricted democratization, although eventually nationalist conflict was accommodated and the regime gradually became less restrictive. Nationalist demands and Basque terrorism in Spain did not affect its classification as a liberal democracy from the first elections in 1977. Therefore no convincing evidence exists to the effect that nationalism was an impediment to democratization.

The regression results for the effects of institutions on democratization (Table 16.8) show that only the system of government and new states had some effect, although of no statistical significance.[29] Parliamentarism increased the degree

[28] The Pearson correlation between cultural heterogeneity and democratization in year seven was −0.062. This is further confirmation that no linear relationship existed between the variables.

[29] The variables for institutions have been coded as follows. In 'system of government', semi-presidentialism is 0, parliamentarism is 1. 'Governmental stability' is coded by the average number of months that governments were in power. The number of 'parties in government' indicates coalitions and their internal fragmentation. 'New state' is a binary variable, with old states as 0, and new independent states as 1.

Table 16.8 *Regression models for the effect of institutions*

Independent variable	Degree of democracy in year 2	Degree of democracy in year 7
Constant	3.193***	2.697***
System of government	−0.664	−0.140
Parties in government (first gov.)	−0.282	—
Parties in government (years 1–6)	—	−0.564
Government stability (first gov.)	0.017	—
Government stability (years 1–6)	—	0.019
New state	0.302	0.692
Signif. F	0.182	0.077
R^2	0.341	0.432
N	19	19

***Statistically significant at 1 per cent.

of democracy by 0.664 in the next year, but its impact became negligible in year seven. New states seemed to be slightly less democratic in year seven than old states. However, what this really indicates is that the pace of democratization was slower: the mean democracy score in year two was 3.1 both for old states and for new ones; in year seven, the respective mean scores were 2.1 and 2.6. Neither the number of parties in government nor the instability of governments were an impediment to democratization: many of the 1999 liberal democracies had a tradition of multiparty and short-lived governments.

The weak effect of the system of government deserves more attention. Our data suggest that a dichotomous variable conceals differences within presidential and semi-presidential regimes. Empirical evidence (Shugart and Carey 1992; Frye 1997; Nichols 1999; Metcalf 2000) shows that presidential systems vary substantially in the degree of powers attributed to the president; the consequences for democratization can thus be very different. In fact, Belarus, our only case of democratic collapse, was a presidential regime with a powerful president, a weak party system, and undisciplined parties. On the contrary, semi-presidential systems with more limited presidential powers and multi-party systems became liberal democracies (Portugal) or did not collapse (Croatia, Moldova). The problem seems to lie in the combination of presidentialism, multipartism, and undisciplined parties (Mainwaring 1993: 225).

CONCLUSIONS

Our analysis of the new regimes that emerged in the European periphery, South and East, has questioned several arguments of democratization theory. Our main variable is the variation in the democratization of the polyarchies. With the exception of Belarus, none of the new regimes reverted to authoritarianism, although their degree of democratization varied substantially. In 1999, Portugal ranked at 1.0 in the Gastil scale; Spain, Poland, Hungary, the Czech Republic, Slovakia, Lithuania, Latvia, Slovenia, and Estonia at 1.5. On the other extreme Belarus ranked at 6.0, Albania at 4.5. We do not study, therefore, what causes the establishment or survival of democracies, nor what makes them work, in comparison to authoritarian regimes.

Our first conclusion is that the experience of the new European democracies shows that the past, neither the nature of the previous regime nor the type of transition, had lasting effects on democratization. It influenced the pace, but only for a few years. That is, after the first elections and for some time, some countries democratized more rapidly than others, but the political outcomes ten years later could be remarkably similar as the pace of late democratizers became much faster in the second half of the 1990s. For instance, once the new governments started to negotiate with the European Union, the Commission indicated in a report in July 1997 its concern over the democratic shortcomings of Romania and, particularly, Slovakia:[30] in 1999, however, Slovakia was as democratic as Hungary, and both ranked as Spain did; Romania was as democratic as Greece.

Our second conclusion is that, once the first elections took place, the more democratic governments achieved more economic growth and less inflation over the following decade. The pattern of growth was more consistent and stable than that of the less democratic regimes. The latter were also reluctant to launch economic reforms, for fear that the liberalization of prices would produce a politically explosive inflation. They could sometimes avoid a sharp, but temporary, increase in prices, but only by postponing it for a brief period and at the cost of future growth. The more democratic regimes were very resilient to economic crises; although these were frequently dramatic, such regimes did not become more restrictive (with only limited caveats for Bulgaria in 1996–9 and Slovakia in 1996–7).

A third conclusion is that, in plural societies, the new regimes were often associated with an increase in nationalist conflict. The more democratic the regimes were, the more likely that nationalist rebellion would exist. However, the regression coefficient of rebellion decreased over time. Also contrary to the diagnosis of Roeder (1999), the effect of nationalist conflict on the degree of democratization was statistically insignificant. In particular, the proportion of the total population that belonged to ethnic or cultural minorities was irrelevant for democratization.

Our fourth conclusion is that variations of the new regimes in the Gastil scale when they were established were statistically irrelevant for the choice of semi-presidential or parliamentary institutions. The coefficients suggest, however, that the latter were more likely, the more democratic the regimes were. Initial differences in democratization seem to have had no effect either on the number of parties in power,

---

[30] 'Only one applicant state—Slovakia—does not satisfy the political conditions laid down by the European Council' (European Commission 1997: 4).

or on the durability of incumbents. Conversely, parliamentary institutions and old states appear to have facilitated more democratic regimes, although the results are not statistically significant. But what probably limited more democratization was the coexistence of strong presidents, a fragmented party system, and weak parties. New states only slowed down the process.

Our final comments refer to the relationship between the new regimes and European integration. Negotiations with the European Union privileged the ten Central and East European countries whose Gastil scores ranked them as 'liberal democracies': Poland, the Czech Republic, Hungary, Lithuania, Latvia, Estonia, Slovenia, Bulgaria, Romania, and Slovakia. Of these, Bulgaria was on the borderline in 1999, with a score of 2.5. The average score of the ten countries was 1.6. Six other countries were outside the queue: Albania, Croatia, Ukraine, Belarus, Moldova, and Macedonia. These countries were all ranked as 'illiberal democracies', and their average score in 1999 was 4.0. In fact, political criteria seem to have been more important for the European Union than economic ones. Bulgaria had in 1999 only 22 per cent of the EU average per capita income in purchasing power parities; Latvia and Romania had 27 per cent. The group of the ten 'liberal democracies' had a better average growth rate than the group of six 'illiberal democracies', both over the decade (-0.36 per cent per year vs -3.5 per cent) and in 1999 (1.5 per cent vs 0.25 per cent). But the differences are only due to the catastrophic economic performance of Moldova and Ukraine in the second group. The rates of growth of Bulgaria (-3.5 per cent), Latvia (-4.1 per cent), and Lithuania (-3.3 per cent), all in the first group, were no better over the decade than that of the second group; they were worse than the rates of Croatia, Macedonia, and Albania.

We know that the European Community was a crucial political and economic reference for politicians in the new democracies. Vaclav Havel described it as 'the unprecedented, historical dimension of European reunification' (interview in *Le Monde*, 19 November 1998). It is not easy to assess what effect this had on the political and economic transformations of the Central and East European countries. Initiatives of the European Union such as the Phare and Tacis Democracy Programs are difficult to evaluate (ISA Consult 1997), and the volume of investment in, and trade with, the Central and East European countries has varied greatly. But the criteria of the European Union for inclusion and exclusion in negotiations must be clarified. Is Ukraine too important for Russia to become part of an integrated Europe? Is Albania too poor? We must note that, at the beginning of the decade, the democracy scores for Slovenia, Lithuania, Latvia, or Estonia were the same as those for Ukraine, Macedonia, or Belarus. These countries were ranked as more democratic than Romania. If the European Union successfully promoted democratization in some of these countries with the 'conditionality' of negotiation, why other European countries cannot benefit from such influence needs to be explained by politicians.

Democracy and Participation

Appendix 16.1 *The evolution of democracy scores in the European periphery*

Country	1974	1975	1976	1977	1978	1979	1980	1981	1982	1983
Greece	2	2	2	2	2	2	2	1.5	1.5	1.5
Portugal		4	2	2	2	2	2	1.5	1.5	1.5
Spain				2	2.5	2	2.5	2.5	1.5	1.5
	1990	1991	1992	1993	1994	1995	1996	1997	1998	1999
Albania	(7)	4	3.5	3	3.5	3.5	4	4	4.5	4.5
Belarus	(4.5)	4	3.5	4.5	4	5	6	6	6	6
Bulgaria	3.5	2.5	2.5	2	2	2	2.5	2.5	2.5	2.5
Croatia	(4.5)	3.5	4	4	4	4	4	4	4	4
Czech Rep	(2)	(2)	(2)	1.5	1.5	1.5	1.5	1.5	1.5	1.5
Estonia	(4.5)	2.5	3	2.5	2.5	2	1.5	1.5	1.5	1.5
Greece	1.5	1.5	1.5	2	2	2	2	2	2	2
Hungary	2	2	2	1.5	1.5	1.5	1.5	1.5	1.5	1.5
Latvia	(4.5)	2.5	3	3	2.5	2	2	1.5	1.5	1.5
Lithuania	(4.5)	2.5	2.5	2	2	1.5	1.5	1.5	1.5	1.5
Macedonia	(4.5)	n.a	3.5	3	3.5	3.5	3.5	3.5	3	3
Moldova	(4.5)	4.5	5	5	4	4	3.5	3.5	3	3
Poland	2	2	2	2	2	1.5	1.5	1.5	1.5	1.5
Portugal	1.5	1	1	1	1	1	1	1	1	1
Romania	5.5	5	4	4	3.5	3.5	2.5	2	2	2
Slovakia	(2)	(2)	(2)	3.5	2.5	2.5	3	3	2	1.5
Slovenia	(4.5)	2.5	2	1.5	1.5	1.5	1.5	1.5	1.5	1.5
Spain	1	1	1	1.5	1.5	1.5	1.5	1.5	1.5	1.5
Ukraine	(4.5)	3	3	4	3.5	3.5	3.5	3.5	3.5	3.5

Source: Freedom House.

Appendix 16.2   *The evolution of political rights scores in the European periphery*

Country	1973	1974	1975	1976	1977	1978	1979	1980	1981	1982	1983
Greece	7	2	2	2	2	2	2	2	1	1	1
Portugal		5	5	2	2	2	2	2	1	1	1
Spain				5	2	2	2	2	2	1	1
	1989	1990	1991	1992	1993	1994	1995	1996	1997	1998	1999
Albania	7	7	4	4	2	3	3	4	4	4	4
Belarus	6	5	4	4	5	4	5	6	6	6	6
Bulgaria	7	3	2	2	2	2	2	2	2	2	2
Croatia	5	5	3	4	4	4	4	4	4	4	4
Czech Rep	6	2	2	2	1	1	1	1	1	1	1
Estonia	6	5	2	3	3	3	2	1	1	1	1
Greece	1	1	1	1	1	1	1	1	1	1	1
Hungary	4	2	2	2	1	1	1	1	1	1	1
Latvia	6	5	2	3	3	3	2	2	1	1	1
Lithuania	6	5	2	2	1	1	1	1	1	1	1
Macedonia	5	5	3	3	3	4	4	4	4	3	3
Moldova	6	5	5	5	5	4	4	3	3	2	2
Poland	4	2	2	2	2	2	1	1	1	1	1
Portugal	1	1	1	1	1	1	1	1	1	1	1
Romania	7	6	5	4	4	4	4	2	2	2	2
Slovakia	6	2	2	2	3	2	2	2	2	2	1
Slovenia	5	5	2	2	1	1	1	1	1	1	1
Spain	1	1	1	1	1	1	1	1	1	1	1
Ukraine	6	5	3	3	4	3	3	3	3	3	3

Source: Freedom House.

Democracy and Participation

Appendix 16.3   *The evolution of civil liberties scores in the European periphery*

Country	1973	1974	1975	1976	1977	1978	1979	1980	1981	1982	1983
Greece	5	2	2	2	2	2	2	2	2	2	2
Portugal		3	3	2	2	2	2	2	2	2	2
Spain				3	2	3	2	3	3	2	2
	1989	**1990**	**1991**	**1992**	**1993**	**1994**	**1995**	**1996**	**1997**	**1998**	**1999**
Albania	7	6	4	3	4	4	4	4	4	5	5
Belarus	5	4	4	3	4	4	5	6	6	6	6
Bulgaria	7	4	3	3	2	2	2	3	3	3	3
Croatia	4	4	4	4	4	4	4	4	4	4	4
Czech Rep	6	2	2	2	2	2	2	2	2	2	2
Estonia	5	4	3	3	2	2	2	2	2	2	2
Greece	2	2	2	2	3	3	3	3	3	3	3
Hungary	3	2	2	2	2	2	2	2	2	2	2
Latvia	5	4	3	3	3	2	2	2	2	2	2
Lithuania	5	4	3	3	3	3	2	2	2	2	2
Macedonia	4	4	4	4	3	3	3	3	3	3	3
Moldova	5	4	4	5	5	4	4	4	4	4	4
Poland	3	2	2	2	2	2	2	2	2	2	2
Portugal	2	2	1	1	1	1	1	1	1	1	1
Romania	7	5	5	4	4	3	3	3	2	2	2
Slovakia	6	2	2	2	4	3	3	4	4	2	2
Slovenia	4	4	3	2	2	2	2	2	2	2	2
Spain	1	1	1	1	2	2	2	2	2	2	2
Ukraine	5	4	3	3	4	4	4	4	4	4	4

Source: Freedom House.

Appendix 16.4 *The evolution of growth during the first years of democracy (real GDP growth as % change on previous year)*

Country	Year 1	Year 2	Year 3	Year 4	Year 5	Year 6	Year 7	Year 8	Year 9	Year 10
Albania	−27.70	−7.20	9.60	9.40	8.90	9.10	−7.0	8.0	8.0	
Belarus	−9.64	−7.64	−12.59	−10.37	2.81	11.4	8.3	1.5		
Bulgaria	−9.12	−8.45	−7.27	−1.48	1.82	2.86	−10.14	−7.0	3.5	0.0
Croatia	−2.09	−8.0	5.98	6.8	6.0	6.5	2.3	−0.5		
Czech Rep	−0.6	3.2	6.4	3.84	0.3	−2.3	0.0			
Estonia	−21.17	−8.51	−1.79	4.25	3.98	10.6	4.0	0.0		
Greece	−3.64	6.05	6.36	3.43	6.70	3.69	1.75	0.06	0.39	0.40
Hungary	−3.50	−11.89	−3.06	−0.58	2.95	1.49	1.34	4.6	5.1	3.0
Latvia	−34.86	−14.87	0.68	−0.85	3.37	8.6	3.6	1.5		
Lithuania	−21.26	−16.23	−9.77	3.29	4.75	7.4	5.2	0.0		
Macedonia		−9.1	−1.73	−1.20	0.77	1.5	2.9	0.0		
Moldova	−29.10	−1.20	−31.20	−1.40	−7.80	1.3	−8.6	−5.0		
Poland	−11.60	−6.97	2.63	3.80	5.20	7.05	6.08	6.9	4.8	3.5
Portugal	−4.35	6.90	5.60	2.82	5.64	4.59	1.62	2.14	−0.17	−1.88
Romania	−5.70	−12.92	−8.78	1.53	3.94	7.12	3.91			
Slovakia	−3.70	4.92	6.92	6.55	6.5	4.4	1.8			
Slovenia	−5.40	2.80	5.30	4.10	3.5	4.6	3.9	3.5		
Spain	2.84	1.46	0.04	2.21	−0.13	1.54	2.16	1.5	1.7	3.2
Ukraine	−9.94	−14.23	−22.93	−12.15	−10.01	−3.2	−1.7	−2.5		

Source: World Bank.

Appendix 16.5 *The evolution of growth between 1990 and 1999 (real GDP growth as % change on previous year)*

Country	1990	1991	1992	1993	1994	1995	1996	1997	1998	1999
Albania	−10.00	−27.70	−7.20	9.60	9.40	8.90	9.10	−7.0	8.0	8.0
Belarus		−1.16	−9.64	−7.64	−12.59	−10.37	2.81	11.4	8.3	1.5
Bulgaria	−9.12	−8.45	−7.27	−1.48	1.82	2.86	−10.14	−7.0	3.5	0.0
Croatia		−18.89	−2.09	−8.0	5.98	6.8	6.0	6.5	2.3	−0.5
Czech Rep	(−1.4)	(−15.9)	(−8.0)	−0.6	3.2	6.4	3.84	0.3	−2.3	0.0
Estonia		−8.00	−21.17	−8.51	−1.79	4.25	3.98	10.6	4.0	0.0
Greece	0.03	3.01	0.51	0.23	2.19	2.03	2.60	3.2	3.0	
Hungary	−3.50	−11.89	−3.06	−0.58	2.95	1.49	1.34	4.6	5.1	3.0
Latvia		−10.41	−34.86	−14.87	0.68	−0.85	3.37	8.6	3.6	1.5
Lithuania		−5.67	−21.26	−16.23	−9.77	3.29	4.75	7.4	5.2	0.0
Macedonia				−9.1	−1.73	−1.20	0.77	1.5	2.9	0.0
Moldova		−17.50	−29.10	−1.20	−31.20	−1.40	−7.80	1.3	−8.6	−5.0
Poland	−11.60	−6.97	2.63	3.80	5.20	7.05	6.08	6.9	4.8	3.5
Portugal	4.38	2.34	2.52	−1.11	2.24	2.85	3.18	3.7	3.5	
Romania	−5.70	−12.92	−8.78	1.53	3.94	7.12	3.91			
Slovakia	(−1.4)	(−15.9)	(−8.0)	−3.70	4.92	6.92	6.55	6.5	4.4	1.8
Slovenia		−8.90	−5.40	2.80	5.30	4.10	3.5	4.6	3.9	3.5
Spain	3.74	2.27	0.69	−1.16	2.22	2.73	2.27	3.5	3.8	
Ukraine		−8.67	−9.94	−14.23	−22.93	−12.15	−10.01	−3.2	−1.7	−2.5

Source: World Bank.

Appendix 16.6 *The evolution of inflation during the first years of democracy (year 1–9)*

Country	Year 1	Year 2	Year 3	Year 4	Year 5	Year 6	Year 7	Year 8	Year 9
Albania	35.50	193.10	85.00	21.50	8.00	12.70	33.10	20.30	1.80
Belarus	971.20	1,190.90	2,219.60	709.30	52.70	63.90	73.20		
Bulgaria	23.80	338.50	91.30	72.90	96.20	62.10	123.10	1,082.60	22.20
Croatia	632.50	1,483.62	197.33	3.95	4.34	3.70	5.90		
Czech Rep	20.80	10.00	9.10	8.90	8.40	10.60			
Estonia	1,078.20	89.60	47.90	28.90	23.10	11.10	10.60		
Greece	26.90	13.36	13.31	12.16	12.53	19.04	24.87	24.46	20.92
Hungary	28.97	34.23	22.95	22.45	18.87	28.30	23.49	18.40	14.20
Latvia	951.20	109.10	35.70	25.00	17.70	8.50	4.70		
Lithuania	1,020.50	410.10	72.00	39.50	24.70	8.80	5.10		
Macedonia	1,505.50	353.10	121.00	16.90	4.10	3.60	1.00		
Moldova	1,308.00	1,751.00	486.40	29.90	23.50	11.80	7.70		
Poland	555.38	76.71	45.33	36.86	33.25	26.79	20.15	15.10	11.70
Portugal	20.41	18.25	27.11	22.70	23.63	16.62	20.04	22.73	25.11
Romania	5.10	170.20	210.70	256.20	137.10	32.20	38.80	154.90	59.30
Slovakia	23.10	13.40	10.00	6.00	6.20	6.70			
Slovenia	207.30	31.70	21.00	13.50	9.90	8.40	7.90		
Spain	24.54	19.77	15.66	15.55	14.55	14.41	12.17	11.28	8.81
Ukraine	1,209.60	4,734.90	891.20	376.70	80.20	15.90	10.60		

Source: World Bank.

Appendix 16.7 *The evolution of inflation between 1990 and 1998*

Country	1990	1991	1992	1993	1994	1995	1996	1997	1998
Albania		35.50	193.10	85.00	21.50	8.00	12.70	33.10	20.30
Belarus		98.60	971.20	1,190.90	2,219.60	709.30	52.70	63.90	73.20
Bulgaria	23.80	338.50	91.30	72.90	96.20	62.10	123.10	1,082.60	22.20
Croatia		122.22	632.50	1,483.62	197.33	3.95	4.34	3.70	5.90
Czech Rep			20.80	10.00	9.10	8.90	8.40	10.60	
Estonia		202.00	1,078.20	89.60	47.90	28.90	23.10	11.10	10.60
Greece	20.40	19.47	15.87	14.41	10.92	8.94	8.19	5.50	
Hungary	28.97	34.23	22.95	22.45	18.87	28.30	23.49	18.40	14.20
Latvia		172.20	951.20	109.10	35.70	25.00	17.70	8.50	4.70
Lithuania		216.40	1,020.50	410.10	72.00	39.50	24.70	8.80	5.10
Macedonia		114.90	1,505.50	353.10	121.00	16.90	4.10	3.60	1.00
Moldova		114.40	1,308.00	1,751.00	486.40	29.90	23.50	11.80	7.70
Poland	555.38	76.71	45.33	36.86	33.25	26.79	20.15	15.10	11.70
Portugal	13.37	11.35	8.94	6.80	4.92	4.12	3.12	2.40	
Romania	5.10	170.20	210.70	256.20	137.10	32.20	38.80	154.90	59.30
Slovakia			23.10	13.40	10.00	6.00	6.20	6.70	
Slovenia		115.00	207.30	31.70	21.00	13.50	9.90	8.40	7.90
Spain	6.72	5.93	5.92	4.57	4.72	4.68	3.56	2.00	
Ukraine		94.00	1,209.60	4,734.90	891.20	376.70	80.20	15.90	10.60

Source: World Bank.

Appendix 16.8 *The evolution of unemployment during the first years of democracy (year 1–9)*

Country	Year 1	Year 2	Year 3	Year 4	Year 5	Year 6	Year 7	Year 8	Year 9
Albania	8.9	27.0	22.0	18.0	12.9	12.3	14.9	17.6	
Belarus	0.5	1.3	2.1	2.7	4.0	2.8	2.3		
Bulgaria	1.8	11.1	15.6	16.4	12.8	11.1	12.5	13.7	12.2
Croatia		17.8	16.6	17.3	17.6	15.9	17.6	18.6	
Czech Rep	3.5	3.2	2.9	3.5	5.2	7.5			
Estonia	1.6	5.0	5.1	5.0	5.6	4.6	5.1		
Greece	2.1	2.3	1.9	1.7	1.8	1.9	2.7	2.2	4.0
Hungary	1.7		9.9	12.1	10.9	10.4	10.5	10.4	
Latvia	2.3	5.8	6.5	6.6	7.2	6.7	9.2		
Lithuania	3.6	3.4	4.5	7.3	6.2	6.7	6.9		
Macedonia	26.8	30.3	33.2	37.2	39.8	42.5			
Moldova	0.7	0.7	1.0	1.4	1.5	1.7	1.9		
Poland	—	14.3	16.4	16.0	14.9	13.2	10.3	10.4	
Portugal	4.4	6.2	7.3	7.9	7.9	7.6	5.1	7.3	7.2
Romania	1.3		8.2	10.4	10.9	9.5	6.6	8.8	10.3
Slovakia	14.4	14.8	13.1	12.8	12.5	15.6			
Slovenia	—	13.3	15.5	14.2	14.5	14.4	14.8	14.6	
Spain	5.3	7.1	8.8	11.6	5.4	14.4	16.3	17.5	20.3
Ukraine	0.3	0.4	0.3	0.6	1.5	2.8	4.3		

Source: World Bank.

Appendix 16.9 *The evolution of unemployment between 1990 and 1998*

Country	1990	1991	1992	1993	1994	1995	1996	1997	1998
Albania			27.0	22.0	18.0	12.9	12.3	14.9	17.6
Belarus			0.5	1.3	2.1	2.7	4.0	2.8	2.3
Bulgaria			15.6	16.4	12.8	11.1	12.5	13.7	12.2
Croatia			17.8	16.6	17.3	17.6	15.9	17.6	18.6
Czech Rep			2.6	3.5	3.2	2.9	3.5	5.2	7.5
Estonia			1.6	5.0	5.1	5.0	5.6	4.6	5.1
Greece			7.9	8.6	8.9	9.2	9.6	9.6	9.3
Hungary			12.3	12.1	10.9	10.4	10.5	10.4	9.1
Latvia			2.3	5.8	6.5	6.6	7.2	6.7	9.2
Lithuania			3.6	3.4	4.5	7.3	6.2	6.7	6.9
Macedonia			26.8	30.3	33.2	37.2	39.8	42.5	
Moldova			0.7	0.7	1.0	1.4	1.5	1.7	1.9
Poland			14.3	16.4	16.0	14.9	13.2	10.3	10.4
Portugal			4.2	5.7	7.0	7.3	7.3	6.8	4.9
Romania			8.2	10.4	10.9	9.5	6.6	8.8	10.3
Slovakia			10.4	14.4	14.8	13.1	12.8	12.5	15.6
Slovenia			13.3	15.5	14.2	14.5	14.4	14.8	14.6
Spain			18.4	22.7	24.1	22.9	22.2	20.8	18.8
Ukraine			0.3	0.4	0.3	0.6	1.5	2.8	4.3

Source: World Bank.

PART V

PUBLIC POLICY

17

The Politics of Regulation and European Regulatory Institutions

GIANDOMENICO MAJONE

REGULATION AND DELEGATION OF POWERS

A distinctive feature of the modern regulatory state is the extensive delegation of powers to politically independent institutions: agencies, boards, commissions, tribunals. This delegation of legislative powers to unelected policy makers has always been somewhat problematic from the point of view of democratic theory. The key normative problem is, in Richard Stewart's words, how 'to control and validate the exercise of essentially legislative powers by administrative agencies that do not enjoy the formal legitimation of one-person, one-vote election' (Stewart 1975: 1688).

The American regulatory state has grappled with this issue for more than a century, and regulatory legitimacy is becoming an increasingly important political problem also in Europe, both at national and Community levels (Majone 1998, 1999). In the United States the 'non-delegation doctrine' was the first attempt to resolve the normative problems raised by the emergence of a modern system of administrative regulation. For several decades the doctrine enjoyed such widespread acceptance that it came to be regarded as the traditional model of administrative law. The model conceives the regulatory agency as a mere transmission belt for implementing legislative directives in particular cases. Vague, general, or ambiguous statutes create discretion and thus threaten the legitimacy of agency action. Hence, when passing statutes Congress should decide all questions of policy and frame its decisions in such specific terms that administrative regulation will not entail the exercise of broad discretion by the regulators (Stewart 1975: 1675–6).

The non-delegation doctrine had already found widespread acceptance when the first institutionalization of the American regulatory state, the Interstate Commerce Commission, was established by the Interstate Commerce Act of 1887. The Act, with its detailed grant of Authority, seemed to exemplify the transmission-belt model of administrative regulation. However, the subsequent experience of railroad regulation revealed the difficulty of deriving operational guidelines from general standards. By the time the Federal Trade Commission was established in 1914, the agency received essentially a blank cheque authorizing it to eliminate unfair competition. The New

Deal agencies received even broader grants of power to regulate particular sectors of the economy 'in the public interest'. Since 1935, courts have usually deferred to agency interpretations of law whenever the statute is ambiguous. According to a view which finds considerable support in recent cases, agencies should be given the benefit of every doubt because of their superior accountability and expertise. In the important *Chevron* case (1984), the Supreme Court said that the courts should defer to agency interpretations of law unless Congress had directly addressed the precise question at issue.

The delegation problem is considerably more complicated in the European Community/European Union (EC/EU). Here one must distinguish between external delegation and internal delegation. The first type denotes the transfer of rule-making powers to outside bodies, including the member states and bodies not named in the treaties. Internal delegation is the transfer of executive powers from the Council of Ministers to the Commission. In the case of delegation to bodies other than Community institutions, the leading decision of the European Court of Justice (ECJ) is *Meroni v. High Authority* (Case 9/56). In this old case, which arose under the European Coal and Steel Community Treaty, the Court ruled that the High Authority possessed only very limited power to delegate to outside bodies. Clearly defined executive powers may be delegated provided their exercise is subject to strict rules based on objective criteria; discretionary powers involving extensive freedom of judgment may not be delegated (Hartley 1988). The legal services of the European Commission maintain that this 'Meroni Doctrine' remains 'good law', that it applies *mutatis mutandis* to all European Treaties, and that it acts as an insuperable barrier to the delegation of decision-making powers to institutions not named in the European Treaties. A growing number of legal and policy analysts, however, consider this conclusion to be more an excuse to avoid surrendering regulatory powers presently held, however tenuously, by the Commission, than a genuine constitutional argument (Majone 2000).

The situation is quite different for the delegation of powers from the Council to the Commission. The only provision in the original Treaty of Rome expressly concerned with internal delegation was Article 155. This Article merely required the Commission to exercise the powers delegated to it by the Council, but contained no express authorization for such delegation. Explicit authority is now provided by Article 145 (new Article 202) of the EC Treaty. According to this Article the Council *must* delegate implementing powers to the Commission. In a number of important cases from the 1970s, the ECJ interpreted the term 'implementation' rather broadly, covering rule making of a general type, such as making directives to complete a framework directive or regulation. Thus, in *Köster* (Case 25/70) the Court was asked whether there were any limits to the delegation of powers to the Commission. It answered that only general principles of Community policy cannot be delegated. Extensive discretionary powers may be delegated, provided the enabling provisions lay down the basic principles governing the matter in question. More recent cases, such as *Germany v. Commission* (Case C 240/90), confirm the general impression that the Court is prepared to accept a large measure of discretion in the case of internal delegation.

In sum, both in the United States and in Europe, constitutional doctrines against delegation unravelled because the practical case for allowing regulatory discretion is overwhelming. Hence it is impossible to study the politics of regulation without first understanding why political principals choose to delegate rule-making powers.

THE DECISION TO DELEGATE

Any delegation of powers creates an 'agency problem' because of the possibility that the agents will not comply with the policy preferences of the principal. Hence principals will delegate certain tasks or functions to agents only if the expected benefit from doing so exceeds expected agency costs. These are the costs incurred during the effort to induce the agents to implement faithfully the principals' objectives, and the losses which principals sustain where they are not able to control their agents perfectly. Agency costs include the costs associated with selecting the executives of the agencies and monitoring their compliance, the costs of using corrective devices (rewards, sanctions, and legislative direction), and the cost of any residual non-compliance that produces a difference between the policy enacted and what is implemented.

Agency problems can be addressed in a number of ways. For example, the same level of compliance can be achieved with less monitoring if *ex post* rewards and sanctions are made more effective at aligning the incentives of the agents with the principals' policy preferences. Similarly, neither monitoring nor incentive devices are as important if it is possible to appoint agency executives who share the objectives of the principals. From a normative viewpoint, the objective of institutional design is to identify the mix of selection, monitoring, and *ex post* incentive and correction devices that will reduce agency problems at lowest cost to the principals, given the decision to delegate in the first place (Horn 1995).

What about the benefits of delegating powers to a regulatory agency? First, it should be noted that the main institutional alternatives to regulatory agencies are government departments (or, in the case of the European Commission, Directorates General), control by Courts, or self-regulation. A number of factors may influence the placing of new regulatory tasks on agencies rather than allocating them to existing departments, or giving more work to courts. In some cases, the new activities may not match the already existing duties of departments or courts. In other cases, functions are thought likely to be better administered if they are the sole or central interest of a specialized agency, rather than a peripheral matter dealt with by someone whose attentions are primarily directed elsewhere.

The increasing technical and scientific complexity of many regulatory issues has also led to the establishment of agencies which are seen as expert in these substantive matters. The required expertise might have been developed inside existing departments or courts, however the need for expertise is often found in combination with a rule-making, decision-making, or adjudicative function that is thought to be inappropriate for a government department or court (Baldwin and McCrudden 1987: 4–5). Moreover, a department is often seen as not able to provide the independence from government needed in some of these applications of expertise. Delegation of rule-making powers to agencies may also be useful where constant fine-tuning of the rules or standards, and quick adaptation to technical progress are required. As the experience of technical standardization in the EC prior to the New Approach demonstrates, a collegial body, such as the Council of Ministers, often cannot justify devoting the time needed to these matters, or else, they simply cannot act quickly enough.

Agencies' separateness from government may also make them a preferred mechanism for co-opting certain groups into the decision-making process. This seems to have been an important consideration in the creation of some European agencies such as the European Foundation for the Improvement of Living and Working Conditions and the European Agency for Health and Safety at Work. On the other hand, agencies' separateness from government facilitates their capture by the regulated interests, according to some scholars.

A rough calculation of benefits and costs may be sufficient to determine whether or not to delegate powers to a separate agency. Delegation is not a binary variable, however. It may vary in scope, in precision of regulatory objectives, in the level of agency independence. All these determinations have important consequences for the structure of benefits and costs. Thus, a broad delegation reduces decision-making costs since the legislators do not have to invest resources in working out the details of regulation, but it increases the cost of controlling the agency's discretion. Again, a high level of agency independence increases the credibility of long-term policy commitments by reducing the influence of political considerations in agency decision making, but it increases the risk that the agency will not comply with the policy preferences of its principals. In fact, the single most important dimension along which regulatory institutions vary is the degree of independence from the political process. The relation between delegation and agency independence is analysed more precisely in the following sections, using the concept of political property rights.

POLITICAL PROPERTY RIGHTS

We start with a few general definitions. Property rights are the rights of individuals to the use of resources. It is common to distinguish three categories of property rights: user rights—the rights to use an asset; the right to earn income from an asset; and the right to transfer permanently to another party ownership rights over an asset. Property rights are often *partitioned*, that is, several people may each possess, at the same time, some portion of the rights to use an asset. For example, A may possess the right to grow wheat on a piece of land, and B may possess the right to walk across it (Alchian 1977: 133). Finally, property rights are *attenuated* when the state imposes some limits on individual rights to use, earn income from, and exchange assets (Eggerston 1990: 38).

In the light of these definitions it is possible (and, as we shall see, heuristically useful) to think of the rights to exercise public authority as a species of property rights: political property rights. The first thing to observe is that in a democracy political property rights are always attenuated. This is because democracy is a form of government *pro tempore* (Linz 1998). The time limit inherent in the requirement of elections at regular intervals, which is one of the main arguments for democracy, implies that the policies of the current majority can be subverted, legitimately and without compensation, by a new majority with different and perhaps opposing interests.

As Terry Moe writes:

In democratic politics ... public authority does not belong to anyone. It is simply 'out there', attached to various public offices, and whoever succeeds under the established rules of the game in gaining control of these offices has the right to use it. While the right to exercise public authority happens to be with existing office holders today, other political actors ... may gain that right tomorrow, along with legitimate control over the policies and structures that their predecessors put in place. (1990: 227)

Because political property rights are attenuated, creating a situation of political uncertainty, electorally accountable policy makers lack the means of making credible long-term policy commitments. This credibility problem of democratic principals is not new, of course, but it is particularly serious today. Growing economic and political interdependence among nations has the effect of weakening the impact of policy actions on the home country and strengthening their impact on other countries. Thus domestic policy is increasingly projected beyond national boundaries, but it can achieve its intended objectives there only if it is credible.

Some years ago, Theodore Lowi forcefully reminded political scientists that legitimate use of coercion is *the* intrinsic governmental feature. He wrote that 'Governmentalization of a function—that is, passing a public policy—is sought because the legitimacy of its sanctions makes its social controls more surely effective' (Lowi 1979: 37). Indeed, even a nearly worthless currency can be made a legal tender by legislative fiat—but only inside the national borders. Similarly, a policy lacking credibility can be enforced by coercive means, but only domestically and only at high transaction costs. In sum, because of the growing interdependence of nations it is increasingly costly, or even impossible, to use coercive power as a substitute for policy credibility, and policy makers realize this. Hence the growing tendency to delegate policy-making powers to politically independent institutions. Delegation to such institutions is in fact the best strategy available to political principals for making credible long-term policy commitments (Majone, 2001). By delegating responsibility for monetary policy to an independent central banker, for example, the commitment to price stability becomes much more credible: the central banker does not have the incentive to deviate from the optimal long-run policy for short-run political gains.

As was noted in the previous section, however, delegation is not a binary variable. Following Horn (1995) we may represent it as varying continuously between $D = 0$ ('no delegation') and $D = 1$ ('full delegation'). Delegation to regulatory agencies usually corresponds to intermediate values $(0 < D < 1)$, but in order to understand the logic of delegation it is necessary to examine also the extreme cases.

The case $D = 0$ corresponds to a situation where the principals have concluded that in a particular policy area, the costs of delegation are greater than the benefits.

For example, legislatures usually write out all the details of tax law, rather than delegating the task to an agency. Apparently, the political benefits of doing so are greater than the reduction in decision-making costs which delegation would make possible. The case $D = 1$ is more interesting from the perspective of this paper. Murray Horn (1995) refers to it as 'full delegation' without, however, giving a precise definition of this expression. In terms of the concepts developed in the preceding pages, we can interpret 'full delegation' as the complete, and in some cases irrevocable, transfer of certain political property rights (possibly including elements of national sovereignty) to an independent institution.

It should be noted that when $D = 1$, the delegate is something more than a mere agent. An agent is not ordinarily the owner of property for the benefit of the principal. When property is transferred to a person who is supposed to manage it for the benefit of a third party, we do not have an agency but a fiduciary or trusteeship relation. In Anglo-American law a trust is a situation where the owner of some property, the 'settler', transfers it to a 'trustee', with the stipulation that the trustee should not treat it as her own property but manage it for the benefit of the 'beneficiary', who could be the settler himself. A full delegation of powers in the area of monetary policy, for example, may be viewed as a transfer of political property rights in this area by the government (the settler) to an independent central bank (the trustee) for the benefit of the government itself, whose commitment to price stability thereby becomes more credible. In this model, the transfer of political property rights is the guarantee of the bank's independence. The guarantee is particularly strong when the legal basis of the transfer is not a statute, which could be changed by a new majority, but a constitutional provision such as the Treaty of Maastricht in the case of the European Central Bank. Such a transfer is the political analogue of the irrevocable character of most ordinary trusts.

The same model can be used to analyse the transfer of elements of national sovereignty from the member states of the European Union to the European level. In areas directly related to market integration, the Community has acquired *exclusive* competence, so that national action is simply impermissible, and each Community legislative act 'bites off an area previously within national competence and pre-empts national action in the area concerned' (Weatherill 1995: 137). Under total harmonization, for example, once EC rules have been put in place, a member state's capacity to apply stricter rules by evoking the values referred to in Article 36 of the Treaty of Rome—the protection of the health and life of humans, animals, and plants, and the preservation of national cultural treasures—is excluded. In other words, the regulatory powers of the member states—their political property rights in areas covered by total harmonization—have been completely and irrevocably transferred to the European level.

Where Community competence is exclusive, member states can only advance their interests through the European institutions, rather than unilaterally or collectively. Although the area of exclusive competence is fairly limited, here the European institutions enjoy autonomous powers. In particular, the Commission is not an agent but a trustee of the member states where it exercises certain powers expressly granted to it by the treaties, such as agenda setting, ensuring compliance with EC law, or issuing directives and decisions, without Council's approval, under Article 86(3) (ex Article 90(3)) of the EC Treaty. On the other hand, the Commission *is* an agent when it exercises implementing powers delegated to it by the Council. This is the case of 'internal delegation' discussed in the first section.

Thus, the Commission can be either an agent or a trustee of the member states according to the purpose of delegation. The purpose of internal delegation is to reduce the costs and improve the quality of decision making in the Council. In fact, the Single European Act *required* the Council to delegate implementing powers to the Commission. This requirement was part of the same effort to enhance the efficiency of Community decision making that also introduced qualified majority voting for internal market legislation. By contrast, the powers of agenda setting and of monitoring compliance with European law have been delegated to the Commission in order to enhance the credibility of the member states' commitment to European integration. But this objective cannot be achieved unless the Commission has more autonomy than is normally granted to an agent. The latter's task is simply to carry out the directives of the principals, not to monitor their behaviour or to initiate policy.

Having discussed some of the consequences of the attenuation of political property rights in a democracy, what are the consequences of the partitioning of the same rights?

Partitioned Political Property Rights

Full delegation, in the sense specified above of a complete transfer of certain political property rights to an independent institution, is an important but special case. In the general case $(0 < D < 1)$, delegation involves a partitioning of political property rights among several institutions, each of which possesses some portion of the right to exercise public authority in a given policy domain. In the case of competition policy, for example, the power to approve, disapprove, or impose conditions on a proposed merger is usually partitioned among national competition authorities and courts, one or more departments of government, the European Commission, and in some cases even the US anti-trust regulators.

The EC/EU probably provides the most interesting examples of the general phenomenon. This is because most Community competences are not exclusive but are shared with the member states. Thus, while the external powers of federal governments are typically broader than their purely domestic powers, the external powers of the EC, and specifically its power to conclude agreements with third countries, are even more limited than its internal powers.

Strictly speaking, the Community is exclusively competent to act externally only with respect to association agreements, and to commercial policy in the sense of Article 133 (ex Article 113) of the EC Treaty. The European Court of Justice has construed the scope of this Article rather narrowly. According to Opinion 1/94, the concept of commercial policy is restricted to trade in goods and to cross-border services. In this Opinion the Court ruled against the Commission, which has argued that the EC was exclusively competent to conclude the Uruguay Round agreements. The ECJ found that the subject matter, which also included agreements on trade in services and on trade-related aspects of intellectual property rights, extended beyond the areas covered by exclusive Community competences under Article 133; it mandated Community and member states to cooperate closely. Other opinions of the Court confirm that in the area of external relations, shared or mixed competence is much more likely to be found than exclusive competence (Weatherill 1995: 142–4). Also in the area of regulation the trend towards greater sharing of competences with the national governments is unmistakable. The evolution of the regulatory policies since the 1980s has progressively restricted the role of total harmonization which, it will be recalled, excludes the regulatory sovereignty of the member states.

The intrinsic difficulty of harmonizing the laws and regulations of countries with different legal, administrative, and political systems, as well as mounting opposition to what many member states considered excessive centralization, finally convinced the Commission that the powers granted by Article 100 had to be used so as to interfere as little as possible with the regulatory autonomy of the national governments. The emphasis shifted from total to 'optional' and 'minimum' harmonization. Optional harmonization aims to guarantee the right of free movement of goods while permitting the member states to retain their traditional forms of regulation for goods produced for the domestic market. A particular form of optional harmonization is provided by the fourth paragraph of Article 100a (now Article 95) of the EC Treaty. This article introduced qualified majority voting for internal market legislation, but the member states were not prepared to give up their veto power, under Article 100, without some weakening of total harmonization.

Hence Article 100a (4) provides that: 'If, after the adoption of a harmonization measure by the Council acting by a qualified majority, a Member State deems it necessary to apply national provisions on grounds of major needs referred to in Article 36, or relating to protection of the environment or the working environment, it shall notify the Commission of these provisions'. The national provisions are valid once the Commission has verified that they are not a means of arbitrary discrimination or a disguised restriction on trade. Thus Community harmonization does not necessarily exclude the possibility of regulatory action by the member states, where this is shown to be justified (Weatherill 1995: 150–1). Article 100a (4) specifies the permissible grounds for setting national rules that differ from the Community standard, and introduces a system of controls involving the Commission as well as the other member states. Neither restriction applies to the method of minimum harmonization. Under minimum harmonization the national governments must secure the level of regulation set out in a directive, but are permitted to set higher standards, provided of course that the stricter national rules do not violate Community law. It should be noted that the areas where minimum harmonization is the rule—environment, consumer protection, health and safety at work—are not at the core of market integration. By contrast, regulations dealing with the safety or other aspects of traded goods—that is, with products rather than production processes—are usually totally harmonized since they directly affect market integration.

The movement away from exclusive competence and total harmonization is actually accelerating. Since Maastricht the continuous accretion of powers to the

Community is no longer on the political agenda. Article 5 of the EC Treaty, which enacts the principles of attribution of powers, subsidiarity, and proportionality, effectively rules out of court the notion of a Community continuously moving the boundary posts of its own competence (Dashwood 1996: 113). In particular, the Maastricht Treaty defined new competences in a way that actually limits the exercise of Community powers. For example, Article 126 provides a new legal basis for action in the field of education but the measures the EC can take in this field are limited to 'incentive measures' (e.g. programs such as ERASMUS) and non-binding recommendations. Any harmonization of national laws and regulations is explicitly excluded. Similarly, Article 129 creates specific powers for the Community in the field of public health, but the competence is highly circumscribed as subsidiary to that of the member states. Harmonization is again ruled out, even though the Article states that health protection requirements shall form a constituent part of the other EC policies. The other provisions of the Maastricht Treaty, defining new competences in such areas as culture, consumer protection, and industrial policy, are similarly drafted. In sum, rather than rely on implicit competences, whose limits seemed out of control, the Treaty opted for an explicit grant that sets narrow limits to the modes of action and the reach of such policies; the value of the delegation variable has been set fairly close to the limiting case $D = 0$. With the partial exception of public health, the member states have followed the same approach in the Amsterdam Treaty.

THE FUTURE OF EUROPEAN REGULATION

The developments just discussed, as well as the general tone of the most recent proposals of institutional reform, point in the direction of a significant redistribution of powers among European institutions—with potentially serious consequences for the future of the EC-style regulation. The Commission seems to be the major loser from this reallocation of political property rights. Consider how its monopoly of legislative initiative has been progressively weakened. Since the Maastricht Treaty the Commission must share this power with the member states in matters relating to the second and third 'pillar' of the European Union—the common foreign and security policy and cooperation in justice and home affairs, respectively. Moreover, in the important policy areas where the European Parliament (EP) is a co-legislator, the Commission's power of initiative is seriously limited since the Council and the EP can agree on a measure different from the Commission's proposal, without even the need of a unanimous vote in the Council. Again, the right given to the EP to request the Commission to 'submit any appropriate proposal on matters on which it considers that a Community act is required for the purpose of implementing this Treaty' (Article 192 of the EC Treaty) comes close to a true right of legislative initiative.

The real threat to the traditional role of the Commission as a politically independent regulator, however, comes from the progressive parliamentarization of the Community executive—a process which, ironically, is supposed to improve its democratic legitimacy. The idea of reducing the democratic deficit of the EC policy-making process

(EP?)

by assigning a larger role to the European Parliament, and in particular by involving the EP in the appointment of the Commission is not new. However, the procedure introduced by the Treaty of Amsterdam contains a number of radical changes not only with respect to previous practices, such as the custom of the newly appointed President of the Commission to be heard by the EP's enlarged Bureau, but also with respect to the Maastricht Treaty. If under Article 158 of this Treaty the national governments could nominate a new Commission President only after consulting the EP, now the nomination must be approved by Parliament. Moreover, the President and other members of the Commission are subject to a vote of approval by the EP, as in classical parliamentary systems.

The link between the EP's term of office and that of the Commission is another significant institutional innovation. Since a newly elected Parliament takes part in nominating the Commission, any changes in the EP's composition can be reflected at the Commission level. Not surprisingly, influential parliamentarians such as Gil Robles, the former President of the EP, openly advocate a 'parliamentary Commission', the composition and programmes of which would reflect the will of the current majority. In fact, the difficulties surrounding the appointment of the Santer Commission showed that the EP intended to influence the distribution of portfolios among Commissioners.

The process of parliamentarization has been accelerated by the crisis of March 1999, leading to the resignation of the Santer Commission, and by the extended committee hearings of individual members of the Prodi Commission. Henceforth it will be virtually impossible for an individual commissioner to remain in office against the wish of the majority of the EP. These developments amount to a deep transformation of the relationship between the EP and the Commission. The Commission will be fully accountable to the Parliament, whose influence will be felt in all its activities, whether administrative or legislative. In their desire to reduce the EU's democratic deficit, the framers of the Amsterdam and Maastricht Treaties have radically modified the balance of power between Commission and Parliament.

Arguably, an increasing level of politicization of EC policy making becomes unavoidable as more and more tasks involving political discretion are shifted to the European level. These new competences, and the problems connected with the next enlargement, not only increase the administrative tasks of the Commission, but also emphasize the Commission's political responsibilities. In this context the demand for a greater role for the EP becomes understandable. At the same time one should not be blind to the risks which politicization entails for the credibility of EC regulatory policies (Majone 2000).

As we saw earlier, in a parliamentary regime political property rights are attenuated since the policies of the current majority can be subverted by a new majority with different policy preferences. This creates a situation of political uncertainty, where politically accountable policy makers lack the means of making credible long-term commitments. For this reason a growing number of countries delegate regulatory policy making to agencies operating at arm's length from government. The delegation of regulatory powers to some agency distinct from the government itself is best understood as a means whereby governments can commit themselves to regulatory strategies that would not be credible in the absence of such delegation (Gatsios and Seabright 1989).

Also the framers of the founding treaties knew that the commitment of the member states to European integration would lack credibility without the delegation of important powers to independent supranational institutions. Thus Article 157 (2) of the Treaty of Rome states: 'The members of the Commission shall, in the general interest of the Communities, be completely independent in the performance of their duties. In the performance of these duties they shall neither seek nor take instructions from any Government or from any other body ... ' The progressive parliamentarization of the Commission not only departs from the spirit, if not from the letter, of the treaty, but raises in acute form the issue of the consistency and credibility of EC regulatory policies. The delegation of powers for regulatory bodies distinct from the Commission itself, or at least enjoying significant decisional autonomy, would provide the most effective solution to the consistency and credibility problem under the new political conditions prevailing in the Union.

As previously mentioned, delegation of powers to independent European agencies has been impeded, in part, by a narrow reading of Article 4 of the Treaty of Rome. This article lists the various European institutions, and states that each of them must act 'within the limits of the powers conferred upon them by this Treaty'. This has been interpreted as a general prohibition on the establishment of additional bodies, so that nothing short of a treaty revision would allow for the creation of truly independent agencies. The ECJ, with its Meroni doctrine, has slightly eased the consequences of such a reading of the Treaty, thus allowing the Commission to delegate certain of its executive functions to bodies not named in the Treaty, but such delegation is subject to severe limitations. At any rate, this so-called Meroni doctrine is totally out of step with the development of European regulatory policies. Lip-service notwithstanding, it has de facto been overruled. It is true that the agencies created in the early 1990s—such bodies as the European Environment Agency, the European Agency for the Evaluation of Medicinal Products, and the European Agency for Safety and Health at Work—have not been granted formal independence. However, their creation suggests a large functional need not satisfied by the existing institutions. Their very existence confirms that the Commission, as well as the member states, are becoming increasingly aware of the severe mismatch between the increasingly specialized functions of the Community and the administrative instruments at its disposal (Majone 2000).

THE POLITICS OF INSTITUTIONAL CHOICE

It is tempting to think that the creation of European agencies with autonomous powers of rule making, adjudication, and enforcement would represent the optimal solution to the current regulatory problems of the Union. This solution is suggested by efficiency considerations, as well as by the experience of countries like the United

States. It is supported by leaders of European industry in various areas of regulation, from air traffic control to food safety. For example, Anthony Burgman, co-chairman of the Anglo-Dutch multinational, Unilever, has advocated a powerful and independent European Food Safety Agency on the model of the US Food and Drug Administration. A strong European agency would streamline the testing and introduction of new food products which is now left to the member states, and help restore consumers' confidence after such episodes as the dioxin food scare in Belgium and the bovine spongiform encephalopathy (BSE) crisis in the United Kingdom.

Burgman is aware that national governments would probably oppose the loss of powers to a centralized agency, but he warned that the absence of a powerful EU-wide agency could leave European customers at the mercy of US food producers (*Financial Times*, 7 September 1999: 2). However, the proposal for an independent European Food Authority advanced by the new White Paper on food safety of the European Commission (Commission 2000*b*) falls far short of what Anthony Burgman and other industry leaders would have liked. The Authority is supposed to monitor developments, touching upon food safety issues, provide scientific advice, collect and analyse information, and communicate its findings to all interested parties. Thus it would be responsible for risk analysis and risk communication, but would have no regulatory powers. Once more, bureaucratic inertia and vested interests, at national and European levels, have prevented the emergence of much needed institutional innovations.

This and many similar examples show that political actors are well aware that institutional choices have significant consequences for the context and direction of policy. They are prepared to invest considerable resources in order to influence such choices in their favour, so that issues of institutional design are caught up in politics as much as issues of policy. As Terry Moe (1990: 127) writes: 'however grand and lofty the policies that emerge from the political process, it is virtually guaranteed that the bureaucratic arrangements that go along with them, are the product of compromise and thus, in part, are designed by opponents to ensure that the policies are not achieved'. In the context of institutional choice, political compromise means that opposing groups have a direct say in how an agency and its mandate are constructed. Political compromise offers a chance for the opponents of the new policies to have a say in the design of the implementing agencies, and thus to impose structures that make effective performance difficult to achieve. This simple political model of institutional choice helps us to understand the origin and particular organizational design of a body like the European Environment Agency.

The European Environment Agency (EEA) has been established by the Council Regulation No. 1210/90 of 7 May 1990. Article 20 of the Regulation states: 'No longer than two years after entry into force of this Regulation ... the Council shall decide on further tasks for the Agency ... ' The possible new tasks include: associating the EEA in the monitoring of the implementation of Community environmental legislation, in cooperation with the Commission and existing competent bodies in the member states; awarding environmental labels to environmentally friendly products, services, and technologies; establishing criteria for assessing environmental impacts 'with a view to application and possible revision of Directive 85/337/EEC'. These three tasks were some of the demands of the advocates of a more powerful environmental agency. Their inclusion in the revision clause of the enabling statute is an important part of the political compromise which made the creation of the EEA possible. All member states, political parties and European institutions voiced support for the proposal of an environmental agency at the European level, made by Jacques Delors, the Commission President, in January 1989. However, this general agreement concealed deep divisions concerning specific structural choices, especially those concerning the regulatory powers and effective autonomy of the new agency.

The European Parliament (EP), green parties, and some top Commission officials (such as Commissioner Ripa di Meana, head of the Directorate General for the environment which at the time was called DG XI) wanted a body with regulatory 'teeth'. In varying degrees all member states opposed the idea that the agency could monitor the implementation of European environmental legislation by national regulators, preferring to restrict its task to the collection and coordination of environmental information, and to networking with other research institutions at national, European, and international levels. The position of the majority of the Commission officials was rather ambivalent. On the one hand, officials like Laurens Jan Brinkhorst, at the time Director General of DG XI, were concerned about the criticism of industry and of some member states, especially Great Britain, that DG XI proposals were not grounded in 'good science'. They were even more concerned by the poor implementation of environmental directives at the national level, and realized that having accurate, comparable, and more credible data on the quality of the environment in the member states was an important step towards improving implementation of EC environmental legislation. Thus the idea that the EEA could become a sort of inspectorate of national environmental inspectorates, along the lines of the existing Fisheries Inspectorate, had a number of influential supporters in the Commission, as well as in the EP. On the other hand, DG XI was reluctant to surrender regulatory powers to an agency operating at arm's length. Commissioner Ripa di Meana, initially a supporter of an independent EEA, realized that the Treaty of Rome, interpreted in the light of the Meroni doctrine, probably prevented the delegation of decision-making powers to a new body, and called the attention of the EP to this legal impediment. The Commission proposal of 21 June 1989 outlined four functions for the new agency: (a) coordinate the enactment of EC and national environmental policies; (b) evaluate the results of the environmental measures; (c) provide modelling and environmental forecasting techniques; (d) harmonize processing and storage of environmental data to facilitate information exchanges with other international organizations. Being aware of the opposition of the member states to the inspectorate model, the Commission did not propose any inspection tasks for the EEA.

This proposal was quite distant from the EP's 'ideal point'. The fact that Beate Weber, the rapporteur of the Environmental Committee, travelled to Washington, DC to gain first-hand knowledge of the US Environmental Protection Agency, suggests the model of regulatory agency that European parliamentarians had in mind.

Between November 1989 and February 1990 Frau Weber drafted an opinion which sought to extend the role of the agency beyond that envisaged by the Commission and the Council. The Environmental Committee maintained that the EEA should be given power to inspect and police environmental abuses, and enforce EC environmental regulations along the lines of the inspection teams that monitor compliance with European fishing and competition rules. The Committee also argued that the agency should carry out environmental impact assessments on certain projects funded by the European Community, both inside the Community and in non-EC countries, and that it should be given the task of developing a Community green label for environmentally-friendly products. The EP further believed that the agency should be autonomous from the Commission. Also the composition of the management board of the EEA—the body which sets priorities for the work of the agency—became a point of contention. According to the EP, environmentalist groups should be represented on the board, along with representatives from the member states, the Commission, and the EP itself, and the board should be allowed to take decisions by majority vote.

Comparing the preferences of the main political actors—member states, EP, Commission—with the provisions of Council Regulation 1210/90, one sees that the member states clearly won the contest over institutional choice. The main task assigned to the agency is to provide the Community and the member states with the objective information needed for framing and implementing sound and effective environmental policies and, in particular, 'to provide the Commission with the information that it needs to be able to carry out successfully its tasks of identifying, preparing, and evaluating measures and legislation in the field of environment' (Article 2). The wording is sufficiently vague, however, that it is not clear whether the agency would be allowed directly to influence policy formulation, for example, by evaluating alternative proposals for regulatory measures, as suggested by its executive director. In fact, until now the EEA has not been allowed to carry out research that is directly policy relevant.

Furthermore, the Regulation fails to clarify the relationship between the agency and the Commission, on the one hand, and the national environmental regulators, on the other. The decisive influence of the member states is also revealed by the composition of the management board, which consists of one representative of each member state, two Commission representatives, and two scientific personalities designated by the European Parliament. The executive director of the EEA is appointed by the management board, on a proposal from the Commission, and is accountable to the board for the activities of the agency. As already noted, the main concession to the advocates of an agency with real regulatory powers is contained in Article 20 of the enabling regulation, but this is simply a promise to reconsider certain competences of the EEA in the future. So far, the agency has not been given any significant role in the EC regulatory process. Political compromise has produced an institutional design characterized by uncertain competences, unresolved conflicts, and failure to deal with the serious implementation problem of Community environmental regulation.

CONCLUSION

In a democracy policy is supposed to be made by electorally accountable leaders. When these leaders decide to delegate important powers to politically independent institutions such as central banks or regulatory bodies operating at national, European, or international level, they solve one problem—how to make credible long-term policy commitments—but they simultaneously raise a new one: the problem of accountability. Whether this dilemma can be resolved depends to a large extent on one's understanding of democracy.

Political philosophers distinguish two different conceptions of democracy, both compatible with Abraham Lincoln's notion of 'government of the people, by the people, for the people'. The first, represented by the majoritarian or populistic model of democracy, tends to concentrate all political power in the hands of the current majority. According to this conception, majorities should be able to control all of government, and thus to control everything that politics can touch. By contrast, the non-majoritarian (or Madisonian, after James Madison) model of democracy aims to share, disperse, delegate, and limit power in a variety of ways. The overriding objective is, to use Madisonian language, to protect minorities against the 'tyranny of the majority' and to create safeguards against 'factionalism'—the usurpation of government by powerful and self-interested groups. In particular, delegation of powers attempts to restrain majority rule and discretionary policy by placing public authority in the hands of officials who have limited or no direct accountability to either political majorities or minorities.

Within the non-majoritarian model of democracy—which is just another name for constitutional democracy—reliance upon qualities such as expertise, credibility, fairness, or independence has always been considered more important than reliance upon direct political accountability—but only for some limited purposes. The legitimacy of independent institutions in a constitutional democracy depends crucially on how precisely those purposes are defined. This is because accountability by results cannot be enforced when the objectives are either too vague or too broad.

The main task delegated to regulatory agencies is to correct market failures so as to increase aggregate welfare. This implies, *inter alia*, that regulatory instruments should not be used for redistributive purposes. Regulatory policies, like all public policies, have redistributive consequences. However, for the regulator such consequences should represent potential policy constraints rather than policy objectives. Only a commitment to the maximization of aggregate welfare, and to accountability by results, can legitimize the political independence of regulators. By the same token, decisions involving significant redistribution of resources from one social group to another cannot legitimately be taken by independent experts, but only by elected officials or by administrators directly responsible to elected officials.

From the perspective of the positive theory of regulation, the influence of politics on regulatory policies and institutions appears to be pervasive, as shown, for example, by the discussion in the previous section. From a normative perspective, however, it is equally clear that 'political' solutions complex regulatory problems tend to be unstable—since they can always be subverted by a new majority—and because of their inefficiency, they can undermine the legitimacy of the political system. However difficult to draw in practice, the distinction between policy and politics—or, more precisely, between efficiency-enhancing and redistributive policies—is an essential element of constitutional democracy. The delegation of powers to independent regulatory institutions is one way of emphasizing this distinction and thus strengthen the democratic process.

18

From Industrial Policy to a Regulatory State: Contrasting Institutional Change in Britain and France

MARK THATCHER

Britain and France are *frères enemis* in economic policy: as European nations, they compete over financial outcomes and successful policies. They offer a rich source of evidence to ask broader questions about economic policy making, particularly over the role of national institutions. On the one hand, the two countries are subject to similar regional political, technological, and economic forces, yet on the other, they enjoy differing state traditions and institutions.

The present chapter compares industrial policy and economic regulation in Britain and France in order to consider national capacities to alter institutions and policy norms. Analyses of the period between 1945 and 1980 have claimed that French policy makers enjoyed much greater innovatory capacities than their British counterparts. They use industrial policy as an example to support their views. Yet the reverse held true in the 1980s and 1990s: Britain was able to introduce more comprehensive reforms, and did so with less difficulty and earlier than France. It moved decisively towards a 'regulatory state', whereas France followed the same direction of change but at a slower, more hesitant pace, without adopting a new rationale for state action. The chapter analyses how and why this was so from a historical institutionalist perspective before drawing some more general conclusions about institutional change.

NATIONAL INNOVATORY CAPACITIES AND INDUSTRIAL POLICY IN BRITAIN AND FRANCE 1945–80

Historical institutionalist analyses argue that national institutions—both formal structures and less formal policy norms and state traditions—are long-standing and differ among countries. National institutional differences lead to dissimilarities in policies, the processes of decision making, economic performance; they also influence the nature and path of change in policies and institutions (Hall 1986; Thelen and Steinmo 1992; Hall and Taylor 1996; Immergut 1998; Peters 1999; Thelen 1999). The focus of the present chapter is on institutional change, both of formal structures and of the norms of policy. Existing institutions influence national innovatory capacities.

Hence countries differ in their ability to introduce reforms. Institutional factors that are important for change and national innovatory capabilities can be grouped under four headings: state structure; links between the state and society; the structure of society; state traditions (cf. Hall 1986, 1983; Cortell and Peterson 1999).

The structure of the state, particularly the form of the executive and legislature, rules governing relations between political leaders and their officials, and the number of veto players/points in making decisions, affects the ability of political leaders to formulate policies (cf. Weaver and Rockman 1991; Immergut 1992; Tsebelis 1995). The structure of state–society relations influences the leverage that policy makers have over non-governmental interests and the capacity of the two to cooperate; important features include the extent of interpenetration between public and private sectors, and the existence of mechanisms for collaboration between them. The structure of society, including the extent of fragmentation of private actors and their resources, affects the balance of power between state and society. Finally, nations have differing state traditions and policy styles that influence the acceptance of state leadership and power (Dyson 1980; Richardson 1982).

Comparison of Britain and France offers a valuable illustration of differences in national innovatory capacities. France has appeared much better able to change than Britain, thanks to its institutions (Hayward 1976; Hall 1983, 1986). Its political system has allowed political leaders to mobilize resources to overcome inertia. Under the Fifth Republic, the presidential system concentrated power around a single individual, who could call upon direct legitimacy, traditions of strong personalities, and appropriate personnel, including a well-trained civil service and a large Elysée staff (Wright 1989). Although the French state was marked by internal divisions and rivalries, notably between *corps*[1] and among ministries and bureaux, in selected areas focused political leadership could overcome such obstacles, aided by an activist 'policy style' (Hayward 1982). The *grands corps* provided a group of well-trained leaders that spanned politics, administration, and, increasingly big business. Relationships between the state and private firms were constant and intimate, aided by the expansion of '*pantouflage*' between them. The private and public sectors were linked and could work closely together. France had a tradition of a strong state, and norms that encouraged and lauded a '*dirigiste*' state (Dyson 1980). 'Civil society' was weak and pressure groups were often 'pressured groups' (Hayward 1983).

Britain suffered from a weak state, with its nineteenth century suspicion of state action (Dyson 1980). It lacked effective mechanisms for political leadership. The British Prime Minister was surrounded by powerful potential rivals and lacked a proper Number 10 staff. Whitehall civil servants were cut off from industry, not only by lack of movement between the two but also by education and social snobbery (Weiner 1981). There were few mechanisms for cooperation between them. Civil society was strong and powerful lobbies could block change. In particular,

---

[1] On entering public service, officials join a *corps* or group, to which they often remain attached throughout their lives, even if they leave public service; the *corps* operates as a form of professional 'family' with close links and aid among its members; the most prestigious and powerful corps are known as the *grands corps*.

powerful financial interests of 'the City' hindered an activist industrial policy (Hall 1986). The trade unions were able to mobilize support but were too divided to act as effective partners in attempts to build corporatist agreements on wages, prices, investment, and employment. Finally, state traditions ran counter to activist public action; instead, a strong skepticism, if not outright hostility, existed towards a strong state.

Industrial policy illustrated how dissimilar institutions in Britain and France influenced change (Shonfield 1965; Hayward 1976; Hall 1983, 1986; Mény and Wright 1987). Industrial policy between 1945 and 1980 appeared to show the greater innovatory capabilities available to French policy makers even in the face of powerful forces for continuity. France was able to establish a planning process, with the Commissariat du Plan, which provided impetus to alter policy and a capacity to influence investment and priorities, in both the public and private sectors (Stoléru 1969; Hayward and Watson 1975). As part of its 'state-led capitalist' model of policy (Hayward 1983; Schmidt 1996), French policy makers reorganized key markets through *grands projets industriels* in fields such as telecommunications, aerospace, railways, and energy (Stoffaës 1983; Muller 1989; Cohen 1992; Thatcher 1999). The *grands projets* involved large-scale, long-term, and sustained public investment, applying financial instruments developed for such purposes, and constant close interaction between policy makers and suppliers. French firms, public and private, developed world leads in new technologies such as nuclear power, high-speed trains, digital telecommunications, and jets. Policy makers were able to select, promote, and indeed create (by reorganizing sectors via mergers and exchanges of activities) 'national champion' firms such as CGE/Alcatel, Thompson, Dassault, and Aerospatial.

In contrast, institutional innovation was extremely difficult in Britain. Changes in state ownership (both privatization and increased nationalization) encountered powerful opposition from employees/trade unions or the private sector—for example, after 1945, the only major industry to be privatized in Britain was steel, whilst the Labour government's attempts to extend public ownership between 1974 and 1979 were very controversial and largely abandoned. Promises to 'roll back the state' and allow much greater play for the market by cutting public expenditure and ending support for 'lame duck' industries were quickly dropped when faced with rising unemployment and industrial unrest (e.g. the U turns performed by Edward Heath's Conservative government between 1970 and 1974). Attempts to copy the French planning institutions produced a pale imitation (Hall 1986). The government seemed unable even to reorganize key sectors or select national champions—for example, it spent twenty years failing to reduce the numbers of telecommunications manufacturers from three to two (Cawson *et al.* 1990; Thatcher 1999). Most government activity seemed to be reacting to crises in declining industries, such as in the motor industry and shipbuilding, and even here, with little success (Grant 1989). Government and industry relations (including with public sector firms) were marked by a much greater distance than in France. The main British success story, the financial sector, was largely left to informal regulation led by private organizations such as those in the City and Lloyds of London. The interests of the City were uppermost in policy, seen, for example, in attempts to maintain the exchange rate at all costs and squeezes on public spending; other industries suffered from the consequences of a large, powerful financial sector (Hall 1986).

By the late 1970s, the contrasts between British and French industrial policy appeared to be well established. Whereas France could adapt and innovate, Britain suffered from much greater inertia (Hayward 1976; Hall 1983, 1986). When economic crisis occurred in the 1970s and early 1980s, the two countries adopted different strategies of adaptation (Dyson 1983). The French state followed a much more *dirigiste* activist strategy, in contrast to the more reactive British one (Machin and Wright 1985; Cawson *et al.* 1990; cf. Cohen 1992).

REFORM IN BRITAIN, OBSTACLES IN FRANCE: MOVES TOWARDS A REGULATORY STATE IN THE 1980s AND 1990s

Major changes in the institutions of industrial policy were introduced in Britain and France during the 1980s and 1990s. Long-standing structural features of the state and policy norms were altered. The two countries moved towards a 'regulatory state' (cf. Majone 1996). In industrial policy, this involved four key features: privatization of state-owned enterprises; liberalization—that is, ending state monopolies; 're-regulation'—that is, establishing rules governing competitive supply; establishing or strengthening independent/semi-independent regulatory bodies.

However, the move towards a 'regulatory state' differed between the two countries. The reforms were marked by a reversal of the relative capacities for change of the British and French states. British policy makers were able to introduce large-scale institutional changes; they did so quickly and sometimes in the face of powerful opposition. In contrast, their French counterparts were obliged to proceed at a slower pace and to offer substantial concessions to opponents. Moreover, they had difficulty legitimating reforms, which were often introduced covertly and/or only in response to apparently overwhelming pressures. The strategies of French policy makers spoke of profound ambivalence about the changes being introduced. The policy style of the 1980s and 1990s thus became British boldness, but French hesitancy.

Sweeping privatization was introduced in Britain (cf. Richardson 1994; Heald 1988; Vickers and Wright 1988; Vickers and Yarrow 1988; Feigenbaum *et al.* 1999). Conservative governments after 1979 began with limited sales of public corporations in competitive markets—for instance, British Petroleum, British Aerospace, and Amersham International. Thereafter they moved to other sectors with very long-standing state ownership, notably the utilities—for example, BT, the CEGB, regional water companies, and British Gas. The Labour government after 1997 continued to sell off remaining state assets, even turning to part privatization of the air traffic control system (Nats). The pace and extent of change were remarkable: by 2001, there were almost no publicly owned suppliers of industrial and financial goods and services. Privatization extended to domains financed by the public sector—for instance, the Private Finance Initiative (PFI) involving private financing, construction, and operation of public facilities such as hospitals, roads, and buildings; the provision of public services such as management of education, legal services, and refuse collection were contracted out to private companies.

Privatization was introduced by governments in the face of determined opposition. Employees and trade unions in public corporations took industrial action—for example, the sale of a majority stake in BT was met with a lengthy strike, as were contracting out measures. During the 1980s, the Labour Party promised to reverse most privatizations. Public opinion was hostile to several major sales (e.g. the water companies and railways) and expert opinion was sceptical about private ownership of 'natural monopolies'. The sales were a radical break with decades of institutional stability—telecommunications operators had been totally state-owned since 1912; municipal ownership of gas, water, and electricity dated from the nineteenth century. Despite these obstacles, governments were able to extend privatization rapidly, transforming the extent of state ownership in under twenty years.

New regulatory frameworks replaced long-standing arrangements such as state monopolies or informal regulation. Sectoral regulatory bodies were established; they were created by statute and were semi-independent from the government. The most prominent were in the utilities (Thatcher 1998; Prosser 1997)—for example, the Offices of Telecommunications (Oftel), the Office of Gas Supply (Ofgas), the Office of Electricity Regulation (Offer),[2] and the Office of Rail Regulator. Even in the previously hallowed domain of the City, statutory regulation was introduced: the Financial Services Authority was created and the supervisory powers of the Bank of England were transferred to the FSA in 1997. Regulators were given many powers, notably to enforce licences and standards, to modify licences, and to ensure that competition was 'fair' (Prosser 1997; Thatcher 1998). A host of legal rules replaced state monopolies in the utilities and informal codes of behaviour in financial services. Thus, for instance, suppliers in the utilities and many financial markets were obliged to obtain licences and meet requirements (set out in the licences and/or legislation) over matters such as quality, interconnection, complaints procedures, accounting norms, and prices (to name but a few of the areas covered).

The norms of state action in Britain saw a shift away from protecting national champions and rescuing 'lame ducks' towards liberalization, competitiveness, and rule-based state action. Private firms found they could not count on government protection against predators from abroad. Takeovers were accepted and sometimes led by governments. Potent symbols of British industry such as British Leyland/Rover were sold off to foreign companies and takeovers of large companies, including the privatized electricity and water companies or large banks, by overseas firms were not resisted by the government. Competition became the centrepiece of policy. It was a key criterion in decisions over takeovers. Sectoral regulators frequently stated that their overriding aim was to encourage competition, this being the best way to promote consumer interests (see, for instance, Carsberg 1989). In the late 1990s, the Competition Commission and utility regulators were given new powers to impose heavier penalties for anti-competitive behaviour.

---

[2] Merged in 2000 to form Ofgem—the Office of Gas and Electricity Markets.

These changes did not mean de-politicization, but rather a modification in the form of government action. Its role was to restructure regulation and the state, notably in privatizing, establishing regulatory bodies, determining their powers and resources, issuing licences, and extending competition. Regulatory agencies became key actors in setting the new norms centred around competition, thanks to their expertise, statutory powers, and specialization (Thatcher 1998). Individual ministerial interventions in the decisions of suppliers became rarer; the most frequent occasions concerned mergers and takeovers, but even here, in 2000, the Secretary of State for Trade and Industry, announced that he would follow the recommendations of the Office of Fair Trading (OFT) and Competition Commission save in exceptional circumstances. Although ministers appointed heads of regulatory bodies, the personnel chosen were rarely party politicians, and in the late 1990s, procedures such as public advertisements for posts began. Moreover, once appointed, regulators have enjoyed a considerable degree of separation from ministerial intervention, aided by the protection of judicial review.

Privatization in France was slower, more limited, and more ambivalent than in Britain (Zahariadis 1995; Feigenbaum *et al.* 1999). Following the Left's victories in 1981, large-scale nationalizations were undertaken, but these were curtailed in 1983 as the government turned to an austerity programme and sought to ensure that publicly owned firms became profitable (Barreau *et al.* 1990; Smith 1995; Schmidt 1996, 1997). The Chirac Government of 1986–8 undertook a large-scale privatization programme (Zahariadis 1995; Bauer 1988), mostly of financial enterprises, but its defeats in the 1988 Presidential and parliamentary elections and Mitterrand's 'ni-ni' pledge in 1988 (neither more nationalizations nor privatizations) represented a brake on change (Dumez and Jeunemaître 1994). Privatizations accelerated after the Right returned to government in 1993, although they remained focused on financial enterprises. In the 1997 parliamentary elections, the Left promised to end privatizations; in practice, the Jospin Government accelerated sales, but the decisions were made *sotto voce* and in response to intense pressures rather than as an explicit strategy of reforming the state.

Privatizations were delayed and limited by strong opposition, especially by trade unions and employees. In sensitive cases, sales took the form of partial openings of capital and employees were given guarantees as to their employment status. Thus, for example, the partial privatization of France Télécom in 1997 took several years to achieve, in the face of several strikes; a statutory limit (of 49 per cent) was placed on it; existing employees were allowed to keep their civil service status and recruitment of employees as civil servants was to be continued until 2002 (Thatcher 1999). 'Hidden privatizations' were used—for instance, suppliers which remained fully state-owned such as EdF, SNCF, or La Poste, established subsidiaries to cooperate with private sector firms and to expand abroad. Several suppliers formed international joint ventures or alliances with private companies (e.g. Air France and Delta Airlines in the 'Skyteam' alliance). Privatizations were often presented by Left and Right as reluctant responses to inexorable and overwhelming outside forces: EC 'imposed' competition; the need for international alliances; fiscal constraints;

the financial needs of publicly owned firms. The result was that, by 2001, France had moved hesitantly towards away from the previous model of public ownership of sectors towards a patchwork: in contrast to Britain, state ownership remained in domains such as telecommunications, electricity and gas, the railways, and airlines (Coen and Thatcher 2000).

Liberalization took place in France, but it too arrived later and was more limited than in Britain. Thus full competition in telecommunications only took place in 1998 (and even so, in practice, was difficult), and competition in energy supply was limited. Traditional price-setting arrangements in the private sector, often involving state approval, were ended and general competition regulation was strengthened (Albert 1992), but government ministers retained many important formal powers (for instance, over prices or universal service), as well as influence through state ownership of suppliers. Liberalization attracted opposition, especially from parts of the political Left, trade unions, and the employees of state suppliers. External justifications were generally needed for ending monopolies and state support schemes. This applied even though public enterprises and their monopolies were increasingly facing difficulties in sustaining their monopolies (due to desires to internationalize, cost pressures, and supra-national regulation) and were engaging in preparations for competition such as tariff re-balancing and internationalization (cf. Quélin 1994; Bauby 1997; Rouban 1997; Cauchon 1998; Thatcher 1999). The most common method was for France to wait for EC-wide requirements, which were then presented as 'imposed' by Brussels and which acted as a 'catalyst' for change (cf. Cohen 1996; Henry 1997; Rouban 1997; Commissariat du Plan 2000; Le Galès 2001a). This approach applied even when competition was in the interests of French suppliers and users. Thus for instance in electricity, liberalization offered opportunities rather than threats to Électicité de France (EdF): it enjoyed low-cost nuclear-generated electricity (given the write-off of fixed costs) which it supplied to other countries; it was able to engage in takeovers of foreign suppliers, such as British regional electricity companies. Yet although the threat of EC legal action provided an important justification for reform, the Jospin Government was unable to pass legislation in 1999–2000 to open up part of the electricity sector to competition due to opposition by the PCF in parliament, missing EC deadlines. Re-regulation developed alongside liberalization, but its objectives were confused, attempting to combine 'fair and effective competition', protection of *service public*, and offering covert support for 'national champions', public and private. Thus in telecommunications, electricity, and railways, universal service obligations sat uneasily with attempts to move prices closer to costs, to protect certain groups of users, to ensure that the French incumbent maintained its dominant position whilst also ensuring that France met its EC obligations and opened its market sufficiently to permit French firms to enjoy reciprocal access to overseas markets (Chevallier 1997; Henry 1997). No overall hierarchy of principles emerged. Competition jostled with rival views of *service public*.

New regulatory bodies were created but the process took place later in France and more slowly than in Britain. Semi-independent agencies were created for telecommunications, broadcasting, the railways, electricity, the stock exchange, and general competition. Nevertheless, the degree of independence enjoyed by the agencies was limited. Appointments were highly politicized: typically, the President and the heads of the two houses of Parliament each nominate members of regulatory bodies such as those for telecommunications and broadcasting (the ART—Autorité de Régulation des Télécommunications—and the CSA—the Conseil Supérieur de l'Audiovisuel). The individuals chosen have frequently had clear links with political parties.

Previous norms of protecting national champions and obstructing entry by foreign firms also evolved, but slowly and ambivalently (Schmidt 1996; Hayward 1997). When necessary, vast sums of public money were pumped into loss-making firms to prevent their collapse; the most spectacular examples were the Crédit Lyonnais, whose cost to the state rose to 140 billion francs, and firms in the electronics industry (Bolloc'H-Puges 1991). Policy makers sought to prevent foreign takeovers through state leadership or at least participation in restructuring. Thus privatization was justified by the need to create viable national champions, transform them into 'international players', and protect them from takeovers (cf. Bauer 1988; Maclean 1997). '*Noyaux durs*' of core shareholders were created for privatized firms, themselves often linked by cross-shareholdings, to protect them from predators. During the 1990s, policy makers sought to create European or international champions through mergers of French firms to establish much larger entities and alliances and takeovers of overseas companies (Hayward 1997). Thus, for example, the Jospin Government sold Aerospatial to Matra in order to create EADS, and in the car industry the government during the 1990s sought to partner Renault with Volvo. In telecommunications the alliance between France Télécom and Deutsche Telekom was a central objective of policy for most of the 1990s (Thatcher 1999). In the financial sector, the government and Banque de France have sought to establish several large-scale French banks (for instance, encouraging mergers/takeovers between the BNP, Paribas, and the Société Générale, or Indosuez and the Crédit Agricole).

Yet in contrast to the rhetoric of policy and often out of the limelight, practices altered and France moved hesitantly away from supporting its traditional industrial policy. Ailing state firms such as the Crédit Lyonnais, once restored to financial balance, were sold off. The creation of strong French firms was frequently a precursor to alliances with foreign ones—for example, in aerospace and banking. Overseas companies were accepted as equal or junior partners, or as sources of investment in selected sectors of manufacturing. In banking, attempts by officials failed to create a three-way merger between Paribas, BNP, and la Société Générale in 1999 to keep out entrants such as the German firm Allianz. (However, a two-way merger of BNP and Paribas took place.) Takeovers by foreign companies remained rare, especially hostile ones, but by the 1990s became possible (e.g. Allianz's 1998 takeover of AGF—Assurances Générales de France—or HSBC's acquisition of CCF in 1999).

One reason for slow changes in norms was the increasing gap between rhetoric and the reality of policy (Cohen 1996; Hayward 1997; Schmidt 1997). Whilst in practice France moved away from its previous *dirigiste* policies (Schmidt 1997; Wright 1997*a*), politicians and policy makers continued to claim that the state could and should lead industrial restructuring and promoting French firms (cf. Esambert 1992). Difficulties with traditional industrial policies were ascribed to external impositions arising from globalization, 'unrestrained liberalism', and the European Union (Guersent 1996; Dauba 1997; Duharcourt 1997). The principles of *service public* were defended and indeed proclaimed as a 'French specificity' (Boiteux 1996). On the Right, politicians such as Jacques Chirac and Alain Juppé rapidly abandoned references to liberalism; Chirac campaigned in the 1995 presidential elections on the theme of the 'social fracture'. The major proponent of liberalism, Alain Madelin, resigned as Finance Minister after only a few months in office in August 1995. On the Left, political leaders promised to preserve an activist state in the face of globalization and the European Union. Yet in practice, French policy makers adapted industrial policies, accepting and often welcoming opportunities to do so and move away from increasingly ineffective strategies of subsidising failing firms and attempting to create 'national champions'.

Thus by 2000, Britain and France had both altered their institutions of industrial policy. Both had moved towards a 'regulatory state'. They had privatized, liberalized, established semi-independent regulators, and re-regulated. The norms of policy had altered. However, change had been more far-reaching in Britain than France. Opposition had been greater in France, and had been more effective in delaying and limiting change and in forcing concessions. Moreover, French policy makers showed great ambivalence about reform: changes were justified by necessities such as the EC or internationalization, and were often introduced covertly, whilst the norms of policy continued to be public service, the promotion of (inter)national champions, and a strong state leadership. Why was France less able to overcome opposition and alter formal and informal institutions, leaving it ambiguous and hesitant in the 1980s and 1990s, whereas Britain embraced change? The question is particularly interesting as it marked a reversal of the situation between 1945 and 1980.

EXPLAINING DIFFERENCES IN NATIONAL INNOVATION IN THE 1980s AND 1990s

No single factor can explain the greater innovation in the move from industrial policy towards a regulatory state seen in Britain than in France during the 1980s and 1990s. Rather, several interlocking factors contributed, using similar explanatory factors as those applied to analyse innovatory capacities before 1980: the structure of the state, state–society links, the structure of society, and state traditions. The four categories permit comparison with the situation before the 1980s when France had greater innovatory capacities than Britain.

The Structure of the State and Political Leadership

Powerful presidential leadership was one of the keys to France's greater innovatory capacities before 1980. However, the presidency was weakened during the 1980s and 1990s, revealing dependence on political leadership and the importance of potential veto points in France. In contrast, Britain experienced strong political leadership, which showed how the British state could lead radical changes.

Throughout the 1980s and 1990s, Britain had single party majority governments that adopted strategies of moving towards a regulatory state. The Conservative Party believed that it derived political advantages from privatization, including electoral support for 'popular capitalism' and focusing debate on its vision of a smaller state. From the 1990s, 'New Labour' sought to be the 'party of business' and leave behind its 'old fashioned big state' position. Once internal party agreement had been secured, governments were able to pass legislation and faced few veto players (cf. Tsebelis 1995). In practice, party leaderships were able to exercise powerful discipline and prime ministers such as Margaret Thatcher and Tony Blair enjoyed great power. There were few constitutional restrictions on legislation: the House of Lords delayed and amended many regulatory changes but could not prevent a determined government pressing ahead, and the courts played little role in restricting governments. Strong political leadership allowed governments to make unpopular changes, such as the water, rail, and air traffic control privatizations, and to overcome opposition from trade unions and public sector employees. It also meant that government could pursue large-scale reforms openly.

In contrast, for much of the 1980s and 1990s, the French 'dyarchy' of President and government was divided and weak. Thus the privatizations of the Chirac and Balladur Governments (1986–8 and 1993–5) were introduced under *cohabitation* with forthcoming presidential elections in which the prime ministers were candidates (Dumez and Jeunemaître 1994). Mitterrand warned against controversial privatizations and used his powers to block sales by decree in 1986, forcing the Chirac Government of 1986–8 to pass primary legislation, a difficult task given its narrow parliamentary majority. Divisions within Right and Left placed constraints on bold reform, as opponents from the same political wing manoeuvred for advantage. Thus, for instance, Mitterrand's long-standing feud with Michel Rocard (Prime Minister 1988–90) hampered change, and Chirac and Balladur were rival presidential candidates in 1995. Even between 1995 and 1997, when the Right held both the presidency and majorities in parliament, there was a nationalistic, strong state faction within the RPR led by Philippe Séguin that was hostile to Alain Juppé's Government. The 'Plural Left' government after 1997 was constrained by Jospin's election promises in 1995 and 1997, by factions within the Socialist Party, and by its reliance on the Communist Party for its parliamentary majority. Constitutional constraints were much stronger than in Britain. The 1986 Law on privatizations established a Valuations Commission that set minimum prices for shares, whilst notions of *service public* that were well anchored within French legal and political doctrines limited liberalization and privatization, especially in the utilities (Chevallier 1997; Rouban 1997).

The weaknesses of French political leadership hampered the introduction of a clear direction and rationale for change. Reforms had to be accepted by numerous veto players and allowed their opponents greater opportunities for resistance. Policy makers often had to negotiate patiently, prepare opinion for change, and/or wait for external justifications for reform such as financial crisis or EC requirements.

The Structure of Relationships between Governments and Firms

Whereas before 1980 the weakness of institutional links between policy makers and firms cramped industrial policy in Britain, the gap between them aided the move towards a regulatory state in the 1980s and 1990s. Interests within and outside the state realized that they had much to gain and little to lose from institutional reform. The drawbacks of the public sector were important in privatization in Britain. Within Whitehall, the nationalized industries were seen as a millstone, and a 'bureau-shaping' explanation of the sales points to the advantages for senior policy makers of offloading unrewarding technical decisions onto private companies and regulators, leaving Whitehall with grander 'strategic' matters (Dunleavy 1986). The managements of nationalized industries became increasingly restless in the 1970s and 1980s when faced with cuts in their expenditure and 'political interference' by Whitehall over matters such as prices and profit targets. They were particularly concerned about investment: due to arcane public sector accounting rules, no distinction was made between current and capital spending, so that public sector borrowing targets in the 1970s and 1980s were often achieved by reducing the investment plans of nationalized industries (Redwood and Hatch 1982; Likierman 1988). Moreover, constant alterations in investment targets to meet fiscal and electoral 'fine tuning' damaged medium-term planning. Initially, the managements of nationalized industries were sceptical or opposed to sales, but they were won over by the advantages of the private sector, notably the promise of greater freedom from Whitehall control, higher investment, and the abandonment of most break-up plans, not to mention sharp increases in their incomes once in the private sector. The privatization of BT in 1984 served as an influential example. It was sold as an integrated entity, despite pressure by Mrs Thatcher to break it up, and was then able to raise capital expenditure, profits, and management salaries.

The separation of state and industry discouraged ad hoc interventions in the internal decisions of suppliers by politicians and Whitehall civil servants. After privatization, specialized semi-independent regulators, such as Oftel, Ofwat, the Environment Agency, and Ofgem became central actors in regulation (Thatcher 1998). They had greater technical expertise than ministers and civil servants. Much of their power lay in determining and altering suppliers' licence conditions, which became more explicit and detailed. They established reputations as non-party partisan bodies. Private-sector interests supported the principle of independent regulators (even if they disagreed with some of their substantive decisions) in order to increase regulatory certainty and stability.

For British governments, reliance on regulation and separation from suppliers brought advantages, whereas attempts to 'take charge' of industrial policy carried costs and risks. They were able to leave politically and technically difficult matters to regulatory agencies: for instance, price re-balancing whereby cross-subsidies were unwound or dealing with the aftermath of pensions mis-selling. In contrast, their lack of links to industry discouraged specific interventions and encouraged action through regulatory agencies. This was clear when Labour returned to government in 1997.

Its attempts to 'take charge' of the rail industry largely failed, even in the hands of an avowed 'interventionist' like John Prescott. Ministers found that they lacked the expertise and instruments to act effectively alone—for instance, they could not prevent fare increases nor 'make the trains run on time' even by meetings at Downing Street—and their claims rapidly attracted media ridicule. Rather, it was necessary and advantageous to rely on the regulators (the Franchising Director and the Office of Rail Regulator, which was replaced by a new Strategic Rail Authority in 2001). Government could play a role, but it was by altering the regulatory structure, appointing new heads of the regulatory agencies, and cooperating with them.

In France, strong links between industry and the state constrained moves away from traditional industrial policy after 1980. Elected politicians believed that continued intervention through traditional industrial policy offered benefits, whilst disengagement was difficult. Firms, public and private, supplied jobs, money, and rewards. The scandals involving the oil company Elf that emerged in the late 1990s provide the most extreme example of the exchange of mutual favours: the company engaged in selling oil, provision of arms to France's African contacts, and funding of political parties and of politicians (and their mistresses). Moreover, large industrial groups such as Vivendi (formerly La Générale des Eaux) or Bougyues had interests across many sectors, including the media, which made it difficult for governments to keep them at a distance. (Fewer equivalents exist in Britain except perhaps the Murdoch group.) When politicians publicly admitted that they could not act, they lost popularity; thus Jospin's comment that 'l'Etat ne peut pas tout' in response to closure of a factory by Michelin in 1999 led to a barrage of criticism. Locally rooted politicians were expected to bring in firms and jobs to their town and constituency.

For private and public suppliers, ties to the executive also offered advantages. State-owned companies faced fewer investment constraints than their British counterparts (thanks to rules that 'de-budgetized' capital expenditure and instruments that permitted them to borrow on private capital markets) and indeed enjoyed certain advantages (e.g. they could borrow at favourable rates thanks to government guarantees). Their employees were either civil servants (for instance, in France Télécom and La Poste) or enjoyed similar status (for instance, in EdF/GdF and SNCF). They appeared highly successful, both in economic terms and in their 'social model' that reconciled efficiency and the pursuit public interest goals such as universal service or the protection of the poor (Boiteux 1996; Rouban 1997; Saussois 1997). Most managers of state-owned companies were political appointees or part of a group of top managers who went from one part of the public sector to another and whose careers were built on their personal networks. They were able to undertake 'grands projets' and obtain subsidies thanks to close ties with their political masters and government civil servants (Cohen 1992; Henry 1997; Suleiman and Courty 1997). Privatization represented a threat to the security of employees and a break with patterns of a lifetime for heads of public-owned suppliers.

Networks of formal and informal links that stretched across public and private sectors made it difficult to move towards arm's length regulatory relationships between officials and firms. In particular, the existence of powerful *grands corps* and the many channels whereby governments, firms, and other interests engaged in close inter-dependent relationships limited the move to a regulatory state. Private national champions maintained close relationships with elected and unelected officials. Many of the heads of large private companies were closely identified with certain politicians (e.g. Francois Pinault and the Dassault family were close friends of Chirac); even Socialist ministers such as Martine Aubry or Dominique Strauss-Kahn had previously been employed by national champion firms. Such companies used their networks of relationships to lobby policy makers and obtain advantages in matters such as takeovers, the allocation of licences, or public sector contracts. Thus, for example, in television, the licensing of Canal Plus in 1985 and the sale of TF1 to Bouygues in 1986/7 were the basis of the profitability of these privately owned companies. In the aerospace industry, the Jospin Government sold its share in Aerospatiale to Matra at below market value in order to create a French national champion that was large enough to be a partner in the European industry.

Independent regulators were rarer and established later than in Britain. Their role was circumscribed by continuing state–supplier links. Firms lobbied elected politicians directly, using links of *corps* and previous employment. Sometimes firms were directly represented in regulatory commissions—for example, in the takeover bids for the Société Générale and Paribas, decisions were taken by a banking committee the CECEI (Comité des établissements de credit et des enterprises d'investissement) whose members included the Governor of the Bank of France and representatives of the financial community. For their part, state regulators appeared partisan: their members were generally political appointees. They lacked the resources, including reputations for impartiality, to prevent ad hoc interventions by elected and unelected officials. Thus for instance, when the ART pressed for a 'beauty contest' rather than an auction for third generation mobile licences, it was seen as favouring the interests of key French suppliers; after much lobbying of the government and presidency, the licensing method was decided by an internal tussle within the government between the Finance and Telecommunications ministries. Even privately owned firms felt the power of political pressure. They were often dependent on political support against takeovers or management changes. Governments were closely involved in creating the 'hard core' shareholders at the heart of privatized companies. There were complex structures of share cross-holdings and debts, including by state firms, together with political and personal links between senior businessmen and politicians. As a result, processes of restructuring or even replacing managers (in private firms as well as public ones) frequently saw the involvement of elected and unelected public officials.

The Structure of Society

The 1980s and 1990s revealed much stronger obstacles to moves towards a regulatory state in France than in Britain. In the former, organized interests and unorganized protests represented significant barriers to abandoning the institutions of traditional industrial policy. Interests opposed to change in the latter were either defeated or became proponents of reform.

In Britain financial institutions in the City became supporters of regulatory reforms from which they gained. They embraced privatization which provided lucrative work for an army of bankers, lawyers, accountants, and advisers. They welcomed new regulatory bodies that offered greater certainty for investors and limited ad hoc government interventions. They were obliged to accept increased state regulation of their own activities after scandals such as those involving Lloyds 'names', insider trading (e.g. the 'Guinness affair' involving the mid-1980s takeover battle for Distillers), and pensions miss-selling in the 1990s. Increased state action to formalize arrangements appeared to be essential in response to court cases and public pressure. The main opponents of privatization and liberalization, trade unions and public sector employees, suffered a series of reverses that reduced their political power, from new legislation that restricted their strike activities to the failed long miners' strike of 1984. When confronted with privatization, closures, foreign takeovers, and reduced government subsidies, at most, the unions were able to delay or reduce changes (e.g. in the motor industry); at worst, they were straightforwardly defeated (notably in sales of the utilities).

In contrast, French public sector trade unions and employees acted as a major block on reforms. Privatization and liberalization were delayed for long periods or abandoned in the face of strikes, and governments were repeatedly forced to make major concessions. Thus, for instance, the sales of banks were put back or altered. In telecommunications, despite the wave of privatizations, it took four years to sell a minority share in France Télécom and the government had to promise not only that existing employees could keep their civil service status but also that more *functionnaires* would be hired until 2002. Apparent dangers to social rights and privileges from reform triggered industrial action and public protests that were often effective—for instance, strikes by the railway workers in 1995 or France Télécom staff in 1993. Fear of strikes and protests constrained governments, especially when weakened by other events or facing elections in the near future; hence the Chirac Government's reform plans largely ended in 1987 after street protests whilst the Juppé Government drew back from change after the 'autumn of discontent' of 1995. Although financial interests gained from reforms such as privatization, they were weaker than their British counterparts and were often comfortable with traditional close and interdependent relationships with the public sector.

State Traditions, Public Rhetoric, and Practical Experience

During the 1945–80 period, state traditions and public discourse in France had been in harmony with a *dirigiste* industrial policy and had aided reforms that expanded its scope, whereas in Britain they ran counter to activist industrial policies and hindered them. However, in the 1980s and 1990s, long-standing British traditions and discourse fitted well with moves towards a regulatory state, whereas the reverse was true in France. Moreover, the experiences of post-war industrial policy were interpreted differently in the two countries, with implications for the ease of institutional changes.

Despite the existence of a large state and the power of Keynesian ideas, a strong strand of nineteenth century liberalism persisted in Britain after 1945 (cf. Brittan 1975; Richardson 1982). A powerful discourse in favour of a smaller state continued: for instance, even in the 1940s and early 1950s, the Conservatives promised to 'set the people free' and Harold Wilson offered a 'bonfire of controls', whilst in the 1970 general election, the Conservatives under Heath again sought to reduce the size and scope of the state. Thus 'Thatcherite' policies of privatization, liberalization, and a 'retreat of the state' were far from new: the ground had been prepared and they formed part of an existing debate.

By the 1980s, post-war industrial policies in Britain were largely viewed as unsuccessful by much of political, academic, and popular opinion. Nationalized industries had low standing and were criticized for their inflexibility, low productivity, and poor quality, whilst politicians were criticized for constant short-term interference (cf. Pryke 1981). Such experiences aided attacks on existing institutional structures and norms of public ownership, monopoly, and ministerial control. Moreover, their replacements harked back to earlier, rival traditions that had been overshadowed by post-1945 institutions but which had continued to exist. Reforms that appeared to 'roll back the state' and take power away from interfering politicians meshed well with the British tradition of suspicion of state activity. Semi-independent regulatory bodies were not entirely new: regulatory commissions had been developed in the nineteenth century (Foster 1992; Foreman Peck and Milward 1994). Similarly, the virtues of competition and attempts to introduce it even into 'natural monopolies' (for instance through franchising) dated from at least the previous century.

France lacked a strong 'neo-liberal' tradition; on the contrary, 'Colbertism' and dirigism were the dominant inheritance in terms of ideas (Cohen 1992; Schmidt 1996). Moreover, during the twentieth century and especially after 1945, the expanded role and functions of the state had been increasingly accepted, whereas 'neo-liberal' economic ideas were very unfashionable. Within the Right, de Gaulle and his heirs lauded a strong state, as did most of the Left. In contrast, political figures who supported neo-liberal doctrines, such as Alain Madelin, were isolated figures, often seen as mavericks. The Right's flirtation with economic liberalism in the mid-1980s was limited and brief. Thus moving away from traditional industrial policies centred on state action and close relationships with firms ran counter to both inherited economic paradigms and the dominant political discourses of Left and Right (Schmidt 1997).

Interpretations of the success or failure of past industrial policies also differed greatly from those in Britain. State action was seen as having been highly beneficial— for example, the period 1945–75 was referred to as the 'thirty glorious years'. Policies of supporting national champions, planning, and financial aid had led to public success stories particularly in 'high tech' industries such as aerospace (Aerospatiale), the railways (SNCF's development of the TGV), or digitalization of telecommunications (Cohen 1992). The nationalized industries were seen as valuable organizations whose *service public* missions needed to be protected against dangers such as the EC, competition, and foreign takeovers (Dauba 1997; Duharcourt 1997; Saussois 1997).

They enjoyed high public esteem. For instance, the strikes of November/December 1995 in public transport against the Juppé Government's reorganization plans were aided by considerable popular support. Moving towards competition and regulation appeared to involve abandoning past successful industrial policies (Cohen 1996). Yet these perceptions were often at odds with the reality, which by the 1980s was one of increasing difficulty for the traditional French industrial policy model, notably the *grand projet* and publicly owned enterprises providing *services publics* (Cohen 1992; Chevallier 1997; Henry 1997; Rouban 1997; Cauchon 1998). The result was conflict between rhetoric and perceptions of past successes of traditional industrial policies, and attempts to alter institutions and norms in response to new pressures in the 1980s and 1990s.

CONCLUSION

During the 1980s and 1990s, both Britain and France moved away from industrial policies of the 1945–8 period. They privatized public enterprises, ended state monopolies, created and strengthened independent/semi-independent regulators, and set up a host of rules governing supply. Britain exhibited a greater capacity to innovate and move towards a regulatory state than France. It reformed earlier, to a greater extent, and more decisively; the rationale of a regulatory state was widely accepted by 2000. In contrast, changes in France were later, more piecemeal, and undertaken hesitantly. There was often a gap between the rhetoric of an activist *dirigiste* industrial policy and the reality of a gradual slippage towards a regulatory state.

Britain's greater innovatory capacities than France's ran counter to the experience of 1945–80, when it appeared to be constrained and unable to undertake bold industrial policy reforms (Hayward 1976; Dyson and Wilks 1983; Hall 1983, 1986). The same institutional factors that were used to explain the relative capabilities of the two countries before 1980 have been applied to the 1980s and 1990s, when they operated in the opposite direction than in the 1945–80 period. Thus the structure of the state, links between it and society, and the organization of society, together with state traditions, all favoured greater innovation in Britain than in France after 1980.

What implications can be drawn for historical institutionalist analysis of change from the findings? The case chosen is particularly apposite given that leading historical institutionalist work on Europe has been based empirically on economic and industrial policy and/or Britain and France (cf. Hall 1983, 1986, 1989; Hayward 1986). The central conclusion must be that the effects of institutional structures on innovation are not fixed. Rather, they interact with other factors which change over time. The case studied here points to three such factors. The first is the presence of strong political leadership. Britain saw a succession of Conservative governments between 1979 and 1997, all of which enjoyed parliamentary majorities and most of which were led by a formidably effective leader, Margaret Thatcher; at the same time, the opposition was divided and weakened. After 1997, the position was reversed. In France, there were several periods of *cohabitation*, Right and Left were very divided, several governments lacked decisive parliamentary majorities, and the timing of parliamentary and presidential elections meant that there were many periods in which political leaders were waiting on a proximate electoral contest.

Past experiences also create a dynamic process that interact with state traditions. In Britain, the industrial policies of the 1945–80 period were seen as failures, whereas in France they were often perceived as successful. It was therefore easier for British policy makers to alter policies and institutions, whereas their French counterparts had to avoid appearing to abandon recipes that had worked. At the very least, the experiences of the 1945–80 period constrained modification of the public rhetoric of policy making in France, which in turn facilitated opponents of change and hindered its exponents.

Perhaps the most important factor, however, is the 'fit' between national institutions and the direction of reform. French institutions were more suited to developing an activist industrial policy than British ones, thanks both to state traditions and to discourse and structural factors such as state–society linkages. However, the organization and traditions of the British state, together with the structure of society and its links with the state, were well matched to a regulatory state. In contrast, the French equivalents did not fit well with the reforms of the 1980s and 1990s. Hence the type of change also matters: national institutions may hinder one type of reform but be much better suited to facilitating another type. Innovatory capacity is not a fixed matter but varies according to the match between institutions and the changes sought.

19

Monetary Policy and the Euro

LOUKAS TSOUKALIS

On 1 January 1999, eleven countries of the European Union (Austria, Belgium, Finland, France, Germany, Ireland, Italy, Luxembourg, the Netherlands, Portugal, and Spain) entered the final stage of EMU, which subsequently led to the replacement of the national currencies by the euro. They were joined by Greece on 1 January 2001. On the other hand, the citizens of Denmark decided in a referendum held in September 2000 to stay out. As for Sweden and the United Kingdom, their participation in EMU will also depend on the outcome of referenda to be held in the future.

Money is at the heart of national sovereignty, the currency being a key symbol of nationhood, while monetary policy and the exchange rate constitute important instruments of economic policy. The EMU promises to be one of the most important events—arguably, the most important—in the history of European integration, with extensive economic and political ramifications. If anything, it could be compared to the common foreign and security policy (CFSP) of the Union. And we would then need to explain why monetary integration has reached the final (and irreversible?) stage, while the CFSP still remains more of a procedure than a policy.

Monetary integration in Europe has a long and chequered history, starting with the very cautious handling of monetary matters by the authors of the Treaty of Rome and ending with the complete transfer of power in the conduct of monetary policy to the European level. Money has always been highly political and it has also been frequently used as an instrument for wider political objectives, even though markets and economic fundamentals have not always obliged by adjusting themselves to the exigencies of high politics. It is likely to prove different this time round.

This chapter will trace briefly the history of European monetary integration. It will then examine the politics and economics of the Maastricht Treaty and EMU; the convergence criteria and the transition to the final stage; and the institutional structure provided for in the treaty. It will conclude with the main outstanding issues, drawing on the experience of the first two years of life with the euro, and the prospects for the future.

THE EARLY HISTORY

The first twenty years after the establishment of the European Economic Community (EEC) in 1958 were characterized by much talk and little action as regards monetary policy. The debate did, however, help to prepare the ground for the more substantial phase of monetary integration, which started with the setting up of the European Monetary System (EMS) in 1979.

The Treaty of Rome contained very little in terms of binding constraints in the field of macroeconomic policy. There was clearly no intention to set up a regional currency bloc. The Bretton Woods system provided the international framework and the US dollar the undisputed monetary standard. Moreover, Keynesianism was still at its peak. This meant that national governments were zealous in retaining the independence of their monetary and fiscal policies for the pursuit of domestic economic objectives, and a heavy armoury of capital controls was considered as an acceptable price to pay for this independence.

Interest in monetary integration grew during the 1960s, largely in response to the increasing instability in the international system and the perceived need to insulate Europe from the vagaries of the US dollar. But this apparent interest was not translated into much action. Defining a common policy towards the United States and the dollar proved to be a major stumbling block.

The situation seemed to change in December 1969, when the political leaders of the Six adopted for the first time the target of a complete EMU. It was a political decision reached at the highest level, and it was directly linked to the first enlargement of the Community and the further deepening of integration. It was also the first important example of a Franco-German initiative. But solemn decisions taken at the highest level did not in the end prove strong enough to survive the adverse economic conditions of the 1970s. EMU became the biggest non-event of the decade. After 1974, what was left of the ambitious plan for EMU was a limited exchange rate arrangement from which the majority of EC currencies stayed out (Tsoukalis 1977).

However, interest in developing a regional currency bloc never disappeared. And this led to the establishment of the EMS in March 1979, the product of another Franco-German initiative from which only the British decided to abstain. The EMS was a renewed attempt to establish a system of fixed, even though periodically adjustable, exchange rates between EC currencies. Concern about the proper functioning of the common market was combined with the desire to preserve common agricultural prices. On the other hand, the initiative for the creation of the EMS was linked to the expectation that there would be no substantial reform of the international monetary system, and hence no prospect of a return to some form of exchange rate stability in the future.

Exchange rate stability was to be backed by an increased convergence between national economies, with the emphasis clearly placed on inflation rates. The EMS was considered as an important instrument in the fight against inflation, and its creation meant an implicit acceptance by the other EC governments of German policy priorities. The experience of the 1970s was seen as validating the German combination of an uncompromising anti-inflationary stance combined with a strong currency option. The EMS was also intended as a defensive mechanism against US 'benign neglect' as regards the dollar. Last but not least, the EMS was directly linked to the wider project of European integration. It was seen as a means of strengthening Europe economically and politically through closer cooperation, at a time when US leadership was seen as waning. Once again, monetary integration was partly—and in a rather vague manner—used by its supporters as an instrument for political ends; and this largely explains why the British chose to stay out (Ludlow 1982).

The EMS prepared the ground for the much more ambitious project of EMU. Between 1979 and 1992, when all hell broke loose in exchange markets, it was characterized by an increasing stability of exchange rates (see Gros and Thygesen 1998). Greater stability in nominal exchange rates inside the exchange rate mechanism (ERM) was achieved largely through a gradually accelerating convergence of inflation rates downwards. Price convergence and intra-ERM exchange rate stability relied basically on monetary policies and the almost exclusive use of short-term interest rates for exchange rate stabilization purposes. Price convergence, coupled with the growing credibility of stability-oriented policies, brought about the gradual convergence of nominal long-term interest rates downwards.

The ERM operated for many years as a system of fixed, but adjustable, exchange rates. Adjustments, soon the product of collective decisions, became smaller and less frequent as price convergence grew. Central banks made use of a combination of different instruments whenever bilateral exchange rates came under attack. Those instruments included changes in short-term interest rates, foreign exchange interventions, and capital controls, especially in countries such as France and Italy, which were later to abandon this policy instrument in the context of liberalization. Realignments were usually considered as an instrument of last resort. The everyday management of the system was left to central bankers, relying as much on informal networks as on established EC institutions and committees, and most notably the Committee of Governors of Central Banks.

Monetary stability was, however, also directly linked to the asymmetrical nature of the EMS. Asymmetry in a system of fixed (even if periodically adjustable) exchange rates is manifested in terms of an unequal distribution of the burden of intervention and adjustment, and also of influence in the setting of policy priorities. Despite special provisions, such as the creation of the divergence indicator intended precisely to prevent this, the EMS operated all along in an asymmetrical fashion, thus following the earlier example of the snake. The asymmetry of the EMS related in turn to the central role of the Deutschmark (DM).

Asymmetry is not always bad, at least in economic terms. The EMS enabled countries, such as Italy, with a weak track record in terms of monetary stability, to borrow credibility by pegging their currencies to the DM. Participation in the ERM thus provided a convenient external constraint and strengthened the hand of institutions and interest groups inside countries fighting for less inflationary policies. This largely explains the popularity of the system with most central bankers, contrary to their earlier expectations. On the other hand, the asymmetry of the EMS became less acceptable in times of recession and growing unemployment, when the other European countries tended to adopt a less benign view of German leadership (see Giavazzi and Pagano 1988; de Grauwe 2000).

EMU: THE PRIMACY OF HIGH POLITICS

The debate on EMU was initially revived by the single market, although no binding commitment had been undertaken in the Single European Act (SEA) of 1987. An attempt was made, mostly by the Commission, to present EMU as the logical continuation of the single market programme, with exchange rates as another non-tariff barrier to be eliminated. This was again an example of the neo-functionalist strategy and the logic of spill-over, with integration in one area of economic activity creating the forces which lead to the extension of integration efforts in other areas. In the late 1980s, the EMS was still remarkably stable and Euro-euphoria was at its peak; hence the urgency felt in some European circles to win political commitment to the next stage of integration while the conditions remained favourable.

Monetary union would be the final and irrevocable confirmation of the reality of the single European market, and of a unified European economy. A common currency was seen as the means of welding national economies together; but also, very importantly, the means of accelerating the movement towards political union. And then came the breakdown of the old political division of the European continent, bringing down with it the communist regimes in Central and Eastern Europe as well as the disintegration of the Soviet Union. It also brought with it the unification of Germany, which finally acted as a powerful driving force for EMU.

For many people in Paris and Brussels in particular, the change of the European political scene called for a stronger Community and also a Community which would provide a stable and secure framework to contain a larger Germany. Money once again served as the main instrument. Wider balance of power considerations were thus added to what used to be an old and deep French concern with the asymmetrical character of the existing EMS, while most of the other EU countries had apparently reconciled themselves with the limitations on their monetary sovereignty.

Earlier initiatives in the field of European monetary integration had been largely motivated by external preoccupations; the instability of the dollar and US policies of 'unbenign neglect' had served as powerful federalizing factors in Europe. This was not true of the various initiatives which finally led to the new treaty provisions adopted at Maastricht for the establishment of EMU—or, at least, not to the same extent as in the past. True, the reform of the monetary system was not on the cards and the lack of unity among European countries remained an important factor behind the asymmetry in the international system. But this asymmetry was then less evident, the US Administration did not adopt the aggressive stance of its predecessors, and intra-ERM exchange rates appeared at the time less vulnerable to the gyrations of the dollar. Perhaps less preoccupation with external factors was also a sign of the new collective confidence of the Europeans.

The decision to liberalize capital movements, taken in 1988 as part of the single market programme and also a long-established German pre-condition for any progress towards EMU, provided the catalyst. The combination of fixed exchange rates and free capital movements meant that national monetary autonomy would have to be abandoned (Padoa-Schioppa 1994: ch. 6). This is also the main argument on which the Commission strategy was later based, another example of the Commission trying to make full use of functional spillover.

Money was thus once again at the centre of European high politics and commitment to monetary union was almost indistinguishable from the more general commitment to European unification. A new intergovernmental conference (IGC) was called to prepare the necessary treaty revisions for a complete EMU. Another IGC on political union quickly followed suit, political union being seen, at least initially, as an adjunct to the EMU project. During the negotiations, the economic and political desirability of EMU was not seriously put in question. This matter was supposed to have been already settled. The policy decision had been taken at the highest political level, and only British representatives were ready to express their doubts in public. The other doubters, and they did exist in significant numbers in the other countries, kept a low profile. They preferred to concentrate on specific problems instead of challenging the main principles and objectives. After all, much of the work had already been done by committees of experts. There was very little public debate on the subject of EMU prior to the signing of the Treaty, and one important reason was that it was still considered a matter for the cognoscenti.

The driving force for the relaunching of monetary union came from Paris, and to a lesser extent, Rome and Brussels. French governments had always been in favour of fixed exchange rates. They had never believed in the stability or efficiency of financial markets, which were often caricatured as a den of Anglo-Saxon speculators. For France, the move towards a complete EMU would help to end the asymmetrical nature of the existing system and would therefore secure for the country a stronger say in the collective conduct of European monetary policy. Last but not least, money provided the instrument for integrating the German giant more tightly into the Community system. Those objectives were largely shared by the Italians. As for the Commission, under the Presidency of Delors, it saw in EMU the consolidation of the internal market and the further strengthening of European political construction. It was the inevitable next step in the process of integration. The Commission provided valuable support, even though it played only a very limited role during the actual negotiations.

Initially, the Germans showed very little enthusiasm: the government and the central bank were happy with the status quo and any move towards monetary union was perceived, quite rightly, as leading to the erosion of Germany's independence in the monetary field. In purely economic terms, there was in fact precious little advantage for the Germans in a monetary union, assuming, of course, that some kind of regional currency arrangement which helps to contain the overvaluation of the DM can be taken for granted. For most of the period of the EMS, the main gain for the Germans was the stability of exchange rates for approximately half of the country's external trade and the gain in competitiveness. This has always been a very important consideration, clearly more important for politicians and industrialists than for central bankers (see CEPR 1995). On the other hand, there is no doubt that an EMS in which Germany sets the monetary standard was infinitely better for the Germans than a monetary union in which they would have to share with others the power to run monetary policy.

What finally tipped the balance was the perceived need to reaffirm the country's commitment to European integration in the wake of German unification. This is how the matter was presented in Paris. Thus, the German decision (Chancellor Kohl's to be precise) to proceed with EMU was highly political (Garrett 1994). Kohl spoke of economic and monetary integration as a matter 'of war and peace in the 21st century' (quoted in *Financial Times*, 19 October 1995), a statement indicative of his approach to the subject. The combination of different factors, namely the relative weight of the country, its high reputation in terms of monetary stability, especially among European central bankers, and its strong preference for the status quo, strengthened enormously the negotiating power of Germany, thus enabling it in most cases to impose its own terms with respect to the transition and the contents of the final stage of EMU (Dyson 1994; Dyson and Featherstone 1999).

Arguing that European integration can best be explained as a series of rational choices made by national leaders, with the emphasis on economic interests, Moravcsik argues that 'the outcomes of distributive conflict … consistently reflected the preferences of Germany—the country with the tightest domestic win-set and the most to give up in the monetary negotiations'. And he continues: 'the choice of institutions reflected above all the need for credible commitments, in particular Germany's desire to "lock in" a guarantee of low inflation by creating an autonomous ECB' (1998: 386). Although Moravcsik tends to underestimate the role of high politics in the shaping of German policy, he has correctly identified the key role of Germany in those negotiations. The monetary area is where German power has been most pronounced. This should change after the entry into the final phase, hence the attempt made by the Germans to exact as high a price as possible for allowing this to happen. They argued that they only wanted to make sure that the new European currency would be at least as stable and strong as the Deutschmark, and the German public seemed wholeheartedly to support this argument.

Once a Franco-German agreement had been reached on the subject of EMU, the process appeared almost unstoppable, thus repeating earlier patterns of European decision making. Italy was supportive, and it also provided much of the intellectual input. The Dutch shared much of the economic scepticism of the Germans, but their margin of manoeuvre was extremely limited. Belgium and Luxembourg were fervent supporters, although Belgium was at the same time extremely concerned in case a strict application of the convergence criteria kept it outside the privileged group, because of its very high public debt; Denmark felt almost like a natural member of the European currency area, although its politicians were not at all sure whether they would be able to carry the population with them into a monetary union; hence the 'opt-out' protocol.

The main concern of the other Southern countries was to link EMU to more substantial budgetary transfers and also to avoid an institutionalization of two or more tiers in the Community. As for Ireland, it benefited from the transfers and felt more secure than its Southern brethren that it would be among the first to obtain an entry ticket into the final stage. It would, however, have preferred that the other island separating it from the Continent would also join, since so much of its trade is still done with it.

Britain remained the only country where the government, itself internally divided, expressed grave doubts about the desirability and feasibility of EMU, on both economic and political grounds (Talani 2000). The situation had apparently changed little since 1979. Realizing its isolation, the Conservative government made a conscious effort to remain at the negotiating table, and it sacrificed Mrs Thatcher in the process. It made alternative proposals, as part of the diversionary tactics employed, which failed to make much of an impression on the other partners. In the end, it reconciled itself with an 'opt-out' provision in the treaty.

Central bankers, who are absolutely crucial for the successful implementation of the EMU project, had been closely involved from an early stage, notably through their participation in the Delors Committee and subsequently in the drafting of the European Central Bank (ECB) statutes. They were also responsible for the everyday running of the EMS. In contrast, domestic interest groups, parliaments, and the wider public played hardly any role during the negotiations. For the large majority of member countries, EMU became a political issue only after the signing of the Treaty, and popular reactions then came as an unpleasant surprise to most politicians. The Maastricht Treaty is an absolutely remarkable case study of elite driven integration; even against the opposition of several national elites in a European system in which the crucial decisions are supposed to be taken by unanimity.

CONVERGENCE CRITERIA AND TRANSITION TO EMU

The new Treaty on European Union was signed in Maastricht in February 1992. It provided for the establishment of EMU in three stages. The first stage, which started formally in July 1990, was aimed at improving both monetary and non-monetary cooperation within the existing institutional framework and also achieving the complete liberalization of capital movements. The inclusion of all currencies in the narrow band of the ERM was the other important objective of the first stage. Unfortunately, markets thought differently; thus, instead of consolidation, there was a breakdown of the old ERM during the first stage.

For the second stage, starting on 1 January 1994, convergence according to the criteria set by the new treaty was the main objective. Furthermore, the Committee of Governors of Central Banks would be replaced by the European Monetary Institute (EMI) which would make the necessary technical preparations before the entry into the final stage. This did not, however, involve any formal transfer of monetary sovereignty.

The most crucial part of the transitional arrangements related to the conditions to be fulfilled at the beginning of the third and final stage. The latter would start with the irrevocable fixity of the exchange rates of those currencies participating in it, to be followed by the 'rapid introduction' of the single currency which would replace national currencies. The definition of speed, moving from irrevocably fixed exchange rates to a single currency, was to be decided later. According to the treaty, the European Council would decide on the basis of reports from the Commission and the EMI whether each individual country fulfils the conditions for admission to the final stage.

According to the treaty, the third stage would begin on 1 January 1997 only if a simple majority of member countries were found to fulfil those conditions. Otherwise, the third stage would start on 1 January 1999 at the latest, irrespective of how many member countries were found to fulfil the necessary conditions at the time; again the European Council was to decide on each case on the basis of qualified majority. Those failing the test would remain in 'derogation' and, to all intents and purposes, they would be excluded from the new institutional framework. Their case would, however, be examined at least every two years. Voluntary 'opt-outs' were added to provisions for temporary derogations, thus turning EMU into a new kind of experiment with variable speed and multi-tier forms of integration. Because the United Kingdom refused to commit itself in advance to participating in the final stage of EMU, it secured an 'opt-out' protocol which left the decision for a future government and parliament. Denmark chose a softer version of 'opting out': in this case, the relevant protocol referred to the holding of a referendum prior to Denmark's participation in the final stage.

The conditions for admission to the final stage, otherwise known as convergence criteria, are quite explicit and concentrate exclusively on monetary variables. The first convergence criterion refers to a sustainable price performance, defined in the attached protocol as a rate of inflation which does not exceed that of the three best performing member countries by more than 1.5 percentage points. The second relates to the sustainability of the government financial position: the actual or planned deficit should not exceed 3 per cent of GDP, while the accumulated public debt should not be above 60 per cent of GDP. With respect to this criterion, the wording of Article 104c of the treaty (Article 104 after the Amsterdam revision) leaves some margin for manoeuvre: it allows for higher deficits as long as they have been declining 'substantially and continuously' or are considered to be 'exceptional and temporary'; and it also allows for higher government debt on the condition that the latter is 'sufficiently diminishing and approaching the reference value at a satisfactory pace'. The wording is thus vague enough to allow room for interpretation.

Exchange rate stability is the third criterion: the national currency must have remained within the 'normal' fluctuation margins of the ERM for at least two years prior to the decision about the final stage, without any devaluation and without any severe tension. Since the widening of the bands in August 1993, 'normal' is generally understood to mean the existing margins of the ERM, namely plus or minus 15 per cent from the central rate. The fourth criterion refers to the durability of the convergence: the average nominal interest rate on long-term government bonds has been chosen as the appropriate indicator and it should not exceed that of the three best performing member states by more than two percentage points.

The convergence criteria have been criticized on many grounds (see e.g. de Grauwe 2000). They are mechanistic, some of them arbitrary and, perhaps, also superfluous. On the other hand, they completely ignore real convergence. In economic terms, they could be viewed at best as a very rough (and also ephemeral) indicator of the stability orientation of countries to be admitted into the final stage. This could, arguably, influence the credibility of EMU and the ECB. Economic convergence as a pre-condition for EMU is an old 'economist' argument,[1] which also happened to receive wide support in a country like Germany. The convergence criteria were meant (by the Germans) to restrict, at least for some time, the number of countries allowed into the final stage. Economics is an inexact science, and politics the art of the possible; hence the very imperfect product of Maastricht.

The treaty met with little applause from European societies and international markets alike. What proved to be an agonizing process of ratification of the treaty coincided with the turmoil in the exchange markets, and the two became mutually reinforcing. Strong speculative pressures in 1992–3 forced a series of realignments inside the ERM, the withdrawal of two currencies, and finally the abandonment of the old narrow bands of fluctuation, not to mention the big losses incurred by central banks. They certainly did not augur well for the success of the EMU project. Hardly anybody would have dared to predict at the time that the final stage of EMU would in fact begin on 1 January 1999, with eleven (and later twelve) countries participating in it. This became possible due to a dramatic transformation of the political and economic climate during the intervening period. The road leading to EMU was shaped by the continuous interaction between governments, markets, and societies. Governments operate at both the national and the European level (the subnational level being hardly relevant in the case of monetary policy), while financial markets are international and societies stubbornly national.

During the transition to EMU, most governments, acting separately or through European institutions, showed an absolutely remarkable commitment to this goal, not only in words but also in deeds. A number of important decisions were taken by successive European Councils, including most notably the plan for the changeover to the single currency, following the introduction of the final stage. Activity at the European level was continuously backed by political statements pointing to the inevitability of EMU and the appropriate macroeconomic policies which aimed at satisfying the convergence criteria. In this respect, the role played by Chancellor Kohl was absolutely decisive. The transition to EMU survived important changes of government in different member countries, which in itself says very much about the degree and cross-party nature of the political commitment in most EU countries, and hence about the solidity of the project.

Also encouraged by the significant improvement in the economic environment, markets gradually began to believe in EMU. This helped to create a virtuous circle: the decline in inflation and budget deficits led to exchange rate stability and a reduction

---

[1] For the old debate between 'economists' and 'monetarists', see Tsoukalis (1977).

deflationary policies

in nominal and real interest rates, both short and long, which in turn contributed to a further reduction in inflation and budget deficits.

European societies did not show the same degree of conviction or enthusiasm about EMU. This is perhaps understandable, since EMU was identified, at least in several countries, with deflationary policies at times of high unemployment, which hardly helped to make it an object of love for European citizens. In others, it was mainly perceived as leading to a substantial loss of national sovereignty, even though this loss of national sovereignty may be more a question of appearance than substance.

During the transition, opinion polls did, however, regularly register clear majorities for the Union as a whole in favour of EMU; and those majorities were increasing as the big day approached (Tsoukalis 2000). The change in countries like Germany and the Netherlands, which had started with very low levels of public support for EMU, was quite dramatic. This may serve as an interesting lesson about the ability of politicians to shape, as opposed to simply following, public opinion. If, for example, the German government had taken early opinion polls on EMU too seriously, the whole project would never have materialized.

The highest popular support for EMU appeared in countries with strong pro-integration majorities and/or high propensity to inflation and debt accumulation. Italy and Greece are the best examples, with very high levels of popular support for EMU; the rest of Southern Europe, together with the Benelux countries, followed closely. On the other hand, negative attitudes continued to prevail in Denmark, Sweden, and the United Kingdom until the end of the transition to EMU, although the balance of opinion had become more favourable during the intervening period. Not surprisingly, these were also the countries where the governments had decided to postpone the decision, presumably hoping for a further shift in the future of public attitudes in favour of EMU. The trend of rising public support for EMU did not continue after the entry into the final stage. In fact, exactly the opposite happened in most countries. The apparent disillusionment with EMU was directly linked to the weakness of the euro in international exchange markets, although this may very well prove to be temporary and reversible.

POSTMODERN ARCHITECTURE

The treaty provides for a complete centralization of monetary policy, while fiscal policy remains highly decentralized and the European political system even more so. This combination has no precedent in history. The architects of Maastricht have produced a complex design of arguably postmodern inspiration, which seems to defy the laws of gravity. Time will, of course, be the ultimate judge.

In EMU, national currencies of participating countries have been replaced by the new single currency, having previously coexisted with the euro as only a virtual currency and tied to it and between themselves with the irrevocably fixed exchange rates for a period of three years (1999–2001). The ECB located in Frankfurt has been given exclusive responsibility for the conduct of European monetary policy, including foreign exchange operations and the management of foreign reserves. Its primary objective is the maintenance of price stability, while other objectives, such as financial stability and high employment, are clearly meant to be secondary. The ECB is independent and strongly protected from political interference; it is also, in practice, largely unaccountable. It follows closely the German model of a central bank, although even more so because of the lack of a corresponding political authority at the European level. It is governed by a six-member Executive Board, consisting of the President, the Vice-President, and four other members appointed by the European Council for an eight-year non-renewable term; and the Governing Council in which the members of the Executive Board as well as the governors of the twelve participating national central banks take part.

The Governing Council is the main decision-making body, deciding by simple majority on interest rates, reserve requirements, and the provision of liquidity in the system. The simple majority rule clearly gives excessive weight to the small members, but the principle is that governors of national central banks are not meant to represent national interests; and this principle applies even more so to the members of the Executive Board. The refusal to publish minutes of the proceedings and the way members of the Governing Council have voted is also meant to protect governors from political pressure. National legislation has also been changed to ensure the independence of national central banks. European monetary policy has been very consciously entrusted to the experts. Thus, EMU implies not only the transfer of power from the national to the European level, but also for most countries the transfer of power from elected representatives to technocrats. At the centre of the system, there are six members of the Executive Board, setting the policy agenda and implementing decisions by giving instructions to the national central banks. The decision-making system of EMU is the closest to a federal structure that can be found in the Union.

The ECB has the exclusive right to authorize the issue of money. It is not permitted to lend to governments: any form of 'monetary financing' of governments is prohibited and so is any 'bailing out' of indebted governments and other public institutions. Provision has also been made for a future role of the ECB with respect to the prudent supervision of financial institutions, although this will have to be authorized eventually by the Council. On the other hand, the treaty allows the Council of Economics and Finance Ministers (ECOFIN) a role in the exchange rate policy of the Union, notably in the negotiation of international agreements and the formulation of 'general orientations', thus leaving the formulation of exchange rate policy and the division of responsibilities between the ECB and ECOFIN somewhat unclear.

The Maastricht Treaty did not create any new institution for the conduct of fiscal policies, which remain a national responsibility, nor is there any mention of fiscal federalism which might lead to the creation of a much bigger EU budget. Only the Economic and Financial Committee has been born out of the ashes of the old Monetary Committee, with the main task of preparing the work of ECOFIN (the Committee of Economic and Finance Ministers). The treaty did, however, make provisions for the strengthening of existing mechanisms of multilateral surveillance, while also attempting to define in some detail what constitutes 'economically correct' behaviour. On the basis of a recommendation made by the Commission, ECOFIN will draft each year 'the broad guidelines of the economic policies of the Member States and of the Community' (Article 99—ex Article 103), although those guidelines are still generally seen as a kind of 'soft' coordination of national policies. The first public reprimand of the budgetary policy of a member country, namely Ireland, issued by ECOFIN in January 2001 could be interpreted as a willingness to add some real bite to those broad guidelines.

There are in fact much stricter provisions for the profligate members, which have been introduced through the so-called excessive deficit procedure (Article 104—ex Article 104c, and the attached protocol). The ceilings of 3 per cent for public deficits and 60 per cent for public debt in terms of GDP, adopted as part of the convergence criteria for admission to the final stage of EMU, will be used as reference values for the assessment of national budgetary policies.

On the basis of reports prepared by the Commission, which is thereby given the role of a watchdog, ECOFIN will decide by qualified majority whether a situation of excessive deficit exists in a member country. A whole range of measures would then be available to the Council, from public recommendations to the imposition of fines. Following strong pressure from Germany, the Council adopted the Stability and Growth Pact in June 1997. It is meant to give real teeth to the excessive deficit procedure agreed earlier at Maastricht, while also making it more stringent. The Stability and Growth Pact was consistent both with the economic orthodoxy of the time, laying the emphasis on fiscal consolidation, and with the political balance of power inside the Union, especially in monetary affairs (see Eichengreen and Wyplosz 1998). It came under severe criticism in late 2002 in the context of economic recession.

ECONOMIC RISKS AND POLITICAL STAKES

The detailed provisions of the treaty, and the meticulous preparations which preceded the entry into the final stage of EMU, have left some fundamental questions unanswered. The Maastricht package was a political bargain, which deliberately left for later negotiation many of the wider ramifications of monetary union. Some of them will be discussed below (see e.g. Cameron 1997; Frieden 1998; Obstfeld and Peri 1998; Crouch 2000; de Grauwe 2000; Dyson 2000).

The European Union is not an optimal currency area; far from it. There are no adequate adjustment mechanisms, such as large budgetary transfers, flexible labour markets, and high labour mobility, to act as effective substitutes for the exchange rate. There is already a large body of literature as to how countries may be able (or not) to cope with the so-called asymmetric shocks in the context of monetary union and what the effects in terms of employment and output may be.

If economic cycles remain unsynchronized among individual economies within the euro-zone, the costs of the 'one-size-fits-all' monetary policy will be uneven. This has been abundantly clear during the first two years of EMU, when the needs in terms of stabilization policy of the fast growing European periphery were very different from those of the slow moving core. It was unavoidable that the ECB would give much greater weight to economic trends in Germany, France, or Italy, rather than those in Ireland or Portugal in deciding on the conduct of monetary policy for the euro-zone.

The ECB faced an extremely difficult task in taking over responsibility for the conduct of monetary policy for the euro-zone as a whole. It had to build its own credibility in the markets, and in so doing it risked ending up as more German than the Bundesbank in its pursuit of price stability. The weakness of the euro vis-à-vis the dollar during much of the early period of EMU did not make things easier. According to a CEPR report, the ECB displayed more flexibility than had been generally expected, although at the expense of transparency in its monetary policy (CEPR 2000). And there were often problems of coordination in the public statements made by European central bankers and finance ministers, which certainly did not help in boosting confidence in the new currency.

In a monetary union, there are strong arguments for greater flexibility of fiscal policy, to serve as an instrument of adjustment at the national and regional level. On the other hand, there is a risk of free-riding by national, or even regional, governments operating under the shield of the Union, assuming, of course, that markets cannot be relied upon to provide an effective restraint on government overspending (and undertaxing). The treaty provisions, and the Stability and Growth Pact which followed, were aimed essentially against 'free-riders' in the future monetary union. Their effectiveness and political feasibility, however, remain to be tested. As for the possible deflationary bias of the Pact, this is undoubtedly a controversial issue among economists.

Behind the institutional structure established to manage the single currency lies the political issue of who is to determine macroeconomic priorities for the European Union as a whole, and how (Allsopp and Vines 1998; Eichengreen 1998). There is as yet no mechanism for this. The guidelines for the coordination of national policies are generally considered too broad to have any noticeable effect on national economic strategies. However, the public reprimand of Ireland by ECOFIN in 2001 for an expansionary fiscal policy (even with a large budget surplus in a booming economy) suggests that the coordination mechanism provided for in the Maastricht treaty may prove to be less 'soft' than most people had anticipated.

The pressure for more effective coordination of fiscal policies, and macro-economic policies in general, for the euro-zone as a whole has come mostly, although not exclusively, from France. The Euro Group, which is the new name of the informal council of economics and finance ministers of the countries participating in EMU and meeting before ECOFIN, may end up appropriating for itself most of the real functions of the latter. What would then become of ECOFIN? The strengthening of the Euro Group may eventually provide a political counterweight to the bankers, thus creating the conditions for a real dialogue between economics and finance ministers and the ECB. The EMU could then end up being Europe's answer to the globalization and inherent instability of financial markets by restoring some of the effectiveness of macroeconomic policy, which has been irretrievably lost at the national level

(Fitoussi 1995; Tsoukalis 1998). After all, the European Union is still a relatively closed economy in trade terms, very similar to the United States. Excluding intra-EU trade, the external trade of the Union in goods is still around 10 per cent of GDP, almost the same as that for the Unites States. Some elements of Keynesianism could therefore be resurrected in the context of EMU; although, admittedly, this is something not envisaged by the authors of the Treaty on European Union, nor is it very compatible with current economic orthodoxy.

The link between monetary and economic union has long been debated among economists. The MacDougall Report in 1977, reflecting the continuing influence of Keynesianism, suggested that a larger common budget would be needed (MacDougall *et al.* 1977). The Padoa-Schioppa Report of 1987, working within the constraints of the new economic orthodoxy, was more cautious on this issue (Padoa-Schioppa *et al.* 1987). The EU budget remains very small, and with no provision for a stabilization function. Nor is there much support in most member states for a large common budget.

Holding the two intergovernmental conferences in parallel in 1990–1 was meant to stress the link between EMU and political union. The Treaty on European Union, however, delivered little of substance on political union; and the Treaties of Amsterdam and Nice, which followed, have contributed precious little to the correction of the democratic deficit of the Union. We are going to have another try with the Convention and the new intergovernmental conference that should follow; indeed, the last try before the new enlargement. The emergence of a central bank without a corresponding political authority has led some analysts to portray catastrophe scenarios not only for EMU but also for the European Union as a whole, if there is a recession in one or more of the big countries of the euro-zone, and if the ECB is perceived as not responding adequately to popular demands for more expansionary policy (Feldstein 1997). Although such scenarios may stretch the point too far, there is clearly a problem of legitimacy with European institutions in general, and the ECB in particular. With the deepening of integration, the indirect legitimacy acquired through the democratic process within member states, on which they have so far drawn, may no longer prove sufficient. Independent central banks, in Germany or elsewhere, have always been able to draw on the reservoir of legitimacy of the nation-state, but there is no equivalent as yet at the European level. European policy makers seem to have left it to a future recession to test whether EMU will act as the catalyst for further political union, or whether monetary policy has been completely decoupled from political authority.

Monetary union carries implications for a wide range of other policy domains, some not yet drawn into the EU framework, others already subject to EU regimes. The regulation of financial markets is an obvious field for spillover, especially given the rapid restructuring in this sector, partly a consequence of the move towards a single currency. This is already an important issue on the EU agenda, raising questions about the kind of regulation as well as about the division of powers between European and national institutions, and between independent agencies and democratically accountable bodies. Questions of tax harmonization, or of the prevention of harmful tax competition, have been a hot issue for some time. Taxes on capital, which is more mobile than labour across frontiers, are a particular concern to many EU governments. Short of adopting minimum rates at the European level, tax competition will force rates downwards, thus shifting the tax burden onto the less mobile factors of production, and most notably labour. How does one reconcile national fiscal autonomy with increasingly European and global markets?

The growing number of cross-border mergers and acquisitions is fast changing the corporate map of Europe. This will also have implications for EU competition policy. On the other hand, the loss of the exchange rate as a policy instrument at the national level, and the lack of any sizeable inter-country budgetary transfers to act as shock absorbers, will place the burden of adjustment on labour markets. Hence the emphasis has shifted to promoting greater flexibility in labour markets and social policies, even though definitions of flexibility differ widely and so still do national models of capitalism. The Lisbon summit of March 2000 has introduced the so-called 'open method of coordination', relying mainly on benchmarking and peer pressure, as an alternative to traditional rule-based integration. It is as yet too early to tell whether anything substantial will come out of it.

Until the launching of the final stage of EMU, its external dimension had been largely ignored (for exceptions to this rule, see Portes and Rey 1998; Bergsten 1999). Monetary union should imply a single external representative, but finance ministers of the major EU states are accustomed to playing a role on the international stage. The European Council has so far decided that the President of the Euro Group will, together with the President of the ECB, represent the countries of the euro-zone in meetings of the Group of Seven (Eight, when Russia takes part), alongside—not instead of—colleagues from the larger member governments. Logically, the separate national representations of EU countries in international financial organizations, such as the International Monetary Fund (IMF), should in time give way to a single European representation. But the weak legitimacy of the European Union, and the national sensitivities of the larger members, may make this a long-term prospect. The issue of common representation begs the question of what the external policy of EMU would be and how that might be defined.

This also relates to the exchange rate of the euro against other international currencies. The first two years after the introduction of the euro were characterized by a large depreciation of the new currency with respect to the US dollar. This depreciation was largely explained in terms of different market expectations regarding growth prospects on the two sides of the Atlantic and also in terms of interest rate differentials. Although being yet another example of overshooting in financial markets, possibly to be followed by a movement in precisely the opposite direction if and when the US economy goes into recession, the depreciation of the euro in 2000–1 was also not unrelated to the difficulties experienced by European policy makers (be they central bankers or finance ministers) to present a coordinated, not to mention unified, stance.

The launch of EMU has opened up more than ever before the prospect of a multi-tier EU, assuming that some countries decide to stay outside this most important manifestation of economic integration; and the accession of new countries can only complicate matters further. The institutionalization of different tiers of membership may in the end prove the only way of reconciling this new phase of deepening of integration with economic and political diversity in an ever larger Union.

European monetary integration already has a long history. Earlier proposals had sketched out a broader programme of parallel policies and institutional development than that which the European Union accepted in the 1990s. The narrower agenda set out in the Treaty on European Union in some ways made agreement easier, but at the cost of leaving to be settled later a large number of politically sensitive issues—some potentially explosive.

The Treaty on European Union, and subsequent developments through the 1990s, have been strongly influenced by prevailing economic ideas, most notably the belief that there is no trade-off between inflation and unemployment. This is the 'stabilization state' referred to by Dyson (2000). If and when economic conventional wisdom changes, then treaties and institutions will have to face a difficult test of flexibility and endurance. The ECB, at the centre of the new institutional architecture, will be tested most severely. It remains to be seen whether it will by then have found a credible political interlocutor in the form of a revamped ECOFIN. Debate about macroeconomic choices, and about the balance between the instruments of economic policy, has been at the heart of national politics since the Second World War. Some of those choices and instruments have now been transferred to the EU level, without the parallel institutions for generating a Europe-wide debate.

EMU is indeed a high-risk strategy. There is a serious economic risk involved in the irrevocable fixing of exchange rates, while other adjustment mechanisms are still very weak and economic divergence persists. Arguably, the instability of currency markets, combined with the high degree of openness of individual EU economies, left European policy makers with little choice. There is also a political risk linked to the legitimacy deficit of the Union. And there is no easy exit option if things go wrong. There is, however, the other side of the coin. If EMU works, it will most likely bring with it a much stronger and more integrated EU, in both economic and political terms. After all, the history of European integration has been marked by bold initiatives, which seemed to provide easy targets for various categories of Eurosceptics. On most occasions, it was the latter who finally had to adjust to the ever-changing European reality.

20

Recasting European Welfare States

MAURIZIO FERRERA, ANTON HEMERIJCK, AND
MARTIN RHODES

INTRODUCTION

Recent years have seen a proliferation of literature analysing the past, present, and prospective future of the welfare state. There have been several key phases of development. First, in the early 1990s, Gosta Esping Andersen (1990) altered our understanding of the institutional underpinnings of welfare state diversity in Europe with his analysis of the 'three worlds'—or regimes—of welfare capitalism: the social democratic (the Scandinavian countries), the liberal (the United Kingdom and Ireland), and the conservative corporatist (Austria, France, the Benelux countries, and Italy). The three main principles for a theoretical specification of the welfare state in this analysis were the position of the citizen vis-à-vis the market (the less dependent on the market, the more citizenship was 'de-commodified'); how this status of citizenship modified social stratification (i.e. class position); and the relationship between state, market, and the family in social provision.

This analysis did not go uncontested. In particular it was attacked for its neglect of the role of gender in shaping welfare systems (e.g. Lewis 1992, 1993; followed by a proliferation of high quality studies of the gender dimensions of welfare states); second for its neglect of the distinctiveness of southern European countries within the 'conservative group' (Leibfried 1993; Castles 1995; Ferrera 1996; Rhodes 1997); and third for problems relating to the methodology of comparative type construction (see Castles 2001 for a survey and discussion). Nevertheless, and recognizing the import of these critiques, most welfare state analysis since that date has been shaped to one extent or another by Esping-Andersen's seminal contribution.

More recently, there have been several new steps forward. One came with Esping-Andersen's own deeper exploration of welfare state adjustment in the 1980s and 1990s (Esping-Andersen 1996) and his (partial) embrace of the feminist critique in his (1999) analysis which brought the role of gender and the family to centre stage. In the meantime, of course, our understanding of these issues has been greatly advanced by numerous in-depth analyses of gender and particular types of welfare system (e.g. Sainsbury 1996; O'Connor et al. 1999; Daly 2000; for a review and critique, see Morgan 2001). At the same time, other projects have examined the adjustment of welfare states from the oil shocks of the 1970s through to the 1990s. Scharpf and Schmidt (2000) assembled a group of national and comparative studies in an effort, first, to understand the root causes of persistent high unemployment in European countries, and second to trace their subsequent trajectories of adjustment. Meanwhile, Gallie and Paugram (2000) have improved on our understanding of unemployment, poverty, and social exclusion, while also innovating in terms of regime analysis. Goul Anderson and Jensen (2002) link analysis of changing labour markets and welfare policies and social citizenship. Another team (Pierson 2001*a*) has focused more precisely on the politics welfare state adjustment, covering systems of interest intermediation, parties, elections, political institutions, as well as particular policy domains.

Another, but closely related, stream of research has sought to render more explicit the linkages between cross-national ('models of') welfare state research, and comparative political economy (Goodin *et al.* 1999; Ebbinghaus and Manow 2001; Hall and Soskice 2001). Exploring connections between 'welfare regimes' and 'production regimes' has been of particular concern, especially in countering simplistic understandings of the impact of globalization on social policy and employment (Huber and Stephens 2001). Other projects still have focused on the development of particular policy domains (e.g. Esping-Andersen and Regini 2000 on labour markets; Moran 1999 on health systems; Disney and Johnson 2001 on pensions; Bermeo 2001 on unemployment) or cross-national comparisons of reform (Ferrera and Rhodes 2000*b*; Taylor-Gooby 2001). From these various strands of the literature, we have gained considerable insights into how welfare states function, how they also generate their own 'pathologies of development', and where their strengths and weaknesses of adjustment lie.

As a result of this decade of research, we now understand European welfare states much better than previously. We now know that economists are mistaken to posit a 'big trade-off' (e.g. Okun 1975) between equality and efficiency: some welfare states (Sweden, Denmark) combine the two very effectively, whereas the most unequal systems may also experience low levels of growth and productivity. We also know that the 'globalization' literature is mistaken in positing a convergence of socio-economic systems in reaction to external pressures: in reality, even if government autonomy is limited by free trade, the internationalization of finance and—in Europe—economic and monetary union (EMU), their impact can only be understood alongside (and as subordinate in importance to) the *endogenous* problems of particular welfare states (Garrett 1998*b*; Ferrera *et al.* 2001; Rhodes 2002; Swank 2002). Regarding the latter, we also understand much better now than a decade ago how the nature of employment (and unemployment), social security systems, gender, and the family all interact to create different sets of reform dilemmas and challenges. It is also becoming clearer why some types of welfare state can better accommodate post-industrial change (especially the shift in employment growth from the industrial to the services sector) than others. We now know that some countries share a number of institutional ingredients that are systematically linked, producing a distinct 'logic' of development over time and which, today, pre-structure the reform agenda, in terms of both constraints and opportunities (for a survey and analysis, see Ferrera *et al.* 2000).

In this chapter we present, in synthesis form, some key elements of what is now understood about welfare 'regimes', their respective 'pathologies' of development, their current paths of reform, and the challenges that still confront them. Part one examines welfare state performance thematically, focusing on employment, the scale and shape of social security systems, and distributive outcomes. Part two takes Europe's four 'welfare regimes' and analyses their respective strengths and vulnerabilities. The conclusion considers where the literature on welfare states is likely to go in the future.

WELFARE STATE PERFORMANCE

Europe's welfare states vary enormously in terms of their adjustment problems and reform potential. Before analysing them in some detail, below we briefly assess them in terms of three dimensions of *effectiveness*: (a) employment performance; (b) the level of social security spending, benefits, and services; and (c) distributive outcomes in terms of wage dispersion, income equality, and poverty.

Employment Performance

There is great variation in employment performance across Europe, as shown in Table 20.1. The employment/population ratio ranges from 76 per cent in Denmark to 53 per cent in Italy. Unemployment goes from a low of 2.4 per cent in Luxembourg to a high of 14 per cent in Spain. Cross-national differences in long-term unemployment are even greater (extending from 0.6 per cent in Luxembourg to 6.4 per cent in Italy). But amidst the diversity there is a general trend: countries with employment rates significantly below the average (Germany, Belgium, France, Spain, and Italy) are welfare states of the conservative continental or the Southern regime type. Their strong reliance on payroll taxes to finance social security drives up non-wage labour costs; and all combine modest levels of public and private employment. This is not to say that these welfare states are inevitably stuck in an 'inactivity trap'. The Netherlands and Portugal both have above average employment levels, low unemployment, and modest levels of youth unemployment, and seem to have escaped, to varying degrees, the vicious circle of 'welfare without work'. But the Scandinavian countries of Denmark and Sweden perform best: they firmly take the lead in levels of female, public, and overall employment, and suffer least from long-term and youth unemployment and early (age) exits from the labour market.

Social Security Spending, Benefits, and Services

With respect to levels of social protection (Table 20.2), we again observe tremendous cross-regime variation. Even after suffering considerable turbulence in the 1980s and 1990s, Denmark, Finland, and Sweden continue to be the most generous welfare states with very high levels of spending, especially on social services. The conservative, continental welfare states remain at intermediate levels of generosity and clearly

Table 20.1 *Employment performance in the European Union (2000)*

	Employment rate[a]	Unemployment rate[b]	Long-term unemployment[c]	Female employment rate	Youth unemployment rate[e]	Employment rate, men aged 55–64	Public employment ratios[f]
Denmark	76.3	4.7	1.0	71.6	5.3	54.6	22.7
Finland	67.5	9.8	2.8	64.4	11.2	41.2	14.6
Sweden	73.0	5.9	1.3	71.0	5.5	64.6	21.9
Austria	68.3	3.7	1.0	59.4	2.9	29.2	10.0
Belgium	60.5	7.0	3.8	51.5	6.5	25.0	10.3
France	62.2[g]	9.5	3.8	55.3[g]	7.1	29.3	14.5
Germany	65.4[g]	7.9	4.0	57.9[g]	4.6	37.8	9.3
Luxembourg	62.9[g]	2.4	0.6	50.3[g]	2.5	26.3	—
Netherlands	73.2[g]	2.7	0.8	63.7[g]	3.6	35.3	6.8
Ireland	65.1	4.2	1.7	54.0	3.3	43.8	9.3
United Kingdom	71.2	5.5	1.5	64.6	8.3	50.5	9.5
Greece	55.6[g]	11.1	—	40.9[g]	—	38.4	6.9
Italy	53.5	10.5	6.4	39.6	11.8	27.3	8.9
Portugal	68.3	4.2	1.7	60.3	4.2	51.7	12.0
Spain	55.0	14.1	5.9	40.3	11.4	36.6	7.5
EU-15	63.3	8.2	3.6	54.0[g]	7.8	39.4	11.7

[a]Total employment/population 15–64 years.
[b]Standardized ratio.
[c]Long-term unemployed (12 months and over) as per cent of labour force.
[d]Per cent of population 15–24.
[e]Unemployed as per cent of population aged 15–24.
[f]1998.
[g]Eurostat estimation.

Source: European Commission 2000; OECD 1999a (public employment figures).

spend less on social services than their Nordic counterparts. At the lower end of the scale of social protection we find the liberal Anglo-Saxon and the Southern welfare states, which are lean in terms both of social expenditures and public services.

Distributive Outcomes

Welfare state generosity is also reflected in the distributive performance of the welfare state (Table 20.3). The Anglo-Saxon countries display not only high levels of wage dispersion, but also comparatively high poverty rates and an inegalitarian distribution of disposable household income. The Continental welfare states are by and large located in the middle range, displaying a medium performance in terms of distribution. However, within the sample of Continental welfare states, the spectrum is wide. The Southern welfare states, with average levels of wage dispersion, reveal

Table 20.2 *Level of social security in the European Union*

	Social expenditures in per cent of GDP[a]	Total taxation[b]	Net repl. rate of unempl. benefits[b]	Old age and survivors as per cent of GDP[a]	Active labour market policy[c]	Labour market training[c]	Social exclusion[d] 1995	Family/children as per cent of GDP[a]
Denmark	30.0	52.2	81	11.49	2.01	0.48	1.1	3.90
Finland	27.2	47.3	80	9.38	1.66	0.21	0.4	3.48
Sweden	33.3	53.3	83	13.12	0.87	0.28	0.1	3.60
Austria	28.4	44.4	67	13.69	1.89	1.07	1.5	2.84
Belgium	27.5	46.5	70	11.77	1.23	0.41	0.7	2.34
France	30.5	46.1	79	13.42	0.42	0.09	0.3	2.99
Germany	29.3	37.5[c]	70	12.69	0.44	0.15	0.3	3.03
Luxembourg	24.1	—	84	10.65	0.30	0.01	0.4	3.40
Netherlands	28.5	43.3	85	11.71	1.76	0.22	0.7	1.28
Ireland	16.1	34.8	57	4.01	1.37	0.35	0.5	2.04
United Kingdom	26.8	35.3	68	11.77	0.72	0.21	0.1	2.30
Greece	24.5	40.6	49	12.89	1.29	0.29	0.7	1.98
Italy	25.2	45.0	45	16.13	1.27	0.34	0.6	0.91
Portugal	23.4	34.5	82	9.99	0.35	0.06	—	1.24
Spain	21.6	35.3	75	9.96	1.08	0.01	0.0	0.45
Average	27.7	42.6	72	12.66	1.1	0.27	0.5	2.30

[a] 1998.

[b] 1997. Net replacement rates after tax; average for different family types (single, married couple, couple with two children) and two earnings levels (APW-level and 66.7 per cent of APW level); including unemployment family, and housing benefits in the first month of benefit receipt; it is assumed that waiting periods are met.

[c] 1996.

[d] 1995 data, or latest year available.

Sources: Eurostat 2000*a*; OECD 1999*b*.

strong disparities in income distribution and poverty after taxes and transfers. As discussed below, this is a consequence of their pension-heavy and 'insider-biased' welfare systems and absence of an adequate safety net for young people, single mothers, and the long-term unemployed. Although belonging to the Continental cluster, Belgium, Germany, and the Netherlands reveal a comparatively favourable performance along all three dimensions, coming close to the Nordic welfare states in terms of distributive outcomes.

The overall picture that emerges is that the association between the total burden of taxation and social security contributions (measured as a share of GDP) and employment performance is quite weak. To be sure, Denmark and Sweden, the most redistributive welfare states, with the highest tax burdens, do better in employment terms than the low tax, Anglo-Saxon welfare states of Ireland and the United Kingdom, showing that—contrary to neo-liberal nostrums—high taxes and high levels of employment can go hand in hand. But this association is not borne out by the experience of the Continental welfare states, which display medium-to-high tax rates but just average levels of employment performance. It is only the Scandinavian welfare states, as Scharpf correctly observes, that have 'systematically translated high

Table 20.3 *Distributive performance 1994*

	40 per cent line	50 per cent line	60 per cent line	Gini-coefficient (year)[a]	Wage dispersion D9/D1[b]
Denmark	2.9	6.0	21.4	0.239 (92)	2.86
Finland				0.223 (91)	2.75
Sweden				0.229 (92)	2.78
Austria		12.1			
Belgium		11.4		0.230 (92)	2.79
France	7.7	14.9	24.5	0.324 (89)	4.11
Germany	9.9	15.2	21.4	0.300 (94)	3.84
Luxembourg	6.5	15.4	25.9	0.235 (94)	2.93
Netherlands	4.7	8.8	19.1	0.249 (91)	3.05
Ireland	11.2	21.6	32.9	0.328 (87)	4.18
United Kingdom	12.3	21.3	30.8	0.346 (95)	4.56
Greece	14.8	21.8	29.3		
Italy		12.5		0.255 (91)	3.14
Portugal	17.1	25.2	32.9		4.05
Spain	11.0	19.8	29.1	0.306 (89)	4.04

[a] Lower figures indicate a more egalitarian structure of distribution of disposable income.
[b] D1 refers to the lowest income decile, D9 refers to the highest income decile (latest year available).
Sources: Eurostat 1998; OECD 1996*a*; Gottschalk and Smeeding 1998.

tax revenues into high levels of publicly financed social services'—and therefore high (and apparently sustainable) levels of public employment (Scharpf 2000*a*: 132). The medium-to-high tax Continental welfare and the moderate-tax Southern welfare states have the lowest employment scores, due less to the level of taxation, but more so to their methods of social security financing. In this respect, the heavy reliance on social security contributions seems to engender strongly negative employment effects.

This brief appraisal shows how different welfare states vary and how they measure up against our three indicators. Scandinavian welfare states are generous, strongly 'de-commodifying' (to use Esping-Andersen's terms), and expensive (in terms of funding levels). But they also achieve high levels of employment. The liberal welfare states of the United Kingdom and Ireland are lean, rather mean, but have also (at least recently) delivered a respectable (albeit less impressive) employment performance. But their levels of service provision are (often chronically) poor and levels of inequality very high. The conservative continental countries are also expensive, achieve rather less respectable distributive outcomes than their Nordic counterparts, but also register a very poor employment performance. Meanwhile, the Southern welfare systems are much less developed (though they have been rapidly catching up), much less generous, with relatively high levels of inequality and (apart from Portugal) disastrous employment performance. If, as we argue below, these are regime specific problems, then, as we also argue, so too must be the solutions.

WELFARE STATE ADJUSTMENT: REGIME-SPECIFIC STRENGTHS AND WEAKNESSES

Scandinavia: A 'Cost' and 'Jobs' Problem

In the Scandinavian countries, as is well known, social protection is a citizen's right. Coverage is fully universal and everyone is entitled to the same 'basic amounts' when social risks occur. Besides generous income maintenance, these systems offer a wide array of public social services and active labour market programmes, which help sustain high participation rates for both men and women. Their social spending levels have remained by far the highest in Europe throughout the 1980s and 1990s (Table 20.4).

These welfare states are also large employers: in Denmark and Sweden, government employees (largely women, especially in social services) represent more than a fifth of the employed, against an EU average of 12.0 per cent (Table 20.5). These systems embarked on the road to high public employment in the 1960s when financial resources were not a problem. A self-reinforcing mechanism then emerged: the expansion of 'welfare state jobs' encouraged women to enter the labour market,

Table 20.4 *Social protection spending and taxation as a percentage of GDP (Scandinavian countries)*

	Social protection expenditures[a]			Total taxation[b]		
	1990	1993	1998	1990	1993	1998
Sweden	33.1	38.6	33.3	53.7	48.4	52.0
Denmark	28.7	31.9	30.0	47.1	48.8	49.8
Finland	25.1	34.6	27.2	44.7	44.6	46.2
EU-15	25.4	28.9	27.7	39.2	40.3	41.3

Source: [a] Eurostat 2000*a*; [b] OECD 2000: table 3, pp. 67–8.

Table 20.5 *Government employment and labour market participation (Scandinavian countries)*

	Government employment (1998)	Labour market participation rates (1997)*	
		Women	Men
Sweden	21.2	85.8	90.6
Denmark	23.0	83.7	93.2
Finland	14.8	84.7	90.8
EU-15	12.1	71.8	93.4
United States	10.6	—	—
Japan	6.2	—	—

*Persons aged 25–49 years.
Source: OECD 1999; Eurostat 2000*a*.

allowing a 'de-familization' of many caring functions, in turn fostering demand for more services (Sainsbury 1996; Fargion 2000).

General taxation plays a large role in funding of social expenditure, especially in Denmark, where social security contributions only amount to 3 per cent or so of GDP. In Sweden and Finland contributions make up a smaller share of total taxation than in Continental Europe, but are larger than in the United Kingdom or Ireland. Means-tested public assistance is rather circumscribed. The various functions of social protection are highly integrated and the provision of benefits and services is mainly the responsibility of (central and local) public authorities. The only sector outside this framework is unemployment insurance, which is not formally compulsory and is directly managed by the trade unions.

Thanks to their institutional solidity and coherence, these systems have long been regarded as the 'ideal type' welfare state, resting on deep-seated norms of egalitarianism and solidarity. However, the exogenous and endogenous challenges affecting all political economies in recent decades have not left this part of Europe untouched, creating both a 'cost' and a 'jobs' problem. The early 1990s produced a shock in both respects, especially for Finland and Sweden. GDP fell for three consecutive years, budgetary balances worsened dramatically, and unemployment levels deteriorated. The Danish situation was somewhat different from the other two countries—with higher unemployment in the 1980s, but better macroeconomic conditions in the early 1990s (Stephens 1996). The economic crisis and increase in unemployment pushed up social expenditure, which in 1993 reached 36.9 per cent of GDP in Sweden and 34.8 per cent in Finland. The Danish peak was 32.6 per cent in 1994. Throughout the past decade, these countries have been grappling with pressures for cost-containment in their generous social programmes and for labour market reorganization—especially with a view to generating more demand for private sector employment.

Given the high level of popular support for social policies, the reform agenda has been shaped by a pragmatic, problem-solving approach, with no 'grand controversy' on alternative views and scenarios. The principles of universalism have not been significantly questioned, even if this has meant cuts 'across the board' in replacement rates (especially in sickness and unemployment benefits) and of eligibility conditions and benefit duration—a sort of universalism in reverse gear. Some significant steps have been taken towards the 'Bismarckian tradition' in pensions: the link between contributions and benefits has been strengthened by reforms in the 1990s in both Sweden and Finland, a trend that has questioned the maintenance of a basic pension guarantee, independent of labour market status. Besides cost-containment, a second important leitmotiv of reform in the 1990s has been 'activation', giving actual and potential beneficiaries incentives to stay in or find gainful employment. The 'work line'—as it is referred to—has indeed been strengthened, especially in Denmark. The Danish labour market reform of 1994 was one of the most far reaching and comprehensive moves in Europe towards the 'activation' of benefits (Cox 1998).

The reforms of the 1990s have clearly downsized the Scandinavian model, at least in terms of institutional generosity, and have also reorganized its system of incentives. But the underlying architecture of the model remains largely intact: in the words of Stein Kuhnle, 'the Nordic welfare states stood the test' of the 1990s, and have even shown that 'an advanced, universalistic welfare state is not a handicap when a sudden, unexpected economic crisis occurs' (Kuhnle 2000). The architecture of Nordic welfare seems well 'calibrated' for responding to the new risks and needs associated with ageing societies and with the transition to the 'new economy' (Table 20.6). Basic income guarantees provide a safeguard not just against poverty and exclusion, but also against the penalties deriving from spells out of work and broken careers. The availability of a wide array of services allows a more effective response to the caring needs of families and socializes their costs. High rates of labour market participation attenuate financial strains on pension systems. As Table 20.6 also shows, these countries invest more than most in labour market training (a crucial policy for more knowledge intensive economies) and their education expenditure ratios are by far the highest in Europe.

Unresolved problems remain, however, especially regarding private employment creation in the sheltered services sector. This is particularly true for Sweden where such jobs have markedly declined in the 1990s—which can be explained by the sensitivity of less productive services to the high tax wedge, low wage dispersion, and high

Table 20.6 *Public expenditure on selected functions as percentage of GDP*

	Old age and survivors 1998[a]	Education 1995[b]	Family and children, 1998[a]	Active labour market policy[c]	Labour market training[c]	Social exclusion* 1995
Denmark	11.5	8	3.9	1.89	1.07	1.5
Sweden	13.1	7.8	3.6	2.01	0.48	1.1
Finland	9.4	7.3	3.48	1.23	0.41	0.7
United Kingdom	11.8	5.2	2.3	0.42	0.09	0.3
Ireland	4.0	4.7	2.04	1.66	0.21	0.4
Austria	13.7	5.6	2.84	0.44	0.15	0.3
Belgium	11.8	5.7	2.34	1.29	0.29	0.7
Germany	12.7	4.8	3.03	1.27	0.34	0.6
France	13.4	6	2.99	1.37	0.35	0.5
Netherlands	11.7	5.2	1.28	1.76	0.22	0.7
Luxembourg	10.7	4.4	3.4	0.30	0.01	0.4
Italy	16.1	4.7	0.91	1.08	0.01	0.0
Spain	10.0	4.9	0.45	0.72	0.21	0.1
Portugal	10.0	5.8	1.24	0.87	0.28	0.1
Greece	12.9	2.9	1.98	0.35	0.06	—
EU-15	9.4	5.2	1.57	1.2	0.27	0.5

*1995 data, or latest year available.

Source: [a]Eurostat 2000*a*; [b]Eurostat 2000*b*; [c]EC (there may be some overlap with other categories of expenditure).

minimum wages (Iversen and Wren 1998; Scharpf 2000*a*). If it is true that the margins for employment creation in both the public and the private exposed sectors are quite narrow, then the key for solving the 'employment trilemma' lies in the social and political readiness to relax traditional norms of universalism and egalitarianism in wages and job protection. So far, however, *Homo Socialdemocraticus*—to use Esping Andersen's (1999) metaphor—has been very reluctant to take steps in this direction.

The United Kingdom: A Social Exclusion and Poverty Problem

The coverage of social protection in the United Kingdom is highly inclusive, though not fully universal (except for health care): inactive citizens and the employed earning less than a certain threshold have no access to National Insurance benefits. These benefits—which are flat rate—are much more modest than in Scandinavia. Conversely, the range of social assistance and means-tested benefits is much more extensive. Health care and social services are financed through general taxation, but contributions play an important role in the financing of cash benefits. Tax and expenditure levels have remained relatively low (see Table 20.7), and the same is true for public sector employment (9.5 per cent in 1998, compared with an EU average of 11.7 per cent and 10.6 per cent in the United States).

The UK welfare state is usually regarded as the closest European approximation to the 'liberal regimes' of the United States, Australia, and New Zealand with their more modest levels of protection and predilection for targeted provision—a view that is basically correct, with some caveats. Aggregate social spending in the United Kingdom remains well above that of the United States (and just below the EU average—see Table 20.7), the NHS caters to the needs of the whole population, and the range of benefits offered (if not always their amounts) is relatively large. But the institutional logic of the British welfare state is indeed distinct; and over time this has generated specific outcomes and problems and shaped a particular reform agenda (Rhodes 2000*a*, *b*).

The flat-rate nature of 'Beveridgean' benefits and their coverage loopholes (based on earnings thresholds) allowed Conservative governments in the 1980s and 1990s to 'residualize' social protection and expand low-pay, low-skill jobs (see Rhodes 2000*a*). The real value of universal benefits (e.g. basic pensions and child benefits)

Table 20.7 *Social spending and taxation as a percentage of GDP (United Kingdom and Ireland)*

	Social protection expenditures[a]			Total taxation[b]		
	1990	1993	1998	1990	1993	1998
United Kingdom	22.9	29.1	26.8	36.0	33.3	37.2
Ireland	18.7	20.5	16.1	33.6	34.5	32.2
EU-15	25.4	28.9	27.7	39.2	40.3	41.3

Source: [a]Eurostat 2000*a*; [b]OECD 2000: table 3, pp. 67–8.

Table 20.8 *Social assistance expenditure in selected European countries*

	Cash social assistance (% of GDP)		Total social assistance expenditures as % of social security expenditures	
	1980	1992	1980	1992
Germany	1.0	1.6	7.1	11.9
France[a]	0.6	1.3	3.5	6.4
Italy	1.1	1.5	9.1	9.1
Sweden[a]	0.8	1.5	4.6	6.7
United Kingdom[a]	1.8	3.9	21.9	33.0
EU-15	0.9	1.5	7.7	10.2

[a] Including housing

Source: OECD 1996*b*; own calculations.

was left to erode while earnings-related supplements to National Insurance payments were abolished. A barrage of restrictive measures was introduced to tackle unemployment—especially among the young—which culminated in the new *Jobseekers Allowance* in 1996, which limited the duration of benefits and made them conditional on strict 'activation' criteria. The middle classes were encouraged to 'opt out' into non-public forms of insurance (e.g. private occupational pensions after the 1986 reform) and targeted, means-tested benefits expanded rapidly—from 1.8 to 3.9 per cent of GDP between 1980 and 1992, by far the highest level in Europe (Table 20.8).

A second important reform has been the introduction of wage subsidies to supplement low pay. The first 'in-work benefits' were introduced as long ago as 1973 (as Family Income Supplement), but the new Family Credit introduced in 1986 was more generous—in terms of income supplementation and offsets for childcare expenses. It also became more widespread, especially when extended after 1995 to childless couples and single adults as 'Earnings top-ups'. It was thought that the expansion of in-work benefits would help remove the unemployment trap by increasing incomes for those in work without reducing out-of-work incomes. On the employer side, incentives (contribution reductions and exemptions) to hire the low-skilled, long-term unemployed were introduced in 1995 and 1996.

The consequences have been significant. The erosion of universal provision (as well as the market-oriented re-organization of health and social services) has contributed to an avoidance of cost problems, most importantly in long-term pensions liabilities. Wage subsidies have fostered an expansion of private employment and contributed to a remarkable fall in the unemployment rate. Unlike many other European countries, the United Kingdom no longer seems to have a problem of jobless growth.

But inequality and poverty levels have also markedly increased—partly due to the perverse effects of welfare residualization. During the 1980s and 1990s, the nature of British employment and the distribution of earnings have changed considerably. On the one hand, there has been a sharp decline in 'fordist' jobs in manufacturing and

Table 20.9 *Income distribution and poverty in selected European countries*

	Gini-Index		Poverty ratio	
	1983–7	1992–5	1983–7	1992–5
Belgium	22.8	23.0	4.8	5.5
Denmark	25.7	24.0	7.7	6.9
Sweden	22.0	22.9	8.0	7.3
United Kingdom	30.4	34.6	7.0	10.6
United States	34.1	36.9	17.9	17.9

Source: Luxembourg income study website: http://lissy.ceps.lu.

other non-service sectors in the middle range of the earnings distribution. On the other hand, the increase in employment has been concentrated in sectors like banking, finance, and business services where earnings are relatively high, and in hotels, catering, and other services where pay is low. Meanwhile, earnings at the upper end of the spectrum have grown relative to those at the bottom. The result has been a rapid polarization of incomes (Table 20.9—also Table 20.3) (Rhodes 2000a).

The increase in the number of working poor is the other side of Britain's success in job creation. Between 1990 and 1995, the number of working families with children receiving means-tested Family Credit to top up low pay almost doubled. Statistics also show a marked increase in poverty levels. In the mid-1990s, nearly 10 million people in 5.7 million families were dependent on means-tested Income Support compared with 4.4 million in 2.9 million families in 1979 (Johnson 1996; OECD 1998). Recent studies report a worrying decline in income mobility, with growing numbers stuck in a low pay/no pay cycle (Gurumurthy 1999).

With the New Labour government, a distinct reform agenda has emerged in the United Kingdom. While not essentially questioning the functional links between the social policy/employment regime and the economy inherited from its predecessors, the new government has embarked upon a strategy of rationalization in various directions. These include fine-tuning benefit rules to neutralize the various 'traps' created by old and new welfare-to-work schemes, fighting against poverty and social exclusion through an increase in minimum guarantees, tax reforms, and the introduction of new targeted programmes. The NHS is being strengthened and investment in human capital policies increased with a view to upgrading skill levels. As shown in Table 20.6, education expenditure was just below the EU average in the mid-1990s, but spending on labour market training (and, more generally, on active policies) was very modest.

The enhancement of national human capital seems an especially important ingredient of New Labour's 'Third Way' project, which explicitly aims to bring together the inherited neo-liberal design and incentive structure with elements of Scandinavian-style active labour market policy. But will the 'Third Way' succeed in reducing poverty and inequality while preserving the UK economy's recent capacity for employment creation? To some extent, the dilemmas facing the New Labour government are the inverse of those facing the other EU governments. In the solidarity/efficiency trade-off, it is the former that needs to be enhanced in the United Kingdom. The main political challenge for a strategy of 'modernization' is not so much that of overcoming the vested interests of entrenched welfare constituencies (as in much of continental Europe), but the resistance of the general public to paying higher taxes, regardless of their oft recounted willingness to do so in opinion polls (Rhodes 2000*a, b*). So far, the Blair government has tried so solve this dilemma 'by stealth', that is, by finding indirect and invisible ways of spending and taxing. It remains to be seen whether this strategy will continue to be politically feasible and—more importantly—whether it will prove adequate for the tasks at stake.

Continental Europe: High Costs and Low Employment

The 'continental conservative' group includes Germany, France, the Benelux countries, and Austria. Here the Bismarckian tradition centred on the links between work position (and/or family status) and social entitlements is still highly visible both in income maintenance and in health care. Only the Netherlands has altered this tradition by introducing some universal schemes (e.g. in basic pensions). Benefit formulae (proportionate to earnings) and financing (via social security contributions) largely reflect insurance logics, often with different rules for different professional groups. Replacement rates are generous and coverage is highly inclusive (although fragmented); spending and taxing levels are high (Table 20.10).

The occupation-oriented approach is also apparent in the organization and management of social protection. Trade unions and employers' associations actively participate in governing the insurance schemes. The majority of the population is covered by social insurance, through individual or derived rights. Insurance obligations come into effect automatically at the beginning of a gainful job—though in Germany and Austria there is a minimum earnings threshold. Whoever falls through the insurance net in these countries is cushioned by fairly substantial social assistance benefits.

Table 20.10 *Social protection expenditure and taxation in 1998 as a percentage of GDP (Continental Europe)*

	Social protection expenditures[a]	Total tax revenue[b]
Austria	28.4	44.4
Belgium	27.5	45.9
France	30.5	45.2
Germany	29.3	37.0
Luxembourg	24.1	41.5
Netherlands	28.5	41.0
Switzerland	27.9	35.1
EU-15	27.7	41.3

Source: [a]Eurostat 2000*a*; [b]OECD 2000: table 3, pp. 67–8.

In the debates of the 1990s, this type of welfare state has often been seen as generous but perverse—a phenomenon aptly captured by the metaphors of 'frozen fordism' and 'inactivity traps' (Esping Andersen 1996, 1999; Scharpf 1997*a*). Their root cause has been identified in its combination of three characteristics:

- the generosity of insurance-based cash benefits, indicated by high earnings replacement ratios, long benefit durations, and a tendency towards 'institutional stretching' (e.g. the loose application of rules governing disability benefits);
- the mainly 'passive' nature of insurance benefits, with a limited conditionality attached to benefit receipt (e.g. active job search, availability for job offers, etc.) and the low incidence of controls;
- the mainly contributory financing of benefits. The systems of Continental (but also Southern) Europe display a higher ratio of social security contributions to total social expenditure either than the Scandinavian or Anglo-Saxon countries.

The interplay of these three elements has produced a distinctive syndrome. Honouring generous insurance entitlements (especially those of maturing pension systems) has required the maintenance of high contributory rates on the wages of standard workers in the presence of highly protective systems of labour law. This has a number of adverse consequences (Manow and Seils 2000): it has discouraged firms from offering traditional 'fordist' employment; it has created pressures for subsidised early retirement (as shown in Table 20.1, rates of employment among men above fifty-five are now very low); and high social charges have blocked the expansion of private service jobs. Meanwhile, due to fiscal overload, there is little scope for following the Scandinavian route by creating employment in public sector services.

As highlighted by Scharpf (1997, 2000*a*), Continental labour markets are therefore doubly deficient. Like the United States (but unlike Scandinavia) they have relatively low public employment ratios, ranging from 9.3 per cent in Germany to 14.8 per cent in France in 2000. But like Scandinavia (and unlike the United States), they have low employment ratios in sheltered services. In the 'wholesale and retail trade, restaurants and hotels' (ISIC 6 in the OECD classification)—where most of the American 'Mcjobs' of the 1980s and 1990s are concentrated—France and Germany have employment ratios of 10 and 9.4 per cent, respectively, against a US ratio of 16.1 (Austria and the Netherlands fare much better, with ISIC 6 rates at 14.9 and 13.6 per cent, respectively in 1997).

In consequence, most Continental countries registered mounting rates of unemployment in the 1980s and early 1990s (Table 20.11). The challenge of unemployment has been responded to by further expanding passive income maintenance schemes (unemployment, sickness, disability, and early retirement) requiring further increases in social charges. This self-reinforcing upward cost spiral has had a negative impact on low-skilled workers, the young, and women. These systems have also proven ineffective in promoting arrangements to allow women to combine work and family (especially child rearing) responsibilities (van Kersbergen 1995; Esping-Andersen 1999). The result has been an emerging 'bad' equilibrium between low female employment and low fertility—contributing in turn to the growing welfare cost problems.

Public Policy

Table 20.11   *Unemployment and female employment (continental Europe)*

	Unemployment rate			Female employment rate	
	1985	1990	1999	1985	1999
Austria	3.6	3.2	3.7	52.1	59.7
Belgium	10.4	6.7	9.0	39.1	50.2
France	10.2	9.0	11.3	49.3	53.5
Germany	7.2	4.8	8.7	48.9	57.1
Luxembourg	2.9	1.7	2.3	39.7	48.7
Netherlands	8.3	6.2	3.3	40.9	61.3
EU-15	9.9	7.7	9.2	44.7	52.6

Source: European Commission 2000.

This situation has generated a complex reform agenda in the Continental systems, centred on various measures: containing the expansion of social insurance; rationalizing the structure of social spending by trimming pensions and 'passive' benefits; improving and updating family policy; introducing 'active' incentives in short-term cash benefits; reforming labour market rules to overcome the insider/outsider cleavage; and reducing the incidence of social charges. The Dutch reforms in particular have proven quite effective in reversing 'welfare without work' by combining new forms of labour market flexibility with sustained levels of income security and expanding the level of female employment significantly (Table 20.11). But even there, a low rate of activity among men over fifty-five (Table 20.1) and the high level of 'invalidity' beneficiaries reveal the persistence of the problem of unemployment.

In the other countries, adjustment has proven less effective as well as socially and politically turbulent. To take the French case (where unemployment rates, especially amongst the young, have persistently been the highest in the Continental group), the violent street demonstrations against the Juppé plan in 1995 revealed just how difficult welfare reform can be. France has made noticeable progress since the 1990s and its employment performance has been improving in recent years, assisted by higher growth and greater flexibility associated with the 35-hour week reform. But most of the 'structural' changes required are still to be implemented; and its rate of unemployment is still the highest in the continental group, at 9.5 per cent in 2000.

Thus, while Scandinavia has a 'flexibility' problem (in facilitating private service sector employment), and the United Kingdom has mainly a 'security' problem (strengthening basic guarantees for low paid jobs), the Continental countries face a fight on both fronts. A major priority is that of strengthening their relatively solid educational and training systems behind their high-skills systems of production (cf. Table 20.6). However, this is unlikely to generate new and high levels of employment. As argued by various authors (Esping-Andersen 1999; Scharpf 2000a), the most promising way out of the Continental syndrome is via an expansion of services, producing higher female participation rates. But the Bismarckian approach—and especially its social insurance logic—impedes such post-industrial developments: it tends to price low-end services out of the market and is ill-suited, in general, for creating virtuous combinations of flexibility and security. A close link between contributions and entitlements may in fact discourage work mobility and prevent the provision of adequate benefits for the mobile. Thus 'de-frosting' the Bismarckian status quo and eliminating its inactivity traps will definitely require additional policy innovation.

Southern Europe: Uneven Development and Adverse Demographics

The fourth family includes Italy, Spain, Portugal, and Greece. These countries are quite different in terms of economic wealth: while Italian GDP per capita is around the EU average, the other three countries still lie at the bottom of the EU prosperity league—though they are rapidly catching up. Their levels of social protection maturity are also different: the Italian system was created much earlier than the others, and this is reflected in spending and taxation (Table 20.12).

Despite their diversity, they share a number of common institutional traits (Ferrera 1996):

1. In terms of coverage they are mixed, with 'Bismarckian' income transfers (which are occupationally fragmented) alongside 'Beveridgean' universal national health services (although only in Italy and Spain are these complete).
2. Their safety nets are weakly developed: the establishment of guaranteed social minima is recent and uneven.
3. Occupational funds and the social partners play a prominent role in income maintenance, but less so in health care.
4. Social charges are widely used (generating some of the 'inactivity traps' found in Continental Europe), but health and social services are increasingly funded from general taxation.
5. The family is still important and acts as a welfare 'broker' for its members, as revealed by the high incidence of 'extended households' with three or more generations (and/or lateral kin), as well as by the high number of persons over twenty living at home (Table 20.13).

Table 20.12 *Social spending and taxation in Southern Europe as percentage of GDP*

	Social expenditures[a]			Total tax revenue[b]		
	1990	1993	1998	1990	1993	1998
Greece	23.2	22.3	24.5	29.4	31.0	33.7[*]
Italy	24.3	26.2	25.2	38.9	44.2	42.7
Portugal	15.8	21.3	23.4	29.6	31.2	34.2
Spain	20.5	24.7	21.6	33.0	33.5	34.2
EU-15	25.4	28.9	27.7	39.2	40.3	41.3

[*]Tax revenue figure from 1997.

Source: [a]Eurostat 2000a; [b]OECD 2000: table 3, pp. 67–8.

362 Public Policy

Table 20.13 Share of young persons living with their parents in Southern Europe (%)

	20–24 years		25–29 years	
	1987	1996	1987	1996
Greece	63	73	39	50
Italy	81	89	39	59
Portugal	75	80	39	52
Spain	84	90	49	62
EU-15	—	66	—	32

Source: Eurostat 1998: 58.

Table 20.14 Employment performance in Southern Europe

	Employment rate (%) 1999	Female employment rate (%)		Unemployment rate (%) 1999	Youth unemployment rate (%) 1999	Part-time employment (% total employment) 1999
		1985	1999			
Greece	55.0	35.8	40.4	11.7	12.4	6.1
Italy	52.5	32.5	38.1	11.3	12.4	7.9
Portugal	67.4	48.8	59.6	4.5	4.3	11.0
Spain	52.3	25.2	37.3	15.9	12.4	8.3
EU-15	62.1	44.7	52.6	9.2	8.4	17.7

Source: European Commission 2000.

6. Female employment is low (Table 20.14). This is partly due to a distinct 'gender regime' which 'treats women (. . .) principally on the basis of family roles as regards their duties but sends them unprotected onto the market in case of economic need' (Trifiletti 1999: 54).
7. Family benefits and, especially, family services are still relatively underdeveloped (see Table 20.6).

All four systems are characterized by internal disequilibria:

1. Their social transfer systems thus display both peaks of generosity for certain occupational groups and serious gaps in protection for others. In the early 1990s, for example, the 'standard pension' (i.e. the maximum benefit obtainable after a full career as a percentage of the average production worker's wage) was much higher than the EU average (of 75 per cent), ranging from 89 per cent in Italy to 107 percent in Greece. But the minimum non-contributory pension was well *below* the EU average (of 36 per cent) at 8 per cent in Greece, 19 per cent in Italy, 32 per cent in Spain, and 30 per cent in Portugal (EC 1993).

2. 'Insider' and 'outsider' workers have traditionally been separated in terms of guarantees and opportunities, with a middling group of semi-peripheral workers moving backwards and forwards across the line (Moreno 2000).
3. The black economy is very extensive (between an estimated 15 and 30 per cent), posing problems both of efficiency and equity.
4. Employment levels are relatively low and unemployment is high, especially among young people. Portugal does better than the other three in terms of employment and unemployment (Table 20.14). Portugal also has higher levels of educational and especially training expenditures (Table 20.6)—the latter being at their lowest in Italy and Greece—albeit against a background of poor educational standards and literacy rates.

'Catching up' with their more advanced European counterparts has been made difficult by a particularly adverse demographic situation. With their low fertility rates, Southern European populations (especially those of Italy and Spain) are ageing at one of the fastest rates in the world (Table 20.15). In Italy and Greece, pension expenditure absorbs a higher share of total social spending (around 58–60 per cent in the mid-1990s) than in any other European country.

The 1990s saw the initiation of an adjustment process centred on some common measures:

- the ironing out of benefit formulae for privileged occupational groups while upgrading minimum benefits;
- the introduction and consolidation of safety net schemes;
- remedying deficiencies in family benefits and services;
- rationalizing and, in some cases, decentralizing the organizational frameworks and financial incentives of the national health services.

Various 'moralizing' measures have also been introduced to combat corruption, clientelism, tax evasion, and the underground economy. Labour market reform and the promotion of 'national competitiveness' have also acquired increasing policy salience, as attested by the emergence of new social 'pacts' or 'dialogues' between

Table 20.15 *Fertility rates (children per women) in Southern Europe*

	1980	1990	1998
Greece	2.21	1.39	1.30
Italy	1.64	1.34	1.19
Portugal	2.18	1.57	1.46
Spain	2.20	1.36	1.30
EU-15	**1.82**	**1.57**	**1.45**

Source: Eurostat 2000*b*.

governments and social partners (Rhodes 2001). However, these countries have revealed no inclination towards 'social devaluation', or building growth on low social standards (Guillen and Matsaganis 2000). Indeed, the 1990s have seen the Portuguese welfare state expand from around 15 to 24 per cent of GDP. The overall tone of the adjustment debate is that of 'upgrading' social standards to align them with the core group of the EU's continental member states.

The Southern welfare states find themselves on a difficult path of reform. Two developments will prove to be critical for success. The first is the further consolidation of the basic safety net, that is, the floor of tax-financed benefits for individuals and households. The existence of a robust and reliable safety net is a prerequisite for successfully combating poverty and exclusion, as well as cushioning the costs of economic change. Spain and Portugal have already taken some important steps in this direction, but Italy and especially Greece have still to put some basic structures (e.g. a national minimum income guarantee) in place. As shown by Table 20.6, these two countries display the most unbalanced pattern of social expenditure—a pattern that urgently needs incisive policy reform.

The second ingredient for successful modernization is a more rapid expansion of the 'service sector', which might encourage more female employment and reinvigorate fertility. Given financial constraints and cultural norms, the Scandinavian solution of collectivizing family needs in the hands of the state is not a viable option. More feasible would be the promotion of a 'family-serving welfare mix', an amalgam of public regulations and incentives, corporate arrangements, third sector activism, and private entrepreneurship to respond to the needs of the family (and especially women) through the supply of new services in the formal economy. Given the institutional legacies, marked territorial disparities, and the size of the underground economy, the promotion of this new welfare mix and, more generally, the search for a new balance between flexibility and security is no easy task in the South.

CONCLUSION—AND FUTURE DIRECTIONS FOR RESEARCH

The above survey of regime-specific strengths and vulnerabilities reveals how common constraints and the convergent risks of post-industrialism confront different welfare states with divergent problems. Successful adjustment thus requires tailor-made, regime- or country-specific solutions (Ferrera *et al.* 2000; Hemerijck and Schludi 2000). While the Scandinavian countries are primarily faced with a 'cost' problem and a 'flexibility' problem (i.e. creating the conditions for an expansion of private services), the Anglo-Saxon countries continue to face problems of 'security' and 'poverty' in an otherwise strong and expanding labour market. The Continental countries are confronted with the social and employment policy challenge of boosting female employment and shifting from passive income maintenance to secured activation while also maintaining and transforming their all-inclusive pay-as-you-go pension systems. Finally, the Southern welfare states are faced with the most difficult tasks of overcoming the inequities of their employment and social security systems, while also combating the adverse demographic effects of low fertility. The future of welfare state adjustment is therefore less one of convergence than one of path-dependent reform, as policy makers come to terms with the complex legacies of their particular welfare state traditions.

Future research on these issues (at least in the short-to-medium term) is likely to go in several directions. The first will be a further exploration of the political dimensions of welfare reform (see Pierson 2001*a* for the most comprehensive study to date). To quote Pierson (2001*b*: 455), 'there is not a single new politics of the welfare state, but different politics in different configurations'. For just as the problem constellations and reform potential of welfare states can be differentiated by their 'regime' (albeit with due attention paid to their country distinctiveness), so too can their politics of reform. There is already a growing literature on how reform has differed between Westminster systems such as the United Kingdom and New Zealand (where changes have been implemented unilaterally by governments), compared with the 'veto-point heavy' countries of Continental and Southern Europe where reform has to contend with the opposition of vested interests, and often proceeds via negotiation and complex trade offs. In the latter case, 'social pacts', some temporary, others more permanent, are now frequently assisting the welfare state modernization process, as well as in modifying national wage bargaining systems in the EMU member countries (see Iversen *et al.* 2000). How these work, and to what effect, is only now becoming the subject of detailed investigation (Fajertag and Pochet 2000; Molina and Rhodes 2002). Equally, the politics of the broader coalitions that need to be put in place to underpin the reform process—a project spurred forward by the recent work of Pierson (2001*b*)—is also in need of further analysis.

The second direction of future research will be more policy oriented and will focus on the achievement of optimal policy mixes in making welfare states sustainable, both financially and in their capacity to meet effectively with citizens' demands. Policy design is of crucial importance in making health and pensions systems, and social security more generally, affordable, effective, and responsive in a world of demographic change, increasingly differentiated forms of (post-industrial) employment, and shifts in the nature of 'need' and the distribution of social risk across the life course (Ferrera and Rhodes 2000*b*). Increasingly central to such studies are the family and gender dimensions of welfare systems, and debates on the trade-offs involved in boosting female labour market participation while also improving the gender division of labour in the household (Esping-Andersen 1999; O'Connor *et al.* 1999; Orloff 1999). The search for superior policy mixes also raises issues of policy formulation and implementation. Part of the 'design problem' in this regard lies in the effective sequencing of reform—the search, that is, via processes of policy learning and 'puzzling', for effective and legitimate innovations. The work of Hemerijck and Schludi (2000) and Ferrera *et al.* (2000) has already established the basis for this project; and future research in this area is likely also to embrace the normative philosophical tradition of analysis (e.g. Rothstein 2000), as researchers seek to make a contribution to the growing 'epistemic community' of actors mobilized in pan-European policy circles.

Public Policy

Which brings us to the third major area of new research—the nature of European governance in this policy domain. Research on EU level social policy (see Leibfried and Pierson 1995, 2000; Kleinman 2002 for an excellent introduction) has been reinvigorated by the emergence first of the 'Luxembourg process' and the new employment chapter of the Amsterdam Treaty (1997), and the subsequent announcement of a 'concerted strategy for modernizing social protection' at the EU's Lisbon Summit of spring 2000. The latter extended the new policy methods experimented with under the Luxembourg Process and its 'National Action Plans' (benchmarking, monitoring, and peer review) to the wider realm of social policy. Now dubbed 'the open method of co-ordination', this approach relies on 'soft law' rather than directives as a means of enhancing pan-European coordination (Adnett 2001; Hodson and Maher 2001). The first practical steps have been taken in social protection and pensions, with the search for a common if differentiated approach to many of the regime-specific problems dealt with in this article.

These developments open up several new areas for analysis that span a number of disciplines (political science and law) and sub-disciplines (European integration, policy studies) and are therefore highly conducive to inter-disciplinary research (Shaw 2000 points the way forward). Political economy approaches are also likely to make a major contribution, since new forms of coordination are emerging at the European level that link social policy with European fiscal and monetary policy making (under the Cologne Process that addresses the issue of policy inter-dependencies within EMU) (Rhodes 2002; Scharpf 2002). Gradually, the major issues of welfare sustainability and reform addressed in this article are being elevated to the EU level, as the recalibration of the European 'Social Model' shifts to the centre of policy-making attention. The eventual outcomes of this actual and anticipated process of institutional engineering are impossible to predict. But just as the last decade has illuminated much about European welfare states and their contemporary evolution, research in the next decade will inevitably focus on their 'Europeanization' in the emerging 'multi-level' EU polity.

PART VI

THE STATE

21

The Changing European State

WOLFGANG C. MÜLLER

INTRODUCTION

The modern state is an historic phenomenon that has been under constant transformation since its birth in the period of absolutism (Page 1995). In this chapter, I present a framework for analysing changes of the state and map out changes that have occurred in Western Europe since the 1980s. Since the completion of the state's democratization, the most interesting question has traditionally been what it is doing. Answers to this question have led to a number of labels such as 'welfare state' or 'night-watchman state' (i.e. the liberal non-interventionist state). In this chapter, I first suggest six dimensions which together capture the essence of the state. Then I provide an overview of changes in Western Europe since the 1980s along these dimensions.

A FRAMEWORK FOR ANALYSIS

The state is here regarded as a set of political institutions that hold the monopoly of the means of physical violence. In contrast to actors, institutions have no preferences and preferences are required to decide which tasks the state should take on and which not. In the early days of the modern state the monarch and the landed nobility were the driving forces in shaping the state. Later they were forced to share power with the new bourgeois classes and eventually—in the age of mass politics—all citizens had the chance to participate in shaping the state. More specifically, it is political parties that structure elections and occupy the positions in which political authority is vested. However, they are influenced not only by the preferences of the citizens but also those of various social and economic interests (interest groups, important business firms), other states, and supra-national organizations. Specific preferences are often derived from objective conditions, that is, challenges and opportunities that exist in a given situation. These include international relations, economic conditions, demographic developments, and technological innovation. Finally, the shaping of the state is highly path-dependent. This means that the state is shaped by decisions of the past, which are often very difficult to reverse. The status quo always has an advantage for at least two reasons. First, changing structures and procedures of large and complex organizations is always costly and risky. Second, existing structures are defended not only by those interests which had been driving forces in their creation, but also by new ones, which, in effect, were created through these structures. Thus, to provide one example, the welfare state is defended not only by its clients and their political representatives but also by the welfare bureaucracy and its political allies.

The emphasis of this chapter will be on the state, not on the forces that shape it. More specifically, I am concerned with changes of the state that can be identified in at least six dimensions (see also Grande 1997).

Levels of state activities. One can still speak of 'the state' if certain activities are legitimately carried out (or, at least, decided upon) at the subnational and supranational levels. What is important is that there is a constitutional delegation to these levels and a chain of command that allows decisions reached there to be implemented, in the last consequence, with the help of the nation state's monopoly of legitimate physical violence. Thus it is possible to identify different levels of state activity: subnational, national, European Union (EU), and even beyond Europe (NATO). State change occurs by shifting responsibilities and/or authority from one level to another, for example, from the nation state to the European Union.

State responsibilities. At any given time the state assumes responsibility for providing certain 'goods' to its citizens. While the precise combination of these 'goods' differs over time and between countries, they include external and internal security, the rule of law (guaranteeing personal freedom, private property, enforcement of contracts), a common (official) language, education, a common currency, transportation systems, information systems, energy supply, food supply (a state function mainly limited to crisis times in its extensive form), social security, a strong economy, a clean and healthy environment, the market (business competition), and democracy (political participation rights, party competition). To some extent these 'goods' are causally linked with each other. Thus the absolutist state introduced (forced upon its citizens) a common language and education in order to allow for effective external security (an army with soldiers who could be commanded in one language) and a strong economy. In this dimension, change means to add new responsibilities to the state's load, redefine, or eliminate old ones.

Modes of production. The state can use different production modes for the 'goods' the provision of which fall under its responsibility. (a) The state can act as sovereign and can honour its responsibilities through a special state apparatus. For example, external security is guaranteed by the military, internal security by police forces, and the rule of law by the judiciary. (b) The state may, however, delegate some of its obligations to special agencies, such as a central bank or regulatory bodies. Of course, the judiciary was the first of these (largely) independent institutions, though the separation of powers has remained imperfect in many countries. In establishing such agencies and their goals the state acts as sovereign, but there is no direct line of command between the government of the day and the agencies. This type of institutional design allows the agencies to carry out their tasks without interference from the government of the day. The intended consequence is to gain credibility that the 'goods' (e.g. monetary stability) are indeed provided, even if this is inconvenient in the short term.

(c) Finally, the state can act through state-owned companies. Here the state may still partially act as sovereign. This is the case when the state establishes monopolies, which in turn have special duties (e.g. serving all parts of the country, or to contain the abuse of the products, as is sometimes the case with alcohol, tobacco, and gambling). In other cases the state is just the owner of firms that participate in truly competitive markets (e.g. commercial banking, industry). These firms have no share of state sovereignty. The state, in its role as sovereign, should treat them just like their private-owned competitors; for instance when implementing tax or environmental regulations, and as state-owned firms they should not enjoy a competitive advantage when bidding for public contracts. (In practice, however, state firms often enjoy preferential treatment by the government or administration.) State change in this dimension means to place different weights on these three production modes, or to abandon one or more of them.

Resources. In the state provision of 'goods', one or more of the following resources are used: laws, personnel, and money. Laws are a unique resource of the state. As Richard Rose (1984: 63) has put it very well, 'any organization can raise and spend money and employ people to produce goods and services', but only the state 'can enact laws, which tell people what they can and cannot do, and regulate social life'. One of the problems with laws, of course, is that they are self-enforcing only to some extent and need enforcement mechanisms when they conflict with societal norms and/or interests. Speed limits, for instance, may be enforced by police patrols or with the help of automatic radar cameras. Hence, law enforcement requires personnel and equipment, and both cost money. Yet, there are limits to the enforceability of laws and (fortunately) some political goals can never be achieved by fiat in Western democracies (e.g. an increase of the birth rate). Therefore the state offers incentives for the 'right' kind of behaviour and they are mostly material rewards. In other words, the state tries to 'bribe' its citizens to behave in certain ways (e.g. make investments, raise children, drive environmental-friendly cars, take out private pensions and health insurance). Hence, money is required to pay for the incentives and personnel is required for the administration of these schemes. In this dimension change means to alter the mix of resources used for meeting the responsibilities the state has taken on. It is closely linked to what I have called 'production modes' and 'responsibilities'.

Finance. Whatever resources the state employs to provide its 'goods', money is required. This, in turn, can be raised by a wide range of different taxes, by fees (payments for specific state services), by income from state-owned firms, and, at least temporarily, by borrowing. Hence, another dimension to identify state change draws on the relative importance of these four ways of financing state activity and changes within each of them. Of particular relevance are changes in the tax system, which provides the bulk of state income. Here, change can occur, for instance, by shifts from property to income taxation, or from income to consumption taxation.

Steering of state activities. Finally, state activities can be organized either by rules which govern the process of making and implementing decisions, or by defining the outputs to be produced. Clear rules for the administrative process, as exemplified in the Weberian bureaucratic model, have always been a hallmark of the modern state.

The underlying theory is that it is clear from the outset how to achieve the substantive goals of the state and/or that the behaviour of agents is a goal in itself (e.g. transparency of administrative conduct). Change in this dimension would be a shift from classic process-oriented bureaucracy to output-oriented forms of steering state activities.

TRENDS IN WESTERN EUROPE SINCE 1980

The explicit emphasis is on identifying trends which are general European, or, at least to identify causes which exercise a uniform pressure on Western European states. In each case, there are leaders and latecomers, and responses to uniform pressures are likely to be similar though not identical.

Level of State Activities

Western Europe has seen a great number of important shifts in state responsibilities from one level to another since the 1980s. More specifically, authority has been shifted from the nation state both downwards, to the subnational level, and upwards, to the European Union.

The most sweeping shift to the subnational level has occurred in Belgium, which has followed a gradual path toward devolution, with a fully federal constitution adopted in 1993. Spain has given considerable autonomy to a great number of its regions and, at least under minority governments depending on the support of ethnic minority parties, works like a federal state. France has engaged in considerable decentralization in the 1980s and Swedish local governments have become increasingly autonomous of the central government in their implementation of the welfare state. Since 1997, devolution in the United Kingdom established directly elected assemblies in Scotland and Wales (see Strøm et al. 2002).

The dynamics of Europeanization have been even greater (see chapter by Hurrell and Menon). The South European enlargement of the 1980s was followed by the EFTA enlargement of the 1990s and it now seems very likely that the first group of Central and East European countries will join the European Union before 2005. Moreover, Iceland, Liechtenstein, and Norway have become European Economic Area (EEA) countries, effectively accepting European authority over a large number of policy areas. Hence, for many European countries a further layer of statehood was added and competences were transferred upwards to the European level.

Yet, the European Community not only grew in size but also fundamentally transformed itself. Beginning with a 1985 White Paper, the single market strategy was completed with the Single European Act (SEA) of 1992. It was soon followed by the Economic and Monetary Union (EMU) initiative, which was formally accepted with the Maastricht Treaty, in force since 1993. The dynamics of the single market and the convergence criteria, to be met by EMU countries (i.e. low inflation, low government deficit and debt, stable interest rates), have, in effect, taken away core policy competencies from the EMU member states and have shifted them to the European level

Table 21.1 *Europeanization of government authority, 1950–2001*

Issue arena (number of issues)	1950	1957	1968	1970	1992	2001
Economic (15)	1	1.4	2.2	2.4	2.7	3.4
Sociocultural (5)	1	1.2	1.8	2.0	1.8	2.6
Politico-constitutional (4)	1	1	1.5	1.8	2.0	2.8
International/external security (4)	1	1	1.8	2.0	2.8	4.0

Source: Calculated from Table 1 in P. Schmitter (1997: 403–4) 'The Emerging Europolity and its Impact Upon Natural Systems of Production', in Hollingworth, J. R. and Boyer R. (eds.). Contemporary Capitalism, Cambridge University Press, reproduced by kind permission.

(Dinan 1994; Moravcik 1998). The SEA also introduced qualified majority voting in the Council of Ministers for a number of important policy areas. Subsequent developments, including the 2000 Nice Treaty, have added to that list of policy areas and practice shows increasing use of this decision rule rather than traditional unanimity (Galloway 2001: ch. 5).

In an interesting attempt to capture the dynamics of the expansion of EC authority in a nutshell, Schmitter (1997: 403–4) has identified four issue arenas and a total of twenty-eight issue categories. He provides Europeanization scores for each of them for six selected years. In so doing he employs a five points scale, where 1 means 'All policy decisions at national level', 2 'Only some policy decisions at EC level', 3 'Policy decisions at both national/EC level', 4 'Mostly policy decisions at EC level', and 5 'All policy decisions at EC level'. The twenty-eight issue categories are not of equal importance and the five points scheme is not an interval scale. Hence, strictly speaking, the data should not be further aggregated. However, for heuristic reasons this may nevertheless be useful. Table 21.1 reports Schmitter's Europeanization mean scores for the twenty-eight issue categories grouped in his four issue arenas. The figures display a clear trend towards Europeanization. While individual issue classifications are not undisputed, the overall picture is generally considered accurate (Pollack 2000*b*: 523). Despite the commitment to the principle of subsidiarity in the EU Treaty, the 1990s have not seen a decline of EU regulations; hence regulatory Europeanization is likely to continue (Pollack 2000*b*).

State Responsibilities

Since the 1980s Western European states have considerably changed their responsibilities. Rather than attempting to provide a full account of state responsibilities, I discuss those which had been most contested in the post-war period, beginning with industrial ownership.

The comprehensive privatization programme in Britain under Margaret Thatcher, that with some delay was followed by most European governments, has introduced a new orthodoxy with respect to the state's role in the economy. Accordingly, the state now generally denies that running commercial banks and industrial firms is one of its tasks, irrespective of how state ownership was initially legitimized (Wright 1994*a*;

Boix 1998). Western European states have also largely withdrawn from the allocation of loans and subsidies to the private sector (Verdier 2000).

The picture is more complex when it comes to the provision of infrastructure. While the state has largely withdrawn (or is ready to do so) from the ownership role in telecommunications, it does not deny responsibility for the provision of telecom services. Rather the state's withdrawal from the ownership role is accompanied by a commitment to ensure effective competition, the maintenance of some public services, and the protection of privacy (Grande 1994). With respect to railway systems, the situation seems similar with respect to the state's ambitions; however, the private sector is less willing to step in at conditions that are considered socially acceptable and politically viable.

While microeconomic intervention of the government is now largely discredited, the state remains responsible for macroeconomic stabilization (Majone 1997: 141–2). Yet, things have changed substantially since the heyday of Keynesian demand management in the 1970s (Müller 1994). First, the state's ambition level is reduced with respect to both the precision and effects of intervention. No one believes any longer in the state's capacity for 'fine tuning' the economy and guaranteeing specific desired outcomes. Hence the state cannot provide jobs, it can only help to bring about conditions favourable to investment so that the creation of jobs through the market becomes more likely. Given the long-standing state vs. market conflict, it seems paradoxical that the liberal state's traditional function of providing (or protecting) the market has been revived since the 1980s. This new orthodoxy still leaves room for disagreement about the most important goals and the means to achieve them.

Since 1945 the state has assumed responsibility for providing welfare to such an extent that the term 'welfare state' was coined to label OECD states in general and Western European states in particular. Protagonists of the fully fledged welfare state have tried hard to show that it is in decline since the 1980s. Yet, budget figures for the OECD countries until the early 1990s showed no decline in welfare expenditure, only a reduction of its growth (Stephens *et al.* 1999; Lane and Ersson 1999: 331–3). The 'decline of the welfare state school' is not satisfied with this finding. First, they claim that the growth of social spending has remained lower than the growth of GDP, hence it can be labelled 'relative decline' (Clayton and Pontusson 1998). Second, they provide qualitative evidence for significant benefit cutbacks and the downsizing of welfare programmes. Tálos and Falkner (1994), based on their study of seven European welfare systems, report 'shrinking coverage' of social security systems and 'increased risk of poverty'. Stephens *et al.* (1999) report major cutbacks even before the mid-1980s in the United Kingdom, the Netherlands, and Denmark, and cuts in individual welfare programmes in a number of countries. Ferrera and Rhodes (2000) have marshalled a wealth of evidence, generally in line with the claim that, notwithstanding the expansions of individual programmes, welfare cutback is the imperative since the 1990s. While all comparative studies are careful to point to considerable differences between states, these may be interpreted as time-lags in adaptation as much as the results of fundamentally different challenges and resulting strategies (Damgaard *et al.* 1989: 190–1). Third, these studies claim that the need for welfare 'increased greatly' and hence more welfare services would be required to maintain the level of welfare provision (Stephens *et al.* 1999). In line with this claim, Iversen and Cusack (2000) demonstrate that most European countries suffer from the dein-dustrialization of employment, mainly caused by productivity growth in the agricul-tural and industrial sectors that could not be absorbed by equivalent growth of the service industries. This, in turn, means greater expenditure for unemployment and pension benefits, a trend that is further strengthened by demographic developments in most European societies, in particular the population's ageing. Overall, Stephens *et al.* (1999: 191) conclude, 'by the late 1980s and early 1990s a picture of wide-spread cuts emerges, in some cases at least of considerable magnitude'.

Finally, the state's role in environmental protection has certainly increased since the 1980s. First, environmental concerns have become more widespread among European citizens (Nas 1995). Second, environmental and ecological problems have become more visible if not more pressing, as exemplified by global warming and BSE. While there are ups and downs—inversely related with the business cycle—in paying tribute to these concerns in actual policy making, the overall trend is toward more state intervention, even at the international level. Given the trans-national character of environmental problems, it is easy to understand why policies at the EU level and even attempts at trans-continental agreements (such as the Kyoto agree-ment on reducing the output of carbon monoxide) are particular important in this policy area.

Production Modes

Of the three production modes the state can employ to provide its 'goods' one is clearly in retreat: state-owned companies are now generally considered ineffective and inefficient. Their microeconomic performance too often had been a disaster; the achievement of goals other than profits is hard to measure and it is even harder to enter them in an equation explaining profits or losses; and, finally, there are reasons to believe that state-owned firms had often been captured by politicians and trade unions, serving the special interests of these groups rather than laudable public aims (Majone 1996; for a particularly telling case see Meth-Cohn and Müller 1994). Where they still exist, state-owned firms are reminders of the past, and often only the problems associated with getting rid of them have allowed them to survive.

In a number of publications and in this book Giandomenico Majone (1994*a*, 1996, 1997) has forcefully argued that the regulatory state is on the rise. This argu-ment has important implications for several of the dimensions of the state discussed in this chapter. While it will figure prominently also in the subsequent sections, here the discussion is confined to its relevance for the production modes of the state. Given the problems with state-owned firms and the scarcity of financial resources (see below), the state turns to regulatory policies. This strategy is compatible with both of the remaining production modes. The state can make rules, from the most general to very specific ones, by parliament or government and implement them through its bureaucracy. Alternatively, the state can delegate the making of more detailed rules to special agencies, vested with public authority. Given that the demands on rule making are 'best met by flexible, highly specialized organizations enjoying considerable autonomy in decision making' (Majone 1997: 152), the state indeed turns to independent regulatory agencies. In several European countries highly specialized agencies have taken over the regulation of 'emerging markets', that is, economic sectors that previously were characterized by 'natural' monopolies held by state-owned firms (e.g. electricity supply, telecommunications, railway systems). And such change is under way in more states and economic sectors.

Independent agencies are certainly important from the point of view of state responsibilities. Yet, they are less so from the point of view of the manpower devoted to various production modes. From this perspective, production by the classic state apparatus remains by far the most important production mode. However, even here important changes can be noticed (see below under 'Steering of state activities').

Resources Employed

Money was always a scare resource of the state. Incumbents as a rule have much more ideas on spending than the state can (or should) afford to pay for. The scarcity of money makes personnel also a scare resource. There has always been demand for more teachers in the classrooms, nurses in the hospitals, and policemen in the streets. If anything, it has become more difficult for the state to respond to these demands since the 1980s. On the one hand limits to revenue generation have become more narrowly drawn, in particular since the mid-1990s (see next section). On the other hand, fulfilling long-standing obligations—such as to provide pensions and health care—have become much more expensive. For these reasons the 'classic' resource of the state—the law—gains in relative importance for undertaking new tasks. Rule making is less affected by budgetary constraints since the costs of regulation are borne to a large extent by the private sector (Majone 1997: 149).

This perspective of the 'rise of the regulatory state' (Majone 1994a) seems at odds with the claim of many governments to conduct a policy of deregulation (Hancher and Moran 1989). However, deregulation in European practice has not meant the undoing of all state intervention but rather 'a combination of deregulation *and* re-regulation' (Majone 1997: 143).

It is one thing to say that using laws does not place a great burden on the state budget, but it is quite a different thing to claim that regulation achieves its objectives. While regulation itself may be cheap, its implementation against resistance can be very costly, both in terms of budgets and legitimacy. Regulations that can become effective only through intensive 'police patrol' oversight are unattractive solutions. Hence, regulators may prefer to rely on 'fire alarm' oversight. This, in effect, means leaving the oversight to interested third parties, for example, interest groups, who raise the alarm if rules are not observed (McCubbins and Schwartz 1984). Unfortunately, third parties may find it beneficial to raise false alarms in an attempt to benefit their cause. Therefore, third party reliance is useful only under specific conditions. Building on Lupia and McCubbins (1994), who were interested in specifying the conditions under which legislators can learn from the actions of bureaucrats whether these are in line with their preferences, the conditions for the credibility of 'fire alarms' are: costly action of those who raise the alarm and the potential loss of reputation for false alarms. Costly action means, for instance, the collection of data on the breach of environmental laws. The potential loss of reputation for false alarms requires permanent actors in a specific policy area who may lose more in the long run by false alarms than they can possibly gain in the short term. In this sense environmental organizations that provide expertise, sometimes bolstered with results from independent laboratories, and which want to 'remain in business', can help make regulation effective.

A step further away from the Leviathan is the 'negotiating state' (Scharpf 1997*b*: 200–5). Here potential regulation is merely a threat to overcome resistance. Regulation will be issued only if the ends of regulation cannot be met by other means. One form that has been long known is self-organization 'in the shadow of the state'. In such cases, a common interest in a sector exists and the threat of state regulation allows overcoming the collective actor problem. Hence interests agree to, and observe, rules that are in their common interest. A more recent feature of the 'negotiating state' is to substitute contracts and agreements between the state and private actors for legislation. In 1996, 300 such agreements in the environmental policy area were in force in the EU member states, with more being signed each year (Mol *et al.* 2000). With respect to both faces of the 'negotiating state' there are important differences between countries. While 'self-organization in the shadow of the state' goes together with corporatist traditions, Germany and the Netherlands lead with regard to the 'voluntary approach'. However, it seems that the ideas have spread to other countries.

Generation of Resources

Capital income from state-owned firms has seldom been an important source of state revenue and given the politics of privatization this source is likely to disappear altogether. However, returns from privatization have made relevant contributions to state income in some European states since the 1980s (Boix 1998: 84). Of course, this income has a one-off character and at some point everything that can be sold will have gone. And compared to the overall state budgets, even comparatively substantial privatization returns were hardly more than a drop in the ocean. In contrast to privatization returns, fees (i.e. charges for specific state services) can be expected to increase. This is in line with the New Public Management modernization of the state administration (see next section). Nevertheless, the modern state has remained and is likely to remain predominantly a 'tax state'.

The conditions for taxation and state borrowing have fundamentally changed since the 1980s. The liberalization of financial markets, beginning in the 1970s, has significantly changed the conditions under which states generate income through taxation (Moran 1994; Simmons 1999). The removal of practically all hurdles for international capital transfers allows financial capital to select among worldwide opportunities even for short-term investments. Since the creation of the EMU, the member states have also lost the option of correcting a loss of international competitiveness through adjustments of the exchange rate. Hence national systems of taxation have become vulnerable to the extent that they reduce the attractiveness of the national economy to mobile capital. In other words, under the pressure of international tax and investment competition, states ought to cut taxes on capital. Rather than taxing capital, governments could be expected to turn to tax bases that are 'relatively immune to international tax competition', that is, taxes on consumption, social security contributions, and taxes on income from labour (Scharpf 2000*a*: 201). However, things are more complex: governments also need to consider the potential impact of tax increases on the cost of labour and hence on employment. For this reason 'they ought to cut taxes on labour inputs and on the consumption of services' (Scharpf 2000*a*: 212). Moreover, under the constraint of international financial markets and EMU convergence criteria, European states ought to reduce public sector deficits. In practice, most EMU countries have achieved balanced or even budget surpluses (that are aimed at contributing to reduce state debt) by the beginning of the twenty-first century. European states could comply with these economic imperatives by raising personal income taxes, indirect taxes on mass consumption, and taxes on immobile capital such as private homes. But while these options 'might be economically innocuous, they have been politically unpalatable in most cases' (Scharpf 2000*a*: 212).

Given this complexity it is not surprising that empirical analyses, covering the period until the late 1980s or early 1990s, have not found more than a 'modest downward pressure on the taxation of business' as a consequence of the rise in international trade openness (Swank 1998: 691; see also Quinn 1997).

Steering of State Activities

A major shift has occurred with regard to the steering of state activities in Western democracies over the last two decades. It is a shift from classic bureaucracy, placing the emphasis on process steering, to New Public Management (NPM). As Vincent Wright has put it, NPM 'has become a new policy fashion or fad, a pervasive *Zeitgeist* diffused by international bodies' (1994*b*: 108). The NPM includes the setting of measurable (or at least verifiable) performance standards, output control, the breakdown of monolithic bureaucracies into single-purpose units with separate budgets, greater competition in the public sector, and private sector styles of management practice (Wright 1994*b*; Hood 1996; Majone 1997: 146; Lane 2000; Peters 2001*d*: chs 8 and 9). Most of these features diverge from the principles or practice of classic bureaucracy. In Europe, the NPM revolution is most advanced in Britain. Under the 'Next Steps' programme, the unified civil service was reorganized after 1988 by the separation of agencies from ministries. The ministries remain in charge of setting the overall goals, providing the broad outlines of the agencies' organization, and monitoring the agencies. The agencies, in turn, have great autonomy with respect to how to provide their services (which include the running of prisons, providing child support, and running laboratories). Compared to bureaucracies, agencies can be run cost-efficiently and, whenever their tasks allow, they are obliged to tender their

Table 21.2 *New public management emphasis in Western European states in the 1980s*

Low	Medium	High
Germany	Austria	Sweden
Greece	Belgium	United Kingdom
Spain	Denmark	
Switzerland	Finland	
	France	
	Ireland	
	Italy	
	Netherlands	
	Norway	
	Portugal	

Source: Hood (1996: 277, 280).

services to commercial customers (Gains 1999). Some of those agencies which offer services that appeal to the market have already been privatized in Britain and elsewhere.

Table 21.2 shows that most Western European states had begun to reform their administrations according to the principles of NPM in the 1980s. Then, only Sweden and the United Kingdom belonged to the group of states internationally leading in the NPM revolution (along with New Zealand, Australia, and Canada). In the meantime several other European states have radicalized their NPM emphasis. In the new century Switzerland and Austria, for instance, have placed themselves among the states with a strong emphasis on NPM.

CONCLUSION

I have identified six dimensions along which changes of the modern state can be analysed and I have summarized some trends under each of these categories which have occurred since the 1980s. To be sure, these trends have not occurred simultaneously in all Western European countries nor have they had the same impact everywhere. Diverse preferences of the political actors, in particular political parties, national peculiarities in terms of economic and political challenges, and different national paths of development before the 1980s, account for the lack of uniformity. Yet, there are clear limits to divergence and sooner or later these trends affect all countries. Nevertheless, it is unlikely that the modern state of the twenty-first century will have a uniform outlook all over Europe.

22

The Changing European State: Pressures from Within

PATRICK LE GALÈS

Vincent Wright's main interest was in the state, both as an historian and as a political scientist. While working in France, this admirer of the Jacobin state enjoyed searching for archives in the most remote French prefecture which went hand to hand with his research on the Council of State in Paris. In Italy, Spain, or France he was always interested in the diversity of those countries and in the ways in which the state constructed and managed a political order. However, he was no conservative and did not use his sharp mind to defend a frozen representation of the nation-state. Among the first, with his close friends Yves Mény, Jack Hayward, or Sabino Cassese, he passionately engaged in exploring changing forms of the state faced with the dynamics of European integration, changing markets and firms, and the rise of regions and cities. To explain the changing forms of the state, Vincent put forward the dynamic combination of the following factors: the economic recession, a paradigm shift in favour of the market, changing forms of politics, globalization, Europeanization, liberalization, technological progress, decentralization and fragmentation, reforms of the public sector, and a different political agenda. However, he never lost sight of the achievements of the state form and its capacity for restructuring, hence his famous recourse to a series of paradoxes which he loved to present to puzzled students and colleagues alike.

This chapter deals with bottom up pressures on the state. Although Wright enjoyed nothing better than giving a hard time to his students working on regions or cities, he had a profound interest in the ways in which those subnational governments managed their relationship with the state in the new environment. In the 1980s, his edited volume with Yves Mény (Mény and Wright 1985b) and then the special issue of West European Politics he edited with Rod Rhodes in 1987 were essential points of reference to move out of the 'centre–periphery paradigm' and to engage in systematic comparative work. However sceptical he might have been, he had no doubt that the dynamic of cities and regions in Europe was cumulative and self-sustaining, that is, 'the genie appears to be out of the bottle'.

The chapter focuses on the challenges that cities and regions are posing to the nation state in Western Europe, rather than the rise of 'meso-government' in Europe. It analyses three sets of pressures (the fragmentation of the policy process, the competition for resources, the legitimacy of the nation state) and the role they play in the transformation of the state.

FRAGMENTATION OF THE STATE AND PUBLIC POLICY:
IS THE STATE BECOMING IMPOTENT?

The state has lost its claimed monopoly in public policy (although that monopoly was never complete). Local and regional governments are more involved in policy making. However, pressures and contradictions limiting state capacity also apply at that level (Wright 1998*b*). They contribute to the fragmentation of the policy process and the mosaic of public policy making in Europe, hence raising the salience of issues of policy coordination.

Local and regional governments are more differentiated within the political system and therefore contribute to the fragmentation of the state and of the public policy process. However, they face the same contradictions as the state in terms of the multiplication of actors, increasing demands, and deterritorialized networks. As Wright once wrote: 'Today... regional government is increasingly a prisoner of the traditional demands of the nation-state: to manage contradictions and elaborate legitimate forms of governance. Governance requires the coordination of multiple levels of inter-dependencies in a complex framework, and includes not only official politico-administrative actors, but also a vast series of economic and social actors, both public and private, that manage, control... and are members of networks which in some cases, exceed official political boundaries' (Wright 1998*b*: 48).

A large body of research has by now emphasized the twofold fragmentation of the state and the policy process both from the sociology of organizations and the public policy approaches. It appears fragmented into a myriad of organizations (agencies, networks, individuals, differentiation of political arena) where public policies do not work in terms of hierarchies or coherent policy stages but rather in terms of negotiation, flexibility, and ad hoc arrangements, sometimes suggesting a dissolution of the state. This fragmentation also has a multi-tier dimension: the European Union, the international, and, as far as we are concerned, subnational levels of governments.

More than thirty years ago, Pressman and Wildavsky stressed the illogicality of policy implementation in Oakland (Pressman and Wildavsky 1973). Starting from a crisis of governability, a different body of literature underlined the resistance of subsystems of societies to state steering and their self-organizing capacity: policy networks, sectors, social actors, and subnational territories (Kooiman 1993; Mayntz 1993, 1999). Subnational levels of government play an increasing role in public policy.

A first point to mention is related to the slightly limited margin of financial manoeuvre. Central governments are always willing to associate other levels to contribute financially to public policy schemes. Everywhere in Europe, the financing of public policies involve complex transfers and cooperation between central and local governments. In a country such as France, where the state was once the main provider of resources and expertise, it often seems that it is largely impoverished and unable to push forward its own priorities. Local and regional authorities pay for universities and different public policies (on top of their own functions and policies)... but demand a say in the process. The rise of yet another buzzword—'partnership'—was first used to describe cooperation between public and private actors. But in many countries, it also encompasses wide-ranging cooperation between public actors at different levels (Benington and Geddes 2001). The whole issue of the coordination of public policy involves various schemes to bring together different level of governments. Policy instruments addressing this question are on the rise, for instance contracts, pacts, and partnership. The development of new policy tools provides evidence of the ambiguities and dynamism of public policies. It attempts to redefine public policy in a rather flexible way in order to face ill defined problems, to cope with heterogeneous goals, or to manage different types of networks (Kickert *et al.* 1997). At the micro-level, policy processes reveal fragmentations, adjustments between representations, goals, and policies which are made through interactions on a day-to-day basis, pro-gressive elaboration of some views of general interests, institutionalization of collec-tive action (Lascoumes and Le Bourhis 1998; Le Galès 2002).

Second, subnational levels of government now have more resources, more legitim-acy, more room for manoeuvre within European governance in the making. Public policies and their impacts are becoming more important to legitimise representative governments (output legitimacy in Scharpf's terms (2000*b*)). Local and regional gov-ernments alike have become keen to manage services and to launch public policies in order to gain more legitimacy within the political system which, these days, is not favourable to representative government.

Cities and regions have become more or less involved in the European institution-alization dynamic. Their representatives have learned new roles, repertoires, and modes of action. They have found legitimacy on this larger playing field of European multi-level governance (Jeffrey 1997; Hooghe and Marks 2001), which has increased their room for manoeuvre in relation to the state. Bartolini insists that the form of the modern state, 'the case in which a strongly differentiated internal hierarch-ical order manages to control the external territorial and functional boundaries—and to correspondingly reduce exit options—so closely as to insulate domestic structuring processes from external influence...is simply the contingent historical result of a specific configuration' (1998: 9). Beyond the most clear-cut cases of exit (secession), Europeanization offers regions and cities a relative capacity to escape the constraints and hierarchies of the national political system—that is, partial exit. There is an almost automatic risk that engagement in challenging this national order will increase. The state's capacity to structure its territory is being questioned. However, no local authority can really completely escape the national territory, although there are some exceptional cases. As Bartolini reminds us, looking at the areas that interest us, capacities for exit are shared very unequally between cities and regions. Cities and regions that have the most interest in and capacities for escaping the constraints of the system represent the greatest potential threat to the state's authority; they may therefore gain additional capacities to influence changes in the balance of power and the system, in favour of the simple fact of having potential possibilities for exit, however limited. Emphasizing internal political structuring processes, linked with the formation of boundaries (political, economic, and cultural), may create a fertile setting to better understand the dynamics of Europeanization and their consequences for cities. One should, however, keep in mind the deep diversity of European state experience which renders perilous any generalization.

Europeanization processes have potentially very destabilizing effects on regions and cities. At first, Europe represented an international stage for cities and their elected representatives; it gave a form of recognition, a new political legitimacy for representing citizens beyond the state's borders, with possibilities for integrating horizontal and vertical networks and bypassing the state, and with access to new resources—in other words, new room for manoeuvre and new opportunities for political entrepreneurs. Europe seemed to represent modernization, the culture of a new generation of elected representatives.

The second stage saw the constraining, destabilizing effects of this European governance come fully to light. The criteria that have to be observed in order to obtain funding seem even more rigid and strict than those pertaining to national programmes. Behind flexible networks and forms of interdependence lie complex rules, the difficulty of exerting pressure on choices, and the constraints of coalitions and networks. Elected representatives have finally discovered the limits of their activities, norms that seem to have come upon them like a bolt from the blue. Thus, the European integration dynamic has a destabilizing effect because of the uncertainties associated with it.

Third, local and regional governments aim at improving the living conditions of their citizens and the general prosperity of their territory (Goldsmith and Wollmann 1992) through public policies and the delivery of services. They have become involved in the fields of welfare, urban regeneration or economic development, culture, environment. The territory—a city, a locality, a region—may appear as a possible integrating factor in a fragmented policy-making process. Thanks to their territorial roots, 'new economic and social policies' may be more democratic, more transparent, more effective, more long term, and more coherent. In social policy in particular, subnational territories appear as a potential support for a new generation of renovated public policies. Unfortunately, even if it offers a mobilizing myth and some important potential, it often fails to provide such support (Balme *et al.* 1999; Le Galès 2001*b*; Stoker 2000). On the one hand, the rise of partnerships and their activities are indicative of attempts to territorialize public policies through an integrated horizontal approach. On the other hand, there are also cases either of de-territorialization of actors or of local adaptation of programmes and policies, whose logic, as well as legal and financial constraints, are still determined at the central or European level.

Regional and local government and governance-building are about the development of subnational political arenas which allow political leaders to behave as political entrepreneurs and to aggregate different networks. There are plenty of examples demonstrating that subnational governments are present in a number of networks, are learning new rules of the political game, and in some cases, certain sectors and certain countries, we can see the structuring of urban or regionalized forms of governance (Keating and Loughlin 1997; Balme 1996; Keating 1998). These forms are still extraordinarily limited and the pressure from market forces is compelling different actors to demand horizontal coordination, indeed political structuring, in order to protect themselves from the destructuring caused by markets (Bagnasco and Le Galès 2000).

Meanwhile, politicians involved in the making of territorialized modes of governance play an important political role. In fragmented environments, the question of leadership becomes more important (John 2001). The restructuring of the public sector leads to increased confusion in public policies and the fragmentation of urban governments (Pierre 2000), hence the growing interest in issues of leadership, management, coordination, and governance (Borraz *et al.* 1994; Stoker 2000). Both in order to integrate and to represent networks of actors and interests, political leaders develop a repertoire of action. The personalization of power in democracies also impacts on the subnational level. As the national level is less central to structuring the political system, regional and local leaders can articulate values, norms, and expectations of groups and individuals within a given system. Within a multi-level European governance in the making, local and regional leaders are more involved: 'Leadership constructs meaning: the meaning of a community or collective action; the meaning of member participation; the meaning of the place of this community or collective action in society. It builds bridges, translates, imparts values, incarnates principles' (Borraz 2000). Leaders are part of the institutionalization of local and regional governments. It follows that they may exert more pressure on the state, contest its legitimacy, use vertical and horizontal networks to bypass the national political order.

In recent years, high profile political leaders have emerged and challenged the legitimacy of the state, have competed with it and have tried to play a role in Europe in order to secure resources and influence within and beyond the state. The Catalan leader Pujol and the Barcelona Mayor Maragall have frequently done so. In Italy, the president of the Lombardy region Formigoni or the former mayor of Venice Cacciari have articulated views and political projects which are far from coinciding with the Italian state. Even in Sweden, the Mayor of Stockholm is putting forward ideas which challenge classic Swedish universalism. The same is true for the Scottish and Welsh Parliaments, some French mayors, or German *Länder* presidents.

COMPETING FOR FINANCES, THE THREAT OF THE IMPOVERISHED STATE

In a context of Europe in the making and economic forces evading the nation state, the latter has lost part of its monopoly, not its importance. Subnational levels of government are gaining room for manoeuvre, limited possibilities to exit the disciplines of national systems, and therefore can negotiate more forcefully their share of public resources. Those pressures constitute a permanent challenge to the nation state and may threaten, in some cases, the redistributive role of the state.

More Resources at the Local and Regional Levels

In the post-war period, a common trend of state expansion dissimulated a wide variety of modes of territorial organization within states: the dual state in the United Kingdom, the Jacobin centralist state in France, the ponderous but not so effective

Italian state, the social democratic, egalitarian Scandinavian state, federal Germany and its sophisticated egalitarian form of federalism, authoritarian regimes in Spain, Portugal, and Greece for a while.

In some of those models, particularly in the North of Europe, powerful municipalities were in charge of implementing welfare services. The accelerated rise of education, health, and social services in the 1960s worried political elites. Anxious to control the growth and rationalize the delivery of those services, they started a process of local government restructuring which lasted for several years in a cooperative manner in Scandinavia or Germany, in a more brutal way in the United Kingdom (Goldsmith and Page 1987). Most countries started at the time some form of weak decentralization (France, Italy) and/or local government restructuring to improve the effectiveness of public spending. The game was played under the strict control of state elites.

Nowadays, the situation has become quite different. In the 1970s and beyond, most states had faced a fiscal crisis which has progressively led to greater or less stabilization of the percentage of state expenditure in relation to the GDP, and to limit the deficit. Pressure from international markets particularly important for the states deepest in debt (such as Belgium, Greece, and Italy where the debt is higher than 100 per cent of GDP), together with the European agreement on deficit reduction, is limiting the room of manoeuvre for the state. Although less spectacular, the rise of local and regional governments in Europe is having a profound impact on public finances. National states have to share some tax revenue and taxing power with subnational governments. Although they keep the major say in the organization of revenue sharing, they have progressively to give up a growing share of the revenue to local and regional governments all over Europe, except in the United Kingdom.

Table 22.1 shows that in all Western European countries but Portugal, more than half of the public investment is now made at the local or regional level. In the Netherlands or in France, local and regional authorities now account for 70 per cent of the public investments. This constitutes a crucial change for public expenditure (Tables 22.2 and 22.3).

In most countries, from 1985 to 1996, local tax kept increasing, however slow and diverse that trend might be. The United Kingdom is, of course, the remarkable exception to this trend as the figures declined from 3.8 to 1.4 per cent. At one extreme, where local tax is important such as in Denmark or Sweden, they have risen by nearly 2 per cent of GDP. At the other extreme where they used to be low, they have risen from about one to two per cent of GDP in Portugal or Italy, and these figures are rising. France is in an intermediary position from 3.8 to 4.7 per cent of GDP. The slow rise of local taxation is often strengthened by a redistribution of tax which takes into account the local level with once again major variation between Denmark and Sweden, where local government obtained over 30 per cent of all fiscal revenues, and the United Kingdom, Ireland, and Greece, where this figure is below 5 per cent.

In terms of revenue raising and sharing, the context in which the cooperation/competition between various levels of government takes place is making the choice more acute and politically contested. This takes two different forms which

Table 22.1 *Local share of gross fixed capital formation in total GFCF for 1996 in Europe*

		Local GFCF national GFCF as % of public services	Local GFCF, GFCF in as % of public services
Germany	Länder	2.2	20.5
	municipalities	6.6	62.1
Austria	Bundesländer	1.6	13.8
	municipalities	7.4	63.5
Belgium		4.0	58.9
Denmark		6.2	63.6
Spain		10.3[a]	59.3
Finland		8.6	50.9
France		12.6	71.8
Greece		No figures available	No figures available
Ireland		10.9[a]	80.1
Italy		8.8	66.9
Netherlands		10.1	74.2
Portugal		7.4[b]	47.9
United Kingdom		5.3	59.3
Sweden		10.2	54.2

[a]1995; [b]1992.

Source: Local authorities in figures 1998, DGCL, Ministry of the Interior.

Table 22.2 *Fiscal revenue of different public administrations*

	Federal state or central administration	State	Local authorities	Social security
Austria	52.7	9.3	10.2	27.8
Belgium	36.7	23.3	4.9	35.1
Germany	29.4	22.0	8.0	40.6
Denmark	64.9		11.9	44.1
Finland	52.6		22.2	25.2
France	43.6		10.6	45.8
Greece	68.8		1.1	30.1
Ireland	86.8		2.0	11.2
Italy	58.8		11.7	29.5
Luxembourg	68.1		6.3	25.6
Netherlands	56.5		3.0	40.5
Portugal	67.0		6.1	26.9
Spain	48.0		17.0	35.0
Sweden	58.1		30.8	11.1
United Kingdom	63.0		13.3	23.7

Source: OECD Economic outlooks, 2001.

Table 22.3   *'Degree of financial autonomy, in terms of the relationship of tax to total non-borrowing income'* *(Gilbert 1999: 163)*

EU member state	Local authority spending in % of GDP (1995)	Degree of local fiscal autonomy
Denmark	33	49
Sweden	28.7	60
Finland	23	43
Netherlands	19.1	8
Italy	13.7	25
Spain (excl. Autonomous regions)	7.2	30
Austria	12	5
Luxembourg	11.7	32
Germany	10	20
United Kingdom	10	14
France	9.2	54
Belgium	7.4	35
Ireland	5.4	16
Portugal	3.7	7
Greece	2.1	

constitute different challenges, if not a serious threat to the nation state. First, politically dynamic regions and cities are demanding more resources. Second, in some cases, they want to limit the redistribution within the nation state to keep a higher share of revenues, hence threatening the major redistributive role of the welfare state. Significantly, associations of urban mayors have flourished in Germany in the mid-1990s, in Britain with the Core Cities groups, in Italy with the movement of the cities, in France, Spain, and now the six cities of Finland have done the same. In all cases those organizations express an interest different from the traditional redistribution within the welfare system, emphasizing the needs of cities' inhabitants and the crucial role of the cities for the competitiveness of the countries.

The slow rise of local, regional, and federal government in Europe was bound to have some fiscal impact. Revenue sharing has always been a crucial demand from local and regional authorities, eager to start their own programmes and policies. In Scandinavia, powerful municipalities have gained from the apparently ever increasing welfare state . . . until the crisis of the early 1990s. In Italy, in the 1990s, several laws have given greater political legitimacy to the mayors, the *sindici*, who became directly elected. The new administrative function of 'city manager' also went in the same direction of enhancing local public policies and the delivery of services. Within a context of tight fiscal centralization, those mayors, who became major political figures in Cattania, Venice, Naples, Rome, and Palermo, were bound to ask for more resources to go together with their new political legitimacy. The mayors of large cities having to deal with increased social polarization and the pressure of economic competition sought to obtain more resources from the state to deal with the urban problems. In a different context, the same applies: in Stockholm, Lille, or Stuttgart, where mayors have been actively seeking more resources from the state. If the model of the elected mayor gains as much ground as expected in the United Kingdom, following the London example, one would expect those new political figures to compete more vigorously for funds.

In Spain, the Autonomies, now quasi-federal states, have pursued a similar strategy. Since the return of democracy, led by the historical Autonomies of Catalonia and the Basque country, they systematically asked for more resources and became powerful political actors. In Belgium, the long and complex process of differentiation between Flanders and Wallonia also required the sharing of taxing and spending power at the expense of the Belgian central state. In Italy, the long march of the regions has gone hand to hand with the increase in the resources at their disposal. The new law in 1997 has considerably increased their general powers. Ongoing discussion about forms of federalism or decentralization in Italy include important transfers of resources and powers to subnational levels of government. Once officially created in 1982 with taxing powers, French regions were, fiscally speaking, the most dynamic level of government in France until the 1990s: raising tax to hire employees, chief officers, and to develop public policies.

The process of European integration also fuels this dynamic up to a point. European programmes concerning regions and local authorities (mainly within the structural funds framework) often require nation states to match European funds. Although they usually try their best to maximize the use of European money, or even to use those funds to finance their own programmes, their gate-keeping role is limited by the fact they do not exert strict control over the content of development programmes. Central government funds are to some extent more biased towards the financing of local and regional development programmes, legitimized by the European Union, entering more or less within the priorities of national governments.

This long term trend of increasing resources for subnational governments is not uniform and masks large variations among and within countries. It is not just the result of the pressures from within the state, but also the result of the strategy of state elites. Already in the early 1980s, Mény and Wright had clearly shown that decentralizing the management of cuts and shortages was a popular move among nation states' elites. In Scandinavia, Finland, and France, for instance, decentralization reforms, or the making of a regional level of cooperation, was instrumental to decentralize the responsibility of managing the restructuring of hospitals, to limit the growth of social services, and to accumulate indicators to restructure health policy.

Beyond taking advantage of such a movement in order to be able to concentrate on other issues and to escape part of the political pressure, nation states in Europe are usually able, when required, to impose their fiscal choice at the expense of local and regional governments. The United Kingdom has shown this at length. Even in the process of the devolution of power to Scotland and Wales, a key point was to limit very narrowly the spending powers of the newly elected parliaments and governments. The same, or even stricter, budgetary discipline applies to the Mayor of London, and will probably apply to future elected mayors of large cities and non-elected regional assemblies. London's tight control on public spending which developed under the Thatcher period also became a New Labour credo. To meet the Maastricht criteria to enter the Euro club, Italy increased taxes but required sub-national governments to reduce expenditure. At the time of welfare cuts in the second part of the 1980s in Denmark, municipalities had to bear the brunt. When Finland was badly hit by the economic crisis of 1992, it led to a dramatic recentralization of public finances at the expense of municipalities. Last but not least, the reunification of Germany led to a massive transfer of funds to former East Germany: *Länder* and municipalities had to pay for a large part of those transfers. In other words, in times of crisis, nation states still have the political resources and legitimacy to impose fiscal discipline and cuts on reluctant local and regional governments. It remains that entrenched within the state, local and regional authorities constitute a powerful lobby competing for public resources. They exert a constant pressure to control a higher proportion of fiscal resources, hence strengthening the financial power of the state within a context where tax increases do not seem a popular option.

Challenging State Redistribution

Competing for public expenditure is one thing; competing to raise its taxes or to keep a larger share of the main tax is another. In the past two decades, the challenges to the state from regional or quasi-federal governments has taken a different turn which reveals a powerful logic of decreasing state control. The term 'neo-regionalism' aims at capturing the mix of political entrepreneurialism and identity led regional mobilization in a context of strong economic growth (Balme 1996; Keating and Loughlin 1996). The spatial logic of economic growth seems to benefit large urban areas, cities, and some dynamic local economies in Italy, Germany, or Scandinavia.

Catalonia in Spain epitomizes the dreams and fears of many in Europe. Holding the balance of power first in favour of the Gonzalez Socialist government and then for the Aznar Conservative government, the Catalan leader Pujol negotiated period after period more fiscal and political advantages. It seemed at the time a never ending process which would progressively give Catalonia greater political and fiscal autonomy at the expense of the Spanish state. The fiscal argument was central and not without paradox. Although Catalan leaders figured prominently in Brussels to defend regional policy in favour of southern European countries and regions in the name of social cohesion, they did not accept those arguments in Spain. By contrast, in the name of autonomy, they defended fiscal egoism and attacked welfare state redistribution in favour of Spain's poorest regions in the South. During the transitional period, national grants to Autonomies used to depend on the cost of services transferred. From 1987 to 1991, the government included socioeconomic criteria in the calculation of Autonomous Communities' share of the state's tax incomes. As the Socialist government needed their support to secure a majority, the Catalans negotiated a share of 15 per cent of income tax for Autonomous communities, health financing reforms, and debt coordination mechanisms. In 1997, the newly elected centre right Aznar government needed the Catalans to secure a majority in parliament. Autonomous

Communities obtained a share of 30 per cent of income tax (Gallego 2000). In 2000, Aznar's greater political success (majority) in the general elections and by contrast Pujol's narrow success in Catalonia has stopped this process. The central government in Madrid is trying to restrict in a variety of ways the autonomy of the Autonomous Communities, and Catalonia in particular. What is at stake is not the end of the Spanish state, because Catalan political leaders have claimed they do not want their independence, but want to stay within Spain in Europe. However, West European states contribute massively to the reduction of inequalities (less so in the United Kingdom, of course). The Catalan dynamic put that redistributive role at risk, together with its homogenizing role in society.

To a lesser extent, the Italian case reveals a similar dynamic. As Diamanti (1995) has shown at length in the case of the Northern League, the rhetoric of its leaders and its members (mainly small firm entrepreneurs) demands greater autonomy for a mythic 'Padania' in the North, from the corrupt Italian state and from transfers in favour of the Mezzogiorno. Within the European Union and facing increased economic competition for firms, they argue that they cannot pay for inefficient state services. Again, the threat is not so much against the existence of the state as such, but may lead to forms of federalism which allow increased differentiation in terms of culture, education, and services, but would also prevent fiscal and social redistribution, hence dramatically reshaping the role of the state. In that sense, and in that sense only, one could imagine a 'hollow state' scenario. The dynamics of neo-regionalist movements, or of the rich as is sometimes said, clearly encompasses a resistance towards public redistribution in favour of the poorest regions within the nation state.

That sort of pressure also exists in Germany (Benz and Goetz 1996). It was once the country of cooperative federalism where a sophisticated system of joint policy making (*Politikverflechtung*) went hand to hand with a strong commitment to maintain uniformity between the *Länder*. The complex system of horizontal and vertical revenue sharing and tax redistribution proved very effective in limiting inequalities in Germany. This system is under intense pressure, so much so that Germany may be evolving towards a system of 'competitive federalism' where each *Land*, and particularly the most powerful among them such as Bavaria, is showing discontent with existing arrangements. The European integration process has clearly destabilized them together with existing inter-dependence between levels within Germany. Faced with ongoing Europeanization processes they cannot control, persistent fiscal pressure to support the reconstruction, and a federal state which enjoys new room for manoeuvre, the *Länder* seem to question the uniformity principle, to put more emphasis on the defence of their own interest and economic prosperity. If that trend towards competitive federalism grows, that may limit the ability of the centre to coordinate the *Länder*, or even put a ceiling on redistributive mechanisms as argued by Bavaria.

Last but not least, in Belgium, several observers have claimed that the large debt, together with the monarchy, are the sole remaining obstacles to splitting the country between Flemish and Walloons. Again, the dynamics of federalization have clearly gained over the past three decade at the expense of the central state, as the two quasi federal states have gained more powers and resources. They also tend to diverge more and more in various ways including policy making.

In that complex interplay between powerful regions, quasi federal states, federal states, and the centre, the United Kingdom is nowadays quite intriguing, particularly in Scotland. On the one hand, Scotland is another case of nation without a state which has historically been integrated into the United Kingdom. The emotional reopening of the elected Scottish Parliament in the summer 1999 in Edinburgh marked an important step in the revival of Scotland as a political community. On the other hand, Scotland is not such a rich region. The transfers of public money go from England to Scotland. Another step towards more autonomy may lead to severe cuts in public spending... unless the North Sea oil revenues that the Scottish National Party would like to claim are transferred to Scotland, a move which would radically change the fiscal rules of the game between Scotland and the United Kingdom.

THE DEREGULATION OF IDENTITY STRUCTURING

In more differentiated, more individualized societies, which are party to globalization processes, national society, viewed from the perspective of the nation, no longer has a monopoly over structuring identities; this (according to Badie 1999) is leading to 'deregulation of the identity market' and the proliferation of alternatives on offer—ethnic, religious, sexual, and particularly urban and regional identities. In Europe, regional and urban actors take great pleasure in representing themselves as new 'imagined communities' (Smouts 1998), in reconciling reinvented tradition with the future. In so far as cities and regions have room for manoeuvre in national societies, where the groups and actors that make up the societies define themselves partly in relation to globalized processes (sanction, mobilization, resource allocation), regions and cities have become one space among others, a space for social regulation and for identity-based mobilization.

The making of European nation states and national societies took several centuries. Most authors now stress the diversity of the populations to start with and the diversity of the processes, the complex fitting of local interests and national rules, the slow social and cultural integration. Anthropologists, social historians, and sociologists alike underline the time dimension in the long process of building a nation, including the most centralized cases. For sociologists, the nation state is usually defined in the terms of Weber and Gellner (i.e. a bounded monopoly of legitimate violence, administration, and culture), but national society includes the interrelationship of a modern industrial economy, a national class structure, a set of national institutions, rules, values, organized interests (political parties, churches, welfare states, economic interests), and infrastructures (Touraine 1990). All of these were more or less in place at the end of the nineteenth century. The post-1945 decades marked the completion of national modern industrialized European societies, although many characteristics were to be found elsewhere. Thanks to television, national cultures became dominant and national languages triumphed nearly everywhere. Regional differences were on the way out thanks to massive redistribution, national labour markets, the strength of national institutions, and integrating factors, as well as mass consumption. Society meant national society.

National societies and nations are challenged in particular by the pressure from local and regional mobilization. In most areas of social life (work, family, consumption, education, leisure, politics, religion) social science research tends to stress the following points: individualization, fragmentation but also rearticulation of groups, autonomy towards institutions, differentiation, pluralization, individualization, detraditionalization, deinstitutionalization. These processes are often put forward under the heading of the fragmentation of societies (Mingione 1991; Dubet and Martucelli 1998) and the apparent ever increasing autonomy of individuals toward national institutions. Hence the story of national political parties, national economic interests, national churches, national armies (military industrial complex), but also welfare states and school systems are facing increased pressure in most European countries. That does not mean they are disappearing. But national institutions which used to structure societies, organize interactions, provide social links, representations, norms, social practices, are less and less able to impose their logic on regions or cities. They are part of this differentiation process.

The question of the level of social organization has been raised at the infra-national level. At the time of the triumphant modern nation state in the 1960s, countervailing forces started to appear which used localities and regions to contest national homogenizing tendencies: new social movements, regionalist movements . . . While regions and localities were seen less as constraints for individuals, thanks to social and geographic mobility, regions became increasingly significant for the formation of social groups, the invention or reinvention of identities, solidarities within or against the nation state. While national symbols started to lose their significance in the face of the uncertainties and variability of economic relations, the state became less central. Local and regional cultures became codes for the satisfaction of needs for self-expression and identity. In view of the erosion of (more or less) integrated national societies and major institutions which structure national societies (parties, unions, churches . . .), it could be assumed that other levels of structuring of social groups are likely to have a greater importance. Research on localities in Italy, France, and the United Kingdom has shown how social groups can be formed in the framework of conflicts or local collective action, because all social groups clearly do not have the same type of attachment to or interests in a locality. Progressively in the United Kingdom (it was always more the case in Italy), the sociology of social groups and classes took local and regional dynamics into account in the creation of these social groups. By contrast to the North of Europe, the South of Europe is characterized by a greater emphasis on the territorialization of social and political structures. Trigilia's classic work on political subcultures in the third Italy illustrates the point, but there are many examples in Spain, Germany, or Italy (Trigilia 1986).

In Europe, the dynamic of infra-national territories was first led by cultural minorities which resisted the homogenizing forces of nation states and/or which were economically losing ground within the national economy. As was mentioned before, not many states were homogenous to start with. 'In most states, national integration is incomplete since distinct cultures, identities, traditions, histories, and myths subsist' (Keating 1998: 44). However, if the renaissance of regionalism and localism has often been interpreted in cultural terms, the question is not to know whether the rediscovery of local cultures stems from the need to express identity: this may be the case, without it having much effect on social organization. As Bagnasco suggests, drawing on the Italian case, economies are less and less able to consider themselves in isolation: a cultural and a political idiosyncrasy can endure only by being associated with an economy that can withstand the free market (cases of neo-regionalism, Catalonia, Bavaria, or the so-called Padania for instance).

The revival of identity-seeking claims perhaps count less in Western Europe in explaining regional and local mobilization than the (offensive and defensive) reaction to globalization processes. The reinforcement of subnational, territorial, political mobilization is pushed by the need to face the destructuring of local and regional societies, bearing in mind, on the one hand, globalization processes and, on the other, rivalries among subnational territories. Social groups, organized interests, and institutions mobilize collective projects, reinvent local identities, and organize governance regimes, in order to resist politically, culturally, and economically, or in order to adapt to globalization processes.

National societies have not disappeared in Europe. They remain crucial for most individuals and groups. However, national societies face acute processes of internal differentiation and fragmentation together with the development of cross-national networks and levels of interdependence. The second part of the equation of the nation state is also under pressure.

A last set of pressures comes from violent nationalist movements, which are a direct challenge to the authority of the state and the political order. The Basque country in Spain and Corsica in France tell a story of long term political violence, which at times seems rather desperate. In both cases, the state has reacted through political negotiation and/or quasi-permanent war with illegal nationalist organizations.

CONCLUSION

We can agree with Poggi (1996) that the reshaping of the state, along the lines we have sketched above, seems to mark the beginning of 'a new phase of the state story' and perhaps, as an indirect outcome, the end of a cycle for the state. This cycle began in the second half of the nineteenth century, and was marked by the structuring of the state and its growth, which seemed to be unlimited. In this context, regions and cities, whatever the room for manoeuvre in their particular contexts, found themselves operating within the centre–periphery paradigm, within hierarchies and national policies, in a political space dominated by the nation-state. This is no longer the case. Closely interconnected processes of reshaping the state, and Europeanization, are rendering this view obsolete. Cities and regions, even with Brussels' support, are not about to replace the state. However, the central state's grip has been loosened, and

Europe is witnessing increasingly unstable inter-governmental relations, with the cooperation/competition model giving way to the creation of networks. This reshaping of the state should not be confused with weakening. Retreat may actually allow state elites (finance ministries naturally spring to mind) to pursue their main objectives, and to impose changes by acting on the various levels of government. Most central governments have been able to make use of 'the constraints of Europe', which they have been active in developing, in order to impose reforms on national social actors. Conversely, many decentralization reforms have allowed central governments to 'decentralize penury', giving regions the responsibility of managing scarcity and painful restructuring.

Subnational governments are part of a complex European governance within which states are reorganizing themselves. The key question as far as the state is concerned is: will regions or federal states be able to 'exit' from the nation state? Is there any risk of dismantling the state? Self-sustained process of regional autonomy seeking are not easy to stop. Although the central government in Spain and the United Kingdom is now clearly fighting back and trying to limit the autonomization of Catalonia and Scotland, it is hard to know what the future holds. The federalization processes in Belgium, the United Kingdom, Spain, and to a lesser extent Italy, may lead one day to the secession of one of the leading European regions. The Scottish dynamic is particularly interesting. However, none is explicitly searching for an army or police force. One should therefore expect continuous tensions and pressures from federal states or quasi-federal states and regions on the status quo. The extent of the 'exit' strategies remains to be seen.

23

International Relations, International Institutions, and the European State

ANDREW HURRELL AND ANAND MENON

Comparativists have often tended to study politics within states as if their external environment was an irrelevance (notable exceptions include Gourevitch 1978; Katzenstein 1978). However, the nation states of Western Europe do not exist in a political vacuum. Rather, they interact within an international environment that exercises a powerful influence over both their very nature and their relationships with one another, an influence that could hardly have been made clearer than by the aftermath of the terrorist attacks in the United States of September 2001.

This chapter takes a broad look at the impact exerted by international economic and political pressures on patterns of government and governance in Europe. It assesses the degree to which, as a consequence of the end of the Cold War and of the forces of globalization, these pressures are changing, and considers the implications of such change. We argue in Section 1 that the profound impact of the external environment on the character of the European state has been all too evident—despite the internalist tendencies of so much comparativist scholarship. Moreover, West European states continue to confront several external challenges to the stability that has, since the Second World War, characterized their half of the Old Continent.

The first of these comes from the continued development of the very forces of liberalization that have played such an important role in Europe's recent past, changes that, for the sake of convenience, can be categorized under the heading of 'globalization'. The revolutionary impact of globalization has dominated a great deal of the political debate on the changing external environment and has generated a considerable academic literature—although one of extremely variable quality. Globalization, it is confidently asserted, is transforming world politics, fundamentally altering the character of the nation state, the content and meaning of sovereignty, the policies that states are able to pursue, and their capacity to act as both the primary focus for human loyalties and as the principal institution for legitimate political order. In Section 2 we examine some of the major aspects of this debate as it relates to the European state, but remain sceptical. We suggest that those accounts of globalization that emphasize the dramatically declining ability of European states to frame and pursue their own policy preferences run well in advance of the available empirical evidence. Not only are many of the supposed systemic determinants of national action far less powerful and uniform than is often supposed, but also their impact on nation states is patchy, with national governments still enjoying significant room for manoeuvre in designing public policies. It is not the case, in other words, that the international economic environment systematically determines even the actions, let alone the properties, of its most important constituent units.

If the reality of globalization runs in advance of the evidence, what other features of the external environment may be important? The second set of challenges comes from the international political system—from the emergence of the United States as the single superpower; from the collapse of the Soviet Union; and from the changing character of the security problems facing Europe. An emphasis on these changes can be found most prominently in the writings of US neo-realists who asserted that the end of the Cold War would inevitably result in Europe returning to its geopolitical and conflictual 'historic norm'. In Section 3 we show why such extreme predictions have been proved wrong but nevertheless argue that the neo-realist emphasis on the international political system is, in a fundamental sense, correct. Changes in the international political system are more significant than the much-hyped revolutionary impact of globalization—or, more accurately, it is on geopolitics in the context of globalization that we should focus. This is not because these changes lead inevitably back towards a pattern of competition, anarchy, and conflict. It is rather because international political change has had an important impact on the relationship between the politico-economic and politico-security spheres, bringing distributional politics among states and within European and transatlantic political and economic institutions more firmly back into the centre ground. The resulting (and still unresolved) dilemmas affect many aspects of European politics, but can be observed with most clarity in the debates concerning EU enlargement and European security cooperation.

The external environment has also changed in a further way that merits close attention—the rise and consolidation of international institutions. Europe and the North Atlantic area constitute the most densely institutionalized region on earth and we would expect this to have important implications for the character and functioning of the European state. We argue that institutions do indeed play a crucial role in both the economic and security domains. On one side, the relationship between international cause and national effect is mediated by profoundly different national institutional structures and political landscapes; on the other, regional and international institutions often serve as mechanisms by which states can mitigate the effects of international constraints and can seek to influence dominant systemic norms and practices. Yet international institutions are neither simple reflections of the underlying distribution of state power (as most neo-realists insist), nor a framework for new patterns of governance that subsume or supersede the nation state (as some liberals argue). Even within the most densely institutionalized part of the world, European states retain effective, albeit highly unequal, control over the institutions that they have created. At the same time, far from replacing the traditional world of interstate competition with something more benign, institutions provide an arena for competitive politics and the quest for relative gains.

INTERNATIONAL RELATIONS AND THE STATE IN
HISTORICAL CONTEXT

The character of the European state—what it is, what purposes it seeks to promote, and its capacity to promote them—has long been shaped by external factors and by changing patterns of power and dominance in the international system. War and political conflict played key roles in the process of state formation and the intellectual tradition analysing the links between state-making and war-making stretches from Machiavelli and Hintze to, more recently, Anderson (1974) and Tilly (1975). Even more compelling than the links between conflict and state-formation are those between geopolitics and the emergence and power of political nationalism, with images of the collective self and foreign 'other' flourishing on the battlefield as nowhere else. Moreover, as both Weber and Marx recognized, the unparalleled dynamism of European capitalist industrialization was fuelled by the tensions that existed between increasing market integration on the one hand and continued political fragmentation and inter-state conflict on the other. Finally, as much recent work has argued, European political thought and our stock of ideas about the state and political order within the state were very closely connected to both European imperial expansion overseas and to patterns of war and peace within Europe (Hont 1994; Rothschild 1995; Tuck 1999).

In the twentieth century, many of the most significant changes in the character of the European state were driven by developments in the international system. Thus the vast expansion of state power and state function was closely bound up with the geopolitical conflicts of the period from 1870 to 1950 and with the transnational ideological confrontation between liberalism on the one hand and fascism and communism on the other. With the advent of large-scale war, the range of state agencies and ministries increased, budgets and levels of taxation soared, and the scope and range of legislation expanded. It is only within the context of these systemic pressures that we can understand the shifting boundaries between politics and the market, between public and private spheres, and the emergence of new understandings of the responsibilities of the state to its citizens as reflected in both an expanded conception of social rights and, of course, the rise of the welfare state. Thus Michael Howard has emphasized the way in which warfare and welfare went hand in hand (Howard 1991: 156; see also Beloff 1984; Eley 1995; Ferguson 2001).

If we focus on the period after 1945, it is hard to exaggerate the extent to which the evolving character of West European politics was intertwined with the Cold War international system. It was within the framework of the Cold War that economic recovery gathered pace, that democratic governments were established in hitherto unpromising parts of Europe (such as Italy, Germany, and later Spain, Greece, and Portugal), that regional and transatlantic institutions were created and consolidated, and that increasingly non-militarized societies sustained a regional security community with historically low levels of military expenditure. It is important, of course, to avoid painting an excessively rosy image of the Cold War years, and to recall both its intrinsic dangers and the repression and suffering to which the division of Europe gave rise. Nevertheless, the fact remains that the Cold War years were immensely favourable to the states of Western Europe, compared both to their own past and to all other regions of the world, with the exception of North America.

The crucial role played by international economic factors in shaping the character of the twentieth century European state is equally evident. New economic ideas emerged in the wake of the Great Depression that came, in turn, to be embodied in new supporting political coalitions. Institutions and what we would today term 'transnational policy networks' played a major part in diffusing ideas and thus building consensus regarding the desirability of increasing state intervention in domestic economies and societies (Ikenberry 1992). Above all, when we compare it to the immediate past and to other plausible counterfactual possibilities, the post-1945 international *political* settlement was *economically* extremely favourable to Western Europe. An auspicious balance of political forces inside the United States bolstered European policies and preferences (as Nixon put it in 1971: 'we are all Keynesians now'). Crucially, the geopolitical imperatives of the Cold War and the sheer extent of America's wealth and power led Washington to provide large amounts of aid to Western Europe, to take the lead in constructing and stabilizing a set of far-reaching liberal economic institutions, to accept the logic of 'embedded liberalism' (state activism and welfarism at home, combined with relative openness abroad), and, at least up until 1971, to adopt a broad and generally long-term view of its own economic interests.

Throughout the twentieth century, then, states have had to respond to, and been shaped by, forces emanating from outside their borders. So what of the external challenges—economic and political—that confront them today?

GLOBALIZATION AND THE EUROPEAN STATE

Contemporary debates surrounding globalization are couched in terms of novelty and transformation. But the core themes are old ones, and there is a long tradition exploring how changing external economic constraints act upon nation states. Adam Smith was only one of a number of eighteenth and nineteenth century writers to anticipate the rise of globalization and to predict its potentially revolutionary impact (Rothschild 1999; see also Garrett 1998a: 793–95). Such themes were revived in the late 1960s and early 1970s, when writers on interdependence and modernization prefigured many of the arguments used today by globalization theorists. It was widely argued that the rapid expansion of international trade and investment, the increased awareness of ecological interdependence, the declining utility of military power, and the increasing power of non-state actors—transnational corporations (TNCs), religious organizations, and terrorist groups—constituted a systemic shift that would increasingly undermine the traditional role and primacy of nation states (Cooper 1968; Vernon 1971; Nye and Keohane 1977). As Morse wrote at that time: changes 'in the structure of the global economy have resulted in a withering of the ability of governmental control of certain activities presumed to be *de jure* within the domain of governments' (Morse 1972: 23). Such thinking also sparked a wave of interest in the relationship between international relations and domestic politics. A number of detailed studies appeared analysing the interaction between the international economy and domestic political structures and economic policies (Gourevitch 1978; Katzenstein 1978).

The 1970s interdependence literature faded under pressure from two sources. First, the reappearance of superpower confrontation in the form of the second Cold War appeared to justify those who took a more Hobbesian view of international life, a view dominated by the spectre of military confrontation rather than by the promise of economic exchange and interdependence. Second, within academia, statists and realists responded vigorously to interdependence theorists' claims, arguing, for example, that TNCs were closely tied to states and to patterns of inter-state politics (Gilpin 1975, 1987); that the state was still the most important institution of international order (Bull 1977, 1979); that the utility of military power had not declined; and, most important of all, that the international political system, with its dominant logic of power balancing, remained the most important element of any theory of international politics (Waltz 1979). In the face of such criticism, many liberals moved away from the broader claims about systemic change and focused instead on the narrower question of how, and under what conditions, regimes and institutions could emerge and become effective (Krasner 1983; Keohane 1984, 1989; Rittberger *et al.* 1993).

With the end of the Cold War, however, academic interest shifted back to the role of external or global economic factors, this time under the broad heading of 'globalization'. Indeed, globalization has increasingly been understood as the most important external influence both on the character of European states and societies and on inherited patterns of regional governance. It is far from easy to gather together the wide variety of meanings attached to the term. At one level, at least, it appears simple. Globalization refers to the complex set of processes leading to a dramatic increase in the density and depth of economic, ecological, and societal interdependence, where 'density' refers to the increased number, range, and scope of cross-border transactions, and 'depth' to the degree to which interdependence affects, and is affected by, the ways in which societies are organized domestically (Hurrell and Woods 1995). (It is impossible here to review the vast body of literature on globalization, but, for useful contributions, see Clark 1999; Held *et al.* 1999; Hirst and Thompson 1999; Held and McGrew 2000; Lechner and Boli 2000; Scholte 2000; Woods 2000).

Much of the muddle and inconclusiveness of the globalization debate stem from ambiguities inherent within the concept itself. Sometimes globalization is presented as a causal theory; sometimes as a collection of concepts, mapping (but not explaining) how the changing global system is to be understood; and sometimes it is understood as a particular kind of discourse or ideology. There are also important distinctions to be made between economistic readings of globalization that stress increased inter-state transactions and flows of capital, labour, goods, and services; and social and political readings that stress the emergence of new forms of governance and authority, new arenas of political action ('deterritoralization' or the 'reconfiguration of social space'), or new understandings of identity or community. Within economistic readings, we might further distinguish between the traditional focus on inter-state economic transactions on the one hand, and broader shifts in transnational production-structures and the emergence of new kinds of deterritorialized markets on the other. Distinctions can also be drawn between globalization, internationalization, westernization (or Americanization), and modernization. And, particularly relevant to this chapter, we must distinguish between the claim that globalization should be seen as the continuation of deep-rooted historical processes and the view that contemporary globalization represents a critical break point or fundamental discontinuity in world politics (for strong claims of discontinuity see Strange 1996; Castells 1998; Beck 2000).

Perhaps the single most important idea arising from the globalization debate is that of the rapidly growing disjuncture between the concept of the self-contained sovereign state, the dynamics of the contemporary global economy, and the increasing complexity of world society. Indeed, the debate has breathed new life into many core liberal claims about the changing character of world politics, claims regarding: the multiple and ever-increasing links that exist between societies, many of which are either beyond direct government control or can only be controlled with tremendous difficulty; the consolidation of the role of diverse actors, such as corporations and Non-Governmental Organizations (NGOs); the increasing irrelevance of military power as a solution to key problems on the international agenda, such as how to promote global financial stability or tackle climate change; and the contradictions inherent in building a theory of international relations around discrete nation states, each of which can be assumed to have a clear set of 'national interests' (Nye and Keohane 2000). There are three broad categories of claim that globalization is having a deep, perhaps revolutionary, impact.

In the first place, it is widely argued that globalization is eroding the 'the authority, legitimacy, policymaking capacity, and policy-implementing effectiveness of the state' (Cerny 1995: 621). According to such analyses, certain sets of economic policy tools have ceased to be viable and European states are under growing pressure to adopt pro-market policies. The increasing power of financial markets forces governments to pursue macroeconomic policies that meet with market approval (Frieden 1991; Pauly 1995). As Garrett puts it, summarizing arguments he goes on to challenge, governments 'are held to ransom by the markets, the price is high, and punishment for non-compliance is swift' (1998a: 793). Increasing levels of trade intensify this pressure, as governments seek to avoid policies that might harm business, such as heavy taxation or high interest rates. Furthermore, footloose multinational companies are quick to punish governments that stray from the path of economic righteousness by exercising their exit option. As a consequence, the range of policy choices open to governments is, it is claimed, dramatically reduced. Social democratic parties in particular have to adjust their policy proposals: left-of-centre economic programmes, with their traditional focus on the public sector and generous state welfare provisions, tend to trigger the wrath of both multinationals and the markets (Scharpf 1991: 274–75; Rodrik 1997). Overall, the logic behind such accounts is remarkably similar to that underpinning the arguments of political neo-realists: functional necessity and systemic pressures will lead all states to behave in similar ways; the international system constrains governments into becoming more alike, increasingly depriving them of autonomy.

A second cluster of arguments concerns the degree to which processes of globalization have created the conditions for an activist global or transnational civil society, subsuming, or at least relativizing, the dominance of state-based 'Westphalian' politics. The physical infrastructure of increased economic interdependence (new systems of communication and transportation) plus the impact of new technologies (satellites, computer networks, etc.) have made it more costly and difficult for governments to control flows of information, while simultaneously facilitating the diffusion of values, knowledge, and ideas across national boundaries. The phrase 'transnational civil society' refers to those self-organized intermediary groups that are relatively independent of both public authorities and private economic actors; that are capable of taking collective action in pursuit of their interests or values; and that act across state borders. Theories of globalization have laid particular emphasis on the role played by NGOs, social movements, and transnational coalitions. The analytical focus of much of this work has been on transnational networks—for example, knowledge-based networks of economists, lawyers, or scientists; or transnational advocacy networks which act as channels for flows of money and material resources and, more critically, of information and ideas (for illustrative work from different perspectives see Wapner 1995; Keck and Sikkink 1998; Falk 1999).

A third line of argument suggests that it is institutional enmeshment, rather than economic transactions or the 'reconfiguration of social space', that has most constrained the West European state. According to this view, a vast array of rules, laws, and norms that are promulgated internationally affect almost every aspect of how states organize their societies domestically. Indeed, one of the most notable features of the Seattle protests and of recent World Trade Organization debates concerning contentious issues such as Genetically Modified Organisms (GMOs) and beef-hormones, was the belated realization amongst both European public opinion and European politicians of just how far-reaching these processes of legal and institutional enmeshment had become. Proponents of this view focus on emerging patterns of global or multi-level governance. They highlight the tremendous growth in the number of international organizations; they point to the vast increase in both the number of international treaties and agreements and the scope and intrusiveness of such agreements; and they suggest that important changes are occurring in the character of the international legal system, such as the appearance of 'islands of supranational governance' (such as the European Union or the dispute settlement procedures of the WTO); the blurring of municipal, international, and transnational law; and the increased importance of informal, yet norm-based, governance mechanisms, which are often built around complex transnational and transgovernmental networks (Teubner 1997; Cutler *et al.* 1999; Slaughter 1999).

Contrary to the debates of the 1970s and to popular images (Ohmae 1995), the cornerstone of the argument for change is not that the state is disappearing but rather that globalization is reconstituting the state and repositioning it within the broader pattern of global politics. How might we respond to such claims? First, it is critical to consider the methodological difficulties involved. Different authors have employed contrasting methodologies to examine the extent and impact of globalization. From 'large *n*' studies, using aggregate data (Garrett 1998*b*), to purely qualitative, single-country studies (Schmidt 1996; Cohen 1996), the range of academic work is huge.

Each methodology, of course, has its own advantages and disadvantages. The use of conceptual tools derived from economics, notably the assumption of economic rationality, certainly allows for parsimony in the construction of theoretical accounts, but their use can also imply an insensitivity to national and institutional context. As Boyer puts it, many theorists assume that 'the globalization of finance, labour, technologies, and products proceeds so that each nation comes to resemble a small- or medium-size firm in an ocean of pure and perfect competition' (Boyer 1996: 30). Similarly, aggregate data taken from many countries may provide a useful way by which to identify general trends, but is a less effective means of identifying those attitudinal changes which often act as precursors to shifts in behaviour and eventually policy outcomes. A further methodological problem concerns the difficulties involved in accurately identifying the causal chains that produce outcomes. Thus, even if globalization apparently militates in favour of deregulation at the national level, such deregulation may in fact be triggered, not by international, but domestic pressures, such as lobbying by business and financial institutions (Sobel 1994).

Additionally, it is worth noting that the scholar's task is further complicated by the fact that governments of all ideological complexions are prone to blame external pressures for policy change, pleading, in defence of unpopular policies, a need to respond to the pressures imposed by the international economy. Hence it has become common to use globalization and the 'pathology of over-diminished expectations' to which it has given rise (Hirst and Thompson 1999) as a convenient cover for the difficulty of maintaining domestic political support for redistributive or welfare policies—a technique perfected in France to justify adherence to the principles of the Maastricht convergence criteria in the face of high unemployment and growing public unrest. Separating rhetoric and reality is a difficult yet unavoidable task facing those interested in discerning the true impact of globalization on the states of Western Europe.

Second, there are empirical grounds for scepticism. Part of the sceptical riposte repeats (almost verbatim) the arguments of the later-1970s, urging would-be transformationists to consider the interdependence and transnationalism of earlier periods and especially of the decades before 1914 (see Hirst and Thompson 1999; Krasner 1999; Sutcliffe and Glyn 1999). Others have questioned the extent to which national economies have in fact become globalized (Krugman 1995; Wade 1996; Garrett 1998*a*). Equally it is far from clear that globalization has transformed economic policy management and is leading to policy convergence around pro-market economic and regulatory policies (Schulze and Ursprung 1999); that firms are inevitably opposed to interventionist government policies (Garrett 1998*a*; Goodhart 1998); that states can no longer effectively tax capital or fund welfare states (Swank 1998); that they are being forced to abandon desired labour, health, or environmental standards in a desperate race to the bottom (Drezner 2001); or, finally, that globalization is clearly associated with rising levels of social and economic inequality

(Goldthorpe 2001). It is clearly not possible to survey these debates in any detail. Nor is it necessary to agree on all of these issues with the arch-sceptics. For the purposes of this chapter it suffices merely to stress that, whilst many of the challenges of globalization are very real, they do not point in a single direction and certainly do not provide secure grounds for accepting the claim that some sort of deep change or transformation is underway, eroding the foundations of the European state and of the European regional order.

Finally, states themselves are not passive players. Globalization has been driven not by some unstoppable impersonal logic of technological innovation, but by specific sets of state policies, backed by specific political coalitions. Nor does globalization inevitably push governments towards declining state activism (Weiss 1998, 1999). Even where liberalizing effects can be attributed to globalization, it is not always the case that this implies state 'retreat'—as in the process by which privatization and deregulation have involved very significant degrees of re-regulation (Müller and Wright 1994: 8–9). Whilst old-style mercantilism built around the state as producer and national champions may have faded, the new geopolitics of globalization has come to involve a wide range of state initiatives from education policy to transport and information technology infrastructure. Thus states have not simply accepted the loss of their traditional role. Rather, as 'with virtually all social trends, those adversely affected must be expected to react; they will not necessarily do so with great success, but they may be able to do enough to disturb or divert the main lines of change' (Crouch, this volume). Equally, whilst pro-globalization coalitions can emerge, globalization can also lead to increased pressure on government to provide some level of protection against the economic and social dislocations arising from increased external vulnerability. Moreover, a great deal of the work cited above has highlighted the importance of national institutions in shaping how the impact of globalization will be felt (e.g. on the welfare state) and in determining the success of state responses to globalization.

It is also important to underscore the key role that international institutions play in the politics of globalization. States and markets cannot be viewed as necessarily in opposition. All markets, but especially complex global markets, depend on a dense set of rules and norms, on secure systems of property rights and of contract, and on civil order that only states can provide. Financial markets can impose huge costs on states, but the operation of the global financial system depends on an institutionalized inter-state order with well-respected rules and with national economies that are under the control of reasonably well-functioning states (Evans 1997). In addition, liberals have correctly stressed the extent to which globalization and increased interdependence create ever-increasing demand for international institutions. It is both an everyday intuition and the stuff of countless speeches and articles that globalization creates problems that can only be solved by stronger, deeper, and more effective forms of international cooperation. Now, as we have seen, transformationists suggest that the existence of an ever-denser and more intrusive set of regional and global institutions leads to increased legal and normative enmeshment, emptying traditional claims to sovereignty of any real content and dramatically undermining the policy autonomy of states over an expanding range of issues. Against this, two arguments can be made. First, the standard statist rebuttal—that international institutions themselves constitute a critical part of the response that states have made to globalization. But second, and much more import-ant, that the impact of globalization on a state or a group of states will be critically determined by their relative capacity to shape and structure those same institutions. It is this relative power that is fundamental to the politics and geopolitics of globalization.

Much of what is understood as globalization in fact involves the intensification of interdependencies at the regional rather than the global level, and the balance between globalization and regionalization is struck differently in different parts of the world (Oman 1999). Europe, however, is particularly well placed. On one side, the process of economic regionalization, of regional integration, and of institution-alized political regionalism is more deep-rooted and more intensive than in any other part of the world. This means that it is by engaging in the regional integration process that European states can seek to reposition themselves and to adapt to the pressures of economic globalization. Indeed the European Union provides us with a clear example of the ways in which states use international institutions to serve their own ends, and gain relative advantage over their competitors. Historically, as Milward and others argue, the EC can be understood as a means of reinforcing states that were weakened at a particular historical moment (Milward 2000). Subsequently, whilst agreeing to pool and delegate sovereignty within the European Union, its member states have continued to shape its development and to argue, primarily amongst themselves, about whose preferences—in both policy and institutional terms—its development should reflect. It is no surprise that, as European integration increasingly impinges upon national policies and national politics, member states are arguing more fiercely than ever between themselves over who wins and loses in spe-cific policy areas. Simultaneously they are attempting, by means of instruments such as the so-called Lisbon process—under which Heads of State and Government enjoy, through the European Council, an unprecedented degree of control over the devel-opment of EU economic and social policies—to lessen the ability of supranational agents such as the Commission to set the agenda for such policies.

But if one side of state-repositioning looks inward, the other looks outward, and concerns the capacity of the European Union to influence the norms and rules by which the globalized economy and global political system operate. There are three principal arenas for action, in all of which European states are relatively well posi-tioned. First, there is the traditional world of inter-state bargaining, regime creation, and international legal regulation in such forums as the WTO, the G8, and the OECD. Here one of the most important consequences of the development of the European Union has been to consolidate its external role in such institutions. It is of course the case that influence will vary according to the problem-structure, the power-structure, and the institutional characteristics of the particular issue. European preferences may win out within the WTO but fail to make any headway on international financial reform. Furthermore, US hegemony in the post-Cold War world clearly poses particu-lar difficulties and problems. But these are hardly novel problems, and, whilst the United States does have many veto and some exit options, its hegemony is far from unlimited. There is, then, no need to make optimistic assumptions about the EU's external economic or political clout. The issue is whether the capacity of Europe and the European Union to influence the global rules of the game has undergone some dramatic reduction compared to the 1970s (or the 1940s). It has not. Indeed a plausible case could be made that its potential power has increased significantly.

A second means of influencing the ground-rules of globalization is through the externalization of national or regional rules, norms, and practices, either as a result of market pressures or with the assistance of state power (e.g. as in the case of the extraterritorial application of US law). Indeed one of the most important aspects of the new regionalist mercantilism is precisely the capacity to set the rules for larger and larger blocs that then become the standard to which other players have to adapt (cf. Crouch, this volume, who describes the 'new mercantilism, or at least a version of national champions strategy compatible with an era of deregulation, as governments and leading firms engage in technical diplomacy on behalf of their chosen standard'). Again, there are major challenges both from the United States itself and from the United States' turn towards economic regionalism (first with North American Free Trade Area and now with the Free Trade Area of the Americas process). But here too Europe has real options, as the case of privacy rules for the Internet suggests.

The third means of influencing the ground-rules of globalization concern the ability to construct transnational and transgovernmental coalitions and to play network politics. A very great deal of norm creation takes place in and around transnational regulatory networks, involving state bureaucracies, international institutions, epistemic communities of scientists and specialists, representatives of firms and corporate associations, and advocacy NGOs. This is not a neutral, technical arena of specialist deliberation but an arena of contestation and unequal power. But it is an arena of governance in which Europe has the capacity to act effectively—partly because it has many players and partly because it is an aspect of governance in which Europe, through its own integrationist history, has been a pioneer.

It is, therefore, all too easy to exaggerate the scale and uniformity of international pressures on contemporary European states. The most strident claims for transformation in the role of the state run far in advance of the empirical evidence, underplay the variation of national responses, and neglect the extent to which external changes are mediated by institutions at the national level, by European-level institutions, and by multilateral institutions over which European states and the European Union have significant influence. Globalization has certainly posed challenges to the European state; changes in the global economy and in transnational civil society have impacted on European states and will continue to do so. But the notion of any kind of structural transformation or of a fundamental recasting of the ways in which the global economy affects the character of the European state is difficult to sustain. What, then, of the international political system?

THE EUROPEAN STATE AND THE INTERNATIONAL POLITICAL SYSTEM

As we suggested at the beginning of this chapter, the post-1945 changes in the character of the European state were closely bound up with the transformation of regional international relations, the successful development of regional institutions, and the emergence of a secure security community in Western Europe. Economic and political success was the product of a particular set of permissive international conditions.

In the first place, the great European transformation depended on the existence of a common external threat together with superpower protection against that threat, embodied in an alliance that, from the mid-1950s, became increasingly militarized and institutionalized. For all the recurrent crises within the Alliance, NATO cemented the historic shift in US (and also British) commitment to Western Europe, created a community of fate constructed around extended nuclear deterrence, and served as a magnet for new members (Greece and Turkey in 1952, West Germany in 1955, Spain in 1986). This acceptance of almost total security dependence on the United States was one of the essential compromises on which the success of European cooperation and integration was built. Indeed it is possible to argue that this success was made possible by the fact that the immensely difficult task of politico-military cooperation could be left to one side.

Second, stable European institutional structures depended on a solution to the 'German problem'. European integration was a response both to the Cold War and to the problem of German unification that had bedevilled Europe since 1870. If European integration was pressed from outside by the threat of the Soviet Union on the one side and by the hegemonic leadership of the United States on the other, it was also explicitly promoted as a means of managing German power. Although the division of Germany mitigated the fears of other Europeans, it certainly did not remove them. Europe needed German economic power to fuel post-war recovery and German military power to counter the Soviet threat. Indeed the specific project of regional *integration* arose precisely as the preferred means of dealing with this problem: permitting rearmament and economic rehabilitation by tying a semi-sovereign Germany into an integrated network of institutions in both the economic (EC) and military (NATO/WEU) fields. From Germany's perspective, regionalism provided the essential multilateral cover under which it could first of all re-establish its diplomatic position and recover its sovereignty and, having done so, re-establish its influence (Garton Ash 1994).

Third, the shift towards regional cooperation was bound up with decolonization, a process that ended the previously unparalleled European dominance over the rest of the world. Decolonization reduced even the strongest of the imperial powers to second-rank power status, had a profound impact on states' domestic societies and politics, and resulted in states reorienting their foreign policies and foreign economic relations back firmly towards their European neighbours (with Britain's hankering after the 'special relationship' with the United States being the most important exception to this trend). This enforced adaptation was far from smooth and unproblematic and varied from country to country; but it remains one of the most important ways in which a changing international context affected the character of the European state.

Finally, the Cold War cemented the boundaries of Europe. 'European' integration was in reality only sub-regional integration between a small group of countries with compatible values and similar economic and security policies. This both facilitated the process of regional rapprochement and integration and meant that difficult decisions regarding Eastern Europe could be left aside. Whilst the rhetoric of a reunified Germany and of a reintegrated East was maintained, the division suited most West Europeans and was a central element of what many took to be the stability of the post-1945 European order (DePorte 1986). It gave Western Europe '... the peculiar advantage of never having to worry, from 1951 to 1989, about the implications of trying to incorporate into "Europe" the even poorer lands to the East' (Judt 1996: 41). The Cold War also dictated the nature of relations with important parts of the periphery, ensuring a close military relationship with Turkey and the continued involvement of Spain, Portugal, and Greece with the 'West', despite their authoritarian politics.

 Given all of this, it was natural for many commentators to predict that the end of the Cold War would have important and unsettling implications for Western Europe. Neo-realists such as Mearsheimer (1990) and Waltz (1993) argued, first, that both the western alliance and European institutions were bound to erode in the absence of a clear, joint external threat; second, that the unparalled extent of US hegemony was inherently unstable and that this asymmetry of power would sooner or later provoke balancing behaviour, including from Washington's erstwhile allies (Layne 1995); and finally, that European nation states would increasingly look to their own security interests with, at the extreme, a rearmed and assertive Germany leading a race 'back to the future'. In short, changes in the international political system would lead eventually, if gradually, to a return within Europe and across the Atlantic of the realist norm: anarchy, strategic rivalry, and security competition that would be mitigated, if at all, not by international institutions but by balances of power or hegemonic ordering.

Such analyses, however, neglect or misconstrue a number of fundamental factors. In the first place, they neglect the qualitative changes that had taken place in the character of politics in Western Europe and the degree to which European states and societies appeared deeply reluctant to revert to the neo-realist 'norm'. The classical imperatives, whether of material gain, of security and fear, or of doctrine and ideology, that produced the major wars of the nineteenth and twentieth century and the need for military power appear to have receded. Mercantilist impulses may well persist but these are not readily susceptible to use of military power, nor do they obviously threaten to create military conflict. Despite the urgings of neo-realist theorists, emerging 'Great Powers' such as Germany seem remarkably reluctant to take on the military trappings of their traditional forebears. In such cases the balance between welfare and security goals has shifted and states enjoy all sorts of other ways to promote their interests and objectives. Profound domestic changes and altered external circumstances have led to very different definitions of national interest and, more fundamentally, of identity. It is true that Germany has moved towards greater military involvement and a rethinking of its broader political role. But the elements of continuity in the notion of Germany as a civilian power with an attachment to multilateralism, supranational integration, and constraining the use of force through national and international norms are still more pronounced (Rittberger 2001).

Second, neo-realists neglect the continued success and density of institutions within Europe. Indeed, the end of the Cold War coincided, not with the erosion but with a deepening and expansion of the European Union. Europe remained the most densely institutionalized region on earth and was consistently viewed in the 1990s not only as a 'security community' (Adler and Barnett 1998), but also as the prime example of a region where understandings of sovereignty have been transformed (Ruggie 1993; Waever 1995; Linklater 1999), and supranational governance extended (Sandholtz and Stone Sweet 1998). The European Union constitutes not merely a security community amongst its own members, but also a powerful and prosperous core to which peripheral states no longer respond by balancing power, but rather by aspiring to membership.

Third, European states are firmly embedded in a broader security community covering the North Atlantic area, and perhaps encompassing the OECD world. There are many theoretical takes on the durability of NATO (for a review see Duffield 2001). Yet whether viewed in terms of institutionalist theory or in narrower terms of power and state interest, NATO is as an institution that has a unique range of military assets (in its elaborate and complex joint planning, intelligence, and force structures); that embodies a dense transnational security network; that can rely on an effective decision-making process (combining hegemonic aspects, a range of well-established informal norms, and the veneer of unanimity and consensus); and, finally, that reflects the continued foreign—as opposed to security—policy interests of a range of states, including the United States, Britain, and Germany.

Finally, it is important to highlight the particular nature of the United States as a hegemonic power. In part this has to do with its democratic values and the degree to which these are shared by its European allies. In part, it has to do with the characteristics of American power and the degree to which its reliance on coercive and military power is balanced by a wide range of soft power instruments and shaped by its particular ideological traditions. In part, it reflects the degree to which US external power is balanced by the nature of its domestic political system, the decentralized structure of which provides numerous points of access to competing groups.

These arguments provide good grounds for rejecting the extreme 'back to the future' predictions favoured by some neo-realists. Some liberals suggest that the foundations of the post-1945 liberal international order are secure. As Ikenberry puts it:

By the end of the 1990s, the United States possessed unrivalled military and economic power, but the other major states have not sought to move away from or balance against American power. Nor has the level of conflict between the United States and its allies increased since the end of the Cold War. On the contrary, the scope and density of intergovernmental relations between the industrial democracies has actually expanded. The logic and stability of the Western order—crystallized in the late 1940s—is still evident today. (2001: 218)

And yet it is too easy to slip into an unguarded liberal optimism. Liberal theorists, in turn, tend to downplay both the pressures and effects that flow from the international system and exaggerate the degree to which international institutions have overcome the primacy of traditional competitive politics. Institutions do matter and institutional development has gone further in Europe than in any other part of the world. Yet this should not lead us to devalue the continued centrality of the West European state, nor to neglect the continued importance of distributional conflict, nor, indeed, to ignore the ongoing tensions that exist between the highly developed European legal order and its political and power-political foundations. Even within this allegedly post-sovereign political space, interstate competition, geopolitics, and security concerns continue to influence the calculations of governments and to shape patterns of institutional development.

Whilst there is no denying that interstate politics in Western Europe have been 'tamed' in comparison to their turbulent past, institutions have not simply replaced inter-state conflict, but have often come to constitute new arenas for it. This is a true of NATO as it is of any other institution. Consistent attempts by Paris to create alternative, European structures, or to reshape NATO from within stemmed from a desire to address what Paris perceived as its lack of relative influence, and hence ability to shape outcomes within that institution. From the time of de Gaulle onwards, France made this struggle for distributional advantage within the organization the focal point of its NATO policies—witness how Chirac's efforts to ensure European control over NATO's southern command derailed what had previously been a hugely successful diplomatic initiative to bring France back within the integrated military commands. The European Union has also increasingly become prey to such squabbles. From the public fears voiced by smaller member states about bullying tactics employed by their larger partners, to often poisonous disputes about specific pieces of legislation—such as the long awaited European company statute—to Franco-German quarrels over the policy content of Economic and Monetary Union, distributional conflict has taken centre stage. It is hard to deny that, in many senses, the Union 'exemplifies a distinctly modern form of power politics' (Moravcsik 1998: 5; Menon 2001*b*).

Moreover, and here we disagree fundamentally with the seminal work of Moravcsik (1998), geopolitics (ignored in most liberal accounts of the development of international institutions in favour of an emphasis on the internal dynamics of such institutions), plays a fundamental role in shaping the development of international institutions. The genesis of EMU cannot be explained without reference to French desire to ensure that a united Germany was firmly tied into the European institutional structure. But it is the issues of institutional enlargement and European security that provide the clearest evidence that, even in an archetypal zone of peace and institutional density, military geopolitical concerns have not gone away.

Enlargement has been central to European institutional developments over the past decade. Even if a security community has been created within a given region, stability will depend crucially on what happens around its boundaries; hence the central strategic justification for European Union and NATO enlargement with its accompanying rhetoric about the impossibility of remaining an island of peace in a troubled sea. The idea has been to manipulate both the prospect of eventual membership and the creation of specific criteria for admission in order to lock surrounding states into policies that are deemed to promote stability: economic liberalization, human rights and democracy, and changes in military structure and organization (through North Atlantic Cooperation Council, Partnership for Peace, and Euro-Atlantic Partnership Council in the case of NATO, and through various association, pre-membership agreements, and negotiations for membership in the case of the European Union).

The enlargement issue is critical because of the unresolved dilemmas to which it gives rise and because these dilemmas in turn raise unsettling questions for liberal understandings of regional pacification. First, there is the dilemma over boundaries. The liberal logic of inclusion finds it hard to cement outer boundaries. Indeed, in an important sense it depends on the denial that such boundaries exist, because to fix boundaries is necessarily to define insiders and outsiders and to separate friends from potential foes.

The second dilemma concerns the management of the periphery. Whilst enlargement is viewed as a solution to many of the security and economic problems of peripheral states, it can also be a threat and a challenge. States joining a well-established regional institution are more likely to find themselves constrained by it than those who are already members; the social and economic changes required for membership can be immensely disruptive; and the very power of a dynamic and prosperous region can provoke disturbing changes in the social structures and political arrangements of neighbouring states.

The third dilemma is the institutionalist one: how to provide for effective decision making in a community of twenty-five or thirty states? If expansion continues, how can Europe prevent the resulting institutions from being so loose, so lacking in effectiveness, reflecting such a thin sense of community, that their 'institutionalization' provides the thinnest of thin cloaks for older power political practices? Liberal theories suggest that this will necessarily require deeper institutionalization and a reduction in the veto power of national governments. But if this does not happen, then the only logical alternative is a return to forms of institutionalized governance in which unequal power and hierarchy play a more central role. The persisting doubt, therefore, is that enlargement will dilute the very socializing pressures and tight institutional binding that has been so important in the post-1945 process of regional pacification.

Finally, whilst geopolitical concerns have been central to the debate over institutional enlargement, they have also played a major role in shaping the other set of discussions that have increasingly come to preoccupy European leaders—the relationship between the European Union and security and defence issues. Now that the end of the Cold War has called into question not only NATO's continuing utility but, more importantly, the continued commitment of the United States to that institution, even traditionally highly pro-NATO states such as Britain have accepted the need for the European Union to move beyond its status as a civilian power. Yet incorporating defence will create severe problems for the European Union. For one thing, there is the question of how effectively the fifteen will manage to take defence-related decisions. Europe still highlights the enormous difference between the unthinkability of war, not fighting against each other, on the one hand, and the idea of fighting for each other on the other. Even if a common interest is perceived, it may be extremely difficult to forge a common policy in the face of conflicting interests, competing prescriptions, and collective action problems between member states.

In particular the use of military power in response to security challenges whose origins lie in civil wars, ethnic conflict, or state collapse raises politically divisive questions as to the definition of state interests and the precise objectives that should be sought. Hence it is not surprising that contemporary security threats, such as those arising in the Balkans, have tended not to cement regional alliances as in the past, but rather to place enormous strain on regional cohesion or consensus.

Second, the European Security and Defence Policy (ESDP) provides cause for concern for those anxious to see the European Union remain an effective forum for inter-state cooperation in Europe. Whatever its flaws, the European Union has been a remarkably successful experiment in such cooperation. The fifteen member states are enmeshed in a previously unimaginable network of negotiation on virtually every aspect of public policy. Within the Union, the culture is very much one of bargaining, of trade-offs, of openness, and of a system backed up by the force of law and policed by the supranational institutions. The problem is that attempts to introduce institutions for dealing with defence may threaten this culture. Defence is a specific kind of policy sector which is simply not amenable to the kind of treatment to which the other core sectors of Union competence are routinely exposed, such as log-rolling, trade-offs across issues, or transparency (Menon 2001*a*). Institutionally, the marginalization of the Commission in matters pertaining to the ESDP, to a degree as yet unmatched, threatens not only the effectiveness of the ESDP by dislocating it from other elements of the EU's external policies, but also the institutional unity of the EU system. The decision to expand the Council secretariat to incorporate the EU's military staff may have implications not only for the ability of this organization to carry out its other tasks effectively, but also for its relations with the Commission, of which it could conceivably come to be viewed as a rival.

All this is not to say that the institutional solution chosen for defence will not work. It is simply to point out that the way in which the shifting international political environment has forced an issue not previously dealt with by the European Union onto its agenda may have far-reaching consequences for that institution, which forms the centrepiece of what some have seen as Europe's post-Westphalian system.

CONCLUSION

All states are embedded within a complex social order in which it is conventional to make distinctions between the 'domestic' and the 'international', and between three external 'arenas' of social action: the international political system, the international and transnational economy, and transnational civil society. But such categories are at best only rough approximations and always run the risk of neglecting or misunderstanding the links that run between the external and the internal and amongst the three arenas that constitute global politics. This chapter began by underscoring the obvious point that the character of the European state and of all existing European states was inextricably bound up with particular and historically contingent patterns of both regional and global international relations. It went on to suggest that many of the features of the European state that are politically taken for granted, and that dominate academic writing, were functions of the transformation of European international relations in the period that followed the Second World War. This is true of many aspects of the domestic political agenda—the dominance of considerations of social welfare and economic development, the decreasing militarization of European societies, the rise of new forms of identity politics, and the decline in extremist political forces. And it is also the case in terms of the character of the regional security complex that has emerged within western Europe and the construction of a complex institutionalized polity that is the one clear example of a group of states moving 'beyond Westphalia' (although the character of that polity remains highly contested).

In considering contemporary challenges to this inherited picture, we looked first at the claims surrounding the concept of globalization and concluded, somewhat sceptically, that arguments for a deep or structural transformation were overblown. Yes, many of the changes discussed by globalization theorists are significant. But such changes do not fall outside what one might see as a pattern of 'normal change', nor are they unprecedented. Yes, many forces do work to reduce the autonomy of states (or at least of particular states) and do reconstitute the operational meaning of sovereignty. But the available evidence is often ambiguous and many globalizing pressures work in precisely the opposite direction, pushing towards the reassertion of state power, either individually or through regional or international institutions. By contrast, we suggested that change in the international political system has already had an important impact on the character and stability of the regional order in Europe. Living in a unipolar world, dealing with the geopolitical imperatives of enlargement, and having to face up to the return of high politics and defence have been central to state policies in the 1990s and to the institutional development of Europe. They pose fundamental dilemmas for European states and for the European regional order that are unlikely to go away.

Finally, we acknowledge the importance of institutions in understanding the character of the European order, but seek to steer between the neo-realist rhetoric of eternal recurrence and the liberal belief in institutions as paths towards political transcendence. It is not the case that the institutions that litter the West European international landscape have signalled the end of traditional competitive international politics between these states. Rather, as our brief discussions of both NATO and the European Union have sought to show, member states continue to vie for relative influence and distributional benefits within them, much as they always have. Nor have institutions succeeded in sheltering states completely from the impact of pressures imposed by the international political system. Both the debates about enlargement and the ongoing saga of the ESDP serve to illustrate that international politics still matter, and should still be of interest to students of both the international institutions and the states of Western Europe. Compared to their own past and to all other regions of the world, West European international institutions have tamed the international jungle. At the same time, that jungle remains quintessentially political, and one in which interstate political conflict and concerns for relative power and influence remain central.

Conclusion

Governing Europe

ANAND MENON

In his preface, Jack Hayward explains how Vincent Wright would have handled writing a conclusion such as this, and how, in particular, Vincent would have sought 'to compensate for the divergences between authors by incorporating as much as possible of their diversity into his comprehensive comparative analysis'. Quite a trick to pull on the co-editor charged with concluding this volume.

The aim of this chapter is far more modest than those Vincent would have set himself. It is, quite simply, to tease out the major themes that have reappeared throughout the book. In doing so it addresses six questions:

- What are the most striking features of the picture of contemporary West European politics painted in the preceding pages?
- To what extent has there been convergence between West European states?
- How can one go about accounting for continued divergences between political systems confronted by similar pressures?
- How has the European Union affected the political landscape in Western Europe?
- How serious are the problems of legitimacy confronting West European political systems?
- How do different methodological approaches impact upon our understanding of West European Politics?

The answers to these questions are neither clear nor straightforward. The various chapters not only address different issues, often from different perspectives, but also on occasion come to different conclusions regarding the same phenomena. What is apparent from the brief discussion that follows, however, is the richness, diversity and vibrancy of the subfield to which Vincent contributed so much.

The author would like to thank Jack Hayward, Sid Tarrow, and particularly Hussein Kassim for detailed and perceptive comments on an earlier version of this chapter.

GOVERNING EUROPE

Change

If the chapters in this volume carry a single message, it is that to study how Western Europe is governed is to shoot at a rapidly moving target. All the contributors emphasize how politics in the various West European nation states is constantly evolving.

Several of the contributions—notably by Goetz, Cassese, and Peters—underline the importance of the evolution of public administrations over the last couple of decades. They stress in particular those changes associated with the New Public Management (NPM). Across Western Europe, though to varying extents, at varying paces, and with varying implications, this new philosophy has wrought significant and substantive changes via its emphasis on, among other things, agencification, the centrality of value for money considerations, marketization and customer orientation. Traditional patterns of trust in the bureaucracy as an institution have been eroded. The ethos of competition has challenged traditional Weberian notions of a professional and dedicated cadre of public officials, and the lines between politics and administration have become more than ever blurred.

In addition to such ideologically driven developments, the increasing sectorization, differentiation, and complexity of policy making have altered styles of bureaucratic action, leading to an ever-increasing emphasis on coordination, negotiation, and compromise. Indeed, evolution is inherent in the very nature of contemporary European administrative systems. Goetz argues that there exists within them a permanent and dynamic tension between politicization and bureaucratization, the balance between the two constantly shifting, but never settling.

Administrative reforms are an integral part of an overall process of evolution affecting both the nature and the role of the state in Western Europe. For some, such as Rod Rhodes, this process represents a veritable revolution. Taking as his point of reference the British government, and particularly the durable and, as he claims, misleading notion of the Westminster system, he points to several areas of radical change, involving the 'hollowing out' of the British state, as well as its increasing fragmentation and segmentation. The delegation of certain traditional government functions to agencies is an area of particular concern to several of the contributors, in terms not only of its impact on the role, nature, and indeed *raison d'etre* of the state, but also its implications for democratic accountability in European political systems (see below).

The state also increasingly confronts external challenges. Hurrell and Menon argue that, whilst many of the claims about the impact of globalization are exaggerated, West European nation states nevertheless find themselves significantly constrained by the workings of the international *political* system. Perhaps more significantly, states are losing their monopoly over public policy to other actors. Regions, as Le Galès illustrates, are becoming involved in areas such as welfare and the environment, while the European Union has become not only increasingly active in ever more policy domains, but also far more visible, and hence politically salient, in the domestic politics of the member states.

As the core institutions of government and governance have evolved, so too have both their relations with society, and the nature of that society itself. Yves Mény provides striking figures about the decreasing levels of trust in, and declining appreciation of the need for, political parties. And he argues that it is this increasing dissatisfaction with parties that has spawned what many see as a legitimacy crisis confronting many, if not most, European political systems. Moreover, as parties represent the crucial link between public opinion and governing institutions, their apparent decline has had important consequences in terms of the growth in, and changing nature of, the social protest movements discussed by Sid Tarrow.

Political parties themselves have had to adapt to shifting and increasingly intense pressures upon them. They have reformed their organizational structures, becoming more dominated by small cadres of committed professionals, and turning themselves into 'electoral-professional parties'. In so doing, they have moved away from a civil society that seems increasingly distrustful of, not to say hostile towards, them, and into closer relations with the state. Thus, 'not only are parties moving towards the state and away from civil society, but also a party's leadership is becoming more remote from the party itself' (Smith, this volume).

Changing public perceptions of political parties are mirrored by attitudes towards politics and politicians more generally. Profound cynicism about what politicians have to offer was encapsulated in the slogans used by many between the two rounds of voting in the 2002 French presidential election: 'vote for the crook, not the fascist'. Moreover an atmosphere of economic crisis, along with high levels of unemployment in many West European states, have rendered examples of corruption more intolerable than ever. The backlash has taken many forms, from the obsession with sleaze that, under the Major government, gripped the British press and political scene, to protest votes at elections that have (finally) alerted mainstream politicians to the threat posed by the extreme right,[1] to the new-found activism of the French media and judiciary in the quest to root out instances of wrongdoing. To parody Majone's discussion of political property rights, there is a general and growing belief that, unlike economic property rights, their holders should not enjoy the ability to earn income from them.

Ironically, this hardening of attitudes has coincided with corruption itself becoming more common and more complex, as political parties seek different ways of funding their increasingly expensive activities. Even in Britain, where the kinds of unofficial levy imposed on business by political parties in France and Germany has not existed, recent newspaper reports alleging favours for donations, and the sudden, if somewhat abortive, interest in the idea of public funding for political parties underline the extent to which the growing cost of politics has led to the need for parties to think hard about strategies for generating income.

Finally, as political and administrative structures, their links with society, and societal attitudes towards them have shifted, so too have the outputs of politics—the

---

[1] Even if the reaction has often been to steal the agenda of the extreme right, rather than to challenge its arguments.

public policies which shape the lives of the citizens of Western Europe. The European Union has represented a fundamental shift in the nature of the political opportunity structure confronting actors and this alone has been significant in helping to redefine the policy agenda, reshape policy structures, and introduce new public policy agendas. The most obvious area of innovation has been the euro, with European leaders confronting the challenge of how best to formulate a macroeconomic policy for twelve very different economies. Yet even in more traditional sectors, at the level of the nation state, evolutions are underway. Ferrera, Hemerijck, and Martin Rhodes illustrate how the very different welfare policies of the various West European states have come under pressure, and will face increasing pressures to reform. Mark Thatcher outlines the profound changes in industrial policy that occurred during the 1980s, involving privatization, liberalization, reregulation, and the establishment or strengthening of independent or semi-independent regulatory bodies.

Political Science and Political Change

As its subject matter has developed so, too, has the discipline of political science had to adapt. As Cassese points out, a central theme of many of the chapters in this volume—administrative reform—only became a subject in its own right this century. Previously, owing both to the limited size of bureaucracies and the lack of need to distinguish between politics and administration, the concept would have been meaningless. Now, however, things are very different, as administrations have grown, and the lines between politics and administration have become increasingly blurred (with officials, for example, coming to play an ever greater role in providing policy advice, and in policy implementation). Similarly, Tarrow explains how political science has for most of its recent history 'relegated the study of popular protest movements to sociology—or worse, to abnormal psychology'. Yet he talks now in terms of the possible emergence of a movement society, with social movements as a perpetual element of modern life, employed by more diverse constituencies and within the reach of conventional politics.

Perhaps the most acute challenge confronting the discipline is the relocation of much authority away from nation states. Political science is not alone in struggling to deal with an issue that is, for example, beginning to trouble sociologists (Crouch 2001). Yet it, too, faces a pressing need to address the fact that the nation state, for so long the basis of its analyses, is not only constrained, but also shaped by exogenous forces (Hurrell and Menon, this volume). The state now has to coexist alongside other layers of governance and authority, which have laid claim to some of its core functions. And the impact of the external environment continues to make itself felt. In the light of issues as diverse as the terrorist attacks of 11 September, the imposition of US steel sanctions on Europe, the creation of the International Criminal Court, or the resignation of the Dutch government due to much earlier events in the Balkans (to name but a few obvious examples), it is simply not enough for political scientists to invoke the deus ex machina of external pressures, to refer casually to 'exogenous shocks', or 'critical junctures', or whatever the current intellectual fashion might be. National politics is part of a global system; and each interacts, to varying degrees, with the other in a more systematic and sustained way than is often assumed (Hurrell and Menon, this volume).

The fact that changes in the 'real world' provide pressure for change in the ways that political scientists conceive of it does not mean that they agree on the need for, or necessary extent of, any concomitant evolutions in the discipline. Thus while Andeweg discusses differing approaches to the study of government, Rod Rhodes, in typically iconoclastic fashion, questions whether the term should be used at all, arguing that 'the literature on governance explores how the informal authority of networks supplements and supplants the formal authority of government'. Rhodes emphasizes in particular the way in which elected British governments have become locked in relations of mutual dependence with powerful groups, a development which, in his opinion, deprives the notion of government of much, if not all, of its analytical utility.

Such terminological differences are not merely a question of semantics. If governments, believing the myths about the strength of the executive, adopt a 'command operating code', this 'builds failure into the design of the policy' (Rhodes, this volume). Thus, whilst academics undoubtedly are often guilty of using excessive amounts of jargon and of deliberate obfuscation, this should not be taken to imply that all their terminological squabbles are irrelevant to those outside the academy.

Scholarly disputes are not, of course, limited to questions of terminology. The contributors reveal several areas of ongoing debate about the nature of West European politics. Both Tarrow and Mény emphasize the importance of what they see as a possible decline in the role of political parties as at least a partial explanation for the rising importance of social protest movements and corruption, respectively. Tarrow attributes the rise in number of public interest groups to the decline of parties, and cites the residual strength of party affiliations in Europe as the reason why such movements have risen more slowly on the Old Continent than they have in the United States.

Yet Gordon Smith offers a salutary warning to those too eager to assume that parties are in decline. For one thing, the supposed 'golden age' of mass political parties was both a far more recent phenomenon than is generally suggested and not as real as is often supposed. Moreover, in contesting overly simplistic claims about voter turnout, electoral volatility, and the rise of protest parties—on both empirical grounds and in terms of their actual significance as indicators of decline—he makes it clear that the jury is still very much out on this crucial issue. Not inconsequentially, he is also at pains to point out that there is 'no necessary link between the fortunes of liberal democracy and the role played by political parties'.

Evolution vs Revolution

This cautionary note should alert us to the dangers of excessive haste in discarding the old in favour of the new. Change is a fundamental element of all the accounts presented in this volume—Smith himself admits that parties are under threat and that their future is far from assured. Yet at least two qualifications should be made. First, the pace of change is not always as rapid as eager heralds of a new age in politics might wish us to believe. As Page points out, perhaps we should 'reserve judgement about the applicability of europeanization as homogeneity for a few more decades until the processes on which it is based might be expected to have had time to make a more noticeable impact on European political systems'. We are witnessing evolution, not revolution, and evolution takes time.

Second, it is important to avoid the trap of faddism. A case in point is the way in which scholars have approached the question of the role of the state. Political scientists have long made sport of proclaiming—all too hastily—its demise. Thus, in the mid-1980s, American political scientists saw fit to bring back in a state that, for European observers, had never really gone away. Such trends in the literature were all too redolent of the way in which scholars of an earlier generation had—again wrongly as it turns out—proclaimed that European integration was taking us 'Beyond the Nation State' (Haas 1964). Currently, as Hurrell and Menon observe, there is no shortage of observers willing to proclaim that the state is in terminal, and irreversible, decline.

Yet consider the facts. Certainly, the modern European state is under pressure. However, as Müller reminds us, it 'is a historic phenomenon that has been under constant transformation since its birth'. Change, in other words, is not necessarily synonymous with decline. Moreover, the state, like all institutions, has traditionally shown a marked capacity to react to new circumstances and to emerging pressures upon it. Crouch reminds us that, the forces of globalization notwithstanding, states have managed to find new ways of doing what they always have—assisting national economic performance—only now, the chosen method is through engaging in technical diplomacy alongside leading firms in a quest to have national standards adopted internationally (see also Hurrell and Menon, this volume). Note, too, that political parties, partly in response to increasing societal indifference, partly to the increasing demands—particularly financial—upon them, have turned to the state for salvation—hardly indicative of a moribund form of political and social organization. Likewise, Tarrow makes the point that states still retain significant power over borders, and hence can act as effective brokers between subnational actors and international institutions. Finally, if the aftermath of the events of 11 September revealed anything, it was that the state is widely perceived as the ultimate guarantor of both internal and external security—whatever its actual capacity to perform these two tasks.

Less tangibly, though no less importantly, the state as a form of political organization remains the crucial referent for politicians and political scientists alike. This is most clearly (and, as argued below, most unhelpfully) the case in discussions about the European Union. Both the academic literature and the pages of the quality press are replete with suggestions for reform of the Union based on the assumption that the solution to its problems lie in making it more state like. Thus there are those who want to provide it with a constitution, whilst others debate the optimal nature of its putative army. Moreover, the more the state devolves its functions to subnational and supranational institutions, the more debates about democracy seem to focus on the fact that the state, or organizational and institutional forms that resemble it, are the only ways of providing democratic legitimacy (see below). Finally, of course, and one of the fundamental problems confronting the European Union insofar as its democratic credentials are concerned, is the fact that states remain the primary object of the loyalty of their citizens.

For all the emphasis on change within this volume, therefore, we should avoid exaggeration. Evolutionary trends have not reconfigured West European politics to the point where traditional labels and concepts are necessarily anachronistic. They do, however, necessitate that political scientists are willing to conceive of familiar phenomena in new and creative ways.

TOWARDS CONVERGENCE?

Pressures

The authors in this volume have identified a number of common pressures that are affecting politics in Western Europe today. These pressures are responsible for many of the developments outlined in the previous sections, and are held by some, because they affect all West European states, to be laying the basis for convergence between their political systems. Before examining these claims in more detail, it is worth briefly considering the various drivers of change.

Andrew Hurrell and Anand Menon distinguish between the economic and political pressures emanating from the international system. They argue that, whilst international factors have always impinged upon, and continue to affect, politics within nation states, the impact of globalization has tended to be exaggerated. In contrast, they make the claim that the international political system, for so long ignored or underplayed by comparativists as an independent variable explaining political developments within states, has exerted a profound impact on such developments.

Perhaps the most widely cited (in this volume) exogenous factor affecting politics in Western Europe is the European Union. All contributors to this volume are at pains to at least mention it as a catalyst for change, though they are far from unanimous about the nature of the changes it has wrought. Thus while Müller is convinced by many of the claims made by those who emphasize the profound transformative effects of europeanization, Page is far more circumspect, and at pains to argue that such effects are far from obvious. Hurrell and Menon, approaching the question from a different angle, argue that institutions such as the European Union in fact empower states, enabling them better to resist, and to shape, the pressures exerted by the international environment.

A third factor is the changing nature of politics and, particularly, of public policy. On the one hand, policy has become more specialized and technical in nature. Specialization has created incentives for politicians to delegate certain functions to agencies, particularly where, as Majone points out, complex policies developed alongside the need for rule making or adjudicative functions—tasks inappropriate for an existing government department or court. Recent years have also witnessed the emergence, and increasing salience, of 'cross-cutting issues that do not fit neatly into existing departmental structures' (Goetz). Crouch argues that technological change serves to blur the boundaries between economic sectors, 'bringing together technologies and processes which were once seen as different'. As a consequence, the 'idea of economic sectors ... is ... becoming elusive'.

Technological change has also impacted upon politics in other ways. Most notably, the Internet and mass media have facilitated communication both within and between states, and represent an organizational resource in the hands of ordinary citizens. This was perhaps most striking in terms of their contributions to the seismic events in Eastern Europe in the late 1980s, but they have also impacted in the West, allowing organizers of protest movements to use mobile phones and Internet sites to organize their activities, and allowing for the creation of virtual movements (Tarrow, this volume). Technological change has also helped to bring about and reinforce the phenomenon known as globalization by, for instance, allowing for the free movement of massive sums of capital instantaneously across borders, a development which itself has had a profound impact on politics in Western Europe.

A further driver of change has been financial. Cassese highlights financial pressures as one of the key drivers of administrative reform, as states, increasingly active in the areas of education, health, social security, and promoting employment, have found themselves overextended. Like all the factors listed in this section, financial concerns are themselves both an independent and dependent variable. Thus, whilst helping to drive many of the developments discussed by the contributors—such as welfare state retrenchment, or privatization, or the policy mix chosen for EMU—they are themselves driven by others: the pretensions of subnational governments to pursue policies of their own choosing; the opposition of rich, powerful regions to redistribution to poorer areas; or the convergence criteria agreed to in the Maastricht Treaty.

Social change, sometimes underplayed by political scientists increasingly fascinated with institutional accounts, is another variable helping to determine the nature, direction, and pace of change in West European politics. Gordon Smith argues that the lower intensity of social class and denominational barriers, coupled with rising educational levels and a loosening of social bonds, have conspired to engender falling levels of identification with individual parties. In a similar vein, Sid Tarrow points to the importance of generational (or as he puts it, biological) factors which led to the student and new left movements of the late 1960s bequeathing a reservoir of activists who continued to have an impact on politics in the decades that followed.

A final factor that has accounted for change has been dissatisfaction with public sector performance. Cassese argues that this created incentives for experimentation with new forms of administrative organization. More broadly, under the impact of the kinds of pressures listed above, governments, accustomed to making extravagant promises, found themselves increasingly unable to deliver even on their more modest ones. Consequently, as Mény puts it, 'political leaders who used to increase the expectations of citizenry are now pleading everyday their own incapacity to satisfy them'. While doing so, and while they foster what Hirst and Thomson (1999) have described as a 'pathology of over-diminished expectations', they have increasingly delegated core functions—such as the regulation of public service industries or the conduct of monetary policy—to other actors, thereby dissociating themselves from responsibility for what are increasingly constrained policy options available at the national level.

Continued Divergence

Confronted with so many common pressures, it seems intuitively reasonable to expect the various European states to have reacted and been shaped in similar ways by them. It is indeed possible to identify some clear elements of convergence, or at least of convergent trends in different countries. Privatization and deregulation have spread across the continent; steps to tackle welfare reform are everywhere being taken; chief executives are becoming more powerful; interest groups more prone to lobby the European Commission; parties more professional; regions more assertive; administrations more marketized; politicians less trusted.

Yet for all this, what is most striking are not instances of convergence but rather the fact that, despite such pressures, the various national systems have remained, in many crucial respects, stubbornly different. Moreover, they have responded in very different ways to the pressures upon them. Thus, Crouch points out that the reaction of private actors to the pressures of globalization has been varied. The decomposition of membership of interest associations has been most marked in the United Kingdom, whilst in France 'the neo-liberal challenge is paradoxically strengthening neo-corporatist initiatives, which emerge as less unacceptable alternatives than the former *etatisme*'. Similarly, public sector reform in France has not involved *services publiques* (post, gas, electricity, rail), all of which have been privatized across the Channel.

When confronted with precisely the same problem, individual states retain a capacity—indeed a proclivity—to respond in different ways. Take the need for them both to adjust to the demands of EU membership, and to seek appropriate and effective ways of influencing EC decisions. Despite Cassese's claim that 'public administrations are moving towards a European model, imposed by the European Community (and later by the European Union)', recent research on the coordination of national policies towards the EU reveal that marked differences continue to characterize the various national systems in place (Kassim *et al.* 2000*b*, 2001).

The same can be said of another phenomenon that is all too often treated as uniform across western Europe: the recognition by national legal authorities of the principal of the supremacy of European Union over national law. Paul Craig's chapter underlines not only the fragility of the acceptance of this principle, but also the various different bases upon which it has been—tentatively—accepted in the member states—ranging from the highly *communautaire* approach adopted in Belgium to the more circumspect legal reasonings used in states like France and Germany.

Divergences persist, therefore, but, in an era of flux and evolution, they cannot be encapsulated by simple stereotypes. Certainly, the role of the state has been altered more radically in Britain than in France. Yet, its decreasing role in the latter case does not imply a fullscale, coherent retreat from its previous activism in socioeconomic affairs. The Blair government is currently engaged in a massive programme of investment into Britain's (public) health service, whilst the role of the state in managing the rail transport network is as yet far from settled. In discussing what he sees as misleading claims about the unitary nature of the British state, Rod Rhodes warns against utilising convenient shorthands simply because they are generally understood, convenient, and short. The point is well taken.

Explaining Continued Divergence

How, then, are we to explain this relative absence of convergence? The first cluster of possible explanations concerns the nature of the pressures themselves. As Hurrell and Menon point out in the case of globalization, exogenous forces acting upon nation states are sometimes not as far-reaching as claimed, may operate unevenly, and in some cases are themselves the product of state action, with the inevitable result that their impact on states varies.

Moreover, the various pressures identified above act upon West European countries in numerous different, and often contradictory ways, creating multiple pressures for different kinds of response. Thus, executives are confronted with challenges ranging from budgetary pressures, to their 'hollowing out'— 'from above (e.g. by international interdependence), from below (by marketization and networks), and sideways (by agencies)' (Rhodes, this volume). Simultaneously, however, they face new demands upon them and a potentially growing role (Heywood and Wright 1997). Little wonder, then, that different states choose to react in different ways.

The other side of any explanation of continued divergence, however, concerns the nature of the various nation states themselves. Page points out that, even if ideas travel, 'once they disembark that is only the beginning of the story'. The first filter through which they must pass is that of the history and traditions of the system they are entering. According to Vincent Wright, the 'biggest decision-maker in any political system is the past.' (Wright 1978: 229–30). Several authors in this volume concur. Page stresses path dependence—arguing that starting points limit the range of alternatives open even to policy makers who wish to respond to the pressures upon them. Mueller too is at pains to emphasize the inherent advantages enjoyed by the status quo over putative alternatives because not only are structures and procedures difficult to change, but they are reinforced by the support of those with a stake in their survival. Ferrera, Hemerijk, and Rhodes also make the point that chosen policies develop a logic of their own, and that these logics are crucial determinants of the ways in which states adjust or react to external pressures or stimuli. Thus the problems confronting the United Kingdom are the inverse of those found elsewhere in Europe, that country having achieved greater efficiency at the cost of solidarity. The lessons of the chapter on welfare state reform are that the existing policy mix matters, and that adjustment often requires regime specific solutions.

National differences also stem from the different political and administrative opportunity structures in place. Mark Thatcher is at pains to emphasize the importance of different domestic arrangements in place in Britain and France in explaining their divergent reactions to pressures upon their traditional industrial policies. Moreover, different opportunity structures provide leverage for different kinds of policies: thus, whereas 'before 1980, the weakness of institutional links between policy makers and firms cramped industrial policy in Britain, the gap between them aided the move towards a regulatory state in the 1980s and 1990s' (Thatcher, this volume).

Nor is it only state structures that matter. Danish corporatist arrangements have become so much more effective than their Swedish counterparts in recent times because, whilst the Swedish economy is dominated by multinationals who might, under the influence of globalization, increasingly eschew such national arrangements, the SMEs which predominate in Denmark may have found their dependence on the interest representation system there enhanced (Crouch, this volume). Similarly, France, unlike Britain, remained within the European Monetary System in the early 1990s despite repeated interest rates hikes necessitated by a rapidly appreciating mark because the majority of French homeowners are on fixed rate mortgages and were therefore relatively unaffected. The low level of capitalization of the Paris bourse provided another incentive for French elites to pursue a policy of high interest rates that was absent in other West European states.

The fact is that nation states are very different. And these differences in turn condition their varying reactions to even identical pressures. Perhaps one of the most revealing passages in this book appears in the chapter by legal scholar Paul Craig, who expresses puzzlement as to why political scientists should be surprised to find time lags or variations between the adoption of EU legal supremacy amongst the member states. Yet these should not be a source of mystery, as '[c]ourts are not machines. Legal systems are not identikit computers. The forces which operate in legal systems are diverse and eclectic. There is no reason to expect uniformity in this respect'.

Finally, divergence can be explained by the fact that institutions, when subjected to external or internal pressures, have the capacity to adapt. Thus, states have used institutions to empower themselves; have discovered creative new ways of promoting economic growth despite the constraints of the global economy; and have reformed their own structures in such a way as to cope with the increasing financial burdens upon them. The move towards a greater use of regulation is at least partly a creative response to the resource pressures that have affected all governments. As Müller points out, the state is thereby using the one resource—law making ability—that is neither scarce nor threatened with scarcity.

The absence of convergence should not, therefore, come as a surprise. Indeed, as Crouch puts it, in the face of numerous more or less uniform and powerful drivers for change, the 'diversity of [national] contexts and past experiences is helping to create a new diversity'.

THE EUROPEAN DIMENSION

As mentioned above, the European Union is referred to more often than any other single factor as a catalyst of change in West European politics. Nugent and Paterson describe the development of the EU political system as the 'single most striking feature of government and politics in the modern era', and there is a large literature on 'europeanization' that, with varying degrees of enthusiasm, has tended to proclaim that the European Union is bringing about seismic changes in the nature of politics within the various member states. Caution should be exercised, however, when assessing such claims, not least because recent empirical studies suggest that the Union has had only a highly limited impact on politics within the member states (Hix and Goetz 2000*b*).

Many studies of europeanization conceptualise the relationship between the European Union and member states as being 'top down'; the former acts, while the latter adjust to those actions. This, however, is to fundamentally misunderstand the nature of the Union. Rather than the member states being separate from, and hence prey to, the exogenous influence of, the European Union, the 'defining characteristic of the Union as a system of collective governance is rather the enmeshing of the national of the European or *the embedding of the national in the European*' (Laffan *et al.* 2000: 74, emphasis added). Or, as Helen Wallace puts it:

Most of the policy-makers who devise and operate EU rules and legislation are from the member states themselves. They are people who spend the majority of their time as national policy-makers, for whom the European dimension is an extended policy arena, not a separate activity. Indeed much of EU policy is prepared and carried out by national policy-makers and agents who do not spend much, if any, time in Brussels. (Wallace 2000: 6–7)

Member states, their officials, and their representatives, permeate an EU system that was created, and is still dominated, by them (Kassim this volume; Kassim and Wright 1991). The European Union is as much a venue as an actor in its own right. In its former guise, it serves as an arena within which member states fight to impose their own preferences on each other. By this reading, the European Union can be viewed as an institutionalized form of inter-state conflict, with member states competing to ensure their own preferences are adopted as policy at the European level, as Mazey and Richardson underline in the cases of health and safety and the EU Charter of Fundamental Rights, and Tsoukalis stresses in the case of the triumph of German preferences in debates about the shape of EMU. In delegating functions to supranational institutions, member states are not so much risking, allowing those institutions to impose change on them, as gambling on their ability to impose their own preferences on those institutions, allowing them to export these to their partners. Delegation, by this reading, represents the 'institutionalization of partiality' (Menon 2002).

The member states play an important, indeed the most important, role in shaping developments within the Union. In the areas particularly of constitutional amendment, but also the passing of day to day legislation, high thresholds of member state support are required for the Union to act (Moravcsik 2001: 173–4). And their dominance of the system is, if anything, increasing (Kassim and Menon 2003). Majone (this volume) argues that not only was the Commission a net loser during recent processes of institutional reform, but also that the member states have taken steps to reassert control over the Union as a whole. The principles of subsidiarity and proportionality have helped limit the extent to which the accretion of powers to the EC is possible; the member states dominate in the second and third pillars; specialized new agencies—such as the European Environment Agency—have been created as a result of bargaining between member states and in such a way as to ensure their continued influence within them.

The highly circumscribed autonomy of the European Union from member state influence is one of many reasons why it is misleading to view the Union as a state, or nascent state. Lowi (cited by Majone, this volume) informs us that the legitimate use of coercion is the intrinsic feature of government. The Union, however, has next to no coercive power, and recent moves to introduce the use of very modest fines against governments that do not respect their treaty obligations has served, if anything, merely to reinforce this claim. Moreover, if, as Müller claims, another defining feature of the state is its ability to pass laws and implement them, then here again the Union exhibits several shortcomings. For one thing, the supremacy of European over national law is, as Craig argues, not as assured as one might suppose. For another, the very nature of the legal methods relied upon by the Union illustrates its weakness rather than its strength. The preference for the use of directives, with the need for transposition into national law via national legislation, is one of the reasons why the homogenizing effects of membership are relatively limited. And directives are a necessary choice because of the need to respect the sensibilities of the member states, and because of the lack of resources at the centre.

To claim that the European Union is not, and is not about to become, a state is not to deny the utility of comparing it with states. Indeed, in many respects, the Union exhibits, in almost caricatural form, many of the phenomena identified by the contributors in the various national contexts. The elusiveness of any identifiable locus of ultimate authority; increasing fragmentation and sectorization; a pressing need for improved coordination; a blurring of the lines between politics, regulatory institutions, and administration; a distance between politicians and citizens; the problems inherent in the delegation of core policy functions to unelected agencies; consequent concerns about democratic legitimacy. Given the similarity of the issues confronting them, comparison between the EU and the state can yield valuable insights about the working of each.

Yet to use comparison between the European Union and the state as a methodological tool should not be to equate them, or to assume that solutions designed for one are appropriate for the other. Forder (2001) argues that the latter fallacy represented a significant problem when it came to the institutional design of the ECB and plans for the move towards Economic and Monetary Union. Because the European Union lacks many of the features of a state, because it is an entity comprised of sovereign member states, it is simply not appropriate to assume that institutional forms and normative assumptions designed and intended for states are appropriate for the Union. Nowhere is this more apparent than in debates about legitimacy and democracy.

DEMOCRATIC LEGITIMACY AND EUROPEAN GOVERNANCE

Many of the chapters in this volume allude to the problems of democratic legitimacy that exist in contemporary Western Europe. Before turning to these, it is worth remembering that democracy 'is the product of an evolving process in which the institutions and ideals of representative government adapt to recurring challenges' (Hall, this volume). The past fifty years have witnessed 'subtle but pervasive shifts in the configuration of European democracy' (*ibid.*). Thus, notions concerning what democracy can and should entail are not immutable or absolute, but have developed along with the politics to which they are applied.

Several developments lead the contributors to question the effectiveness of traditional mechanisms of ensuring democratic legitimacy. Both Goetz and Rhodes voice concern about the rise of agencies, and particularly about the tendency, especially in Britain, to hold their chief executives accountable before parliamentary committees. This has undermined a core element of the traditional system within which an unelected bureaucracy reported to ministers who in turn were responsible before parliament. A second and related trend identified by the contributors has seen the administrative reforms' of the 1980s and 1990s increasing reliance on the actions of consumers of governmental activities for enforcing accountability. Whilst this certainly provides a means of redress for these consumers by leaving open to them an exit option it also, as Peters puts it, has the potentially rather less salutary effect of 'divorcing the state—hence accountable politicians—from direct responsibility'.

A third trend challenging established notions of democratic accountability is the increasing specialization of government activities. Hall points out that it has become extremely difficult for politicians to supervise semi-independent agencies, simply because of the specialized work they carry out. Moreover, the increasing proclivity on the part of governments to endow such agencies with considerable autonomy limits the practical means open to politicians to exercise effective oversight. As Mény puts it, the popular pillar of democracy has become weaker at the expense of the constitutional pillar, which constitutes the checks and balances necessary to avoid the danger of rule by the tyranny of the majority. Thus the new institutions of economic regulation—or often deregulation—are not accountable to the population in the same way as are those political leaders who once controlled the economy.

The problems raised by delegation are, if anything, far more acute at the European level. For one thing, its scale has arguably been much greater. In Majone's terms, the relationship between member state principals and the European Central Bank is less that of principal–agent, and more that of settler and trustee, in that it is based upon a constitutional settlement which is consequently almost impossible to unpick. The weakness of mechanisms of principal control of the ECB and Commission is striking even in comparison to many delegated agents in domestic political settings: the role and functioning of these (including the Bundesbank) can generally be changed by normal legislation.

The whole issue of democratic control is more problematic at the European level, because popular or political protest is one step still further removed from the source of discontent. Tsoukalis describes a complex institutional design in monetary policy which 'seems to defy the laws of gravity'. Consequently, he points to the potential problems if the ECB is not seen to be responding adequately to problems in some of the member states.

The potential problems of democratic accountability at the EU level therefore mirror, if in more extreme form, those to be found within the member states. Because of the proclivity on the part of many commentators to treat the Union as a state, or state in the making, much of the debate about this issue has focussed on ways to address problems at the Union level by making it more like a state. Thus Decker (2002), having begun his analysis by pointing to the important differences between the EU and the nation state, goes on, somewhat paradoxically, to propose making it more state-like by taking steps to provide its citizens with the kind of identity on which majoritarian politics in the member states are based, as a precursor to making the Commission president directly elected.

Such proposals are flawed both practically and conceptually. First, a response to perceived problems of legitimacy at the European level based on recreating state structures, in order to relocate sites of representative democracy, raises all manner of awkward problems associated with the disinclination of citizens simply to shift their sense of allegiance. As Fritz Scharpf (1998: 9) puts it:

Given the historical, linguistic, cultural, ethnic and institutional diversity of its member states, there is no question that the Union is very far from having achieved the 'thick' collective identity that we have come to take for granted in national democracies—and in its absence, institutional reforms will not greatly increase the input-oriented legitimacy of decisions taken by majority rule.

More compellingly, and paradoxically, the fundamental problem with many of the ideas for EU reform that claim to take their cues from the national level is that they pervert the lessons learnt in the national context. Proposals to render the Commission more democratically accountable raise the question as to what policy-related functions require such accountability. Moravcsik (2001) argues that a crucial feature distinguishing the EU from traditional federal states is its relative lack of competence over core areas of public policy (and of interest to electorates). Thus whilst Paterson and Nugent are right in asserting the importance of EU citizenship, the EU flag, and, most importantly, the euro, what they fail to point out is that in the crucial areas of education, culture, infrastructure, redistribution, and defence, the Union enjoys little if any real capacity for effective action. Interestingly, what this means is that EU activity is largely confined to areas where delegation to non-majoritarian institutions is the norm in the member states themselves (Moravcsik 2001: 183–4).[3]

Delegation in these areas, both in member states and in the EU, often occurs precisely in order to shelter agencies from the vicissitudes of democratic politics. Majone (this volume) whilst admitting that the 'delegation of legislative powers to unelected policy makers has always been somewhat problematic from the point of view of democratic theory', defends it (1999), arguing that such delegated institutions are necessary

---

[3] Whilst this fact is certainly salient, particularly when it comes to understanding the shortcomings of many of the criticisms levelled at the European Union for being less democratic than the member states, it is important not to make the mistake of which Michael Moran accuses Majone—of resorting to the 'dubious functional argument' that 'since non-majoritarian institutions are preferred "everywhere" they must be accepted as the outcome of social fate' (Moran 2002: 403).

to provide credible commitments and overcome problems of time inconsistencies inherent in the actions of politicians with an eye perpetually on the next election. Crucially, the policies pursued by such institutions are legitimated by their effectiveness and efficiency. Because elected politicians are now less than ever able either to make credible commitments (not least because they cannot threaten coercion outside their own borders, and politics is increasingly transnational), or to understand the issues at stake in contemporary politics, then effective policy more and more requires delegation to specialists who are precisely unaccountable directly to the electorate.

Fritz Scharpf (1998) has drawn a distinction between input and output legitimacy in assessing the European Union. Democratic self-determination, he insists, requires that choices made by the given political system be driven by the authentic preferences of citizens. This suggests a chain of accountability linking those governing to those governed. It is input legitimation, or government by the people. But democratic self-determination also demands that those exercising political power are able to achieve a high degree of effectiveness in meeting the expectations of the governed. The democratic process is, for Scharpf, an 'empty ritual' without such delivery—output legitimacy or government for the people. Scharpf argues vigorously and persuasively that although the Union is regularly and (to some extent) justifiably criticized for deficiencies in input legitimacy, too little attention is paid to the inadequacies of states when judged from the standpoint of output legitimacy. This tends to breed an inflated assumption of the claim of states to legitimacy. Scharpf's key point is that in at least some policy areas it may be possible to conceive of the European Union as capable of legitimation by reference to its output, even if input legitimation is lacking.

One problem of basing remedies to the perceived absence of democracy at the European level on ideas generated for member states is that they will hamper the ability of the supranational institutions—particularly the Commission—to deliver effective policies. This is all the less justifiable in an era when it is clear that few if any of the member states intend to allow the Commission ever again to take up the highly political role of strategic agenda setter for the European Union that it briefly enjoyed in late 1980s and early 1990s. An institution that has increasingly seen its area of competence restricted to bureaucratic and regulatory activities should, more than ever, therefore, be judged by criteria of output legitimacy. Such an approach could also bear fruit in the national context. Scharpf's claims concerning output legitimacy are mirrored, to some extent, by Peters, who discusses in his chapter the current tendency within national administrations to invoke 'the values of performance and quality management'. Emphasis is thereby placed on what government produces for citizens. This can in turn be viewed as a way of renewing the link between government and notions of public interest that had been undermined by the ethos of the NPM.

A further shortcoming of attempts to model solutions to the EU's democratic problems on those adopted in nation states is their tendency to overlook the fact that multiple levels of political authority coexist on the continent. Yves Mény points out that a striking difference between the nature of multi-tiered political authority in the United States and in Western Europe in that, whilst the institutional element of democracy is very strong at the national level in the United States, this is compensated for by the strength of the popular component at the local/state level. Certainly the constitutional rather than popular pillar of democracy predominates at the EU level, but this is far less the case at the national level. A democratic 'division of labour' between the two major levels (or some more complex split between regional, national, and subnational) may represent a way of building a coherent democratic whole, without the need to impose standards of complete input and output legitimacy on each level.

The European Union was created, and has developed, as a means of providing solutions to the negative externalities arising from heightened interdependence between the advanced mixed economies of Western Europe. This applies in particular to the realm of market creation at the European level. Importantly, quite apart from the economic efficiencies involved in this undertaking, the EU also, by providing a level of economic regulation at the transnational level, is in some senses providing a degree of representation to those deprived of it within a purely nationally based system. Thus is can be seen as a correction to national political processes that are unaligned with the range of interests—domestic and particularly foreign—that are themselves affected by national decisions taken in an increasingly transnational regional economy (see Menon and Weatherill 2002). The very existence of a layer of political and regulatory action above the nation state can therefore be seen as beneficial in and of itself in age of intense transnational activity.

Certainly, viewing output legitimacy as an essential ingredient of legitimacy as a whole creates problems in its own right. Majone and Scharpf both argue that efficiency criteria are limited in their applicability, with Majone in particular insisting that it is only effective in areas where economic efficiency as a whole can be improved, as opposed to questions of redistribution. However, by placing the European Union in wider context, and seeing it as part of an overall West European system within which its actions are legitimized in terms mainly of their output legitimacy will, at the least, act as palliative to the misleading assumptions that all too often have flowed from seeing it as an autonomous system in its own right.

METHODOLOGICAL ISSUES

West European nation states, in contrast to the European Union, have traditionally—as in the current volume—been studied from a comparative perspective. Yet comparison can be carried out using many different kinds of methodological approach. And the approaches adopted can shape the picture that emerges. Andeweg, who would have delighted Vincent Wright by his use of a matrix, illustrates thereby how certain kinds of approach have traditionally focussed on certain kinds of question. One's choice of methodology, in other words, affects the choice of research question.

It also, of course, affects the nature of one's findings. Nowhere is this clearer than in the different views presented in this volume of the importance of history in shaping the present and the future. Whilst the majority of contributors see history's role as significant, the results of the statistical analysis carried out by Alonso and Maravall strongly imply that the past played no role in shaping the transitions to democracy in southern, central, and eastern Europe. Whilst Alonso and Maravall provide food for thought for those who see history as the most important determinant of both the present and the future, two things should be noted about their analysis. First, the past works in various ways, and takes various forms. Different countries have different reference points when it comes to their own histories. If the West German obsession with inflation stemmed from the events of the early 1920s, French political leaders are more likely to take their cues from 1789 than they are from the Fourth Republic. To find that previous regime type does not affect the nature of democratization is not to say that history played no part in the process or the outcome. Second, the statistical method employed by Alonso and Maravall precludes the identification of several of the ways in which history might have a role to play. More qualitative studies have revealed the tremendous weight of history (Gildea 1996) in shaping the present.

This is not in any way to downplay the significance of the conclusions at which Alonso and Maravall arrive. At the very least, they invite us to consider more carefully exactly how the past influences the present, and how important such an effect might be. Their analysis points to the need for more rigour than is present in many Historical Institutionalist accounts in specifying the precise causal mechanisms through which the past influences the present. The fundamental lesson we can learn is that only 'by applying several theoretical perspectives to the same research question can we improve our understanding of both that research question, and of the strengths and weaknesses of the various theoretical perspectives'. As Andeweg's matrix implies, using different methodologies to test the same hypothesis is something that happens all too rarely in political science.

Methodological proclivities also shape the kinds of questions asked by scholars. As Andeweg again points out, rational choice scholars working on executive–bureaucratic relations have tended to focus on the top down element of that relationship. Despite its 'scientific' pretensions, even rational choice is prone to be based on largely implicit normative assumptions. The literature on delegation pays relatively little attention to the issue of legitimacy.[4] Partly, this is because it was derived from, and continues to be applied to, settings where legitimacy is not an issue—notably the relationship between shareholders and managers, or that between employers and employees. Partly, too, scholars who employ the concepts associated with delegation tend, implicitly at least, to base their work upon the assumption that the principal is vested with some form of legitimate authority, and that the agent can only be deemed to be acting legitimately if its preferences do not diverge from those of the principal (Elgie and Jones 2000).

Such assumptions however are problematic. As Peters points out, the willingness of German bureaucrats during the Nazi period to follow the commands of their political masters hardly validates the notion that the demand for faithful service by their agents is invariably legitimate. Yet even in less extreme situations, to assume that the fundamental problem of a contractual relationship is to ensure legitimate principal control is sometimes to miss the point. As the preceding section argued,

---

[4] For surveys of this literature, see Elgie and Jones 2000; Doleys, 532–53; Kassim and Menon (2002).

delegation is sometimes more a matter of insulating agents from principals to secure the achievement of policy goals than of ensuring 'legitimate' oversight by those principals (Elgie and Jones 2000; Kassim and Menon 2002; Menon and Weatherill 2002). And if output legitimacy is considered an important component of the overall legitimacy of a political system, then this at the very least casts doubt upon such implicit assumptions concerning the inherent legitimacy of the principals.

More generally, methodological choice is related to world views. It is not unreasonable to posit that rational choice could be seen as an academic equivalent and soulmate of marketization in the real world. Its harsh world of contracts, prices, bargaining, strict hierarchies, clear inter-institutional boundaries, and strategic choice stands in stark contrast to the human science 'narrative' of Rhodes, with its emphasis on trust rather than contracts, on informal authority, on blurred boundaries between institutions, and the absence of effective hierarchies.

Finally, the reverberations of the debate about method do not end within the scholarly world. The assumptions on which policy choices are made colour the nature of those choices. Peters warns against the dangers of accepting rational choice assumptions based on economic benefit and efficiency for several reasons. First, because emphasizing notions of efficiency and economy may compromise notions of a public interest as 'the values of the public are more diverse and often focussed on quality of services rather than on their costs'. Second, he points out that notions of rationality may mean something quite different to economic efficiency. Finally, as Cassese underlines, administrations are very different from private enterprises, being generally much larger and also, because regulated by laws, unable to reform themselves.

Vincent Wright himself was scathing in his criticism of the simple application of assumptions derived from the study of economics to that of politics. As he remarked when discussing the New Public Management (1998a: 137—cited in Cassese, this volume):

> While it is highly laudable to make government more business-like, it is highly problematic to make it more like business. The public sector has always had to juggle with many conflicting sets of values, including democracy (hence accountability), equity (involving uniformity) and efficiency (minimizing costs). Too much current radical reform of the public sector is obsessed with efficiency, narrowly defined, as is based on a simplistic view of bureaucracy, a naïve view of the market, an idealized view of the private sector, an insensitivity to the hidden cause of reform, and perhaps more fundamentally, a misleading view of the state.

The point here is not that one approach or method is intrinsically better than another. It is simply to underline that the choice matters, and may matter in highly significant, practical ways, and that the choice of approach will affect the nature of the research and of its findings.

CLOSING REMARKS

So what emerges from this survey of politics and government in Western Europe? Truth be told, it is a picture that Vincent Wright would have recognized and much appreciated. It is one of change and instability; of contradictory pressures on diverse and diffuse actors and institutions, of uncertainty about appropriate normative criteria by which to judge politics, of complexity surrounding the notion even of what Europe now is. Vincent would have delighted in the proliferation of Zanzibars (see Hayward, this volume), obdurately resisting determined attempts by political scientists to stuff them into inappropriate analytical boxes.

Of course the picture presented here has been far from complete. In retrospect, the editors should have included chapters dealing with the politics of race, immigration, and citizenship—ever more pressing issues on the agendas not only of all European governments, but also of the European Union. Moreover, enlargement of the European Union will not only challenge our notions as to what 'Europe is', but will fundamentally alter the nature of politics on the Old Continent. Not only will enlargement force a new raft of comparative cases upon those preparing or proposing comparative volumes such as this, but it will also affect the ability of the European Union to carry out its tasks—and hence to influence developments within its member states—whilst conceivably reinforcing concerns, within the Western side of the continent at least, about migration and the future of redistributive national policies.

Methodologically, we have eschewed discussion of an increasingly vibrant approach to the study of politics. Whilst, for some, the existence of certain 'objective' exogenous pressures implies a suitable response from affected actors, Hay and Rosamund argue that it is 'the ideas that actors hold about the context in which they find themselves, rather than the context itself which informs the way in which actors behave' (2002: 148). To accept that ideas and world views act as prisms through which actors interpret the world around them is to adopt a fundamentally different approach to the study of politics to that adopted by virtually all of the contributors to this volume.

We have, however, seen enough to concur with Vincent's typically provocative and striking assertion that studying government in Western Europe:

as in any complex society...is rather like peering down a dimly-lit kaleidoscope, held in a gently inebriated hand; after a while it is possible to distinguish some of the more significant pieces, but the pattern is ever changing and is sensitive to the slightest shudder. Furthermore, there are pieces that remain in obstinate obscurity.

The contributors to this volume have cast light on several of these obscure pieces. One can only imagine how much greater its overall insights would have been had they been shaped by Vincent's hand.

Bibliography

Abélès, M., Bellier, I., and McDonald, M. (1993). *Approche Anthropologique de la Commission Européenne*, Unpublished report for the Commission.

Aberbach, J. D., Putnam, R. D., and Rockman, B. A. (1981). *Bureaucrats and Politicians in Western Democracies*. Cambridge, MA: Harvard University Press.

Adler, E. and Barnett, M. (1998). *Security Communities*. Cambridge: Cambridge University Press.

Adnett, N. (2001). 'Modernizing the European Social Model: Developing the Guidelines'. *Journal of Common Market Studies*, 39(2): 353–364.

Alberoni, F. (1968). *Statu nascenti*. Bologna: Il Mulino.

Albert, J.-L. (1992). *La Politique Française de la Concurrence*. Lyon: Presses Universitaires de Lyon.

Alchian, A. (1977). *Economic Forces at Work*. Indianapolis, IN: Liberty Press.

Allan, T. R. S. (1997). 'Parliamentary Sovereignty: Law, Politics and Revolution'. *Law Quarterly Review*, 113: 443–452.

Allison, G. T. and Zelikow, P. (1999). *Essence of Decision; Explaining the Cuban Missile Crisis*, 2nd edition. New York: Longman.

Allsopp, C. and Vines, D. (1998). 'The assessment: macroeconomic policy after EMU'. *Oxford Review of Economic Policy*, 14(3), Autumn.

Almond, G. and Verba, S. (1963). *The Civic Culture: Political Attitudes and Democracy in Five Nations*. Princeton, NJ: Princeton University Press.

Alonso, S. (2000). *Élites y Masas. Un Análisis de la Perestroika y las Huelgas Mineras*. Madrid: Centro de Investigaciones Sociológicas.

Alter, K. (1998). 'Explaining National Court Acceptance of European Court Jurisprudence: A Critical Evaluation of Theories of Legal Integration', in A.-M. Slaughter, A. Stone Sweet, and J. H. H. Weiler (eds), *The European Court and National Courts, Doctrine and Jurisprudence*. Oxford: Hart Publishing.

Althusser, L. (1984). *Essays on Ideology*. London: Verso.

Altvater, E. (1999). 'The Relation of Material and Formal Democracy', in I. Shapiro and C. Hacker-Cordón (eds), *Democracy's Edges*. Cambridge: Cambridge University Press.

Alvarez, M., Garrett, G., and Lange, P. (1991). 'Government Partisanship, Labor Organization and Macroeconomic Performance'. *American Political Science Review*, 85: 2.

Andersen, S. S. and Eliassen, K. A. (1991). 'European Community Lobbying'. *European Journal of Political Research*, 20(2): 173–187.

Anderson, B. (1991). *Imagined Communities*. London: Verso.

Anderson, P. (1974). *Passages from Antiquity to Feudalism and Lineages of the Absolutist State*. London: New Left Books.

Andeweg, R. B. (1988). 'Centrifugal Forces and Collective Decision-Making: The Case of the Dutch Cabinet'. *European Journal of Political Research*, 16: 125–151.

——(1993). 'A Model of the Cabinet System: The Dimensions of Cabinet Decision-Making Processes', in J. Blondel and F. Müller-Rommel (eds), *Governing Together*. London: Macmillan, pp. 23–42.

——(1995). 'The Reshaping of National Party Systems'. *West European Politics*, 18(3): 58–78.

Andeweg, R. B. (1996). 'Elite-Mass Linkages in Europe: Legitimacy Crisis or Party Crisis?', in J. Hayward (ed.), *Élitism, Populism, and European Politics*. Oxford: Oxford University Press.

——(1997a). 'Collegiality and Collectivity: Cabinets, Cabinet Committees and Cabinet Ministers', in P. M. Weller, H. Bakvis, and R. A. W. Rhodes (eds), *The Hollow Crown*. London: Macmillan, pp. 58–83.

——(1997b). 'The Netherlands: Coalition Cabinets in Changing Circumstances', in J. Blondel and F. Müller-Rommel (eds), *Cabinets in Western Europe*, 2nd edition. Basingstoke: Macmillan, pp. 52–73.

——and Nijzink, L. (1995). 'Beyond the Two-Body Image: Relations between Ministers and MPs', in H. Döring (ed.), *Parliaments and Majority Rule in Western Europe*. Frankfurt: Campus, pp. 152–178.

Arendt, H. (1958). *The Origins of Totalitarianism*. Cleveland and New York: Meridian Books.

Armingeon, K. (1986). 'Die Bundesregierungen zwischen 1949 und 1985. Einer Forschungsnotiz über Ausbildung und Berufe der Mitglieder der Bundeskabinette in der Bundesrepublik Deutschland'. *Zeitschrift für Parlamentsfragen*, 17: 25–40.

Armstrong, J. A. (1973). *The European Administrative Elite*. Princeton: Princeton University Press.

Aucoin, P. (1994). 'Prime Minister and Cabinet', in J. P. Bickerton and A. G. Gagnon (eds), *Canadian Politics*, 2nd edition. Peterborough: Broadview Press.

Ayberk, U. and Schenker, F.-P. (1998). 'Des lobbies européens entre pluralisme et clientelisme'. *Revue Française de Science Politique*, 48(6): 725–755.

Badie, B. (1999). *Un monde sans souveraineté*. Paris: Fayard.

Bagehot, W. (1993) [1867]. *The English Constitution*. London: Fontana.

Bagnasco, A. and Le Galès, P. (eds) (2000). *Cities in contemporary Europe*. Cambridge: Cambridge University Press.

Bakema, W. E. and Secker W. P. (1988). 'Ministerial Expertise and the Dutch Case'. *European Journal of Political Research*, 16: 153–170.

Baldwin, R. and McCrudden, C. (1987). *Regulation and Public Law*. London: Weidenfeld and Nicolson.

Balme, R., Faure, A., and Mabileau, A. (eds) (1999). *Politiques locales et transformations de l'action publique locale en Europe*. Paris: Presses de Sciences Po.

Balme, R. (1996). 'Pourquoi le gouvernement change-t-il d'échelle?', in: R. Balme (ed.), *Les politiques du néo-régionalisme*. Paris: Economica.

——Faure, A., and Mabileau, A. (eds) (2000). *Politiques locales et transformations de l'action publique locale en Europe*. Paris: Presses de Sciences Po.

Barber, J. D. (1992). *The Presidential Character: Predicting Performance in the White House*, 4th edition. Englewood Cliffs: Prentice-Hall.

Barber, L. (1995). 'The Men Who Run Europe'. *Financial Times*, 11–12(3): 1995.

Barker, C. (2001). 'Robert Michels and the "Cruel Game"', in C. Barker, A. Johnson, and M. Lavalette (eds), *Leadership and Social Movements*, ch. 2. Manchester: Manchester University Press.

Barreau, J., Dufeu, J., Guilloux, P., Hardy, J., Le Nay, J., and Mouline, A. (1990). *L'Etat Entrepreneur*. Paris: l'Harmattan.

Barry, B. (1975). 'Political Accommodation and Consociational Democracy'. *British Journal of Political Science*, 5 (October): 477–505.

Barthes, R. (1981). 'The Discourse of History'. *Comparative Criticism*, 3: 7–20.

Bartle, I. (1999). 'Transnational Interests in the European Union: Globalization and Changing Organization in Telecommunications and Electricity'. *Journal of Common Market Studies*, 37(3): 363–383.

Bartolini, S. (1998). *Exit Options, Boundary Building, Political structuring*, EUI working paper, SPS 98(1), Florence: European University Institute.

—— and Mair, P. (1990). *Identity, Competition and Electoral Availability: The Stabilisation of European Electorates, 1885–1985*. Cambridge: Cambridge University Press.

Barzelay, M. (2001). *The New Public Management*. Berkeley: University of California Press.

Bauby, P. (1997). 'Services publics: des modèles nationaux à une conception européenne'. *Politiques et Management Public*, 15(3): 107–122.

Bauer, M. (1988). 'The Politics of State-directed Privatisation: the Case of France 1986–1988'. *West European Politics*, 11(4): 49–60.

Baylis, T. A. (1989). *Governing by Committee*. Albany: SUNY Press.

Beck, T., Clarke, G., Groff, A., Keefer, P., and Walsh, P. (2000). *New Tools and New Tests in Comparative Political Economy. The Database of Political Institutions*. Washington, DC: The World Bank, Development Research Group, Policy Research Working Paper 2283.

Beck, U. (1986). *Risk Society*. Cambridge: Polity.

—— (1998). *Was ist Globalisierung?*. Frankfurt am Main: Campus.

—— (2000). *What is Globalization?*. Cambridge: Polity.

Beer, S. H. (1974). *Modern Political Development*. New York: Random House.

—— (1982*a*) [1965]. *Modern British Politics*. London: Faber.

—— (1982*b*). *Britain Against Itself*. New York: Norton.

Bekke, H. J. G. M. and van der Meer, F. (eds) (2000). *Civil Service Systems in Western Europe*. Cheltenham: Edward Elgar.

Bell, D. (1960). *The End of Ideology*. Glencoe, IL: Free Press.

—— (1973). *The Coming of Post-Industrial Society*. New York: Basic.

Bellier, I. (1995). 'Une culture de la Commission européene? De la rencontre Des cultures et du multilinguisme des fonctionnaires', in Y. Mény and J.-L. Quermonne (eds), *Politiques Publiques en Europe*. Paris: L'Harmattan, pp. 49–60.

Beloff, M. (1984). *Wars and Welfare: Britain 1914–1945*. London: Arnold.

Bender, B. (1991). 'Whitehall, Central Government and 1992'. *Public Policy and Administration*, 6(3): 13–20.

—— (1996). 'Coordination of European Union Policy in Whitehall'. Unpublished lecture at St. Antony's College, Oxford.

Benhabib, S. (1999). 'Citizens, Residents and Aliens in a Changing World: Political Membership in the Global Era'. *Social Research*, 66(3): 709–744.

Benington, J. and Geddes, M. (eds) (2001). *Partnership in Europe*. London: Routledge.

Bennett, A. J. (1996). *The American President's Cabinet: from Kennedy to Bush*. London: Macmillan.

Bennett, R. (1999). 'Business Routes of Influence in Brussels: Exploring the Choice of Direct Representation'. *Political Studies*, 53(4): 1044–1073.

Bennett, R. J. and McCoshan, A. (1993). *Enterprise and Human Resource Development*. London: Paul Chapman.

—— Krebs, G., and Zimmermann, H. (eds) (1993). *Chambers of Commerce in Britain and Germany and the Single European Market*. London: Anglo-German Foundation.

Benveniste, G. (1972). *The Politics of Expertise*. Berkeley: Glendessary Press.

Benz, A. and Goetz, K. (eds) (1996). *A New German Public Sector? Reform, Adaptation, Stability*. Aldershot: Darmouth.

Berger, S. (ed.) (1981). *Organizing Interests in Western Europe*. New York: Cambridge University Press.

—— and Dore, R. (eds) (1996). *National Diversity and Global Capitalism*. Ithaca: Cornell University Press.

Bergman, T. and Raunio, T. (2001). 'Parliaments and Policy-Making in the European Union', in J. Richardson (ed.), *European Union Power and Policy-making*. London: Routledge, pp. 115–134.

Bergsten, C. F. (1999). 'America and Europe: Clash of the Titans?'. *Foreign Affairs*, 78(2), March/April.

Bermeo, N. (2001). *Unemployment in the New Europe*. Cambridge: Cambridge University Press.

——and Nord, P. (2000). *Civil Society Before Democracy*. New York: Rowman and Littlefield.

Betz, H.-G. (1994). *Radical Right-Wing Populism in Western Europe*. New York: St. Martin's Press.

Blair, T. (1996). *New Britain: My Vision of a Young Country*. London: Fourth Estate.

——(1998). *The Observer*, 31 May.

Blais, A. and Dion, S. (eds) (1991). *The Budget-Maximizing Bureaucrat. Appraisals and Evidence*. Pittsburgh: University of Pittsburgh Press.

Block, F. (1987). *Revising State Theory*. Philadelphia: Temple University Press.

Blondel, J. (1985). *Government Ministers in the Contemporary World*. London: Sage.

——(1991). 'Cabinet Government and Cabinet Ministers', in J. Blondel and J. L. Thiébault (eds), *The Profession of Government Minister in Western Europe*. London: Macmillan, pp. 5–18.

——(1997). 'Introduction: Western European Cabinets in Comparative Perspective', in J. Blondel and F. Müller-Rommel (eds), *Cabinets in Western Europe*, 2nd edition. Basingstoke: Macmillan, pp. 1–17.

——and Cotta, M. (eds) (1996). *Party and Government. An Inquiry into the Relationship between Governments and Supporting Parties in Liberal Democracies*. London: Macmillan.

————(eds) (2000). *The Nature of Party Government: A Comparative European Perspective*. Basingstoke: Palgrave.

Blondel, J. and Müller-Rommel, F. (eds) (1993). *Governing Together. The Extent and Limits of Joint Decision-Making in Western European Cabinets*. London: Macmillan.

————(eds) (1997). *Cabinets in Western Europe*, 2nd edition. London: Macmillan.

——and Nousiainen, J. (2000). 'Governments, Supporting Parties and Policy-Making', in J. Blondel and M. Cotta (eds), *The Nature of Party Government*. Basingstoke: Palgrave. pp. 161–195.

——and Thiébault, J. L. (eds) (1991). *The Profession of Government Minister in Western Europe*. London: Macmillan.

Blondiaux, L. (1998). *La fabrique de l'opinion: une historie sociale des sondages*. Paris: Seuil.

Bogdanor, V. (1996). 'The European Union, the Political Class and the People', in J. Hayward (ed.), *Élitism, Populism, and European Politics*. Oxford: Oxford University Press.

Boiteux, M. (1996). 'Concurrence, réglementation et service public'. *Futuribles*, 205: 39–58.

Boix, C. (1998). *Political Parties, Growth and Equality*. Cambridge: Cambridge University Press.

Bolloc'H-Puges, C. (1991). *La Politique Industrielle Française dans l'Electronique*. Paris: (l)'Harmattan.

Bomberg, E. and Peterson, J. (2000). 'Policy Transfer and Europeanisation: Passing the Heineken Test?'. *Queen's papers on Europeanisation*, (2) (Belfast).

Bornstein, S., Held, D., and Krieger, J. (eds) (1984). *The State in Capitalist Europe*. London: Allen and Unwin.

Borraz, O., Bullman, U., Hambleton, R., Page, E., Rao, N., and Young, K. (1994). *Local leadership and Decision-making: France, Germany, the US and Britain*. London: LGC communications.

Börzel, T. and Risse, T. (2000). 'When Europe Hits Home: Europeanization and Domestic Change'. *European Online Papers*, 4(15), http://eiop.or.at/eiop/texte/2000-015a.htm.

Bowles, N. (1999). 'Studying the Presidency'. *Annual Review of Political Science*, 2: 1–23.

Boyer, R. (1996). 'The Convergence Hypothesis Revisited: Globalization but Still the Century of Nations?, in S. Berger and R. Dore (eds), *National Diversity and Global Capitalism*. Ithaca: Cornell University Press.

Boyer, R. (1998). 'The Changing Status of Industrial Relations in a More Interdependent World', in T. Wilthagen (ed.), *Advancing Theory in Labour Law and Industrial Relations in a Global Context*. Amsterdam: North-Holland.

—— (2000). 'The Unanticipated Fallout of European Monetary Union: An essay on the Political and Institutional Deficits of the Euro', in C. Crouch (ed.), *After the Euro*. Oxford: Oxford University Press.

Brans, M. (1992). 'Theories of Local Government Reorganization: An Empirical Analysis'. *Public Administration*, 70(3): 429.

Brehm, J. and Gates, S. (1999). *Working, Shirking and Sabotage: Bureaucratic Response to a Democratic Public*. Ann Arbor: University of Michigan Press.

Bribosia, H. (1998). 'Report on Belgium', in A.-M. Slaughter, A. Stone Sweet, and J. H. H. Weiler (eds), *The European Court and National Courts, Doctrine and Jurisprudence*. Oxford: Hart Publishing.

Brinton, C. (1938). *The Anatomy of Revolution*. New York: Norton.

Brittan, S. (1975). 'The Economic Contradictions of Democracy'. *British Journal of Political Science*, 5: 129–159.

Brown, A. (ed.) (1984). *Political Culture and Communist Studies*. London: Macmillan.

—— and Gray, J. (eds) (1977). *Political Culture and Political Change in Communist States*. New York: Holmes & Meier.

Brubaker, R. (1996). *Nationalism Reframed*. Cambridge: Cambridge University Press.

Brunsson, N. and Olsen, J. P. (1993). *The Reforming Organization*. London and New York: Routledge.

Brzezinski, Z. (ed.) (1969). *Dilemmas of Change in Soviet Politics*. New York: Columbia University Press.

Buchanan, J. M. and Tullock, G. (1962). *The Calculus of Consent: Logical Foundations of Constitutional Democracy*. Ann Arbor: University of Michigan Press.

Budge, I. and Keman, H. (1990). *Parties and Democracy: Coalition Formation and Functioning in Twenty States*. Oxford: Oxford University Press.

Bührer, W. (2000). 'Auf dem Weg zum Korporatismus?—Der Bundesverband der Deutschen Industrie in zeitgeschichtlicher Perspektive', in W. Bührer and E. Grande (eds), *Unternehmerverbände und Staat in Deutschland*. Baden-Baden: Nomos.

—— and Grande, E. (eds) (2000). *Unternehmerverbände und Staat in Deutschland*. Baden-Baden: Nomos.

Buitendijk, G. and Van Schendelen, M. P. C. M. (1995). 'Brussels advisory committees: a channel of influence'? *European Law Review*, 20(1): 37–58.

Bull, H. (1977). *The Anarchical Society: A Study of Order in World Politics*. London: Macmillan.

—— (1979). 'The State's Positive Role in World Affairs'. *Daedalus*, 108(4): 111–123.

Bulmer, S. and Burch, M. (1998). 'Organising for Europe: Whitehall, the British State and European Union'. *Public Administration*, 76: 601–628.

—— and Wessels, W. (1987). *The European Council. Decision Making in European Politics*. London: Macmillan.

Burch, M. and Holliday, I. (1996). *The British Cabinet System*. London: Prentice Hall Harvester Wheatsheaf.

Burley, A.-M. and Mattli, W. (1993). 'Europe before the Court'. *International Organization*, 47(1): 41–76.

Burnham, J. and Maor, M. (1995). 'Converging Administrative Systems: Recruitment, Training and Role Perceptions'. *Journal of European Public Policy*, 2(2): 185–204.

Butler, D. and Stokes, D. (1969). *Political Change in Britain*. London: Macmillan.

Butt-Philip, A. (1985). *Pressure Groups in the European Community.* London University Association for Contemporary European Studies, Occasional Papers, No. 2.

Byers, M. (ed.) (1999). *The Role of Law in International Politics: Essays in International Relations and International Law.* Oxford: Oxford University Press.

Cabinet Office (2000). *Wiring It Up. Whitehall's Management of Cross-Cutting Policies and Services. A Performance and Innovation Unit Report.* London: Stationery Office.

Caiden, G. E. (1999). 'Administrative Reform. Proceed with Caution'. *International Journal of Public Administration,* 22(6): 819.

Calhoun, C. (1995). '"New Social Movements" of the Early Nineteenth Century', in M. Traugott (ed.), *Repertoires and Cycles of Collective Action.* Durham, NC: Duke University Press, pp. 173–216.

Cameron, D. (1984). 'Social Democracy, Corporatism, Labor Quiescence and the Representation of Interest in Advanced Capitalist Societies', in J. A. Goldthorpe (ed.), *Order and Conflict in Contemporary Capitalism.* Oxford: Oxford University Press, pp. 143–78.

——(1997). 'Economic and Monetary Union: Imperatives and Third-stage Dilemmas'. *Journal of European Public Policy,* 4.

Campbell, C. (1993). 'Political Executives and Their Officials', in A. W. Finifter (ed.), *Political Science: The State of the Discipline II.* Washington DC: APSA, pp. 383–406.

Canovan, M. (1981). *Populism.* New York: Harcourt Brace Jovanovitch.

Caporaso, J. *et al.* (1997). 'Does the European Union Represent an n of 1?'. *ECSA Review,* X(3): 1–5.

Cargill, C. (1996). *Open Systems Standardization: a Business Approach.* Englewood Cliffs: Prentice-Hall.

Carsberg, B. (1989). 'Injecting Competition into Telecommunications', in C. Veljanovski (ed.), *Privatisation and Competition.* London: IEA.

Cartabia, M. (1998). 'Report on Italy', in A.-M. Slaughter, A. Stone Sweet, and J. H. H. Weiler (eds), *The European Court and National Courts, Doctrine and Jurisprudence.* Oxford: Hart Publishing.

Cassese, S. and Wright, V. (eds) (1996). *La recomposition de l'Etat en Europe.* Paris: La Découverte.

Castells, M. (1997). *The Power of Identity.* Oxford: Blackwell.

——(1996; 2nd edition 2000). *The Rise of Network Society.* Oxford: Blackwell.

——(1998). *End of Millennium.* Oxford: Blackwell.

Castles, F. (1995). 'Welfare State Development in Southern Europe'. *West European Politics,* 18(2): 291–313.

—— (2001). 'Reflections on the Methodology of Comparative Type Construction: Three Worlds of Real Worlds?' *Acta Politica,* 36(2): 140–154.

Cauchon, C. (1998). 'Le modèle public à la recherché d'une nouvelle regulation: un procesus engagé mais non abouti à la SNCF'. *Politiques et Management Public,* 16(4): 19–40.

Cawson, A., Holmes, P., Webber, D., Morgan, K., and Stevens, A. (1990). *Hostile Brothers.* Oxford: Clarendon Press.

CEPR (Centre for Economic Policy Research) (1995). *Flexible Integration.* London: CEPR.

—— (2000). *One Money, Many Countries: Monitoring the European Central Bank—2.* London: CEPR.

Cerny, P. G. (1995). 'Globalization and the Changing Logic of Collective Action'. *International Organization,* 49(4): 595–625.

——(1999). 'Globalization and the Erosion of Democracy'. *European Journal of Political Research.*

Chapman, B. (1959). *The Profession of Government: The Public Service in Europe*. London: Allen & Unwin.

Chevallier, J. (1997). 'Regards sur une évolution'. *L'Actualité Juridique —Droit Administratif*, 20 juin: 8–15.

Christiansen, T. (2001). 'The Council of Ministers: the Politics of Institutionalised Intergovernmentalism', in J. Richardson (ed.), *European Union: Power and Policy-making*. London: Routledge, pp. 135–154.

Christoph, J. B. (1992). 'The Effects of Britons in Brussels: the European Community and the Culture of Whitehall', Paper presented at the annual Meeting of the Midwest Political Science Association. Chicago, 9–11 April.

Cini, M. (1997). 'Administrative Culture in the European Commission: the Cases of Competition and Environment', in N. Nugent (ed.), *At the Heart of the Union: Studies of the European Commission*. London: Routledge.

Civil Service (1968). *Report of the (Fulton) Committee 1966–68*, (1). London: HMSO.

Claeys, P., Gobin C., Smets, I., and Winand, P. (eds) (1998). *Lobbying, Pluralism and European Integration*. Brussels: Brussels European University Press.

Clark, I. (1999). *Globalization and International Relations Theory*. Oxford: Oxford University Press.

Clayton, R. and Pontusson, J. (1998). 'Welfare-State Retrenchment Revisited'. *World Politics*, 51: 67–98.

Clemens, C. and Paterson, W. E. (eds) (1998). *The Kohl Chancellorship*. London: Cass.

Cm 2811 (1995). *Department of National Heritage Annual Report 1995*. London: HMSO.

Cm 4310 (1999). *Modernising Government*. London: The Stationery Office.

Coen, D. (1996). 'The Large Firm as a Political Actor in the European Union', Ph.D. thesis. Florence: European University Institute.

——(1997). 'The Evolution of the Large Firm as a Political Actor in the European Union'. *Journal of European Public Policy*, 4(1): 91–108.

——(1999). 'Business Interests and European Integration', Paper presented at the conference, 'Organised Interests in the European Union: Lobbying, Mobilisation and the European Public Area', at Nuffield College, Oxford, 1–2 October 1999.

——and Thatcher, M. (eds) (2000). 'Utilities Reform in Europe'. *Current Politics and Economics of Europe* (Special issue) 9(4).

Cohen, E. (1995). 'France: National Champions in Search of a Mission', in Hayward, J. (ed.), *Industrial Enterprise and European Integration*. Oxford: Oxford University Press.

——(1992). *Le colbertisme 'high tech'*. Paris: Hachette.

——(1996). *La Tentation Hexagonale*. Paris: Fayard.

——and Bauer, M. (1985). *Les Grandes Manoevres Industrielles*. Paris: Belfond.

Cohen, S. (1985). *Rethinking the Soviet Experience: Politics and History Since 1917*. Oxford: Oxford University Press.

Cohen, S. (2000). 'Social Solidarity in the Delors Period: Barriers to Participation', in C. Hoskyns and M. Newman (eds), *Democratizing the European Union: Issues for the Twenty first Century*. Manchester: Manchester University Press, pp. 12–38.

Cole, A. and Drake, H. (2000). 'The Europeanisation of the French Polity', *Journal of European Public Policy*, 7(1): 26–43.

Collins, R. (1986). *Weberian Sociological Theory*. Cambridge: Cambridge University Press.

Commissariat du Plan (2000). *Services Publics en réseau: perspectives de concurrence et nouvelles regulation*. Paris: Commissariat du Plan.

Commission of the European Communities (1995). *Report On the Operation of the Treaty of European Union*. SEC (95) 731 Final, 10.5.95.

—— (2000*a*). *Reforming the Commission: A White Paper*, 2 parts, Brussels: Commission (1 March).

—— (2000*b*). *White Paper on Food Safety.*

Committee of Independent Experts (1993*a*). *First Report on Allegations Regarding Fraud, Mismanagement and Nepotism in the European Commission*. Brussels: European Parliament, 15 March.

—— (1993*b*). *Second Report on Reform of the Commission: Analysis of Current Practice and Proposals for Tackling Mismanagement, Irregularities and Fraud*, vols. 1 and 2. Brussels: European Parliament.

Constas, H. (1958). 'Max Weber's Two Conceptions of Bureaucracy'. *American Journal of Sociology*, 63: 400–409.

Converse, P. E. (1969). 'Of Time and Partisan Stability'. *Comparative Political Studies*, 2: 139–171.

Converse, P. and Dupeux, G. (1962). 'Politicization of the Electorate in France and the United States'. *Public Opinion Quarterly*, 261: 1–23.

Cooper, A. H. (1996). *Paradoxes of Peace*. Ann Arbor: University of Michigan Press.

Cooper, Richard N. (1968). *The Economics of Interdependence: Economic Policy in the Atlantic Community*. New York, McGraw-Hill.

Corbett, R., Jacobs, F., and Shackleton, M. (2000). *The European Parliament*, 4th edition. London: John Harper Publishing.

Cortell, A. P. and Peterson, S. (1999). 'Altered States: Explaining Domestic Institutional Change'. *British Journal of Political Science*, 29: 177–203.

Cotta, M. (1991). 'Conclusion', in J. Blondel and J. L. Thiébault (eds), *The Profession of Government Minister in Western Europe*. London: Macmillan, pp. 174–198.

Court of Auditors (1992). 'Special Report No. 3/92 concerning the Environment together with the Commission's replies'. *Official Journal*, 92/C245/01, Vol. 35, 23 September.

Cox, A. (1986). *The State, Finance and Industry*. Brighton: Wheatsheaf.

Cox, R. H. (1998). 'From Safety Net to Trampoline: Labour Market Activation in the Netherlands and Denmark'. *Governance: An International Journal of Policy and Administration*, 11(4): 397–414.

Craig, P. (1991). 'United Kingdom Sovereignty after *Factortame*'. *Yearbook of European Law*, 11: 221–255.

—— (1992). 'Once Upon a Time in the West: Direct Effect and the Federalization of EEC Law'. *Oxford Journal of Legal Studies*, 12: 453–479.

—— (1998). 'Report on the United Kingdom', in A.-M. Slaughter, A. Stone Sweet, and J. H. H. Weiler (eds), *The European Court and National Courts, Doctrine and Jurisprudence*. Oxford: Hart Publishing.

—— (2000*a*). 'Britain and the European Union', in J. Jowell and D. Oliver (eds), *The Changing Constitution*, 4th edition. Oxford: Oxford University Press.

—— (2000*b*). 'Public Law, Political Theory and Legal Theory'. *Public Law*, 211–239.

—— and de Burca, G. (1998). *EU Law, Text, Cases and Materials*, 2nd edition. Oxford: Oxford University Press.

Cram, L. (1993). 'Calling the Tune without Paying the Piper? Social Policy Regulation: the Role of the Commission in European Community Social Policy'. *Policy and Politics*, 21(2): 135–146.

—— (1994). 'The European Commission as a Multi-Organization: Social Policy and IT Policy in the EU'. *Journal of European Public Policy*, 1(2): 195–217.

—— and Richardson, J. (2001). *Policy Styles in the EU*. London: Routledge.

Crossman, R. H. S. (1972). *Inside View, Three Lectures on Prime Ministerial Government*. London: Cape.

Crouch, C. (1993). *Industrial Relations and European State Traditions*. Oxford: Oxford University Press.

—— (1994). 'Beyond Corporatism: the Impact of Company Strategy', in R. Hyman and A. Ferner (eds), *New Frontiers in European Industrial Relations*. Oxford: Blackwell.

—— (1996). *The Social Contract and the Problem of the Firm*, EUI Working Paper RSC No. 96/46. Florence: European University Institute.

—— (1998). 'The Globalized Economy: An End to the Age of Industrial Citizenship'?, in Wilthagen, (ed.), *Advancing Theory in Labour Law and Industrial Relations in a Global Context*. Amsterdam: North Holland.

—— (1999). *Social Change in Western Europe*. Oxford: Oxford University Press.

—— (2000a). 'National Wage Determination and European Monetary Union', in C. Crouch (ed.).

—— (ed.) (2000b). *After the Euro: Shaping Institutions for Governance in the Wake of European Monetary Union*. Oxford: Oxford University Press.

—— (2001). 'Breaking open black boxes: The Implications for Sociological theory of European Integration', in A. Menon and V. Wright (eds), *From the National State to Europe? Essays in Honour of Jack Hayward*. Oxford: Oxford University Press.

—— and Farrell, H. (2001). 'Great Britain: Falling through the Holes in the Network Concept', in C. Crouch, P. Le Galès, C. Trigilia, and H. Voelzkow (eds), *Local Production Systems in Europe: Rise or Demise?* Oxford: Oxford University Press.

—— and Pizzorno, A. (eds) (1978). *The Resurgence of Class Conflict in Western Europe*. London: Macmillan.

Crozier, M., Huntington, S., and Watanuki, J. (1975). *The Crisis of Democracies*. New York: New York University Press.

Cutler, A. C., Haufler, V., and Porter, T. (1999). *Private Authority and International Affairs*. Albany: State University of New York Press.

Daalder, H. (1987). 'Countries in Comparative European Politics'. *European Journal of Political Research*, 15/1.

—— (1992). 'A Crisis of Party?'. *Scandinavian Political Studies*, 15: 269–288.

Dahl, R. (1956). *A Preface to Democratic Theory*. Chicago: Chicago University Press.

—— (1961). *Who Governs?* New Haven: Yale University Press.

—— (1971). *Polyarchy*. New Haven: Yale University Press.

—— (1982). *Dilemmas of Pluralist Democracy*. New Haven: Yale University Press.

Dahrendorf, R. (1967). *Society and Democracy in Germany*. New York: Doubleday.

Dalton, R. (1988). *Citizens Politics in Western Democracies*. Chatham: Chatham House Publishers.

—— (1994). *The Green Rainbow: Environmental Groups in Western Europe*. New Haven and London: Yale University Press.

—— (1996). *Citizen Politics: Public Opinion and Political Parties in Advanced Industrial Democracies*, 2nd edition. Chatham, NJ: Chatham House.

Dalton, R. J. and Kuechler, M. (eds) (1990). *Challenging the Political Order*. New York: Oxford University Press.

—— and Wattenberg, M. P. (eds) (2000). *Parties without Partisans: Political Change in Advanced Industrial Democracies*. Oxford: Oxford University Press.

Daly, M. (2000). *The Gender Division of Welfare: the Impact of the German and British Welfare States*. Cambridge: Cambridge University Press.

Damgaard, E., Gerlich, P., and Richardson, J. J. (eds) (1989). *The Politics of Economic Crisis*. Aldershot: Avebury.

Dashwood, A. (1996). 'The Limits of European Community Powers'. *European Law Review*, 21: 113–128.

Dauba, M. (1997). 'Services publics: évolutions récentes et enjeux nouveaux'. *La Pensée*, 310: 19–28.

Davis, R. H. (1997). *Women and Power in Parliamentary Democracies: Cabinet Appointments in Western Europe 1968–1992*. Lincoln: University of Nebraska Press.

de Bassompierre, G. (1988). *Changing the Guard in Brussels. An Insider's View of the Presidency*. New York: Praeger.

Debbasch, C. (1988). *National Administration and European Integration*. Paris.

De Burca, G. and Scott, J. (2000). *Constitutional Change in the EU, From Uniformity to Flexibility?* Oxford-Portland Oregon: Hart Publishing.

Decker, F. (2002). 'Governance Beyond the Nation State: Reflections on the Democratic Deficit of the European Union'. *Journal of European Public Policy*, 9: 2.

de Grauwe, P. (2000), *Economics of Monetary Union*, 4th ed. Oxford: Oxford University Press.

Dehousse, R. (1998). *The European Court of Justice: the Politics of Judicial Integration*. London: Macmillan.

De la Gueriviere, J. (1992). *Voyage à l'Intérieur de l'Eurocratie*. Paris: Le Monde Editions.

della Porta, D. (1995). *Social Movements, Political Violence and the State: A Comparative Analysis of Italy and Germany*. Cambridge and New York: Cambridge University Press.

—— 'Social Movements and Representative Democracies at the Turn of the Millenum: The Italian Case', unpublished paper, University of Florence, Italy.

della Porta, D. and Reiter, H. (eds) (1998). *Policing Protest: The Control of Mass Demonstrations in Western Democracies*. Minneapolis and London: University of Minnesota Press.

Denham, J. (1999). Speech to the CIPFA/Public Management and Policy Association Conference on an 'An Epidemic of Zones: Illness or Cure'? International Conference Centre, Birmingham.

De Noriega, A. E. (1999). 'A Dissident Voice: The Spanish Constitutional Court Case Law on European Integration'. *European Public Law*, 5: 269–299.

DePorte, A. W. (1986). *Europe between the Superpowers: The Enduring Balance*, 2nd edition. London: Yale University Press.

Derlien, H.-U. (1994), 'Karrien, Tätigkeitsprofil und Rollenverständnis der Spitzenbeamten des Bundes-Konstanz und Wandel'. *Verwaltung und Fortbildung*, 22(4).

Derlien, H.-U. (1999). 'On the Selective Interpretation of Max Weber's Theory of Bureaucracy', in P. Ahonen and K. Palonen (eds), *Dis-Embalming Max Weber*. Jyvaskyla: Sophi Press.

—— (2000). 'Germany: Failing Successfully'? in H. Kassim, B. G. Peters, and V. Wright (eds), *The National Co-ordination of EU Policy: the domestic level*. Oxford: Oxford University Press, pp. 54–78.

De Swaan, A. (1973). *Coalition Theories and Cabinet Formation*. Amsterdam: Elsevier.

De Winter, L. (1991). 'Parliamentary and Party Pathways to the Cabinet', in J. Blondel and J. L. Thiébault (eds), *The Profession of Government Minister in Western Europe*. London: Macmillan, pp. 44–69.

—— Timmermans, A., and Dumont, P. (2000). 'Belgium: On Government Agreements, Evangelists, Followers and Heretics', in W. Müller and K. Strom (eds), *Coalition Governments in Western Europe*. Oxford: Oxford University Press, pp. 300–355.

De Witte, B. (1984). 'Retour a Costa. La primauté de droit communautaire à la lumière du droit international'. *Revue trimestrielle de droit européen*.

de Zwann, J. W. (1995). *The Permanent Representatives Committee: Its Role in European Union Decision-Making*. Amsterdam: Elsevier.

—— (1996), *The Permanent Representatives Committee: Its Role in European Union Decision Making*. Amsterdam: Elsevier.

Diamanti, I. (1995). *La lega, gegrafia, storia e sociologia di un nuovo soggetto politico*. Rome: Donzeilli.

Diamond, L. (1999). *Developing Democracy: Toward Consolidation*. Baltimore and London: Johns Hopkins University Press.

Diani, M. (1995). *Green Networks: A Structural Analysis of the Italian Environmental Movement*. Edinburgh: University of Edinburgh Press.

DiMaggio, P. J. and Powell, W. W. (1991*a*). 'Introduction', in P. J. DiMaggio and W. W. Powell (eds), *The New Institutionalism in Organizational Analysis*. Chicago: University of Chicago Press.

—— (1991*b*). 'The Iron Cage Revisited: Institutional Isomorphism and Collective Rationality', in P. J. DiMaggio and W. W. Powell (eds), *The New Institutionalism in Organizational Analysis*. Chicago: University of Chicago Press, pp. 63–82.

—— (1983). 'The iron cage revisited: institutional isomorphism and collective rationality in organizational fields'. *American Sociological Review*, 48(1): 47–60.

Dimitrakopoulos, D. (1997). *Beyond Transposition: a Comparative Inquiry into the Implementation of European Public Policy*, PhD Thesis, University of Hull.

Dinan, D. (1994). *Ever Closer Union?*. Basingstoke: Macmillan.

—— (1999). *Ever Closer Union: An Introduction to European Integration*. Basingstoke: Macmillan.

—— (2000). 'Governance and Institutions 1999: Resignation, Reform and Renewal'. *Journal of Common Market Studies, Annual Review*, 1999/2000: 25–42.

Direction Générale des Collectivités locales. (1999). *Les collectivités locales en chiffres*. Paris: la Documentation française.

Disney, R. and Johnson, P. (eds) (2001). *Pension Systems and Retirement Imcomes across OECD Countries*. Cheltenham: Edward Elgar.

Dogan, M. (ed.) (1975). *The Mandarins of Western Europe*. New York: Halsted.

—— (ed.) (1989). *Pathways to Power. Selecting Rulers in Pluralist Democracies*. Boulder: Westview.

Dogan, R. (1997). 'Comitology: Little Procedures with Big Implications'. *West European Politics*, 20(3): 31–60.

Doleys, T. (2000). 'Member States and the European Commission: Theoretical Insights from the New Economics of Organization'. *Journal of European Public Policy*, 7(4): 532–553.

Dolowitz, D. and Marsh, D. (1996). 'Who Learns What from Whom? A Review of the Policy Transfer Literature'. *Political Studies*, 44(2): 343–357.

Donnelly, M. (1993). 'The Structure of the European Commission and the Policy Formation Process', in S. Mazey and J. J. Richardson (eds), *Lobbying in the European Community*. Oxford: Oxford University Press.

Downs, A. (1967). *Inside Bureaucracy*. Boston: Little, Brown and Company.

Drescher, S. (1987). *Capitalism and Antislavery: British Mobilization in Comparative Perspective*. Oxford and New York: Oxford University Press.

Drezner, D. W. (2001). 'Globalization and Policy Convergence'. *International Studies Review*, 3(1): 53–78.

Dubet, F. and Martucelli, D. (1998). *Dans quelle société vivons-nous?*. Paris: Le Seuil.

Dudley, G. and Richardson, J. (1999). 'Competing Advocacy Coalitions and the Process of "Frame Reflection": a Longitudinal Analysis of EU Steel Policy'. *Journal of European Public Policy*, 6(2): 225–248.

Due, J., Madsen, J. S., Jensen, C. S., and Petersen, L. K. (1994). *The Survival of the Danish Model*. Copenhagen: DJØF.

Duffield, J. S. (1998). *World Power Forsaken: Political Culture, International Institutions, and German Security Policy after Unification*. Stanford: Stanford University Press.

—— (2001). 'Transatlantic Relations after the Cold War: Theory, Evidence, and the Future'. *International Studies Review*, 2(1): 93–115.

Du Gay, P. (2000). *In Praise of Bureaucracy: Weber, Organization, Ethics*. London: Sage.

Dubbins, S. (2002). *Towards Euro-Corporatism: A Study of Relations between Trade Unions and Employers' Organisations at the European Sectoral Level*, unpublished PhD thesis, European University Institute, Florence.

Duharcourt, P. (1997). 'Les enjeux de la modernisation des services publics'. *La Pensée*, 310: 5–18.

Dumez, H. and Jeunemaitre, A. (1994). 'Privatization in France 1983–1993', in V. Wright (ed.), *Privatization in Western Europe: Pressures, Problems and Paradoxes*. London: Pinter.

Dunleavy, P. (1986). 'Explaining the Privatisation Boom: Public Choice Versus Radical Approaches'. *Public Administration*, 64: 13–34.

—— (1991). *Democracy, Bureaucracy and Public Choice*. Hemel Hempstead: Harvester Wheatsheaf.

—— (1995). 'Reinterpreting the Westland Affair; Theories of the State and Core Executive Decision Making', in R. A. W. Rhodes and P. Dunleavy (eds), *Prime Minister, Cabinet and Core Executive*. London: Macmillan: pp. 181–218.

—— and Rhodes, R. A. W. (1990). 'Core Executive Studies in Britain'. *Public Administration*, 68: 3–28.

Duverger, M. (1954). *Political Parties: Their Organization and Activities in the Modern State*. London: Methuen.

—— (1980). 'A New Political System Model: Semi-Presidential Government'. *European Journal of Political Research*, 8: 165–187.

Dyson, K. (1980). *The State Tradition in Western Europe*. Oxford: Martin Robertson.

—— (1983). 'The Cultural, Ideological and Structural Context', in K. Dyson and S. Wilks (eds), *Industrial Crisis*. Oxford: Martin Robertson.

—— (1994). *Elusive Union: The Process of Economic and Monetary Union in Europe*. London and New York: Longman.

—— (2000). *The Politics of the Euro-Zone*. Oxford: Oxford University Press.

—— and Featherstone, K. (1999). *The Road to Maastricht*. Oxford: Oxford University Press.

Ebbinghaus, B. and Hassel, A. (1999). 'The Role of Tripartite Concertation in the reform of the welfare state'. *Transfer*, 1–2: 64–81.

—— and Manow, P. (2001). *Comparing Welfare Capitalism: Social Policy and Political Economy in Europe, Japan and the USA*. London: Routledge.

Eckstein, H. (1961). *A Theory of Stable Democracy*. Princeton: Princeton Center for International Studies.

—— and Gurr, T. (1975). *Patterns of Authority*. New York: Wiley.

Eder, K. (1993). *The New Politics of Class: Social Movements and Cultural Dynamics in Advanced Societies*. London: Sage.

Edwards, G. (1996). 'National Sovereignty vs. Integration? The Council of Ministers' in J. Richardson (ed.), *The European Union: Power and Policy Making*. London: Routledge, pp. 127–147.

Edwards, P., Hall, M., Hyman, R., Marginson, P., Sisson, K., Waddington, J., and Winchester, D. (1998). 'Great Britain: from Partial Collectivism to Neo-liberalism to Where?', in Ferner and Hyman (eds), *Changing Industrial Relations in Europe*. Oxford: Blackwell.

Egeberg, M. (1995). 'Bureaucrats as Public Policy-Makers and their Self-Interests'. *Journal of Theoretical Politics*, 7: 157–167.

—— (1999). 'The Impact of Bureaucratic Structure on Policy Making'. *Public Administration*, 77(1): 155–170.

—— and Sætren, H. (1999). 'Identities in Complex Organisations: A Study of Ministerial Bureaucrats', in M. Egeberg and P. Lægreid (eds), *Organizing Political Institutions*. Oslo: Scandinavian University Press, pp. 96–108.

Eggertsson, T. (1990). *Economic Behavior and Institutions*. Cambridge: Cambridge University Press.

Ehrmann, H. (1957). *Organized Business in France*. Princeton: Princeton University Press.

Eichengreen, B. (1998). 'European Monetary Unification: A *Tour d'horizon*'. *Oxford Review of Economic Policy*, 14(3), Autumn.

—— and Wyplosz, C. (1998). 'The Stability Pact: More than a Minor Nuisance?'. *Economic Policy*, No. 26, April.

Eisenstadt, S. N. (1965). *Essays on Comparative Institutions*. New York: John Wiley.

Elder, N. C. M. E. and Page, E. C. (2000). 'Sweden. The Quest for Coordination', in B. Guy Peters, R. A. W. Rhodes, and Vincent Wright (eds), *Administering the Summit: Administration of the Core Executive in Developed Countries*. Basingstoke: Macmillan.

Eley, G. (1995). 'War and the Twentieth-Century State'. *Daedalus*, 124(2): 155–174.

Elgie, R. (1993). *The Role of the Prime Minister in France, 1981–1991*. London: Macmillan.

—— (1995). *Political Leadership in Liberal Democracies*. London: Macmillan.

—— (1998). 'The Classification of Democratic Regime Types: Conceptual Ambiguity and Contestable Assumptions'. *European Journal of Political Research*, 33: 219–238.

—— and Jones, E. (2000). 'Agents, Principals and the Studies of Institutions: Constructing a Principal-Centered Account of Delegation', University of Nottingham, Working Documents in the Study of European Governance, No. 5, December.

Eliassen, K. A. and Kooiman, J. (eds) (1993). *Managing Public Organizations*. London: Sage.

Ellul, J. (1964). *The Technological Society*. New York: Vintage.

Enkegren, M. (1996). 'The Europeanisation of State Administration'. *Cooperation and Conflict*, 31(4): 387–415.

Ersson, S. and Lane, J.-E. (1998). 'Electoral Instability and Party System Change in Western Europe', in P. Pennings and J.-E. Lane (eds), *Comparing Party System Change*. London: Routledge.

Ertman, T. (1998). 'Democracy and Dictatorship in Inter-War Europe Revisited'. *World Politics*, 50(3): 475–505.

Esambert, B. (1992). 'L'Etat et les entreprises', in R. Renoir and J. Lesource (eds), *Où va l'Etat? La souveraineté économique et politiqe en question*. Paris: Le Monde Editions.

Esping-Andersen, G. (1990). *The Three Worlds of Welfare Capitalism*. Cambridge: Polity.

—— (ed.) (1996a). *Welfare States in Transition: National Adaptations in Global Economies*. London: Sage Publications.

—— (1996b). 'After the Golden Age? Welfare State Dilemmas in a Global Economy', in G. Esping-Andersen (ed.), *Welfare States in Transition: National Adaptations in Global Economies*. London: Sage, pp. 1–31.

—— (1999). *Social Foundations of Post-industrial Economies*. Oxford: Oxford University Press.

—— and Regini, M. (eds) (2000). *Why Deregulate Labour Markets?*. Oxford: Oxford University Press.

European Commission (1992a). *Increased Transparency in the Work of the Commission*. Brussels, 2 December, SEC (92) 2274 final.

—— (1992b). *An Open and Structured Dialogue between the Commission and Special Interest Groups*. Brussels, 2 December, SEC (92) 2272 final.

—— (1993). *Openness in the Community*, Communication to the Council, the Parliament and the Economic and Social Committee. Brussels, 2 June. COM(93) 258 final.

—— (1997). *For a Stronger and Wider Union*, Agenda 2000, vol. I (Doc. 97/6), Strasbourg.

—— (1999) *Discussion Paper on the Commission and Non-Governmental Organizations*. Brussels: Commission.

European Commission (2000). *Employment in Europe*. Brussels.

European Council (1999). *Presidency Conclusions. Helsinki European Council, 10 and 11 December 1999*, Council of the European Union website.

—— (2000). *Presidency Conclusions* (Santa Maria da Feira, 19–20 June). Brussels: General Secretariat of the Council.

Eurostat (1998). *Social Portrait of Europe*. Brussels.

—— (2000*a*). *Statistics in Focus: Social Protection in Europe: Theme 3-15/2000*. Brussels.

—— (2000*b*). *The Social Situation in the European Union 2000*. Brussels.

Evans, G. and Manning, N. (2001). *Policy Management at the Center of Government: Symptoms and Cures*. Manuscript, March 2001.

Evans, P. (1997). 'The Eclipse of the State?'. *World Politics*, 50 (October).

—— Rueschemeyer, D., and Skocpol, T. (eds) (1985). *Bringing the State Back In*. New York: Cambridge University Press.

Everling, U. (1994). 'The Maastricht Judgment of the German Federal Constitutional Court and its Significance for the Development of the European Union'. *Yearbook of European Law*, 14: 1–19.

—— (1996). 'Will Europe Slip on Bananas? The Bananas Judgment of the Court of Justice and National Courts'. *Common Market Law Review*, 33: 401–437.

Eyre, S. and Lodge, M. (2000). 'National Tunes and a European Melody? Competition law Reform in the UK and Germany'. *Journal of European Public Policy*, 7(1): 63–79.

Fajertag, G. and Pochet, P. (eds). *Social Pacts in Europe—New Dynamics*. Brussels: European Trade Union Institute/Observatoire Social Européen.

Falk, R. (1999). *Predatory Globalization*. Cambridge: Polity.

Falkner, G. and Nentwich, M. (2000). 'The Amsterdam Treaty: The Blueprint for the Future Institutional Balance?', in K. Neunreither and A. Wiener (eds), *European Integration After Amsterdam. Institutional Dynamics and Prospects for Democracy*. Oxford: Oxford University Press, pp. 15–35.

Falkner, G., Wolfgang, C. M., Eder, M., Hiller, K., Steiner, G., and Trattnigg, R. (1999). 'The Impact of EU Membership on Policy Networks in Austria: Creeping Change Beneath the Surface'. *Journal of European Public Policy*, 6(3): 496–516.

Fargion, V. (2000). 'Timing and the Development of Social Care in Europe', in M. Ferrera and M. Rhodes (eds), *Recasting European Welfare States*. London: Frank Cass, pp. 59–98.

Favell, A. (1998). *Philosophies of Integration*. London: Macmillan.

Feigenbaum, H., Henig, J., and Hamnet, C. (1998). *Shrinking the State*. New York: Cambridge University Press.

—— (1999). *Shrinking the State. The Political Underpinnings of Privatization*. Cambridge: Cambridge University Press.

Feldblum, M. (1999). *Reconstructing Citizenship: the Politics of Nationality Reform and Immigration in Contemporary France*. Albany: State University of New York Press.

Feldstein, M. (1997). 'EMU and International Conflict'. *Foreign Affairs*, vol. 76, No. 6, Nov./Dec.

Ferguson, N. (2001). *The Cash Nexus: Money and Power in the Modern World 1700–2000*. London: Allen Lane.

Ferner, A. and Hyman, R. (eds) (1998). *Changing Industrial Relations in Europe*. Oxford: Blackwell.

Ferrera, M. (1996). 'The Southern Model of Welfare in Social Europe'. *Journal of European Social Policy*, 6(1): 17–37.

—— and Rhodes, M. (eds) (2000a). *Recasting European Welfare States*. London: Frank Cass (also a special issue of *West European Politics*, 23(2): 2000).

——and Rhodes, M. (2000b). 'Building a Sustainable Welfare State', in M. Ferrera and M. Rhodes (eds), *Recasting European Welfare States*. London: Frank Cass, pp. 257–282.

Ferrera, M., Hemerijck, A., and Rhodes, M. (2000). *The Future of Social Europe: Recasting Work and Welfare in the New Economy*. Lisbon: CELTA/Ministério do Trabalho e da Solidariedade.

—— (2001). 'The Future of the European "Social Model" in the Global Economy'. *Journal of Comparative Policy Analysis*, 3(2): 163–190.

Finer, S. E. (1970). *Comparative Government*. London: AllenLane, The Penguin Press.

—— (1997). *The History of Government from the Earliest Times*, vols. I–III. Oxford: Oxford University Press.

—— Bogdanor, V., and Rudden, B. (1995). *Comparing Constitutions*. Oxford: Clarendon Press.

Fishman, R. (1990). 'Rethinking State and Regime: Southern Europe's Transition to Democracy'. *World Politics*, 42: 422–440.

Fitoussi, J. P. (1995). *Le débat interdit: Monnaie, Europe, Pauvreté*. Paris: Arlea.

Flanagan, S. C. (1987). 'Value Change in Industrial Society'. *American Political Science Review*, 81: 1303.

Flora, P. and Heidenheimer, A. J. (eds) (1981). *The Development of Welfare States in Europe and America*. New Brunswick and London: Transaction Books.

Foley, M. (1993). *The Rise of the British Presidency*. Manchester: Manchester University Press.

Forder, J. (2001). 'Image and Illusion in the Design of EMU', in A. Menon and V. Wright (eds), *From the Nation State to Europe: Essays in Honour of Jack Hayward*. Oxford: Oxford University Press.

Foreman-Peck, J. and Millward, R. (1994). *Public and Private Ownership of British Industry 1820–1990*. Oxford: Clarendon Press.

Foster, C. (1992). *Privatisation, Public Ownership and the Regulation of Natural Monopoly*. Oxford: Blackwell.

Foucault, M. (1977). *Discipline and Punish*. New York: Pantheon.

Frances, J. *et al.* (1991). 'Introduction', in G. Thompson *et al.*, *Markets Hierarchies and Networks: The Co-Ordination of Social Life*. London: Sage.

Freedom House (1999). *Freedom in the World*. New York: Freedom House.

Frieden, J. A. (1991). 'Invested Interests: The Politics of National Economic Policies in a World of Global Finance'. *International Organization*, 45(4): 425–451.

Frieden, J. (1998). *The New Political Economy of EMU*. Oxford: Rowman & Littlefield.

Friedrich, C. J. (1962). *The Public Interest*. New York: Atherton.

—— and Brzezinski, Z. (1956). *Totalitarian Dictatorship and Autocracy*. New York: Praeger.

Frowein, J. (1988). 'Solange II'. *Common Market Law Review*, 25: 201–206.

Frye, T. (1992). 'Ethnicity, Sovereignty and Transitions from Non-Democratic Rule'. *Journal of International Affairs*, 45: 599–623.

Frye, T. (1997). A politics of Institutional Choice: Post-Communist Presidencies in *Comparative Political Studies*, 30:5.

Gabel, H. L. (ed.) (1987). *Product Standardization and Competitive Strategy*. Amsterdam: Elsevier.

Gabriel, O. and Hoffman-Martinot, V. (eds) (1999). *Démocraties Urbaines*. Paris: L'Harmattan.

Gains, F. (1999). 'Implementing Privatization Policies in "Next Steps" Agencies'. *Public Administration*, 77: 713–730.

Gaja, G. (1990). 'New Developments in a Continuing Story: The Relationship between EEC Law and Italian Law'. *Common Market Law Review*, 27: 83–95.

Gallego, R. (November 2000). *The Dynamics of Autonomous Communities, Paper for the Conference of City Regions in Europe*, London.

Gallie, D. and Paugam, S. (eds) (2000). *Welfare Regimes and the Experience of Unemployment in Europe*. Oxford: Oxford University Press.

Galloway, D. (2001). *The Treaty of Nice and Beyond*. Sheffield: Sheffield Academic Press.

Gamble, A. (1990). 'Theories of British Politics'. *Political Studies*, 38: 404–420.

Gamson, W. (1990). *Strategy of Social Protest*, 2nd revised edition. Belmont, CA: Wadsworth.

Garrett, G. (1992). 'The European Community's Internal Market'. *International Organization*, 46(2): 533–560.

—— (1994). 'The Politics of Maastricht', in B. Eichengreen and J. Frieden (eds), *The Political Economy of European Monetary Unification*. Boulder, CO, San Francisco, and Oxford: Westview.

—— (1995a). 'The Politics of Legal Integration in the European Union'. *International Organization*, 49(1): 171–181.

—— (1995b). 'From the Luxembourg Compromise to Codecision: Decision Making in the European Union'. *Electoral Studies*, 14(3): 289–308.

—— (1998a). 'Global Markets and National Politics: Collision Course or Virtuous Circle?'. *International Organization*, 52(4): 787–824.

—— (1998b). *Partisan Politics in the Global Economy*. New York: Cambridge University Press.

—— and Tsebelis, G. (1996). 'An Institutional Critique of Intergovernmentalism'. *International Organization*, 50(2): 269–299.

Garrett, G. and Weingast, B. (1993). 'Ideas, Interests and Institutions: Constructing the EC's Internal Market', in J. Goldstein and R. Keohane (eds), *Ideas and Foreign Policy*. Ithaca: Cornell University Press, pp. 173–206.

Garton Ash, T. (1994). *In Europe's Name: Germany and the Divided Continent*. London: Vintage.

Gatsios, K. and Seabright, P. (1989). 'Regulation in the European Community'. *Oxford Review of Economic Policy*, 5: 37–50.

George, A. L. and George, J. L. (1956). *Woodrow Wilson and Colonel House*. New York: John Day.

Gerbet, P. (1992). 'La Haute Autorité de la Communauté Européene du Charbon et de l'Acier', in 'Early Europan Community Administration', *Yearbook of European Administrative History 4*. Baden-Baden: Nomos Verlagsgesellschaft, pp. 11–30.

Gerhards, J. and Rucht, D. (1992). 'Mesomobilization: Organizing and Framing in Two Protest Campaigns in West Germany'. *American Journal of Sociology*, 98: 555–595.

Gerth, H. and Mills, C. W. (eds) (1946). *From Max Weber*. New York: Oxford University Press.

General Secretariat of the Council of the European Union (1996). *Council Guide*. I, Presidency Handbook. Luxembourg: Office for Official Publications of the European Communities.

Giavazzi, F. and Pagano, M. (1988). 'The Advantage of Tying One's Hand: EMS Discipline and Central Bank Credibility'. *European Economic Review*, 32: 1055–1082.

Giddens, A. (1990). *The Consequences of Modernity*. Cambridge: Polity.

—— (1998). *The Third Way*. Cambridge: Polity.

—— (1999). *Runaway World: How Globalization Is Shaping Our Lives*. London: Profile.

Giddings, P. (1995). *Parliamentary Accountability: A Study of Parliament and Executive Agencies*. Basingstoke: Macmillan.

Gilbert, G. (1999). *L'autonomie financière des collectivités locales est-elle en question?, Les 2ème entretiens de la Caisse des Dépôts et Consignations*, La tour d'Aigues, Editions de l'Aube.

Gildea, R. (1996). *The Past in French History*. New Haven: Yale University Press.

Gilpin, R. (1975). *US Power and the Multinational Corporation*. New York: Basic Books.

—— (1987). *The Political Economy of International Relations*. Princeton: Princeton University Press.

Giugni, M. G. McAdam, D., and Tilly, C. (eds) (1998). *From Contention to Democracy*. Oxford and Lanham MD: Rowman and Littlefield.

Goetz, K. H. (1997). 'Acquiring Political Craft: Training Grounds for Top Officials in the German Core Executive'. *Public Administration*, 75(4): 753–775.

—— (1999). 'Senior Officials in the German Federal Administration: Institutional Change and Positional Differentiation', in E. C. Page and V. Wright (eds), *Bureaucratic Elites in Western European States: A Comparative Analysis of Top Officials in Eleven Countries*. Oxford: Oxford University Press, pp. 147–177.

—— (2000a). 'European Integration and National Executives: A Cause in Search of an Effect?'. *West European Politics*, 23(4): 211–231.

—— (2000b). 'The Developement and Current Features of the German Civil Service System', in H. A. G. M. Bekke and F. M. van der Meer (eds), *Civil Service Systems in Western Europe*. Cheltenham: Edward Elgar, pp. 61–91.

—— and Hix, S. (eds) (2000). *Europeanized Politics?* A special issue of *West European Politics*, 23: 4.

—— and Margetts, H. Z. (1999). 'The Solitary Centre: The Core Executive in Central and Eastern Europe'. *Governance*, 12(4): 425–453.

—— and Wollmann, H. (2001), 'Introduction'. *Journal of European Public Policy*, 8(6).

Göhler, G. (1994). 'Politische Institutionen und ihr Kontext', in idem G. Göhler, *Die Eigenart der Institutionen: Zum Profil politischer Institutionentheorie*. Baden-Baden: Nomos.

Goldsmith, M. and Klausen, K. (eds) (1997). *European integration and local government*. Cheltenham: Edward Elgar.

Goldstein, J. and Keohane, R. (1993). 'Ideas and Foreign Policy: an Analytical Framework', in J. Goldstein and R. Keohane (eds), *Ideas and Foreign Policy: Beliefs, Institutions and Political Change*. Ithaca: Cornell University Press, pp. 3–30.

Goldstein, R. (1983). *Political Repression in 19th Century Europe*. London: Croom Helm.

Goldthorpe, J. A. (ed.) (1984). *Order and Conflict in Contemporary Capitalism*. Oxford: Oxford University Press.

—— (2001). 'Globalization and Social Class'. *Mannheimer Vortrage 9*.

—— and Hirsch, F. (eds) (1978). *The Political Economy of Inflation*. London: Martin Robertson.

Gomez, R. and Peterson, J. (2001), 'The EU's Impossibly Busy Foreign Ministers "No One is in Control"'. *European Foreign Affairs Review*, 6: 53–74.

Goodhart, D. (1998). 'Social Dumping within the EU', in D. Hine and H. Kassim (eds), *Beyond the Market: The EU and National Social Policy*. London: Routledge.

Goodin, R. E., Headey, B., Muffels, R., and Dirven, H.-J. (1999). *The Real Worlds of Welfare Capitalism*. Cambridge: Cambridge University Press.

—— and Klingemann, H.-D. (1996). *A New Handbook of Political Science*. Oxford: Oxford University Press.

Gordon, M. (1971). 'Civil Servants, Politicians and Parties: Shortcomings in the British Policy Process'. *Comparative Politics*, 4 (October): 29–58.

Gorges, M. J. (1996). *Euro-corporatism? Interest Intermediation in the European Community*. Maryland: University Press of America.

Gottschalk, P. and Smeeding, T. (1997). 'Cross-National Comparisons of Earnings and Income Inequality'. *Journal of Economic Literature*, 35: 633–687.

Gourevitch, Peter A. (1978). 'The Second Image Reversed: International Sources of Domestic Politics'. *International Organization*, 32: 881–912.

Goul Anderson, J. and Jensen, P. H. (2002). *Changing Labour Markets, Welfare Politics and Citizenship*. Bristol: The Policy Press.

Grabbe, H. (2000). 'The Sharp Edges of Europe: Extending Schengen Eastwards'. *International Affairs*, 76(3): 519–536.

Grande, E. (1994). 'The New Role of the State in Telecommunications: An International Comparison'. *West European Politics*, 17(3): 138–157.

——(1997). 'Auflösung, Modernisierung oder Transformation? Zum Wandel des modernen Staates in Europa', in E. Grande and R. Prätorius (eds), *Modernisierung des Staates?* Baden-Baden: Nomos.

Grant, W. (1989). *Government and Industry. A Comparative Analaysis of the US, Canada and the UK*. Aldershot: Edward Elgar.

Graubard, S. (ed.) (1964). *The New Europe*. Boston: Beacon Press.

Gray, J. (1998). *Endgames*. Cambridge: Polity Press.

Greenwood, J. (1997). *Representing Interests in the European Union*. London: Routledge.

——(2002a). *Inside the EU Business Associatons*. Basingstoke: Palgrave.

——(2002b). *The Effectiveness of EU Business Associations*. Basingstoke: Palgrave.

——and Aspinwall, M. (eds) (1998). *Collective Action in the European Union*. London: Routledge.

Greenwood, J., Grote, J. R., and Ronit, K. (eds) (1992). *Organized Interests and the European Community*. London: Sage Publications.

Grémion, P. (1976). *Le Pouvoir périphérique*. Paris: Editions du Seuil.

Gros, D. and Thygesen, N. (1998). *European Monetary Integration*, 2nd edition. London and New York: Longman.

Guersent, O. (1996). 'La Régulation des services publics en Europe: comment maîtriser les mutations de l'économie mondiale?'. *L'Année Européenne*, 1996: 192–198.

Guillen, A. M. and Matsaganis, M. (2000). 'Testing the 'Social Dumping' Hypothesis in Southern Europe: Welfare Policies in Spain and Greece during the Last 20 years'. *Journal of European Social Policy*, 10(2): 120–145.

Guizot, F. P. G. (1846). *The History Of Civilization From The Fall Of The Roman Empire to the French Revolution*, vol. 1 (trans William Hazlitt). London: David Bogue.

Gurumurthy, R. (1999). 'Tackling Poverty and Extending Opportunity'. *Political Quarterly*, 70(3): 335–340.

Haas, E. (1958). *The Uniting of Europe, Political Social and Economic Forces 1950–57*. Stanford: Stanford University Press.

——(1964). *Beyond the Nation State: Functionalism and International Organisation*. Stanford: Stanford University Press.

Haas, P. (1992). 'Introduction: Epistemic Communities and International Policy Coordination'. *International Organization*, 46(1): 1–37.

Haas, P.M. (1998). Compliance with EU Directives: Insights from International Relations and Comparative Politics. *Journal of European Public Policy*, 5(1): 17–37.

Hall, P. A. (1983). 'Policy Innovation and the Structure of the State: The Politics-Administration Nexus in France and Britain'. *The Annals*, 466: 43–59.

——(1986). *Governing the Economy*. Cambridge: Polity Press.

——(1999). 'Social Capital in Britain'. *British Journal of Political Science*, 29(3): 417–461.

——and Franzese, R. (1998). 'Mixed Signals: Central Bank Independence, Coordinated Wage-Bargaining and European Monetary Union'. *International Organization*, 52(5): 502–536.

——and Soskice, D. (eds) (2001). *Varieties of Capitalism*. Oxford: Oxford University Press.

——and Taylor, R. (1996). 'Political Science and the Three New Institutionalisms', XXXXIV/5.

Hammond, T. A. (1996). 'Formal Theory and the Institutions of Governance'. *Governance*, 9: 107–185.

Hancher, L. and Moran, M. (eds) (1989). 'Deregulation in Western Europe'. Special Issue. *European Journal of Political Research*, 17(2).

Hardiman, N. (2000). 'Social Partnership, Wage Bargaining and Growth', in B. Nolan, P. J. O'Connell, and C. T. Whelan (eds), *Bust to Boom? The Irish Experience of Growth and Inequality*. Dublin: Institute of Public Administration.

Harding, A. (1997). 'Urban Regimes in a Europe of Cities?'. *Urban and Regional Studies*, 4(4).

Hartley, T. C. (1988). *The Foundations of European Community Law*, 2nd edition. Oxford: Clarendon Press.

Hartley, T. (1999). *Constitutional Problems of the European Union*. Oxford: Hart Publishing.

Harvey, B. (1993). 'Lobbying in Europe: the Experience of the Voluntary Sector', in S. Mazey and J. J. Richardson (eds), *Lobbying in the European Community*. Oxford: Oxford University Press.

Hay, C. and Rosamund, B. (2002). 'Globalisation, European integration and the discursive construction of economic imperatives'. *Journal of European Public Policy*, 9(2).

Hay, R. (1989). *The European Commission and the Administration of the Community*. Luxembourg: Office for Official Publications of the European Communities.

Hayes-Renshaw, F. and Wallace, H. (1995). 'Executive Power in the European Union: the Functions and Limits of the Council of Ministers'. *Journal of European Public Policy*, 24(4): 559–582.

——— (1997). *The Council of Ministers*. Basingstoke: Macmillan.

Hayward, J. (1976). 'Institutional Inertia and Political Impetus in France and Britain'. *European Journal of Political Research*, IV.

—— (1982). 'Mobilising Private Interests in the Service of Public Ambitions: The Salient Element in the Dual French Policy Style', in J. Richardson (ed.), *Policy Styles in Western Europe*. London: Allen and Unwin.

—— (1983). *Governing France: The One and Indivisible Republic*, 2nd edition. London: Weidenfeld and Nicolson.

—— (1986). *The State and the Market Economy. Industrial Patriotism and Economic Intervention in France*. Brighton: Wheatsheaf.

—— (ed.) (1995). *The Crisis of Representation in Europe*. London: Cass.

—— (ed.) (1996). *Elitism, Populism and European Politics*. Oxford: Oxford University Press.

—— (1997). 'Changing partnerships: Firms and the French state'. *Modern and Contemporary France*, 5(2): 155–165.

—— (1999). 'British Approaches to Politics: the Dawn of a Self-Deprecating Discipline', in J. Hayward, B. Barry, and A. Brown (eds), *The British Study of Politics in the Twentieth Century*. Oxford: Oxford University Press.

——and Page, E. C. (eds) (1995). *Governing the New Europe*. Oxford: Polity.

——and Watson, M. (eds) (1975). *Planning, Politics and Public Policy: The British, French and Italian Experience*. London: Cambridge University Press.

——and Wright, V. (1998). 'Policy Co-ordination in West European Core Executives', ESRC unpublished end of award (L124251013) report.

—— (2002). *Governing from the Centre: Core Executive Co-ordination in France*. Oxford: Oxford University Press.

Hazareesingh, S. and Nabulsi, K. (2000). 'The Ambivalent Jacobin: Vincent Wright as an Historian of Modern France'. *Modern and Contemporary France*, 8.

Heald, D. (1988), 'The United Kingdom: Privatisation and its Political Context'. *West European Politics*, 11(4): 31–49.

Heclo, H. (1974). *Modern Social Politics in Britain and Sweden*. New Haven: Yale University Press.

—— and Wildavsky, A. (1974). *The Private Government of Public Money*. London: Macmillan.

Heidenheimer, A. J., Johnston, M., and Levine, V. T. (eds) (1989). *Political Corruption, A Handbook*. New Brunswick, NJ: Transaction Publishers.

Héritier, A. (1997). 'Market-Making Policy in Europe. Its Impact on Member-State Policies. The Case of Road Haulage in Britain, the Netherlands, Germany and Italy'. *Journal of European Public Policy* 4(4): 539–555.

Heisler, M. (1974). 'Patterns of European Politics: The "European Polity Model" ', in M. Heisler (ed.), *Politics in Europe: Structures and Processes in some Postindustrial Democracies*. New York: David McKay.

Held, D. (1987). *Models of Democracy*. Cambridge: Polity Press.

—— (1995). *Democracy and the Global Order*. Cambridge: Polity Press.

Held, D. and McGrew, A. G. (2000). *The Global Transformations Reader: An Introduction to the Globalization Debate*. Cambridge: Blackwell.

—— *et al.* (1999). *Global Transformations: Politics, Economics, Culture*. Cambridge: Polity Press.

Hemerijck, A. and Schludi, M. (2000). 'Sequences of Policy Failures and Effective Policy Responses', in F. W. Scharpf and V. Schmidt (eds), *Welfare and Work in the Open Economy: vol. I—From Vulnerability to Competitiveness*. Oxford: Oxford University Press, pp. 125–228.

Hennessy, P. (1992). *Never Again*. London: Jonathan Cape.

—— (1996). ' "Shadow and Substance": premiership for the twenty-first century', Gresham College, Rhetoric Lectures, Lecture 6, 5 March 1996.

Henry, C. (1997). *Concurrence et services publics dans l'Union Européenne*. Paris: Presses Universitaires de France.

Hentic, I. and Bernier, G. (1999). 'Rationalization, Decentralization and Participation in the Public Sector Management of Developing Countries'. *International Review of Administrative Sciences*, 65: 197–209.

Herdegen, M. (1994). 'Maastricht and the German Constitutional Court: Constitutional Restraints for an Ever Closer Union'. *Common Market Law Review*, 31: 235–249.

Herf, J. (1984). *Reactionary Modernism*. New York: Cambridge University Press.

Héritier, A. (1996). 'The Accommodation of Diversity in European Policy-Making and its Outcomes: Regulatory Policy as a Patchwork'. *Journal of European Public Policy*, 3(2): 149–167.

—— (1999). *Policy-Making and Diversity in Europe*. Cambridge: Cambridge University Press.

—— Knill, C., and Mingers, S. (1996). *Ringing the Changes in Europe*. Berlin: de Gruyter.

Heywood, P. and Molina, I. (2000). 'A Quasi-Presidential Premiership: Administering the Executive Summit in Spain', in B. G. Peters, R. A. W. Rhodes, and V. Wright (eds), *Administering the Summit: Administration of the Core Executive in Developed Countries*. Basingstoke: Macmillan, pp. 110–133.

Heywood, P. and Wright, V. (1997). 'Executives, Bureaucracies and Decision-Making', in M. Rhodes, P. Heywood, and V. Wright (eds), *Developments in West European Politics*. Basingstoke: Macmillan, pp. 75–94.

Hill, K. A. and John, E. H. (1998). *Cyberpolitics: Citizen Activism in the Age of the Internet*. Oxford and Lanham, MD: Rowman and Littlefield.

Hine, D. (2001). 'Constitutional Reform and Treaty Reform in Europe', in A. Menon and V. Wright (eds), *From the Nation State to Europe?* Oxford: Oxford University Press.
——and Kassim, H. (1998). *Beyond the Market. The European Union and National Social Policy.* London: Routledge.
Hintze, O. (1962). *Staat und Verwaltung.* Göttingen: Vandenhoeck und Ruprecht.
Hirschman, A. (1970). *Exit, Voice and Loyalty.* Cambridge, MA: Harvard University Press.
——(1982). *Shifting Involvements: Private Interest and Public Action.* Princeton, NJ: Princeton University Press.
Hirst, P. and Thompson, G. (1996). *Globalization in Question.* Cambridge: Polity.
——(1999). *Globalization in Question: The International Economy and the Possibilities of Governance.* 2nd edition. London: Polity.
Hix, S. (1998). 'The Study of the European Union II: The "New Governance" Agenda and its Rivals'. *Journal of European Public Policy*, 5(1): 38–65.
——(1999). *The Political System of the European Union.* Basingstoke: Macmillan.
——and Goetz, K. (2000*a*). 'Introduction: European Integration and National Political Systems'. *West European Politics*, 23(4): 1–26.
——(eds) (2000*b*). *Europeanised Politics? European Integration and National Political Systems. West European Politics* (Special Issue), 23(4) October.
Hodson, D. and Maher, I. (2001). 'The Open Method as a New Mode of Governance: The Case of Soft Economic Policy Coordination'. *Journal of Common Market Studies*, 39(4): 719–746.
Hoffmann, S. (1982). 'Reflections on the Nation-State in Western Europe Today'. *Journal of Common Market Studies*, 21: 21–38.
——*et al.* (1963). *In Search of France.* Cambridge, MA: Harvard University Press.
Hofstede, G. H. (1984). *Culture's Consequences: International Differences in Work-Related Values.* Beverly Hills: Sage.
Holstein, W. J. (1990). 'The Stateless Corporation'. *Business Week*, May 14, 98–100.
Hont (1994). 'The permanent crisis of a divided mankind'. *Political Studies*, XLII (Special Issue).
Hood, C. C. (1976). *The Limits of Administration.* London: John Wiley.
——(1996). 'Exploring Variations in Public Management Reform of the 1980s', in H. A. G. M. Bekke, J. L. Perry, and T. A. J. Toonen (eds), *Civil Service Systems in Comparative Perspective.* Bloomington: Indiana University Press.
——*et al.* (1999). *Regulation Inside Government: Wastewatchers, Quality Police and Sleazebusters.* Oxford: Oxford University Press.
Hooghe, L. (1996). *Cohesion Policy and European Integration.* Oxford: Oxford University Press.
——and Marks, G. (2001). *Multilevel Governance and European Integration.* Lanham, MD: Rowman and Littlefield.
Horn, M. J. (1995). *The Political Economy of Public Administration.* Cambridge: Cambridge University Press.
Hough, J. (1977). *The Soviet Union and Social Science Theory.* Cambridge, MA: Harvard University Press.
Howard, M. E. (1991). *The Lessons of History.* Oxford: Oxford University Press.
Huber, E. and Stephens, J. D. (2001). *Development and Crisis of the Welfare State: Parties and Policies in Global Markets.* Chicago: University of Chicago Press.
Huber, J. (1996). *Rationalizing Parliament.* New York: Cambridge University Press.
——(2000). 'Delegation to Civil Servants in Parliamentary Democracies'. *European Journal of Political Research*, 37: 397–413.
Hull, R. (1993). 'Lobbying Brussels: A View From Within', S. Mazey and J. Richardson (eds), *Lobbying in the European Community.* Oxford: Oxford University Press, pp. 82–92.

Huntington, S. P. (1984). 'Will More Countries Become Democratic?'. *Political Science Quaterly*, 99(2): 193–218.

—— (1991). *The Third Wave. Democratization in the Late Twentieth Century*. Norman and London: University of Oklahoma Press.

—— and Domínguez, J. I. (1975). 'Political Development', in Fred I. Greenstein and Nelson W. Polsby (eds), *Handbook of Political Science (III Macropolitical Theory)*. Reading, MA: Addison-Wesley.

Hurrell, A. and Woods, N. (1995). 'Globalisation and Inequality'. *Millennium*, 24(3): 447–470.

Hyman, R. (1998). 'Industrial Relations in Europe: Crisis or Reconstruction?'. in Wilthagen (ed), *Advancing Theory in Labour Law and Industrial Relations in a Global Context*. Amsterdam: North Holland.

Ignazi, P. (1992). 'The Silent Counter-Revolution: Hypotheses on the Emergence of Extreme Right-Wing Parties in Europe'. *European Journal of Political Research*, 22: 3–34.

—— (1996). 'The Crisis of Parties and the Rise of New Political Parties'. *Party Politics*, 2: 549–565.

Ikenberry, G. J. (1992). 'A world economy restored: expert consensus and the Anglo-American postwar settlement'. *International Organization*, 46(1): 289–321.

—— (2001). *After Victory: Institutions, Strategic Restraint, and the Rebuilding of Order after Major Wars*. Princeton: Princeton University Press.

Imig, D. and Tarrow, S. (eds) (2001). *Contentious Europeans: Politics and Protest in a Europeanizing Polity*. Lanham MD: Rowman and Littlefield.

Immergut, E. M. (1992). *Health Politics: Interests and Institutions in Western Europe*. Cambridge: Cambridge University Press.

—— (1998). 'The Theoretical Core of the New Institutionalism'. *Politics and Society*, 25(1): 5–34.

Inglehart, R. (1977). *The Silent Revolution: Changing Values and Political Styles among Western Publics*. Princeton: Princeton University Press.

—— (1997). *Culture Shift in Advanced Industrial Society*. Princeton: Princeton University Press.

ISA Consult (1997). *Evaluation of the Phare and Tacis Democracy Programs (1992–97)*. Sussex University: European Institute.

Iversen, T. and Cusack, T. R. (2000). 'The Causes of Welfare State Expansion'. *World Politics*, 52: 313–349.

Iversen, T. and Wren, A. (1998). 'Equality, Employment and Budgetary Restraint: The Trilemma of the Service Economy'. *World Politics*, 50: 507–546.

Iversen, T., Pontusson, J., and Soskice, D. (eds) (2000). *Unions, Employers and Central Banks: Macroeconomic Coordination and Institutional Change in Social Market Economies*. Cambridge: Cambridge University Press.

Jacoby, J. (1973). *The Bureaucratization of the World*. Berkeley: University of California Press.

Jacoby, W. (2000). *Imitation and Politics. Redesigning Modern Germany*. Ithaca and London: Cornell University Press.

Janis, I. L. (1982). *Groupthink; Psychological Studies of Policy Decisions and Fiascos*, 2nd edition. Boston: Houghton Mifflin.

Jann, W. (1997). 'Public Management Reform in Germany: A Revolution without a Theory'? in W. J. M. Kickert (ed.), *Public Management and Administrative Reform in Western Europe*. Cheltenham: Elgar.

Jeffrey, C. (ed.) (1997). *The Regional Dimension of the European Union*. London: Frank Cass.

Jensen, H. J. and Knudsen, T. (1999). 'Senior Officials in the Danish Central Administration: From Bureaucrats to Policy Professionals and Managers', in E. C. Page and V. Wright (eds),

Bureaucratic Elites in Western European States: A Comparative Analysis of Top Officials.
Oxford: Oxford University Press, pp. 228–248.

John, P. (2001). *Local Governance in Europe*. London: Sage.

Johnson, P. (1996). 'The Assessment: Inequality'. *Oxford Review of Economic Policy*, 12(1): 1–14.

Jones, G. W. (ed.) (1991). *West European Prime Ministers*. London: Cass.

Jordan, G. and Richardson, J. (1979). *Governing under Pressure: the Policy Process in a Post-Parliamentary Democracy*. Oxford: Martin Robertson.

Josselin, D. (1996). 'Domestic Policy Networks and European Negotiations. Evidence from British and French Financial Services'. *Journal of European Public Policy*, 3(3): 297–317.

Judt, T. (1996). *A Grand Illusion? An Essay on Europe*. London: Penguin Books.

Kaarbo, J. and Hermann, M. G. (1998). 'Leadership Styles of Prime Ministers: How Individual Differences Affect the Foreign Policymaking Process'. *Leadership Quarterly*, 9: 243–263.

Kanter, R. M. (1972). *Commitment and Community*. Cambridge MA: Harvard University Press.

Karl, T. L. and Schmitter, P. (1991). 'Modes of Transition in Latin America, Southern and Eastern Europe'. *International Journal of Social Science*, 128: 269–284.

Kassim, H. (2000*a*). 'The National Co-ordination of EU Policy: Confronting the Challenge', in H. Kassim, B. G. Peters, and V. Wright (eds), *The National Co-ordination of EU Policy: The Domestic Level*. Oxford: Oxford University Press, pp. 235–264.

—— (2000*b*). 'The National Co-ordination of EU Policy: Must Europeanisation Mean Convergence'? Paper presented at PSA 2000 Conference, London, April.

—— (2001). 'The United Kingdom. The Fine Art of Positive Co-ordination', in H. Kassim, A. Menon, B. G. Peters, and V. Wright (eds), *The National Co-ordination of EU Policy: the European Level*. Oxford: Oxford University Press

—— and Menon, A. (eds) (1996). *The European Union and National Industrial Policy*. London: Routledge.

—— Menon, A. (2002). 'Rethinking the Application of Principal-agent Models to the EU: Member States and the European Commission'. *Journal of European Public Policy*, 9: 6.

—— and Menon, A. (2003). 'The Principal-Agent Approach and the Study of the European Union: Promise Unfulfilled? in E. Jones and A. Verdun (eds) 'Political Economy and the Study of European Integration; Special Issue of *Journal of European Public Policy*, 10: 1.

—— and Menon, A. (2003). 'EU Member States and the Prodi Commission', D. Dimitrakopoulos (ed), *The Prodi Commission*. Manchester: Manchester University Press.

—— and Wright, V. (1991). 'The Role of National Administrations in the Decision-making Processes of the European Community'. *Rivista Trimestrale di Diritto Pubblico*, 832–850.

—— Peters, B. G., and Wright, V. (2000*a*). 'Introduction', in H. Kassim *et al.*, *The National Co-ordination of EU Policy: The Domestic Level*. Oxford: Oxford University Press, pp. 1–21.

—— (eds) (2000*b*). *EU Policy Making*. Oxford: Oxford University Press.

—— Menon, A., Peters, G., and Wright, V. (eds) (2001). *The National Co-ordination of EU Policy Making: The EU Level*. Oxford: Oxford University Press.

—— and Peters, B. G. (2001), 'Conclusion: Coordinating National Action in Brussels – A Comparative Perspective' in Kassim *et al.*, *The National Co-ordination of EU Policy*. Oxford: Oxford University Press.

Katz, R. S. (1986). 'Party Government: A Rationalistic Conception', in F. G. Castles and R. Wildenmann (eds), *Visions and Realities of Party Government*. Berlin: Walter de Gruyter.

—— and Mair, P. (eds) (1994). *How Parties Organize: Change and Adaptation in Party Organizations in Western Democracies*. London: Sage.

Katz, R. S. (1995). 'Changing Models of Party Organization: The Emergence of the Cartel Party'. *Party Politics*, 1: 5–28.

Katzenstein, P. (1978). *Between Power and Plenty: Foreign Economic Policies of Advanced Industrial Countries*. Madison: University of Wisconsin Press.

—— (1985). *Small States in World Markets*. Ithaca: Cornell University Press.

Kavanagh, D. and Seldon, A. (2000). 'The Power Behind the Prime Minister: The Hidden Influence of No. 10', in R. A. W. Rhodes (ed.), *Transforming British Government. vol. 2. Changing Roles and Relationships*. London: Macmillan.

Keating, M. (1998). *The New Regionalism in Western Europe: Territorial Restructuring and Political Change*. Cheltenham: Edward Elgar.

—— (2000). *New Regionalism in Western Europe*. Aldershot Hants.: Edward Elgar.

—— and Loughlin, J. (eds) (1996). *The Political Economy of Regions*. London: Frank Cass.

Keck, M. and Sikkink, K. (1998). *Activists Beyond Borders: Advocacy Networks in International Politics*. Cornell: Cornell University Press.

Keohane, R. O. (1984). *After Hegemony: Cooperation and Discord in the World Economy*. Princeton: Princeton University Press.

—— (1989). *International Institutions and State Power*. Boulder: Westview Press.

—— and Hoffmann, S. (eds) (1991). *The New European Community*. Boulder, CO: Westview Press.

Kerremans, B. (2000). 'Belgium', in H. Kassim, B. G. Peters, and V. Wright (eds), *The National Co-ordination of EU Policy: The Domestic Level*. Oxford: Oxford University Press.

Kickert, W., Llijn, E. H., and Koppenjan, J. (eds) (1997). *Managing Complex Networks*. London: Sage.

Kindleberger, C. (1969). *American Business Abroad*. New Haven: Yale University Press.

King, A. (ed.) (1969). *The British Prime Minister*. London: Macmillan.

—— (1975a). 'Overload: Problems of Governing in the 1970s'. *Political Studies*, 3.

—— (1975b). 'Executives', in: F. I. Greenstein and N. W. Polsby (eds), *Handbook of Political Science, vol. 5: Governmental Institutions and Practices*. Reading, MA: Addison-Wesley, pp. 173–256.

—— (1976). 'Modes of Executive-Legislative Relations: Great Britain, France, and West Germany'. *Legislative Studies Quarterly*, 1: 11–36.

—— (1981). 'The Rise of the Career Politician in Britain and its Consequences'. *British Journal of Political Science*, 11: 249–287.

Kingdon, J. (1984). *Agendas, Alternatives and Public Policies*. New York: Harper Collins.

—— (1990). *The Civil Service in Liberal Democracies*. London: Routledge.

Kirchheimer, O. (1966). 'The Transformation of the Western European Party Systems', in J. LaPalombara and M. Weiner (eds), *Political Parties and Political Development*. Princeton: Princeton University Press, pp. 177–200.

Kirchner, E. and Swaiger, K. (1981). *The Role of Interest Groups in the European Community*. Aldershot: Gower.

Kirkpatrick, J. J. (1982). *Dictatorships and Double Standards*. New York: Simon & Schuster.

Kitschelt, H. (1986). 'Political Opportunity Structures and Political Protest: Anti-Nuclear Movements in Four Democracies'. *British Journal of Political Science*, 16: 57–85.

—— Marks, G., Lange, P., and Stephens, J. (eds) (1999). *Change and Continuity in Contemporary Capitalism*. Cambridge: Cambridge University Press.

Kitts, J. A. (1999). 'Profit in Exodus: Age Dependence in Mortality of American Communes, 1609–1965'. American Sociological Association annual meeting.

—— (2002). *Community Ecology: Organizational Dynamics and the Mortality of American Communes, 1609–1965*. Ithaca, New York: Cornell University Dissertation.

Kjær, P. and Pedersen, O. K. (2001). 'Translating Liberalization: Neoliberalism in the Danish Negotiated Economy', in J. L. Campbell and O. K. Pedersen (eds), *The Rise of Neoliberalism and Institutional Analysis*. Princeton: Princeton University Press.

Kjellberg, A. (1998). 'Sweden: Restoring the Model?', in Ferner and Hyman (eds), *Changing Industrial Relations in Europe*. Oxford: Blackwell.

Klandermans, B., Kriesi, H., and Tarrow, S. (eds) (1988). *From Structure to Action*. Greenwich, CT: Jai Press.

Kleinman, M. (2002). *A European Welfare State? European Union Social Policy in Context*. London: Palgrave.

Knill, C. and Lenschow, A. (1998). 'Coping with Europe: The Implementation of EU Environmental Policy and Administrative Traditions in Germany and Britain'. *Journal of European Public Policy*, 5(4): 595–514.

Knudsen, T. (2000). 'How Informal Can You Be? The Case of Denmark', in B. G. Peters, R. A. W. Rhodes, and V. Wright (eds), *Administering the Summit: Administration of the Core Executive in Developed Countries*. Basingstoke: Macmillan, pp. 153–175.

Kohler-Koch, B. (1996). 'Catching up With Change: The Transformation of Governance in the European Union'. *Journal of European Public Policy*, 3(3): 359–380.

——(2000). 'Unternehmensverbände im Spannungsfeld von Europäisierung und Globalisierung', in W. Bührer and E. Grande (eds), *Unternehmerverbände und Staat in Deutschland*. Baden-Baden: Nomos.

——and Eising, R. (eds) (1999). *The Transformation of Governance in the European Union*. London: Routledge.

Kohn, H. (1967). *The Idea of Nationalism*. Toronto: Macmillan.

Kokott, J. (1996). 'German Constitutional Jurisprudence and European Integration'. *European Public Law*, 2: 237 and 413–436.

——(1998). 'Report on Germany', in A.-M. Slaughter, A. Stone Sweet, and J. H. H. Weiler (eds), *The European Court and National Courts, Doctrine and Jurisprudence*. Oxford: Hart Publishing.

Komorita, S. S. (1984). 'Coalition Bargaining'. *Advances in Experimental Social Psychology*, 18: 183–245.

Kooiman, J. (ed.) (1993). *Modern Governance*. London: Sage.

Koole, R. (1996). 'Cadre, Catch-All or Cartel: A Comment on the Notion of the Cartel Party'. *Party Politics*, 2: 507–523.

Koopmans, R. (1995). 'A Burning Question: Explaining the Rise of Racist and Extreme Right Violence in Western Europe', unpublished paper, Wissenschaftszentrum Berlin.

Kornai, J. (1992). *The Socialist System*. Princeton: Princeton University Press.

Korte, K.-R. (2000). 'Solutions for the Decision Dilemma: Political Styles of German Chancellors', *German Politics*, 9(1): 1–22.

Krasner, S. D. (1983). *International Regimes*. London: Cornell University Press.

——(1999a). *Sovereignty*. Princeton: Princeton University Press.

——(1999b). 'Globalization and Sovereignty', in D. A. Smith, D. J. Solinger, and S. C. Topik (eds), *States and Sovereignty in the Global Economy*. London: Routledge, 34–52.

Krieger, J. (1999). *British Politics in the Global Age*. New York: Oxford University Press.

Kriesi, H. (1999). 'Movements of the Left, Movements of the Right: Putting the Mobilization of Two New Types of Social Movements into Political Context', in Gary Marks *et al.* (eds), *Continuity and Change in Contemporary Capitalism*, ch. 14. New York and Cambridge: Cambridge University Press.

——(1996). 'The Organizational Structure of New Social Movements in a Political Context', in D. McAdam, J. McCarthy, and M. Zald (eds), *Comparative Perspectives on Social Movements*. New York and Cambridge: Cambridge University Press, pp. 152–184.

—— Koopmans, R., Duyvaendak, J.-W., and Giugni, M. G. (1995). *The Politics of New Social Movements in Western Europe*. Minneapolis: University of Minnesota Press.

Krugman, P. (1995). 'Growing World Trade: Causes and Consequences', in *Brookings Papers on Economic Activities*, pp. 327–362.

Kuhnle, S. (2000). 'Challenged, but Viable. The Scandinavian Welfare States in the 1990s', in M. Ferrera and M. Rhodes (eds), *Recasting European Welfare States*. London: Frank Cass, pp. 209–228.

Kumm, M. (1999). 'Who is the Final Arbiter of Constitutionality in Europe?: Three Conceptions of the Relationship between the German Federal Constitutional Court and the European Court of Justice'. *Common Market Law Review*, 36: 351–386.

Laffan, B. (1997). *The Finances of the European Union*. Basingstoke: Macmillan.

—— O'Donnell, R., and Smith, M. (2001), *Europe's Experimental Union. Rethinking Integration*. London: Routledge.

—— (2001). 'National Co-ordination in Brussels: The Role of Ireland's Permanent Representation', in H. Kassim, A. Menon, B. G. Peters, and V. Wright (eds), *The National Co-ordination of EU Policy: The European Level*. Oxford: Oxford University Press.

—— O'Donnell, R., and Smith, M. (2000). *Europe's Experimental Union. Rethinking Integration*. London: Routledge.

Lagroye, J. and Wright, V. (eds) (1979). *Local Government in Britain and France: Problems and Prospects*. London: Allen and Unwin.

Lane, D. (1976). *The Socialist Industrial State*. London: George Allen & Unwin.

Lane, J.-E. (2000). *New Public Management*. London: Routledge.

—— and Ersson, S. (1999). *Politics and Society in Western Europe*. London: Sage.

Lange, P., Irvin, C., and Tarrow, S. (1989). 'Phases of Mobilization: Social Movements in the Italian Communist Party since the 1960s'. *British Journal of Political Science*, 22: 15–42.

LaPalombara, J. (1964). *Interest Groups in Italian Politics*. Princeton: Princeton University Press.

Lascoumes, P. (1997). *Elites irrégulières. Essai sur la Délinquance d'affaires*. Paris: Gallimard.

—— (1999). *Corruptions*. Paris: Presses de Sciences Po.

—— and Le Bourhis, J. P. (1998). 'Le bien commun comme construit territorial, identités d'action et procédures'. *Politix*, 42.

Lasswell, H. D. (1948). *Power and Personality*. New York: Norton.

Laver, M. (1998). 'Models of Government Formation'. *Annual Review of Political Science*, 1: 1–25.

—— and Schofield, N. (1990). *Multiparty Government*. Oxford: Oxford University Press.

Laver, M. and Shepsle, K. A. (eds) (1994). *Cabinet Ministers and Parliamentary Government*. Cambridge: Cambridge University Press.

—— (1996). *Making and Breaking Governments; Cabinets and Legislatures in Parliamentary Democracies*. Cambridge: Cambridge University Press.

Laws, Sir J. (1995). 'Law and Democracy'. *Public Law*: 72–93.

Layne, C. (1995). 'The Unipolar Illusion: Why New Great Powers will Rise', in M. E. Brown, S. M. Lynn-Jones, and S. E. Miller (eds), *The Perils of Anarchy: Contemporary Realism and International Security*.

Lechner, F. J. and Boli, J. (eds) (2000). *The Globalization Reader*. Oxford: Blackwell.

Lee, J. M., Jones, G. W., and Burnham, J. (1998). *At the Centre of Whitehall: Advising the Prime Minister and Cabinet*. Basingstoke: Macmillan.

Le Galès, P. (2001*a*). 'Est Maître des lieux celui qui les organise. How rules change When National and European Policy Domains Collide', in N. Fligstein, W. Sandholtz, and A. Stone (eds), *The Institutionalisation of Europe*. Oxford: Oxford University Press.

—— (2001*b*). 'Les politiques locales', in J. Caillosse and D. Renard (eds), *Villes, droit et politiques publiques*. Paris: LGDJ.

—— (2002). *European Cities, Social Conflict and Governance*. Oxford: Oxford University Press.

—— and Lequesne, C. (eds) (1998). *Regions in Europe. The Paradox of Power*. London: Routledge.

Leibfried, S. (1993). 'Towards a European Welfare State?', in C. Jones (ed.), *New Perspectives on the Welfare State in Europe*. London: Routledge, pp. 133–156.

—— and Pierson, P. (1995). *European Social Policy: Between Fragmentation and Integration*. Washington DC: The Brookings Institution.

—— (2000). 'Social Policy: Left to Courts and Markets?', in H. Wallace and W. Wallace (eds), *Policy-Making in the European Union*, 4th edition. Oxford: Oxford University Press.

Leiserson, M. (1966). 'Factions and Coalitions in One-Party Japan: An Interpretation Based on the Theory of Games'. *American Political Science Review*, 62: 770–787.

Lepsius, M. R. (1997). 'Institutionalisierung und Deinstitutionalisierung von Rationalitätskriterien', in G. Göhler (ed.), *Institutionenwandel* (Leviathan Sonderheft 16), Opladen: Westdeutscher Verlag.

Lequesne, C. (1993). *Paris-Bruxelles: comment sefait la politique européenne de la France*. Paris: Presses de la Fondation Nationale des Sciences Politiques.

Lewin, M. (1988). *The Gorbachev Phenomenon: A Historical Interpretation*. Berkeley: University of California Press.

Lewis, J. (1992). 'Gender and Welfare Regimes'. *Journal of European Social Policy*, 2: 159–171.

—— (ed.) (1993). *Women and Social Policies in Europe: Work, Family and the State*. Aldershot: Edward Elgar.

—— (1998). 'Is the "Hard Bargaining" Image of the Council Misleading? The Committee of Permanent Representatives and the Local Elections Directive'. *Journal of Common Market Studies*, 36(4): 457–477.

—— (1999). 'Administrative Rivalry in the Council's Infrastructure: Diagnosing the Methods of Community in EU Decision-making'. Paper delivered at the Sixth Biennial ECSA International Conference, 2–5 June 1999.

Liegl, B. and Müller, W. C. (1999). 'Senior Officials in Austria', in E. C. Page and V. Wright (eds), *Bureaucratic Elites in Western European States: A Comparative Analysis of Top Officials*. Oxford: Oxford University Press, pp. 90–120.

Lijphart, A. (1977). *The Politics of Accommodation*. Berkeley: University of California Press.

—— (ed.) (1992). *Parliamentary versus Presidential Government*. Oxford: Oxford University Press.

—— (1999). *Patterns of Democracy; Government Forms and Performance in Thirty-Six Countries*. New Haven: Yale University Press.

Likierman, A. (1988). *Public Expenditure*. Suffolk: Penguin.

Lindberg, L. (1963). *The Political Dynamics of European Economic Integration*. Stanford: Stanford University Press.

Lindblom, C. (1977). *Politics and Markets*. New York: Basic Books.

Linklater, A. (1999). *The Transformation of Political Community: Ethical Foundations of the Post-Westphalian Era*. Cambridge: Polity Press.

Linz, J. J. (1973). 'Opposition in and under an Authoritarian Regime: the case of Spain' in R. Dahl (ed). *Regimes and Oppositions*. New Haven: Yale University Press.

Linz, J. J. (1990). 'The Perils of Presidentialism'. *Journal of Democracy*, 1: 51–69.

—— (1998). 'Democracy's Time Constraints'. *International Political Science Review*, 19: 19–37.

—— and Stepan, A. (1992). 'Political Identities and Electoral Sequences: Spain, the Soviet Union and Yugoslavia'. *Daedalus*, 121(2): 123–139.

Linz, J. J. (1996). *Problems of Democratic Transition and Consolidation: Southern Europe, South America, and Post-Communist Europe*. Baltimore: Johns Hopkins University Press.

Lipset, S. M. (1959). 'Some Social Requisites of Democracy: Economic Development and Political Legitimacy'. *American Political Science Review*, 53.

—— and Rokkan, S. (eds) (1967). *Party Systems and Voter Alignments*. New York: Free Press.

—— and Schneider, W. (1983). *The Confidence Gap*. New York: Free Press.

—— Trow, M., and Coleman, W. (1956). *Union Democracy*. New York: Free Press.

Llewellyn, D. T. (1997). *The Economics of Mutuality*. London: Building Societies Association.

Long, T. (1995). 'Shaping Public Policy in the European Union: a Case Study of the Structural Funds'. *Journal of European Public Policy*, 2(4): 672–679.

Lord, C. (2000). *Legitimacy, Democracy and the EU: When Abstract Questions Become Practical Policy Problems*, One Europe or Several, ESRC Programme, Policy Paper 03.

Lowe, R. and Rollings, N. (2000). 'Modernising Britain, 1957–64: A Classic Case of Centralisation and Fragmentation?', in R. A. W. Rhodes (ed.), *Transforming British Government. Vol. 1. Changing Institutions*. London: Macmillan.

Lowi, T. J. (1964). 'American Business, Public Policy, Case Studies and Political Theory'. *World Politics*, 16(4): 677–715.

—— (1971). *The Politics of Disorder*. New York: Norton.

—— (1979). *The End of Liberalism*, 2nd edition. New York: W.W. Norton.

Lübbe-Wolff, G. (2001). 'Effective Environmental legislation—on different philosophies of pollution control in Europe'. *Journal of Environmental Law*, 13(1): 79–87.

Ludlow, P. (1982). *The Making of the European Monetary System*. London: Butterworths.

Luebbert, G. (1986). *Comparative Democracy; Policy Making and Government Coalitions in Europe and Israel*. New York: Columbia University Press.

Lupia, A. and McCubbins. (1994) 'Learning From Oversight: Fire Alarms and Police Patrols Reconstructed'. *Journal of Law, Economics and Organization*, 10: 96–125.

MacCormick, N. (1993). 'Beyond the Sovereign State'. *Modern Law Review*, 56: 1–18.

—— (1995). 'The Maastricht-Urteil: Sovereignty Now'. *European Law Journal*, 1: 259–66.

—— (1996). 'Liberalism, Nationalism, and the Post-Sovereign State'. *Political Studies*, 44: 553–567.

—— (1999). *Questioning Sovereignty. Law State and Nation in the European Commonwealth*. Oxford: Oxford University Press.

MacDougall, D. *et al.* (1977). *Report of the Study Group on the Role of Public Finance in European Integration*. Brussels: Commission.

Machin, H. and Wright, V. (eds) (1985). *Economic Policy and Policy Making under the Mitterrand Presidency, 1981–1984*. London: Pinter.

MacIntyre A. (1983). 'The Indispensability of Political Theory', in D. Miller and L. Siedentop (eds), *The Nature of Political Theory*. Oxford: Clarendon Press.

Maclean, M. (1997). 'Privatisation, Dirigisme and the Global Economy: an end to French Exceptionalism'? *Modern & Contemporary France*, 5(2): 215–228.

Madgwick, P. (1991). *British Government: The Central Executive Territory*. New York: Philip Allan.

Magone, J. (2001). 'The Portuguese Permanent Representation in Brussels: The Institutionalization of a Simple System', in H. Kassim, A. Menon, B. G. Peters, and V. Wright (eds), *The National Co-ordination of EU Policy: The European Level*. Oxford: Oxford University Press.

Maher, I. (1996). 'Limitations on Community Regulation in the UK: Legal Culture and Multilevel Governance'. *Journal of European Public Policy*, 3(4): 577–593.

Mainwaring, S. (1993). 'Presidentialism, Multipartism and Democracy: the Difficult Combination'. *Comparative Political Studies*, 26(2): 198–228.
——(1998). 'Party Systems in the Third Wave'. *Journal of Democracy*, 9(3): 67–81.
——and Shugart, M. S. (1997). 'Juan Linz, Presidentialism and Democracy: A Critical Appraisal'. *Comparative Politics*, 29: 449–471.
Mair, Peter (1995). 'Political Parties, Popular Legitimacy and Public Privilege'. *West European Politics*, 18(3): 40–57.
——(2000). 'The Limited Impact of Europe on National Party Systems'. *West European Politics*, 23(4): 27–51.
——and van Biezen, I. (2001). 'Party Membership in Twenty European Democracies, 1980–2000'. *Party Politics*, 7: 5–23.
Majone, G. (1991a). 'Cross-national Sources of Regulatory Policy-making in Europe and the United States'. *Journal of Public Policy*, 11(1): 79–106.
——(1991b). *Market Integration and Regulation: Europe after 1992*, European University Institute Working Papers, SPS No. 91/10. Florence: European University Institute.
——(1993). *Deregulation or Re-regulation? Policymaking in the European Community Since the Single Act*. Working Paper, SPS 93/2. Florence: European University Institute.
——(1994a). 'The Rise of the Regulatory State in Europe', in W. C. Müller and V. Wright (eds), *The State in Western Europe: Retreat or Redefinition?* London: Frank Cass: 77–101.
——(1994b). *Understanding Regulatory Growth in the European Community*. Working Paper SPS 94/17. Florence: European University Institute.
——(1996). *Regulating Europe*. London: Routledge.
——(1997). 'From the Positive to the Regulatory State: Causes and Consequences of Changes in the Mode of Governance'. *Journal of Public Policy*, 17: 139–167.
——(1998). 'Europe's "Democratic Deficit": The Question of Standards'. *European Law Journal*, 4: 5–28.
——(1999). 'The Regulatory State and Its Legitimacy Problems'. *West European Politics*, 22: 1–24.
——(2000). 'The Credibility Crisis of Community Regulation'. *Journal of Common Market Studies*, 38: 273–302.
——(2001). 'Two Logics of Delegation: Agency and Fiduciary Relations in EU Governance'. *European Union Politics*, 2: 103–122.
Manning, N. et al. (1999). *Strategic Decision Making in Cabinet Government: Institutional Underpinnings and Obstacles*. Washington, DC: The World Bank; Sector Studies Series.
Manow, P. and Seils, E. (2000). 'The Employment Crisis of the German Welfare State', in M. Ferrera and M. Rhodes (eds.), *Recasting European Welfare States*. London: Frank Cass, pp. 137–160.
Maravall, J. M. (1997). *Regimes, Politics, and Markets*. Oxford: Oxford University Press.
March, J. G. and Olsen, J. P. (1989). *Rediscovering Institutions; The Organizational Basis of Politics*. New York: Free Press.
Marks, G. et al. (1996). 'Competencies, Cracks, and Conflicts', in G. Marks et al. *Governance in the European Union*. London: Sage.
——Scharpf, F. W., Schmitter, P. C., and Streeck, W. (1996). *Governance in the European Union*. London: Sage.
——Marks, G., Hooghe, L., and Blank, K. (1996). 'European Integration From the 1980s: State-Centre v Multi-level Governance'. *Journal of Common Market Studies*, 4(3): 34–78.
Marsh, D. and Rhodes, R. A. W. (1992). *Policy Networks in British Government*. Oxford: Oxford University Press.

Marsh, D., Smith, M. J., and Richards, D. (2000). 'Bureaucrats, Politicians and Reform in Whitehall: Analysing the Bureau-Shaping Model'. *British Journal of Political Science*, 30: 461–482.

Massenet, M. (1975). *La nouvelle gestion publique—pour un Etat sans bureaucratie*. Paris: Editions hommes et technique.

Mattli, W. and Slaughter, A.-M. (1998). 'The Role of National Courts in the Process of European Integration: Accounting for Judicial Preferences and Constraints', in A.-M. Slaughter, A. Stone Sweet, and J. H. H. Weiler (eds), *The European Court and National Courts, Doctrine and Jurisprudence*. Oxford: Hart Publishing.

Maurer, A. and Wessels, W. (2001). 'The German Case: A Key Moderator in a Competitive Multi-Level Environment', in H. Kassim, A. Menon, B. G. Peters, and V. Wright (eds), *The National Co-ordination of EU Policy: The European level*. Oxford: Oxford University Press.

Mayer, N. (1999). *Ces Français qui votent FN*. Paris: Flammarion.

Mayhew, D. R. (1991). *Divided We Govern; Party Control, Lawmaking, and Investigations 1946–1990*. New Haven: Yale University Press.

Mayntz, R. (1993). 'Governing Failures and the Problem of Governability', in J. Kooiman and R. Mayntz, *La teoria della governance: sfide e prospettive*. Rivista Italiana di scienza politica, vol. XXIX, n.1.

——and Scharpf, F. W. (1975). *Policy-Making in the German Federal Bureaucracy*. Amsterdam: Elsevier.

Mazey, S. (1992). 'Conception and Evolution of the High Authority's Administrative Services (1952–1956): From Supranational Principles to Multinational Practices', in 'Early European Community Administration'. *Yearbook of European Administrative History 4*. Baden-Baden: Nomos, pp. 31–49.

Mazey, S. (1995). 'The Development of EU Equality Policies: Bureaucratic Expansion on Behalf of Women? *Public Administration*, 73(4): 591–609.

——(1998). 'The European Union and Women's Rights: From the Europeanization of National Agendas to the Nationalization of a European Agenda?'. *Journal of European Public Policy*, 5(1): 131–152.

——and Richardson, J. J. (1992a). 'British Pressure Groups in the European Community: The Challenge of Brussels'. *Parliamentary Affairs*, 45(1): 92–107.

——(1992b). 'Environmental Groups and the EC: Challenges and Opportunities'. *Environmental Politics*, 1(4): 109–128.

——(eds) (1993a). *Lobbying in the European Community*. Oxford: Oxford University Press.

——(1993b). 'Interest Groups in the European Community', in J. J. Richardson (ed.), *Pressure Groups*. Oxford: Oxford University Press, pp. 191–213.

——(1994). 'Policy Coordination in Brussels: Environmental and Regional Policy'. *Regional Politics and Policy*, 4(1): 22–44.

——(1995). 'Promiscuous Policymaking: The European Policy Style'? in C. Rhodes and S. Mazey (eds), *The State of the European Union, vol. 3. Building a European Polity?* Boulder: Lynne Rienner and Longman Publishers, pp. 337–360.

——(1996). 'The Logic of Organization: Interest Groups', in J. J. Richardson (ed.), *European Union: Power and Public Policy-Making*. London: Routledge, pp. 200–215.

——(1996) 'Agenda-Setting, Lobbying, and the 1996 IGC', in G. Edwards and A. Pijpers (eds), *The European Union and the Agenda of 1996*. London: Pinter.

——(1997). 'Policy Framing: Interest Groups and the 1996 Inter-Governmental Conference'. *West European Politics*, 20(3): 111–133.

——(1999). 'Interests', in L. Cram, D. Dinan, and N. Nugent (eds), *Developments in the European Union*. London: Macmillan, pp. 105–29.

—— (2001). 'Institutionalising Promiscuity: Groups and European Integration', in W. Sandholtz and A. Stone Sweet (eds), *The Institutionalisation of European Space*. Oxford: Oxford University Press.

Mazlish, B. (1973). *In Search of Nixon*. Baltimore: Penguin.

McAdam, D. (1982). *Political Process and the Development of Black Insurgency 1930–1970*. Chicago, IL: University of Chicago Press.

—— (1983). 'Tactical Innovation and the Pace of Insurgency'. *American Sociological Review*, 48: 735–754.

—— (1988). *Freedom Summer*. Chicago: University of Chicago Press.

—— (1999). 'The Biographical Impact of Activism', in G. Marco, D. McAdam, and C. Tilly (eds), *How Social Movements Matter*. Minneapolis and London: University of Minnesota Press, pp. 119—148.

—— S. Tarrow, and C. Tilly, (2001). (eds) *Dynamics of Contention*. New York and Cambridge: Cambridge University Press.

—— McCarthy, J. D., and Zald, M. N. (1996). *Comparative Perspectives on Social Movements*. Cambridge: Cambridge University Press.

McCarthy, J. and Zald, M. (eds) (1987). *Social Movements in an Organizational Society*. New Brunswick, NJ: Transaction.

McCormick, J. (1999). *Understanding the European Union: A Concise Introduction*. Basingstoke: Macmillan.

McCubbins, M. D. and Schwartz, T. (1984). 'Congressional Oversight Overlooked: Police Patrols Versus Fire Alarms'. *American Journal of Political Science*, 2: 165–179.

McDonald, M. (1997). 'Identities in the European Commission', in N. Nugent (ed.), *At the Heart of the Union: Studies of the European Commission*. London: Routledge.

McKenzie, R. B. and Tullock, G. (1975). *The New World of Economics: Explorations in Human Experience*. Homewook III: Richard Irwin.

Mearscheimer, J. (1990). 'Back to the Future: Instability in Europe after the Cold War'. *International Security*, 15(5).

Melucci, A. (1985). 'The Symbolic Challenge of Contemporary Movements'. *Social Research*, 52: 789–815.

—— (1989). *Nomads of the Present*. London: Hutchinson Radius.

Menon, A. (2000). 'France', in H. Kassim, B. G. Peters, and V. Wright (eds), *The National Co-ordination of EU Policy: The Domestic Level*. Oxford: Oxford University Press, pp. 78–98.

—— (2001*a*). 'In Lieu of a Conclusion', in A. Menon and V. Wright (eds) *From the Nation State to Europe?* Oxford: Oxford University Press.

—— (2001*b*). 'The French Administration in Brussels', in H. Kassim, A. Menon, B. G. Peters, and V. Wright (eds), *The National Co-ordination of EU Policy: The European Level*. Oxford: Oxford University Press.

—— (2001*c*). 'Sectoral Determinants of International Cooperation: Defence Policy and the European Union', Paper Presented at the European University Institute. Florence, March.

—— (2001*d*). 'Organizations and Institutions: Member States and the European Union', Paper Presented to the APSA Annual Conference, San Francisco, August–September 2001.

—— (2002). 'Member States and International Institutions: Institutionalising Inter-governmentalism in the European Union'. Unpublished article.

—— and Hayward, J. (1996). 'States, Industrial Policies and the European Union', in H. Kassim and A. Menon (eds), *The European Union and National Industrial Policy*. London: Routledge, pp. 267–290.

Menon, A. and Weatherill, S. (2002). 'Legitimacy, Accountability and Delegation in the European Union', in A. Arnull and D. Wincott (eds), *Legitimacy in the European Union After Nice*. Oxford: Oxford University Press.

Menon, A. and Wright, V. (1998). 'The Paradoxes of "Failure": British EU Policy Making in Comparative Perspective'. *Public Policy and Administration*, 13(4): 46–66.

Mény, Y. (1992). *La corruption de la République*. Paris: Fayard.

—— (1996). 'Corruption "fin de siècle": changement, crise et transformation des valeurs'. *Revue internationale des sciences sociales*, 149: 359–370.

—— and Surel, Y. (2000). *Par le peuple, pour le peuple—Les Démocraties et le populisme*. Paris: Fayard.

—— and Wright, V. (eds) (1985a). *La crise de la sidérurgie européenne, 1974–1984*. Paris: PUF.

—— —— (eds) (1985b). *Centre-periphery Relations in Western Europe*. London: Allen and Unwin.

—— —— (eds) (1987). *The Politics of Steel: Western Europe and the Steel Industry in the Crisis Years (1974–1984)*. Berlin: de Gruyter.

Metcalf, L. K. (2000). 'Measuring Presidential Power'. *Comparative Political Studies*, 33(5): 660–685.

Metcalfe, L. (1992). 'After 1992: Can the Commission Manage Europe'? *Australian Journal of Public Administration*, 51(1): 117–130.

—— (1988). 'Institutional Inertia Versus Organizational Design: European Policy Coordination in the Member States'. ECPR Paper, Rimini.

—— (2000). 'Reforming the Commission'. *Journal of Common Market Studies*, 38(5): 817–842.

Meth-Cohn, D. and Müller, W. C. (1994). 'Looking Reality in the Eye: The Politics of Privatization in Austria', in V. Wright (ed.), *Privatization in Western Europe*. London: Pinter.

Meyer, D. S. and Tarrow, S. (eds) (1998). *The Social Movement Society: Contentious Politics for a New Century*. Lanham, MD: Rowman & Littlefield.

Michels, R. (1915). *Political Parties: A Sociological Study of the Oligarchial Tendencies of Modern Democracy*. New York: Collier Books.

Miliband, R. (1969). *The State in Capitalist Society*. New York: Basic Books.

Mills, C. W. (1956). *The Power Elite*. New York: Oxford University Press.

Milward, A. S. (2000). *The European Rescue of the Nation State*, 2nd edition. London: Routledge.

Mingione, E. (1991). *Fragmented Societies*. Oxford: Blackwell.

Moe, T. M. (1990). 'Political Institutions: the Neglected Side of the Story'. *Journal of Law, Economics and Organization*, 6: 213–253.

Mol, A. P. J., Lauber, V., and Liefferink, D. (eds) (2000). *The Voluntary Approach to Environmental Policy*. Oxford: Oxford University Press.

Molina, I. (2000). 'Spain', in H. Kassim, B. G. Peters, and V. Wright (eds), *The National Co-ordination of EU Policy: The Domestic Level*. Oxford: Oxford University Press, pp. 114–140.

Molina, O. and Rhodes, M. (2002). 'Corporatism: The Past, Present and Future of a Concept'. *Annual Review of Political Science*, vol. 5.

Mommsen, W. J. (1974). *The Age of Bureaucracy*. Oxford: Blackwell.

Monar, J. (2000). 'Justice and Home Affairs', in G. Edwards and G. Wiessala (eds), *Journal of Common Market Studies, Annual Review 1999/2000*: 125–142.

Montagu-Harris, G. (1926). *Local Government in Many Lands*. London: DS King.

Moore, B. (1966). *Social Origins of Dictatorship and Democracy*. Boston: Beacon.

Moran, M. (1994). 'The State and the Financial Services Revolution: A Comparative Analysis'. *West European Politics*, 17(3): 158–177.

—— (1999). *Governing the Health Care State: A Comparative Study of the United Kingdom, the United States and Germany*. Manchester: Manchester University Press.

—— (2002). 'Review Article: Understanding the Regulatory State'. *British Journal of Political Science*, 32: 391–413.

Moravcsik, A. (1991). 'Negotiating the Single Act: National Interests and Conventional Statecraft in the European Community'. *International Organization*, 45(1): 19–56.

—— (1993). 'Preferences and Power in the European Union: A Liberal Intergovernmentalist Approach'. *Journal of Common Market Studies*, 31(4): 473–524.

—— (1998). *The Choice for Europe: Social Purpose and State Power from Messina to Maastricht*. Ithaca: Cornell University Press.

—— (2001). 'Federalism in the European Union: Rhetoric and Reality', in K. Nicolaidis and R. Howse (eds), *The Federal Vision: Legitimacy and Levels of Governance in the United State and the European Union*. Oxford: Oxford University Press.

Moreno, L. (2000). 'The Spanish Development of Southern European Welfare', in S. Kuhnle (ed.), *Survival of the European Welfare State*. London: Routledge, pp. 146–165.

Morgan, K. (2001). 'Gender and the Welfare State: New Research on the Origins and Consequences of Social Policy Regimes'. *Comparative Politics*, 34(1): 105–124.

Morse, Edward L. (1972). 'Transnational Economic Processes', in Robert O. Keohane and Joseph S. Nye (eds), *Transnational Relations and World Politics*. Cambridge, Mass: Harvard University Press.

Morth, U. (2000). 'Competing Frames in the European Commission—the Case of the Defence Industry and the Equipment Issue'. *Journal of European Public Policy*, 7(2): 173–189.

Mosca, G. (1939). *The Ruling Class*. New York: McGraw Hill.

Mossberger, K. (2000). *The Politics of Ideas and the Spread of Enterprise Zones*. Washington, DC: Georgetown University Press.

Muller, P. (1989). *Airbus, l'Ambition européenne: Logique d'état, logique de marché*. Paris: l'Harmattan.

Müller, W. C. (1994). 'Political Traditions and the Role of the State'. *West European Politics*, 17(3): 32–51.

—— (2000b). 'Conclusion: Coalition Governance in Western Europe', in idem (eds), *Coalition Governments in Western Europe*. Oxford: Oxford University Press, pp. 559–592.

—— and Strøm, K. (eds) (1999). *Policy, Office or Votes? How Political Parties in Europe Make Hard Decisions*. Cambridge: Cambridge University Press.

—— (eds) (2000a). *Coalition Governments in Western Europe*. Oxford: Oxford University Press.

—— and Wright, V. (eds) (1994). 'The State in Western Europe: Retreat or Redefinition'? *West European Politics*, 17(3).

Murphy, T. V. and Roche, W. K. (eds) (1997). *Irish Industrial Relations in Practice*, 2nd edition. Dublin: Oak Tree Press.

Nas, M. (1995). 'Green, Greener, Greenest', in J. W. van Deth and E. Scarbrough (eds), *The Impact of Values*. Oxford: Oxford University Press.

Nedelmann, B. (1995). 'Gegensätze und Dynamik politischer Institutionen', in B. Nedelmann (ed.), *Politische Institutionen im Wandel*. Opladen: Westdeutscher Verlag, pp. 15–40.

Négrier, E. and Jouve, B. (eds) (1998). *Que gouvernent les régions en Europe?* Paris: L'Harmattan.

Neumann, S. (ed.) (1956). *Modern Political Parties*. Chicago: Chicago University Press.

Nichols, T. M. (1999). *The Russian Presidency*. New York: St. Martin's Press.

Niskanen, W. A. (1971). *Bureaucracy and Representative Government*. Chicago: Altine Atherton.

—— (1991). 'A Reflection on *Bureaucracy and Representative Government*', in A. Blais and S. Dion (eds), *The Budget-Maximizing Bureaucrat*. Pittsburgh: University of Pittsburgh Press, pp. 13–31.

Norris, P. (1999). *Critical Citizens*. Oxford: Oxford University Press.

Norton, P. (ed.) (1998). *Parliaments and Governments in Western Europe*. London: Cass.

——(2000). 'Barons in a Shrinking Kingdom: Senior Ministers in British Government', in R. A. W. Rhodes (ed.), *Transforming British Government. vol. 2. Changing Roles and Relationships*. London: Macmillan.

Nugent, N. (2001). *The European Commission*. Basingstoke: Palgrave.

——(2003). *The Government and Politics of the European Union*, 5th edition, Basingstoke: Macmillan.

Nunberg, B. (1999). *The State After Communism: Administrative Transitions in Central and Eastern Europe*. Washington, DC: The World Bank.

Nye, J. S. and Keohane, R. O. (1977). *Power and Interdependence: World Politics in Transition*. Boston: Little, Brown.

——(2000). 'Globalization: What's New? And What's Not (And So What?)'. *Foreign Policy*, 118: 104–112.

Oakeshott, M. (1975). 'On the Character of a Modern European State', *On Human Conduct*. Oxford: Clarendon Press.

Obstfeld, M. and Peri, G. (1998). 'Regional Non-adjustment and Fiscal Policy'. *Economic Policy*, April.

O'Connor, J. (1973). *The Fiscal Crisis of the State*. New York: St. James Press.

—— Orloff, A., and Shaver, S. (1999). *States, Markets, Families: Gender, Liberalism and Social Policy in Australia, Canada, Great Britain and the United States*. Cambridge: Cambridge University Press.

O'Donnell, G. (1996). 'Illusions about Consolidation'. *Journal of Democracy*, 7(2): 34–51.

Offe, C. (1984). *Contradictions of the Welfare State*. Cambridge, MA: MIT Press.

——(1984). *Disorganized Capitalism*. Cambridge, MA: MIT Press.

——(1985). 'New Social Movements: Challenging the Boundaries of Institutional Politics'. *Social Research*, 52: 817–868.

——(1990). 'Reflections on the Institutional Self-Transformation of Movement Politics: A Tentative Stage Model', in R. Dalton and M. Kuechler (eds), *Challenging the Political Order*. Oxford and New York, NY: Oxford University Press.

——(1996). 'Designing Institutions in East European Transitions', in R. Goodin (ed.), *The Theory of Institutional Design*. Cambridge: Cambridge University Press.

——(1999). 'How Can We Trust Our Fellow Citizens'? in M. E. Warren (ed.), *Democracy and Trust*. New York: Cambridge University Press, pp. 42–88.

Offerle, M. (1998). *Sociologie des groupes d'intérêt*. Paris: Montchrestien.

OECD (1996*a*). *Employment Outlook*. Paris: OECD.

OECD (1996*b*). *Social Assistance in OECD Countries: Synthesis Report*. Paris: OECD.

OECD (1998). *OECD Economic Surveys: United Kingdom*. Paris: OECD.

OECD (1999*a*). *Employment Outlook*. Paris: OECD.

OECD (1999*b*). *Benefit Systems and Work Incentives*. Paris: OECD.

OECD (2000). *Revenue Statistics (Statistical Compendium)*. Paris: OECD.

Ohmae, K. (1985). *Triad Power: the Coming Shape of Global Competition*. New York: Free Press.

——(1991). *The Borderless World: Power and Strategy in the Interlinked Economy*. New York: Harper Collins.

——(1995). *The End of the Nation State*. New York: Free Press.

Okun, A. M. (1975). *Equality and Efficiency: The Big Trade Off*. Oxford: Blackwell.

Olsen, J. P. (1997). 'European Challenges to the Nation State', in B. Steunenberg and F. van Vught (eds), *Political Institutions and Public Policy*. Amsterdam: Kluwer Academic Publishers, pp. 157–188.

Olson, M. (1982). *The Rise and Decline of Nations: Economic Growth, Stagflation and Social Rigidities*. New Haven: Yale University Press.

Oman, C. (1999). 'Globalization, Regionalization and Inequality', in A. Hurrell and N. Woods (eds), *Inequality, Globalization and World Politics*. Oxford: Oxford University Press.

O'Nuallain, C. and Hocheit, J.-M. (1985). *The Presidency of the European Council of Ministers*. London: Croom Helm.

Osborne, D. and Gaebler, T. (1992). *Reinventing Government*. Reading, MA: Addison Wesley.

Osieke, E. (1977). 'Ultra Vires Acts in International Organizations: The Experience of the International Labour Organization'. *British Yearbook of International Law*, 48: 259–80.

——(1983). 'The Legal Validity of Ultra Vires Decisions of International Organizations'. *American Journal of International Law*, 77: 239–256.

Padgett, S. (ed.) (1994). *Adenauer to Kohl: The Development of the German Chancellorship*. London: Hurst.

Padoa-Schioppa, T. (1994). *The Road to Monetary Union in Europe: The Emperor, the King, and the Genies*. Oxford: Clarendon Press.

——*et al.* (1987). *Efficiency, Stability, and Equity*. Oxford: Oxford University Press.

Page, E. C. (1985). *Political Authority and Bureaucratic Power*. Brighton: Harvester.

——(1990). 'British Political Science and Comparative Politics'. *Political Studies*, XXXVIII/3.

——(1991). *Localism and Centralism in Europe, the Political and Legal Bases of Local Self-Government*. Oxford: Oxford University Press.

——(1992). *Political Authority and Bureaucratic Power; a Comparative Analysis*, 2nd edition. New York: Harvester Wheatsheaf.

——(1995). 'Patterns and Diversity in European State Development', in J. Hayward and E. C. Page (eds), *Governing the New Europe*. Cambridge: Polity Press.

——(1997). *People Who Run Europe*. Oxford: Clarendon Press.

——and Goldsmith, M. (eds) (1987). *Central and Local Government Relations, a Comparative Analysis of West European Unitary State*. London: Sage.

——and Wright, V. (eds) (1999*a*). *Bureaucratic Elites in Western European States*. Oxford: Oxford University Press.

——(1999*b*). 'Conclusion: Senior Officials in Western Europe', in E. C. Page and V. Wright (eds), *Bureaucratic Elites in Western European States: A Comparative Analysis of Top Officials*. Oxford: Oxford University Press, pp. 266–279.

Panebianco, A. (1988). *Political Parties: Organization and Power*. Cambridge: Cambridge University Press.

Panitch, L. (1981). 'Trade Unions and the Capitalist State: Corporatism and its Contracitions'. *New Left Review*, 125 (Jan–Feb.): 21–44.

Papadopoulos, I. (2001). 'How does Direct Democracy Matter? The Impact of the Referendum on Politics and Policy Making', in J.-E. Lane (ed.), *The Swiss Labyrinth: Institutions, Outcomes and Redesign*. London: Frank Cass.

Pareto, V. (1935). *The Mind and Society*. New York: Harcourt, Brace.

Pasquino, P. (1998). 'Constitutional Adjudication and Democracy: Comparative Perspectives: USA, France and Italy'. *Ratio Juris*, 11: 38–50.

Pauly, L. (1995). 'Capital Mobility, State Autonomy and Political Legitimacy'. *Journal of International Affairs*, Winter, pp. 369–388.

Pederson, T. (2000). 'Denmark', in H. Kassim, B. G. Peters, and V. Wright (eds), *The National Co-ordination of EU Policy: the Domestic Level*. Oxford: Oxford University Press, pp. 219–234.

Pederson, W. D. (ed.) (1989). *The 'Barberian' Presidency. Theoretical and Empirical Readings*. New York: Lang.

Pedlar, R. H. and Schaefer, G. (1996). *Shaping European Law and Policy. The Role of Committees and Comitology in the Political Process.* Maastricht: European Institute of Public Administration.

—— and Van Schendelen, M. P. C. M. (eds) (1994). *Lobbying the European Union: Companies, Trade Associations and Issue Groups.* Aldershot: Dartmouth.

Perez-Dias, V. (1993). *The Return of Civil Society.* Cambridge, MA: Harvard University Press.

—— (2000). 'Globalization and Liberal Tradition'. Analistas Socio-Politicos Research Paper 35b, Madrid.

Perrineau, P. (1988). 'Front National: l'écho politique de l'anomie urbaine'. *Esprit*, March–April, pp. 22–38.

—— (1997). *Le symptome Le Pen.* Paris: Fayard.

Pestoff, V. A. (1991). *The Demise of the Swedish Model and the Resurgence of Organized Business as a Major Political Actor.* Stockholm: University of Stockholm, Department of Business Administration.

—— (1995). 'Towards a New Swedish Model of Collective Bargaining and Politics', in C. Crouch and F. Traxler (eds), *Organized Industrial Relations in Europe: What Future?*. Aldershot: Avebury.

Peters, B. G. (1986). 'Burning the Village: The Civil Service under Thatcher and Reagan'. *Parliamentary Affairs*, January.

—— (1991). 'The European Bureaucrat: the Applicability of *Bureaucracy and Representative Government* to Non-American Settings', in A. Blais and S. Dion (eds), *The Budget-Maximizing Bureaucrat.* Pittsburgh: University of Pittsburgh Press, pp. 303–353.

—— (1992). 'Bureaucratic Politics and the Institutions of the European Community', in A. M. Sbragia (ed.), *Euro-Politics, Institutions and Policy-Making in the 'New' European Community.* Washington, DC: The Brookings Institute, pp. 75–122.

—— (1994). 'Agenda Setting in the EU'. *Journal of European Public Policy*, 1(1): 9–26.

—— (1996). *The Future of Governing: Four Emerging Models.* Lawrence: University of Kansas Press.

—— (1997*a*). 'Bureaucrats and Political Appointees in European Democracies: Who's Who and Does it Make Any Difference?', in A. Farazmand (ed.), *Modern Systems of Government: Exploring the Role of Bureaucrats and Politicians.* London: Sage, pp. 232–254.

—— (1997*b*). 'The Commission and Implementation in the European Union: Is There an Implementation Deficit and Why'?, in N. Nugent (ed.), *At the Heart of the Union. Studies of the European Commission.* Basingstoke: Macmillan, pp. 187–202.

—— (1999). *Institutional Theory in Political Science. The 'New Institutionalism'.* London: Pinter.

—— (2001*a*). *The Future of Governing*, 2nd edition. Lawrence, KS: University of Kansas Press.

—— (2001*b*). 'Implicit and Explicit Contracts: Congress and Administrative Reform', in Y. Fortin (ed.), *Contracts and Legislatures.* Brussels: IIAS.

—— (2001*c*). 'The Anglo-American Administrative Tradition', in J. Halligan (ed.), *Anglo-American Administrative Systems.* Cheltenham: Edward Elgar.

—— (2001*d*). *The Politics of Bureaucracy*, 5th edition. London: Routledge.

—— and Goetz, K. H. (1999). *Institutional Theory and Political Executives: Creating Executive Organizations in East and West.* Paper presented at the Conference on Institutional Theory in Political Science, University of Strathclyde.

—— and Pierre, J. (2000). 'Citizens Versus the New Public Manager: The Problem of Mutual Empowerment'. *Administration and Society*, 22: 9–28.

—— and Wright, V. (1996). 'Public Policy and Administration, Old and New', in R. E. Goodin and H.-D. Klingemann (eds), *A New Handbook of Political Science*. Oxford: Oxford University Press, pp. 628–641.

—— Rhodes, R. A. W., and Wright, V. (eds) (2000a). *Administering the Summit: Administration of the Core Executive in Developed Countries*. Basingstoke: Macmillan.

—— —— (2000b). 'Staffing the Summit—the Administration of the Core Executive: Convergent Trends and National Specificities', in Peters *et al.* (eds), *Administering the Summit: Administration of the Core Executive in Developed Countries*. Basingstoke: Macmillan, pp. 3–22.

Peterson, J. (1991). 'Technology Policy in Europe: Explaining the Framework Programme and Eureka in Theory and Practice'. *Journal of Common Market Studies*, 39(3): 269–290.

—— (1995). 'Decision-Making in the EU: Towards a Framework for Analysis'. *Journal of European Public Policy*, 2(1): 69–93.

—— and Bomberg, E. (1999). *Decision-Making in the European Union*. Basingstoke: Macmillan.

Petriccione, R. (1986). 'Italy: Supremacy of Community Law over National Law'. *European Law Review*, 11: 320–327.

Pfiffner, J. P. (1996). *The Strategic Presidency; Hitting the Ground Running*, 2nd edition. Lawrence: The University Press of Kansas.

Pharr, S. and Putnam, R. (eds) (2000). *Disaffected Democracies*. Princeton: Princeton University Press.

—— (forthcoming), *Why Western Citizens Don't Trust their Governments*. Princeton: Princeton University Press.

Pierre, J. (ed.) (2000). *Debating Governance. Authority, Steering and Democracy*. Oxford: Oxford University Press.

Pierson, P. (1996). 'The Path to European Integration: A Historical Institutionalist Account'. *Comparative Political Studies*, 29(2): 123–164.

—— (ed.) (2001a). *The New Politics of the Welfare State*. Oxford: Oxford University Press.

—— (2001b). 'Coping with Permanent Austerity: Welfare State Restructuring in Affluent Democracies', in P. Pierson (ed.), *The New Politics of the Welfare State*. Oxford: Oxford University Press, pp. 410–456.

Piven, F. F. and Cloward, R. (1977). *Poor People's Movements: Why They Succeed, How They Fail*. New York, NY: Vintage Books.

—— —— (1992). 'The Normalization of Movements', in A. Morris and C. Mueller (eds), *Frontiers of Social Movement Theory*, ch. 13. New Haven, CT: Yale University Press.

Plottner, J. (1998). 'Report on France', in A.-M. Slaughter, A. Stone Sweet, and J. H. H. Weiler (eds), *The European Court and National Courts, Doctrine and Jurisprudence*. Oxford: Hart Publishing.

Pochet, P. (ed.) (1999). *Monetary Union and Collective Bargaining in Europe*. Brussels: Peter Lang.

Poggi, G. (1978). *The Development of the Modern State. A Sociological Introduction*. London: Hutchinson.

—— (1996). 'Une nouvelle phase de l'Etat', in S. Cassese and V. Wright (eds), *La recomposition de l'Etat en Europe*. Paris: La Découverte.

Poguntke, T. and Scarrow, S. (eds) (1996). 'The Politics of Anti-Party Sentiment'. *European Journal of Political Research* (Special issue), 29: 257–400.

Polanyi, K. (1957). *The Great Transformation*. Boston: Beacon Press.

Polidano, C. (1999). 'The Bureaucrat Who Fell Under a Bus: Ministerial Responsibility, Executive Agencies and the Derek Lewis Affair in Britain'. *Governance*, 12(2): 201–229.

Pollack, M. (1994). 'Creeping Competence: The Expanding Agenda of the European Community'. *Journal of Public Policy*, 14(2): 95–145.

—— (1997). 'Delegation, Agency and Agenda-Setting in the European Community'. *International Organization*, 51(1): 99–134.

—— (2000a). 'The Commission as an Agent', in N. Nugent (ed.), *At the Heart of the Union: Studies of the European Commission*, 2nd edition. Basingstoke: Macmillan, pp. 111–130.

—— (2000b). 'The End of Creeping Competence? EU Policy-Making Since Maastricht'. *Journal of Common Market Studies*, 38: 519–538.

—— and Hafner-Burton, E. (2000). 'Mainstreaming Gender in the European Union'. *Journal of European Public Policy*, 7(3): 432–456.

Pollitt, C. (1993). *Managerialism and the Public Services: Cuts or Cultural Change in the 1990s*, 2nd edition, Oxford: Blackwell.

—— and Bouckaert, G. (2000). *Public Management Reform. A Comparative Analysis*. Oxford: Clarendon Press.

Portes, R. and Rey, H. (1998). 'The Emergence of the Euro as an International Currency'. *Economic Policy*, 26: 307–343.

Poulantzas, N. (1972). 'The Problem of the Capitalist State', in R. Blackburn (ed.), *Ideology in the Social Sciences*. London: Fontana, pp. 238–253.

Pressman, J. L. and Wildalvsky, A. B. (1973). *Implementation*. Berkeley: University of California Press.

Preston, M. (1998). 'The European Commission and Special Interest Groups', in P. Claeys, C. Gobin, I. Smets, and P. Winnand (eds), *Lobbying, Pluralism and European Integration*. Brussels: Brussels European University Press.

Prewitt, K. and McAllister, W. (1976). 'Changes in the American Executive Elite; 1930–1970', in: H. Eulau and M. M. Czudnowski (eds), *Elite Recruitment in Democratic Polities*. New York: Sage.

Prosser, T. (1997). *Law and the Regulators*. Oxford: Clarendon Press.

Pryke, R. (1981). *The Nationalised Industries: Policies and Performance since 1968*. Oxford: Robertson.

Przeworski, A. and Limongi, F. (1997). 'Modernization: Theories and Facts'. *World Politics*, 49: 155–183.

—— and Sprague, J. (1986). *Paper Stones*. Chicago: University of Chicago Press.

—— and Wallerstein, M. (1982). 'The Structure of Class Conflict in Democratic Capitalist Societies'. *American Political Science Review*, 76: 215–238.

—— Stokes, S. C., and Manin, B. (eds) (1999). *Democracy, Accountability and Representation*. New York: Cambridge University Press.

—— Alvarez, M., Cheibub, J. A., and Limongi, F. (1996). 'What Makes Democracies Endure?'. *Journal of Democracy*, 7(1): 39–55.

—— (2000). *Democracy and Development. Political Institutions and Well-Being in the World, 1950–1990*. New York: Cambridge University Press.

Pujas, V. and Rhodes, M. (1999). 'Party Finance and Political Scandal in Italy, Spain and France'. *West European Politics*, 22(3): 41–63.

Putnam, R. D. (1993). *Making Democracy Work*. Princeton: Princeton University Press.

—— (ed.) (2002). *Democracies in Flux*. Oxford: Oxford University Press.

Quelin, B. (1994). 'La Déréglementation en Marche'. *Revue d'Économie Industrielle*, 68(2): 107–116.

Quinn, D. (1997). 'The Correlates of Change in International Financial Regulation'. *American Political Science Review*, 91: 531–551.

Radaelli, C. (1999). 'The Public Policy of the European Union: Whither Politics of Expertise'. *Journal of European Public Policy*, 6(5): 757–776.

Radin, B. A. (1998). 'The Government Performance and Results Act (GPRA): Hydra-Headed Monster or Flexible Management Tool?'. *Public Administration Review*, 58: 307–316.

Randall, V. (1997). 'Childcare Policy in the European States: Limits to Convergence'. *Journal of European Public Policy*, 2000, 7(3): 346–368.

Raunio, T. and Hix, S. (2000). 'Backbenchers Learn to Fight Back: European Integration and Parliamentary Government', in K. H. Goetz and S. Hix (eds), *Europeanised Politics? European Integration and National Political Systems*. London: Frank Cass.

Raz, J. (1998). 'On the Authority and Interpretation of Constitutions: Some Preliminaries', in L. Alexander (ed.), *Constitutionalism*. Cambridge: Cambridge University Press.

Redford, E. (1969). *Democracy in the Administrative State*. New York: Oxford University Press.

Redwood, J. and Hatch, J. (1982). *Controlling Public Expenditure*. Oxford: Basil Blackwell.

Recchi, E. (1996). 'Parliamentary Recruitment and Consociationalism in the First and Second Italian Republics'. *West European Politics*, 19(2): 340–360.

Reich, R. (1991). *The Work of Nations*. New York: Knopf.

—— (1996). 'Judge-made Europe à la Carte'. *European Journal of International Law*, 7: 103–111.

Rein, M. and Schon, D. (1991). 'Frame-reflective Policy Discourse', in P. Wagner, C. Hirschon Weiss, B. Wittrock, and H. Wollman (eds), *Social Sciences and Modern States: National Experiences and Theoretical Crossroads*. Cambridge: Cambridge University Press, pp. 262–289.

Reiter, H. L. (1989). 'Party Decline in the West: A Sceptics View'. *Journal of Theoretical Politics*, 1: 325–348.

Reynaud, J.-D. (1975). *Les Syndicats en France*. Paris: Seuil.

Rhodes, M. (2000a). 'Restructuring the British Welfare State: Between Domestic Constraints and Global Imperatives', in F. W. Scharpf and V. Schmidt (eds), *Work and Welfare in Open Economies: vol. 2—Diverse Responses to Common Challenges*. Oxford: Oxford University Press, pp. 19–68.

—— (2000b). 'Desperately Seeking a Solution: Social Democracy, Thatcherism and the "Third Way" in British Welfare'. *West European Politics*, 23(2): 161–186.

—— (2001). 'The Political Economy of Social Pacts: "Competitive Corporatism" and European Welfare Reform', in P. Pierson (ed.), *The New Politics of the Welfare State*. Oxford: Oxford University Press, pp. 165–194.

—— (2002a). 'Globalisation, EMU and Welfare State Futures', in E. Jones, P. Heywood, and M. Rhodes (eds), *Developments in West European Politics*. London: Palgrave.

—— (2002b). 'Why EMU is—or May Be—Good for European Welfare States', in K. Dyson (ed.), *European States and the Euro: Europeanization, Variation and Convergence*. Oxford: Oxford University Press, pp. 305–333.

Rhodes, R. A. W. (1981). *Control and Power in Central-Local Relations*. Farnborough: Gower.

—— (1988). *Beyond Westminster and Whitehall*. London: Unwin-Hyman. Reprinted Routledge, 1992.

—— (1994). 'The Hollowing Out of the State; the Changing Nature of the Public Service in Britain'. *Political Quarterly*, 65: 138–151.

—— (1997a). *Understanding Governance*. Buckingham: Open University Press.

—— (1997b). ' "Shackling the Leader"? Coherence, Capacity and the Hollow Crown', in P. M. Weller, H. Bakvis, and R. A. W. Rhodes (eds), *The Hollow Crown*. London: Macmillan, pp. 198–223.

—— (1999) [1981]. *Control and Power in Central-Local Government Relationships*. Farnborough: Gower. New edition (Aldershot: Ashgate).

Rhodes, R. A. W. (2000*a*). 'Public Administration and Governance', in J. Pierre (ed.), *Debating Governance*. Oxford: Oxford University Press.

—— (ed.) (2000*b*). *Transforming British Government, vol. 1. Changing Institutions, vol. 2. Changing Roles and Relationships*. London: Macmillan.

—— (2001). 'Unitary States', in N. J. Smelser and P. B. Baltes (eds), *International Encyclopaedia of the Social and Behavioural Sciences*. Oxford: Pergamon.

—— and Dunleavy, P. (eds) (1995). *Prime Minister, Cabinet and Core Executive*. London: Macmillan.

—— Bache, I., and George, S. (1996). 'Policy Networks and Policy-Making in the European Union: A Critical Approach', in L. Hooghe (ed.), *Cohesion Policy and European Integration: Building Multi-Level Governance*. Oxford: Oxford University Press.

Rials, S. (1977). *Administration et Organisation 1910–1930*. Paris: Beauchesne.

Richards, D. (2000). 'The Conservatives, New Labour and Whitehall: A Biographical Examination of the Political Flexibility of the Mandarin Cadre', in K. Theakston (ed.), *Bureaucrats and Leadership*. Basingstoke: Macmillan, pp. 91–117.

Richardson, J. J. (ed.) (1982). *Policy Styles in Western Europe*. London: Allen and Unwin.

—— (1994). 'The Politics and Practice of Privatisation in Britain', in V. Wright (ed.), *Privatization in Western Europe. Pressures, Problems and Paradoxes*. London: Pinter.

Richardson, J. J. (ed) (1996). 'Policy-Making in the EU: Interests, Ideas and Garbage Cans of Primeval Soup', in J. Richardson (ed.), *European Union: Power and Policy-Making*. London: Routledge.

—— (2000). 'Government, Interest Groups and Policy Change'. *Political Studies*, 48(5).

—— and Jordan, A. G. (1979). *Governing Under Pressure*. Oxford: Martin Robertson.

Riggs Fuller, S. and Aldag, R. J. (1997). 'Challenging the Mindguards: Moving Small Group Analysis Beyond Groupthink', in P. 't Hart, E. K. Stern, and B. Sundelius (eds), *Beyond Groupthink. Political Group Dynamics and Foreign Policy-Making*. Ann Arbor: University of Michigan Press, pp. 55–93.

Riker, W. (1962). *The Theory of Political Coalitions*. New Haven: Yale University Press.

Rintala, M. (1984). 'The Love of Power and the Power of Love: Churchill's Childhood'. *Political Psychology*, 5: 375–390.

Ritchie, E. (1992). 'The Development of *Cabinets* within the High Authority', in 'Early European Community Administration'. *Yearbook of European Administrative History 4*. Baden-Baden: Nomos, pp. 95–106.

Rittberger, B. (2000). 'Impatient Legislators and New Issue Dimensions: A Critique of Garrett and Tsebelis "Standard Version" of Legislative Politic'. *Journal of European Public Policy*, 7(4): 554–575.

Rittberger, V. (2001). *German Foreign Policy Since Unification: Theories and Case Studies*. Manchester: Manchester University Press.

—— *et al.* (1993). *Regime Theory and International Relations*. Oxford: Clarendon Press.

Rochon, T. (1998). *Culture Moves: Ideas, Activism and Changing Values*. Princeton, NJ: Princeton University Press.

Rodrik, D. (1997). *Has Globalization Gone Too Far?* Washington, DC: Institute for International Economics.

Roeder, P. (1999). 'Peoples and States after 1989: The Political Costs of Incomplete National Revolutions'. *Slavic Review*, 58(4): 854–883.

Rokkan, S. (1970). *Citizens, Elections, Parties: Approaches to the Comparative Study of the Process of Development*. Oslo: Universitetsforlaget.

Rosamond, B. (2000). *Theories of European Integration*. Basingstoke: Macmillan.

Rose, R. (1981). *Do Parties Make a Difference?* London: Macmillan.

—— (1984). *Understanding Big Government.* London: Sage.

—— (1985). *Public Employment in Western Nations.* Cambridge: Cambridge University Press.

—— (1991). 'Comparing Forms of Comparative Analysis'. *Political Studies*, XXXIX/3.

—— (1993). *Lesson-drawing in Public Policy: A Guide to Learning Across Time and Space.* Chatham, NJ: Chatham House Publishers.

—— (1995). 'Mobilizing Demobilized Voters in Communist Societies'. *Working Papers*, no 76. Madrid: Juan March Institute.

—— and Peters, B. G. (1978). *Can Government Go Bankrupt?* New York: Basic Books.

Ross, G. (1995). *Jacques Delors and European Integration.* Cambridge: Polity Press.

Roth, G. (1963). *The Social Democrats in Imperial Germany: A Study on Working-Class Isolation and National Integration.* Totowa, NJ: Bedminster.

Rothschild, E. (1995). 'What is Security?'. *Daedalus* (Summer 1995).

—— (1999). 'Globalization and the Return of History'. *Foreign Policy*, 115: 106–116.

Rothstein, B. (1998). 'Breakdown of Trust and the Fall of the Swedish Model'. Paper presented to the Seminar on the State and Capitalism since 1800, Harvard University, December.

—— (2000). *Just Institutions Matter: The Moral and Political Logic of the Universal Welfare State.* Cambridge: Cambridge University Press.

Rouban, L. (1997). 'La crise du service public en France: l'Europe comme catalyseur'. *Culture et Conflits*, 28: 99–124.

Rueschemeyer, D., Stephens, J., and Stephens, E. H. (1992). *Capitalist Development and Democracy.* Chicago: University of Chicago Press.

Ruggie (1993). *Multilateralism Matters: The Theory and Praxis of an Institutional Form.* New York: Colombia University Press.

Ruzza, C. and Schmidtke, O. (1993). 'Roots of Success of the Lega Lombarda'. *West European Politics*, 16(2): 2–23.

Sabatier, P. (1988). 'An Advocacy Coalition Framework of Policy Change and the Role of Policy Orientated Learning Therein'. *Policy Sciences*, 21: 128–168.

Sainsbury, D. (1996). *Gender, Equality and Welfare States.* Cambridge: Cambridge University Press.

Salvati, M. (1981). 'May 1968 and the Hot Autumn of 1969: The Responses of Two Ruling Classes', in S. Berger (ed.), *Organizing Interests in Western Europe.* Cambridge and New York: Cambridge University Press, pp. 329–363.

Sandholtz, W. and Stone Sweet, A. (1998). *European Integration and Supranational Governance.* Oxford: Oxford University Press.

Sandholtz, W. and Zysman, J. (1989). '1992: Recasting the European Bargain'. *World Politics*, 42: 1–30.

Sartori, G. (1976). *Parties and Party Systems.* Cambridge: Cambridge University Press.

Sasse, C. *et al.* (1977). *Decision-Making in the European Community.* New York: Praeger.

Sasse, C., Poullet, E., Coombes, D., Deprez, G. (1997). *Decision Making in the European Community.* New York: Praeger.

Saussois, J.-M. (1997). 'La fin de l'exception française'. *Revue Française de Gestion*, 115: 57–68.

Savoie, D. J. (1994). *Reagan, Thatcher, Mulroney: In Search of a New Bureaucracy.* Pittsburgh: University of Pittsburgh Press.

Saward, M. (1997). 'In Search of the Hollow Crown', in P. M. Weller, H. Bakvis, and R. A. W. Rhodes (eds), *The Hollow Crown.* London: Macmillan, pp. 16–36.

Scarrow, S. E. (2000). 'Parties without Members? Party Organization in a Changing Electoral Environment', in R. J. Dalton and M. P. Wattenberg (eds), *Parties without Partisans: Political Change in Advanced Industrial Societies.* Oxford: Oxford University Press.

Scarrow, S. E., Webb, P., and Farrell, D. M. (2000). 'From Social Integration to Electoral Contestation: The Changing Distribution of Power within Political Parties', in R. J. Dalton and M. P. Wattenberg (eds), *Parties without Partisans: Political Change in Advanced Industrial Societies*. Oxford: Oxford University Press.

Scharpf, F. W. (1991). *Crisis and Choice in European Social Democracy*. Ithaca, NY: Cornell University Press.

——(1994). 'Community and Autonomy: Multi-Level Policy Making in the European Community'. *Journal of European Policy*, 1(2): 219–242.

——(1997a). *Combating Unemployment in Continental Europe*. Florence, EUI, Robert Schuman Centre Working Paper, no. 97/3.

——(1997b). *Games Real Actors Play*. Boulder, CO: Westview Press.

——(1999). *Governing in Europe: Effective and Democratic?* Oxford: Oxford University Press.

——(2000). 'The Viability of Advanced Welfare States in the International Economy: Vulnerabilities and Options'. *European Review*, 8(3): 399–425.

—— and Schmidt, V. (eds) (2000). *Work and Welfare in Open Economies, vols. 1 and 2*. Oxford: Oxford University Press, pp. 19–68.

Scharpf, F. W. (2002). 'The European Social Model: Coping with the Challenges of Diversity'. Paper presented to the 40th Anniversary Conference of the *Journal of Common Market Studies*, European University Institute. Florence: Italy, 11–13 April.

Schedler, A. (1998). 'What is Democratic Consolidation'? *Journal of Democracy*, 9(2), 91–107.

Schilling, T. (1996). 'The Autonomy of the Community Legal Order—An Analysis of Possible Foundations'. *Harvard International Law Journal*, 37: 389–409.

Schmidt, M. G. (1996). 'When Parties Matter: a Review of the Possibilities and Limits of Partisan Influence on Public Policy'. *European Journal of Political Research*, 30: 155–183.

Schmidt, S. K. (1997). 'Sterile Debate and Dubious Generalisations: European Integration Theory Tested by Telecommunications and Electricity'. *Journal of Public Policy*, 16(3): 233–271.

——(2000). 'Only an Agenda Setter? The European Commission's Powers Over the Council of Ministers', *European Union Politics*, 1(1): 37–61.

——(2000). 'Only an Agenda Setter? The European Commission's Power Over the Council of Ministers'. *European Union Politics*, 1(1): 37–61.

Schmidt, V. A. (1996). *From State to Market? The Transformation of French Business and Government*. Cambridge: Cambridge University Press.

——(1997). 'Running on Empty: the End of *Dirigisme* in French Economic Leadership'. *Modern & Contemporary France*, 5(2): 229–241.

Schmitter, P. (1974). 'Still the Century of Corporatism'. *Review of Politics*, 36: 85–131.

——(1994). 'Dangers and Dilemmas of Democracy'. *Journal of Democracy*, 5(2): 57–74.

——(1997). 'The Emerging Europolity and Its Impact Upon National Systems of Production', in J. R. Hollingsworth and R. Boyer (eds), *Contemporary Capitalism*. Cambridge: Cambridge University Press.

—— and Brouwer, I. (2000). 'Promozione e Protezione della Democracia. Il Concetto, le Ricerche, la Valutazione'. *Rivista Italiana di Scienza Politica*, 2: 187–226.

—— and Grote, J. (1997). *The Corporatist Sisyphus: Past, Present and Future*, Working Paper SPS 97(4). Florence: European University Institute.

—— and Lehmbruch, G. (eds) (1979). *Trends Toward Corporatist Intermediation*. Beverly Hills: Sage.

Scholte (2000). *Globalization: A Critical Introduction*. Basingstoke: Macmillan.

Schulze G. and Ursprung, H. (1999). 'Globalisation of the Economy and the Nation State'. *The World Economy*, 22(3): 295–352.

Schumpeter, J. (1942). *Capitalism, Socialism and Democracy.* New York: Harper.

Scully, R. (1997). 'The European Parliament and the Co-decision Procedure: a Re-assessment'. *Journal of Legislative Studies*, 3(3): 58–73.

Searing, D. D. (1994). *Westminster's World. Understanding Political Roles.* Cambridge: Harvard University Press.

Secker, W. P. (1991). *Ministers in Beeld; de Sociale en Functionele Herkomst van de Nederlandse Ministers (1848–1990)*, (with a summary in English). Leiden: DSWO Press.

Secretariat General of the Council of the European Union (1997). *Council Guidexs: vol. I. Presidency Handbook.* Luxembourg: Office for Official Publications of the European Communities.

Selden, S. (1996). *The Search for Representative Bureaucracy.* Armonk, NY: M.E. Sharpe.

Self, P. (1977). *Econocrats and the Policy Process: The Politics and Philosophy of Cost-Benefit Analysis.* London: Macmillan.

—— (1993). *Government by the Market?* Macmillan: Westview.

Sellers, J. (2002). *Governing from Below. Urban Politics and Post-Industrial Economy.* Cambridge: Cambridge University Press.

Sharpe, L. J. (ed.) (1993). *The Rise of Meso Government in Europe.* London: Sage.

Shaw, J. (2000). *Social Law and Policy in an Evolving European Union.* Oxford and Portland: Hart Publishing.

Sherrington, P. (2000). *The Council of Ministers: Political Authority in the European Union.* London: Pinter.

Shonfield, A. (1965). *Modern Capitalism.* London: Oxford University Press.

Shugart, M. (1996). 'Executive-Legislative Relations in Post-Communist Europe'. *Transition*, 13: 355–365.

—— and Carey, J. M. (1992). *Presidents and Assemblies.* New York: Cambridge University Press.

Siaroff, A. (2000). 'Women's Representation in Legislatures and Cabinets in Industrial Democracies'. *International Political Science Review*, 21: 197–215.

Siedentop, L. (2001). *Democracy in Europe.* New York: Columbia University Press.

Siedentopf, M. and Ziller, J. (1988). *Making European Policies Work.* London: Sage.

Simmons, B. A. (1999). 'The Internationalization of Capital', in H. Kitschelt, P. Lange, G. Marks, and J. D. Stevens (eds), *Continuity and Change in Contemporary Capitalism.* Cambridge: Cambridge University Press.

Skach, C. (1999). *Semi-Presidentialism and Democracy.* D.Phil. Thesis, University of Oxford.

Skalnik Leff, C. (1999). 'Democratization and Disintegration in Multinational States: the Breakup of the Communist Federations'. *World Politics*, 51(2): 205–235.

Slaughter, A.-M. (1992) (1999). 'Governing the Global Economy Through Government Networks', in M. Byers (ed.), *The Role of Law in International Politics: Essays in International Relations and International Law.* Oxford: Oxford University Press, pp. 177–205.

Smith, G. (1972), *Politics in Western Europe. A Comparative Analysis.* London: Heinemann.

Smith, G. (1990). 'Core Persistence and Party System Change', in P. Mair and G. Smith (eds), *Understanding Party System Change in Western Europe.* London: Frank Cass.

—— (1999). 'Seeking to Understand European Politics', in H. Daalder (ed.), *Comparative European Politics. The Story of a Profession.* London: Pinter.

Smith, M. J. (1990). *The Politics of Agricultural Support in Britain: the Development of the Agricultural Policy Community.* Aldershot: Dartmouth Press.

Smith, M. J. (1999). *The Core Executive in Britain.* London: Macmillan.

Smith, R. (1995). *The Left's Dirty Job. The Politics of Industrial Restructuring in France and Spain.* Pittsburgh: University of Pittsburgh Press.

Smouts, M. C. (1998). 'Region as a new imagined community?', in P. Le Galès and C. Lequesne (eds). *Regions in Europe: the paradox of power*. London: Routledge.

Sobel, A. (1994). *Domestic Choices, International Markets: Dismantling National Barriers and Liberalizing Securities Markets*. Ann Arbor: University of Michigan Press.

Soysal, Y. (1994). *Limits of Citizenship*. Chicago: University of Chicago Press.

Spanou, C. (2001). 'Permanent Challenges? Representing Greece in Brussels', in H. Kassim, A. Menon, B. G. Peters, and V. Wright (eds), *The National Co-ordination of EU Policy: The European Level*. Oxford: Oxford University Press.

Spence, D. (1993). 'The Role of the National Civil Service in European Lobbying: The British Case', in S. Mazey and J. Richardson (eds), *Lobbying in the European Community*. Oxford: Oxford University Press, pp. 47–73.

——(1995). 'The Co-ordination of European Policy by the Member States', in M. Westlake (ed.), *The Council of the European Union*. London: Cartermill Publishing.

—— (2000). 'Plus ça change, plus c'est la même chose? Attempting to Reform the European Commission'. *Journal of European Public Policy*, 7(1): 1–25.

Spierenberg, D. (1979). *Proposals for Reform of the Commission of the European Communities and Its Services*. Brussels, Commission of the European Communities.

Stepan, A. and Skach, C. (1993). 'Constitutional Frameworks and Democratic Consolidation'. *World Politics*, 46: 1–22.

Stephens, J. D. (1996). 'The Scandinavian Welfare States: Achievements, Crisis and Prospects', in G. Esping-Andersen (ed.), *Welfare States in Transition: National Adaptations in Global Economies*. London: Sage Publications, pp. 32–65.

——Huber, E., and Ray, L. (1999). 'The Welfare State in Hard Times', in H. Kitschelt, P. Lange, G. Marks, and J. D. Stevens, (eds), *Continuity and Change in Contemporary Capitalism*. Cambridge: Cambridge University Press.

Stevens, A. and Stevens, H. (2001). *Brussels Bureaucrats? The Administration of the European Union*. Basingstoke: Palgrave.

Stewart, R. (1975). 'The Reformation of American Administrative Law'. *Harvard Law Review*, 88: 1667–1813.

Stillman, R. J. (1991). *Preface to Public Administration: A Search for Themes and Direction*. New York: St. Martin's.

Stoffaës, C. (1983). *Politique Industrielle*. Paris: Les Cours de Droit.

Stoker, G. (ed.) (2000). *The New Politics of British Local Governance*. Basingtoke: Macmillan.

Stoleru, L. (1969). *L'Impératif Industriel*. Paris: Éditions du Seuil.

Stone Sweet, A. (1998). 'Constitutional Dialogues in the European Community', in A.-M. Slaughter, A. Stone Sweet, and J. H. H. Weiler (eds), *The European Court and National Courts, Doctrine and Jurisprudence*. Oxford: Hart Publishing.

——(2000). *Governing with Judges: Constitutional Politics in Europe*. Oxford: Oxford University Press.

Strange, S. (1996). *The Retreat from the State: the Diffusion of Power in the World Economy*. Cambridge: Cambridge University Press.

Streeck, W. (1995). 'From Market-Making to State-Building: Reflections on the Political Economy of European Social Policy', in S. Leibfried and P. Pierson (eds), *European Social Policy*. Washington: Brookings, pp. 359–441.

—— and Schmitter, P. (1985). 'Community, Market, State-Association?', in *Private Interest Government: Beyond Market and State*. Beverly Hills: Sage.

——(1991). 'From National Corporatism to Transnational Pluralism: Organised Interests in the Single European Market'. *Politics and Society*, 19(1): 133–164.

Strøm, K. (1990). *Minority Government and Majority Rule.* Cambridge: Cambridge University Press.

—— (2000). 'Parties at the Core of Government', in R. J. Dalton and M. P. Wattenberg (eds), *Parties without Partisans: Political Change in Advanced Industrial Societies.* Oxford: Oxford University Press.

—— Müller, W. C., and Torbjörn, B. (eds) (2003). *Delegation and Accountability in Parliamentary Democracies.* Oxford: Oxford University Press.

Suleiman, E. (1974). *Politics, Power and Bureaucracy in France.* Princeton: Princeton University Press.

—— (ed.) (1984). *Bureaucrats and Policy-Making.* New York: Holmes and Meier.

—— and Courty, G. (1997). *L'Âge d'or de l'État.* Paris: Éditions du Seuil.

Surel, Y. (2000). 'The Role of Cognitive and Normative Frames in Policy Making'. *Journal of European Public Policy,* 7(4).

Sutcliffe, B. and Glyn, A. (1999). 'Still Underwhelmed: Indicators of Globalization and their Misinterpretation'. *Review of Radical Political Economics,* 31(1): 111–132.

Sutherland, P. (1992). *Report to the Commission by the High Level Group on the Operation of the Internal Market. The Internal Market after 1992. Meeting the Challenge.* Brussels: EU Commission.

Swank, D. (1998). 'Funding the Welfare State: Globalization and Taxation of Business in Advanced Market Economies'. *Political Studies,* 46: 671–692.

—— (2002). *Diminished Democracy? Global Capital, Political Institutions, and Policy Change in Developed Welfare States.* Cambridge: Cambridge University Press.

Taggart, P. (1996). *The New Politics and the New Populism.* New York: St. Martin's Press.

Talani, L. S. (2000). *Betting For and Against EMU.* London: Ashgate.

Tálos, E. and Falkner, G. (1984). 'The Role of the State within Social Policy'. *West European Politics,* 17(3): 52–76.

Tarrow, S. (1989). *Democracy and Disorder: Protest and Politics in Italy, 1965–1975.* Oxford and New York: Oxford University Press.

—— (1994). *Power in Movement.* Cambridge: Cambridge University Press.

—— (1998a). *Power in Movement: Social Movements and Contentious Politics,* 2nd edition. Cambridge and New York: Cambridge University Press.

—— (1998b). 'Social Protest and Policy Reform: May 1968 and the *Loi d'orientation*', in M. Giguni, D. McAdam, and C. Tilly (eds), *From Contention to Democracy.* Lanham, MD: Rowman and Littlefield, pp. 31–56.

—— (2001). 'Transnational Politics'. *Annual Review of Political Science* 4.

Taylor-Gooby, P. (2001). *Welfare States Under Pressure.* London: Sage Publications.

Teubner, G. (ed.) (1997). *Global Law without the State.* Aldershot: Dartmouth.

'T Hart, P. (1994). *Groupthink in Government: A Study of Small Groups and Policy Failure.* Baltimore: Johns Hopkins University Press.

Thatcher, M. (1998). 'Regulation, Institutions and Change: Independent Regulatory Agencies in the British Privatised Utilities'. *West European Politics,* 21(1): 120–147.

—— (1999). *The Politics of Telecommunications.* Oxford: Oxford University Press.

Theakston, K. (1999). *Leadership in Whitehall.* Basingstoke: Macmillan.

—— (ed.) (2000). *Bureaucrats and Leadership.* Basingstoke: Macmillan.

Thelen, K. (1999). 'Historical Institutionalism in Comparative Politics'. *The Annual Review of Political Science 1999.*

—— and Steinmo, S. (1992). 'Historical Institutionalism in Comparative Politics', in S. Steinmo, K. Thelen, and F. Longstreth (eds), *Structuring Politics. Historical Institutionalism in Comparative Analysis.* Cambridge: Cambridge University Press.

Thiébault, J. L. (1991*a*). 'The Social Background of Western European Ministers', in J. Blondel and J. L. Thiébault (eds), *The Profession of Government Minister in Western Europe*. London: Macmillan, pp. 19–30.

——(1991*b*). 'Local and Regional Politics and Cabinet Membership', in J. Blondel and J. L. Thiébault (eds), *The Profession of Government Minister in Western Europe*. London: Macmillan, pp. 31–43.

Thies, M. F. (2000). 'On the Privacy of Party in Government: Why Legislative Parties can Survive Party Decline in the Electorate', in R. J. Dalton and M. P. Wattenberg (eds), *Parties without Partisans: Political Change in Advanced Industrial Societies*. Oxford: Oxford University Press.

Tilly, C. (ed.) (1975). *The Formation of Nation States in Europe*. Princeton: Princeton University Press.

——(ed.) (1978). *From Mobilization to Revolution*. Reading, MA: Addison Wesley.

——(ed.) (1990). *Coercion, Capital, and European States, AD 990–1990*. Oxford: Basil Blackwell.

——(ed.) (1995). *Popular Contention in Great Britain, 1758–1834*. Cambridge, MA: Harvard University Press.

Timmermans, A. and Andeweg, R. (2000). 'The Netherlands: Still the Politics of Accommodation'? in W. C. Müller and K. Strøm (eds), *Coalition Governments in Western Europe*. Oxford: Oxford University Press, pp. 356–398.

Tivey, L. (1988). *Interpretations of British Politics*. London: Harvester Wheatsheaf.

Touraine, A. (1985). 'An Introduction to the Study of Social Movements'. *Social Research*, 52: 749–788.

Touraine, A. (1990). 'Existe-t-il encore une société française'. *Tocqueville Review*, vol. 11.

Trifiletti, R. (1999). 'Southern European Welfare Regimes and the Worsening Position of Women'. *Journal of European Social Policy*, 9(1): 49–64.

Trigilia, C. (1986). *Grandi partiti e piccole imprese. Comunisti e democrastiani nelle regioni a economia diffusa*. Bologne: Il Mulino.

——(1990). *Nested Games. Rational Choice in Comparative Politics*. London: University of California Press.

Tsebelis, G. (1994). 'The Power of the European Parliament as a Conditional Agenda-Setter'. *American Political Science Review*, 88: 128–142.

——(1995). 'Decision-Making in Political Systems: Comparisons of Presidentialism, Parliamentarism, Multicameralism, and Multipartyism'. *British Journal of Political Science*, 25: 289–325.

Tsoukalis, L. (1977). *The Politics and Economics of European Monetary Integration*. London: Allen and Unwin.

——(1998). 'The European Agenda: Issues of Globalization, Equity and Legitimacy'. *Jean Monnet Chair Papers*. Florence: European University Institute.

——(2000). 'Economic and Monetary Union: Political Conviction and Economic Uncertainty', in H. Wallace and W. Wallace (eds), *Policy Making in the European Union*. Oxford: Oxford University Press, 2000.

Tuck, R. (1999). *The Rights of War and Peace: Political Thought and the International Order from Grotius to Kant*. Oxford: Oxford University Press.

Tuytschaever, F. (1999). *Differentiation in European Union Law*. Oxford–Portland, Oregon: Hart Publishing.

Udy, S. (1959). ' "Bureaucracy" and "Rationality" in Weber's Theory'. *American Sociological Review*, 24: 791–795.

Van Deemen, A. M. A. (1989). 'Dominant Players and Minimum Size Coalitions'. *European Journal of Political Research*, 17: 313–332.

van der Meer, F. and Raadschelders, J. (1999). 'The Senior Civil Service in the Netherlands: A Quest for Unity', in E. C. Page and V. Wright (eds), *Bureaucratic Elites in Western European States: A Comparative Analysis of Top Officials*. Oxford: Oxford University Press, pp. 204–228.

van Kersbergen, K. (1995). *Social Capitalism: A Study of Christian Democracy and the Welfare State*. London: Routledge.

Van Roozendaal, P. (1992). *Cabinets in Multi-Party Democracies: The Effect of Dominant and Central Parties on Cabinet Composition and Durability*. Amsterdam: Thesis Publishers.

Van Schendelen, M. P. C. M. (ed.) (1993). *National Public and Private EC Lobbying*. Aldershot: Dartmouth Press.

—— (1996). ' "The Council Decides": Does the Council Decide?'. *Journal of Common Market Studies*, 34(4): 531–548.

—— (1998). 'Prolegomena to EU Committees as Influential Policymakers', in M. P. C. M. Van Schendelen (ed.), *EU Committees as Influential Policymakers*. Aldershot: Ashgate, pp. 3–22.

—— (1999). *EU Committees as Influential Policymakers*. Aldershot: Ashgate.

Verba, S., Nie, N., and Kim, J. (1978). *Participation and Political Equality*. New York: Cambridge University Press.

Verdier, D. (2000). 'The Rise and Fall of State Banking in OECD Countries'. *Comparative Political Studies*, 33: 283–318.

Verheijen, A. J. G. (2000). *Administrative Capacity Development: A Race Against Time?* The Hague: Scientific Council for Government Policy, Working Documents 107.

Verheijen, T. (ed.) (1999). *Civil Service Systems in Central and Eastern Europe*. Cheltenham: Edward Elgar.

Vernon, R. (1971). *Sovereignty at Bay: The Multinational Spread of US Enterprises*. London: Longman.

Vickers, J. and Yarrow, G. (1987). *Privatization: an economic analysis*. Cambridge, Mass.: MIT Press.

Vickers, J. and Wright, V. (eds) (1988). 'The Politics of Privatisation in Western Europe'. *West European Politics*, 11(4).

—— —— (eds) (1989). *The Politics of Privatization in Western Europe*. London: Frank Cass.

Visser, J. and Hemerijck, A. (1997). *A Dutch 'Miracle'*. Amsterdam: Amsterdam University Press.

Vogel, S. (1996). *Freer Markets, More Rules*. Ithaca, NY: Cornell University Press.

Wade, H. W. R. (1955). 'The Basis of Legal Sovereignty'. *Cambridge Law Journal*, 172–197.

Wade, R. (1996*a*). 'Globalization and its Limits: Reports of the Death of the National Economy are Greatly Exaggerated', in S. Berger and R. Dore (eds), *National Diversity and Global Capitalism*. Ithaca: Cornell University Press.

Wade, Sir W. (1996*b*). 'Sovereignty—Revolution or Evolution'? *Law Quarterly Review*, 112: 568–575.

Waever, O. (1995). 'Europe since in 1945: Crisis to Renewal''. in Wilson, K. and van der Dussen, J. (ed). *The History of the Idea of Europe*. London: Routledge.

Wallace, H. (1973). *National Governments and the European Communities*. London: Chatham House/PEP.

—— (1990). 'Making Multilateral Negotiations Work', in W. Wallace (ed.), *The Dynamics of European Integration*. London:Pinter/Royal Institute of International Affairs, pp. 213–228.

—— (2000). 'The Institutional Setting: Five Variations on a Theme', in H. Wallace and W. Wallace (eds), *Policy-Making in the European Union*, 4th edition. Oxford: Oxford University Press.

—— and Wallace, W. (1996). *Policy-Making in the European Union*, 3rd edition. Oxford: Oxford University Press.

Wallace, H. and Wallace, W. (2000*a*). 'Analysing and Explaining Policies', in H. Wallace and W. Wallace (eds). *Policy Making in the European Union*. Oxford: Oxford University Press, 4th edition, pp. 65–81.

—— —— (2000*b*). 'The Institutional Setting: Five Variations on a Theme', in H. Wallace and W. Wallace (eds). *Policy Making in the European Union*, 4th edition. Oxford: Oxford University Press, pp. 3–38.

Wallerstein, I. (1974). *The Modern World System*. New York: the Academic Press.

Walsh, K. and Stewart, J. (1992). 'Change in the Management of Public Services'. *Public Administration*, 70: 499–518.

Waltz, K. (1979). *Theory of International Politics*. London: Addison, Wesley.

—— (1993). 'The Emerging Structure of International Politics'. *International Security*, 18(2), Fall.

Walzer, M. (1971). *The Revolution of the Saints: A Study in the Origins of Radical Politics*. New York: Atheneum.

Wapner, P. (1995). 'Politics Beyond the State'. *World Politics*, 47: 3 (April).

Warsaw, S. A. (1996). *Powersharing: White House-Cabinet Relations in the Modern Presidency*. Albany: SUNY Press.

Warwick, P. (1994). *Government Survival in Parliamentary Democracies*. Cambridge: Cambridge University Press.

Waterman, R. W. and Meier, K. J. (1998). 'Principal–Agent Models: an Expansion'? *Journal of Public Administration Research and Theory*, 8: 173–202.

Weatherill, S. (1995). *Law and Integration in the European Union*. Oxford: Clarendon Press.

Weaver, R. K. and Rockman, B. A. (eds) (1991). *Do Institutions Matter?*. Washington, DC: Brookings.

—— —— (eds) (1993). 'When and How do Institutions Matter'? in R. K. Weaver and B. A. Rockman (eds), *Do Institutions Matter? Government Capabilities in the United States and Abroad*. Washington DC: Brookings, pp. 445–461.

Weber, M. (1962). 'Bureaucracy', *Essays in Sociology*, translated by H. H. Gerth and C. Wright-Mills. Oxford: Oxford University Press.

—— (1968). *Economy and Society*. Berkeley: University of California Press.

—— (1972). *Wirtschaft und Gesellschaft*, 5th edition. Tübingen: JCB Mohr.

Weiler, J. H. H. (1981). 'The Community System: The Dual Character of Supranationalism'. *Yearbook of European Law*.

—— (1991). 'The Transformation of Europe'. *Yale Law Journal*.

—— (1995*a*). 'Does Europe Need a Constitution? Reflections on Demos, Telos and the German Maastricht Decision'. *European Law Journal*.

—— (1995*b*). 'The State über Alles, Demos, Telos, and the German Maastricht Decision', in Ole Due *et al.* (eds), *Festschrift für Ulrich Everling*.

—— (1997). 'To Be a European Citizen: Eros and Civilization'. *European Journal of Public Policy*, 4: 495–519.

—— (2000). *The Constitution of Europe*. Cambridge: Cambridge University Press.

—— and Haltern, U. R. (1996). 'The Autonomy of the Community Legal Order—Through the Looking Glass'. *Harvard International Law Journal*, 37: 411–448.

Weiss, L. (1998). *The Myth of the Powerless State*. Ithaca: Cornell U.P.

—— (1999). 'Globalization and National Governance: Autonomies or Interdependence'? in K. Booth, M. Cox, and T. Dunne (eds), *The Interregnum: Controversies in World Politics 1989–1999*. Cambridge: Cambridge University Press.

Weller, P. M. and Bakvis, H. (1997). 'The Hollow Crown: Coherence and Capacity in Central Government', in P. M. Weller, H. Bakvis, and R. A. W. Rhodes, *The Hollow Crown*. London: Macmillan, pp. 1–15.

Bibliography

481

—— Bakvis, H., and Rhodes, R. A. W. (eds) (1997). *The Hollow Crown: Countervailing Trends in Core Executives*. London: Macmillan.

Wessels, W. (1990). 'Administrative Interaction', in W. Wallace (ed.) *The Dynamics of European Integration*. London: Pinter/Royal Institute of International Affairs, pp. 213–218.

—— (1997). 'An Ever Closer Fusion? A Dynamics Macropolitical View on Integration Processes'. *Journal of Common Market Studies*, 35(2): 267–299.

Westlake, M. (1995). *The Council of the European Union*. London: Cartermill Publishing.

Westney, E. (1987). *Imitation and Innovation. The Transfer of Western Organizational Patterns to Meiji Japan*. Cambridge Mass: Harvard University Press.

White, H. (1973). *Metahistory*. Baltimore: John Hopkins Press.

—— (1978). *Tropics of Discourse*. Baltimore: John Hopkins Press.

Wiener, M. (1981). *English Culture and the Decline of the Industrial Spirit*. Cambridge: Cambridge University Press.

Wilke, H. A. M. (1985). *Coalition Formation*. New York: Elsevier.

Wilthagen, T. (ed.) (1998). *Advancing Theory in Labour Law and Industrial Relations in a Global Context*. Amsterdam: North Holland.

Williams, P. (1964). *Crisis and Compromise*. London: Longman.

Williams, S. (1991). 'Sovereignty and Accountability in the European Community', in R. Keohane and S. Hoffmann (eds), *The New European Community*. Boulder, CO: Westview, pp. 155–76.

Wilson, Sir Richard (1998). 'Modernising Government: The Role of the Senior Civil Service'. Speech, Senior Civil Service Conference, October.

Wilson, W. (1887). 'The Study of Administration'. *Political Science Quarterly*, 2: 197–222.

Wincott, D. (2001). 'The Court of Justice and the European Policy Process', in J. Richardson (ed.), *European Union Power and Policy-Making*. London: Routledge.

Winkler, J. (1976). 'Corporatism'. *European Journal of Sociology*, 17(1): 100–136.

Winter, D. G. (1987). 'Leader Appeal, Leader Performance, and the Motive Profiles of Leaders and Followers: a Study of American Presidents and Elections'. *Journal of Personality and Social Psychology*, 52: 196–202.

—— (1995). 'Presidential Psychology and Governing Styles: A Comparative Psychological Analysis of the 1992 Presidential Candidates', in S. A. Renshon (ed.), *The Clinton Presidency; Campaigning, Governing, and the Psychology of Leadership*. Boulder: Westview, pp. 113–134.

Wishlade, F. (1993). 'Competition policy, cohesion and the co-ordination of regional aids in the European Community'. *European Competition Law Review*, 14(4): 143–150.

Wollmann, H. and Goldsmith, M. (1992). *Urban Politics and Policy: A Comparative Approach*. Oxford: Blackwell.

Wollmann, H. (2000). 'Local government systems: from historic divergence towards convergence? Great Britain, France and Germany as comparative cases in point', *Environment and Planning C: Government and Policy*, 18(1): 33–55.

Woods, N. (2000). *The Political Economy of Globalization*. Basingstoke: Macmillan.

Worms, J.-P. (1965). 'Le Préfet et ses notables'. *Sociologie du travail*, II.

Wright, V. (1965). *The Basses-Pyrénées from 1848 to 1870. A Study in Departmental Politics*. University of London, PhD thesis.

—— (1972). *Le Conseil d'Etat sous le Second Empire*. Paris: A. Colin.

—— and Le Cléré, B. (1973). *Les Préfets du Second Empire*. Paris: A. Colin.

—— (1974). 'Politics and Administration in the Fifth French Republic'. *Political Studies*, XXII/1.

—— (1978). *The Government and Politics of France*, 1st edition. London: Hutchinson.

—— (1984), *Continuity and Change in France*. London: Allen and Unwar.

Wright, V. (1989). *The Government and Politics of France*, 3rd edition. London: Unwin, Hyman.

—— (1990). 'The Administrative Machine: Old Problems and New Dilemmas', in P. Hall, J. Hayward, and H. Machin (eds), *Developments in French Politics*. Basingstoke: Macmillan.

Wright, V. (1993). 'The President and the Prime Minister: Subordination, Conflict, Symbiosis and Reciprocal Parasitism?', in J. Hayward (ed.), *De Gaulle to Mitterrand. Presidential Power in France*. London: Hurst.

—— (ed.) (1994*a*). *Privatization in Western Europe*. London: Pinter.

—— (1994*b*). 'Reshaping the State: Implications for Public Administration'. *West European Politics*, 17: 102–134.

—— (1996*a*). 'The Development of Public Administration in Britain and France: Fundamental Similarities Making Basic Differences'. *Yearbook of European Administrative History*, 8: 305–219.

—— (1996*b*). 'The National Co-ordination of European Policy-Making: Negotiating the Quagmire', in J. J. Richardson (ed.), *European Union: Power and Policy-Making*. London: Routledge, pp. 148–169.

—— (1997*a*). 'La fin du dirigisme'. *Modern and Contemporary France*, V/2.

—— (1997*b*). 'The Paradoxes of Administrative Reform', in W. Kickert (ed.), *Public Management and Administrative Reform in Western Europe*. Aldershot: Edward Elgar.

—— (1998*a*). 'Reshaping the State: the Implications for Public Administration', in C. Amirante and A. Cattanio (eds), *Efficienza, Trasparenza e Modernizzazione della pubblica amministrazione in Europa*. Rome: Università di Roma La Sapienza, pp. 137–157.

—— (1998*b*). 'Intergovernmental Relations and Regional Government in Europe: A Sceptical View', in P. Le Galès and C. Lequesne (eds), *Regions in Europe, the Paradox of Power*. London: Routledge.

—— (1999). 'The Path to Hesitant Comparison', in H. Daalder (ed.), *Comparative European Politics. The Story of a Profession*. London: Pinter.

—— (2000). 'The Fifth Republic: From the *Droit de l'État* to the *État de droit*', in R. Elgie (ed.), *The Changing French Political System*. London: Cass.

—— and Hayward, J. (2000). 'Governing from the Centre: Policy Co-ordination in Six European Core Executives', in R. A. W. Rhodes (ed.), *Transforming British Government. vol. 2. Changing Roles and Relationships*. London: Macmillan, pp. 27–46.

Wyszomirski, M. J. (1989). 'Presidential Personnel and Political Capital: From Roosevelt to Reagan', in M. Dogan (ed.), *Pathways to Power*. Boulder: Westview, pp. 45–73.

Zacher, M. (1992). 'The Decaying Pillars of the Westphalian Temple', in J. Rosenau and E-O. Cziempel (eds), *Governance without Government: Order and Change in World Politics*. Cambridge: Cambridge University Press.

Zahariadis, N. (1995). *Markets, States, and Public Policy*. Ann Arbor: University of Michigan Press.

Zald, M. N. (2000). 'Ideologically Structured Action'. *Mobilization*, 5: 1–16.

Zielonka (2000). 'Should Europe Become a State in the Future State of Europe?', in M. Leonard (ed.), *The Future Shape of Europe*. London: The Foreign Policy Centre.

Zulegg, M. (1997). 'The European Constitution under Constitutional Constraints: The German Scenario'. *European Law Review*, 22: 19–34.

Zysman, J. (1983). *Governments, Markets and Growth*. Ithaca: Cornell University Press.

Index